MW00366233

TALAAT PASHA

CONTENTS

Acknowledgments ix

Prologue xi

1 Istanbul, 1915: A Revolutionist Heading an Empire   1

Married with a Cause   1

"On first impression, this is a lucid mind" (April 1915)   5

*Fraught but in Top Form: Toward a Communion
in Crime*   12

Relying on Germany   17

"The people are the garden, we are its gardener"   22

*"Revolutionist Statesmanship," Imperially Biased:
A Prototype*   25

Bridging a Post-Ottoman Century   30

2 Patriotic Rebellion and Networking against
Sultan Abdulhamid II   35

From Edirne in European Turkey, 1870s   37

Exiled to Salonica   42

Conspiratory Organization in Salonica and Beyond   46

Talaat's Lead on the Road to the 1908 Revolution   51

Under the Shadow of Dr. Nâzım and
Dr. Bahaeddin Şakir 55

3 A Komiteci and the Challenge of Parliamentarism
(1908–11) 61

The Ottoman Spring 65

Against Counterrevolution: Empowering the
Central Committee 69

From Hidden to Semipublic Politics: Talaat as
a Minister 73

Sobered, Disturbed, Depressed: A Crisis for Talaat
and the Ottoman Future 81

A New Friend: Ziya Gökalp, Prophet
of Messianist Turkism 98

4 Alignment toward War and Dictatorial CUP
Power (1911–14) 107

CUP's Crises, Fall, and Radical Recalibration 110

War-Prone, Revanchist, High-Risk: Talaat Retrieves
the CUP from Its Nadir 121

Putsch, January 1913 130

Revolutionists at the Reins of the Empire 136

Edirne 1913: The Baptism of Committee Rule 141

Truth Test: Challenged by the Armenian Question 151

Negotiating Reforms Backed by Europe 157

Strange Spring, 1914: Reform and Peace or War
and Cataclysm? 165

Rûm Removal: A Cataclysmic Success 173

Talaat Pasha

FATHER OF MODERN TURKEY, ARCHITECT OF GENOCIDE

HANS-LUKAS KIESER

PRINCETON UNIVERSITY PRESS

PRINCETON & OXFORD

Published by Princeton University Press,
41 William Street, Princeton, New Jersey 08540

In the United Kingdom: Princeton University Press,
6 Oxford Street, Woodstock, Oxfordshire OX20 1TR

press.princeton.edu

Jacket image courtesy of Granger

ISBN 978-0-691-15762-7
Library of Congress Control Number: 2017963959

British Library Cataloging-in-Publication Data is available

This book has been composed in Arno Pro

Printed on acid-free paper. ∞

Printed in the United States of America

10 9 8 7 6 5 4 3 2 1

5 Total-War Gamble, Domestic Demolition,
Biased Nation Building   181

*European War: "End and Revenge" of the Eastern
Question?*   186

*For Turan's Sake, by German Will: Attack instead
of Reform*   196

Polarizing and Reframing the East   203

*Embracing War, Concentrating Power:
Toward Talaat's Dictatorial Rule*   210

Depressed by Defeat, Galvanized by Gallipoli   220

Exploit: "The Armenian Question no longer exists"   232

*Mirroring and Managing Anti-Christian Forces
in the East*   248

*Leading Assimilation, Plunder, Extermination,
Nation Building*   258

*Victor, Noah, National Father: A Wide-Ranging
Radiance*   277

Talaat, Palestine, and Zionism   295

6 Triumph and Fall, Lies and Resilience
(1917–21 and After)   315

Grand Vizier Talaat Pasha's "New Turkey"   320

Defiant Revolutionists, Troubled Wilhelminians   331

Faltering British Rule: A Matrix for Defiance   344

*Imperialisms Face Utopia, Dystopia: Sykes-Picot,
Balfour, Brest-Litovsk*   354

*From a Summer in Denial in Istanbul to Truth
in Berlin—and Resignation*   369

German Asylum: Keeping on the Struggle   381

Antiliberal International of Revolutionists   395

Death—and Afterlife—in Germany and Turkey   403

Talaat's Long, Strong Shadow   411

Epilogue   425

Notes   429

Bibliography   489

Index   503

ACKNOWLEDGMENTS

I AM HAPPY to extend many thank-yous first.

This study is based on a variety of sources from many archives in different languages. Excellent research assistance by Serhat Bozkurt, Dikran Kaligian, Martina Narman-Berli, Raymond Kévorkian, Mehmet Polatel, Ozan Ozavci, Thomas Schmutz, and Vahé Tachjian has enabled me to efficiently process data from Ottoman, Armenian, German, Austrian, British, and Israeli archives.

In an early phase, the support of Osman Kavala from Anadolu Kültür in Istanbul was critical to my successfully starting the research. (This outstanding friend and philanthropist is nowadays, in late 2017, unjustifiably imprisoned in Erdogan's Turkey.) Later, as a fellow of the Australian Research Council at the Centre for the History of Violence at the University of Newcastle, Australia, I enjoyed generous means for research, the necessary freedom of mind, and a welcoming, dynamic environment among the historians in Newcastle to elaborate and write my study of Talaat Pasha.

During the many years in which this analysis took shape, I profited from discussions with students in seminars, auditors of talks, and conference participants. Together with my colleagues, I organized several specific workshops and conferences about the "Ottoman cataclysm" (the last and seminal decade of the Ottoman Empire in which Talaat played an outstanding role) at the Universities of Basel and, foremost, Zurich, largely sponsored by the Swiss National Research Foundation and partly by the University of Newcastle. I thank the supportive team at the Department of History at the University of Zurich, where I taught for fifteen years, namely Fatima Leine and Barbara Welter Thaler, and Maurus Reinkowksi, director of the Middle Eastern Studies at the University of Basel.

I benefited from rich feedback on my manuscript by the anonymous reviewers at Princeton University Press, as well as by my historian colleague Margaret L. Anderson; Philip Dwyer, the director of the Centre for the History of Violence in Newcastle; Taner Akçam, Turkish pioneer of Armenian Genocide studies and helpful friend; my doctoral student Thomas Schmutz; my colleague in philosophy Markus Stepanians (University of Bern); Ronald G. Suny; Ümit Kurt; and Johannes Houwink ten Cate. I had the privilege of working with a great team at Princeton University Press and a superbly supportive editor, Brigitta van Rheinberg. Thanks go also to my cartographer, Shane Kelley, and, emphatically, to my copy editor, Cathy Slovensky, as well as to Mark Bellis, production editor, and Amanda Peery, associate editor.

This book is dedicated to all those affected by, but resilient to, political patterns in Turkey that must be traced back to Talaat Pasha, the driving force and architect of the first single-party experience in the twentieth century.

I would also like to dedicate this book to my family. My wife and our sons made sure that my immersion in a demanding historical exploration went hand in hand with attentiveness to daily life, the present and the future.

I express my heartfelt thanks to all those who helped me and contributed to bringing this study to a good end.

PROLOGUE

WHO WAS MEHMED TALAAT (1874–1921), and why might we call him a first founder of the Turkish nation-state even before Kemal Atatürk?

The last powerful grand vizier (a sort of prime minister) ruling the Ottoman Empire, Talaat was also a partisan heading the so-called Committee of Union and Progress (CUP), a former underground organization. He acted from within the latter's secretive Central Committee: not top-down but as a living hub, through networks of party, state, and co-opted agents in the provinces of the empire. Architect of the 1915 genocide in synergy with forces in the committee and in the provinces, he also pioneered demographic engineering in Asia Minor with other non-Turkish groups of the empire while simultaneously initiating modernist-nationalist reforms.

He thus became a founding father of a post-Ottoman Turkish nationalist polity. Talaat had concentrated power during the Balkan Wars and World War I by operationalizing elements of a new messianic nationalism (Muslim pan-Turkism, also called Turanism), framed by his influential Central Committee friend Ziya Gökalp. Gökalp's nationalism in the 1910s was openly imperial and politically Muslim, in contrast to its later version adopted by the Kemalists and Atatürk, himself a spiritual child of Gökalp.

Talaat was not a late nineteenth-century socialist revolutionary who had started believing in new futures for humanity—failing in his methods, and, in deeper analysis, also vision—but a revolutionist obsessed by empire and nation, the main references of far right-wing thought in twentieth-century Europe. In this spirit, he led the ultimate destruction of the Ottoman social fabric in 1915. Although his imperial goals were thwarted, he had prepared the way for the establishment of unrestricted Turkish sovereignty and a Turkish national home in Asia Minor. This book revises the traditional view of a Young Turk triumvirate throughout the 1910s and the marginalization of Ottoman actors in the history of a larger Europe. It reinstates agency to these actors, reconstructs the Ottoman capital, Istanbul, as a diplomatic hub in the early 1910s, and highlights the lasting magnitude of Talaat's policy. Of the same age and, since 1910, an acquaintance of Winston Churchill, Talaat represented Turkish-Islamic might in a period of bellicose confrontation with the British Empire.

Until now, no scholarly biography of Talaat Pasha has been available, although his legacy is present in powerful patterns of government and political thought, as well as in the name of many streets, schools, and mosques dedicated to him in and outside Turkey.[1] Talaat Pasha was a quintessential "political animal" of the modern twentieth-century Middle East. In the eyes of his admirers in Turkey today, and throughout the twentieth century, he was a great statesman, skillful revolutionary, and farsighted founding father, whereas for Ottoman Christians who survived World War I, he was principally the organizer of destruction, dispossession, and extermination. This was also true, in part, for Kurds. Kemal Atatürk "rested on Talaat's shoulders."[2]

Applying an inside perspective of the Ottoman Empire and its capital, Istanbul, this biography reinstates Mehmed Talaat as a major political figure of twentieth-century history who set the course for decades to come. He was the last powerful leader of the Ottoman Empire. He and his fellows cataclysmically revolutionized state and society from within, thus largely disrupting Ottoman tradition in politics and in social life, which was until then multireligious. The most influential ruler in the Middle East of the 1910s, when Asia Minor (Anatolia), Iraq, and Syria (including Lebanon and Palestine) were still part of the Ottoman Empire, Talaat led the first single-party experience of the twentieth century.

He stood at the reins of an endangered state that was formally still ruled by a sultan-caliph ("caliph" is a Muslim ruler deemed to be a successor of Muhammed). Not an aloof, single dictator, and far from being omnipotent, Talaat acted from within a conspiring committee that had established a party regime staunchly committed to saving the state, Islam, and the Turks. He succeeded in managing communication, balancing factions, and, although himself a civilian, getting along well with young officers.

Rejecting the entrenched view of the Young Turk leadership as an ongoing triumvirate, this study assesses it as a temporary constellation of 1913–14 (see chap. 4, sec. "Negotiating Reforms"). From then on, Talaat was more than a primus inter pares, both in domestic and foreign politics, thus politically superior to Enver Pasha (see ibid.). Confusion regarding this point misses the regime's architecture and the crucial nexuses that led to the Republic of Turkey.[3]

The CUP, the Young Turk power organization, directed the sultan and made him a representative figure after the Young Turk Revolution of 1908. Guided by Talaat, it established a single-party regime in 1913 while simultaneously starting what it considered to be a national struggle of salvation for a Turkey freed from foreign influence, from which an explicit narrative of national salvation began. It thus inaugurated the first founding period of a post-Ottoman nation-state marked by modern dictatorial patterns and the sidelining of the sultanate-caliphate, though it maintained an imperial spirit throughout the 1910s in its understanding of sociopolitical hierachies. This is true even for its Kemalist successors, after the sultanate-caliphate was definitively abolished in early 1924.

This study therefore calls the committee's mentality "imperially biased," and a main obstacle for real democracy, although its politics demolished the Ottoman social fabric and thus the empire. In this vein, Talaat became the direct forefather of a post-Ottoman Turkey based on radical nationalism ("Ata-türk" means the "Turks' father or progenitor"). Importantly, Atatürk's predecessor Talaat still embraced the power of political Islam, thus making the return of religious hegemony for Kemalists a constant threat and, in a post-Kemalist era, almost inevitable. Public history and political culture in the Republic of Turkey did not disavow Talaat's legacy but welcomed it officially in the 1940s, after silence during Atatürk's lifetime.

Together with his fellows, Talaat led the Ottoman Empire into World War I and jihad—he understood the whole war as a jihad[4]—and began to transform Asia Minor into a Turkish national home, that is, a "Turkey for the Turks," as a contemporary slogan read. When World War I was lost and the committee was dissolved, informed Germans rightly argued that Talaat was "too strong, on the whole, to simply disappear" in contrast to other, more ephemeral CUP figures.[5] Talaat's shadow eventually not only emerged and is imprinted on the founding history of the Turkish nation-state, the present Republic of Turkey, but also lingers in a modern confrontation between East and West, Ottoman-Muslim, and Christian powers and traditions. This contemporary polarization informs an alternative understanding of World War I, centered in Istanbul, seat of the Ottoman sultanate-caliphate, and emphasizes victory against the West at Gallipoli.

The Ottoman capital constitutes a main hub, cause, and factor of war itself, and Talaat was the man who was most identified with, most committed to, and most influential in determining the course of the Ottoman state during the last decade of its existence. He was involved in all critical decision making. He and his circle mirrored the forces around them, the zeitgeist and the contemporary system of powers. Tying Europe to an Ottoman cataclysm already in action, they anticipated and shaped the seminal catastrophe of Greater Europe, or, in the terminology of this book, "larger Europe" of the 1910s (Europe, Russia, and the Ottoman world).

Talaat's era, the so-called second constitutional period of the Ottoman state, keeps on "failing to be historicized,"[6] at least in public history, because of unbroken implicit and explicit identifications with actors and positions of that era that remain entrenched in the political culture. Successful efforts at comprehensive historicization are therefore critical in order to acquire a healthy distance and to face new futures in and with Turkey. In the first edition of Talaat's memoirs in 1946, the foreword states that Talaat "was one of a few rare statesmen whom Turkish history produced. Among the Ottoman grand viziers, this great Turkish leader had reached his high position thanks to his patriotism, honesty, intelligence and assiduity. . . . I bow respectfully before the great presence of the late Talaat Pasha."[7] To this day, Talaat's memoirs have seen many reeditions in this same spirit, indicating that many—including the Turkish state and polity—still stand under his spell and shadow.

In chapter 1, this book opens amid Talaat's most salient actions in the first year of World War I. This chapter introduces main topics of Talaat's biography, referring in several places to in-depth treatment and documentation that is explored in later chapters (see chaps. 2–6). These chapters proceed generally in chronological order, apart from two thematic sections (see chap. 3, sec. "A New Friend" and chap. 5, sec. "Talaat, Palestine, and Zionism"). Discussion of research and historiographical issues permeate the entire narrative and the endnotes.

TALAAT PASHA

1

Istanbul, 1915: A Revolutionist Heading an Empire

IT WAS SPRING 1915. Let us zoom in on the office of Talaat Bey, the minister of the interior, in the building known as the Sublime Porte, the seat of the government in the historical center of the European side of the Ottoman capital, Istanbul—then often still referred to by its historical name, Constantinople.

Married with a Cause

Talaat was bulky but not fat, a tall man with wide shoulders, a broad face, black eyes, bushy eyebrows, and black hair (which turned gray in 1918). Physically and mentally, he was an imposing figure. His office was a big and relatively light room, particularly notable for the several telephones on his desk. At times he also gave his orders from the telegraph in his home office.

He was married to Hayriye Hanım and had no children (he had learned from his doctor that he could not father a child; see chap. 3, sec. "Sobered, Disturbed, Depressed"). He lived instead in a symbolic marriage—or passionate concubinage—with his cause: Make Turkey strong again! Somewhat puzzlingly, he asserted himself as a Muslim of Turkish descent, a "son of empire," *and* a patriotic revolutionist. "We must win back our old strength, our old influence," he told the Germans in late 1915.[1] He and his friends pursued a "great national ideal," as they called it, informed by Ottoman imperial glory and contemporary ethnoreligious nationalism (not the socialism inspired by Marx nor the universal positivism in Auguste Comte's sense).

Theorists of modern revolutions might therefore identify Talaat as an imperially biased right-wing revolutionary (or rather "revolutionist," in the terminology of this study, and to be distinguished from a value-based right-wing stance). Psychologists, in turn, might find him addicted to power—compensation, perhaps, for having been deprived of children and family. Power was "the dearest thing that he had known," he confessed a few days before being killed in Berlin in 1921, adding that "one could have too much of a good thing."[2] He was the only grand vizier who ascended, step-by-step, to power from below—from subversive opposition to continuous membership in parliament and ministries in different cabinets. From summer 1913, Mehmed Talaat (both names are forenames; Ottoman Muslims did not have surnames) was the actual head of the government, even if he was promoted to grand vizier, with the honorific title of "Pasha" only in 1917. Before, he was only "Bey."

He owed his predominance to his strong position within the Committee of Union and Progress (CUP), a primarily conspiratoral party organization directed by the Central Committee. It had its headquarters on Nur-i Osmaniye Street, a few minutes' walk from the Sublime Porte on one side and the Hagia Sophia cathedral (transformed into a mosque after the Turkish conquest of Constantinople in 1453) and the Sultanahmed Mosque on the other, and next to the house in the Yerebatan neighborhood where Talaat lived with his wife. *Komiteci* (or *komitacı*) is the Turkish name for a member of a conspiratory committee of revolutionists. The CUP was the foremost organization within a broad Young Turk movement that had begun as an opposition force against Sultan Abdulhamid II, the last ruling sultan of Ottoman history. Talaat's cause was the Central Committee's cause and—as he, at least, maintained—the cause of "the people," the Turkish nation, and of Islam.[3]

After their putsch in 1913, the CUP Central Committee alone dictated politics and the allocation of ministries. When the committee had organized the Young Turk Revolution of 1908 (see chap. 2, secs. "Talaat's Lead on the Road" and "Under the Shadow"; chap. 3, sec. "The Ottoman Spring"), it could only partly control politics. In the aftermath of the autocratic rule of Sultan Abdulhamid II, it had been inclined to democracy. The CUP then had even allied with the main Armenian party, the Armenian Revolutionary Federation (ARF). Publically, then, both groups pursued the common goal of establishing constitutional rule.[4] A longtime Central Committee member and an experienced administrator, Talaat used his networks to concentrate power, to impose policies, and to organize action. It was he who had principally prepared the putsch of 1913; the same is true for the reconquest of Edirne in the same year during the Second Balkan War, which won him and the CUP huge prestige among patriots.

Ever since his childhood in Edirne (the early Ottoman capital in European Turkey), Talaat had an emotional attachment to the Selimiye Mosque (see chap. 2, sec. "From Edirne"). It recalled past glory, although the mosque's sponsor, the late sixteenth-century sultan Selim II ("the drunkard"), stood for imperial decadence. His grandfather and namesake, Selim I "the grim" (*yavuz*), however, provided a strong role model for the Young Turks and served as the party's patron saint. In a similar vein, the Young Turks, most of whom hailed from the Balkans, understood themselves as superior "sons of conquerors" (Evlad-ı Fatihan), within a geography that had remained largely Christian.[5] Tellingly, after his forefathers' conquest of Western Asia Minor and the Balkans, in the early sixteenth century, Selim I had not only conquered Eastern Asia Minor, Syria, and Egypt but also waged war against domestic adversaries called Kızılbaş, today better known under the general designation of Alevis.

Alevis did not (and do not) identify with orthodox Sunni or imperial Islam but did have sympathies with premodern Shiite Iran, and had connections to Bektashi heterodoxy, a well-established religious network in the early Ottoman world.[6] Talaat's nation, in contrast, was tantamount to Turkish-speaking Muslims relying on the Ottoman state. But while his political roots lay in the Ottoman power organization based on Selim I's achievements, Bektashism played a role even for Talaat, since its *tekke* (cloisters) had offered a safe niche for dissidents under Abdulhamid and cultivated a more liberal spirit than the Sunni orthodoxy that the sultan demanded. After the ascendance of Turkish nationalism in the early 1910s, a few CUP intellectuals tried to co-opt Alevis and Bektashis, purporting that they were the true bearers of Turkishness in language and in habits, who had resisted assimilation to the surrounding Kurdish tribes and to Arab- and Persian-influenced imperial culture. But this modestly successful CUP flirtation with Alevism scandalized conservative Sunni Muslims.[7]

War and the patriotic call to fight for the nation is political tender in times of crisis, if enough people follow the call. Talaat had applied this maneuver during a deep CUP crisis on the eve of the Balkan Wars in September 1912, for Edirne's reconquest in 1913, and again in July 1914 (see chaps. 4 and 5). Then, a small group around him decided to use Europe's July crisis as a chance to approach Germany and to conclude, finally (after several frustrated attempts in the months and years before), an alliance with a European Great power. Talaat embraced war as a game-changer, although this was a gamble with high stakes and even higher risks.

The secret treaty on 2 August 1914 demanded active war from Turkey. Henceforth, an ambitious world war agenda dominated politics. Although the German-speaking war minister Enver Pasha, an iconic military hero of the 1908 revolution, appeared as the figurehead during these plots, Talaat pulled the strings. Contrary to traditional wisdom, he was not less in command of the CUP's notorious paramilitary forces than Enver. This "Special Organization" prepared a war of conquest into the Caucasus and actually made raids from August 1914 onward. He was also centrally involved in the proposition to the German ally in October 1914 to launch a naval attack on the Black Sea to provoke open war with Russia. Only then did the world know for sure of the Turkish-German alliance. In his memoirs, written in 1919, Talaat misleads the reader to believe that he was not aware of the planned aggression. What he wrote after defeat served as a vindication in his larger, ongoing political struggle in exile (see chap. 6).[8]

"On first impression, this is a lucid mind" (April 1915)

Behind the desk at the Ministry of the Interior in mid-April 1915 was a forty-one-year-old man who impressed his freshly arrived German visitor, journalist Emil Ludwig, with his energy, willpower, and the striking aura of a self-made man.[9] Talaat was very active, yet at the same time, he was apparently friendly and approachable. He signed documents and made telephone calls while carrying on his conversation with Ludwig. From time to time, secretaries entered and exited the room. Talaat's smile and charm, even under stress, were famous. Upon meeting Talaat for the first time, Ludwig (soon to gain renown as biographer of powerful politicians) already had a penetrating view of the man: "At first sight this is a lucid mind. But behind it, within him, there is a subdued daemonic temper chained up."

A British deputy who had known Talaat from a few encounters wrote in 1921, shortly after the former grand vizier was killed in Berlin, "I only know that he was, in himself, fearless, and anyone who, like myself, only knew him superficially found him to be kindly and with a singular charm."[10] Interacting within the function of his political goals, Talaat often joked, in cold blood, about unresolved issues or, enjoying his power, at times teased his CUP friends and ministers.[11] He had the ability to quickly spot psychological weakness in people, including European diplomats, yet he knew little beyond the universe of the CUP, the political home that he had guided since late 1912. In meetings, he was convivial and sociable, his personality dominating the situation.

Indeed, behind the smile was a brain that planned, constructed, and carried out what would be called one of the most monstrous political acts of the twentieth century: the extermination of the Ottoman Armenians. Many others have noted Talaat's charm and his capacity to humor the people who came to him. At times he combined this charm with melancholy— the melancholy of a man presiding over a crumbling empire— which made him likable, particularly to the Germans, and mollified even angry friends in his presence. For Talaat, sadness served as a weapon. In addition to this, he was an emotional person and wept at times, for example, at a ceremony in a soldier cemetery or after the death of Sultan Mehmed V.[12] Sly, perhaps, rather than intelligent and farsighted, he possessed the emotional and social qualities of a networker, a strong instinct for power, and an excellent memory, which tended toward the vengeful. "Why did we enter the war?" Talaat asked rhetorically, in order to shape Ludwig's flattering report in the *Berliner Tageblatt* (*Berlin Daily*); he answered his own question with a CUP mantra: "We had to reestablish our independence, and we were sure that we would achieve this best at Germany's side."

More than the other Great powers, Wilhelminian Germany was attracted, politically and culturally, to Turkey.[13] During the war, Germany was ready to adopt a laissez-faire approach vis-à-vis Turkey's men of radical action and demolitionist domestic policy, at times fascinated by them. Germany's interest in re-empowering Ottoman Turkey—and its noninterference in its ally's domestic policies—were essential for Talaat's designs. This was particularly true in order to have "a free hand" in what he called "the national struggle for survival" against his fellow Armenian citizens.[14] Social Darwinism—a belief in a deathly "fight for survival," as interpreted from Darwinist notions like "survival of the fittest" and applied to human society—played a seminal role during World War I in general and for CUP members in particular.

On 24 April 1915, Talaat sent circulars to his provincial governors and a long telegram to Enver, the vice commander of the Ottoman army. (The sultan was the nominal commander.) In them, Talaat defined the current domestic situation as a general Armenian insurrection. He evoked the specter of a Russian-backed Armenian autonomy in Eastern Asia Minor, where Turkey risked losing the war. Neither his circulars nor his memoirs mention that he and his friends had prepared and started the war in the East in August 1914 (see chap. 5).[15] Their aim? To restore Turkey's strength and full sovereignty, abolish internationally monitored reforms for the crisis-ridden Kurdish-Armenian eastern provinces, and reconquer territory lost decades ago in the Caucasus and beyond.

Since the mid-nineteenth century, in the eastern provinces unrest had accompanied lack of security and justice. Diplomacy called the issue "the Armenian Question" and considered it an essential part of the modern "Eastern Question": What could or should be the future of the Ottoman Empire—which is the future of the Near East—and what should Europe do about it?[16] A main stumbling block for any easy answers was the Ottoman non-Muslims' demand for equality. It met fierce opposition by local lords and Sunni leaders, particularly in Eastern Asia Minor, where non-Muslims were still regarded as *zimmi*, obliged to respect Muslim hegemony in state and society. The Armenians, the most vocal group demanding reforms, were denigrated as agents of foreign Christian powers who wanted to rule over them. Young Armenian activists spread ideas of social revolutionary change, sought foreign backing, and began to coordinate self-defense tactics. About 100,000 Armenians, mostly men, were massacred in 1895, and roughly another 20,000 in April 1909, by gangs organized in mosques who connived with or were supported by state officials and local notables. Islamist discourse by various authorities—as an honest, though solitary, Kurdish historian in the 1970s reminded us—had publicly incited Muslims to kill the *gavur* (non-Muslim) en masse and made killing a duty to the *ummah* (community of Muslims).[17]

To forestall collapsing entirely within its periphery, the state had to conspire with and co-opt violent reactionary forces. The

Great powers, in turn, lacked viable common ground and failed to act. They were paralyzed, not only by imperialist competition but also by their fear that the collapse of the state would lead to dangerous geostrategic conflicts and seriously affect their economical investments and interests. Ottoman diplomacy under Sultan Abdulhamid II exploited this constellation, and the state did not prosecute domestic mass crimes, which he had largely condoned, except for their repercussions abroad.[18] During World War I, the situation further worsened. Though the government had signed a reform plan for Eastern Asia Minor in February 1914, war and German acquiescence allowed Talaat to suspend it, and, by the end of 1914, to abrogate it completely.

Talaat had convinced himself that reforms would ultimately lead to the region's autonomy and possibly to territorial loss, as in the recent case of Macedonia. (In that case however, Talaat's purposeful warmongering during autumn 1912, as well as long-standing deficits in the administration, had played a role.) The loss of almost all of European Turkey in 1912–13 had converted him and his friends into radical partisans of a fresh Turkish nationalism. This new current dismissed any residual belief in Ottoman multinational coexistence and claimed Asia Minor as a "Turkish home/homeland" (Türk Yurdu), and let itself simultaneously become obsessed by Ziya Gökalp's expansive vision of "Turan." It assumed the successful assimilation of non-Turkish Muslims, particularly Kurds, but not of Ottoman Christians. Such ambitious goals of social transformation, as well as imperial restoration and expansion, could only be achieved through war. Dreams of conquest toward Turan via the Caucasus region were extremely popular among young elites, foremost military officers, from August 1914, but saw catastrophic frustration in late 1914. They were revived, however, when czarist Russia collapsed in 1917.

On 24 April 1915 Talaat decided to end the Armenian Question once and for all, after meeting with CUP friends and receiving suggestions from young, radical governors in the East during the days and weeks before (see chap. 5). Although quite open to the Armenians after the constitutional revolution of 1908, he now fanatically hated and deeply feared them as the main obstacle to his personal ambitions and a Turkish future that he no longer conceived as related to the principles of the Ottoman constitution. In his circular, he ordered the arrest of the Armenian elite. Actually, he was suspicious of all non-Muslim groups with political projects, and of the Zionists as well. During dinner with US ambassador Henry Morgenthau on the same day, he expressed the conviction that "they [the Zionists] are mischievous" and that "it is their [the CUP rulers'] duty to get rid of them." The German ambassador Hans von Wangenheim told Morgenthau three days later that "he would help Zionists but not Armenians."[19] And, in fact, Germany protected Jews but not Armenians. With his 24 April 1915 orders, Talaat even surrendered former political friends to interrogation, torture, and, in most cases, murder. Before killing those arrested, the security apparatus, a part of his ministry, extorted confessions to prove that there was a general Armenian conspiracy.[20] In fact, there was no conspiracy. But in Talaat's calculated conspiracy theory, which was spread during spring 1915, there was.

Many former political companions, now victims, could not believe that Talaat had become their persecutor. It was to him that they appealed for help as they were led to trial and death.[21] The lawyer and writer Krikor Zohrab, his longtime political partner and an internationally renowned Ottoman cross-bench deputy, had been exempted from the arrests of Saturday night,

24 April 1915. Together with the Armenian patriarch and two other representatives, he visited Talaat on Sunday morning and urged him to liberate the prisoners, but found him inflexible: "All Armenians who verbally, by written word, or by their actions have worked or can one day work for the construction of Armenia are considered enemies of the state."[22] A day later, Zohrab sent Talaat a memorandum in which he complained that not only had the original statement wrongly indicated that those arrested would be released but that no news could be obtained on those arrested.[23]

Like his Central Committee friend Ziya Gökalp, a very influential spiritual father of Turkish nationalism, Talaat embraced a state-centric Muslim Turkism, refused the idea of a social contract, and rejected regionally rooted democracy. Instead, both men favored unitary, authoritarian centralization. Gökalp's modernizing ideology, called "idealism" (*mefkûrecilik*, from Gökalp's seminal term *mefkûre*, "ideal") by its adepts, was in fact political messianism. Underestimated, and almost overlooked by historians, except for twentieth-century Armenian scholars,[24] the alliance of Talaat and Gökalp played a seminal role in the cataclysmic disruption of the late Ottoman Middle East. It impacted Europe, especially Germany, where Gökalp was praised as the ingenious founder of Turkish nationalism and a great historic figure.

Radical party politics was combined with transformative political thought (Gökalp) and practice (Talaat) during the Ottoman cataclysm. Fragile seeds of a more modest but consensual and pluralist state- and nation-rebuilding plan based on Ottoman constitutionalism were thus destroyed. German orientalists of the early interwar period noted both Gökalp's implication in Islamist reform currents and that he was simultaneously a Turkish enthusiast who had "got drunk ... with the ideal of the 'great eternal country Turan.'" Orientalists turned into Turcologists, and many positively greeted nationalism based on Islam and Turkdom, thus banishing from their discipline the hitherto most important contributors to Ottoman Turcology in Europe: the Armeniens. Gökalp was rightly recognized as the spiritual father of Turkish nationalism and praised as a master of a "popular philosophy" that had "proved itself so brilliantly during the last war."[25]

Fraught but in Top Form: Toward a Communion in Crime

On 27 May 1915, Emil Ludwig visited Talaat a second time.[26] Talaat's frame of mind was excellent. Two and a half months before, quite the contrary had been the case. But the first Ottoman victory that thwarted an attack on Istanbul—Churchill's attempted naval breakthrough at the Dardanelles on 18 March—had greatly lifted the mood of a government that, during winter 1914–15, had suffered heavy defeats in the Caucasus, Northern Iran, Southern Iraq, and at the Suez Canal. The press of the Entente countries and neutrals were then vocal in their pleas for internationally protected Armenian autonomy.[27] The victory on 18 March 1915 against the Entente inspired CUP "brothers" (as they mutually called themselves) not only with a new self-reliance but also with an arrogant and brutal chauvinism, as the Austrian general Joseph Pomiankowski, a frequent companion of Enver Pasha, noted.[28]

Chauvinism then merged with daredevilry. Determination crystallized among the CUP radicals in the capital and in the eastern provinces; they decided that this was the opportune moment to end the Armenian Question by terminating

Armenian existence. Talaat produced security arguments regarding the eastern front against Russia. The main underlying reason given for the action, however, was the will to "free" Asia Minor from any Armenian claims. In a comprehensive strategy of the war, in which the imperial revolutionists perceived interior and exterior fronts, he was confident of achieving a bone-crushing victory against the domestic adversary. He had embraced total war as a total war–jihad since August 1914 and understood it to be waged on all sides. He had already achieved tremendous success in June 1914, when CUP gangs expelled more than 150,000 Orthodox Christians (so-called Rûm), Ottoman citizens from the region of İzmir, at the Aegean to the near islands and then Greece. By mid-July 1915, he boasted as having "accomplished more in three months about crushing the Armenians than Abdul Hamid could do in thirty-seven years."[29]

In May 1915, everybody was busy with the struggle for the Ottoman capital. Only a few hours after mass arrests had commenced, the Entente had begun to invade Gallipoli on the morning of 25 April 1915. While the Ottoman army resisted successfully, the repelling of Entente forces was led by German generals and supported by German experts and submarines. During an interview with Ludwig, Talaat showed himself to be utterly self-confident: "Nobody will break through the Dardanelles." He did not fear Italy's possible entrance into war or the outbreak of war in the Balkans. He felt sure of winning his "domestic war" against not only the Rûm but also the Armenians. He had already sent a letter on 16 May to the grand vizier that detailed how his Ministry of the Interior had settled more than 250,000 Muslim refugees at the places from which the Rûm had been expelled. Talaat was becoming a pioneering demographic engineer, as his notebook, with his fastidious statistical accounting, testifies.[30]

Talaat also exhibited utter self-confidence regarding global history, as is evident in his introduction to the Ottoman translation of Karl Helfferich's analysis of how World War I had broken out. In this piece, dated 14 May 1915, the Ottoman leader entirely identified with the view on contemporary history of this academically trained and sharp-tongued advocate of German *Weltpolitik* and a future leader of the German Far Right. Conveniently for Talaat, Treasury secretary Helfferich, with apodictic certainty, blamed Russia for the war and declared France and Britain complicit, while the Central powers only defended themselves against arsonists of the Entente. "In this way, the responsibilities become fully evident; in my opinion, there is not even any task left to later historiography," Talaat concluded. Two years later, Grand Vizier Talaat was offered a reception in Helfferich's house in Berlin.[31] They had known each other well since the aftermath of 1908, when Helfferich, former director of the Anatolian Railway and now chairman of the Deutsche Bank, and journalist Paul Weitz organized propaganda and, in Helfferich's words, "baksheesh," besides "advances ad libitum" to persuade the CUP. It had initially shown reserve vis-à-vis Germany because of its courtship of Sultan Abdulhamid II.[32]

After the attack on the Armenian elite, Talaat prepared the main act: to send an entire people group into the desert in Syria. The day before Ludwig's second visit, Talaat had delivered a long letter to Grand Vizier Said Halim, a CUP member but less influential than Talaat and Enver. This letter on 26 May 1915 presents the evacuation of the Armenians as a comprehensive and definitive solution of a vital question for the Ottoman state. While the long sentences are tortuous to read, their authoritative articulation leaves no room for doubt concerning Talaat's goal of pursuing a project that breached the constitution and Ottoman laws, even if it feigned a resettlement of the removed people, the protection of their rights, and a limited removal from war zones (he then already intended the country-wide removal of the Armenians).[33]

Urged on by Enver and Talaat, the cabinet decreed a provisional law on 27 May that permitted the army to "crush any opposition" and, in case of suspicion, to "dispatch individually or collectively, and to resettle elsewhere, the inhabitants of villages and towns."[34] It did not name the Armenian target, in contrast to a much more detailed decree of 30 May. This decree again bore Talaat's mark and repeated whole passages from his 26 May letter.[35] He acted in defiance of the Entente declaration on 24 May 1915, which warned the members of the Ottoman government that they would be held personally responsible for "crimes against humanity." (This is the first time the term was used in high politics.)[36] Talaat reacted to this international admonition by extending the responsibility to the whole cabinet, thus producing a fundamental communion in crime.

Talaat often acted before he informed his peers or sought the consent of formal superiors or the cabinet as a whole, and before laws were made that sanctioned the deeds. On 18 and 23 May, he had already instructed the governor of Erzurum and the governors of Van and Bitlis—three provinces included in the reform plan signed in February 1914—to chase the Armenian population toward the south. At the same time, he had briefed the governors on the resettlement of Muslim refugees from the lost Balkan provinces into the houses that the Armenians had "abandoned."[37] Hence, during three months, beginning in the East, caravans of Armenian women, children, and men (those not drafted) dragged their way through Asia Minor. They were exposed to privation, spoliation, massacre, and repeated rape of women and children, girls and boys. Most men in the East were killed before departure. The comprehensive spoliation of the Armenians profited the state materially, but it also enriched notables, a great number of neighbors, and occasional robbers. Crime went hand in hand with the corruption of a countrywide miscreant regime.

That Thursday, 27 May 1915, as Ludwig left Talaat's office, he saw twenty or so employees prostrating themselves for prayer. Although Talaat could rarely join in due to lack of time, he participated in the public prayers (*namaz*) on Friday. According to his wife, every morning he recited the Al-Fath (Victory or Triumph), the forty-eighth surah in the Koran. At times there are elements of pious rhetoric in his diverse letters, although little elaboration. In discussions with the sheykhulislam (the head of the religious administration) Mustafa Hayri, who was also a member of the CUP's Central Committee, he insisted that he was a good Muslim. He had been the first to approvingly shake the hand of the *fetva* commissioner after the latter had read the legal document (*fetva*) written by Hayri declaring jihad on 14 November 1914. He both identified with and used Islam to support his power, even in April 1909, when he had extorted a *fetva* in order to dethrone Abdulhamid (see chap. 3).[38]

Hayri was at odds with Talaat's radicalism and rudeness, but, like a small number of other CUP representatives who felt similarly, was neither able nor willing to confront him seriously. In contrast to Hayri, Talaat did not see the salvation of the precarious state by a reformed Muslim union. He preferred to transform state and society simultaneously, as suggested by the ideas of Gökalp. In the Central Committee, Hayri accused Gökalp of putting Turkism over Islam and resented the fact that this adversary enjoyed more influence than he did.[39] According to Gökalp's vision, leaders had to cull bad elements from society and graft on new ones. Once the renewed society acquired Western science and civilization, it would not only realize the superiority of Islam and the Turkish race and culture but also become a unitary body, a country in which, in Gökalp's words, "every individual has the same ideal, language, habit, religion. . . . Its sons ache to give their lives at its frontier!"[40]

Gökalp proclaimed a messiah named "Turan," which did not stand for a person but for a compelling myth of an "enormous and eternal fatherland," to be conquered across the Caucasus. In the first months of World War I, Turan galvanized young, "idealist" CUP officers into a pan-Turkist conquest of the Caucasus and beyond. They felt it their mission to save Turkic Muslims from Russia's yoke. In various rhymes Gökalp proclaimed jihad and his shrill prophecy in early August 1914: "Russia will collapse and be ruined / Turkey will expand and be Turan!"[41] All too quickly, exalted Turan turned into a frustrated monster after the disaster of Enver's Caucasus offensive at Sarıkamış in January 1915. "The road to Turan," however, remained suggestive and present, also in telegrams of Talaat's subordinates.[42]

Relying on Germany

The term "genocide" did not exist before the lawyer Raphael Lemkin coined it. After years of campaigning by Lemkin, "genocide" entered the legal vocabulary of the United Nations General Assembly on 9 December 1948 as General Assembly Resolution 260 (the Convention on the Prevention and Punishment of the Crime of Genocide). Lemkin's original inspiration in pursuing legal means to prosecute war criminals was inspired by the actions of Talaat, the demolitionist at the head of the Ottoman Empire who had anticipated genocide by actually committing it. Talaat used the Armenian genocide to form a united Turkish-Muslim body and polity in Asia Minor. Lemkin learned essential information about Talaat while following the trial of his assassin, Soghomon Tehlirian, in Berlin in 1921 (Tehlirian was found not guilty and released). Supported by German friends and in coordination with Mustafa Kemal (Atatürk), who led the Turkish nationalist struggle for Asia Minor after war defeat, Talaat had continued to agitate in Europe after escaping Ottoman postwar justice against war criminals (see chap. 6).[43]

Before "culling bad elements from society," that is, destroying a stigmatized people, a critical barrier had to be overcome in spring 1915: possible German interposition. Potential shocks to the alliance had to be tamped down until the deed became irreversible and, according to the military logic of alliance, Germany fully invested in denying or downplaying what had happened. On 31 May 1915, one day after his detailed removal decree, Talaat sent Enver to the German ambassador Wangenheim. Enver was not only German-speaking and the darling of the German press and court but also the intimate friend of the Turkish-speaking captain Hans Humann, a frequent interlocutor, advisor, critic of Wangenheim, and Turcophile hard-liner. In very polite and trivializing terms, Enver demanded understanding for the need and support of the project "to evacuate a few subversive families from centers of insurrection." A few Armenian schools and newspapers would also be closed, but Turkey's existence, dear to Germany and German ambitions to *Weltgeltung* (global standing), was at risk. Wangenheim acquiesced.[44]

On 1 June 1915, Krikor Zohrab, a member of parliament once thought to be on excellent terms with Talaat, asked Talaat and Midhat Şükrü (Bleda), a Central Committee member and the CUP's secretary-general, one last time for an explanation of the arrests and the anti-Armenian policy.[45] Talaat retorted that he didn't need to give an account for anything to anybody. "But to me, in the status of an Armenian deputy," Zohrab insisted.

As a response to a power-holder who detached himself from basic human norms, this answer was proof of a personality still anchored in an Ottoman constitutional period that was now to be irrevocably revoked, together with Ottoman society itself. One day later, Zohrab was arrested by order of Talaat and sent to Diyarbekir, ostensibly for court-martial, but he was brutally assassinated on the road by CUP killers. On the road from the Baghdad hotel in Konya, Zohrab had sent Talaat a long, heart-breaking but dignified and well-pondered letter. It stands to this day as a monument of a man with spirit—an outstanding Armenian author, arguably the best Ottoman-speaking orator in the parliament—wanting to live versus being eager to kill for power.[46]

Wangenheim soon regretted his rapid acquiescence to Enver, but Talaat had won the time he needed to set into motion the administrative machine of deportation. The collective targeting of Armenians released and spurred anti-Christian hate and cupidity in broad parts of society—though not everywhere. Yezidis and Alevis in remote regions, and individuals in different places, offered asylum. On 10 June 1915, the German vice-consul in Mosul reported to Wangenheim horrible massacres of deportees from the neighboring province of Diyarbekir. A high number of corpses and cut body parts floated on the Tigris.[47] Immediately, Wangenheim interrogated Talaat, who answered, "We liberate ourselves from the Armenians to be a better ally for you, freed from weakness induced by a domestic enemy." Below, on the same page on which Humann reports these words, he added his own opinion: "The Armenians are now exterminated grosso modo because of their conspiracy with the Russians. This is hard, but useful."[48]

Humann gives a foretaste of an exterminatory National Socialism that has more to do with the German experience and perception of genocide in Turkey than popular history has revealed.[49] Anti-Semite and anti-Levantine, he identified with the "idealism," ambition, and methods of his powerful friend Enver. Wilhelminian elites largely cherished the idea that a systematically reempowered Turkey would be the key to German hegemony in Europe and Western Asia, and consequently to German global power. Humann used his relations and coproduced myths of German and Turkish power to boost his own career. Though from a cultivated and cosmopolitan family, during World War I (and afterward) he admired brutal energy and will in the service of national power. Wangenheim got on his nerves when "all the time lamenting [about the treatment of the Armenians], much to the disadvantage of our political interest," now that the ambassador understood the comprehensive dimension of the extermination. The paradox between culture and nature in social Darwinist terms penetrated much of the contemporary German elite. An expert on Turkey and a friend of the Armenians, Johannes Lepsius stood for the other side.[50]

Soon thereafter, Wangenheim, the representative of the Wilhelminian empire in Istanbul, who had had reasons to deem himself superior to Talaat, collapsed. Strokes killed him in October, after he had finally tried to convince himself of the inevitability of Talaat's policy and even proposed, inspired by proposals of Zionist Alfred Nossig's circle, to replace the removed Armenians with Jews from Poland. Nevertheless, he had never consented to more than limited removals; thus, German diplomacy remained, in principle, committed to the return of the Armenian survivors and restitution of their property.[51] Even if at first against his will, Wangenheim had made the Turkish-German war alliance his own project—a product of haste, emergency, and gamble. Committee advances after mid-July 1914 had offered Germany the sudden possibility of having Turkey at its side. This shaped German war psychology and planning for the future, while, in late July, war was still only a possibility, not a reality. Hence, both governments depended on each other in a mutual war gamble. Thereafter, Wangen-heim courted the CUP men of action, but for "higher" strategic reasons; he ignored the warnings and cries for help from the Armenian side since late 1914. He had himself written the draft for the apologetic Ottoman answer to the Entente declaration of 24 May 1915. Joint propaganda efforts of denial intensified in August 1915 and continued until 1918. It took until 2016 for German politics to acquire the maturity to officially call the 1915 deed by its name.[52]

In terms of political strategy, Talaat's Turkey was advantaged, because Germany's aspiration to dominance in Europe and *Weltgeltung* remained based on vague concepts. It cherished the idea of a German Central Europe with a zone of influence reaching into the Ottoman world and beyond. Only after the collapse of czarist Russia did it refocus on Eastern Europe. In contrast, right from the eve of World War I, Talaat possessed a concrete, minimal goal: the preservation of CUP power and the establishment of national sovereignty, at least in a secure Turkish-Muslim home in Asia Minor. Despite defeat in World War I, Turkey achieved this goal under Mustafa Kemal Pasha, defied Western diplomacy, and was therefore envied by its former senior partner.[53] Muhittin Birgen (1885–1959), one of Talaat's former counselors and journalistic mouthpieces, wrote in the 1930s, "If Talaat, who died as a Turk, would today again wake up and see Turkey, he would not be sad at all that he had died already at a young age!" For him, Talaat had accomplished the all-decisive conversion from an Ottoman to a modern Turk-ish and Muslim identity, the precondition for a restored Turk-ish sovereignty.[54]

"The people are the garden, we are its gardener"

Talaat became grave when Ludwig asked him, during a third visit on 18 August 1915, if the persecution of the Armenians would not damage the economy. He answered, "Yes, a bit. But we will rapidly replace the empty spots with Turks." Then he talked of proof of a general conspiracy. "We are not cruel, only energetic."[55] (As ever, they conversed in French, the global language of education, culture, and diplomacy in the early twentieth century, and also in the late Ottoman world.) In fact, Asia Minor had by this point largely lost its most educated, industrious, and agriculturally productive population. "The people are the garden, we are its gardener," Gökalp had stated before the war. In retrospect, Midhat Şükrü justified the extermination by what he called the contagious mental illness of the Armenians. Others, such as military doctor Mehmed Reşid, the governor of Diyarbekir and Talaat's direct subordinate, compared the Armenians to bandits and microbes to be eliminated.[56]

Talaat promoted radicals and corrupt subordinates, and transferred or demoted those in his administration who dared to help the persecuted people or who refused his orders. Though relying on these subordinates to promote his policies, he cultivated for himself the image of an incorruptible patriot. In contrast, several governors, notables, and Muslim leaders preserved their humanity, and a few therefore lost their lives. But all in all, they were a small minority.[57] Within the Central Committee, Talaat allowed the extremist members to have the upper hand, notably, the military doctors Selanikli Nâzım and Bahaeddin Şakir. When Mehmed Cavid, his close companion for a decade, came back to Istanbul in August 1915 after several months in Europe, he was deeply appalled by the "monstrous murder and enormous dimension of brutality that Ottoman history had never known

FIGURE 1: Not yet grand vizier, but boss in party and government, Talaat
in late summer 1915, with Alfred Nossig and Halil and Enver Pasha (from
Alfred Nossig, *Die Türkei und ihre Führer* [Halle: Otto Hendel, 1916]).

before, even in its darkest periods. . . . You managed to destroy
not only the political existence but the life itself of a whole
[Armenian] people," he silently accused the committee—in
his diary.[58] Beyond this confession, Cavid was not able to react
against the dominance of his political friend and, also, did not
know all the facts, because Talaat communicated discreetly,
being the soul and architect of the whole scheme.

The foolhardy removal of the Armenians, allegedly for the
benefit of "the nation," strengthened Talaat's position and
prestige. Henceforth, he was deemed the savior of the fatherland, the "man of the future," even a prophet. "You are Noah /
You, if you were not, this nation would be orphaned," Gökalp
rhapsodized in the CUP newspaper *Tanin* on 14 September
1915. Churchill, by contrast, had failed miserably, forcing the
Dardanelles to take Istanbul, and resigned from the Admiralty

(the leadership of the Royal Navy). "There is more blood than paint on these hands . . . All those thousands of men killed. We thought it would be a little job and so it might have been if it had been done the right way," he said mid-August 1915, while painting, to a friend who feared that "Churchill might go mad" after his catastrophic failure.[59]

The political elite in Berlin, the German press, and a large segment of the public—from majoritarian socialists to liberals and the militaries—also took Talaat for a respectable, if not admirable, leader, but in any case, "the most interesting and most important statesman of Turkey." From 1915 onward, panegyrics about him appeared in the German press. But when Ludwig visited Talaat several times in early 1916, even before returning to Europe, his faith in beneficial cooperation between both countries had faded, although his reports still repeated set propagandistic phrases. After one year under Talaat's reign, Ludwig was alienated. He found the foundations of state and society "totally different" in both countries. He warned readers to "beware of unrealizable expectations that would contradict why we help a [Turkish] nation to recover power, so that Turkey becomes the master in its own house."[60] In summer 1918 only, the chancellor let Cavid and Talaat know that, as minister of finances Cavid relates, he was "saddened to see that the money which Germany had given us [Turks] was used to annihilate Christians; [and that] this was part of the actual problems" between both governments.[61]

Faced with Talaat's charm, many Germans revealed schizophrenic attitudes that went hand in hand with a specific Wilhelminian orientalism and, in consequence, a form of moral defeatism. Count Johann Heinrich Bernstorff, German ambassador in Istanbul from 1917 and, seemingly, an upright liberal—afterward a member of parliament in the Weimar Republic for the German Democratic Party—is a case in point. An exile in Switzerland, in 1936 he published his memoirs, which offer important insights and edifying remarks but lack analytical penetration and honesty. He contended that "a dainty blend of skepticism and slight cynism increased the charm of this [Talaat's] appealing personality" of "full integrity" and that he "learned to venerate and love" Talaat. Yet, in the same paragraph, he emphasized Talaat's complicity in "the Turkish sin" (Bernstorff's term for the crime against the Armenians) and quoted him as saying, when he had asked him about the Armenians, "What do you want? The question is finished. There are no more Armenians." Contemporary correspondence shows that Ambassador Bernstorff did not distinguish between facts and propagandistic lies, thus blaming victims with easily assimilated sterotypes—an aspect largely concealed in his memoirs.[62]

"Revolutionist Statesmanship," Imperially Biased: A Prototype

Historically, it is time to understand coherencies and to be clear about evidence. Talaat must be considered a true pioneer. He instigated the first single-party experience in the twentieth century and imperial *komitecilik* (politics by a revolutionist committee heading an empire). He spearheaded violent demographic engineering commensurate with radical ethnic nationalism and knew how to use jihad to this effect. He went decidedly further than politically ambitious young men of the Balkans in the late nineteenth and early twentieth centuries who were haunted and informed by Bulgarian and "Serbian ghosts."[63] Overall histories of World War I remain Eurocentric as long as they do not integrate the dynamics of the Ottoman

FIGURE 2: Talaat at the height of his power in his hotel in Brest-Litovsk, early 1918 (Wienbibliothek im Rathaus, Tagblattarchiv).

1910s, when the international hub of Istanbul was a proactive mirror of issues, ideas, and political patterns that would dominate in larger Europe.

Talaat's political biography suggests that he understood genocide as a highly asymmetrical form of total war at home, one that "compensated" for international weakness.[64] An important background to his cataclysmic and demolitionist policy was the loss of Ottoman territory, power, and sovereignty, which had been almost continuous since the late eighteenth century. The diminution of the empire's reach resulted in hundreds of thousands of *muhacir*—Muslim refugees and migrants—mostly from the Balkans and the Caucasus, who had experienced persecution or been subjected to non-Muslim, primarily Russian, rule. Defeat and loss in the Balkan Wars inflicted by former Ottoman subjects in 1912–13 had an immediate toxic impact on Ottoman political circles. The "sons of conquerors" (Evlad-ı Fatihan) reacted with aggressive propaganda of victimhood and revenge blended with conspiracy theories.

Ottoman society since the late medieval era had been poly-ethnic and multicultural, although the state itself—its officials and leaders—had been Sunni Muslim since the sixteenth century. Christians and Jews had enjoyed autonomy, wherever they lived in the empire, in civil, cultural, and educational affairs, including family law, but had little say in the affairs of the state. In the modern era, the hierarchical Ottoman fabric underwent a deep crisis when faced with Western ideas of equality and nationalism. The Ottoman reformers introduced the principle of egalitarian Ottoman plurality in the mid-nineteenth century, at a time when there was still slavery in the United States and Europeans governed, very unequally, their home countries and their colonies. When faced with nationalist separatism and final loss on the Balkans, however, the constitutional principle of egalitarian pluralism appeared to be utopian, even to some of its initial supporters.

In its place, Talaat chose homogeneous Turkish-Muslim "unity" without Christians in order to secure Turkish-Muslim sovereignty and to save the core of imperial rule. Thus, he failed to uphold, or willingly renounced, the principles of the 1908 constitution, the basis of a modern social contract, in order to turn Asia Minor into a national home of Muslim Turks by means of coercion and mass violence. The CUP's successors were able to pursue this minimal goal successfully, even after defeat in World War I, thanks to the apogee of Talaat's policy: the destruction of Asia Minor's Armenians in 1915–16 and its posthumous completion in the mandatory population exchange of the 1923 Lausanne Treaty. International diplomacy, then, sanctioned both the previous expulsions of Ottoman Greek Orthodox Christians (Rûm) and, implicity, the genocide of 1915–16. It endorsed Talaat.

Against this backgound, Talaat might be called a radical nationalist and an imperially biased revolutionist, and his policy during World War I a paradigmatic precursor to even more radicalized policies of this type in Central Europe in the years to come. It is not the use of force and its partly rational finality that distinguishes this type of extreme violence from the violence in Europe's colonizing enterprise since the sixteenth century. What marks the distinction is the inclusion of an elusive imperial mythology that its perpetrators pursued in what they considered a Darwinian total war–jihad with the exterior *and* the interior of their state and society. The largely resentful character of their violence stemmed from accumulated feelings of victimhood and compensating myths of ethnoreligious superiority. These myths were reembedded in Islamism and the new "Turkism" (Turkish nationalism), including pan-Turkism, of the early twentieth century, which Gökalp spread most seminally.

Once he became a more visible dictator in 1917, Talaat's appearance, in uniform or not, was comparatively restrained. A carefully managed public image presenting a prophet-like, popular, but ingenious leader, surrounded by other gifted CUP individuals, now joined what had formerly been the dominant institutional cult of the Central Committee. (Traditional scholarship generally emphasizes only this institutional cult of the pre-1912 era.) But there was no personality cult around Talaat comparable to that of the European dictators who followed him. Nevertheless, in the historical area of larger Europe, Talaat opens the age of extremes and the Europe of the dictators.[65] That many people described him as an engaging and approachable person, even as an outstanding statesman of his time, is a telling indicator of the zeitgeist. To approach Talaat successfully, a study must go beyond narratives of identification (by nationalists, Islamists, contemporary Germans, or anti-Western anti-imperialists) and avoid misidentification.

Contemporaries Churchill and Talaat were well acquainted with each other. Both were ambitiously dedicated to empires that were to last only a few years in one and a few decades in the other. Imperial bias is a crucial factor and feature of the cataclysmic decade studied here, and it applied to Ottoman, German, French, Russian, and British politics. Nevertheless, Britain still stood for a liberal worldview and individual rights, while Talaat's Turkey pioneered patterns of a new age of extremes that erased individuality. Talaat and illiberal leaders after him acted in the name of an all-encompassing, abstract victimhood of their "people," "nation," "class," or, in the case of the CUP, "Islam."

After Talaat's fall, Lenin, Stalin, Mussolini, and Hitler led empires. All claimed to be backed by domestic majorities—"the people," "the working class"—and to fight ruthless exploitation by foreign political, economical, and military powers that they saw allied to or in sympathy with domestic agents. In this way they justified systematic persecution of ostracized domestic groups. Ostracism happens in concrete, although deep-rooted, contexts: Hitler became an almost total Jew-hater after World War I, Talaat a foremost political Armenian-hater after the First Balkan War. Exploitation of an industrial proletariat, victimhood of Caucasian and ex-Ottoman Muslims, and pervasive post–World War I misery in Germany and Italy were not only rhetorical but real. "Saviors" answered these realities, using stigmatized scapegoats to give easy explanations for the problems in society and to concentrate power rapidly and ruthlessly.

The Ottoman revolutionists born in the European belle epoque did not long seek a modern consensual social contract. For them, ideology, loyalty, and the logics of a conspirational committee prevailed over law and rationality in domestic administration. This attitude, combined with war and genocide, led to a pervasive rupture in the Ottoman world. Atatürk's "revolution" of the 1920s did not make a break from, but built on, the demolitionist groundwork of its predecessors. We might therefore understand party leader and minister Talaat as a prototypical revolutionist for the post-Ottoman world: a partisan statesman whose legacy is traceable not only in Turkey but also, for example, in Iraq's and Syria's Baath Parties. The challenging gap—from a committee-led empire to functioning democratic states that abstain from claims to any supremacy of religious or ethnic groups—is still not bridged.

Bridging a Post-Ottoman Century

Hamid Kapancızâde, a high functionary who had worked in the Ministry of the Interior when it was headed by Talaat, noted: "The affair [i.e., the administration] finally derailed, the grip was lost and the country faced ruin. I witnessed the Pasha [Grand Vizier Talaat, 1917–18] screaming once in despair and helplessness, but these tears did not touch me, because several times he had preferred the hypocrisy and adulation of the [party] men to my vigorous complaints and warnings. The road that he pursued could not produce another outcome." His rule "had preferred war to the life of the nation."[66]

The Kemalists believed that Atatürk discarded the short-comings of Talaat and the CUP. Yet Kemal Atatürk largely endorsed Talaat as his predecessor, not only de facto but also in his approving correspondence with him in 1919–20, when Talaat led Turkey's anti-Entente agitation in Europe from his asylum in Berlin (see chap. 6). Atatürk therefore followed the former legacy and obeyed its logic to a considerable extent and relied on Talaat's staff—although not on Hamid, an early dissident, but on young governors and devoted party members from Talaat's "team." This group accomplished a quite seamless transition of power from Istanbul to Ankara, thus perpetuating patterns, practices, and principles of governance across the country and across generations.[67] Even if Kemalist breaks of the 1920s (foremost, the adoption of a modern Western civil code, the break with sharia, and the refusal of political Islam) remain important, the Republic of Turkey was largely founded on Talaat's groundwork and Gökalp's ideas.

Kemalist Ankara abandoned the CUP's imperial alliance with and dependence on Germany. Mustafa Kemal Pasha, the later Atatürk, claimed distance from the CUP's Islamism and cultural and political Muslim identity. The same is true for Ottoman imperial language. Talaat had mastered this largely artificial imperial idiom that was used in the administration, thanks to a long post-1908 apprenticeship in the parliament and the Ministry of the Interior. Evolved at the court and used in the official correspondence, this language mirrored the imperial hierarchy and effaced individual agency by frequent use of the passive voice. All in all, it emphasized a mighty autocratic state and its sovereign. This understanding did not fundamentally change, either with the factual disempowerment of the sultan in 1909 or with the abolition of the sultanate-caliphate in 1922 and 1924. Kemal Atatürk's fundamental texts of the 1920s are still composed in imperial Ottoman language, and not in his "purified" republican Turkish or Öz Türkçe, which was otherwise problematic, because of his underlying belief in Turkish origins of human language and civilization.

Although there are no easy, direct lines, this biography intends to clarify the critical historical background of today's cataclysms in the Levant. The term "Ottoman cataclysm" is used to lend a novel approach to the last Ottoman decade and to place this era and its actors more firmly in the center, instead of the periphery, of a history of larger Europe. This study analyzes the Ottoman Empire's last dominant actor, his seminal alignments, and the centrality of the hub Istanbul, the Ottoman capital, in the catastrophe of larger Europe (or the "Old World," as seen from overseas). It emphasizes seminal Ottoman developments that, though little noticed, codetermined the last years of Europe's belle epoque. The historical perspective changes considerably if World War I is investigated from the viewpoint of Istanbul and its policy options, which the radical top actors there could embrace. Contemporary Germans knew well that the Ottoman capital was "a hot spot of European policy" and that "any shift of the European balance of power there influenced the relationship of the Great powers."[68]

This study delves into relevant historical context, insofar as it elucidates main points and strands of Talaat's biography, and into plots and factions, as far as they play a role in the larger context, leaving aside encyclopedic data, anecdotes, or epic analyses of internal CUP matters. It privileges the last and least-explored decade of Talaat and the CUP, starting in 1912, in which

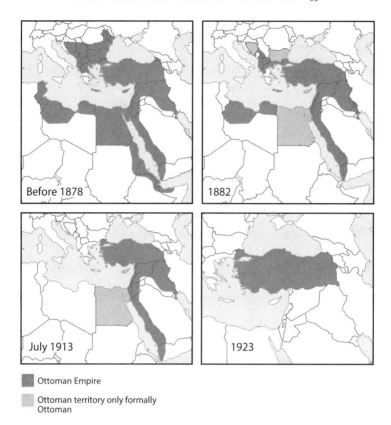

Ottoman Empire

Ottoman territory only formally
Ottoman

MAP 1: The Ottoman Empire before 1878; after 1878; 1913–14 (Egypt was
administered by Great Britain from 1878, but it was still Ottoman before
November 1914; Libya was invaded by Italy in 1911); 1923 (in 1939, the region
of Antakya and Alexandretta in Northwestern Syria was added to Turkey).

he emerged as the leader of the CUP after he had retrieved
the party from its nadir on the eve of the Balkan Wars.[69] He
emerged as a demolitionist builder of a "new Turkey" on shaky
ground, and destruction and extermination, with Talaat at the
helm, are given their due place in this volume. The documents
that Talaat left behind, including his memoirs, leave no doubt
that for the CUP's signature "political animal," the destruction

of the Armenians was crucial. Penetrating knowledge of "the brain and soul behind the persecution of Armenians" (in the words of German ambassador Paul Wolff-Metternich) is a must in terms of unmasking the truth concerning this genocide. War was Talaat's matrix. He and his political friends had embraced it as a main apparatus of their politics from autumn 1912.

It is time to ponder and understand Talaat's entire political biography, including its afterlife, and to overcome a hitherto fractionated and insufficient analysis of CUP rule in the 1910s. It is time to conceive of the 1910s and World War I beyond Eurocentric terms, bringing the Ottoman cataclysm into the framework of a larger Europe. We must see why generations of diplomats had come to believe that the 1923 Near East Treaty of Lausanne had solved the late Ottoman questions, although, endorsing Talaat's legacy, it evidently failed to do so in a constructive way. Concluded by European victors of World War I and Turkish victors of the war for Asia Minor, not by all main groups involved, the Peace of Lausanne endorsed authoritarian rule and the "unmixing of population" according to religion. It seemed to have opened a new chapter for the post-Ottoman world, but instead it perpetuated patterns and principles of Talaat's governance, even making them part of an attractive paradigm for law-breaking radical "solutions" far beyond Turkey.

2

Patriotic Rebellion and Networking against Sultan Abdulhamid II

MANY THINGS MADE Talaat revolt against the situation in which he was born in Edirne in 1874, in a shrinking European Turkey, as did many later CUP members and Kemalists—a politicized male generation born in the late nineteenth century, the European fin de siècle (permeated by the feeling of the near end of an age and civilization). This group was contrived of nearly all young Muslim state employees who were homeless and restless—due to the loss of Ottoman Macedonia in 1913 and the state's decay—and who sought new foundations in an insecure future. Many had lost their fathers early, both physically and symbolically. The revolutionary members (*komiteci*) of irredentist Bulgarian, Serbian, and Greek committees in Macedonia impressed them by their patriotism and their intrepid activism. The young post-Ottoman nation-states, Bulgaria in particular, displayed self-confidence and offered an enviable political model.

The Young Turks, as the Ottoman oppositional party members were called in a broad sense, could not identify with Sultan-Caliph Abdulhamid II. They were negatively fixated on him and despised Hamidism, Abdulhamid's system of government, and his unassertive, artful attitude vis-à-vis Europe. For them, he was a despot, bigot, coward, and, above all, incapable of restoring Ottoman power and Ottoman pride. This was also true for the rebellious youths in Diyarbekir, the eastern opposite of European Turkey, where Ziya Gökalp grew up. After 1909, Gökalp became the ideological master of CUP's Central Committee and Talaat's friend. In the early 1910s, Gökalp's gospel of Turan would give voice to a new patriotic ideal for a disoriented generation of imperial rebels. Before 1908, restoration of power and patriotic pride, along with modern constitutional rule, were the main goals of the opposition against Abdulhamid. Still far from ideological exaltation, it crystallized around the key terms of "liberty," "fatherland," and the "salvation" of the state.

When he was a teenager in Edirne, Talaat profoundly identified with patriotic discourse and subversion. Therefore, he was arrested and then exiled to Salonica, where he excelled as an underground networker. He acquired the identity of a Muslim komiteci who was ready to spill blood in order to save the empire from Hamidism. Before the Young Turk Revolution, he was leading among the founders of the Ottoman Freedom Society, whose significant original name was the (Islamic) Crescent Committee. Though a prominent and imposing committee member in Salonica, Talaat stood in the shadow of Dr. Bahaeddin Şakir's reorganization of the opposition in exile, the Committee of Progress and Union (CPU). Both committees merged in 1907. After the Young Turk Revolution in July 1908, they resurrected the old name of the Committee of Union and Progress (CUP).

Well before Russia, Italy, and Germany, the Ottoman Empire was at the forefront of a radical revolution that led in the interwar period to a "Turkish version of totalitarianism."[1] It was initiated in the early twentieth century by actors in opposition to—then at the reins of—the state. Talaat was the principal actor in this case. He started in the decade before 1908, reached the height of his career during World War I, and fell politically with the Ottoman defeat, after which Mustafa Kemal (Atatürk) took the lead in a Turkey reduced to Asia Minor plus Edirne. Talaat's subversive organization in the months before July 1908 was most successful in the three provinces of Salonica, Manastir, and Kosovo, monitored by the European powers, because international monitoring impaired the otherwise efficient Hamidian repression active in other provinces of Ottoman Europe.

The conspirators needed European presence and sympathy in order to win the infighting against the sultan. Their liberal messages to Europe and the Ottoman non-Muslims largely lacked rootedness and sincerity. Even worse, during the congress of Ottoman opposition parties in late December 1907, Prince Sabahaddin, the main and truly liberal voice in the Young Turk movement, felt compelled to state that "we always refuse interference by foreign states in our interior affairs but prove incapable of implementing reform without foreign interference. Only as long as we shied away from the foreign powers could we protect the Christians living among us. If we had not feared the foreign states, we would have massacred all Christians, in particular, the Armenians."[2]

From Edirne in European Turkey, 1870s

Since the late eighteenth century, the Ottoman Empire had lived a precarious existence.[3] At several points, contemporaries had good reason to believe in its imminent end. The expanding Russian Empire in particular was, and remained, a tremendous adversary. Those involved in European diplomacy referred to the open issue of the Ottoman future as "the Eastern Question." The rise of this complex question paralleled the Western march into modernity and the exploitation of the globe. Since diplomacy could not develop a convincing, comprehensive answer, until World War I the European powers preferred the status quo, along with demands for Ottoman reform. In the Ottoman Balkans (European Turkey), where a majority of Christian lived, they generally backed secession, beginning with Greece in the 1820s.

The empire was a premodern monarchy with a strictly patrilinear, polygamous dynasty in which the sultans' concubines were slaves. Until the seventeenth century, it allowed the killing of brothers or half brothers who did not succeed to their own enthronement, as demanded by reasons of state. Just as any empire, the sultan's empire was based on conquest. In early times (fourteenth century), it also expanded, partly peacefully, with a syncretist (Bektashi) integration of Christian territory from Byzantium. This was notably true in the Balkans in the period before and after Adrianople was made the Ottoman capital (1363–1453) and renamed Edirne. From the sixteenth century, the sultanate opted for Sunni Islam in the state apparatus. Henceforth, religious hierarchy determined politics and the state, and largely excluded non-Sunnis.

At the same time, Christians and Jews, although subordinate, enjoyed a high degree of autonomy as self-organized communities (*millet*, or "nations"), which made the Ottoman realm appear attractive at times for persecuted religious minorities from premodern Europe. From the early eighteenth to the mid-nineteenth century, the Phanariotes, the Rûm from Istanbul, held important positions in the administration yet remained at home in a premodern salvation-historical framework, that is, to serve Ottomans, "under whom God has subjected us for our sins." Stephanos Vogorides (1780–1859), a late representative of similar conservative Christian service for Ottoman unity and dynasty, for instance, took "refuge in the shariᵓa" and the protective "privileges bestowed upon us [oriental Christians] by the shariᵓa," as he wrote at the end of his life.[4] In contrast to the contemporary multiethnic empires of Austria and Russia, the Ottoman state remained founded upon a specific monotheism that excluded equality. Despite the Young Turk Revolution of 1908, this deep-seated feature continued to pervade—and make particularly trenchant—what this book calls the CUP's and Talaat's "imperial bias."

In contrast to Russia and Austria, modern conscription since Tanzimat (Reorganization/Reform) still excluded non-Muslims; from 1909 only, they were principally integrated into the army (and not only exceptionally, e.g., in the navy or medical services).[5] In the nineteenth century, considerable exclusion from global dynamics and ongoing inequality on religious grounds made the Ottoman political condition increasingly unsustainable and nonviable. The sultan and some of the Ottoman elites advocated incisive reforms to prevent collapse after Russian conquests and Napoleon Bonaparte's invasion of the Levant in the late eighteenth century. Muslim refusal of equality seminally merged with a feeling of Muslim and Ottoman geopolitical victimhood. Strong arguments for this feeling, and for resentments against Ottoman non-Muslims, were the Ottoman Capitulations, agreements that originated in the flourishing sixteenth century that gave foreigners privileges in terms of taxes and legal prosecution. From the nineteenth century onward, a considerable number of Ottoman non-Muslims acquired European nationality, thus enjoying these privileges and a better scope of action than fellow Muslims.

Urged by Europe, foremost Britain, the egalitarian reforms of the Tanzimat period (1839–76) largely remained a matter of paperwork, although many Christians, particularly Armenians, gained access to employment by the state. All in all, the combination of a strong Ottoman diversity, including institutionalized millet, with constitutional equality, remained an unachieved utopia, even when the first Ottoman constitution was proclaimed in 1876. Sultan Abdulhamid (r. 1876–1909) suspended the constitution by 1878. He had consented to the introduction of a constitution in order to dispel diplomatic pressures.

In Ottoman and European history, the 1870s were a watershed that introduced loss of faith in universal, supra-ethnoreligious categories of the modern era, hence the rise of ethnic nationalism, Islamism, anti-Semitism, social Darwinism, and the category of race in general. Wars on the Balkans and in the Caucasus, loss of territory, state bankruptcy, famine, and European intervention shook the Ottoman Empire. Misrule and brutality in the Balkans increased diplomatic pressure. During the humiliating Russo-Turkish War of 1877–78, Russian troops advanced almost as far as the Ottoman capital, Istanbul. Hundreds of thousands of muhacir arrived. "Those who have watched the proceedings of the Russians can scarcely doubt that their deliberate object has been to drive the Turkish race out of the provinces they have occupied, and to replace it by the Slav," the British ambassador in Istanbul, Austen Henry Layard, reported.[6]

The Congress of Berlin of 1878 nullified a part of the Russian conquest. Still, the Ottoman Empire had to acquiesce to its loss of important parts of the Balkans to independence (Serbia, Montenegro), autonomy (Bulgaria), or foreign administration (Bosnia-Herzegovina). It lost entirely the provinces of Batumi, Kars, and Ardahan in Southwestern Caucasia. It also warranted full freedom of religion and consented "to carry out without further delay the ameliorations and reforms which are called for by local needs in the provinces inhabited by Armenians, and to guarantee their security against the Circassians and the Kurds" (Art. 61–62). These stipulations were very vague in comparison to those concerning European Turkey.

The 1876 constitution represented the culmination of the Tanzimat. The suspension of the constitution marked the turn to Abdulhamid's authoritarian rule and to an Islamist reorientation of the shrunken empire. If Abdulhamid artfully obstructed reform demands and "permitted" temporary massacres, he did this largely out of the well-founded fear that he risked, at any moment, facing a failed, openly chaotic state. He avoided the risk by co-opting regional forces and conniving with their antiegalitarian—and at times pogromist—attitude. Instead of the Sublime Porte and the magnificent Dolmabahçe Palace, the young sultan made the shielded, secluded Yıldız Palace in Beşiktaş the new power center of the empire, where he alone was to rule.

Talaat was born in 1874 in a middle-class family in Edirne. His father, Ahmed Vasıf, came from a village in the southeastern corner of present-day Bulgaria, lost to Bulgaria in 1878. Vasıf was a *kadı* (religious judge) and thus a state employee of the religious administration subordinate to the sheykhulislam. Talaat, his parents, and his two sisters fled in 1877 before the advancing Russian army from Edirne to Istanbul and turned back after a year.

In Edirne, Talaat went to school until the military secondary school (*askerî rüşdiyesi*), that is, until the age of about sixteen. He left without a certificate because he assaulted one of his teachers, an army officer, and was therefore expelled. His father had died when Talaat was eleven, leaving his family in a difficult situation materially, with Talaat the only male of the family. As an assistant helper in the post office from 1891, and a Turkish teacher in the Alliance Israélite School, he contributed to the breadwinning of the family. At the same school, he learned French.[7] He also learned Greek, first in prison, where he met with Bulgarian and Greek militants, and later from his wife, Hayriye Hanım, who was from Ioannina (Yanya). He may have acquired some knowledge of Bulgarian and Judeo-Spanish as well.[8]

Exiled to Salonica

The teenaged Talaat was deeply impressed by revolutionary, patriotic discourses against Abdulhamid, which he heard from his brother-in-law İsmail Yürükoğlu (or Yürükov), a Turkish- and Bulgarian-speaking journalist-activist who had access to literature that was labeled and taxed as subversive by the palace. An autonomous, conspiratorial group of mostly low-ranking civil and military officers formed around İsmail Yürükoğlu and the Albanian *hoca* (religious teacher) Hâfız İbrahim Efendi in Edirne, among which CUP literature circulated. The police became aware of this circle in summer 1896 and destroyed it. Talaat, an active member, was among the arrested members. In contrast to oppositional graduates of superior schools, they were not exiled to Ottoman Libya but rather imprisoned after a special trial.

In 1889, five students of the Military School of Medicine founded the Committee of Ottoman Union, which soon took the name of the Committee of Union and Progress (CUP; İttihad ve Terakki Cemiyeti) and which had a rapidly growing membership. Even though this committee remained weak in organizational terms, and its members were entirely unexperienced, it soon became a compelling myth, especially for rebellious male youth in state schools of higher education. By the mid-1890s, Abdulhamid felt compelled to repress the movement, and many of its members and sympathizers fled abroad to Switzerland or France.

The early CUP members possessed a strong vision of "a great despotic Satan" and of domestic evil, which needed to be fought in a bloody revolution. At this stage, the hate and resentment were almost entirely directed against the palace and against Hamidian representatives, favorites and spies throughout the country. "We have declared war on those who harass the fatherland from within, and we are sure that we will win. We call to account those who ruin our country, exploit our villages, and cause our enemies to insult our religion and our nation," exclaimed Dr. Mehmed Reşid, one of the founders, who was then also imprisoned in 1897. "The Ottoman element is shrinking. Ottoman land is disappearing piece by piece. Of this, we are witnesses, and we know who the culprits are. In order to make all this evil disappear, in order to rescue our working village dwellers and feed them well, we have declared war on these libertines, these tyrants, these enemies of the fatherland."[9]

Talaat shared this basic feeling of hurt, which evolved into an aggressive stance. He was set free in February 1898 and was then exiled to Salonica. The municipality paid him a salary without duty before he became a postman in July 1898, and, finally, in April 1903, he was promoted to head clerk at the post office directorate. He brought his mother and sisters to Salonica, and they lived together in a small house in the mainly Muslim urban district of Kule Kahveleri.[10] Before its conquest by Greece in 1912, late Ottoman Salonica was a vibrant port city of the empire and the place of an important garrison with about 100,000 inhabitants. Direct railways connected it with Istanbul,

Belgrade, and Vienna, but not yet to Athens in the south. The largest population group of this polyethnic and multilingual city was Sephardic Jews, who constituted half or even more of its inhabitants.[11]

In Salonica, Talaat resumed meeting with subversive contacts and having discussions, dreaming of revolution. Via İsmail Yürükoğlu, in 1901 he began to correspond with Ahmed Rıza, the head of the opposition in exile in Paris. Asked about the establishment of a new and strong subversive network in European Turkey, Talaat gave Rıza a blunt answer in April 1902: "Forget about a strong one today; it would be inconceivable even to establish a weak branch that would operate smoothly." He mentioned İsmail Yürükov, his brother-in-law, as a potential activist. Ironically, this man appears in a 1905 Yıldız Palace document as an agent of the government, as was the case with many early activists turned palace collaborators. We do not know if Talaat became aware of this before the 1908 revolution, when the lists of spies were discovered and used by the CUP as a political means against adversaries.[12]

Talaat amended his rudimentary school education, taking courses during three years at the Salonica Law School. There he met the teacher of economics Mehmed Cavid, who was a year younger than he was. Cavid was a Dönme, that is, outwardly entirely a Sunni Muslim but nevertheless seen as a "crypto-Jew" of the Sabbatean tradition.[13] The group forming around Talaat often met in the Yonyo bar beside the wharf in Salonica and also, at times, in the public park Jardin de Bechtchinar (Beş Çınar Bahçesi). Furthermore, Talaat became a member of the Salonica Freemason lodge Macedonia Risorta in 1903, as did other Young Turk conspirators. He briefly had the idea of founding an "Islamic lodge" free from foreign influence. Masonic lodges, as well as Bektashi *tekke* (monasteries), were places where the men could speak freely without spies listening in.[14]

Toward the end of August 1903, Robert Graves, a young diplomat attached to the British Consulate in Salonica, received "a mysterious request that I would grant an interview to certain Turkish patriots who were in despair at the difficulties threatening their country, and wished to take my advice as to the course which they should pursue. After satisfying myself that this request was a genuine one, and not a trap to compromise me, I agreed to meet these people secretly." Talaat, Mustafa Rahmi (Arslan), Ahmed Cemal (future Pasha), Hacı Âdil, and the Dönme Cavid met with him. They were convinced "that the misrule of the Sultan Abdul Hamid had brought their beloved country to the verge of ruin" and "proposed to put themselves at the head of a revolt against his authority, and asked me what I thought were their prospects of success in carrying the people with them and obtaining some measure of foreign countenance and support."[15]

When the would-be rebels frankly confessed that they lacked organized support in the army, the police, and the government, Graves advised them to abstain from an ill-timed revolt. The meeting took place during the Ilinden-Preobrazhenie Uprising of August–September 1903, which affected the dissidents in two ways: the army officers among them were involved in the brutal repression of the revolt and they were all impressed by the commitment and ideals of the members of the Internal Macedonian Revolutionary Organization (IMRO), their enemies. Mostly Bulgarian Christians, they fought for Macedonian autonomy.

This experience made them long for a "genuine revolution" and enraged them even more against Abdulhamid. What prevailed in the long term, however, and became a popular core element of CUP identity, was hurt Ottoman Muslim pride mixed with resentment against foreign diplomatic intervention. Diplomacy not only critically exposed Ottoman weakness and brutality but also restricted Ottoman sovereignty. The Mürzsteg Agreement of 2 October 1903, a joint Russian and Austrian memorandum, was a consequence of the Ilinden Uprising. Abdulhamid reluctantly accepted it on 25 November. It demanded internationally monitored reforms for better and more regionalist rule, to include the Christians more equally.

Conspiratory Organization in Salonica and Beyond

It took three years for the Salonica dissidents "to transform their scattered activities into an organized effort," as Şükrü Hanioğlu, a leading scholar of the Young Turks in opposition, has outlined.[16] Again, the international context played a role. At the end of 1905, Abdulhamid had been forced to accept international supervision of Macedonia's finances after the European powers had made a humiliating naval show near the island of Lemnos and Mytilene on the Aegean coast.[17]

On 7 September 1906, the patriotic dissidents founded the Crescent Committee (Hilâl Cemiyeti), the regulations of which gave only Muslims access to membership; even Dönme were excluded. Among the founders were several young army officers, including Lieutenant Ömer Naci; Talaat; Mustafa Rahmi, a member of a well-known Salonican family; and Dr. Midhat Şükrü (Bleda), Rahmi's brother-in-law, a graduate from the empire's school for civil servants (Mekteb-i Mülkiye) and the secretary-general of the CUP in the 1910s. In contrast to Ahmet Rıza's men in exile, from the beginning, the group in Salonica emphasized its ideological core of Muslim unity.

This was Talaat's environment, and this team was most effective in the 1908 revolution, finally paving the CUP's road to dictatorial power.

At a second meeting on 18 September 1906 in Midhat Şükrü's house, the organization's name was changed to the Ottoman Liberty Committee (Osmanlı Hürriyet Cemiyeti), and the membership restriction was annulled. Talaat, Rahmi, and the army officer Ismail Canbolad (Canbulat) were elected to the executive body of the committee. Because of his charm, intrepidness, and enduring commitment for the cause, Talaat enjoyed a natural authority and special status among most army officers in and around the committee. "Talaat was more courageous and more reckless than we all; he did not fear the world around him," Midhat Şükrü admitted.[18]

The young captain Mustafa Kemal, the future Atatürk, also played a minor role. As the founder of a four-man Fatherland and Freedom Society in Damascus in 1905, and eager to continue in Salonica, he helped catalyze the foundation of the Ottoman Freedom Society. Kemal must have known Talaat at least by name by early 1906. Secretly back for a few months in his hometown, Salonica, from what he called an exile in Damascus, he was eager to participate in subversive organization. He remained, however, at the margins and was excluded from leadership. Knowingly or not, he prepared other futures from which he was to succeed as the uncontested leader. In 1906, other officers in Macedonia were better positioned than he was. Among them were the adjutant-major Ismail Enver and Enver's uncle, Captain Halil (Kut), both of whom became early members of the new society.

Mustafa Kemal was radically opposed to any foreign influence. He profoundly admired Japan, which had defeated a Russian army in 1905. Many celebrated this military victory,

in Hanioğlu's words, "as the triumph of indigenous modernization" over a West whose might and superiority they deeply
resented. He was certainly not at ease with Islamist connota-
tions (as manifest in the society's initial name). Ömer Naci,
for instance, understood himself as "a soldier for the jihad" and
authored Islamist pamphlets, as did Bahaeddin Şakir and many
others. He also appeared as an early adept of an ethnonation,
and of radical demographic changes to achieve this goal, when
in 1907 he proposed "population changes" that would give "rise
to a Turkish state."[19]

The initiation of a new member to the nascent society was
an impressive secret ritual that combined symbols of komitecilik and Islam in order to inspire total commitment to the
conspiratorial group. Talaat and others officiated as masters of
ceremony. The ritual may have varied; we know, however, the
committee's internal regulations after September 1907. According to these regulations and several memoirs, the ritual bore
a resemblance to initation into a Masonic lodge and the mas-
querade of the Ku Klux Klan or today's "Islamic State." Wearing a red cloak, the candidate was led blindfolded into a room
at committee member Midhat Şükrü's house. The voice of a
masked master of ceremony preached the ideals of the society
to him, and that betrayal meant death. Then his blindfold was
removed and he saw the masked masters of ceremony, who
also wore red gowns.

With one hand touching a Koran and the other a pistol, the
candidate swore his oath of loyalty. Later, if a Christian or a
Jew, he swore on the Bible or the Torah. The password _hilâl_
(crescent) was to be used by the candidate before entering the
house and also, along with other words, when members had
to identify one another. Membership remained secret except
for the leading men. In the same quasi-religious vein, already

before July 1908, the committee in Salonica referred to itself as the "Sacred Committee" (Cemiyet-i mukaddese) and "Kaaba of Liberty" (Kâbe-i hürriyet).[20] The society rapidly won new members and opened a branch in the province of Manastir. Still, it was no supraregional, awe-inspiring revolutionary organization. Talaat likely sent a letter to Nâzım suggesting a fusion of the Ottoman Freedom Society and the Committee of Progress and Union (CPU, so-called temporarily before being renamed the CUP in 1908). Ömer Naci's flight to Paris in spring 1907, and his adherence to the CPU, contributed to a rapprochement. The CPU finally dispatched Nâzım to Salonica in summer 1907 to reach an agreement with the leaders of the Ottoman Freedom Society. Bahaeddin Şakir and Nâzım, both graduates from the Military School of Medicine, dominated the CPU in exile, which had emanated from the CUP of the 1890s. A disciple of the respectable authority Ahmed Rıza, Şakir had built up the new, more activist, and less intellectual CPU from autumn 1905 onward, after his escape from Istanbul.

Both committees merged under the name of CPU by 27 September 1907, with the external center being in Paris and the internal center in Salonica. Talaat, Major Ismail Enver (later Pasha), Captain Ismail Canbolad, Adjutant Major Hafız Hakkı (later Pasha), and barrister Manyasizâde Refik led the internal center. The CPU's common mouthpieces were Şûra-yı Ümmet (Council of the Ummah) in Turkish and Mechveret (consultation) Supplément Français in French.[21]

The merger was a political success for Talaat personally. Two months later, however, he lost his job and was sent to Anatolia. Hüseyin Hilmi Pasha, the Ottoman inspector general of European Turkey, based in Salonica, was more or less aware of Talaat's role, as was the palace. Later a minister of the interior and a grand vizier, Hüseyin Hilmi supervised the provinces of

Salonica, Kosovo, and Manastir. The leading man of the CPU's internal center, however, knew his power well. Thus, the representative of the palace could not implement the relocation after Talaat had demanded an interview, during which he threatened the Pasha with bad consequences. Midhat Şükrü offered his own post as a director of a private Salonician school (which was to take the name of CUP School after July 1908) to his jobless friend.[22]

Macedonia, the extreme west of Asia Minor, and the opposition in exile were overrepresented in the CPU. Anatolia, especially the eastern provinces, was scarcely included. Through a journey by Ömer Naci, member of the external CPU center, Talaat hoped that connections would be forged in Eastern Anatolia and with Armenians, and "henceforth the region there would also become [revolutionary] like Rumelia."[23] Even the Second Congress of Ottoman Opposition parties in Paris in late December 1907, when the CPU and the Armenian Revolutionary Federation (ARF) agreed to ally, did not change the reality that the CPU remained unrooted in the eastern provinces. Due to genuine trust between Prince Sabahaddin and Christians, the Sabahaddin's organization had much better connections there.[24]

Between the ARF and the CPU there was dissension on several issues right from the start. The ARF was and remained a junior partner, even if Dr. Nâzım and Dr. Şakir, the driving forces of activist reorganization, largely emulated structures of the ARF and the IMRO and also created branches of self-sacrificing volunteers (*fedai*). From autumn 1907, they organized Muslim bands in Macedonia to counter Christian guerillas, all in all largely relying on Muslim solidarity, including an alliance with Muslim Albanians. In letters they exalted successful violence and allegedly superior Turkish courage; in a letter dated 15 March 1908, the *Şûra-yı Ümmet* made clear that "we [Muslims] are the sovereigns of this land [Macedonia]."[25]

Talaat's Lead on the Road to the 1908 Revolution

Talaat was well rooted in the subversive Macedonian terrain and well connected with army officers. He knew how to build up solid power relations on crumbly late-Ottoman ground. He knew how the administration worked and how low-ranking and high-ranking officials behaved and reacted. Even if somewhat in the shadow of Nâzım, who did not return to Paris, Talaat was incontestably the engineer of conspiratorial organization in Macedonia and its informal leader, active correspondent, and networker. In risky situations he proved proactive, as in the case of a boyhood friend who recognized the disguised Nâzım in Salonica in summer 1907. He went to his friend's home, drew out a gun, and threatened to kill him if he told anybody about Nâzım.[26]

Talaat and those in and around the internal center worked hard and ambitiously in order to fulfill the expectations that the CPU set upon them with the merger. They succeeded in opening branches in many cities and towns of Macedonia and Albania. Talaat even ventured a trip to Istanbul to strengthen support in the capital.[27] "Our organization has reached a very satisfactory stage around Edirne," he wrote on 12 March 1908 to Paris. "We believe that within two months the organization in Rumelia [European Turkey] will be completed to our best expectation. . . . Definitively, we will soon launch one or two violent actions." In spring 1908, Talaat felt ready to hit hard.[28]

The general mood of the CPU was aggressive, if not martial, by spring 1908, due to growing observation, repression, and arrests by the security forces, as well as because of the international situation. Faced with multiple episodes of lawlessness in Macedonia, since late 1907 the European powers had pressed for a reform of the judiciary and the development of an international gendarmerie, together with the decrease of Ottoman security forces. This would result in a special status, possibly an autonomy, for Macedonia. For the hawks in Paris, this was tantamount to Armageddon, a question of being or not being Turks, to be determined by a final war. They wrote to Talaat on 16 March 1908: "Macedonia's independence means the loss of half of the Ottoman Empire and, therefore, its complete annihilation. . . . Since the Macedonian Question is the Question of the Existence of the Turks, we presume that for a sincere government, it should be preferable to take the chance of a great war instead of losing Macedonia, Rumelia. Alas! What can we expect from this filthy government?"[29]

Abdulhamid's downfall was that he lacked readiness for waging a war that would "kill forty or fifty thousand Europeans." Talaat was actually down to earth compared to the more excitable military doctors turned activists of subversion in Paris, who used feverish rhetoric. The CPU warned the Hamidian authorities that any concession to Europe with regard to reforms in Macedonia would trigger a revolution. Both CPU centers agreed on a memorandum to be presented to European diplomats in Macedonia in May 1908. This memorandum openly stated that the Committee of Union and Progress (this name was well known, in contrast to CPU) wanted to eliminate any foreign interference in its "holy national interests" in Macedonia and elsewhere. At the same time, it stressed a sincere commitment against despotism and for a constitutional government and equality; it made similar declamations tailored for European ears.[30] The CPU ably used—and misused—European references in its struggle against Abdulhamid.

An important trigger for concrete action was the meeting of the English king Edward VII and the Russian czar Nicholas II in Reval, Estonia, in June 1908. CPU people, Talaat in particular, and a broader Ottoman public were anxious that the Great powers might now divide European Turkey under the cover of reforms for solving the Macedonian Question.[31] Talaat then led a plot to assassinate Ömer Nâzım, the garrison commander of Salonica, a loyalist to the palace and the latter's efficient spy against CPU networks. Discussing the plan within a small circle, they agreed that Midhat Şükrü would contact Enver, Commander Nâzım's brother-in-law (whose wife was Enver's sister). Enver fully agreed that murder was called for and that he was ready to actively participate. In the name of the internal center Salonica, Talaat initiated a young *fedai* into assuming the job of a killer. The plot was achieved on 11 June 1908, during King Edward's visit in Reval.[32]

Though called to give account before the authorities in the capital in late June, Enver went to the mountainous region of Tikveš to begin preparing men for guerilla activity, as directed by the internal center. Although Nâzım was not killed, only injured, the bold assault in his private house terrorized the Hamidian establishment and triggered a series of violent actions, including successful assassinations of officials in Macedonia. The snowball effect was resounding, above all, among young officers, whereas high-ranking officers and notables had to remain passive or become accommodating if they wanted to be unharmed under imminent CPU domination. A threatening letter sent by the internal center secured the passive cooperation of Hayri Pasha, field marshal of the Third Imperial Army in Salonica.[33]

On 7 July 1908, a young CPU officer killed the reputed general Şemsi Pasha, whom Abdulhamid had sent to Manastir Vilayet in a forceful last attempt to suppress the revolt. After this shock for the Hamidian establishment, the CPU largely controlled military power in Macedonia—enough to risk an attack on the Ottoman capital and the palace by the end of July, if necessary. On 21 July, the center in Salonica ordered all its branches to prepare a military march to Istanbul if the palace did not reinstall the constitution by 23 July. It and its branches sent telegrams with this ultimatum to the inspector general, the grand vizier, and the palace.[34] Talaat, the impetus driving the actions, was not the full master of the rapidly escalating dynamics in its branches in Macedonia and Albania beginning in early summer 1908. Rebelling army officers, such as Niyazi and Enver, were publicly more visible.

Military might ultimately decided the power balance. The CPU settled on military action and elitist subversion, not popular uprising. Talaat became more populist only in 1912 (see chap. 4). As already touched on in relation to Captain Mustafa Kemal, a cohort of ambitious officers, striving graduates of the War Academy from around 1900, ached to be at the forefront of patriotic action. Nevertheless, in these decisive months before and after the Young Turk Revolution, Talaat, not officers, stood permanently at the political forefront. Since his early days of conspiracy in Edirne, he had learned and knew better than most others how to motivate and deploy young officers for his and the committee's cause.

As demanded, on 23 July the sultan declared the reinstatement of the constitution. The CPU, now renamed CUP, had achieved a splendid victory. Talaat was not only one of its master builders but also present in the metropolis of Salonica, where empire-wide enthusiasm was most manifest. The leaders in Salonica were now no longer merely the internal center but the core itself of the new Central Committee of the CUP. They demanded from the sultan the gift of a mansion at an excellent location in Salonica near Beyazkule. In high spirits, they relocated there by the end of July.[35]

A Salonican Jew wrote this retrospective:

> The delirious joy with which the news of the wresting of constitutional rights from the tyrannous Hamid had been received was unparalleled by any other show of feeling in the history of the country. Peoples yesterday so reserved, so sullenly suspicious of one another, nationalities who for centuries had been nurturing antagonisms and bitter hatreds, had suddenly given themselves up to such spontaneous demonstrations of mutual love and good will that the astounded Westerner who might have been present could not but have been mystified. Greeks, Bulgarians, Turks, Jews, Armenians, and Albanians had literally fallen in each other's arms and with tears of joy had embraced and called each other "Brother." . . . Daily, almost hourly, there were occasions for jubilant demonstrations and singing.[36]

Under the Shadow of Dr. Nâzım and Dr. Bahaeddin Şakir

Talaat, Nâzım, and Şakir were the masterminds of the Young Turk Revolution, all three rooted in the Balkans. Nâzım was four years older and Şakir was one year older than Talaat, and both were superior in terms of education, prestige, and international mobility. Thanks to their leadership in the opposition in exile, they enjoyed revolutionary prominence in many places.

Moreover, Şakir dominated CPU/CUP publication through *Şûra-yı Ümmet*, which he had led since fleeing to Paris. Therefore, we have to assume that these activist military doctors or *éminences grises* (as they were earlier described) had a strong, and at times commanding, influence on Talaat.[37] Even if the balance of power clearly turned in favor of Talaat in 1912–13, both political doctors remained influential in the Central Committee, notably for the anti-Armenian policy of 1915.

Talaat's dependence on others included ideology because neither he nor the CUP had a sound political philosophy. In 1910, however, Gökalp began to prevail as a leading intellectual of both the CUP and the broad movement of Turkism, and became a close and influential friend of Talaat's (see chap. 3). For Talaat, the committee was not only a place of activist power concentration but also of intellectual socialization. He mirrored as much as he managed the forces and discourses in and around the committee, and learned and acted through them.

Because of Talaat's dependence on others, a closer look at the éminences grises is appropriate. Both military doctors were elitist, overpoliticized, and, according to Hanioğlu's convincing analysis, representative of an early Turkism that proudly displayed Muslim identity. Like many politicized contemporaries of similar education in Western Europe, they believed in scientism and had strong ties to social Darwinism, but at the same time they dipped deeply into Islamist rhetoric.[38] Their political language was pamphletic, hyperbolic, inflammatory, Manichean, and repetitive. In a letter to Muslims in the Caucasus, Şakir wrote, "If the poor Muslim nation does not awake and care about its salvation, it will lose its reputation in this world and in the hereafter. Possession and nation, religion and state are perishing. . . . Hurry up, O Muslims, hurry up, heroes, sons of heroes; this is the day. Let us exalt the name of our nation, the glory of our fatherland. The whole world calls us anemic and ignorant. Let us shout out: We demonstrate the contrary to the whole world. We attack them all like roaring lions." In another letter to Muslims in the Caucasus in November 1906, Şakir called Armenians "infidels who are enemies of Islam."[39] The CPU leaders attached much importance to an activist Islamic union and organized ties with Muslims everywhere. Again, Şakir in particular saw "Ottoman greatness" to be a "starting point for the salvation of all Muslims." He believed in Turkish-led pan-Islamism, invoked again and again the specter of the annihilation of Muslim power by the West, and adapted the vocabulary of the Communist Manifesto, saying that "from now on all Muslims will unite and break the chain of slavery around their necks." Apart from references to Turkish leadership and Ottoman myths (again dominant in the ex-CUP-led Islamist International after defeat in World War I) (see chap. 6, sec. "Antiliberal International of Revolutionists"), in many places Şakir's resentful, apocalyptic rhetoric overlaps that of radical Islamists of the early twenty-first century, as is exemplified, for instance, in a pamphlet in July 1907: "In the name of God, the Most Merciful, the Most Compassionate! O Turkish sons! . . . [All] is in flames. . . . Come along, heroes! Let us make our [Muslim] nation prosperous by taking our revenge! God is the Speaker of the Truth."[40]

Since this book perceives the military doctors in question in the same manner as Talaat, that is, as imperially biased revolutionists, it is not surprising that they were socially conservative. They were scared of revolutionary new forms of rule, power sharing, social order, and gender relation, in particular, of futures beyond empire that would include regional autonomies. Prince Sabahaddin and his League of Private Initiative and Decentralization advocated such futures in a critically reformed empire.

They did this in consent with the ARF and other representatives of non-Muslim or non-Turkish groups. This was obvious during the Second Congress of Ottoman Opposition parties in Paris in December 1907.[41] Şakir considered Sabahaddin a traitor and "destroyer of the Ottoman power organization" that Ottoman Christians supported. He reproached him for suggesting the division of the Ottoman realm and the separation of government and caliphate, thus poisoning public opinion. The German Zionist Max Nordau was given a similar answer by Nâzım when inquiring about new perspectives shortly after the 1908 revolution: "Prince Sabahaddin is dead . . . ; his program of decentralization, of autonomous nationalities and provinces, abandoned. The Committee of Union and Progress wants centralization and a Turkish monopoly of power. . . . It wants a unified Turkish nation-state." In summer 1907, Nâzım had written to his friend Şakir that "the Turkish race proved the theory of the survival of the fittest because of its superior characteristics," from which its centuries-old rule originated.[42]

Sabahaddin's non-Muslim friends wanted constitutional rule because a constitutional framework would allow them to share as equals in political life. In contrast, even if they rebelled against and called Abdulhamid a despotic Satan, the CUP leaders felt, like him, attached to an imperial past, tradition, Islam, and—above all—restoration of state power. When asking the notorious late Ottoman question of "how to save the state," they asked in fact "how to save a ruling class of which we are part," thus translating *millet-i hâkime* (ruling nation), a notion of imperial Islam, into an elitist and right-wing weltanschauung. The reinstatement of the constitution and the parliament should first of all reempower the state in this sense. Thus, it was as a tactical alliance only that Nâzım and Şakir sought cooperation with Armenians. Their admiring and feverish emulation of non-Muslim revolutionary activism was mixed with envy, reluctance to share power, and ignorance of history and society in Asia Minor, in particular, Eastern Asia Minor. They originated from the Balkans, where Muslims had become a frustrated minority by the early twentieth century, and looked at other Ottoman issues through Macedonian lenses as proud Balkan Turks (Evlad-ı Fatihan).[43]

Both political doctors' foreign policy ideas, as expressed in the *Şûra-yı Ümmet* and personal correspondence, reflected their anti-Western anger, linked to their Turkish nationalist and pan-Islamist primary references. This anti-imperialism of men who wanted to ensure empire for themselves was directed foremost against Great Britain, Russia, and France, the three major powers in the Triple Entente of 1907. Whereas Talaat seemed to hold some true admiration for Armenian fellows as authentic revolutionaries and audacious operatives in the common opposition against Abdulhamid, they strongly resented the impertinence of non-Muslim "bandits" attacking an Islamic power, even if this power was headed by Abdulhamid, a common adversary. The CUP leaders in general, including Ahmed Rıza, resented European support for Armenian rights and demands—a major issue in Talaat's political life from 1913 onward—and wished for the abrogation of the relevant Article 61 in the Berlin Treaty of 1878.[44]

The CUP's pre-1908 foreign policy ideas shed important light on entrenched attitudes and contextualize and relativize several post-1908 statements and initiatives of CUP representatives toward Europe, especially its alleged Anglophilia. Anglophilia was, on the contrary, what the CUP opinion makers resented regarding Prince Sabahaddin and his group. Sabahaddin made no secret of his pro-British attitude because of his pluralist and federalist vision of the empire and his belief in modern individual responsibility and private initiative, regardless of religious and ethnic affiliation.

The supreme goal of both political doctors from Macedonia, Nâzım and Şakir, was to save a centuries-old empire, in particular, its territorial integrity in the Balkans as of 1878, along with the self-regard and benefits of being Ottoman Muslims. They already behaved as Turkish-Muslim supremacists in the years before 1908, proclaiming the Turks to be superior to all other Ottoman groups. To Ömer Naci, "a person with Turkish blood in his veins," Şakir wrote, "Neither the Armenian nor any other person could be the heir of the bravery left us by a glorious and honorable history of six hundred years."[45] The *Şûra-yı Ümmet* ridiculed Khachatur Malumian, the ARF negotiator at the 1907 Paris Congress, as a quixotic socialist cosmopolite who believed in humankind as one nation and in one home of humankind, the earth.[46]

There was a cleavage between the belief in a global socialist revolution of humanity—even despite its doctrinaire embrace of revolutionary violence—and the inflammatory, panicking, at times hysterical activism of political doctors who spoke for frustrated, anxious imperial elites. While preparing for the 1908 revolution, the latter were fed more by fear of loss and less by a constructive project of an Ottoman society that would offer new, egalitarian ground. A deeper analysis, nevertheless, reveals the connections between the revolutionary violence deemed salutary by believers in radically new social relations and the reactionary fears associated with pretensions of superiority. Even if more pragmatic and flexible than Nâzım and Şakir, and comparatively humble and open-minded before his critical encounter with Ziya Gökalp, Talaat clearly stood in the same current of thought and action.

3

A Komiteci and the Challenge of Parliamentarism (1908–11)

TALAAT ACHIEVED AN important position within the activist reorganization of the Young Turk movement. He was the main organizer of the Ottoman Freedom Society in 1906, which merged with the opposition in exile in September 1907, and therefore the informal head of a dynamic subversion in Macedonia, the main theater of the road to revolution. In July 1908, the activists chalked up a splendid success, imposing their will on Sultan Abdulhamid II. The outcome was, however, not the result of a democratic struggle that involved a larger public or civil society but of infighting in the army and blackmail against representatives of the Hamidian regime.

The method was komitecilik: Central Committee members acted through trusted networks of conspirators, all controlled by a highly disciplined "Holy Committee." They personifed Ittihadism (*ittihadcılık*),[1] that is, the will to reempower the empire and make it modern, centralist, and unitary. Ideologically, they used a mix of Turkism, Islamism, and social Darwinism. With such features, Ittihadists were right-wing revolutionaries even

61

before Gökalp, and obviously so after 1913, once they openly blended ethnoreligion with class struggle.

The Committee of Union and Progress was and remained the strongest political organization of the Young Turk movement from 1908 to 1918. By the end of 1909 it had 360 branches, more than 850,000 members, a majority in the parliament, and ministers in, and commanding influence upon, the government.[2] Many CUP members nurtured a quasi-religious devotion to the "Holy Committee." The members of the Central Committee, at most twenty,[3] perpetuated their pre-1908 secrecy and made the committee a black box for people from the outside, including for diplomats based in the Ottoman capital. Still, there was (already) the weight of personalities: Talaat, Nâzım, and Şakir were the masterminds of the Young Turk Revolution and its heirs in terms of power.

Yet the final and most imposing heir of the 1908 revolution would be Talaat. Within the CUP single-party regime after 1913, he won new scope, concentrating power for himself from the Central Committee, where he was a permanent member, and from the government, in which he became, in summer 1909, the first CUP minister besides the new minister of finances, Cavid. Still, in spring 1912, Central Committee member Mustafa Hayri, seventeen years Talaat's senior, described Talaat as an honest, easily deceivable, and "very naive boy," whom he trusted most among the committee members.[4] Other (marginalized) senior figures of the CUP had by then already experienced Talaat's "capacity" of saying things with a powerful smile but doing something different.[5] Although Hayri gave too rosy a character picture, it is true that in terms of age, education, and prestige, Talaat still stood considerably in the shadow of Şakir, Nâzım, Ahmed Rıza, and a number of other personalities in or outside the committee. Deputy, then minister, Talaat was not yet the decisive politician or the imposing master of the committee. Yet for serious observers, including Louis Rambert, the seasoned director of the Régie des Tabacs, an agency of the international administration of Ottoman debts, in October 1909 Talaat was already "the acknowledged head of the Committee of Union and Progress and the Young Turks."[6]

"No doubt, your patriotism makes you work day and night, and interfere everywhere, even in matters outside of your duty. But this is neither reasonable nor wise," Hayri advised Talaat in July 1912, in a particularly critical moment for the CUP, reflecting on the period since Talaat's first ministry.[7] Out-and-out a komiteci, the green, self-made politician attempted to succeed to the challenge of parliamentarism and a constitutional regime after 1908. He appeared to be, more than other CUP leaders, at the political forefront in parliament and government. He acquired important experiences as a minister of the interior in 1909–11, yet ambitious and expansive, he wanted to achieve too much by himself. For him and his ambitions, the parliamentary system imposed too many restrictions. In 1913, however, again minister of the interior and now a power broker in the vigorously burgeoning single-party dictatorship, he began to be at his best.

By 1910–11, Talaat had gone through a defining personal crisis at the same time that a general crisis hit the CUP, before its near dissolution in fall 1912. After the counterrevolution of April 1909, he had taken responsibility as a minister in an Ottoman capital that remained in a state of emergency. Once faced with populist Islamist rebellion, the young minister staggered and failed to maintain constitutional principles of equality, freedom of the press, and justice in the provincial administrations. The same is true with his handling of movements for autonomy in Albania and Yemen, and particularly of a daunting Hamidian heritage of unpunished crimes, increased by the April 1909 Adana massacres. In the eyes of Nâzım and Şakir, however, the young minister lacked determination in repressing demands for autonomy.

Whereas from the pre-1908 period Nâzım and Şakir's influence on Talaat seems to have prevailed, from late 1909, the new Central Committee friend Ziya Gökalp from Diyarbekir increasingly left his Turkist imprint upon receptive committee friends.[8] Although a pragmatist of the power organization, Talaat needed weltanschauung and fundamental references. Gökalp's ideas were more inspired, innovative, and vigorous than Şakir's vengeful pamphletism, although both obeyed Islamist, Turkist, state-centric, and, by default, empire-centric references. Though mostly vague, Gökalp's ideas suggested far-reaching revolutionary change in contrast to Hayri's focus on a reformed Islamic unity or to a pamphletism that lacked programmatic ideology.

Mainly originating from intracommittee dynamics, Talaat's unsettled political style prevailed when he abandoned hope for democracy after his troubled experiences with post-1908 parliamentarism. He would thereafter rule the imperial administration with an iron fist. He and his friends failed the constitution because, in crisis, their first desire was empire, that is, a restored state whose foundational myths remained untouched and was thus an imperial state dominated by Muslim Turks in the Ottoman tradition. They likely never faced the opportunity nor fully aspired to become familiar with the basics and benefits of egalitarian democracy. This study contends that Gökalp's custom of political thinking and his compelling rhetoric, combined with Talaat's komitecilik, would prove pioneering in the first half of the twentieth century. The stage was now set for a modern right-wing revolution in larger Europe and, with this, elites who were beset by both premodern imperial myths and modernist promises of radical nationalism.

The Ottoman Spring

Talaat's secret travel to Istanbul in spring 1908 had been frustrating, because his attempt to organize subversion there had failed. Everybody in the capital feared the palace and its police. When he came a second time, at the beginning of August 1908, along with Rahmi, Cavid, and Major Ahmed Cemal, they possessed power but still had to implement it. Otherwise, they would squander it to a sultan who was up to every trick in the book. In the first week after the proclamation of the constitution, Abdulhamid had succeeded in representing himself in the capital as a benevolent sovereign whom bad counselors had misinformed. Now he reinstalled "his constitution" of 1876 after solemnly declaring that times were ripe to do so. In the style of bad superiors, he put the entire blame for the flaws of his former regime upon his subordinates.[9]

"The fellow has become even more partisan of liberty than we," Talaat said of their encounter with the sultan. "He did not show any arrogance and haughtiness toward us. He behaved with us like the nearest friend; he even understated his position."[10] Under strong pressure from the CUP, the sultan had to retract his imperial decree of 1 August 1908, which claimed for himself the nomination of the most important ministers. He now had to take those whom the CUP accepted or proposed. "The old fox has become pliable like a glove," Louis Rambert, also a financial counselor of the sultan, noted in his diary. Echoing the mood of the Western colony in Istanbul, he added, "We must admit that hitherto the promoters of the [revolutionary] movement did not commit any mistake. We can be very hopeful for the future." He nevertheless also felt that "from the first days of the constitutional era, an instinctive, unintelligent nationalism hounded the foreign administrations," including the Dette Publique Ottomane (Ottoman Public Debt Administration) and the Régie des Tabacs. Propagandists of this nationalism accused these and other (partly) foreign institutions of "sucking the blood of the people for the profit of foreigners alone."[11]

Lacking competent politicians who would be able to fulfill the duty of ministers, the CUP could not exercise any direct influence on the government before the parliament was reinstalled. Hence, until spring 1909, three centers competed: the palace, the Sublime Porte, and the Central Committee in Salonica, which now commanded an empire-wide party organization. The new grand vizier, Kâmil Pasha, was ambitious and eager to restore power from the palace to his government in the Sublime Porte. He presented himself as, and was considered, a liberal. He reestablished the authority of the ministers and the correspondence of the provincial authorities with the Sublime Porte instead of the palace. It took twenty months until all Hamidian provincial and district governors and ambassadors were exchanged and rejuvenated. In September 1908, Sabahaddin's group founded a liberal party (Osmanlı Ahrar Fırkası). Supported by many journalists, it criticized the Central Committee's ongoing secrecy and interference, saying that this would lead to another despotism.[12]

In early October 1908, diplomatic setbacks seriously troubled the Ottoman spring and its elation. Bulgaria declared its full independence, Austria annexed Bosnia-Herzegovina, and Crete declared its union with Greece. The European powers did not react to this violation of the Berlin Treaty. Even if these territories' status as possessions of the Ottoman Empire was only nominal at this point, these moves made it chillingly clear that the dream of an Ottoman constitutional regime, if ever, had to be implemented in a reduced Ottoman realm. Having written on its banner the struggle against any further dismemberment, the CUP could not cope with shrinkage. It reacted by organizing a boycott of Austrian merchandise, thus politicizing the population and, as further developments revealed, recalling xenophobic ghosts. From the start Talaat was involved in this first of a series of anti-European boycotts. He resented the passivity of the Berlin Treaty's guarantor powers vis-à-vis the breaches regarding the Balkans. He took these and similar instances as an argument against international norms, as becomes evident repeatedly in his 1919 apologia.[13]

The excitation over the annexation spread and included Islamist reactions during the month of Ramadan in October 1908. As an observer, Talaat was with a crowd that Kör Ali, a preacher at a mosque, had led to Yıldız Palace on 7 October. Invoking the sharia, the preacher refused the constitution, movie houses, theaters, and the presence of Muslim women on the street. He addressed the sultan, who appeared at a window with the shout, "My sultan, we want a shepherd. A flock cannot be without a shepherd." The sultan answered that nobody had to worry, as the sharia requirements would be implemented. The CUP, however, pushed for the arrest of Kör Ali, who was executed a few weeks later. Because of suspicions regarding the sultan's use of reactionary forces, the committee transferred loyal military units from Salonica to the capital. Adding to the tension between the military units were tensions inside units between officers who had grown from the ranks and younger men from the military college who were loyal to the CUP.

In mid-October 1908, a Muslim crowd traversed the whole city and, again in Beşiktaş, forced its way through the entrance of a police station, lynched the Greek lover of a Muslim girl who wanted to become a Christian, and injured the girl. Enlightened commentators, such as the journalist Ahmed Midhat, exposed the politico-religious dimension of the crime.[14] Henceforth, after the counterrevolution in April 1909, in particular, religious reaction (*irtica*) and reactionaries (*mürteci*) were a main topic of Turkish history. The CUP and the army on which it relied oscillated between harsh overreaction against and usage of radical Islamic forces in the political sphere. They alternated between haughtiness, fear, and laissez-faire as far as the society and crimes against non-Sunnis were concerned. In this regard, the CUP, including Talaat, remained largely trapped in an interaction with forces from which it could not emancipate itself because it shared with them religiously connoted imperial references and an identity built on these. Even the later Kemalism, which renounced imperial restoration and concentrated power in its new center in Ankara, could not succeed in this emancipation—not for lack of power but for lack of a broadly negotiated and agreed-upon social contract beyond the subliminal references in question.

All male Ottoman nationals older than twenty-five who paid direct taxes could participate at the parliamentary elections in autumn 1908, which revived the enthusiasm for the new era, and which, all in all, went smoothly. The CUP won by an overwhelming majority. On 17 December, 266 deputies, among them Talaat as a representative of Edirne, could inaugurate the parliament, where Abdulhamid was also, reluctantly, present. His secretary read an imperial address that presented the sultan as the author and guarantor of the constitution. A few days later, Ahmed Rıza was elected the president of the parliament and Talaat vice president.

Ceremonious fraternization on the highest level, but lacking trust, continued a few days later during a reception for the deputies at the Yıldız Palace, the seat of the former "great despot" (in the terminology of the Young Turks in opposition). On the sultan's right sat the grand vizier Kâmil Pasha and on his left were Ahmed Rıza and Talaat. Rıza's toast exalted the union of the sultan and his nation at the same table as the "most auspicious moment" for himself and for the peoples of the Levant since the emergence of Islam.[15] For Rambert, Rıza was "a man full of good intentions and attached to general ideas of liberalism and sovereignty of the people, but without penetrating the practical necessities of government." He met Rıza in order to discuss the parliament's negative attitude against the Régie des Tabacs and to establish a contact with Cavid, the CUP's financial expert.[16]

Against Counterrevolution:
Empowering the Central Committee

The CUP dominated the parliament and pressured the government. Talaat was in a leading position both as a deputy and as a Central Committee member. When Kâmil Pasha changed the war and the navy ministers and sent back the troops from Salonica to establish the governmental prerogatives against the occult power from the CUP, he lost the vote of confidence on 12 February 1909. Hüseyin Hilmi Pasha, the former inspector general of Macedonia and now a friend of the CUP, took his place. Now committee control of the government was even tighter, and criticism from both Islamists and liberals intensified. Since Kâmil was rightly considered an Anglophile, British diplomacy was frustrated by the changes. In early April, Talaat, Rıza, and Cavid began to consider the formation of a CUP cabinet.[17]

One of the most vocal liberal critics, Hasan Fehmi of the newspaper *Serbesti* (Liberty), was threatened and then murdered on 6 April 1909, most plausibly by a CUP *fedai*. His funeral on 8 April turned into a crowd of approximately forty thousand people demanding justice. The most visible opposition, however, was that organized by Naqshbandi sheikh Vahdetî, founder of a journal called *Volkan* and of the Society for Muhammadan Unity (İttihad-i Muhammedi Cemiyeti). On the anniversary of Muhammad on 3 April 1909, a huge crowd with green flags gathered, listening to Vahdetî, who castigated the "godless regime."

Against the background of these excitations and of tensions in the army, soldiers and some officers from the rank and file in Istanbul rebelled on the night of 12–13 April, occupied the parliament, and soon controlled the whole capital. Students of *medrese* (Islamic college) joined them in demanding the full implementation of the sharia. "About 8 o'clock . . . the shops close hurriedly. A terrified crowd escapes toward Taksim. Panic reigns as during the Armenian massacres, of which I have seen some samples," Rambert noted on 13 April.[18] The rebels killed several people and pursued prominent CUP members, first among them Talaat and Ahmed Rıza. Aknuni, the chief of the ARF, hid Talaat in his house, and another Armenian did the same for Nâzım after they had first taken cover together with Rıza at another place.[19]

Despite the disorder, about fifty deputies met in the parliament, where a young representative of the rebels demanded the banishment of Ahmed Rıza, Talaat, Cavid, Rahmi, and Hüseyin Cahid (a journalist at the CUP newspaper *Tanin*) from the empire. After breakfeast with Emir Mohammed Arslan (a deputy from Syria) in the Club de Constantinople, Rambert learned that Arslan was bayoneted on the street because he was mistaken for Cahid. A mob destroyed the offices of the CUP papers *Şûra-yı Ümmet* and *Tanin*. Even if not directly involved in the conspiracy, Abdulhamid perked up, again pliable and ready for a reversion. Grand Vizier Hüseyin Hilmi withdrew, and Abdulhamid nominated Ahmed Tevfik to take his place. On 15 April 1909, he declared an amnesty for the rebels, adding, "Thanks to God, our Empire being a Muslim Empire, an imperial rescript has been promulgated ordering that the sacred laws (sheriat [sharia]), which are eternal and sublime, be hitherto observed more precisely."[20]

The CUP had lost its power in the capital. Even if initially also pushed by liberal leaders of the Osmanlı Ahrar Fırkası, the rebellion produced excesses counterproductive to the liberals. Men of the ancien régime filled the new cabinet, as Vahdetî had suggested in an "open letter to His excellency Abdulhamid Han, the caliph of Islam."[21] In the *Volkan*, Vahdetî was enthusiastic, praising jihad, the soldiers' bravery, and the success, at last, of a "legitimate revolution" (*inkılab-ı meşru*) that placed the sharia at the center, with or without a constitution and a parliament. He promised that "a synthesis of Islamic substance with Western civilization would emerge, amazing the whole world."[22] Alas, violence swiftly falsified this enchanting utopia. Anti-Armenian leaders, including governors, army officers, and members of the local CUP branch in Adana, understood the signals from the capital as an opportunity to reenact scenes of the 1895 massacres in order to destroy Christian agility and soft power—again more visible after 1908—and to loot Armenian goods.

Within two weeks after 14 April 1909, Muslim mob violence killed approximately twenty thousand Armenians and destroyed entire urban districts. Social envy, refusal of equality, and the new political visibility of the Armenians all played a role in this horrible hate and destruction.[23] Some of the military units sent to Adana fraternized with the mob instead of swiftly implementing constitutional law and order. "We have got horrible reports from Adana," wrote the director of the Régie. "When the staff of our factory had to flee to Mersin, the soldiers guarding our building killed all Armenians there."[24] In Diyarbekir, Urfa, Mamuretülaziz, Erzurum, and Erzincan, similar scenes were prevented by valiant authorities loyal to the constitution. The situation in Erzican was nevertheless drastic. The soldiers of the garrison had tied Korans to their standards and entered the city, demanding that the Armenians be eliminated and the sharia implemented.[25] Exterminatory Islamism had permeated active parts of the society in Asia Minor since the massacres of the 1890s.

Talaat left his hideout in Istanbul on 16 April 1909, when the new cabinet was formed. Under a pretext, he asked for a leave from the parliament in Istanbul and went to Ayastefanos (Yeşilköy), a place next to Istanbul, in order to reorganize CUP power. He was leading in a commission that wrote martial declarations in the name of the nation and the supreme constitution, while simultaneously derogatorily representing all rebels as self-serving spies and malefactors who misused religion. On 22 April, a national assembly (meclis-i millî) with 100 out of 266 deputies who had followed Talaat met in Ayastefanos. It replaced Abdulhamid with his brother Mehmed Reshad but sent deceptive telegrams to the new grand vizier that Abdulhamid's sultanate was safe, and that the capital was not to be occupied. It enjoyed the ARF's moral support but did not want the latter's active participation at the march on the capital.[26]

In its subversive organization, national discourse, and antiliberal stance, this assembly anticipated the counterparliament in Ankara in 1920. It is safe to say that Talaat, though acting with others, was the main leader in Ayastefanos and determined

Abdulhamid's deposition. The main goal was the reconquest and increase of CUP power, not constitutional rule accompanied by law and order. The Ayastefanos group did not distinguish between liberal criticism of CUP rule and justified pleas of the population on one side and mob violence, demagoguery, and profiteers of disorder on the other. In this vein, it rejected a demand of pardon by the rebels, who were largely back in their quarters by 17 April 1909. Krikor Zohrab, a prominent, independant Armenian deputy and lawyer in Istanbul, had led a delegation from Istanbul to Ayastefanos in order to avoid a bloodbath and to prepare a negotiated solution.[27]

On 23 April 1909, the Action Army under Mahmud Şevket, which had gathered at Ayastefanos, marched to Istanbul with, among Şevket's officers, Mustafa Kemal, later leader of the 1920 countergovernment. The army quickly controlled the situation, declaring a state of emergency that was to last until July 1912, to be quickly reinstalled until 1918. The reconquest of the capital resulted in the death of four hundred soldiers. A high but undetermined number of people were executed in public places after rapid trials. Vahdetî had already fled Istanbul on 18 April and was executed only in July.[28] "A sinister silence reigns in the streets," Rambert wrote on 3 May, and he said there was, "a general unrest . . . many convicted have been shot during the night . . . the hangings go on for several days."[29]

From Hidden to Semipublic Politics:
Talaat as a Minister

Talaat had informally led in Ayastefanos. On 27 April 1909, he led during the close parliamentary meeting on Abdulhamid's deposition under the presidency of Said Pasha, the sultan's former grand vizier. In the days before, the Action Army had conquered Yıldız Palace. Once and for all, Talaat now wanted to eliminate Abdulhamid from politics, but he had to overcome resistance in the parliament and from the sheykhulislam Sahip Molla, who was absent under the pretext of illness. Molla's *fetva* was, however, essential. Calling a meeting so that he could bully Molla face-to-face, Talaat and a delegation got the *fetva* for deposition or withdrawal, upon which the assembly decided for deposition. Talaat instructed Said that the CUP Central Committee wanted Abdulhamid to be exiled to Salonica. He arrived there with his wives, daughters, and a few servants on 28 April.[30]

Tevfik had been urged by Abdulhamid to replace Hilmi, a removal wanted by the putschists. His cabinet did not correspond to the wishes of the CUP, so Talaat "convinced" Tevfik that he had to resign.[31] Most ministers, including Ferid Pasha, the minister of the interior, remained, however, in the new cabinet of Hüseyin Hilmi, but helplessness reigned. Ferid, a close acquaintance of Rambert, asked his Swiss friend to not only write the speech for the new sultan but also one explaining the cabinet program, which would be presented to the deputies. Rambert was aware of—and found unfortunate—the remaining great dissensions between the CUP and the government. Moreover, there was a general will to repression, "to gag the press, to suppress strikes, to suppress the associations' abuses and freedom," but also, by the cabinet, "to save the government from the CUP's interference in the current affairs and the nomination of functionaries." An impotent cabinet and parliament during the rebellion determined that henceforth "dictatorship," as exemplified by Mahmud Şevket's state of emergency, "appeared as an unavoidable eventuality."[32]

As a consequence of the traumatic coup in April, the Central Committee wanted to increase its control and influence. Yet, probably fearful of losing their grip, the éminences grises did not want the "young men" (Cavid, Talaat) to become ministers.[33] They preferred to insert their men as counselors of the ministers, but faced too much resistance in the cabinet and the parliament to implement the idea. Cavid, who already enjoyed prestige as a financial expert, was to assist the "entirely incompetent" finance minister Mehmed Rifat. In June, he succeeded him, becoming the first CUP minister.[34] Yet the committee continued its pressure behind the scenes through Talaat and via "tickets": "In the council of ministers, all is done by small, mysterious tickets. During its meeting . . . Hilmi Pasha is constantly called outside to talk with an emissary of the committee. At any moment, he is given secret instructions or telegrams," Rambert learned from Ferid, who resigned due to pressure.[35] Talaat took Ferid's post in August 1909.

Before entering office, Talaat engaged in his first international experience, thanks to an invitation from the British Parliament offered after the 1908 revolution. He led a parliamentary delegation of seventeen deputies who attended sessions in Westminster, talked with the British prime minister Lord Curzon and foreign minister Edward Grey, and visited several cities. Sir Francis Montefiors, honorary president of the English Zionist Federation, held a luncheon for part of the Ottoman delegation, including Talaat, Dr. Rıza Tevfik, Nissim Mazliah, and Ruhi al-Khalidi (an Arab deputy from Jerusalem). Both Tevfik and Talaat warned that "the political aims of Zionism were not likely to evoke approval in the Turkish Empire."[36]

Talaat communicated all news by telegraph to his political friends in the Ottoman Parliament, where the reception in London was felt as an important recognition. "The deputies of the youngest parliament on their visit to the oldest parliament have met with an extraordinarily warm reception. . . . There is no need to search deeply into the pages of history to see how great this friendship is; we know it is practically a proverb with us: 'The Turk's best friend is the Englishman,'" the Istanbul press wrote.[37] Despite possible British encouragement of the April 1909 rebellion, the CUP leaders still set their hopes—at least publicly—on friendship with Great Britain, since they had known Germany as a friend of the ancien régime. Therefore, officially, Talaat did not follow up on an invitation for a visit to Germany that he had received while in Great Britain, demurring with statements about the fatigue of the delegation. Nevertheless, he visited Berlin and Vienna on the way back from London, since CUP relations with German representatives in Istanbul had already been well initiated (see sec. "Sobered, Disturbed, Depressed" in this chapter). Coming back from Europe as a designated minister in early August, he enjoyed considerable popularity in all circles that were close to the CUP. Politically, for serious observers, he was henceforth known as "the acknowledged head of the Committee of Union and Progress and the Young Turks."[38]

The first hot issue for the new minister, the Adana massacres in April, had been discussed in parliament and dealt with already when he had been in Europe. As a member of the ARF-CUP interparty commission, Talaat was always kept up-to-date, possibly playing a leading part through the telegraph.[39] The former minister of the interior had sent a fact-finding commission to Adana in May. From April to July, the government and most deputies, including those in the CUP, tended to interpret the massacre through Hamidian lenses, that is, by taking at face value the report of the vali (governor) of Adana, Mehmed Cevad, who had himself been involved in the mass crime. He had set a precedent of Armenian provocation and—crucial point—had entirely exonerated the

FIGURE 3: "My collaborators in Turkey: Talaat Bey,
minister of the interior," in Enver Bey's caption (written
on the photo) for Germans in Berlin, where he served as a
military attaché in 1909–11 (Hauptstaatsarchiv Stuttgart).

authorities. However, basic facts became undeniable in July;
hence, the cabinet drew conclusions and ordered the arrest
of leading Muslim perpetrators, including Cevad. Still, many
deputies blocked an open debate, partly out of fear from public
reaction after the April chaos.[40]

The CUP, the ARF, and other representatives, including
Zohrab, therefore acted from a behind-the-scenes arrangement,
simultaneous with Talaat's start as a minister. The influential
CUP member Ahmed Cemal was nominated as the new governor of Adana; the government publicly rejected the argument of
an Armenian provocation, and important funds were provided
to help the victims and reconstruction. Apparently lacking alternatives, and despite voices of warning in their community, the
Armenians attached their constitutional hopes even more tightly
to the CUP, although provincial CUP branches had openly
cooperated with anti-Armenian reactionaries in April and CUP
deputies had proved slow or even unwilling to remove Hamidian glasses. The parliament as a whole had proved incapable of
coming to terms with the mass crime, not least because the even
more comprehensive crimes of the 1890s, including restitution of
goods and land, had still not been addressed and cleared.

Entrenched patterns of denial, along with the refusal of testimony against Muslim perpetrators, still not only dominated
the public space but also characterized CUP members on the
parliamentary commission that dealt with the issue. One of
those responsible for the massacre, a former mufti, had begun
"going here and there and saying that freedom and the Constitution were inventions of the Christians, who are opposed to
the Sharia; in this fashion, he began to stir up the population
and turn them against the Christians and the Constitution,"
reads the report of Agop Babikian (the Armenian member of
the commission), which nevertheless remained concealed.[41]
In his report, Ali Münif (Yeğenağa), Talaat's close friend and
collaborator from 1909 to 1918, used tranquilizing language
that made perpetratorship disappear. His memoirs prove that
already in 1909 he did not consider the Armenians as compatriots and citizens (*vatandaş*) in their full right.[42]

The same is true for Talaat who, in the retrospective gaze of his 1919 apologia, entirely misses Babikian's main points when he refers to him as a proof of Armenian provocation. In his bitter exile in Berlin, Talaat's conspiracy thinking went so far as to pretend that Armenians had wanted to provoke a massacre in order to establish an Armenian autonomy with European help. In 1909, Talaat had been comparably open to Armenians, but he was not ready to face reality, to publish Babikian's report, and thus to prepare a constitutional future based on facts.[43] All in all, the parliamentary handling of the Adana massacre resembles an all-too-familiar chauvinist attitude that can never accept rape as a crime but instead emphasizes provocation by the victim.

On 20 August 1909, the CUP and the ARF concluded an accord on the terms of a reaffirmed cooperation "to save the Ottoman fatherland from separation and division."[44] They "accepted the grievous Adana massacres as a warning admonition" and "decided to work hand-in-hand," to defend the constitution against reactionary movements. Notably, on Armenian insistence, they also agreed on "expanding provincial rights," that is, on paper, on more regionalism in Sabahaddin's sense, even if the CUP had in fact internalized centralism. The 20 August accord did not mention the restitution of land grabbed in the 1890s. This crucial issue of the Armenian Question also challenged Talaat's ministry. He promised to solve it by administrative measures, thus circumventing lengthy and uncertain trials in which non-Muslims were disadvantaged.

Politically, a positive atmosphere of departure had partly returned in late summer and autumn 1909. For the first time, the CUP had its own ministers. They enjoyed a positive image, nationally and internationally. One of them, Talaat, in the eyes of several people already had what it took to become a grand vizier.

"The minister of the interior Talaat Bey . . . is one of the most sympathetic humans one can imagine. His face radiates the most perfect loyalty. He is a nice man [*brave homme*] in the best meaning of this term. But he is also one of the most remarkable among the new persons in Turkish politics, so that he is already conjectured as the future grand vizier," a French journalist wrote.[45]

Instead of receiving submissive visitors, as superiors traditionally did during the Bayram holiday at the end of Ramadan, the ministers Talaat, Cavid, and Bedros Halajian (of public works) left the capital on 14 October 1909, to "come into contact with the population" in the provinces. Edouard Huguenin Pasha (1856–1926) accompanied them. Having worked in many of its regions since 1879, this Swiss-born, Turkish-speaking director of the Anatolian Railway knew Asia Minor better than other high-ranking officials and the Macedonian CUP leaders. "These sirs will realize how much there is to gain in terms of prestige and knowledge of the country, encountering themselves the people and the matters of the provinces. This looks like nothing, but it is a revolution in the habits of the administration. I am greatly pleased," noted Rambert, Huguenin's longtime friend, with whom he met almost daily in Pera, Istanbul's center on the European side. Rambert commented similarly on the sultan's travel to Izmit and Bursa in late October 1909.[46] After a private audience, Rambert described Mehmed V as jovial, good-natured, and friendly. But in all important affairs, the head of a henceforth-reduced sultanate had to obey committee orders.[47]

By mid-December 1909, Rambert and Huguenin still had the impression of a solid and trusted group formed by Hilmi, Cavid, Talaat, and Halajian, whose government was quite authoritarian but unavoidably so in the eyes of most people. They also observed "a very democratic contempt for decorations" among CUP politicians but skeptically predicted that this would probably not last.[48] In this vein, they also seriously questioned the CUP, a "tyrannical organization" in their eyes, but again, perhaps necessarily so for a certain time in the turbulent circumstances. CUP politics excluded minority positions and lacked balancing mechanisms, and thus could not last as a democratic entity in any reasonable assessment. Even if in its 1909 Congress the CUP had decided to be more transparent, to separate its parliamentarian party from the committee and also to waive the secret initiation to membership, this did not develop in reality.

The CUP's behavior in the parliament and cabinet reflected the approach and practices entrenched in the Central Committee. CUP parliamentarians "had to completely sacrifice their personal opinions" except during internal party meetings. Rambert concluded that the CUP had become a highly disciplined *association de salut public* (as known from the French Revolution). Nâzım and Şakir insisted that these were still revolutionary times and that the government must be checked by the committee. In contrast, it seems that by late 1909, Talaat was eager to pass on to more transparent governmental politics, without the secret monitoring by the committee. He was quoted as shouting in the Central Committee, "There cannot be a state within the state!" The éminences grises certainly did not want this, since they would have lost their power, rooted as it was, in their case, in the committee alone.[49]

Sobered, Disturbed, Depressed: A Crisis for Talaat and the Ottoman Future

Unfortunately, the general political mood changed in late 1909. Since July 1908, nothing substantial had been achieved. Unresolved problems accumulated, evidence of "the indecision of

men who do not know how to take and to solve them." Ottoman politics were in the doldrums after Grand Vizier Hilmi
Pasha's withdrawal on 31 December 1909, due to incompabil-
ity between the grand vizier and CUP representatives, according to Rambert, who said, "The young men have the natural
tendency to throw the responsibility on all those who have
played a role in the ancien régime." The committee had pressured Hilmi to evict Gabriel Noradunghian, the minister of
economy and culture, a high-ranking functionary also under
Abdulhamid. Rambert knew the details, since he had had long
talks with both Hilmi and Ibrahim Hakkı Pasha, Hilmi's successor. According to his sources, the committee also considered
withdrawing Talaat from the cabinet, reproaching him for his
bad nominations in the provinces and for being too docile.[50]

A major test for the government and Talaat was unrest in
Albania. A strong Albanist movement wanted to introduce the
Latin alphabet for written Albanian and resented the CUP ideology of centralization in politics and culture. Propaganda against
Albanism blended Islam, Ottomanism, and an Albanian patriotism loyal to the empire. The CUP preferred to maintain the Arabic alphabet (or "Turkish alphabet" in Albanian vocabulary)
and aimed not only at maintaining but also strengthening the
Ottoman language, written in Arabic letters, as the hegemonic
language of a predominantly Islamic empire. If the Albanians
chose Latin letters, they would distance themselves from Istanbul. All population groups, including Sunni Muslims, were represented in the Albanist movement, but it was especially notable
for Bektashis and Christians. A general rebellion in spring 1910,
after the arrests of Albanist leaders, scared Talaat. Far from establishing democracy, the CUP had to rely on regional notables
and the ulema (scholars of the sheykhulislam administration)
or other Islamic networks to maintain power.

Talaat hesitated to use force to disarm the people but was reprimanded by the éminences grises, whose negative outlook on intra-Ottoman autonomies he principally adhered to. He yielded and henceforth CUP politics against autonomist tendencies in Albania were heavy-handed, with the army being used in blanket repressions, aggressive plots, and propaganda, in an effort to further split Albanian society. CUP man (but not Central Committee member) General Ahmed İzzet Pasha, a senior officer of Albanian descent, was sent to Yemen because he bitterly opposed this policy. Though in this study's terminology—imperially biased in a thorough sense—Ahmed İzzet Pasha's bias went hand in hand with paternalistic obligations and Muslim ethics (as in similar cases, e.g., Mustafa Hayri's). "In this issue I have again and again tried to draw Talaat Bey's attention and to explain to him that . . . instead of success by Machiavellian politics, damage would result."[51]

Albania was lost to the empire in 1912 during the First Balkan War. Another essential test was the land question in Eastern Asia Minor, to which I will return. Often called Anatolia, Asia Minor was the place where the empire had originated. It was essential for the Ottoman future, whereas Albania, Palestine, and Yemen were not. In Yemen, insurrection had started in 1904. Imam Yahya was granted autonomous Zaydi-Shiite rule in Northern Yemen in October 1911. In the case of Yemen, right from the beginning of his ministry in summer 1909, Talaat had suspended all autonomy plans and, in September, sent twelve battalions to Yemen to crush rebellion, however, without the desired success.[52]

Regarding Palestine, Talaat stood under considerable pressure from Arab deputies and Zionists. The latter wanted free immigration, the former the prohibition of Jewish mass immigration and land purchase. Talaat decided to renew

Abdulhamid's anti-Zionist restrictions. Petitions had increased after 1908, giving the local, mostly illiterate population a voice via *arzuhalci* (petition writers). Strong-worded petitions, mostly addressed to the Ministry of the Interior, expressed disappointment that the empire turned a blind eye to Zionist activity, which had created a state within the state. A number of Zionists, though not high representatives, declared this to be their goal.[53]

The wisdom not only of hindsight but also of farsighted contemporaries suggests that the empire was, in fact, undeniably overstretched. Overpatriotic, overpoliticized, and state-centric CUP men nevertheless stuck to the dogma of the empire's salvation as a centralist and unitary entity. Major General Imhoff Pasha (Heinrich K. A. Imhoff) critically remarked that the inexperienced minister Talaat "obstinately maintained the plan to bestow Turkey with a tautly centralized, leveling administration," despite experiences that taught the wisdom of a different course.[54] Nâzım and Şakir, strategic leaders of the Central Committee until 1912, proved incapable of setting realistic and farseeing priorities, thus limiting the scope of action of the young CUP ministers they controlled. Imperially biased radical activists, they abhorred considering the necessity of regionalization, a general shakeout and reduction of the empire, while simultaneously refusing Armenian partnership. Wisdom instead of patriotic dogmas would have commanded a peaceful transition to new forms of government in a reduced Ottoman realm. Of this, evidently, Asia Minor would form the core.

German ambassador Adolf Marschall von Bieberstein was unfair when, in a talk with Rambert in early 1910, he acidly disqualified Talaat because of his great "unknown incapacity." As behind-the-scenes leaders, it was the smug éminences grises who foremost failed—as far as viable, rather than cataclysmic, futures were concerned.[55] Let us imagine that in 1910 Talaat had already deployed the organizational genius and energy (remarked upon by Ludwig in 1915) in the eastern provinces, but constructively. He would have had a realistic chance, as CUP governor Celâl testified, to achieve conditions in accordance with constitutional rule. But after 1910–11, this priority lost its appeal. Until then, on the search for constitutional horizons, Talaat had been more open to true reform than many others.

Accustomed to corruption in juridical affairs and to political assassinations, it is, however, unavoidable to state that Talaat probably lacked, early on, the character and courage for fundamental amelioration.[56] The social Darwinist and instrumentally Islamist imprint of Nâzım and Şakir was already present in Talaat's scantily trained and educated mind. These influences continued to determine his policy after 1912, when he emancipated himself in terms of operative power. In some contrast to them, he was less inclined to pursue chimerical goals of a restored or expanding empire put on the road to progress. His appearence was more authentic and less grim than that of the éminences grises, who had the nature of sectarians.[57] Talaat appeared as more jovial, thus his popularity. Nâzım, for instance, in a fierce overidentification with the CUP and the empire, was eager to suppress his Dönme roots, disregarding his origins. This attitude is comparable to that of Leon Trotsky, a contemporary leader of revolutionary socialism in Russia, who refused to cope with and even played down his Jewishness.[58]

Real challenges of Talaat's ministry, embarrassment from within the committee, and bad press contributed to his deep crisis, starting in early 1910. Previously known as calm and jovial, he displayed ever-increasing nervousness, which also affected him in parliament. On different occasions, his new discomposure made him say disturbing, anticonstitutional statements, casting a dark shadow on his political career and the Ottoman future. During the CUP Congress in Salonica in November 1910, interior and financial affairs were avidly discussed and the ministers criticized, to which the young CUP ministers reacted with little self-confidence. Talaat's speech at a CUP meeting in Manastir on 28 August 1910 already proves his precocious loss of trust in constitutional ideals and the fatal perspective that there could "be no question of equality until we succeed in our task of Ottomanizing the Empire."[59]

This statement not only put cooperation on an equal footing with an uncertain future but made it depend on a previous national-imperial Ottomanization blended with Turkification ("Ottomanization" now taking a new, centralist, and Turkist sense). This antiegalitarian recalibration went hand in hand with Talaat's reorganization of the provincial CUP branches. Loyalty to the letter and the spirit of the constitution henceforth played a minor role or no role at all; what counted was the co-optation of local Muslim lords ready to cooperate with the CUP in order to safeguard and consolidate power. If we believe Talaat's 1919 apologia, an ARF memorandum presented to the Socialist International Congress in Copenhagen in late August 1910 had impressed him concerning the Armenian will toward self-defense and organization, and had reverted him to his "primordial" Ottoman Muslim loyalty.[60]

There was a soul in Talaat's breast that cared about the Armenians, and he knew well that cooperation with them was the key for a modern, constitutional Turkey. Armenian international networks and lobbying were, however, tools

FIGURE 4: CUP meeting (1913): Talaat Bey, sitting *(no. 1)*, on his left
Enver Bey, standing *(no. 2)*, Said Halim, sitting *(no. 3)*, Cemal Pasha *(no. 4)*,
Ismail Canbolad *(no. 11)*, and after him, without a number, Midhat Şükrü
(© akg-images, Berlin, Sammlung Archiv für Kunst und Geschichte).

that Talaat and the CUP feared and hated. They could not
accept these means as a necessary lever for realistic politics.
They also feared vocal Islamic opposition and mob violence
organized by regional lords. There was, therefore, another
soul in Talaat—mirroring the mentality of key members in
the committee—that did not believe in equal cooperation
but considered the co-optation of local Muslim forces as the
only possible domestic realpolitik. In contrast to the ARF, the
CUP possessed violent alternatives. The unpunished, unfor-
gotten massacres of the 1890s, even if publicly ostracized in the
Ottoman capital, remained a powerful pattern of destruction
instead of cooperation. It is plausible that in his crisis, Talaat
might already have thought about the option of getting rid of
the Armenians.[61]

Talaat's crisis accompanied a general crisis of the CUP and, interestingly, a turn to Germany in international politics in autumn 1910, the only European partner, in Cavid's words, not to set conditions "inconsistent with the dignity of Turkey." This turn was, however, actively prepared and backed by Ambassador Marschall von Bieberstein since the aftermath of the Young Turk Revolution. During his stay in Istanbul in July 1910, where he met with diplomats and CUP leaders, Churchill experienced "a great sympathy with the Young Turks," and already felt that the Germans had "got the better of our diplomacy there." Karl Helfferich and Paul Weitz, the Istanbul correspondent of the *Frankfurter Zeitung*, made arrangements to print propagandistic materials and, in Helfferich's words, to gather "baksheesh" (bribes), besides "advances *ad libitum*." Helfferich was a codirector of the Deutsche Bank and second director of the Anatolian Railway next to Huguenin, the first director. In contrast to this cosmopolite, Helfferich embraced the German geopolitical interest of the Bagdadbahn (Baghdad Railway). Documents of the Deutsche Bank suggest that in late spring 1909, the CUP was given 100,000 francs for their newspaper *Tanin*. This coincided with Enver's stay in Berlin as a military attaché—he arrived there in March 1909 and was henceforth a staunch admirer of German power—and with the start of journalist Ernst Jäckh's career as an influential propagandist of German-Turkish friendship, even when his CUP friends became dictatorial and radical nationalists in 1913. He contributed substantially to what some contemporaries called *Türkenfieber* (Turk fever) and became himself, from 1914, a propagandist of the common war effort. After a holiday trip to Turkey in 1908, in articles Jäckh had exalted the Young Turk Revolution as a revelation of global reach and prophesied a "Rising Crescent" (title of his seminal, continually reedited book of 1911).[62]

FIGURE 5: Winston Churchill between Talaat Bey and Cavid Bey (both wearing fezzes) during Churchill's private stay in Istanbul in July 1910 (Churchill Archives Centre, Broadwater Collection. Reproduced with permission of Curtis Brown, London, on behalf of the Broadwater Collection).

In 1910, Germany took the opportunity of Cavid's failure to get an important loan in Paris and London. "I consider it eminently important that we not only contract the loan promptly but leave behind the impression of magnanimous generosity," Helfferich wrote on 6 November 1910 to the Deutsche Bank. Thus, Germany markedly, once again, became friends with Turkey. "Financial help comes from Germany," Rambert commented in November 1910, on the result of Helfferich's visit in Istanbul; "the political orientation has deeply changed." Luminary of German *Weltpolitik* (world politics), for a decade Helfferich was a very frequent acquaintance of Cavid, and—via Cavid or directly—of Talaat. During World War I, he became secretary for the German Treasury and vice-chancellor. He is mentioned even more frequently in Cavid's diary than Huguenin, who often participated in financial negotiations, at times as a facilitator. Most of these negotiations were related to the Bagdadbahn, an infrastructural project leading through Asia Minor and Iraq, which was largely financed by the Deutsche Bank. Rambert stood close to Huguenin and Cavid. At times, he dined with them, as on 28 October 1911, when Helfferich and Weitz were additional guests in his home in Beyoglu. In Cavid's diary, only Talaat is more frequently mentioned than Helfferich and Huguenin.[63]

Talaat's crisis also had a personal aspect. In summer 1909, he had married Hayriye, an Albanian girl from Ottoman Yanya (since 1913 Greek) who, like him, did not come from a distinguished family and mostly spoke Greek. After secret medical inquiries around 1911, he had to accept that he could not father a child. He began to say that "the marriage and affectionate adherence to a house could hinder the execution of duties that the ideal demands. If a komiteci nevertheless gets married, he should not have children." He insisted, in the vein of an activist entirely committed to his ideal and duty, that a "komiteci should not think about anybody behind him. If he cared, he would advance only hesitantly." This was in full accord with Ziya Gökalp's blind surrender to duty and ideal. According to Ali Münif, who was the same age, Talaat appeared as if he would not love children but at the same time seemed to envy those who had children.[64] Enver's mother alluded cruelly to Talaat's childlessness when, in mid-July 1914, she leaned on him not to nominate Cevdet, her daughter's husband, as governor of the eastern province of Bitlis because she did not want her to be so far away: "If only you also had a child, then you could understand the fire of my heart."[65]

———

If constitutional rule was implemented in Asia Minor, the 1908 revolution had not been in vain, even if other territories were lost. If the CUP possessed political substance and thus was more than a conspiratorial power organization, it would deploy all its means to realize equality and the rule of law, and to rectify outrageous wrongs from the Hamidian era. Talaat acknowledged that the Armenian demands were justified and that land stolen during the Hamidian period had to be restituted. However, the agrarian question could be solved only if the government committed itself resolutely to this task and did not shy away from confrontation with Muslim lords on the ground.

Yet this was not the case; CUP member Celâl, governor of the province of Erzurum in 1909–11, wrote in retrospect of the decisive lapse of time in Erzurum. He knew the Armenians there were particularly loyal to the constitution and, together with other comparatively weak groups, in need of a solid rule of law against ruthless regional lords. Nevertheless, resolute cooperation with Armenian organizations, though required, was not realized because Talaat lacked the audacity to choose this road. By early 1912, he lacked even the will to spend a serious sum of money to defuse the land problem for a majority of Christian peasants.[66]

As the first CUP minister of the interior, Talaat was the main figure responsible for better administration and for finding a solution to the agrarian question. Celâl judged that Talaat and the whole cabinet failed in this task. Instead of concentrating on basic justice and good government in critical areas, they chose dubious regional lords. The plain constitutional gospel of fairness and justice possessed an appeal for everybody in the provinces and not just for minoritarian Christians and Alevis. This was, however, clearly not the case for important groups whose leaders shared in robbery and exploitation, especially in the land grab of the 1890s, or who patronized their dependents with antiminoritarian and, at times, openly xenophobic Islamism.

Instead of concentrating on the constitutional gospel and its concrete implementation, the CUP affiliated itself with a propagandistic mix of Islamism and Ottoman myths in the tradition of Şakir's pamphletism. After hesitation, Talaat joined this stance. The CUP shied away from a timely confrontation with lords whom, a short time later, it began to appropriate. Moreover, it practiced CUP nepotism. "Capacity, competence and experience no longer play a role, but only the favor of the Committee," the German ambassador Marschall von Bieberstein complained.[67]

In the capital, Armenians, sympathetic CUP leaders, and others still celebrated harmony and cooperation when possible, for example, during a grand ball in Pera Palace in favor of Armenian charity. In the presence of the grand vizier and ministers, Cavid did all he could to encourage people to donate at this ball on 3 March 1910, less than a year after the Adana massacres. Yet in the same week, Adom (alias Harutyun Shahrigian), a leading intellectual of the ARF in Istanbul, published a profoundly sobering book on how to conceive the Ottoman nation. For Adom, Ottomanism was "the collective union of the individual citizens" and ought not to assimilate or dissolve national subunits, as the CUP obviously had already attempted to do. He concluded that the Armenian vision of the Ottoman nation, based on constitutional patriotism, was "greater, more sublime, and more perfect than the one comprehended and yearned for by the narrow[-minded], chauvinist Turkish intellectuals."[68] In the December session of the same year, the socialist deputy of Erzurum, Vartkes Serengülian, gave a "very well done and substantial" summary of the interior situation of Ottoman Turkey—with few signs of hope. Lacking valid alternatives, he nevertheless supported the cabinet.[69]

A parliamentary debate starting on 1 March 1911 and continuing through 16 May mirrored the possibilities and limits of a
fundamental intra-Ottoman debate on global history, monotheism, and urgent problems of late Ottoman society. Talaat
opposed accusations of a CUP-Zionist collusion for loan agreements and immigration. He argued shortly and defensively,
without touching on Zionism. Grand Vizier Hakkı Pasha was
defensive as well, but not at all versed in the topic. The Jewish
deputies appeared evasive, likely because they feared confronta-
tions. The context was suffocating. Emmanuel Karasu (Carasso)
and Nissim Mazliah disclaimed any links to the Zionists, played
down the significance of Zionism, and astutely suggested that
since the Koran had superseded the Torah, there was nothing
for Muslims to fear from biblical prophecies on the restoration
of Israel. "If Zionism is truly damaging for the state, I [will]
entirely agree with the state. . . . Let us burn the Torah for the
state [if necessary]," Mazliah exclaimed on 16 May, without
delving into the topic itself. Critics of Zionism were diverse.
Palestinian deputy Ruhi al-Khalidi was the most erudite among
them. Others mixed imperially biased anti-Jewish views with
serious arguments on motives for autonomy and a Jewish state,
as well as on practices that included land purchase, the exploitation of Ottoman corruption, and far-reaching local self-rule as
practiced by Jewish settlers.[70]

In early March 1911, Talaat stepped back from his ministry, practically forced to do so not only by the opposition but
also by his own crisis, without a compelling, obvious reason.
"Doesn't he exaggerate when he says that he cannot resist longer?" Cavid asked. Halil (Menteşe) took his spot in the ministry, then Celâl. Halil and Talaat were contemporaries and had
first met after the parliament had opened; they also closely
cooperated in the future. A few days after Talaat had resigned,

FIGURE 6: Halil, close CUP friend and Talaat's successor
in early 1911, becoming minister of the interior (from the
Ottoman satirical journal *Cem*, 18 February 1911, 9).

the committee ordered the withdrawal of his CUP ministers
Emrullah Efendi and Bedros Halajian. Cavid bitterly criticized
the decision "to sacrifice" Halajian and to not even give him the
opportunity to resign himself, as Talaat had done. To exclude
the Armenian in a critical time was "tantamount to hurting the
group that is one of the most loyal to us," he confided in his
diary. Cavid, however, lacked the courage and power to confront his CUP friends on this and many other related issues.[71]

Four years before Talaat sent him to death (along with
Zohrab), on 16 May 1911 the Armenian deputy Ohannes Vartkes
Serengülian participated in the final phase of the debate on
Zionism. Talaat listened to the sincere and penetrating speech,

which he only interrupted once. As political friends noted, he admired and envied Vartkes's exemplary attitude of a principled socialist and revolutionary.[72] Vartkes began asking rhetorically if the reason for anti-Jewish discrimination in different countries was a Jewish intention to establish everywhere a separatist kingdom. "I say this because I am a child of the Armenian nation. I fear that the conditions that befell us will also affect the Jews. . . . Thirty years ago, Armenian representatives applied because of [land] seizures, but they were never taken seriously." Unpunished looting and the abduction of women and girls showed how force, not law, reigned over society.

This triggered, Vartkes added, Armenian revolutionary action that mean-spirited groups interpreted as an effort to build up an Armenian kingdom, whence anti-Armenian hate erupted among these groups. Armenians had sweepingly been stigmatized as traitors even before Jews or anyone else. Knowing the sensibility, Vartkes did not explicitly mention the 1890s massacres when he witnessed a fanatic behead his own father. His speech linked the futures of Jews and Armenians—both were formerly religiously protected (*zimmi*) and were subordinate minorities now living in modernizing empires but, in this context, experiencing the threat of pogroms even more. Anti-Armenian violence under Abdulhamid had far outreached the worst anti-Jewish pogroms in Russia. Vartkes criticized the way in which Zionism was now discussed, because mob violence might be aroused. The government should directly be addressed in this case, he argued. Nevertheless, he still hoped for decisive governmental action.

Vartkes insisted on the calamity of societal violence, of which Armenians would again become the first target if tensions escalated in Ottoman society: "If there are turbulences in Palestine or at any other [Ottoman] place, they will again first cut off the heads of Armenians." He appealed to the assembly and the government at last to take seriously the reality of violence instead of doing everything to please majorities in the provinces. Love of humankind, not nationalism, compelled him to emphasize the problem. "The Turks are not brutal," a deputy retorted; "you still want to accuse the Turks with old things." Vartkes responded that murder must be called murder. Feyzi Pirinççizâde, notorious instigator of pogroms and a deputy from Diyarbekir, also queried anti-Armenian violence, as did Halil, now minister of the interior, whom Vartkes had hopefully called as his witness. Halil was entirely evasive, even denialist. "If one or two times a crime has happened, the government has prosecuted and arrested the perpetrators." Asım from Mamuretülaziz warned: "Do not charge the people." Talaat, too, interjected, "If there is anything that the government neglected to do, say it." Vartkes addressed the land issue. Asım responded, "It must be resolved; on this we agree." Vartkes answered, "If we see that day, you will not be happy but destitute."[73] Because he had been a profiteer in 1895, Asım would lose a lot of land.

A considerable factor in Talaat's crisis was his inability to rise to the diversity of conflicting high expectations set upon him. From the Armenian side, it was not only the demand of real constitutional rule but also a remarkable supposition of the ARF (the CUP's ally). They held that Talaat shared the ARF's leftist ideals of society more than most others in the Central Committee. Ahmed Cemal and Hasan Tahsin seemed to join him in this. In contrast, the ARF representatives saw Şakir, Rahmi, and Ahmed Rıza as the right wing of the CUP. In late summer 1909, the ARF had considered Talaat's ministry as being "most[ly] on the left." In this context, it had discussed the introduction of a cantonal federalism according to the Swiss model.[74] In spring

1911, a meeting of the mixed ARF-CUP council, which, since 1910, had helped improve ARF-CUP relations, decided to solve the agrarian question administratively instead of by tribunals, and to organize Armenian village guards, armed by the government. Among the CUP leaders, Cavid and Ömer Naci at least were ready to look at the realities in the East in social terms, thus considering the cleavage between great landowners and peasants in general, Armenians and Kurds, and not always emphasizing ethnoreligious tensions.[75]

Yet in summer 1911, the hope and confidence in common leftist horizons, and trust in general, was lost. The committee was at pains to represent Talaat, "the embodiment of the CUP and target for all who had complaints against the latter body," as "a good Mussulman," who "was not a Freemason" and had nothing to do with "atheism." Thus, three years before World War I, when in Europe the internationalist left capitulated to a nationalist *burgfriede* (party truce) in each country, fragile leftist ideals collapsed for good in the late Ottoman political arena. The self-interested turn of Alexander Helphand Parvus from small but authentic Ottoman socialist circles to the CUP and Turkist organizations is a strong indicator for this approaching dead end of international socialism (the Russian-German socialist Parvus agitated from 1910 to 1915 in Istanbul; see chap. 4, sec. "Rûm Removal"). Fear and the use of Islam prevailed in the CUP, and it began to consider a nationalist alliance with Muslims, thus dropping ideals of social change in favor of a Turkish-Muslim alignment. During the general assembly of the ARF in August 1911, a disillusioned Adom stated that "leftist Talaat assumed" this development and, instead of any self-criticism and soul-searching, pointed to the Armenian side, if there were troubles in the provinces—now simply repeating what biased valis reported.[76]

A New Friend: Ziya Gökalp,
Prophet of Messianist Turkism

Constitutional patriotism originated in the Tanzimât and had grown deep roots in parts of the Young Turk movement—clearly so in Cavid's case and even more clearly for the Armenians who relied existentially on constitutional rule. It was much less rooted, however, in Talaat's, Nâzım's, and Şakir's ideas of socialization, or in that of Mehmed Ziya Gökalp (1876–1924), who settled down in Salonica in 1909. In September 1909, he had come from his hometown Diyarbekir to assist as a delegate of the Diyarbekir CUP branch at the CUP Congress. He became a close acquaintance of the Salonician group and, in 1910, a Central Committee member.[77] He found congenial friends and admirers, founded literary and philosophical journals with them, and, finally based in the capital Istanbul, was the leader of a new school of thought or sect (*tarikat*) of modern Turkism, as Muhittin Birgen, one of his disciples, put it.

Ziya was to be "the spirit" who, after years of ideological vagueness, "gave the CUP a determinate social and political doctrine."[78] According to Gökalp, he inspired an entire young generation in search of ideological orientation by discovering and establishing the salutary ideal of Turan. This was to save them from a general political and mental deadlock that opposed Ottomanism and Islamism in the aftermath of 1908.[79] Talaat became less his disciple than an overarching force that swallowed up fresh shoots from this new tree of knowledge, with whom he frequently discussed issues. At the same time, Gökalp served him as a prophet and appeared as a superior mind, as attested to by a contemporary Turkish historian: "Talaat Pasha and Enver Pasha adored Ziya Gökalp like a holy man [*walī*]. They took every word from him as wonderful wisdom. In every topic, his scientific opinions made him predominant in the Central Committee." In the recollections of Gökalp's daughter, her father had been "Talaat Pasha's closest friend. The Pasha visited us frequently with his friends and talked until late in the night. I was then a child. From time to time I entered the parlor and found my father always standing. He spoke and spoke all the time."[80]

In his new Salonician home, Ziya converted from a 1908 Ottomanism, with sympathy for American federalism, to Turkism, heroic pan-Turkism, and the will to a centralist power organization—the last all based, in his case, on the belief in Muslim supremacy and the emerging new global power of Turkdom. Around 1911 he gave himself the pen name Gök-Alp, meaning "hero" or "warrior of the sky." Along with the Central Committee, he moved to Istanbul in 1912. Gökalp was to have a strong intellectual influence on Talaat, the CUP, and the entire movement of Turkism, including the Turkish nationalism of the Republic of Turkey, and his influence remains evident in the Turkish Islamism of leading figures in today's Justice and Development Party (AKP). Gökalp's impact goes far beyond Şakir's and Nâzım's pamphletism, even if they shared common, basic elements. He is important, not only for the formative intellectual and ideological framing of Talaat's peer group in and around the Central Committee since 1910 but also for the understanding of the eastern provinces, the reform issue, and the Armenian Question. These became main factors of CUP policy from 1913 onward, once Talaat was the actual leader. We need, therefore, to go back to Diyarbekir of the 1890s in order to understand this strand.

The new governmental high school in Diyarbekir, which Ziya attended in the mid-1890s, was a hotbed of antiauthoritarian and anti-Hamidian youth rebellion against despotism, corporal punishments, and brainless religious education. It used the rhetoric of patriotism, revolution, scientism, and sacrifice for the nation. Ziya was influenced by Dr. Abdullah Cevdet, a cofounder of the CUP, who was temporarily sent to Diyarbekir in autumn 1894, where he formed a kind of first CUP nucleus or circle.[81] The young doctor became friends with the seven-years-younger student, who was clearly seeking orientation and new horizons. Ziya was born and raised in a traditional religious environment, but at the same time he was aware of Western science and progress, taught, above all, in missionary and Armenian schools and practiced in hospitals in the region. Another important inspiration for Ziya was a Rûm (Greek Orthodox) high school teacher, an atheist who introduced him to a materialist vision of the world. Depressed and confused when his familiar weltanschauung collapsed, Ziya shot himself in the head on 3 January 1895—but survived.[82]

In a 1922 retrospective, Ziya declared that the quest for supreme truth (*hakikat-i kübra*) preoccupied him during his depressive attacks as an adolescent, and that this quest was accompanied by questions regarding freedom, truth, humanity, and the impact of scientific natural laws on human life and society. He stated that the supreme truth revealed itself to him in the ideal (*mefkûre*) of nation and liberty, and that this healed him.[83] In an epic poem written in early 1913 and entitled "Kızılelma," Gökalp came back to the topic of suicide, taking his former personal affliction as a metaphor for that of the entirety of Turkdom (Türklük). He reinterpreted Kızılelma (red-gold apple), an old Turkish symbol for an appealing object of conquest far beyond existing frontiers, as a cure for Turkdom in its existential grief. In this poem, Kızılelma meant, above all—but not only—cultural, educational conquest, that is, the acquisition of a new, modern Turkish identity.

Ziya represented Kızılelma explicitly as the Turks' self-made messiah (*mehdi*) in their new departure toward Turan and portrayed Turan as a free, "enormous and eternal" fatherland. The notion of Turan suggested a neoimperial expansion and made Gökalp's political thought deeply ambivalent. He believed it was his generation's task—and great ideal (*mefkûre*)—to discover and build up Turan. In comparison, the Turkish home in Asia Minor (Türk Yurdu) was a necessary but small precondition for Turkdom's future. Among Gökalp's magical and messianist notions of the early 1910s, "Turan" was the most suggestive term. It combined a seminal conception of elitist social engineering, which demanded that society must be cropped and cleansed, with new elements engrafted. "The people are the garden, we are the gardeners," read a line in the poem "Kızılelma." This statement could also have been made by Talaat in the Central Committee after 1912.[84]

The teenaged Ziya belonged to a milieu in Diyarbekir in the 1890s that we must grasp in concise terms if we are to understand him as an adult. Anti-Armenian right-wing revolutionism, social envy, and mob violence permeated the society at that time. Diyarbekir's anti-Christian Islamism reacted against a new Armenian self-reliance and the revolutionary currents among Armenian youths. It resented European reform demands based on the Berlin Treaty, and the additional scope of action that the Ottoman Christians had obtained thanks to egalitarian measures of the Tanzimat and new transnational dynamics. In the language of the French vice-consul Gustave Meyrier in 1896 in Diyarbekir, "the Young Turks had convinced the Old Turks to join in finishing off the Christians and, consequently, the sultan, whom they consider[ed] the reason for all evils of the country."[85]

The political atmosphere in Eastern Asia Minor during summer 1893 was tense after Armenians in Sasun had resisted double taxation by the state and by Kurdish tribes. The state reacted against this unheard-of disobedience of non-Muslim subjects by massacring, via the military, more than a thousand villagers, whose houses were also destroyed. This reminded the European powers of the reform demand of the 1878 Berlin Treaty, which had been shelved. Sultan Abdulhamid, however, had to apprehend reactionary revolts if he accepted the elaborate reform plan as proposed in 1895. He feared consequences for the entire region, following the example of the Balkans, and moreover risked losing the acceptance of the Muslims, which he fundamentally needed.[86]

Under European pressure, faced with the evidence of mass crimes in Sasun, Abdulhamid had to acquiesce and sign the reform plan on 17 October 1895. Consequently, in many towns of Eastern Asia Minor, murderous pogroms took place. This was the case in Diyarbekir the first three days of November 1895. According to vice-consul Meyrier, the pogroms were organized by a "party of the Young Turkey [group], composed of twenty leaders or so," of whom he mentions a few, including Pirinçizâde Arif, the mayor of Diyarbekir, maternal uncle of Ziya, and the father of Feyzi.[87] The vali Enis Pasha, a native from Salonica, connived with these leaders and was already known from his former post in Mardin as a fanatical anti-Christian. The appointment of this *mutasarrıf* (district governor) of Mardin to the post of vali in Diyarbekir had raised protests in early October 1895.

According to Meyrier, 1,191 Christians, mostly Armenians in town, were killed during the turmoil, as well as 200 aggressors. Comparatively well organized, the Diyarbekir Christians had tried to defend themselves. Missionaries had taken in 3,000 refugees and the consulate 1,500; 50,000 persecuted Christians of the entire province were in need of food and shelter, and

many girls were abducted, a number of them sold to a slave market in Aleppo.[88] Remarkably, the 1901 correspondence between
Nâzım and İshâk Sükûti (a CUP cofounder born in Diyarbekir)
concerning the 1895 mass violence reports that they were scandalized only by the influence of foreign diplomats in town and
Enis's allegedly insufficient stance against them, and not by the
mass violence.[89]

We know the organizers' ideas of the attacks because immediately after the attacks occurred, on 4 November 1895, they
sent a long telegram, signed by four hundred people, to the
sultan. It exalted Selim I, the conqueror of Eastern Asia Minor
in the early sixteenth century, and defied, in contrast, Sultan
Abdulhamid as an implicitly weak sultan. Those who signed
the telegram represented themselves as true Ottoman Muslims whom the Armenians and foreign powers threatened.
Due to Armenian intrigue, they said, foreign powers interfered
in the eastern provinces and forced the sultan to sign reforms
that would separate the eastern provinces from the empire.
The telegram threatened that more blood would be spilled if
reforms were implemented, and it used propaganda that would
repeat itself in the decades to come: foreign conspiracy against
the fatherland supported by non-Muslim agents; evil reforms
in favor of Armenians; Armenians' intrigue, immorality, and
exploitation; and the praise of centuries-old Muslim tolerance,
but a tolerance that could be revoked at any time in favor of
comprehensive extermination.[90]

In the last years of Hamidian rule, there were a few other
turbulences—although comparatively minor—caused by the
same group of instigators, including Pirinççizâde Arif and, on
other occasions, his nephew Ziya as well. Arif was one of the
new rich of the late Tanzimat who had used the Land Code of
1858 to buy villages. Ziya himself possessed five villages north of

Diyarbekir. This group of Muslim notables wanted supportive and strong authorities but submissive Christians in the villages and in town—surely not equal partners and possibly superior competitors using transnational networks.[91]

After the 1908 revolution, Gökalp founded the CUP Diyarbekir branch that henceforth was dominated by the Pirinççizâde family. He had perhaps become a member of the CUP with Abdullah Cevdet as early as 1894, but he certainly was a member in 1896 while enrolled at the Imperial Veterinary School in Istanbul, where he met Sükûti.[92] During the repression of the opposition in 1896–98, he was arrested like Talaat but released earlier. Without having finished his studies, he returned to his hometown and married the girl whom his family had destined for him. Arif was elected CUP deputy in November 1908 and, after his death in 1909, he was succeeded by his son Feyzi, Ziya's cousin.

After the July 1908 revolution, Ziya was prone to the vision of an "Ottoman America" in the sense of a constitutional and federalist melting pot of diverse ethnic and religious groups based on equality. He denounced explicitly the fantasy of an immense Turan under the authority of a mythic *hakan* (ruler).[93] Nevertheless, a little later this Turan-cum-*hakan* took the place of a *mehdi* in a new Turanist/pan-Turkist gospel. In fact, the brief window of opportunity after July 1908 could not suffice had he wanted to emancipate himself from his formative experiences in Hamidian Diyarbekir. After an Ottomanist interim, he embraced this legacy, embedding and transforming it within a pan-Turkist ideology that exalted heroic will, great rulership, patriotic ideals, and Islamic Turkdom.

The truth-seeking young man Ziya from Diyarbekir had become Gökalp—since 1911 his name as the prophet of a messianist Turkism/Turanism. His conversion coincided with his

new socialization in Salonica. His persuasive talents and cha-
risma as an intellectual mastermind made him influential in the
Central Committee, where he prevailed over others, in particular, the more conservative religious scholar Hayri. A prolific
writer of poetry and prose in relevant journals, particularly in
Türk Yurdu, the main organ of the Turkist movement, by 1912
Gökalp was the spiritual drive of this movement. During the
CUP crisis starting in 1910, both Talaat and Gökalp turned away
from the 1908 democratic utopia. They departed toward a right-
wing revolutionism that was henceforth fed by a compelling
Islamic pan-Turkism: one as its spiritual father, the other its
executor. Both were self-taught and self-made.

The "awakening" of the Turks and Turkic peoples is a main
issue in Gökalp's writings. Yet the essential place of Islam and
of a normative history of religions must also be scrutinized,
since they formed a framework for Talaat's policy. Gökalp read
varied and wide-ranging works of history to support his theses on state, society, and religion. One of his main theses was
inspired by a culturalist zeitgeist that linked Protestantism and
modernity. Astutely, Gökalp represented Protestantism as an
Islamized Christianism. This allowed him to "prove" that Islam
was the most modern and superior religion. He also argued
that Islam had pertinent reasons to sacralize the state instead
of laicizing it. The future belonged to Islam, since the inclusion of both religion and state was its unique advantage. Gökalp
therefore strictly refused the idea of a social contract instead of
sacralized bonds. In the same vein, he castigated the Tanzimat.
He argued that the Tanzimat idea of a constitutional monarchy
emulated the small democratic units formed by non-Muslim
millet—instead of focusing on a strong, corporatist state.
Reorganized after the mid-nineteenth century, the millet were
led by elected assemblies and headed by patriarchs.[94]

For Gökalp, individual rights were subordinated to the state, as he underlines in his poem "Duty": "I do not have rights, interests, and desires / I have my duty, and do not need anything else. . . . I close my eyes / I perform my duty."[95] In connection with his hometown and his relations (notably, his cousin Feyzi), Gökalp codetermined the character and development of the Diyarbekir CUP branch, which evolved into a kind of protofascist CUP outpost in Eastern Asia Minor in the 1910s. Still, in April 1909, many young CUP branches in Eastern Asia Minor, including Diyarbekir, Mamuretülaziz, and Urfa, had resisted reactionary anti-Christian Islamism and contributed to preventing the violence that followed the example of Adana. This changed by 1912, when the Diyarbekir branch not only had affiliated with the local legacy of anti-Western Islamism and anti-Christian mob violence, but was now also part of an intraimperial organization linked to the state. Added to this, it received the new impulses of an Islamic pan-Turkism framed by Gökalp. The empire-wide fame of this son of Diyarbekir was a source of pride.

4

Alignment toward War and Dictatorial CUP Power (1911–14)

TALAAT'S EXPERIENCE OF 1908–11 had caused him to lose not only his confidence in parliamentarian government but also good faith in a more general sense. Undeterred, he resumed working toward his basic goal: to "save the state" in CUP terms, that is, to reestablish a full-fledged CUP-led power organization. Since 1910, Talaat proved by deeds and words that he did not believe in equality, the priority of constitutional government, and law and order to be provided in this framework. Rather, since 1912, he focused on politics that combined komitecilik with public relations and the mobilization of the youth and the common man on the street. This tactic was accompanied by a more aggressive, markedly war-prone ideology and propaganda, along with paramilitary organization. Alignment toward war was therefore a decisive new direction.

This way, by using macrohistorical opportunities, Talaat rescued himself and the CUP from a paralyzing crisis. Three factors played a central role in the pursuit of his goals. The first was the CUP's fall from power in summer 1912 and the First

Balkan War, a crisis that offered him the opportunity to provide renewed—this time war-prone and more public—leadership. The second factor was the emergence of Ziya Gökalp's Islamic Turkism, which gave him, the CUP, and CUP sympathizers more compelling ideological groundwork. A third factor was that Talaat internalized, and now used, the éminences grises' radicalism as an efficient catalyst to combine with audacious political gambling. Henceforth, his tendencies were toward bold action and radical solutions, behavior he had already been versed in during the pre-1908 period. He now lost his reserve and hesitation, which had been part of the parliamentary phase of his life, 1908–11.

Active participation in World War I, in a common gamble with Germany, would make him the incontestable, almost untouchable leader in 1914–18. From late 1912, Talaat was not only a more unifying figure than any other member of the committee but also more popular and visible as a leader in the capital. In this estimation, he even passed Enver, the iconic hero of the 1908 revolution. Yet Enver remained his ongoing close partner in organizing power and for contact with German representatives in 1913–14, along with Ahmed Cemal Pasha, who soon moved to Syria.

From autumn 1912, war, coup d'état, and cooperation with officers allowed Talaat to emerge as the political winner from the crises before. He was henceforth free from the indecision that had restrained him when faced with high-ranking senior figures such as Mehmed Kâmil Pasha, Hüseyin Hilmi, and Mahmud Şevket Pasha, as well as the éminences grises in the committee. Since his youth, Talaat had only reluctantly accepted any authority. From now on, he wanted to impose himself and his political language on a committee that he personified more now than ever. He reinvented himself as a radical and unforgiving

Ottoman patriot who acted publicly in the name of the Ottoman Muslim nation.

Remarkably, this alignment toward nationalist radicalism went hand in hand with a marriage of convenience with Zionism. After the Young Turk Revolution, the Berlin-based Zionist Organization had opened an unofficial branch in Istanbul that could not achieve its hoped-for goals, since the CUP remained reluctant toward anything resembling Jewish autonomy in Palestine. The CUP's more anti-Christian stance after 1912 promised delusory common horizons. Yet the CUP's assumption of international Jewish power, and backing by the Western powers, offered Zionism a limited scope of action in turbulent times (see chap. 5, sec. "Talaat, Palestine, and Zionism").

From summer 1912, Talaat took a new and breathless lead. As we will see in this chapter, he was the paramount mastermind of the January 1913 putsch and of the reconquest of Edirne in July 1913, even if both were implemented in close cooperation with a few others, such as the military figurehead Enver. Although minister of the interior, Talaat led the negotiations for peace with the Balkan states and the reform agreement for the eastern provinces in the second half of 1913. Since late 1912, when the call for such reforms had reemerged in international diplomacy, he looked at the Kurdish-Armenian region as another "Macedonia" to be prevented at all costs. Before brutally readdressing this issue in 1915, in June 1914 he orchestrated the expulsion of Ottoman Christians dwelling on the Aegean coast to make room for the settlement of Muslim refugees from the Balkans. This move, the putsch, and the reconquest of Edirne were striking successes that made Talaat and Enver highly popular among a majority of Ottoman Muslims.

Rambert, who gave a nonpartisan contemporary view from Istanbul, considered the year 1913 an "abominable" period, "a year of disaster, war, extermination, and ruins," asking, "What held 1914 in reserve? It seems impossible that it brings us the renewal . . . The situation created in the Balkans by several international treaties at Lausanne, London, Bucharest, and Constantinople appears still like an artificial, extremely fragile scaffold. All the states and all nationalities have suffered from some violence."[1] Now nearly seventy-five years old, on 1 January 1914, a skeptical Rambert saw the Ottoman future as inseparable from all of Europe's destiny. Most Europeans, in contrast, did not. Up to the present, historiography on World War I has remained surprisingly Eurocentric and has largely left aside the political hub of Istanbul. This hub, however, was essential for Germany's road to war in July 1914, and thus for Europe's seminal catastrophe.

CUP's Crises, Fall, and Radical Recalibration

By spring 1911, Talaat had reached a personal low point: "[Politically] he continued now only as a deputy of Edirne in the parliament. But whereas, formerly, he had won the appreciation of his friends in the parliament through his calm sangfroid and by aptly handling many issues, he had now taken a much more nervous and aggressive posture," Hasan Babacan describes tellingly in his Turkish biography of Talaat.[2] Internal tensions and external attacks threatened the future of the CUP. "Within the Party of Union and Progress the divergences have become dangerous," noted Rambert on 1 March 1911. Seeing danger for the party, Hayri prayed at the end of the same month, "Lord, turn this mischief to peace." In April, a new, clearly conservative party (*hisb-i cedid*) separated from the CUP faction.[3]

Cavid's diary on April 1911 reveals in detail a "most important and vital" issue that Talaat had, at first, hidden from him. A group surrounding the CUP member and colonel Mehmed

Sadık, a hero of the 1908 revolution, had "seduced under the guise of religion a great many among our party members and those whom we trusted most." When Talaat went to talk with Sadık for nearly five hours, there were "always the same fairy tales and nonsense: Freemasonry, Zionism, personalities." Sadık's group suspected, above all, Cavid, Talaat, and Cahid.[4] As a consequence, Cavid resigned on 12 May, whereas Colonel Sadık was sent to Salonica for duty. Immediate breakup was avoided and the programmatic points of the separatists provisionally accepted. Yet the crises continued, and the CUP's influence was shaken. Opposition against the CUP, however, lacked organization, discipline, and, largely, progressive orientation. In Rambert's perception, a less-than-helpful press had become absorbed with declamations and quarrels about great words, incompatible principles, and personal sensitivities. He wished for a common pragmatic, enlightened, and more modest patriotism.[5]

Some European circles in Istanbul expected salvation by a military dictatorship. Meeting mid-September 1911, when Cavid had come back from his travels in Asia Minor, he and Rambert agreed that "everywhere in the country the minds were overexcited." Violence impended when the new parliamentary session in October would begin. Cavid also drew attention to dangerous developments in Eastern Anatolia.[6] Italian aggression against Libya in late September 1911 added to the agitation, which now took on new international dimensions. Public opinion in Italy, too, was overexcited, because of the seemingly excellent opportunity for colonialist expansion; but, evidently, such a conquest "for no other pretext than considerations of a general policy to redraw the map of Africa would have the character of a mere spoliation," Rambert wrote on 24 September 1911. "This is a new big threat at the horizon with a new element of trouble and complications amidst cruel obstacles against which Turkey struggles."[7]

On 28 September, at 2:00 p.m., the Italian ambassador handed down a harsh ultimatum to the Sublime Porte that led to "indescribable confusion." Only Istanbul's ongoing state of emergency prevented excesses. Huge despair and grief reigned in Salonica. A feverishly active Central Committee discussed strategies and published declarations exhorting the people to stay calm. On 29 September 1911, Italy declared war. People in Europe demonstrated "sentimental sympathy" for Turkey, but all European governments had "directly or indirectly participated at the [new] repartition of influences in the Mediterranean." Some deputies in Istanbul boasted that they would succeed in mobilizing twenty thousand Arab fighters against the Italians.[8]

In fact, the CUP and its young officers, first of all Enver and also Mustafa Kemal, were galvanized by the challenge to organize patriotic guerilla resistance. Enver immediately left Berlin, where he had been a military attaché since 1909, for Salonica, where the committee consented to organize resistance in Libya. Enver had been engaged to Naciye Sultan, the niece of Mehmed V, since the aftermath of the 1909 counterrevolution. Therefore, among the Arabs, he enjoyed the prestige of being a relative of the caliph-sultan. In contrast to Talaat, Enver had a penchant for suavity, high society, and caliphal references, even if he would faithfully promise in the committee that all he did first served the common patriotic ideal. In this vein, he had, in fact, been diligent to immolate for the CUP's cause his brother-in-law Nâzım (Ömer Nâzım, not to be confused with the committee member Nâzım) in June 1908.[9]

Immediately after the Italian declaration of war, the Hakkı Pasha cabinet fell. Hakkı was succeeded by Mehmed Said

Pasha. Neither Talaat nor Cavid reentered the cabinet, but their friend Hayri, a future member of the Central Committee, did so. He was given the Ministry of Foundations (*evkâf*). Whereas the grand vizier looked for peace, the CUP insisted on resolute armed resistance in Libya. At the same time, it sought backing from the Entente powers for what it considered its rightful cause. Cavid therefore wrote a letter to Winston Churchill, the newly appointed British minister of the navy, who was Cavid's and Talaat's contemporary. Halide Edib, a former pupil of the American College for Girls—the female figurehead of the Young Turk Revolution and, after 1911, of Turkism—translated the letter into English. The letter asked if the time had come "for a permanent alliance between our two countries." Churchill and Talaat had probably first met when Talaat led a parliamentary delegation to London in July 1909, but for sure when Churchill had gone on holiday to Istanbul in July 1910.

With the letter to Churchill, Cavid and Talaat hoped to address a new First Lord of the Admiralty sympathetic with the CUP cause and their revolt against Italian invasion. Churchill's answer was polite but negative, as instructed by the foreign secretary. The committee members learned that neither Britain nor Germany deemed appropriate an alliance or accord with Ottoman Turkey. At last, as heart-balm for them, in a meeting on 1 November 1911, the German ambassador Marschall von Bieberstein emphasized esteem for the CUP—in contrast to British and French skepticism and enmity but in-line with the marked German rapprochement with the CUP in fall 1910.[10]

"This war becomes an obsession, and nobody knows how to get out," Rambert observed, at the same time pointing to the sharp concurrence between the European powers. They could not act upon Said Pasha's timely appeal for common diplomatic intervention against Italy. A possible future alliance with Italy,

FIGURE 7: Churchill, 1911 (Library of Congress).

and consequently an upheaval of the hitherto existing balance, was at stake. "Little would be needed for plunging the whole of Europe into war."[11] Rambert's perspective from Istanbul on Europe, combined with observations regarding Turkey, was that "a feeling of general unrest affects all minds. The Turks feel threatened from everywhere at the same time." They believed that they must hit back everywhere.[12]

Even if untenable to retain, Tripolitania (Ottoman Libya) had become an absorbing symbol of Ottoman patriotism and militant resistance against imperialist Europe. This unfortunately

FIGURE 8: Talaat, ca. 1910: "His Excellence, Young Turkey's
venerable Talaat Bey Efendi, the energetic and resolute
minister of the interior" (SALT Research, Istanbul).

distracted even bright minds like Cavid's, not only from the
main challenges and back-breaking work at home but also from
fundamental interrogations of Ottoman versions of imperialism. They feared that "to abandon Tripolitania would be a big
moral downfall" for the CUP and would damage it in the eyes
of all Ottomans.[13] Thinking of politics in terms of imperial sovereignty, honor, and central rule, the young men, most of them
from the Balkans, confirmed one or the other in their male

party circles. They projected the same mentality upon society, now framed as a nation, in whose name they spoke. With patriotic fervor, the CUP opened a guerilla front in Tripolitania, while simultaneously losing the struggle for a constitutional Turkey in the capital and in Asia Minor, and with it the groups most loyal to the constitution.

Since summer 1911, dissidents, including Colonel Sadık's circle, who wanted an Ottoman Muslim alignment, and liberal intellectuals and representatives of non-Muslim groups worked in favor of a new and strong party. Even if an independent deputy, the lawyer and Armenian writer Krikor Zohrab, a friend of Cavid's, was an active networker in favor of a liberal alliance. Mid-October 1911, Zohrab, Cavid, Talaat, Halil, Hakkı, Vartkes Serengülian, and Karekin Pastermajian (alias Armen Garo; the last two mentioned here were deputies from Erzurum), were also present. Zohrab insisted that constitutional rule be implemented, since in reality a regime depending on and in favor of the CUP existed, while real pluralism was lacking. CUP interference in the government must stop. The non-Turkish groups felt increasingly alienated by committee chauvinism. A decidedly different policy vis-à-vis these groups was required. Zohrab proposed cooperation and a coalition of the CUP and liberals, since they agreed on many important points.[14]

After a meeting in their Istanbul Nuruosmaniye headquarters, the committee, including Talaat, Cavid, Nâzım, Midhat Şükrü, and Hüseyinzâde Ali, refused to accept Zohrab's proposals. Failed CUP-liberal cooperation and indignation against the Italian invasion coincided with the beginning of a Turkish nationalism organized in the associations Türk Yurdu (Turkish home or homeland) and Türk Ocağı (Turkish hearth). The CUP supported them and identified with them. The movement was also strong among students abroad. Its main journal was

entitled *Türk Yurdu*, the name of the organization abroad. It
pointed to a different direction than that in which a compromise with liberals would have led.[15]

On 21 November 1911, the dissidents founded the party
Freedom and Entente (Hürriyet ve İtilâf) and made Ferid
Pasha their president. The new party won an important seat
for Istanbul in a by-election on 11 December. The aftermath in
parliament was excitement, and newspaper articles were full
of political attacks. For the first time the CUP people feared
losing the upcoming general elections. "They want to do a last
effort . . . dissolve the parliament and have as soon as possible
elections . . . as long as they still possess power and their provincial organization," Rambert commented.[16] On 18 January
1912, the parliament was dissolved; on 22 January, Talaat and
Cavid were again made ministers. In order to better direct the
outcome of the election that spring, Talaat took the Ministry
of Post and Telegraph. He had initially accepted the Interior
Ministry again, but internal opposition arose. As a former post
office clerk in Salonica, Talaat had mastered the communication technology of his time and later equipped his private house
in Istanbul with a telegraph machine.[17]

The CUP won a forced victory in an irregular election (*sopalı
seçim*) that lasted from February to April 1912, in which it used
mob violence and penal action against adversaries. Moreover,
it did not nominate its previous Rûm deputies. When the session began on 18 April, there were only 107 deputies present,
not only because many had not yet arrived but also because,
strangely, the elections still proceeded.[18] The general ambiance
had become increasingly suffocating because of the Islamic or
sharia factor in public life. Both sides tried to use Islam—other
religions did not play a similar role—in their political favor,
even if constitutionally minded representatives from both the

CUP and the Hürriyet ve İtilâf agreed that Islamist reaction was a main danger for the country. Entrenched in rivalry, they lacked the democratic know-how and will to cooperate in order to face this challenge.

A declaration on March 1912 by the conservative sheykhul-islam Abdurrahman Nesib embarrassed them all, because it subjected Muslim women to a strict dress code according to the sharia, to be imposed by the "heads of family" and the courts. Convinced adherents of the constitution from both sides were incapable of jointly reacting against this anticonstitutional grip on society. "If the law, the authorities and the courts penetrate the habits of dressing, what becomes of the principle of individual liberty that is warranted by the constitutions of all civilized states, and by that of Turkey in the first place?" Rambert asked.[19]

The CUP had missed Zohrab's appeal for cooperation, which put into motion an unforgiving race for power. It achieved, in fact, an overwhelming electoral victory, but not for long. Mudslinging from both sides continued. Cavid was accused of having been corrupted by foreign money, "entirely unjustly, in my opinion, because I do not consider him a man of money," Rambert wrote.[20] Talaat was uneasy with Mahmud Şevket Pasha, the war minister, who had not taken timely resolute action against the officers around Sadık, although in early July he introduced a law that prohibited interference in politics by army officers. Talaat disrespectfully urged Mahmud's withdrawal on 9 July, thus affronting parts of the army. The tension rose in and outside the capital. In Albania, an insurrection larger than that of 1910 broke out. Albanian officers revolted, and a number of them escaped from Manastir Vilayet to the surrounding mountains, as Enver and Niyazi had done four years previously.[21]

FIGURE 9: Women in modern dress were looked at with growing
suspicion: "Devil, go and smash her face!" "The [good] days have gone."
"She shall break her neck, won't she?" (*Cem*, 18 February 1911, 9).

In this context of upheaval, in June Sadık founded the
Halaskâr (savior) officer group. According to Lütfi Simavi,
a leading official at the sultan's court, Sadık wrote a letter
on 11 July, in their name, to Halil, the president of the Ottoman Assembly, demanding the immediate dissolution of the

FIGURE 10: "What days have befallen us, oh [my] Sultan, warrior for Islam!"
Turned toward Talaat's friend Halil, who is suspended at "the balance of powers,"
an elderly officer admonishes, "Until you learn [respect before the sultan], you will
write five hundred times [the traditional formula of reverence] until this evening,
to come to reason." With his back against the wall, Halil, then president of the
Ottoman Assembly, remained at this position until the parliament was dissolved
on 5 August, three weeks after the cabinet resigned. From 5 August, the CUP
was completely evicted from the political institutions (*Cem*, 10 August 1912).

parliament. "We do not want to sully ourselves with your filthy
blood . . . If you fail, however, to give evidence that you comply
with our wishes within forty-eight hours, we will discharge our
patriotic duty with perfect determination." This meant that a
strong group in the army demanded a new government cleared
from CUP members. The grand vizier Mehmed Said and his
cabinet resigned on 16 July.[22]

On 21 July, Gazi Muhtar Pasha, a hero of the 1877–88 Russo-
Turkish War, accepted the role of heading a new cabinet with

representatives from outside the CUP, all of them comparatively old and partly made up of men from the old Hamidian
regime. By then, the CUP had lost all governmental power and
risked being politically marginalized within weeks or a few
months. Committee members had to expect penal prosecution. "Everybody was in fear," Cavid wrote.[23] Rumor of flights
spread. There was risk of assassination attempts against public
figures, including Cavid and Talaat. A prompt and unfortunate
amnesty of all figures of the Hamidian regime made the new
government look reactionary right from the start, Rambert
complained.[24]

War-Prone, Revanchist, High-Risk:
Talaat Retrieves the CUP from Its Nadir

Shortly before the crisis reached its apex, Talaat felt that
Mahmud Şevket's forced withdrawal had probably been a
major mistake. He concluded, dissenting with the other committee members, that "we need to mingle anew with the nation
to acquire new force; therefore, we have to withdraw."[25] On 22
July 1912, he published a short article in the newspaper *Sabah*,
in which he portrayed himself as an unabashed, deeply sincere patriot who was more than ever entirely committed to his
nation's welfare.

> Those who identify with the fatherland, who have spent
> the greatest effort for the prosperity and progress of the
> nation, cannot leave the nation and flee to Europe. I declare
> that since the country needs care and concern today more
> than ever, I will not leave, even for a minute, the center of
> the fatherland to go here or there. All malicious news of

this sort has been deliberately fabricated. The deputy of Edirne, Talaat.[26]

This remained the public image and the self-perception that Talaat was to cultivate until the end. "I have certainly only known commitment and sacrifice for what concern for the fatherland and the public safety demanded. In my opinion, there is nobody in the country who has occupied a more useful place in the service of the fatherland than I," he wrote in 1919, at the end of his apologia.[27] On the same day the article appeared in *Sabah*, Cavid wrote in his diary that "the general opinion now considers Union and Progress as broken down and feels great satisfaction from this consideration." The next day he wrote, "They slander Union and Progress as tyrannical. In what an ingrate country do we live, O Lord!" The fall of the CUP was accomplished on 5 August by the dissolution of the parliament and the redeclaration of the state of emergency. Moreover, the committee was completely out of money and thus sought Huguenin's help.[28]

The defeat became even more depressing for the CUP as the ARF terminated its nearly quadrennial alliance by mid-August, although some relations continued. The ARF and the CUP had again concluded an electoral alliance in February 1912 without fixing an explicit proportional representation, as the Hürriyet ve İtilâf had done with its alliance partners. The ARF was very disppointed, when, lacking CUP support, only ten instead of the twenty-three expected deputies were elected (a reasonable 10 percent, out of a total of 283). Since Hürriyet ve İtilâf and its candidates largely lost the forced elections, the Armenians were underrepresented, although they did not lack able candidates. Besides this, there was no progress in the agreed-upon issues of land restitution, supported return of refugees to villages,

FIGURE 11: "Here rests his [Talaat's] chamber. Neither did it itself enjoy peace, nor give comfort to the people. It broke down and left this world. Now the people in the tombs have to endure it. The parliament [is] dying on 23 July 1328 [5 August 1912]" (*Cem*, 10 August 1912).

and village security warranted by local Armenians. Moreover, a promised sum of 12,000 Turkish pounds for Armenian schools still had not been delivered.[29]

In the first days after the Halaskâr insurrection, when Talaat published his short declaration, he had thought of organizing violence against the new order. He even threatened a domestic war, but soon gave up this idea. He and the committee chose a calm proceeding.[30] The CUP Congress, which had met in early September 1911 for the first time in Istanbul, not Salonica, elected in 1912 an unusually high number of twenty-one Central Committee members, among them Talaat, Cavid, Cahid, Hayri,

Nâzım, Halajian, Ali Münif, Ziya Gökalp, and Mithat Şükrü. It decided to continue the political struggle and to prepare for the next elections and thus not to abstain out of protest. This made the government nervous. In order to prevent the CUP's return based on its provincial organization, a purge in the administration was needed, but to do this, the government would need greater determination.[31]

Trapped in an unfortunate rivalry, the CUP involved the government in a race of populism and patriotic defiance in the context of growing tensions with Bulgaria and other Balkan states. At the same time, urgent "administrative matters were completely neglected," the outcome being that "the public avidly complained that the government of the elders was no better than that of the young [Young Turks]." Since March 1912, Bulgaria, Serbia, Montenegro, and Greece had been forming a military Balkan League capable of defeating the Ottoman forces in European Turkey, but by the end of September 1912, not even well-informed observers of current affairs were aware of the alliance.[32] The martial propaganda and military preparation among its neighbors aggrieved Ottoman minds and aroused their pride. On 28 September, Rambert was alarmed that, in an unusual move, the governement "suddenly ordered great military maneuvers in Adrianople and the proximity of the Bulgarian frontier. It is difficult not to see here a provocation," he concluded and worried about Bulgarian reactions. Bulgaria reacted with mobilization.

Talaat and the CUP did all they could to benefit from the tense atmosphere; in fact, they had worked hard to prepare it and to put the government in *zugzwang*. In a long interview in late September 1912, Mahmud Muhtar, the minister of the navy and son of the grand vizier, tried to persuade Talaat toward a peace policy, in particular in the CUP press. Talaat, however, declared that, "in the first place, we are partisans of war ... and we will never give away this strong weapon [of warmongering]." As a principal reason for this, he stated that the CUP was treated unjustly by the new government.[33] On Friday, 4 October, the CUP organized a huge meeting on Sultanahmet Square, where Talaat, Ali Münif, Halajian, Nâzım, Ömer Naci, Emmanuil Emmanuilidis (a Rûm deputy, close to the CUP), and others gave speeches. Talaat and Halajian swung Ottoman flags and shouted "War, we want war!," thus inciting the numerous students from the nearby Darülfünun (Istanbul University) who were in the crowd. They suggested that war alone could save national honor and interests. The students repeated Talaat's "War, we want war!" and added, "Assault on [the Bulgarian town of] Plovdiv, assault on [the Bulgarian capital] Sofia!"[34]

On the next day, 5 October 1912, Hüseyin Cahid wrote, in CUP's mouthpiece *Tanin*, that "there is only one act, one vision that occupies the life and existence of the nation: war, war, war." Cavid alone, a charismatic orator, had the wisdom to absent himself and refuse to speak because "as long as the state had not determined and decided on how to proceed, it was not appropriate to deliver speeches in public places." His diary entry on 3 October mentions an "enormous excitation" and a "war desire" that was difficult to stop. He nevertheless still believed on 7 October that war could be avoided.[35]

By early October 1912, Talaat was again a unifying figure in a committee that had been deeply depressed a few weeks earlier. For the first time, he was now also the mobilizing figure of an entire inflamed, educated youth. He was becoming an enthusiastic, crowd-loving agitator.[36] To set a good example, a day after the big manifestation of 4 October, he prepared to enroll as a voluntary soldier and to buy himself a bayonet.[37] CUP organizers may have arranged that processions of demonstrators, and "groups of volunteers went all over town shouting 'Long live war' and did this in good discipline even in front of foreign embassies."[38] There was a realistic chance that discretion, savvy, and international diplomacy could prevent a war for which the Balkan states were, in fact, prepared. Talaat and the CUP, however, were set on the contrary path. They used poisonous propaganda to achieve new political ground for themselves in Ottoman society, even if at the price of a destructive radicalization. Thus, they largely affected the press and a government that was not sufficiently resilient.

Shortly before the CUP meeting of 4 October 1912, in a move against the CUP, Hürriyet ve İtilâf, the rival party, had also called a meeting in order to inspire resolution and confidence, while simultaneously avoiding martial rhetoric and attacks against the government. The government had certainly acted unwisely by allowing the CUP meeting, and, before, by organizing military maneuvers on the frontier. Moreover, it had manifestly not been able to fully implement the state of emergency. It still struggled in early October to save the situation and, in contact with European diplomats, to commit itself to reform as stipulated in Article 23 of the Berlin Treaty. Notorious, insufficient administration was a main reason for unrest and interference in European Turkey and could serve as a precedent for an anti-Ottoman attack. The experienced foreign minister Gabriel Noradunghian was opposed to war.[39]

The CUP, in turn, exploited Noradunghian's diplomatic move to present itself as the only truly patriotic force and the others as dependent on foreign powers. It inspired, mobilized, and organized the youth on the streets. Thousands of them moved to the Sublime Porte on 8 October, chanting patriotic songs and shouting, "We want war! Long live war! To hell with Article 23!" Finally, Grand Vizier Ahmed Muhtar Pasha and his son, Mahmud Muhtar Pasha, appeared to face the crowd. A student leader, Rambert reports, shouted that "the nation wanted war, not the dismemberment of the empire nor the abandonment of Macedonia." After Ahmed Muhtar's allocution to the students and his reference to past heroism, the crowd shouted that it wanted victories now, not in the past. The chants of the crowd prevented the grand vizier from chiming in again.[40] As a result, the government was even more intimidated. In the morning of the same day, Montenegro had declared war on the Ottoman Empire. Its allies followed after a strange nine-day period of Montenegro's declared war without action.[41]

The Ottoman government was put under compulsion as much from the inside as from the Balkan states. The CUP, large parts of the army, and a vociferous, educated youth wanted war and categorically refused negotiations on reform under European patronage. The Ottoman army, however, was not ready at all. Within a few days in early October, the Sublime Porte had been dragged to the threshold of war, and, nonresilient, had itself slithered into it. Henceforth, it hastened mobilization, requisition, and peace with Italy, achieved on 15 October, although feasible long before this. The European stock exchanges panicked about their oriental stocks and shares. Mediated by Zohrab, there were renewed efforts from Hürriyet ve İtilâf for an alliance between the parties in order to bridge the cleft of the political landscape in times of danger. The CUP, however, looked down on its rival, judging the advances as a sign of weakness or internal rifts.[42] Before the end of October, bad military news reached Constantinople. Consequently, Muhtar's cabinet fell and was replaced by a government under Kâmil Pasha on 30 October 1912.

Both Kâmil and the new minister of the interior, Ahmed Reşid (Rey), were resolute enemies of the CUP.[43] They wanted to achieve a thorough dismantling of the CUP and its provincial power basis. But how to do this in times of an ill-born, half self-inflicted, and, in every sense, catastrophic war? The CUP, with Talaat at its sharp end, did not hesitate to put the whole blame of defeat and loss on the reigning government. What was lacking on both sides, when faced with defeat, was honest self-assessment. In his retrospective, Ahmed Reşid went so far as to lay the main blame for the Balkan War on two Armenians, the CUP's Halajian and his cabinet colleague Noradunghian.[44]

Additionally missing on the CUP side was soul-searching after a vocal campaign that, in scholarly restrospect, had decisively "contributed to the outbreak of the disastrous Balkan Wars."[45] Worse, the warmongering continued unabashed. Some minds pondered ominous new futures: "If Rumeli is lost, the issue of the union of different peoples [ittihâd-ı anasır] will lose its importance, and we will follow a different policy." This meant an Asia Minor–focused policy. Himself incorruptible and well meaning, but subordinate to a committee dominated by others, Cavid was to prove dramatically wrong when insisting that the Rûm of Anatolia would then live "in entire security."[46]

Within two weeks, Ottoman military might had collapsed, and most of European Turkey had been lost. By early November 1912, the myths of Ottoman superiority, Islamic conquest, and the Ottoman Crescent's eternal glory were falsified. War discourse had proved utterly ugly and untrue. "The grief and desolation of the Turks is hard to look at. They bow their heads in gloomy confusion . . . asking themselves what is happening. This is a bad dream, a nightmare, an impossibility," Rambert observed. Thousands of wounded soldiers and tens of thousands of muhacir arrived in the capital. Rambert arranged with the Red Cross, the Istanbul-based journalist Max R. Kaufmann, and other compatriots to provide 50,000 mattresses and care.

Cholera spread. By mid-November, 20,000 or so patients with cholera moved through or lay in the streets, public squares, and mosque courts of Istanbul, among a much higher number of muhacir. Looking at the afflicted people, Rambert could only pray in the indicative mode: "God attends them."[47]

When Rambert talked Régie-related business with Kâmil on 8 November 1912, the latter was hopeful of bringing the war to an end within a few days. After the European powers had refused to impose an armistice, Kâmil sought mediation. Talaat, however, together with Prince Said Halim, a new CUP doyen, had immediately protested. They pleaded for even more war, and so did the newpapers soon after their visit. Renewed warmongering and misleading stories of hypothetical victories replaced soul-searching and a realistic recalibration, and— probably its main purpose—it obstructed the government. At the same time, the newspapers began to lament vehemently that the European powers did not guarantee the status quo as stated in the Berlin Treaty. Talaat's 1919 apologia still echoes this argument and this selective recourse to the Berlin Treaty.[48] The press lay the whole blame for the war on the Great powers, which had allegedly connived with the Balkan states—again suppressing any opportunity for soul-searching.

The events had actually been unfolding very rapidly; still, there were indeed disturbing European contradictions. "Twenty days only separate declarations that are both official, but contradictory. The governments of the Triple Entente had declared still by mid-October in positive terms—not only via press articles, but by explicit notifications to the belligerents— that whatever was the outcome of the war, the victor would not obtain an increase of territory." Analytical minds in Istanbul concluded that now even France and Great Britain agreed on the partition of European Turkey among the victors. Hence, they saw the eventuality of a general European war at the horizon that would obey the maelstrom of the Eastern Question. "A new and little known force has revealed itself. . . . Turkey's power of inertia [in the Balkans] has disappeared. . . . The imbroglio of European politics is complete and we are going to be faced with great historical events." When Talaat stated in 1919 that the world war had emerged from the Balkan Wars, he gave voice to a commonplace that anxious minds in Istanbul had already anticipated in autumn 1912.[49]

Putsch, January 1913

Toward mid-November 1912, the new cabinet increased repression against the CUP, closed its headquarters, and intended to arrest main leaders. Arrested but released already under the former cabinet, Hüseyin Cahid now fled to Europe. Shortly after him, Cavid hid on a French battleship, then traveled to Marseille. Cavid believed in his friend Talaat's "purely faithful and patriotic" service as a soldier at the front line, but this was not so with Talaat's military superior Şükrü Pasha, commander of Edirne. He sent Talaat back to Istanbul because he considered him an agitator in his unit. Although a soldier, Talaat had enjoyed the privileges of an officer. In Istanbul since 5 November and backed by the Central Committee, he resumed visiting members of the adversary cabinet in order to influence the government and inspire changes. However, he had to go underground a few days later.

For a while, Talaat went into hiding in the house of Tahsin's brother-in-law in Arnavutköy (Beşiktaş, Istanbul). There, together, were four people who again closely cooperated in 1915–16: the then valis of Erzurum and Trabzon Hasan Tahsin and Cemal Azmi, the CUP secretary Mithat Şükrü, and

Talaat.[50] Although well known everywhere, Talaat succeeded in hiding because many sympathizers, including among the police, supported him. The government may have preferred to leave him untouched or did not have the courage to arrest him.[51] Theoretically, it could have crushed the CUP for good in those weeks.[52] Hayri, Halajian, Karasu (Carasso), and Kazım, and intellectuals from outside the CUP, such as Abdullah Cevdet and Süleyman Nazif, were among those arrested in late October and in November. The government wanted to prevent any organized popular (including religious) protest movement in case of a peace agreement.[53]

Albanians backed by Austria and Italy declared independence on 28 November 1912. An armistice was signed on 3 December with Bulgaria, Montenegro, and Serbia. Greece stepped out of line, because it wanted to fully conquer the islands of Lesbos (Mytilene), Lemnos, and Chios. Following the armistice, Great power ambassadors and delegations from the Balkan allies met in London to negotiate a final peace.[54] In late December, Talaat could again move freely in Istanbul, invited his friends abroad to come back, and, from December, envisaged a putsch, among other alternatives. Public opinion was again agitated in the capital. Peace negotiations started in London on 16 December 1912.

"Voices from everywhere emphasize an absolute intransigence regarding the possession of Adrianople. One talks about the imminent rupture of the negotiations and the resumption of hostilities," Rambert wrote.[55] Enver had returned from the battlefield. In letters to his friends abroad, Talaat proposed three alternatives: first, a revolution to overthrow "this base government"; second, continuing to supervise the situation; and third, a pact with senior figures, in particular, Nâzım Pasha, the minister of war, against Kâmil, in order to establish a new cabinet.

By late December, Talaat judged the third alternative viable if Nâzım and the army command could be convinced to continue the war rather than surrender Edirne to the Bulgarian army or the islands to Greece. Not all agreed to such a compromise with Nâzım Pasha. Cahid and Cavid favored a new young and radical government, able to inspire new life in the country. The attitude of ("Topal") İsmail Hakkı and Nâzım, two Central Committee members who had also fled to Europe, was similar. At the same time, Cavid considered withdrawing from politics and remaining abroad.[56]

Talaat also visited Ahmed İzzet Pasha, the chief of staff, who had returned from Yemen on 17 November 1912. Yet they could not win him over for a putsch, even if, as Talaat and Hacı Âdil promised, they would make him grand vizier. "I demanded to abstain from revolutionist action during peace negotiations because this would result in perilous conditions."[57] The political atmosphere in Istanbul got worse when, on 23 January 1913, the Sublime Porte had to answer a collective note by the European powers on 17 January regarding the conclusion of peace in the Balkans and demanding the concession of Edirne. On 22 January, it was practically certain that the Porte, backed by an assembly of notables (the parliament was dissolved), would accept all demands on the next day, since it wanted peace. From early January on, expecting peace, the stock exchanges marked a trend reversal; thus, there was a chance that "the period of a never-seen-before industrial boom," as before mid-October 1912, could be resumed.[58]

Rambert, however, made an unusually personal comment in his diary: "It is easy to understand that the states of the Balkans pretend to possess this town [of Edirne], even if it is not yet conquered. The fact, however, that the Great powers unify to coerce Turkey is neither equitable nor conforms to the

principles of neutrality, nor, above all, to the solemn declarations at the beginning of the war. . . . As far as I am concerned,
I am strongly surprised by the duress of the Great powers,
above all, by the cruelly hostile attitude of France."[59] Against
this background, on 23 January 1913, a coup against an Ottoman cabinet ceding to foreign demands could not only count
on broad support at home but also on some understanding in
international circles.

Since early January, Talaat had actively prepared a putsch,
along with an ad hoc group of insiders that included Central
Committee members and others, among them Said Halim, Ziya
Gökalp, Midhat Şükrü, Hacı Âdil, Kara Kemal, Hasan Tahsin,
and Enver. He informed Victor Jacobson, the unofficial Zionist
representative in Istanbul, that a return of the CUP to power
was now possible.[60] Talaat sensed well that others, such as
Hayri and Mahmud Şevket, would not agree on a coup and
would imperil its realization. Enver was decisive for success. He
was not only charged with operative aspects but possessed persuasive qualities in the group's decision making. Moreover, he
exerted influence on the guard at the Sublime Porte, led com-
batant officers needed for the operation, and had good contacts
near the sultan, who must sign for any change of cabinet.

Yet the indisputable political mentor, planner, and authority
during the putsch itself was Talaat.[61] According to his young
and loyal CUP friend Hasan Tahsin (Uzer, 1878–1939) from
Salonica, the putsch had initially been prepared a week earlier
but had to be postponed; Tahsin had by then already organized
hundreds of demonstrators to appear before the Porte.[62] At the
front of a few CUP officers, Enver and Talaat entered the Sublime Porte on 23 January at 2:00 p.m., followed by an organized
group of demonstrators with flags before the exterior gate of
the Porte.

In the building, the ministers prepared to meet. Among them was Huguenin, with a German delegation, to discuss a loan. Nâzım, the war minister, along with some guards, made a stand against the intruders but was shot by Yakub Cemil, one of the officers. Then Talaat and Enver proceeded to the office of the grand vizier. Talaat used harsh and authoritarian words, in contrast to Enver's respectful and reluctant language, with the eighty-year-old Kâmil Pasha, ordering the latter's withdrawal. Kâmil wrote his resignation "in response to a proposal by the military," but they made him correct this to "by the people and the military."[63] Many who had known Talaat only from superficial encounters mentioned his engaging charm. He actually combined charm and intimidation, resolution and brutality, as was clear during the coup and at other occasions.

Talaat governed during and immediately after the putsch, "taking immediately real state power" and "absolute authority over the whole building," first dragoman Weber from the delegation in the building, reported.[64] From the Ministry of the Interior, Talaat sent messages to the provinces, thus immediately shaping public opinion and the attitude within the administration. In his version, Kâmil Pasha's government had decided to leave the entire province of Edirne, as well as the islands, to the enemy, the result of which was an outraged nation that demonstrated before the seat of the government and claimed the cabinet's resignation. His circular telegram ended with the words, "the new government will protect the honor of the nation."[65] Before releasing Weber and the delegation, he made a show of power. "We first had to be presented to and reconnoitered by the dictator Talaat, then only were the exterior gates opened for us." This was after 6:00 p.m. on 23 January 1913.

After the coup, Talaat boasted that with only seventeen men he had subdued the Sublime Porte and summoned everyone to his will.[66] The nation and its alleged emotions were to remain a central tool of Talaat's political discourse, disguising his own will for—and pleasure in—power and masking his penchant for drastic measures and undemocratic but populist politics. Having exploited the patriotic call to war since September 1912, Talaat now renewed it. The CUP may, in fact, have lost power while an adversary government was establishing itself domestically and negotiating compromise and peace internationally, while simultaneously cracking down on the CUP.[67] Even if precarious, Kâmil's government had enjoyed international backing and managed a broad spectrum of political resources—though not the streets or networks of radicals.

Talaat's superiority within the CUP got even stronger after "a putsch that was his creation," CUP member of parliament Emmanuil Emmanuilidis wrote. "Afterward, everybody believed in him as their true head with endless trust."[68] The rupture of the London peace negotiations was the first international consequence of the putsch. The aborted peace of January 1913 was certainly not honorable in patriotic terms. Humbling though it was, and largely pragmatic, the peace of January 1913 would, however, have broken a predilection for war, which led Turkey into disaster in the near future. Henceforth, such war-prone sentiments remained fatally linked to any allegedly patriotic assertiveness that played with tens of thousands of lives. "I give you the holy promise that even if 80,000 Turkish martyrs cover the earth between Adrianople and [the front line of] Çatalca, we prefer heroic death to renouncing Adrianople," Talaat stated.[69]

Both the radical right-wing revolutionist Talaat, soon to be at the reins of imperial power, and a Turkish nationalist discourse fed by Turkism and Ottoman pride emerged from the 1912–13 matrix in Ottoman history. Even if tamed by post–World War

I Kemalism for a few decades, this model remained formative for Turkey up to the present. "National honor" in the sense of 1912–13 remained a cornerstone of political identity. To oppose war for signing a peace treaty and losing territory in order to concentrate on domestic construction was tantamount to signing one's own political death sentence in 1913. Mahmud Şevket Pasha, the new grand vizier by the grace of the committee, knew this well and acquiesced.[70]

Revolutionists at the Reins of the Empire

In early February 1913, the "greatest trouble" still reigned in the capital, and the putschists sought evasion in a renewed war. Shortly before, Kâmil's cabinet had cracked down on its adversaries, whose conspiracy it rightly feared. Now, the CUP leaders "persecuted and imprisoned their political adversaries. That's grotesque. This time, Prince Sabahaddin's friends and supporters are targeted at the first place. Everybody is by turns minister or prisoner," wrote Rambert.[71]

The conservative Central Committee member Hayri resigned from the Ministry of Foundations. Since the new government resulted from agitation and revolution, he argued, it should be composed only of "men of revolution" (*inkılab erbabı*), that is Cavid, Cahid, İsmail Hakkı, Hacı Âdil, Enver, and Cemal, with Talaat as their grand vizier. Hayri agreed with the revolutionaries on the primordial attachment to Islam and Turkdom but not on the methods, that is, komitecilik, including the committee control of the cabinet; nor did he favor the readiness for war. He therefore proposed the dissolution of the CUP. "We [Hayri and Necmettin Molla] came to the conclusion that Talaat, Hacı Âdil, Cavid, and Cahid were a calamity for this nation that they had subdued to their influence. My Lord, preserve this country, amen."[72] By February 1913, the government indeed did not yet function. For example, it could not be accessed to solve Régie-related and public debt–related financial issues. The "only responsive person" was Cavid, who did not yet enter the cabinet but acted like a shadow minister of finance behind the official minister, Mehmed Rifat.

Rambert met Cavid privately in Berlin on 9 March and learned that Mahmud Şevket had not been let in on the putsch, but that afterward Talaat and Enver had urged him to accept the grand vizierate. Regarding the war, the CUP leaders were hopeful that, after having militarily held out since late January, they could inflict the enemies with "a few hard lessons" to save "at least the national honor." In terms of psychology, they were sufficiently farsighted to expect the Balkan allies' incapacity of peacefully dividing the spoils of European Turkey. "The small states will savagely wage war, one against the other. This will be the moment for Turkey to choose its alliances and to descend single-mindedly on one or the other." Even if principally a fond hope, this was a relevant preview of the Second Balkan War, which began in late June, shortly after the peace treaty of London on 30 May 1913. Though Rambert was discouraged about this prospect of war, he was even more depressed when he saw a grandiose military parade in Berlin in memory of national sacrifices against Napoleon, and when he learned of a French project that imposed three years of military service. "[This is a] regress[ion] of civilization toward savagery. To interrupt the studies, the apprenticeship, the life of youth . . . this is an abomination that makes me revolt."[73]

Internal and external tensions accommodated Talaat's political style. He did not enter Mahmud Şevket's cabinet but agitated offstage, urging the cabinet and chief of staff İzzet Pasha to continue the war. Convinced that Talaat pulled the strings, İzzet Pasha addressed important communications with both the new grand vizier and Talaat.[74] Pressing for war became more difficult when Edirne fell on 26 March and the ongoing war devoured resources bitterly needed at many other places within the empire. Talaat networked tirelessly without fear of contact. He even invited the liberal deputy Lütfi Fikri, a leader of Hürriyet ve İtilâf, to enter the government. Fikri was ready to join a "cabinet of national defense" (*müdafaa-i milliye*), if cleansed from "extremists." He compared the committee members to the Jacobins of the French Revolution and bitterly ironized Talaat's heroic saying that "I am even ready to be hanged at the Hagia Sophia," because Talaat expected the same from the whole country. At the end of May, he concluded that Talaat's approach to him and to Sabahaddin had only served to present the liberal dissidents as unwilling to share governmental responsibility: "Always komitecilik, frustrating troubles. . . . A government that starts with murder can never be solid."[75]

The Greek prime minister Venizelos, who enjoyed great popularity after the First Balkan War, was "like our Talaat, a komiteci" who stood or fell according to successful or failed action, answered a former Ottoman Rûm deputy when asked about him. Venizelos was, however, more democratic than Talaat and had not come to power through murder.[76] People in contemporary Greece could publicly raise their voices even in turbulent periods. Not so in Talaat's Turkey. In 1913, the post-putsch regime implemented a much more severe state of emergency than had its predecessor. Its fear of revolt made it ruthless against any adversaries, real or imaginary. Press censorship was pitiless. A great number of arrests and expulsions were not covered by the press. This even disturbed Hüseyin Cahid (Yalçın), committee member, deputy, leading journalist, and owner of the newspaper *Tanin*. In a letter to Talaat in August 1913, he wrote:

> My brother Talaat . . . I had embraced Union and Progress [CUP] with great faith. Union and Progress was for me an ideal. . . . But when I came closer to the reality of things, I saw that this relation [to the CUP] was henceforth not that which I had been looking for. . . . If the loss of big Rumeli cannot awaken us from our embittered mind-set, and if the old stiff [komiteci] understanding remains predominant, then there is plain reason that the country will again be concussed by pains. Just as a stone falls necessarily toward the earth's center, I am entirely convinced that a country that is so carelessly and narrow-mindedly governed must inevitably collapse.[77]

Like Cavid, Cahid felt deeply uneasy with Talaat's komiteci mentality and his lack of demarcation and prudence, but did not turn away from the party despite fundamental criticism. He sold his newspaper to the party in early 1914 but remained loyal.

Backed by the committee, Ahmed Cemal, the former vali of Adana and now military commander of the capital, directed the security operations and the close surveillance of dissidents. His prestige as a tough man of order increased. The empire's general situation worsened under the post-putsch regime. Diverse, small, foreign loans were obtained under exorbitant conditions. All voices of criticism were stifled.[78] A silenced society resigned. "How curious. A revolutionary government is even more favorable to [intrasocietal] agents and spies than a despotic government had been," commented Lütfi Fikri.[79] War at the door of the capital and dramatic international tension deflected attention from unaddressed and growing ruin within

the empire. A general conflagration appeared on the horizon at
the end of April 1913, when Austrian, and perhaps Italian, intervention in the Balkans loomed. Backed by Muslim landowners,
in a temporary agreement with Montenegro and Serbia, and
with Istanbul's schadenfreude, the warlord and CUP associate
Essad Pasha (Toptani) then prepared to make central Albania
an Islamic state under his rule, rivaling the provisional government of Independent Albania under prime minister Ismail
Qemali, founded in November 1912.[80]

Critical minds in the Ottoman capital confided to their diaries that it was the appropriate context in which to establish a
dictatorship without facing resistance.[81] But neither Mahmud
Şevket nor Ahmed Cemal, the manifest military power holder,
had the capacity to do this. On 11 June 1913, Şevket was assassinated. On the same day, Lütfi Fikri stated sharply, but rightly,
"In the full sense of the word, Mahmud Şevket Pasha has committed suicide, and this was decided on the day he accepted the
grand vizierate over the corpse of Nâzım Pasha. I am sure that
this man did not like, for instance, Talaat Bey and his friends.
How could it be that he became, to such a degree, a toy in their
hands and died for this reason?" The assassins were scarcely
related to Talaat, but the latter could make the best out of the
murder. He had never really accepted the authority of Şevket,
who was eighteen years older. Mutual antipathy and reserve had
hindered Talaat's inclusion in the cabinet.

Under the new grand vizier Said Halim,[82] Talaat again
became a minister of the interior. Including Talaat and Halil, the
cabinet was now much more directly dominated by the committee. Nearly ten years older than Talaat, Said Halim stood
closer to the CUP than Şevket but was not a komiteci himself.
Even if he did not possess the influence of Talaat or the éminences grises, he enjoyed prestige as a well-educated prince and

grandson of Muhammad Ali of Egypt. He was more an Islamist than a Turkist. In his later booklet on Islamization, or "becoming Muslim" (İslamlaşmak), he stated that "the salvation of the Muslim peoples" was in "their complete Islamization" and not in Western-style nationalism, while he believed, like Gökalp, in the superiority of Islam as "the most complete religion" and "the highest level of human consciousness."[83]

Şekvet's assassination was followed by a pompous funeral, during which the committee demonstrated its full control and grip of power. Most visible as a leader in the streets, as well as in the government during those critical days, was Talaat. Enver was more guarded.[84] The assassination was an opportunity to repress the opposition once and for all. Prince Sabahaddin and others had to flee. In his post-1918 memoirs, Cemal put the blame for the murder on a broad anti-CUP conspiracy led by Sabahaddin and the latter's associate Nihad Reşad (Belger). This was an ostensible attempt to show the opposition—which temporarily came to power after 1918—as potentially no less bloodstained than the CUP.[85] Although Talaat's anticipation of and acquiescence with Şevket's murder is probable, his involvement is not. Vengeance for Nâzım's assassination, personal and political, with links to oppositional circles, is highly plausible. Ibrahim Temo, a dissident, although a CUP cofounder, had been invited to a preparatory conspirators' meeting but refused to collaborate, because he still considered Talaat a candid patriot. He learned, however, from Captain Kâzım, one of the leaders of the conspiracy, that Talaat had had a plan to murder Temo too.[86]

Edirne, 1913: The Baptism of Committee Rule

The scenario hoped for by the CUP leaders since March 1913 took place. After the London Treaty on 30 May, Bulgaria was not satisfied with its territorial acquisitions in Macedonia. Trusting too much in the strength of its army, it attacked both Greece and Serbia on 29 June. For the committee, this was the moment to reconquer Edirne. For Europe, the renewed war "maintained and increased the commercial marasmus. Impossible to find loans as long as this continues. The Eastern Question keeps all that it promised," Rambert complained. Unduly broken apart, the Pandora's box of Europe's Eastern Question released plain folly, blood, fire, ruins, and extermination, the reasons of which could scarcely be fathomed by contemporaries. "An order is given and these human masses of one and a half million men lunge one at the other."[87]

Even before the January coup, the struggle for the possession of Edirne had become highly symbolic and the litmus test to distinguish Ottoman patriots from alleged defeatists. Military officers competed for the honor to participate in or—better yet—to lead the reconquest of Edirne while the Bulgarian army was busy with other enemies in July 1913. The capital of the young empire five hundred years earlier, Edirne offered a strong imperial reference and link to Ottoman glory. The CUP dealing with Edirne reveals a politicized generation obsessed with empire, at the expense of healthy domestic state building. During the months in which the CUP leaders fixated their eyes excessively on Edirne, essential issues, such as the near collapse of the economy, reform in the eastern provinces, and infrastructure projects, did not get the sustained attention they sorely needed.

By mid-July, the decision making in the new cabinet was taking time and money. Loans were out of reach. In a discussion with most of the ministers in Said Halim's mansion on 18 July 1913, Hayri argued strongly against Talaat, who wanted war. "Let us immediately proclaim war," Talaat put forward. "Excuse

me, but I do not understand your insistence on Edirne," Hayri
replied. He mentioned all of the territories recently lost and
pointed to the military and international risks of a reconquest,
but also to the negative impact of renewed war for the interior.
A majority of ministers were against war. Even the grand vizier
seemed to change his opinion in favor of Hayri. Therefore,
Talaat reacted fiercely.

The opinion of Ahmed İzzet Pasha (the new minister of war
and vice commander of the Ottoman army, the sultan being
the commander) was most critical. As soon as he voiced political reluctance, but confidence as far as the Bulgarian army was
concerned, Talaat took this as a positive vote and thanked
him "in a theatratical and affected manner" for fulfulling the
will of the government, although there was no such approved
will. Finally, when the meeting turned to discussions in small
groups, he intimidated Hayri by saying, "You did badly; resign
and leave." Talaat was in a depressed and aggressive mood. The
next day, Midhat Şükrü and Commandant Cemal approached
Hayri in the name of the committee. They admonished him,
saying that since the majority of the committee wanted war in
order to recover Edirne, he had to yield. Crestfallen, instead
of participating at the decisive cabinet meeting the same day,
Hayri chose to assist at a ceremony in the Dolmabahce Palace.[88]

From start to finish, Talaat was the engine driving Edirne's
reconquest. On 19 July, he ensured the conditions for military
attack by obtaining a loan of 1.5 million pounds from the Régie;
in exchange, he allowed a renewed concession of fifteen years
(thus, he reimplemented dependence on a foreign institution,
a contradiction of his cherished principle of sovereignty). He
drove by car to headquarters to procure the vote of Ahmed İzzet
Pasha. Talaat pressed for a written decision from the cabinet,
obtained it on 19 July, and brought it by car to the sultan. All this

ensured the indispensable conditions in which, on 21 July, Colonel Enver's unit occupied Edirne without combat. This was a flagrant break with the clauses of the London Treaty, for which Bulgaria, however, had set the example.[89] On 25 July, the Friday of the same week, Talaat assisted at the solemn ceremonies in the recovered Edirne Selimiye Mosque. He went by car and returned the same evening by train (an approximately three-hundred-mile round trip), sighing and saying, before his return, "Ah, Sultan Selim, will I really see you again?" Talaat expressed both his concern for a definitive international settlement and his emotional attachment to Selim and Edirne.[90]

The news of Edirne's recovery was received with patriotic enthusiasm in the capital and almost everywhere in the empire. For a large Ottoman public without free press, this success vindicated the political course of the CUP since autumn 1912. Above all, it gave the CUP a new self-assurance. Only now, the committee began to feel more certain of its power at the reins of the empire. Moreover, the success vindicated the radicals, that is, the vocal proponents of war led by Talaat. It marginalized the prudent ones, those who objected that, although craftily and spectacularly, the komiteci Talaat built on sand in terms of political construction. By the end of July 1913, Talaat's consolidation of power and the radical political language associated with this process had largely convinced those in the domestic sphere. Everybody had recommitted to glory and national pride, Rambert reported.[91] Decision making in the capital henceforth followed group dynamics largely dominated by Talaat. Strong figures on his side were Cemal, Enver, and, most visible internationally, Said Halim. The international lesson these men learned from the reoccupation of Edirne was not to take European diplomacy seriously if local power relations allowed active change of a situation. More generally speaking,

"Old Europe" had seriously lost "prestige in the eyes of [the CUP's] Young Turkey," as the Russian chargé d'affaires Gulke-vich in Istanbul put it.[92]

The recovery of Edirne became the starting point of a new history of national salvation. Atatürk, too, was to inscribe him-self into this history when visiting Edirne in 1930, thus symboli-cally aligning with Talaat, although he did not emphasize the Islamic-Ottoman association that prevailed in 1913. Edirne was then called the Kaaba of Honor, and its recovery a victory of the Crescent over the Cross. The city, and the Selimiye Mosque in particular, served henceforth as a place of public celebrations, a subject of speeches and special stamps, and as the destination of a new kind of national-religious pilgrimage. Talaat "trans-formed the city into a major site of popular pilgrimage" that the religious press compared to the hajj to Mekka and Medina. The Ministry of the Interior and the Association of National Defense collaborated in organizing "National Defense" pil-grimage train rides to Edirne, as shown in Eyal Ginio's recent study on the topic.[93] The new militancy and militarization of the CUP, by the way, also expressed itself in a new tradition whereby CUP luminaries outside the army received honorary military ranks. From 1913 to 1918, the "simple soldier" Talaat thus rose, step-by-step, to the rank of a colonel.[94]

———

Remarkably, it was Talaat—not the grand vizier and foreign minister Said Halim—who led the postwar negotiations with the Bulgarians at the Istanbul conference. The negotiations resulted in the agreement of 29 September 1913, which included population exchanges in Macedonia of nearly 100,000 people—half Christians (Bulgarians), half Muslims—from one state to the other. The population exchanges after the Balkan Wars, which already followed the principle of "unmixing" ethnoreligious groups, were modest if compared to those agreed to in the Treaty of Lausanne in 1923; above all, they were not, at least on paper, compulsory.[95] The agreement with Bulgaria put the reconquest of Edirne on safe diplomatic ground, although the treatment of Muslims in Bulgaria remained an issue of conflict. Negotiations with Bulgaria on a military convention succeeded only in January 1914.[96] Talaat also led negotiations with Greece, which resulted in a peace treaty by mid-November.[97] In late 1913, Turkey was in a considerably stronger position than it had been a few months before.

Even if Talaat denied it, he was sponsoring the Albanian movement that wanted to establish Muslim rule. He used a newly established so-called Special Organization (Teşkilât-ı Mahsusa) to stir up Muslim rebellion in the former Ottoman territory and to support a separatist movement in Western Thrace. The Special Organization (SO) was a paramilitary force under Süleyman Askeri, a guerilla leader who had fought in Libya with Enver. Its board or central committee met at the CUP headquarters in Istanbul. Among the SO's board members were Nâzım and Şakir.[98] In this context, the Austrian foreign minister Leopold Berchtold deemed Talaat "dangerous" and felt "alarmed by the latter's prominence" in the agitation.[99]

Just as after the putsch of January, Talaat boasted after the Edirne coup of his bravado and successful gamble. He bragged that within twenty-four hours he had saved the situation. "As far as the [European] powers were concerned, I knew that they would not move, that audacity would impose itself."[100] Yet, in early August 1913, Turkey was still isolated. Defiantly, Talaat and Cemal multiplied declarations such as "possession of Adrianople against everbody, until death, until complete era-sure of military forces!" In fact, they had true angst; at least, Cemal did. "I had the opportunity for an interview with him this afternoon," Rambert wrote on 7 August. "I have found him devastated and completely disoriented. It caused pain to look at him."[101]

A few days earlier, Rambert and Weil had finalized the agreement with the government regarding the concession, had obtained the imperial *irade* (decree) that sanctioned this con-cession, and had disbursed another tranche of the loan of 1.5 million Ottoman pounds, after having paid 300,000 right after Talaat's and Cemal's request of 19 July. Despite this financial injection, national insolvency still loomed. Internationally, Ottoman Turkey's credit was, in every sense, at a record low. It had decreased since the 1913 putsch among the European powers and was at a critical low in August 1913. Analogously, Europe had lost a lot of its prestige within a Young Turkey dom-inated by the CUP. Looking at the Balkans, including chaotic Albania, there was a failure of European diplomacy that impe-rial komitecilik snatched as an opportunity for a wider range of action. Visibly, European diplomacy had bowed before the fait accompli, accepting the accompanying revision of a treaty. Talaat became the champion among the Southeastern Euro-pean pioneers of this new and "promising" political style.[102]

Against this background, in summer 1914, a similar constella-tion was to take a much more comprehensive dimension. Dis-cernible diplomatic success was on the Turkish and Talaat's side since fall 1913. Consequently, "the Turkish government acquired an uncontested prestige among his populations, and Talaat has grown by several cubits."[103] Even if partly sharing concerns about the development of diplomacy, the German attitude in Istanbul appeared significantly different from other powers.

Germany, Abdulhamid's friend, had had to fear for its position immediately after July 1908. This, however, had considerably changed by 1910. After the fall of Kâmil Pasha, a longtime friend of Britain, Germany's relationship with Turkey became even closer. The new ambassador, Hans von Wangenheim, successor of Marschall von Bieberstein in June 1912, was, in Cavid's words, an "utter Turkophile" who, in his first year, however, was skeptical with regard to Turkey's future. He wrongly predicted chaos if Mahmud Şevket fell.[104]

Wangenheim admired the audacity and aplomb of the men who recovered Edirne in July 1913. He felt close to "the entirely new mentality" of the committeemen as compared to former Ottoman politicians. Emphatically, he now gave a more positive view of Turkey's vitality and future than reflected in the general European skepticism.[105] He identified with the pattern of success in the case of Edirne, even if this was in contravention of a treaty, and backed Turkey diplomatically. He later insinuated that Germany would accept a similar Ottoman course of action in the case of the islands of Chios, Lemons, and Lesbos. An alliance with Ottoman Turkey was no longer as strictly excluded as in the months and years before. Wangenheim apparently identified with actionist chauvinism, as expressed in the statement of a director in the Ottoman Foreign Ministry in autumn 1913, saying that the "former fear of laying a finger on a Christian . . . no longer exists. This era is over. Cemal and Talaat want to act, and actually they [do] act."[106]

Wangenheim was fascinated by the men of action in the Central Committee and government, although he admitted that he did not understand how the committee functioned. Nonetheless, he knew important basics after June 1913: "In contrast to Mahmud Şevket, who was a quite independent personality and could entrain his party, Prince Said is to be considered only the first functionary of the committee party." It was clear to him that it was not Said who would "guide the destinies of Turkey, but the strong heads of the committee behind him. Of these, two, Talaat Bey and Halil Bey, have entered the new ministry. Both belong to the radical wing of the party and are regarded as energetic and ruthless nationalists."[107] Citing these characteristics as flattering did not embarrass him; on the contrary, regarding Edirne, he expressed admiration for Talaat's "masterful management" and "coup de maître." He was convinced that there was no alternative to CUP rule. He offered to influence the German press, according to CUP wishes, and to place any pieces they sent him in the newspapers.[108]

As a regular and leading member of the Istanbul Club d'Orient, Rambert observed that by late 1913 the new strongmen and a few young Ottoman diplomats had begun to frequent the club, in particular, for dinner on Thursday evening, before the Muslim holiday on Friday. On 12 December 1913, "we were thirty-five at table," including Halil, president of the Council of State, and Mahmud Bahri Pasha, the minister of the navy. The burly physiques of Talaat, Cemal, and İzzet Pasha at the table reminded him of the "giants of marble . . . who, the head bent forward . . . support on their neck and shoulder" the structure of an empire. Rambert was impressed but ambivalent. Among all these people, "there was not one specimen of the [former] elegant aristocracy. All are upstage who have acquired their high position by sheer hard work. They personify the strength of [imperial] resistance. But nothing in their appearance reveals penetrating thinking, intelligent initiative, or diplomatic finesse. Yet one has to admit that since the [Balkan] war they have saved their country from a definitive collapse . . . and maintained imperial dignity."[109] National and imperial honor or dignity is indeed key to understanding Talaat's cohort.

Vienna

AUSTRIA

Belgrade

SERBIA

ROMANIA
Bucharest

• Silistra

MONTENEGRO
Cetinje
• Scutari
Durazzo • Tirana

ALBANIA
(Independent)

Skopje
(Üsküb)
Bitola
(Monastir)

BULGARIA
• Sofia

• Balchik
• Varna

Black
Sea

Kavála

Salonica

Dedeagatch

• Edirne (Adrianople)

Istanbul

OTTOMAN
EMPIRE

Imbros
Lemnos

Ioánnina
(Yanya)

GREECE

Lesbos

Chios

• Smyrna
(İzmir)

Samos

• Athens

Areas lost by the
Ottoman Empire

Mediterranean Sea

(to Greece)
Crete

Dodecanese I.
(Under Italian
Occupation)

MAP 2: The Ottoman Empire after the Balkan Wars of 1912–13. From *A
Brief History of the Late Ottoman Empire* by M. Şükrü Hanioğlu. Copyright
© 2008 by Princeton University Press. Reprinted by permission.

Truth Test: Challenged by
the Armenian Question

In 1913, Germany stood at a critical threshold with regard to the Eastern Question and its own relationship to the late Ottoman world, globally the most sensitive region. Would the fresh German flirtation with Turkish dictatorship involve stronger mutual engagement and interference in Ottoman interior affairs in favor of constitutional rule? Or, on the contrary, would the unfinished, fragile constitutional democracy of the German Empire lose its political and moral compass in the quagmire of the Eastern Question, and the Armenian issue in particular? Would it lose its soul by too much proximity with crafty imperial komitecilik?

In early 1913, the reform issue of the Armenian Question reemerged in European diplomacy.[110] After the factual end of the Macedonian Question in the Balkan Wars, the Armenian Question stood at the center of Europe's Eastern Question. Germany, for the first time, recognized the reality and relevant history of an issue to be solved by solid reforms. In order to push political friendship under Abdulhamid, it had denied the Armenian massacres and belittled the necessity of reforms in Eastern Asia Minor. In 1913, it wanted both: special friendship with Turkey and reforms. For this reason, for the first time, German diplomacy and friends of Johannes Lepsius, an influential theologian and humanitarian activist from Berlin, began to work hand in hand in an attempted synthesis of German Orientpolitik and German Protestant Orient Mission.[111]

Despite the European diplomatic fiasco in the Balkans in 1913, the CUP regime was internationally still weak regarding the powers before the crisis of July 1914. The international factor therefore counted domestically. If duly introduced, it could determine Turkey's domestic future even against the CUP's fervent will to unchallenged, centralized sovereignty. If Germany cooperated and did not obstruct internationally monitored reforms, the political course of the Ottoman world could be corrected and the committee dictatorship partly neutralized. Armenian representatives attempted to do this. During the Kâmil cabinet in late 1912, they had again demanded the implementation of a reform plan according to Article 61 of the Berlin Treaty. They added an international dimension to renewed reform steps of the cabinet, which, since October 1912, resumed efforts to restore order and solve the land question in the eastern provinces. The cabinet did this after being warned by the Russian foreign minister Sazonov, who had reminded it of the Berlin Treaty.[112] By 18 December 1912, it had prepared a reform plan for the provinces of Van, Bitlis, Diyarbekir, and Mamuretülaziz. One of Kâmil's main ideas was to assign British inspectors as advisers during the implementation of the plan, thus countering Russian pro-Armenian pressure.[113]

Seeking at last a breakthrough after four years of being strung along, on 21 December 1912, the Armenian millet assembly decided to present the reform issue to an international platform. A main excuse—not to act in this case—had repeatedly been the argument of necessary reforms for the whole country, not only a part of it. Based on the 21 December decision, Armenian representatives raised the issue internationally and lobbied in the capitals of the European powers. Main representatives on the international platform were Bogos Nubar Pasha, Zohrab, and the Catholicos of Etchmiadzin Kevork V. The main Armenian political parties (ARF, Hunchak, and Ramgavar) joined for the first time in a common project.[114] The Armenian initiative was not intended to modify the power game in the Ottoman center. Faced with cataclysmic perspectives and a dictatorship, it was first and foremost meant to ameliorate the conditions of life on the ground. Nevertheless, the initiative was potentially a game changer, because it introduced European monitoring. The radicals surrounding Talaat therefore deemed it a fundamental threat to their political goals and resented Armenians' resorting to foreign support as treason. For the Armenians, international guarantee was essential, because trust in true reforms induced by the CUP regime alone would have been, after all, irresponsible.

In the perspective of human rights and dignity, the Armenian resort to diplomacy was the result of a governmental incapacity to provide the basics of egalitarian justice, security, and a solution to the issue of stolen land. Hamid Kapancızâde was a high functionary and close collaborator of Talaat's. He stood on friendly terms with Robert Graves. In 1914 when he went as a governor for the first time in his life to an eastern province (Diyarbekir), he experienced the situation as follows: "I found the place here not only an administratively neglected province, but a [whole] region that was derelict, because subordinate and peripheral. As in many of our provinces, one could scarcely ascertain that the administration of a state had reigned here for centuries." Outside the town, "the lack of administration and the practice of patronage left the rule to local tribes, more precisely, to gangs. Every extortioner who managed to summon forty bandits was a government. . . . If anybody had explained to me in advance this primitive state of affairs that I witnessed in 1914, I would not have believed him, saying that he exaggerates." This was a devastating judgment from a loyal, capable, forthright governor, who, in March 1915, was displaced for his honest assessment of the situation. In his retrospective memoirs, written before his death in 1928, Hamid went so far as to write that "nowhere and never had we become the master and protector of the country. We resided as bad tenants in the countries that we had invaded."[115]

In parallel to the negotiations after the Balkan Wars, mediation continued for reforms in the eastern provinces, which were sorely needed. It was crucial that a domestic peace was based, despite all, on constitutional principles. Talaat played a key role in both streams of negotiations. There was serious concern for the future of Eastern Asia Minor, but for him, the main issue was preservation and reestablishment of central state power. He feared a scenario such as that in Macedonia, which resulted in international control and final loss. At issue for the Armenians were survival, human dignity, and property rights. This was also true for other groups, in particular, Assyrian Christians and Alevis. Armenian and some Assyrian Christians formed the best educated, largely unarmed portion of the provincial population in Eastern Asia Minor.

The political and social opening in the aftermath of the 1908 revolution had not lasted. High-spirited governors of eastern provinces, like Celâl, had been the exception, not the rule. Since 1911, state authorities and local CUP branches sided more and more openly with landlords and the majoritarian Muslim population. If they did not, they had to fear upheaval and complete loss of control. They avoided confrontation with Muslim notables, tribes, and gangs. The unrest, massacres, and urban riots since the 1890s, including Adana in 1909, were still fresh in memory. After four years of a reinstalled constitution, the state had largely proved incapable of implementing egalitarian law. Indeed, as early as 1910, Talaat had postponed and subordinated the principle of egalitarian rule to successful centralization.

By 1913, he followed the same path, but more radically. Against the backdrop of hundreds of thousands of muhacir from the Balkans (to be settled in Asia Minor), he was increasingly prone to drastic measures, including demographic engineering. At issue was no longer constitutional rule but the country-wide implementation of a single-party regime, along with a new agenda. This agenda followed a modified national understanding that not only put off equality with Ottoman Christians but was on the threshold of excluding them for good, since it based "real" belonging to the Ottoman nation on Islam. A resentful kind of Turkish nationalism spread rapidly, taking its force from fervent reaction against "Christian" aggression and injustices, as felt from the West. An intensified organization of Turkism, including an international Turkist Congress in Geneva, and CUP war and atrocity propaganda played determining roles in this process.[116]

In contrast to non-Muslims, non-Turkish Muslims were deemed assimilable to this new understanding of national identity. In its more popular occurrences, this understanding merged with late nineteenth-century Ottoman Islamism. Largely CUP-guided anti-Christian boycotts proved a strong indicator of this development. After Austria-Hungary's annexation of Bosnia-Herzegovina, Bulgaria's declaration of independence, and Crete's unilateral union with Greece in autumn 1908, Muslims found themselves united in their demands for the empire's sovereignty and international security. Boycotts of Austrian, Bulgarian, and Greek businesses and goods extended from Trabzon to Beirut. Large crowds, often numbering in the thousands, protested publicly, burning or tearing up Austrian-made fezzes. By 1910–11, the boycott movement began to target the shops of Christian and Jewish Ottoman citizens as well.[117]

Thus, whereas in 1908 and 1909 the boycotts had been exclusively directed against foreign "Christian states," by 1913 they outright targeted—with an aggressive rhetoric of jihad—Ottoman Christians, especially the Rûm. Ottoman Macedonia was almost entirely lost after the Balkan Wars. The CUP blamed foreign interference and foreign-mandated reforms for this situation. It did not publicly question its own call to war in September 1912, the Ottoman military defeat, or well-known longtime deficits in Ottoman administration. Since late 1913, the CUP saw the Armenians and the Entente powers fabricate a further "Macedonia" in Eastern Anatolia. The CUP branches in the eastern provinces entrenched this perspective in their rhetoric, connecting it with local resentments that had fed the violence of 1895. This legacy, along with the juxtaposition of Armenia and Macedonia, were strong factors in the rapidly growing anti-Armenian stance in the CUP by late 1913.[118]

Illustrating this development was not only Central Committee member Gökalp but also a more general Kurdish unrest. Local power holders, including Kurdish sheikhs and tribal chiefs, feared the restitution of seized Armenian land, which gave Abdurrezzak Bedirhan's attempt at a Kurdish nationalist movement additional momentum in autumn 1913. Intriguingly, Abdurrezzak profited from Russian assistance, which contributed to the CUP's fear of—and mistrust in—Russia during the reform negotiations. If it were to lose local power holders, the CUP government risked losing for good its precarious hegemony over the eastern provinces.[119]

Angry and vengeful mind-sets in Western and Eastern Asia Minor concurred in late 1913 and gave rise to extreme, Islamist, or Turanist anti-Christian hate speech in public. In contrast to the Islamist reaction of 1909, it now came from voices close to, or even within, the CUP (which, while in opposition, had already known similar assonances). A case in point is Hüseyin Kâzım (Kadri), a prolific author, former editor of *Tanin*, provincial governor, and a CUP member of parliament. Based on resentment and a vulgar understanding of Christian theology, he declared war against Christianity, denigrating it as idolatry. The apodictic terms that he used in his 1913 booklet, published under a pseudonym, coincide with those of the "Islamic State" propaganda spread a hundred years later.[120] Talaat himself does not appear to have used similarly extreme rhetoric, but now he knew he could exploit it. His claim to represent the "national will" was based on masses mobilized by a narrative that promised the glorious restoration of Islam.

Negotiating Reforms Backed by Europe

Under international pressure, the cabinet of Mahmud Şevket had continued the reform efforts undertaken by its predecessor, even if there was "obstruction by a few persons in the committee," as Hayri noted.[121] He probably meant Gökalp, Şakir, and Talaat, even if Talaat knew that some compliance was inescapable. In contrast to the previous year, Hayri now occupied a critical stance in relation to "the road chosen by Talaat Bey." He was ready for duty apropos reforms, because he deemed "the land question one of the country's vital questions." His colleagues feared loss of political prestige due to popular Islamic reactions against a commission or temporary peace tribunals, as was proposed. Finally, Hayri, Rahmi, and Necmettin Molla, all prominent CUP members, decided to propose to Talaat that Hayri be nominated as a minister so that he would have sufficient executive power to deal with the land question. (He was, in fact, again made a minister of foundations in late April 1913, but not for action in the East.)[122]

A secret cabinet meeting of 15 April 1913 adopted the idea of a general inspectorate for the eastern provinces and the involvement of British experts, as in the plan of 18 December 1912. It proposed, however, two regions with two separate British-led inspectorates. The anti-Russian construction of the scheme was too evident, and British diplomacy could not accept nominating inspectors general.[123] In June, the unresolved Armenian and reform issue was therefore prominently on the diplomatic table once again. At the end of June, the Russian ambassador distributed a reform plan draft, written by the lawyer and expert on international law André N. Mandelstam, dragoman at the Russian Embassy. It was submitted to a conference of six ambassadors, which was to begin in July, and adopted the idea of one general inspectorate for six eastern provinces under an Ottoman Christian inspector (analogous to the special status of Lebanon) or a European inspector.[124] In response, Talaat, once again minister of the interior, was busy preparing an account emphasizing the governmental position on reform.[125]

During the July 1913 meetings of the conference of ambassadors in Istanbul, represented by their dragomans, Germany supported the Turkish side without considering that Talaat's strategic goal might be obstruction. Since early 1913, Germany's position was aligned with general European diplomacy, that real reform was needed for the Armenians' future in Turkey. Yet this was not a firm conviction, as shown in diplomatic correspondence. In Cavid's judgment, German ambassador Wangenheim lacked any solid and sound opinion on the Armenian issue. General Pomiankowski, too, described a wavering and thus pliable Wangenheim.[126] Once Wangenheim had asserted naively that "the present Turkish government will do all to make the new regime [of reform] succeed in Armenia,"[127] even before a final agreement. Another time he said that "only their conversion to Islam could provide them [the Armenians] rest and security for life and property." He oscillated between conviction that Russia's will concerning Armenian reform was serious and anti-Russian mistrust (which the committee leaders did all they could to encourage).[128] German-Russian discussions established a compromise between Russian and Ottoman drafts in late September.

Once again, Talaat tried to play the British card against Russian influence. He generally operated in a hit-and-run style, using intimidation or friendly surprise of his targets to effect immediate success. In early October 1913, he blindsided two British experts who worked in the government. "Talaat Bey, who was now the dominant personality in the Cabinet, came to see Crawford and me at the Ministry of Finance and made us the following rather startling proposal," Graves reports. Talaat wanted Britons as general inspectors, in this case, David Crawford and Robert Graves. Again, the British government declined.[129]

Cavid himself had many informal talks with German and other diplomats on the reform issue, all of which he reported to Talaat. In turn, Talaat sent him many telegrams and letters, which Cavid summarized in his diary. Fully loyal to Talaat's stance in this case, Cavid used all his persuasiveness to categorically refuse European control and draw Germany more to Turkey's side. He insisted that the CUP was committed to Armenian security and "willing to realize reforms in Armenia [sic]." He deployed a panoply of arguments to show that Armenian propaganda was at fault, Europe was not sincere, and Russia provoked troubles in the eastern provinces. He ridiculed European humanitarian discourse. All turned around the mantra "no European control." "We do not want a new Macedonia to assume shape, and we have no time for European sermons," he preached in one of his interviews with Arthur Zimmermann, undersecretary of the German Foreign Office. "In similar cases, we saw Germany always on our side; now it proceeds together with Russia. This produces a bad impression in our country," he reproached him.[130]

Cavid accepted foreign inspectors as long as the Ottoman government chose them. Talaat did this too, and, moreover, in this case, he had a good sense for elements that the other side wanted to hear in negotiations. As of late November 1913, this meant that inspectors could be chosen from small European countries, that they would be given full authority, and that Ottoman Christians would enjoy proportional representation in provincial councils, in the police force, and in civil service. "We must say to the powers that we will fulfill these points. This declaration from our side will be reckoned as the guarantees that the Armenians want, but it does not mean the acceptance of an obligation." The crucial point was and remained international backing and control of the reforms, that is, a guarantee. This contradicted the CUP's claim to entire sovereignty and not only hurt its pride but substantially restricted Talaat's power.

The claim to foreign guarantee could not, however, be given up in any realistic assessment by the Armenian side, even if their interlocutors resented this. Muhittin Birgen, then a twenty-eight-year-old lead writer for the CUP newspaper *Tanin*, understood himself as belonging to the CUP's left wing, which "backed minority rights and previously had had good relations" with and sympathies for the social democratic ARF. However, his memoirs depict the affront he felt when the ARF explained that "we have no trust in you anymore. We are obliged to demand guarantees by the powers, above all, Russia."[131]

In a late November meeting with Talaat, Halil, Midhat, Vartkes, Halajian, and two other Armenians in Halajian's house, the debate again focused on this point. Talaat conceded all essential points and, in addition to those mentioned, the new laws on the use of regional languages and the autonomy of schools.[132] Full agreement seemed possible. But what was the utility of beautiful promises if trust was lacking and international control was refused? Also, the CUP's left wing prioritized a unitary state of Turkish Muslims and did not sincerely intend to pursue regional Armenian rights. Informal meetings between Talaat and Armenian representatives continued until late December 1913. Still, confidence-building steps were not excluded and, the Armenians hoped, could succeed. Zohrab tried to convince Talaat. On 24 December they met in Halil's house. Zohrab was more ready to compromise than his ARF friends. But still Talaat resisted on the crucial point of Armenian security and a future warranted by other than committee rule. By 26 December, Talaat concluded that the government was better off when negotiating alone with the Great powers.[133]

On 28 December, Cavid invited Vartkes and Zohrab to another debate and, as a result, exclaimed hopefully in his diary that on the matter of the inspectors, "we will be able to agree. The same is true for the issue of guarantees!"[134] This proved presumptuous. On 10 January 1914, Zohrab wrote at last, "To whom could I express my pain?" He referred to what he deemed an essential break with the CUP and found that the ARF should have continued, like him, to informally negotiate with "the Turks" rather than leave all in the hands of Russia and Germany. Krikor Zohrab was a significant nonpartisan figure of post-1908 constitutional Turkey. Like scarcely anyone else, he had believed in a future Turkish-Armenian alignment and felt that something essential had definitively broken down in late 1913 and early 1914.[135]

Cavid, in contrast to Talaat, did not play a power game or a double game, although because of his dependency on Talaat, he sometimes got caught up in such games. Yet he sincerely wanted reforms, not only to satisfy Armenian fellow citizens but to fulfill constitutional rule according to his understanding of political functionality and human dignity. His problem was that he could not acquire nor maintain a critical distance vis-à-vis the CUP except in his diary. Like Talaat, he lived for the committee. He had lost his young wife and had begun writing his diary in 1909 as a reaction to this loss.[136] A year and a half after his hopeful outline on the Turkish-Armenian future, deeply disillusioned, Cavid confessed in his diary in late August 1915, "We have publicly proved . . . that we lack the capacity to rule." By then, all his fervent arguments of 1913 against foreign supervision had revealed themselves as hollow words. Leading his Armenian fellow citizens to death, "we have condemned everything" (connected to CUP rule).[137] This silent cry in the desert did not, however, mark a definitive break from the CUP, because Cavid was neither willing nor able to exit the common political orbit and his dependency on Talaat.

Russian anger at the new German military mission in the Ottoman capital under Otto Liman von Sanders contributed to delaying the finalization of the reform agreement in late 1913. What amplified Russian suspicion was Enver's nomination as a pasha and minister of war in early January 1914. Sazonov regarded him as an ignoble murderer because of Nâzım Pasha's assassination a year earlier.[138] Talaat had used his dominance in the cabinet to elevate Enver and to make Ahmed İzzet Pasha resign. Since early July 1913, he had planned to "bring up a minister of war from us"; since late November, this plan also included appointing Cemal as minister of the navy and Cavid as the minister of finances. (Although Talaat was always Cavid's first committee contact, before World War I Cavid also portrayed Enver in positive and hopeful terms.)[139]

İzzet was ten years older than Talaat, much less war-prone, and had refused to cleanse the military cadre in favor of young CUP loyalists. In his memoirs, transferring responsibility from approved authorities to reckless young CUP revolutionists, thus making it impossible to tame their ambitions, had been "the first and greatest cause in a chain of calamities that led to the World War." Graves, who still worked in the Sublime Porte, judged unambiguously: "The modest young officer [Enver] whom I had known at Salonica five years earlier had not been improved by his rapid rise to power, and could not but be regarded as a dangerous adventurer." Ahmed İzzet Pasha refused Talaat's offer of lifelong vice commandership of the Ottoman army and his insistent, risky offer of becoming the prince of Albania.[140] Talaat always tried to reconcile the opposites in his network of power, entirely unconcerned about principled government.

Now, in early 1914, three men were most visible at the top of the state, whereas in the months before, Talaat and Cemal had ruled in the capital. These young men dominated the Central Committee and used senior CUP figures like Ahmed İzzet, Mustafa Hayri, and Said Halim according to their ideas. Rambert concluded on 8 January: "We are in fact governed by a triumvirate, Talaat, Enver, and Cemal Bey, all men of authority who one feels capable of rash and violent action." This contemporary, afterward often-repeated notion of a triumvirate is true for this precise time frame only.[141]

Germany provided decisive mediation so that a substantial—now, indeed, internationally monitored—reform plan was signed on 8 February 1914 by the grand vizier, Said Halim, and the Russian chargé d'affaires, K. N. Gulkevich. Once the inspectors were chosen, the plan was to be implemented during summer 1914. It had far-reaching consequences for Talaat's administration of domestic affairs. The plan divided seven (not six, as in the first draft) eastern provinces of Asia Minor into northern (Erzurum, Trabzon, Sivas) and southern parts (Van, Mamuretülaziz, Bitlis, Diyarbekir). It put them under the control of two European inspectors, to be selected from neutral

FIGURE 12: Talaat in civilian clothes on the left, Enver and Cemal at the central
forefront during a military ceremony in Istanbul. A so-called triumvirate of
the CUP party and cabinet formed by Talaat, Enver, and Cemal was true
for 1913–14, when all three resided in the Ottoman capital. Yet Talaat was
then already the leading figure politically (SALT Research, Istanbul).

countries. It prescribed publication of laws and official pro-
nouncements in local languages, provided for an adequate proportion of Muslims and Christians in councils and the police
force, and transformed the Hamidiye, an irregular Kurdish cavalry, into cavalry reserves.[142]

By February 1914, for the first time since 1878, international
diplomacy possessed the necessary instruments to make its
point in Eastern Asia Minor. If the international situation did
not change dramatically, the plan must be implemented and
Talaat had to acquiesce. Even if limited to Eastern Asia Minor,
the plan's unmistakable political principles would impact the
entire country. The selection and appointment of two inspectors general took the entire spring. Louis Westenenk from the

Netherlands and Nicolai Hoff from Norway arrived in May, "both anxious to learn from me what life would be like in Erzerum and Bitlis, and in no hurry to take up their posts until they had made the best bargain they could with Talaat for their requirements in the way of salary, official residence, motor-cars, and European secretaries and inspectors," said Graves, who then still worked in the Ministry of the Interior.[143]

Strange Spring, 1914: Reform and Peace or War and Cataclysm?

By spring 1914, for any serious observer of Ottoman affairs, Talaat was the first political figure in the capital. Although a minister of the interior, he also actively led in diplomacy. Was he a domestic and international agent of peace, as he appeared to some contemporaries during the negotiations after the Second Balkan War? Or did he instead play on a broad register of options between reform and revolution, reconciliation and arbitrary cataclysm? Or was he entrenched in the war psychology of a revolutionary komiteci who had achieved spectacular successes by vocally settling on war—for whom war naturally possessed both interior and exterior fronts—and who thus was the right man at the right time to further bank on war?

Soberingly, the second and third questions are true. In theory only, and for people outside the CUP, the catastrophic First Balkan War had been a strong warning against the path of war, and, a fortiori, against the maelstrom of the revanchism that rapidly smothered smarter and more constructive currents.

Since the CUP had internalized war, a Turko-Muslim definition of the Ottoman nation dominated policy. It henceforth determined the predominant understanding of national

(a)

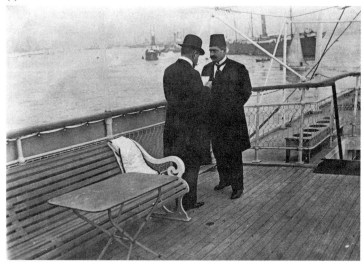

(b)

FIGURE 13: *(a)* Minister of the interior, but also a diplomat: Talaat with
the Romanian government minister Take Ionescu (Wienbibliothek
im Rathaus, Tagblattarchiv) and *(b)* Ionescu's wife, on board the ship
Romania before the quay of Galata (SALT Research, Istanbul).

sovereignty, national security, and national honor. It was steeped in the idea that betrayal by non-Muslims had caused the late Ottoman problems and losses, foremost in the First Balkan War. It is true that, based on mediation by the Romanian minister Take Ionescu,[144] Talaat concluded a peace treaty with Greece by mid-November 1913—but he prepared for war to recover the lost islands. The difficult issues of the islands and of population exchanges had been set apart, unresolved. The victors of the First Balkan War had applied patterns of anti-Muslim ethnic cleansing, to which the CUP reacted with similar patterns that began to take on bigger dimensions. A comprehensive anti-Christian demographic engineering was looming on the horizon by late 1913. The CUP press aggressively claimed that the suffering of the Rûm did not compare to that of the muhacir.[145]

Victimhood became an instrument of propaganda. The logic of negative emotions combined with ethnoreligious stigmatization made an impact upon press and politics, and quickly justified substitutional revenge toward Ottoman Christians. The anti-Rûm policy during the first stage originated directly from the Balkan Wars and concerned Thrace. A number of Ottoman Rûm in Thrace possessed relatives in Greece, were both Ottoman and Greek nationals, and had sympathized with Greece during the Balkan Wars, or even participated as soldiers on the Greek side. Therefore, "Talaat Bey prioritized cleansing the country from the population elements [anâsır] that had revealed themselves as treacherous during the Balkan War," Halil said, summarizing Talaat's new policy as it was crystallizing in late 1913. "The proceeding was like this: Officially the governors and the other functionaries were not involved. The CUP organization would accomplish the task and terrorize the Rûm. . . . In consequence, nearly 100,000 Rûm fled to

Greece without being hurt."[146] As a next step, in spring 1914 and in relation to the unresolved question of the islands, the Rûm living on the Aegean coast were targeted.

Thus, even during and after negotiations with Greece, Talaat had thought of war. In a general sense, war psychology had been paramount among the committee radicals surrounding him since September 1912, yet had started with the outrage against the Italian invasion in autumn 1911. As in the case of Edirne, Talaat was categorical regarding the restitution of the islands of Chios, Lesbos, and Lemnos. This time, early on he had the grand vizier on his side, who urged Wangenheim to be clearly pro-Ottoman in this issue. Yet the German ambassador wished for a Turkish-Greek concord. Despite the peace treaty of November 1913, and against proposals of an exchange with other Aegean islands to be given back by Italy, nonrestitution of Chios and Lesbos meant war for Istanbul. Great effort was therefore undertaken to arm the fleet.[147]

A loan with bad conditions from a French bank allowed the purchase of a British-made dreadnought via Brazil. When the finance minister Rifat hesitated to sign the loan, Talaat, according to Halil, embraced Rifat shouting, "My sir, we are taking back the islands; we have no time to be meticulous." With charming coercion, he caressed him, kissed his beard, brought him to the room where the banker waited, and compelled him to sign. This was a period in which Talaat and the CUP felt themselves to still be on the defensive internationally. All the more, they exhibited a taste for bravado and for war. "The Turks are thinking only of war, as soon as possible, to preserve at least Chios and Lesbos," Rambert noted in late January 1914. The impossibility of getting a reasonable loan while war loomed, however, impeded the military option. Moreover, European diplomacy had decided by mid-January 1914 that the islands would remain Greek. This was an unwise decision in Rambert's eyes, because the islands were "geographically part of Asia Minor's territory. If one honestly wants to conclude peace, causes for constant enmities must be suppressed."[148]

Rambert was referring to systematic Rûm contraband between the islands and the Continent, and also to the security issue, because Chios and Lesbos commanded the naval entrance to the Gulf of İzmir. In the aftermath of the islands' official loss, Talaat tackled the demographical and economical issue head-on at the Aegean coast. He and the radicals among his collaborators understood this issue as a domestic war of salvation. The anti-Rûm policy in Western Asia Minor was diametrically opposed to the political principles applied in Eastern Asia Minor, according to the February 1914 reform plan. Talaat's cleansing policy pursued three main goals: security at the west coast, which separated the newly Greek islands by only a few kilometers; an inexpensive resettlement of Muslim refugees from the Balkans; and politically motivated demographic engineering. These goals all emphasized the crucial aim of a safe Muslim Turkish home in Asia Minor at the expense of the Ottoman Christians. For the CUP, anti-Greek revanchism justified them.

————

Curiously and notably, by April 1914 fundamentally different options and perspectives of an Ottoman future coexisted. There was clearly also a peaceful path. It welcomed, or at least accepted, the outlook of reforms with European involvement. It particularly took into account that Cavid, the minister of finances since March, had succeeded in his negotiations for a substantial French loan of 800 million pounds. From this, the commercial milieu expected a great boost for Turkey and Europe. On 14 April, when Cavid came back to Istanbul from Paris, "all important persons from the political and economic spheres waited for him at the [Sirkeci] train station. A general feeling of relief spread throughout the whole population." On that day, Rambert estimated that "nobody desire[d] to restart war" after the recent experiences. In the months before, the problem of refugees had revealed the misery brought on by war in many places in Western Anatolia and was a heavy financial burden for the state. Most state employees had had to do without or with very small pay for several months.[149]

On 9 May, Talaat surprised the representatives of international Istanbul and many others by leaving for a visit with the Russian czar, Nicholas II, in Livadiya, Crimea, along with Ahmed İzzet Pasha. Many hoped that "this was a sign of general peace and of appeasement in the oriental conflicts." Rambert, too, was amazed. "For the Turks, Russia is the wolf." Yet he expected that Talaat would contribute by "bowing and scraping to the wolf's mouth" to dismantle "the instinctive mistrust of the Ottoman nation vis-à-vis Moscow's empire." In his eyes, Europe's constellation must inspire mistrust in Turkey while it hoped for support. He saw Germany "paralyzed by its alliance with Italy and Austria" and the latter's interests in the Balkans, France "immobilized by a dangerous financial crisis," and Britain "more and more indifferent in regard of oriental affairs." He speculated that the rapprochement with Russia would be a "masterstroke" by Talaat, "the first political personality of the moment." Russia possessed the power to impose solutions in the Balkans and the eastern provinces.[150]

Muhittin Birgen, twenty-nine years old and lead writer of the CUP newspaper *Tanin*, accompanied Talaat. He remembered Talaat as musing a great deal on the journey there, in fear of

FIGURE 14: Talaat returning a salute from a guard of honor
before leaving Istanbul to Livadiya with Ahmed İzzet Pasha,
May 1914 (Wienbibliothek im Rathaus, Tagblattarchiv).

Russian earnestness regarding the reform plan, but he relaxed
on the return because the czar and the Russian foreign minister
Sergei Sazonov had not pressured him but above all had tried
to contain general German influence. Muhittin and Talaat discussed the probability of a general war. Talaat did not openly
reveal to his young collaborator that he had asked Sazonov
about a Turkish-Russian alliance. Sazonov, even if taken by
surprise, according to his own account, was ready to consider
the proposal.[151]

Talaat tested the waters and scarcely believed in the realization of an alliance with Russia. Even if he personally may have
possessed strategic flexibility, he would have faced resistance
from large circles, including pan-Turkists and pan-Islamists
within the CUP who saw the czar as the archenemy of Turkey.
"Look, in this case [of a Turko-Russian alliance], once more

there would be revealed how a wolf fraternizes with the lamb!"
Talaat joked. His paramount wish, as he told Birgen on the journey back, was to "enter the family of Europe." There was a basic
sense of alienation. Belonging to Europe "would assure us the
entrance into the European states' rule of law. Presently, if there
is something like a rule of law, it is only for Europeans. We, like
Asians, Africans, and Australians, are anyway people outside
of and alien to Europe. The main principles of the rule of law
are not [acknowledged as] valid for us. . . . See the annoyance,
wherever we turn and apply, nobody turns his face to us."[152]

Talaat made a fundamentally true, highly relevant point.
But he was to use it, above all, to justify radical politics and
not to build up—if modestly—something new and better that
his people could call their own. The CUP wanted to be fully
sovereign and conserve its own system of values and historical myths, thus actually demarcating itself from the "family of
Europe" to which it aspired to belong. The CUP is best understood by observing its relations with Europe and a West with
which it wanted to be equal, instead of feeling depressingly
inferior in terms of hard and soft power. Thus, the CUP felt
alienated, disrespected, and full of self-pity. If, as a result, its
fundamental structure of action was resentment and defensive-
ness, these actions mirrored and anticipated the faults, failures,
and dark sides of contemporary Europe. There was leverage
for—and confidence in—proactive, daredevil steps since the
CUP's successful coup and the recovery of Edirne.

Talaat was back in Istanbul, when on 14 May 1914 the new
parliament opened. It lacked oppositional forces. "This is a
triumph for Union and Progress. The chamber of deputies is
entirely composed by its creatures," Rambert noted. In the new,
now manifest framework of a single-party regime, the committee continued to deliberate and to make decisions in concert

with the parliament and the cabinet. An experienced minister in the government, Talaat presented his opinions to the government as though they were those of the committee; to the committee his decisions were presented as having been conditioned by the constraints of the government. The result of this duplicity was that nobody could resist his main decisions. In contrast to four years earlier, he no longer had to fear anything from parliamentary discussions.[153]

Rûm Removal: A Cataclysmic Success

The other option in spring 1914 was not peaceful but cataclysmic. It followed the conviction that chaos led to new constellations from which hitherto disadvantaged groups could profit. Obviously, it considered life a fight and believed that war necessarily reproduced itself in the struggles for survival and power. Social Darwinist convictions were the zeitgeist in Europe's era of high imperialism, coinciding with the belle epoque, and were well entrenched in the CUP. They joined expectations of cataclysmic revolutions worldwide.

In contrast to the pacifist strand of socialism, certain revolutionary socialists hoped for world war to trigger a longed-for world revolution. Vocal among those welcoming war was the German Russian socialist Parvus, who had lived in Istanbul since 1910 and had been a co-organizer, with Leon Trotsky, of the 1905 Russian Revolution. First in touch with the small group of mostly Bulgarian and Armenian socialists, Parvus had rapidly sensed where the most promising power dynamics were to be found, and he befriended CUP members and Turkists. He enriched himself as a dealer of arms and foodstuff during the Balkan Wars. Close to the men of the committee and the ideologues of Turkism, he advanced to the informal position of a foreign expert regarding economical issues and published many articles in *Türk Yurdu* and other papers close to the CUP.[154]

Seen from Istanbul in the first half of 1914, a world war was most probable in connection with Turkish-Greek tensions. Moreover, confusion reigned in Albania, where anti-European protesters again demanded the rule of Turkey. In late spring, European diplomacy, particularly Italian and Austrian, was therefore on the edge.[155] What united Parvus with the CUP beyond concrete bargains were resentments against Russia, a disdain of so-called *comprador bourgeoisie*, and war psychology. The "liberation of the economy from the yoke of aliens," among whom Ottoman Christians were definitively counted by early 1914, was a main goal of the CUP and Turkism. By then, not only boycotts but also a largely nonbloody, nonetheless coercive and violent onslaught served the plan of ousting the Rûm. This kind of domestic "war" risked international implications, the first being war with Greece. By early June 1914, international economy and finances reflected the political unrest: "Everybody in the commercial world is in a general and profound anxiety." What aggravated the situation was that in all of Europe, "all wellsprings of public credit are extremely tense," financial expert Rambert noted.[156]

The committee, foremost Talaat, had voted to nominate Mahmud Celâl (Bayar) as the CUP secretary of the İzmir branch in summer 1913. Nine years younger than Talaat, Celâl was a loyal CUP member and nationalist with a marked imperial bias. He wanted to enforce "our rights of rulership against oppositional minorities that were our subjects." Like several other young functionaries under Talaat, Celâl personified the continuity to Atatürk's government, whose minister of economy he became in 1921.[157] Right from the start in 1913, Celâl understood his task, as he writes in his memoirs, as "a war of salvation to liberate the Turkish nation from those who never were from us and never would be from us"; that is, to "Turkify the *gâvur* [non-Muslim] İzmir"; and in particular "to free İzmir's economy from the anational, treacherous, and malicious [Christian] heads and hands." Talaat was the architect— Celâl the local secret executive—of the expulsion of the Rûm to Greece in spring 1914, in which Rahmi, the CUP vali of the province of İzmir, and most subordinate district governors connived or actively participated. Particularly active, including for an early preparatory report, was Mehmed Reşid, the *kaymakam* of the Karesi district in the east of Edremit, north of İzmir.[158]

Reşid's report contains a blend of social frustration and nationalist aversion. During an excursion between 29 July and 7 August 1913, Mehmed Reşid had recorded the state of affairs and projected a future without the Rûm. The dream of a modern administration and infrastructure went hand in hand with the establishment of unrestricted Turkish-Muslim domination. What Reşid perceived was a polarized image: on the one hand, the Rûm, socially envied and viewed less favorably as they were prospering in many places, and on the other hand, the good Muslims, and—in his view—*their* state, to be strengthened at all cost, because they were subject to exploitation and Christian intrigues.[159] Beyond this picture from summer 1913, there was fear in spring 1914 that Greece would actively promote the internationalization of problems of coexistence and administration in a region with many Christians. (Venizelos, prime minister of Greece since 1910, promoted pan-Aegean Hellenism and the "Great Idea" [*Megali Idea*]—the idea of the restoration of Greek rule in parts of Asia Minor.) From such a development, a problem such as the Macedonian Question would arise and provide a lever, and, as in Macedonia, bandits would be used for political purposes. The CUP press emphasized this specter.[160]

Talaat, Enver, Celâl, and others held several secret meetings in Istanbul in May and June 1914 to organize expulsion through doses of terror. A decisive meeting took place in Talaat's house, lasting the entire night, where tangible preparations were made. Young CUP officers were to lead squads on the spot. Not all cabinet members were informed about the scheme—certainly not Cavid, who was again in Europe, nor Hayri.[161] Like many sensitive documents of the committee, Talaat's following order to Rahmi on 14 May 1914 does not appear in the Ottoman state archives (BOA). Its contents are, however, plausible in the light of information provided by the perpetrators themselves and contemporary firsthand reports: "The Rûm living on İzmir's coasts work day and night to implement their Megali Idea. For political reasons, it is necessary to evacuate the Rûm villages and to resettle the Rûm living on Anatolia's coasts . . . If they resist, methods of sorts are needed to make them leave by their own will." As a consequence, in fact, "nearly 200,000 Rûm went to Greece by June 1914," Halil writes.[162]

The expulsion of Aegean Rûm was a terrific success. It was paradigmatic, as well, in its management of information, including public lies, as in its secret combination of gangs, the army, the central government, diplomats, and the central and local branches of the CUP. Talaat again appears as the mastermind and organizational hub of the whole scheme. Starting in early June, he inspected the results of the operation in the regions of Edremit, Aydın, and İzmir, where he arrived before mid-June. He was satisfied that the ousting had succeeded without degenerating into chaos and raising significant resistance. Talaat sent a message to Cavid that all was quiet now. Blindly following his friend's information, Cavid published an appeasing article in the French newspaper Le Temps on 13 June 1914. On 18 June, Grand Vizier Said Halim declared that his vigorous minister Talaat had reestablished order; the previous violence had regrettably, but spontaneously and understandably, emerged from the embittered muhacir. In reality, in almost all cases, organized squads alongside armed bandits purposely created chaos, looted, and sometimes killed.[163]

For experienced observers, the publicity was flimsy. "In reality, they oust[ed] the Greeks," Rambert noted in his diary on 16 June. When, on 18 June, the cabinet invited the ambassadors to send delegates to accompany Talaat and witness efforts at calming the population and stopping emigration, Rambert simply noted, "They disguise the facts. . . . Nobody here [in Istanbul] talks sincerely about what happens." The European powers sent delegates to play lesser parts in the plot, which Talaat performed with them in İzmir from 20 June. He now felt self-confident enough to play with European diplomats. Alone with Russian consul Andrew Kalmykow and vali Rahmi, he confessed, however bluntly, that the "Greeks cannot remain. They are forced to leave. They must go." Looking at him, Kalmykow remembered the decisive expression of Talaat's eyes and the resolute tone of his voice.[164]

Evidently, Talaat failed to inspire confidence in the terrorized people, who continued to flee. This move saved the government a few precious days; otherwise, war with Greece was impending. In case of war, the government would go so far as to also expel the Rûm from Istanbul, thus again inducing incalculable international risks, as Rambert was told. The sultan was moved and upset by what a delegation sent by the Rûm Patriarchate told him and immediately called Talaat. By now a cold-blooded political liar, Talaat swore to the sultan by the name of God and the Prophet—according to palace secretary İhsan, an ear witness—that all news about persecuted Rûm was malicious slander intended to destroy the centuries-old Ottoman state.[165]

The CUP men of action felt triumph after a success that exceeded all expectations. After the oustings in Thrace and on the Aegean coast, they were crafty in their demographic engineering, including public euphemism and diplomatic shows. Enver Pasha joined Talaat in İzmir at the end of June to inspect military exercises. They could savor a crushing victory achieved in a secret war along domestic ethnoreligious lines. In fact, the removal of the Rûm announced another, even larger dimension than that of the Balkan Wars. "The ousting of the Greeks [Rûm] exposes Greece to a much bigger danger, because the Greeks established in Asia [Minor] count several millions," much more than the muhacir from the Balkans. Turkey henceforth pioneered what Rambert already called "an enormous triage of nations. This was foreseeable, because among peoples that exit a horrible war, hates and vengeances make difficult the common life on the same territory."[166] Post-1918 Europe would have to face a deterioration of coexistence that most Europeans had previously thought to be relegated to another world. But it had taken place within the limits of modern Europe, understood as a dense interactional space of (in this book's terminology) larger Europe.

In the immediate aftermath of Talaat's anti-Rûm exploit, the unexpected assassination of Archduke Franz Ferdinand at Sarajevo on 28 June 1914 triggered Europe's July Crisis. This saved the wire-pullers in Istanbul from a possible war with Greece that could have provoked a general war. On 29 June 1914, Talaat was back in the capital, and on 30 June he met with Vramian and Armen Garo, his former political friends of the ARF, in order to discuss again—in spite of everything that had happened—reforms and the issue of the inspectors and their assistants. He was overconfident after the rapid removal of more than 100,000 people. "I am Bismarck," he allegedly said with a smile when Garo reproached him and his closest friends for being drunk with their recent exploits. In Garo's eyes, Talaat had metamorphosed since the coup d'état in January 1913, expressing faith in a future policy of Turkification of the Kurds and alluding to the possibility of removing the Armenians from Ottoman Armenia. "As usual, Talaat was very polite and open," reads Garo's memoir of his last meeting with Talaat on 30 June 1914. Yet, "in the manner of an overconfident person who makes fun of the other, he conjured a satanic smile on his face," as fundamental dissent emerged during the talk.[167]

Istanbul still envisaged war, after Greece had decreed the annexation of the islands. Yet Greece had acquired two new American battleships, whereas Turkey had only one via Brazil. It still waited for ships ordered from Britain. Athens had reasons to be skeptical at lenient statements from Istanbul in early July. If it accepted the removals and integrated the high number of Rûm, peace was conceivable but not at all certain in the long run.[168] The Ottoman government and its broad Turkish public had for a long time, as Rambert put it, "set all their hopes on two dreadnoughts, ordered in England. They were the instruments of revenge against the Greeks, of the islands' reconquest, and of indisputable superiority of the Turkish navy over all small Balkan states. . . . Numbers of troops were massed in Macedonia, targeting Salonica."[169]

On 6 July 1914, the Ottoman Parliament discussed the expulsions, after the Rûm deputy Emmanuil Emmanuilidis had presented the appalling facts. Talaat continued his deception before the deputies. He pretended that spontanous popular boycotts against non-Muslim merchants had motivated many Rûm to emigrate of their own free will. He declared

furthermore that the government lacked the money for building new villages for the muhacir, hence the need to settle them
in Rûm villages. He even insisted on the fact that if he had sent
them to the deserts of Syria and Iraq, as he did a year later with
the Armenians, they all would have died. The misery of the
muhacir thus served as the main justification for the removal of
the Rûm.[170] The Ottoman press covered Talaat's multiple deni-
als of any wrongdoing by the central government in May and
June 1914. After the discussion on 6 July, it attacked Emmanuil
Emmanuilidis to undermine his credibility; the newspaper *Le
Jeune-Turc*, in particular, excelled in doing so.[171] Comparatively
rich in topics, this Istanbul-based, Zionist-sponsored newspaper was devotedly pro-CUP and flattered "His Excellency
Talaat Bey" almost daily.

On 13 July, Talaat assigned Mehmed Reşid to be Inspector
General Hoff's Ottoman assistant, with the rank of vali, in Van.
With his virulent resentments against Ottoman Christians,
Reşid would surely not be a constructive collaborator in the
reforms for Eastern Asia Minor. Reşid, a cofounder of the CUP,
had become a Turkist hard-liner during the Balkan Wars, and a
declared and committed hater of Rûm, though not yet explicity
of Armenians.[172]

5

Total-War Gamble, Domestic Demolition, Biased Nation Building

FOR ISTANBUL, THE murder of Franz Ferdinand, heir to the Austro-Hungarian throne, was not the decisive event that it was for late belle epoque Europe. In the Ottoman capital, there was familiarity with wars, crises, and political assassinations. What changed in Ottoman perception was that Europe, too, now seemed to have comparable times ahead. The misdeed in Sarajevo appeared familiar to Istanbul, and its context, the ex-Ottoman Balkans, was terra cognita for a CUP rooted there.

In contrast, all of Europe was immediately deeply shaken. The assassination had "colossal repercussions in all of Europe," Rambert wrote on 29 June 1914. Since the Balkan Wars, Europe, in particular Austria, had been nervous regarding the political affairs in Southeastern Europe. By 5 July 1914, the stock exchanges had reached a record low. Many feared a general war, but scarcely anybody would have imagined a world war lasting several years. Ill for three weeks, Rambert began to recover and to reorient himself politically on 1 August. He was simply horrified by a diplomacy whose "threatening tone destroys all hope of preserving peace." The murder of Jean

Jaurès, French socialist and antimilitarist member of parliament, shocked him as a frequent visitor to Paris and one deeply critical of French chauvinism. "One must face that an epidemic of madness infests the world."[1]

As far as political gambling in times of crisis and war is concerned, the players in Istanbul were more audacious and hard-boiled than most European politicians. By early summer 1914, Talaat was the strong figure in the government and the committee. Among most Muslims in the country, the CUP enjoyed the prestige of winners, and its domestic power had tightened since the 1913 putsch, the repression of summer 1913, the recovery of Edirne, and the recent success of population removal in favor of Muslim migrants. Thus, a huge contrast existed in this situation in summer 1912. Talaat's partnership with Enver Pasha, minister of war since January 1914, was essential for the hold on the army and Islamist circles. Still in a strong position, Cemal had left Istanbul at the end of June 1914 for a visit in France. There he sought an alliance, but to no avail. In November, he was sent to rule over Syria and to lead the reconquest of Egypt.

Though improved since the aftermath of Edirne's recovery, Turkey's international standing was still weak. Europe's July Crisis offered the opportunity to change established constellations and put Turkey's full strategical weight in the balance. Talaat and the committee appeared inclined to the Entente after 1908, and, according to Cavid's letter to Churchill, particularly so after the Italian invasion of Ottoman Libya. The militant nationalist recalibration in 1912–13 foreclosed this option, although Russia showed some openness during Talaat's visit in Livadiya. Yet, there had been a marked turn to Germany already in 1910, in-line with former Hamidian choices and German support for the CUP since 1909. British foreign policy and its embassy in

Istanbul had remained consistently reluctant. Germany's sea-soned ambassador von Bieberstein, in contrast, had known how to build up relations with the CUP after 1908. Germany's new minister, Hans von Wangenheim, was clearly sympathetic with and even fascinated by the CUP men of action. Since summer 1913, Germany was the most plausible partner, but still far from disposed to an alliance.

After mid-July 1914, a few leading men of the "komiteci gov-ernment" (the executive complex of cabinet and committee) tried their luck and won: nervous Germany accepted the offer of an alliance that Austria, challenged by Serbia, already wanted. Istanbul's backing tipped the scales, emboldening Austria and Germany in late July when general war was possible but not yet real. As a consequence, all issues of the Eastern Question were now implicitly part of the imminent, more inevitable gen-eral war. The spirits were high in Istanbul among the very few who knew about the secret treaty that concluded on 2 August. Those around them caught the spirit without knowing the facts. Immediately, irregular warfare was prepared in the East. It started in September 1914 with raids into the Russian Caucasus and Russian-controlled Northern Iran and made use of jihad even before the jihad declaration of 14 November. This declara-tion intensified the practice and jihad's rhetorical use, the main agents of which were imam (mosque leaders employed by the sheykhulislam administration).[2] Regular Ottoman war began in November.

The German-Ottoman alliance was a product of haste and a sense of emergency, a gamble on both sides, although the sphere of war psychology and politics was less familiar to belle epoque Germany than to the komiteci government. The German Empire, an unfinished constitutional democracy that had tot-tered since the July Crisis, had more to lose. A nerve-wracking, make-or-break war ensued, lasting from August 1914 to fall 1918. The common war had a profound impact on the destinies of both countries in the twentieth century, each depending on the other in a mutual gamble. They shared a determined hope for victory, and even a planned, common postwar future, but largely lacked common fundamentals and basic mutual confidence beyond anti-Entente rhetoric.

World war and a pervasive war psychology offered Talaat room to maneuver, which had been unthinkable before July 1914. He made skillful use of the new opportunities internationally and domestically, and in a continuous bargain with Germany. In contrast to the European theater, war and victory were terms that Talaat also directly related to a domestic agenda. In the end, he succeeded in laying the foundation of an ethnoreligiously cleansed authoritarian state in Asia Minor—despite defeat. Germany, in contrast, fell deeper. For Germany in 1918, temporary democracy after defeat would not suffice to survive the quagmire resulting from the war.

The high Ottoman spirits of early August 1914 gave in to serious disenchantment when confronted with German pressure for rapid military action, and to depression in winter 1914–15, when faced with a series of defeats in the Caucasus, Northern Iran, Southern Iraq, and the Sinai. At the same time, the government struggled with broad desertions in general and guerilla resistance in Eastern Asia Minor in particular. There the reform was annulled, and Islamist (less Turkist than in the capital) war propaganda proved divisive. From August 1914 onward, requisitions hit Christians overproportionally. After the heavy losses of the Sarıkamış campaign and the brutalization of a warfare in the East that included irregulars, the terrain was deeply polarized and ready for radical action in late winter 1915—if ever central rule chose to implement such action.

As discussed in chapter 1, Talaat was in top form from April 1915. While victories at the fronts were scarce and reconquest nonexistent, he pushed again for a crushing "victory" within, as in spring 1914 with the Rûm and Greece. Now radically anti-Armenian, he finished off once and for all the Ottoman social fabric and an ethnoreligious intercommunality that, even if precarious, had briefly flourished again after 1908. He claimed to have erased a thorny issue within the Eastern Question, if not the Eastern Question itself, and to serve the future of Muslims in general and Asia Minor in particular. Muslims in Asia Minor were his nation in the making, to which his ministry systematically transferred the assets of those killed or removed in 1915–16. Armenians, Assyrians, and Rûm were targeted, although not in the same way and degree, or according to the same timetable.

The destruction of Asia Minor's Christians was the most momentous, trenchant, and elaborate act of Talaat's political life. As the brain behind this destruction, he put several ministries, the CUP networks, and all coercive means of the empire and stigmatizing propaganda at its service, while simultaneously unleashing intrasocietal violence, notorious since the 1895 massacres. Openly hailed as a jihad locally, such violence characterized mass crimes against Armenian and Assyrian Christians, not only in Eastern Asia Minor but also in Northern Syria, involving even slave markets for Christian children and women in towns in Mesopotamia.

Although genocide and its impact on Turkey as a whole were not linearly determined from August 1914, it was strongly embedded in the logic and spirit of war, then unleashed. After a journey through Asia Minor in early 1918, Hamid Kapancızâde, a high functionary under Talaat—quoted already several times in this study—who was referred to as "Deli" (Crazy) for his directness, concluded, "The government had preferred war to the life of the [Ottoman] nation. . . . The most productive parts of Anatolia were now turned to desert. The remaining people were condemned to starvation. The misery and wretchedness that we saw during our travel was beyond description and imagination."[3]

European War: "End and Revenge" of the Eastern Question?

Talaat, Enver, Said Halim, and Halil—an ad hoc group of insiders, or "action party" (as Wangenheim called them), within the committee government—used the momentum created by the July Crisis to persuade a European Great power to form an alliance. They realized by mid-July the clear Austrian wish for and need of an alliance in view of the new hot spot in the Balkans, and of the harsh steps Austria desired. Said Halim's meeting with Wangenheim resembled a cautious first approach toward an alliance, without urgency. On 19 July, however, Talaat himself put the German ambassador Wangenheim into *zugzwang* when he gently threatened an alliance with Russia.[4]

Said Halim, Talaat, and Enver put the Austrian ambassador Johann Markgraf von Pallavicini under even more compulsion on 20 July 1914. They not only stressed Ottoman capacity to support the Triple Alliance and the ability to instigate Muslim rebellion in Russia, in particular in Azerbaijan, but they also encouraged Austria to profit from the present and, presumably, last chance to give Serbia a military lesson. They pressured Germany to join Austria in order to intimidate Russia. Talaat probably again chose to use Enver as his front man to achieve the alliance, because, politically, "Enver could not do anything [by himself] if not together with Talaat," as Cavid put it.[5] When

Enver proposed an alliance to Wangenheim on 22 July 1914, the latter still reacted reservedly, as had every European diplomat when faced with similar Ottoman requests. Yet during the march on 23 July, the national holiday of the 1908 revolution, Wangenheim hinted at possible benefits of a Turkish-German alliance, according to Cemal. After reading Wangenheim's report, Emperor Wilhelm signaled on 24 July, a day after the Austrian ultimatum to Serbia, that Germany might henceforth need every gun.[6]

The Ottoman offer was therefore answered positively, the conditions negotiated, and the secret treaty signed on Sunday, 2 August. That morning, Cavid suddenly entered the grand vizier's mansion for a different affair and listened to Said Halim, who loudly read the unsigned treaty. All except Cavid were overjoyed that at long last, they had concluded an alliance with a European Great power. Talaat was ready to enter war, loyal to the letter of the alliance treaty, as he openly stated in his 1919 apologia. Talking in the evening in Enver's house, Cavid felt that "neither Talaat nor Halil had completely understood the treaty that they had decided to sign." On 4 August, Talaat instructed the Ottoman delegates of the Greek-Ottoman commission for population exchange to abstain from any decision.[7] War promised new horizons.

Partly on Cavid's insistence, on 6 August 1914 Wangenheim accepted six far-reaching new conditions added to the 2 August treaty. The same day, the cabinet allowed two German warships to enter the Dardanelles—a dangerous step in terms of neutrality. Among the added conditions were Germany's "help for the abrogation of the Capitulations," the recovery of the islands in the case of successful war with Greece, a German guarantee for Ottoman territorial integrity, and "a small correction" of Turkey's "eastern border, which shall place Turkey into direct contact with the Muslims of Russia." The last item was highly sensitive with regard to the Armenians living in the region. On 5 August, Enver visited the Russian military attaché, suggesting a Turkish-Russian alliance. The move connected with Talaat's proposal of May and served to mask the secret alliance with Germany.[8]

Intense war propaganda manifested the will to—and decision for—war. It began in early August, with the CUP newspaper *Tanin* at the forefront. The propaganda was Islamist and pan-Turkist. It promised the rightful, vengeful uprising of Islam, restorative and expansive conquest, and the emergence of Turan. In a poem in *Tanin* on 8 August, Gökalp wrote, "The lands of the enemy will be ruined! / Turkey will grow and become Turan!" Militarily censored from 7 August, the whole press followed a pro-German line. Again and again, *Tanin* burst in schadenfreude. Under the telling title of "The Turk's Malediction," its 9 August edition welcomed intra-European carnage, because Europe was made responsible for Ottoman problems, while simultaneously identifying the "we" (of the CUP and Turkey) with Islam in general. Divine justice was being implemented; the Turks' woe worked. Gökalp led the anti-European schadenfreude chorus in his poem "Kızıl Destan" (Red Epic) of 8 August: "The land of civilization will be red blood! / Each of its regions will be a new Balkan!" For the CUP prophet Gökalp, jihad had already started, as he wrote on 9 August 1914: "God's will / sprang from the people / We proclaimed the jihad, / God is great."[9]

The government stood under German pressure to provide military capacity and to enter the war as soon as possible, as the treaty demanded and the "action party" was well aware. Partial mobilization began on 1 August and general mobilization on 3 August. Big red posters in the streets called all men between nineteen and forty-five to enlist. The scheme emulated German standards, enjoyed the support of German officers, and was unprecedented in its extent. It included far-reaching requisitions. Preparation for the mobilization had actually started in the last days of July, three and a half months before official entrance into war and the declaration of jihad on 14 November 1914. Over the next four years, the Ottoman Empire conscripted some 3 million men. About a quarter of them died in combat and of disease, half a million deserted, and approximately 250,000 were captured and taken prisoner.[10]

The markedly anti-Entente stance right from the start was fueled by the confiscation on 1 August—shortly before their long-expected delivery—of two Ottoman warships that had been purchased in Britain. The same day, Wangenheim and Enver agreed that the modern German battle cruiser *Goeben* would be an excellent enhancement of Istanbul's anti-Russian offensive strength. By mid-August, this and another German warship, both of which had escaped British pursuit, were integrated into the Ottoman navy, the bigger of them renamed as—what else?—*Yavuz Sultan Selim* (see chap. 1, sec. "Married with a Cause"). The German commander and crew did not change, but they wore Ottoman uniforms. The British confiscation of the aforementioned Ottoman warships on 1 August inspired Enver and Talaat to requisition foreign merchandise.[11]

In a letter on 15 August 1914 to Enver, Churchill, First Lord of the Admiralty, expressed the "personal regard I have for you, Talaat, and Djavid and the admiration with which I have followed your career from our first meeting." These "words of friendship," the letter continued, should motivate Turkey to maintain neutrality, because its author knew nothing about the compelling alliance of 2 August. This, and his confiscation of the battleships, made Churchill's advances illusory. The belle

Der Kaiser in Konstantinopel.
Der Kaiser auf dem „Javus Sultan Selim" („Göben")

FIGURE 15: Kaiser Wilhelm on board the battle cruiser *Yavuz Selim* during a visit in the Ottoman capital in October 1917 (© akg-images, Berlin, Sammlung Archiv für Kunst und Geschichte).

epoque space of mutual communication had definitively collapsed. Frustrated, without an answer from the CUP leaders, Churchill quickly turned angry and bellicose. In a cabinet meeting on 17 August, he already spoke of "sending a flotilla through the Dardanelles."[12]

Leading CUP luminaries were more bellicose. Officially, the Ottoman government declared armed neutrality; in reality, it prepared to wage war as soon as possible. Therefore it started, in early August, to stage a guerilla war in the Russian Caucasus and invited the ARF, its former ally, to join it. Also, in Western Asia Minor, a marked spirit of war prevailed, and war was hastily prepared.[13] The ARF, which met at its Seventh Congress in Erzurum from late July, was approached by committee delegates but balked at these plans and stated that all Armenians should remain loyal to the country in which they lived. Attempts at insurrection in the Caucasus without the ARF nonetheless soon began. Armenian reservation and Cavid's staunch criticism of the alliance attenuated some of Talaat's war enthusiasm by mid-August: "Talaat no longer shows any trace of his former fervor and fire [for immediate war]." Still, as fresh partners of Germany, he and the leading committeemen had won an unequaled self-assurance and confidence.[14]

For connoisseur of political Istanbul Rambert, who also listened to public prayers, three things appeared clear in August 1914: (1) Turkey was actively preparing for war; (2) it stood definitively on Germany's side; and (3) Enver was willing to "commit the big mistake of an untimely attack on the Russian Empire." Like anybody else, Rambert knew nothing of the secret treaty and therefore hoped in vain for a defensive but neutral coalition of Turkey and the Balkan states, including Greece, to fight against any change of the status quo by an aggressor.[15] In contrast, a few leading men—again, not the whole committee government—were now set exclusively on the alliance with Germany and wanted altercation in the Balkans. Yet Talaat tried in vain to draw the Bulgarian ambassador to his side. His and Halil's travels to Bulgaria and Romania failed to persuade their neighbors toward a common war. In contrast to what Rambert hoped, and to Cavid's insistence on neutrality, Talaat embraced the transformative possibilities offered by a general war. Obeying German strategy and his own desire for recoveries in the Balkans, he wanted Bulgaria and Romania to join in warring against Greece, Serbia, and Russia. Yet, on this issue, he returned frustrated in early September.[16]

These first frustrations could be compensated for domestically. Talaat used his new leeway and a burgeoning sovereignty in interior affairs to achieve major CUP goals in September. He abrogated the Capitulations, prohibited foreign postal services, canceled Lebanon's autonomy, and suspended (later annulled)

the reform agreement of 8 February 1914. Although he had not
agreed on this last point, Wangenheim remained silent because
he was anxiously and exclusively fixated on the war effort. The
abrogation of the Capitulations was also a plausible move to a
neutral and distant observer, even if it was not in his personal
interest. "They have failed [regarding the Balkans] to give Turkey all inherent warranties. . . . Why should the Capitulations
be more sacred than the other diplomatic obligations?" Rambert asked two days before actual abrogation, referring to recent
changes on the political map caused by the Balkan Wars.[17]

Although the additions of 6 August 1914 to the alliance treaty
accepted the annulment of the Capitulations, on 9 September
Wangenheim lost his countenance and panicked when faced
with the Porte's unilateral abrogation. He approached Cavid
"with crazy gestures without composure. I thought I was facing
a mad dog. He did not speak but bayed." Wangenheim's basic
anger was that Turkey still did not have joint active war but
had already reaped fruits from the secret treaty. He felt abused,
because since mid-August, he had asked Berlin for patience.
On 9 September, he reported emotionally and wrongly to Berlin that he had limited himself "to a prudent protest" and that
a "criminal" intrigue by the Entente stood behind the abrogation. Inconsistently, on the same day he expressed to Cavid his
fear of harsh reactions by the other powers. For Talaat and the
whole government, the step was an immense success in terms
of popularity and their self-representation as national saviors.
A crowd of about sixty thousand demonstrated its joy on the
central Sultanahmet Square.[18]

Wangenheim was under pressure from Berlin but faced
reluctance in Istanbul.[19] The war had progressed worse than
hoped for. He feared losing Turkey to neutrality or even to
the Entente. Berlin expected him to succeed in bringing about

decisive change by introducing Turkey into war. In this respect, Cavid was not wrong to accuse Germany throughout his diary of having dragged Turkey into war. Yet he lacked critical distance: Talaat, his friend, implicit boss, and leader of Ottoman politics, had foremost advocated war; responsibility could therefore not be thrown on German generals and diplomats alone. Talaat was not less war-prone than Enver, but he preferred to let Enver be the figurehead of advocacy for active war and Germanophilia in Istanbul. Cavid noted, after a talk with Talaat on 6 September 1914, "I said that I saw no interest at all now in making war against Russia, but Talaat, not less than Enver, wants to do so, even if without the Bulgarians!" In communication with Wangenheim two days later, Talaat, "even if bellicose, [still] expected the results" of additional negotiations with Bulgaria.[20]

Istanbul's will to active war was felt throughout the empire from early August 1914, but by outsiders of the CUP often wrongly attributed to Enver alone. In a letter on 16 August 1914, Daniel Thom, a longtime American missionary physician in Mardin, south of Diyarbekir, described the altered situation in his region, which mirrored those of many others in Eastern Asia Minor: "The government has robbed the city, and the country around, of its men, of its animals, of its money, leaving the threshing floors loaded down with a richer harvest than has ever been laid upon, to rot where they are, for lack of men and beasts to tread them out and care for them. The millions that will be lost to the people and the government cannot be estimated. Such suicidal conduct of a government I have not seen, during this variegated life I have lived. . . . Poor Turkey, poor Turkey, going it blindly, with a man at the head of the army, whose name is LIGHT [Enver], but he has certainly turned on the dark slide on his lantern, and is rushing headlong, pell-mell over the precipice, to sure destruction; was there ever such blindness?"[21]

Hasan Tahsin (Uzer), the vali of Van, described in similar though politer terms the economic situation in his province. Van, too, was fully hit by requisition, mobilization, and the challenge to feed those mobilized. In his telegram in mid-September to his superior (Talaat), he demanded financial support and asked about the general political situation, although he got straight to the center's decision for war: "The state of affairs prove that you have decided in favor of war. May God give success and victory." Talaat's answer was straightforward as well: "We wait for the opportune moment." This young and still quite candid high functionary praised the loyalty, support, and goodwill of the Armenians in his province. The mobilization "was completed as in the German army." He was proud to have prepared "30,000 men and 7,000 horses" for, as he was made to believe, imminent war. He drew a rosy picture of pro-Istanbul sympathies, even in Northern Iran, along with unrest in Russian Azerbaijan. "Our paramilitary forces [çetelerimiz] have been equipped from head to toe, given 1,000 pounds, and sent to the border," he wrote to his superior in mid-September.[22]

Tahsin Uzer, one of Enver's cousins who had grown up in Salonica, was—before 1915—an upright, incorrupt CUP representative. As governor of Van, he demonstrated real and successful commitment for the benefit of his province. He showed his own initiative repeatedly, communicated with all groups in the region, and was fully loyal to his superior. In critical times, Talaat could ask him to "sit always before the machine [telegraph], and to stay always in contact and communication." Yet, true to a CUP self-concept of exclusive, imperially biased rule that did not cope with late Ottoman failures, he had detested welcoming Inspector General Hoff into his province in early

August 1914 and hastened the latter's departure. He belonged, like Mahmud Celâl (Bayar) and Mustafa Abdülhalik (Renda), Talaat's brother-in-law, to a group of Talaat's well-educated young men who became instruments of the regime's domestic policy and again reached high positions under Mustafa Kemal Atatürk in the 1920s.[23] This young elite was comprised of proud patriots who were convinced by Istanbul's outlook on history and world affairs, as propagated by the CUP press. Few doubts haunted them.

In an editorial in early September 1914, the CUP paper *Tanin* interpreted the turn to general war as the consequence of a European policy in the Balkans that had not been appreciative enough of Turkey's "loyal and docile watchman's duty" in that region. According to the writer, Talaat's mouthpiece, Europe succeeded in transforming the Balkans but not in maintaining a balance of power. It therefore "tumbled vertiginously down into the abyss of catastrophe within two short years. If there is a moral to recognize in nature and history, we can state that in this way the Eastern Question has very easily and remarkably taken vengeance against Europe and those who are the instruments of Europe." *Tanin*'s quasi-official comment not only took an overconfident position against Europe—and, particularly, Ottoman supporters of the reform plan—but offered proof of a fundamental Ottoman ambition: to end, once and for all, as it stated, the European-made "sinister" Eastern Question itself.

Since autumn 1913, the Armenian Question had been the most salient element of the Eastern Question. The editorial foretold that the Eastern Question "will be removed to history at the end of this war together with the era that ends in 1914. A new era will start after the war for Europe and the whole world; it will not see again an Eastern Question. Since it is not yet possible to determine how this will be resolved, let us only say this: Among the foreigners who see that we take up arms, there are a number [e.g., Rambert] who ask us sometimes why we bear such great expenses. They want to reproach us that we take action without sufficient preparation; they even opine that we have made a partisan decision. We believe that these individuals do not know history well. The shortest and categorical answer that we can give them, and that forbids any response, is this one: the Eastern Question is being resolved!"[24]

For Turan's Sake, by German Will: Attack instead of Reform

From early August, the insiders in the committee, including the ministers of war and the interior, prepared for war by mobilization and requisitions, but before the official declaration of war in November, they also waged a clandestine campaign in the Russian Caucasus and Northern Iran. Although Enver was at the forefront, Talaat was involved in leading this early scheme of irregular aggression. Close communication with governors and leaders of the Special Organization (SO), along with continuous access to military information, suggests that Talaat possessed a better survey of the whole situation in the East than did Enver. Therefore, it might come as only a momentary surprise that the military records, including SO archives in Ankara (in the ATASE), contain rich correspondence from or to Talaat.[25]

Besides overstrung neoimperial goals originating from a pan-ideology, world war at Germany's side offered the opportunity to abolish not only the reform plan but even the conditions on the ground for this plan. World war promised, moreover, the chance to revise the outcome of the 1878

Berlin Treaty with regard to the Southern Caucasus, that is, the restoration of the provinces of Kars, Ardahan, and Batumi to Ottoman rule.

A strategy that had been germinating since early August looked genial at first sight: to combine the new naval strength in the Black Sea with insurrectional warfare behind the lines, including jihad, and an offensive by the Erzurum-based Third Army for an anti-Russian breakthrough in the Southern Caucasus. Germany would contribute with experts, weapons, and money. A parallel offensive into Northern Iran would support the Caucasian campaign and ensure Ottoman dominance in the whole contiguous region. An expeditionary force would advance even more to the East, to Turan. Due to the weakness of Iran's central government, Northern Iran stood under Russian influence according to the Anglo-Russian Entente that had settled (in 1907) the so-called Great Game between Russia and Britain in Central Asia.

A notice by Gottlieb von Jagow, secretary of state at the German Foreign Office, to Wangenheim on 3 August 1914, saying that "revolutionizing Caucasus would be desired," clarified German expectations right after the conclusion of the alliance. The same evening, the Central Committee decided to use the SO and related paramilitary forces to spy on and organize violence within the enemy's territory, following the example of Western Thrace in late 1913.[26] From early August, Wangenheim was excited and impatient to see Turkish action. He put great hopes on irregular anti-Russian violence. He even gave exaggerated news to the Foreign Office, saying on 6 August that "the revolutionizing of Muslims in Caucasus is up and running."[27] What was true was that emissaries from Istanbul had already been sent to this effect. Jihad and the SO appeared as putative wonder weapons.

Wangenheim understood by mid-August that at least the regular army needed time for more preparation. After initial reluctance in late July, he was now fully committed to war in alliance with Turkey. Until July 1914, though poorly informed and not fully convinced, he had pursued a peaceful prosperity of German-Turkish-Armenian relations based on reform, military cooperation, cultural influence, and economic penetration in relation to the Baghdad Railway (Bagdadbahn) project. As late as 31 July 1914, he believed—rather quixotically—that Germany and Great Britain would "become allies with regard to the defense of Armenia."[28] The ambitious ambassador had plausible reason to hope for the post of German foreign minister after a successful ministry in the diplomatic hub of Istanbul.

Bahaeddin Şakir arrived in Erzurum around 8 August to organize and lead the SO on the ground. Now focusing on the Caucasus, he connected the mission goals with his own pre-1908 Islamist, anti-Armenian propaganda toward the Caucasus. As CUP emissaries, Şakir, Ömer Naci, and Filipeli Hilmi first met with delegates of the aforementioned ARF Congress. The SO leaders had brought with them "several scores of Caucasian and Persian agents. Their aim was to organize an anti-Russian propaganda campaign and struggle in the Caucasus and Northern Persia. Their program involved the total mobilization of the eastern provinces," Simon Vratzian, an ARF delegate at the congress, reported.[29] No less than to Rambert, who was in the capital by mid-August, it was clear to Armenian delegates in Erzurum that the decisive leaders of Turkey wanted anti-Russian war without delay. Moreover, Sempad Saadetian, the Armenian prelate in Erzurum, wrote on 14 August to his patriarch in Istanbul that "there is no doubt that these military preparations are being made in anticipation of a war with Russia."[30]

In early September, Şakir reported to Talaat that the preparations had progressed well and that several cross-border raids had
already succeeded. The Russian army refrained from retaliation
until late October.[31] Composed of tribes, released prisoners,
and local Muslims, the SO was markedly Muslim, even if it had
persuaded a few Christian Georgians to join and a few German
officers were actively involved. Its ideology was pan-Islamist
and pan-Turkist, its concrete motivation often prosaically material, that is, spoliation for its own livelihood, since Talaat did
not send Şakir the means that he repeatedly requested. In his
reports to Talaat, Şakir presented the Armenians as enemies
and pretended that Russia had promised them a principality
consisting of parts of the eastern provinces and the Southern
Caucasus—if they collaborated. By mid-September, Ömer
Naci reported via Tahsin that the organization for Northern
Iran was also ready. Yet the supply of the army in Eastern Anatolia was a mess that depressed the soldiers. Like Tahsin, Naci
thought that the regional Armenians were sympathetic. Talaat,
however, followed Şakir's clearly anti-Armenian line and weltanschauung. He offered him the governship of Erzurum, yet
Şakir preferred to head the SO for his project of conquest.[32]

Talaat communicated closely with the SO leaders, the army,
and his governors. He was well informed and deeply involved
in the SO and military matters—much more than was usual
for a normal minister of the interior. He controlled and influenced them via his committee friend Şakir and the members
of his province administration. It clearly appears from the SO
correspondence with Talaat (now largely available in the documentation of the Ministry of the Interior in the Ottoman state
archives), that contrary to widespread traditional belief, Talaat
was as much in command as Enver, and in equally close communication with the SO.

In a telegram on 6 September to Ömer Naci, Talaat spoke of a beginning invasion in Iran that should cast out all Russian forces, but remarked that Azerbaijan still lacked revolutionary (Islamist/Turkist) organization.[33] A fever of conquest and competition had spread among ambitious patriots who wanted to play a leading role in the scheme of conquest. "In a time when the fatherland is most in need, do not leave Tahsin jobless," Governor Tahsin wrote to Talaat. "For the paperwork of the province, I can leave behind the secretary as my deputy. . . . Let me occupy and rule Azerbaijan."[34] In a similar surge of limitless "patriotism," he proposed a great jihad of all Muslims against Great Britain at the end of September, well before the declaration of jihad by Sheykhulislam Hayri on 14 November, because of Great Britain's dishonorable "will to destroy us."[35] By November 1914, Talaat's committee brother Şakir headed the whole SO (until then divided) for the Caucasus, which then took the name of the Revolutionary Committee of the Caucasus.[36]

Talaat's commitment to the scheme of revolution and conquest went hand in hand with the consolidation of a sweeping anti-Armenian attitude. On 6 September, for the first time, he ordered comprehensive measures against the Armenian leadership in large parts of the country: "The local leaders and instigators of the Armenian political parties pursue ever political aims and do not abstain from spreading evil and abominable deeds against the Ottomans and Ottomanity [Osmanlılık]. They must be surveilled and, as soon as required and ordered, be arrested." The use of such harsh and sweeping language with regard to the Armenians was new for Talaat. It recalled anti-Armenian discourse of the 1890s under Sultan Abdulhamid but was now categorical and concerned almost the whole empire, thus prefiguring Talaat's 24 April 1915 circulars. Osmanlılık no longer meant suprareligious Ottoman communality, as in 1908, but only

Ottoman Muslims. Talaat signed this 6 September 1914 circular himself from the Directorate for General Security (a section of the Ministry of the Interior), and it was sent to the governors of Hüdâvendigâr, İzmit, Canik, Edirne, Adana, Aleppo, Erzurum, Bitlis, Van, Sivas, Mamuretülaziz, and Diyarbekir.[37] Henceforth, it was not only the governors in the East who were on standby for a comprehensive anti-Armenian policy.

In his memoir, the Austrian military attaché Pomiankowski hints at the link between Talaat's will to war at Germany's side and his desire to eliminate the Armenian Question and the reform plan. Following the example of the displacement of the Rûm, he may have even thought already of a giant removal or "amputation" (as Pomiankowski put it) if reconquest and expansion in the East failed.[38] The timing in the East in August–September 1914 is relevant, because it proves Talaat and Enver's proactive war policy. A narrative, therefore, of mutual armament and simultanous guerilla warfare by the SO against Russian-sponsored Armenians, and vice versa, lacks decisive accuracy, and the tale of an SO countercampaign is simply wrong.[39]

The fervor to launch war in the Caucasus blended with impatient German expectations, but realities fell short of projects and reports. In early September, for example, the Ottoman ambassador reported from Berlin that a force of 317,000 men— army and SO taken together—stood ready at the frontier to invade the Caucasus.[40] The attitude of the Russian army was defensive, whereas many Armenians hoped for salvation by Russia in the case of war. Only in late September, when the secret services had learned about the Turkish-German treaty, did foreign minister Sazonov acquiesce to Illarion Vorontsov-Dashkov, the governor of the Caucasus, arming Armenians and establishing volunteer regiments formed by Ottoman Armenians who had fled to Tbilisi. In a letter on 30 August, after a staff memorandum of 29 August on the arming of Ottoman Armenians, Sazonov still warned against any anti-Ottoman action before a rupture had taken place. He mentioned the lingering chance of a treaty with Turkey.[41]

The Armenian National Bureau at Tbilisi welcomed Vorontsov-Dashkov's plan for revolt among Armenians in Asia Minor. When returning from Tbilisi, emissaries of Zaven Der Yeghiayan, the Armenian patriarch in Istanbul, reported a joyful atmosphere that was troubling for Armenians in Istanbul. Armenian volunteers were signing up in Tbilisi "to fight against the Turks and liberate Turkish Armenia."[42] There, too, immature political dreams muddled minds. In a novelist's experimental retrospective, in autumn 1914, Gurgen Mahari—a boy of eleven in Van—voiced, shortly after the mid-twentieth century, that the "most terrible thing is that Aram and his friends approve of the policy carried out by their central committee in Tbilisi." He dared to dissect heroic myths, including about Aram Manukian, ARF (Dashnak[tsutiun]) leader in Van: "Their so-called great cause was not honest, because the edifice they had been building had no foundation, because the builders of the cause of 'national liberation' had been inefficient: willfulness and tyranny had been the two-wheeled chariot which Aram called the Dashnak party."[43]

Within the Ottoman Empire, many Armenians did not diguise their sympathies for the Entente. Emotionally, there was already a clear and dangerous front line that traversed most parts of both sides of the Eastern frontier from the Black Sea to Northern Iran before official war started in November. Still comparatively fair-minded, Governor Tahsin reacted to anti-Armenian attitudes in neighboring provinces, and to Talaat's anti-Armenian stance itself in a long telegram in early October 1914. He showed full comprehension of the ARF Congress's decision, saying that the Ottoman Armenians had to side with the Ottoman state but the Caucausian Armenians with Russia. As Van's vali, in his eyes the Armenian behavior entirely conformed to this decision. In Van, Armenians had made more sacrifices for the war tax than had the Muslims. More than anything and anyone else, Armenians worried about the security of life and property. Instead of alienating them, the state should reassure them, by a clear and firm policy, that it was aware of the benefits drawn from its Armenian citizens. It should not follow and exacerbate emotional rifts.

Tahsin complained to Talaat that whereas Van pursued a policy of confidence, the same Armenians, once in the province of Erzurum, were prosecuted and expelled. "These senseless and contradictory opinions amaze us, but above all they amaze the Armenians. . . . We wanted to know why violence is applied against the Armenians in Erzurum. . . . While we promote security here on the basis of facts and evidence, the assemblies of the provinces of Erzurum and Bitlis should not proceed according to defamations based on coffeehouse babble." Yet in a gesture of obedience in advance, and an obligated CUP komiteci show of readiness to implement any instruction, the young governor proposed to his superior at the end, "Which attitude the Porte will ever choose against Armenity [Ermenilik], each province has to adopt it"—in other words, most important was uniformity instead of "contradictory and ridiculous politics" vis-à-vis the Armenians, but not justice based on facts.[44]

Polarizing and Reframing the East

If Talaat could not convince Tahsin of the necessity of harshness against the Armenians in autumn 1914, he had better arguments against the Nestorians. These tribal Christian Assyrians on the Ottoman and Iranian sides of the frontier were no less armed than Kurdish tribes, whereas elsewhere in the Ottoman realm, non-Muslims were generally prohibited to bear arms.

Not only were the Assyrians opposed to being mobilized into the army, as were many Muslims—in particular, Kurds and Alevis—and Christian deserters, but they also represented a risk and hindrance for the attack on Northern Iran. In similar categorical language as his anti-Armenian circular of 6 September, Talaat developed, in a "very urgent" telegram on 26 October to the province of Van, an anti-Assyrian policy of removal and dispersed resettlement. Resettlement and dispersion stood in a long tradition of coercive Ottoman management of nonsubmissive populations and groups (e.g., Alevis) within the Ottoman realm since premodern times. In contrast to the recent Rûm removal, when Talaat sent the "annoying people" to another country via Greece's near islands, he could not alienate and expel Ottoman Nestorians, because they would have strengthened the Christian forces in Iran against the Ottoman invaders.

> Since ever up to the present, the Nestorians are in a situation that arouses suspicion. Once again, in relation to our campaign and final attempts in Iran, they have made clear that they are predisposed to be great agents and instruments of foreign incitements. The government does not trust at all, in particular, the Nestorians in our regions along the border with Iran. Therefore, they must, as a proper punishment, be expelled, removed, and dispersed to appropriate provinces [in Western Anatolia] like Ankara and Konya, where they will henceforth be allowed to stay under the condition that they remain separated, dispersed in Muslim villages, not have more than twenty houses, and do not receive any kind

of governmental support for their resettlement. They have to leave [the province of] Van after the provinces in question have been informed and have accepted the measures.[45]

According to another telegram from Talaat on 29 October, the removal could not be implemented because the means to do so were lacking. This first limited removal scheme demonstrates, nevertheless, relevant elements of planning for the eastern provinces. It proves the interconnection of the early choice of expansive war at the eastern front with considerations of demographic engineering. The addressee of the telegram was actually not Tahsin but Enver's brother-in-law Cevdet, former vice-vali of Van, who had replaced Tahsin by mid-October. However, an accident to Tahsin's daughter deferred his journey to his new post in Erzurum, so that both Tahsin and Cevdet remained present in Van for the time being.[46] Since September, Cevdet had taken SO "bands of volunteers across the border to stir up the Persians against Russia" and to destroy Christian villages. He incited the Muslims "to join in a holy war," reported Clarence Ussher, an American missionary physician in Van who had known Cevdet closely since childhood.[47]

While Tahsin's presence prevented systematic anti-Armenian acts in and around Van in autumn 1914, Şakir and the SO made Armenian life difficult, not only beyond the frontier but also in the province of Erzurum. Extortion of money from Christian citizens and acts of violence on the Erzurum side of the border became frequent, as did anti-Christian raids, rape, and plundering on the other side of the frontier. As a general consequence, society became strongly polarized along religious lines.[48] Talaat was irritated when, during a visit on 7 November 1914, Patriarch Zaven did not merely wish him success in the war that was being declared but expressed concern about anti-Armenian misdeeds in Erzurum, from which he had received alarming reports. Still, Talaat and the other leaders promised "to demonstrate perfect goodwill toward the Armenian people."[49]

The situation worsened when the Ottoman Empire proclaimed war on 10 November and jihad on 14 November. The same day, a well-organized mob of four or five thousand men—swearing, shouting, and cursing Christianity—proceeded from the big Yeni Cami (New Mosque) in the capital to Pera, where it "completely destroyed the interior of the [Armenian-owned hotel] Tokatlian," before demolishing Rûm and Armenian stores and properties; they avoided foreign embassies, except for the Russian consulate. "To me, they looked not only savage, but invincible," said a young, fearful spectator caught in the riot. More than ever, the committee henceforth used urban mobs and pogromist provincial leaders, but did all it could to disguise its destructive "alliances."[50] An outspoken pan-Islamist and pan-Turkist circular by the Central Committee to all CUP branches declared on 11 November 1914 that "the national ideal of our people and country pushes us on the one side to annihilate the Moskowit [Russian] enemy, in order to achieve a natural imperial frontier that includes all our [Turkic] conationals. Religion on the other side pushes us to liberate the Muslim world from the rule of the infidels and to give the adherents of Muhammad independence." *Tanin*, the CUP's mouthpiece, cultivated explicit Islamist propaganda in its edition on 15 November, stressing centuries of oppression that Muslims had to endure from Christian powers. "We wage war for our brothers in faith and race," it stated.[51]

An early SO pamphlet in September 1914 in Northern Iran had already incited Muslims to oust the Christian enemy "from our land."[52] An unhealthy expectation weighed on Hasan İzzet Pasha, the commander of the Third Army in Erzurum, to start

FIGURE 16: Sheykhulislam Hayri Effendi (*center*) during war ceremonies in mid-November 1914; Mehmed Talaat (probably) is at the left from behind. The photo was taken at Ihlamur Kasrı (Ihlamur Pavilion) in Beşiktaş. I thank Mustafa Aksakal for his help in identifying the scene in the photo (photo from Alfred Nossig, *Die neue Türkei und ihre Führer* [Halle: Otto Hendel, 1916]).

the conquest of the Southern Caucasus as soon as possible, but, as a good soldier, he resisted. Therefore, Şakir, Tahsin, and other "idealists" blamed him for his hesitation in telegrams to Talaat and Enver. Enver sent the ambitious and impatient colonel Hafız Hakkı, a committee intimate, to report on the situation. Enver himself left the capital on 6 December to lead the great attack at the eastern front.[53] Enthusiastic young officers responded en masse, hoping to play a role in the ideologically charged campaign. Among them was Rahmi Apak, member of an expeditionary force. "We went to Turan. We were to enter Iranian Azerbaijan to arm the Azeri Turks, then to proceed to Turkestan [vast territory east of the Caspian Sea], to arm the Turks there. Thus we wanted to work for the great cause of Turan."[54]

In a letter on 18 December to his family in Istanbul, Şakir wrote, "With God's help we will soon advance beyond the Caucasus. . . . Pray day and night to the rightful God. The war will come to an end only when we have conquered all of the Caucasus."[55] This proves how seriously they all took the vertiginous Turan project. Later generations and historiographies have tended to downplay or deny this for various reasons by not coming to terms or possibly fathoming political dysfunction and retrospective shame as parts of real history.[56] Local and SO leaders in the East understood the Central Committee guidelines of 11 November 1914 quite correctly when they drew a religious line between friend and enemy without considering the difference between Ottomans and non-Ottomans, combatants and others. They waged war according to a vulgar understanding of sharia, which had also been applied during the Hamidian massacres: Christian property, women, and children were fair prey and men were to be killed. Before the end of 1914, many thousands, mostly villagers, were massacred during an SO advance to Ardanush and Olti, west of Ardahan. Many girls and women were abducted.[57]

Thus, the war at the eastern front rapidly became brutal in autumn 1914. It was ill-conceived and lacked leaders with discipline, settling from the start on an SO with irregulars, among them released criminals and tribes. Armenian and Assyrian militias, who sought and partly obtained help from Russia, were, all in all, defensive but paid the enemies in their own coin where they could. Jihadist propaganda included the promise of loot and Christian girls to secure the SO's local Muslim support. On the other side of the eastern front, which divided communities rather than territories, Armenian and Assyrian militias had internalized anti-Muslim hatred. If they wanted to survive, Christians at the western side of the eastern front had to take sides, because their own state apparently no longer considered them citizens whose life, property, and human dignity were to be protected. In czarist Russia, in contrast, the pro-Orthodox imperial bias remained basically checked by law also during war, as far as Muslims were concerned.

By late 1914, Talaat was disturbed by the developments in Van, where cross-border Armenian activity had begun to respond to state-related coercion and violence. The situation had deteriorated with the start of Cevdet's governorship and the official war. Well aware of Cevdet's aggressive mind-set, of the events in Erzurum, and raids beyond the border, the leading Armenians of Van decided to defend themselves. Therefore, mistrust, tension, and violence also reigned in this province at the end of 1914. Russian intrusion in November, then retreat, followed by indiscriminate anti-Armenian reprisals and acts of Armenian retaliation, contributed to a tense situation.[58]

In a secret and urgent telegram on 30 December 1914, Talaat criticized Cevdet's deputy Şefik and ordered Cevdet to "assure the honor of the government by rapid and categorical measures" in order to "erase and extinguish this militant [Armenian] movement in its beginnings, while it is still possible, before it spreads to the other provinces and districts."[59] In early spring 1915, Rafael de Nogales, an officer in Ottoman service and, from 22 April 1915, leader of the Ottoman forces in Van, witnessed systematic massacres of Armenians by SO men and Kurds on his travels to Van. Among the leading perpetrators in this region was Çerkez Ahmed, a notorious killer. The state had evidently adopted gangs of sophisticated slaughterers who, in retrospect, can be illustrated, by comparison, to those of the twenty-first-century "Islamic State." A leader whom Nogales took to task for his criminal behavior referred to a written order by Cevdet backing his actions. Because the fight for Van, triggered on 20 April 1915, became a main argument for Talaat to start his empire-wide anti-Armenian policy, it is important to be aware of its prehistory.[60]

A final note on the political language of the Ottoman sources analyzed in this and the former section: In accordance with contemporary Europe, but with much more religious emphasis, most sources use sweeping and exclusive notions of belonging. These are, in our case, Islam, Turkdom (Türklük), Armenity (Ermenilik), Christianity, and Ottomanity (Osmanlılık, now reduced to Turko-Muslim imperial belonging). Independent from political frontiers, these terms now largely define the relevant boundaries between "we" and "aliens" during World War I. The same is true, in reaction, for the vocabulary of belonging among Christians who, by late 1914, began to be threatened by extermination—not yet in general but in the eastern war zones. In an already highly problematic region, from early August the committee hawks had implemented war politics, which resulted in a brutal polarization from the Black Sea to Lake Urmiah. Talaat, Enver, and Şakir were the masterminds of the early ideologically charged war in the East.

Embracing War, Concentrating Power: Toward Talaat's Dictatorial Rule

Louis Rambert did not trust the repeated official declarations of neutrality in the capital: "Why then ruin the country by military preparations and an excessive mobilization?" In Istanbul, there were extraordinary army activities and noisy naval excercises day and night that presaged decisive action in early October 1914.[61]

Talaat's ascent after a deep crisis had begun by embracing war logic and public war rhetoric in early autumn 1912. More generally speaking, he had then started to rebuild himself as an integral hawk and to conceive the committee as an organized force fighting in the name of Muslim Turks against interior and exterior enemies. Sociability, charm, and bargaining henceforth served a hawk's policy. By 1912, he had definitively abandoned nonpartisan, consensual negotiation based on the 1908 constitution. Since the recovery of Edirne at the latest, Talaat knew that he succeeded in forming ad hoc insider groups to manipulate both cabinet and committee according to his designs. The July 1914 crisis and the alliance with Germany offered new international dynamics in which he won additional breadth of action and gained even more power, though he now stood under the pressure of German expectations.

Despite Cavid's advice, Said Halim's reluctance, and a firm assertion to the contrary in Talaat's memoirs, Talaat backed, no less than Enver, the official entrance into active war, although, perhaps, more reticently.[62] He knew how to maneuver, in contrast to Enver, a comparably transparent patriot, militarist, and partisan of Germany who, probably sent by Talaat, had tried to deceive the Russian Embassy on 6 August 1914. Talaat's decisive insider group since July 1914 was composed of Enver and Halil. These three men—or action party—met on the evening of 10 October 1914 to promote active war, as demanded by Germany. They succeeded in persuading Cemal, who had initially hesitated. On 11 October, they met Wangenheim to agree to a naval attack against Russia, as suggested by the Germans since early September, for an immediate loan of 2 million Ottoman pounds. Moreover, Germany offered a loan of 5 million pounds starting in 1915.[63]

Against their own public assertions afterward, but in accordance with Cavid's contemporary sense, the insiders proposed and approved the joint German-Ottoman aggression against

Russia on the Black Sea. This move incorporated the Ottoman world into active war at the end of October 1914, when joy and good news of victory against alleged aggression spread immediately in Istanbul. Others felt that soon thereafter, "a secret unrest" reigned over the capital, from which nationals of enemy states were forced to depart in November. Several Ottomans also chose to do so.[64] The second half of October had been hectic and ambivalent, as proven in German diplomatic correspondence, Cavid's diary, and memoirs. From a sober military view, spring 1915 would have been the earliest possible moment for the Ottoman army to enter war. Additional doubts apparently arose even within the action party after Italy had warned Turkey on 23 October to give up its neutrality.

Talaat mirrored as much as he managed his friends, but he also took the lead in cases of doubt—and generally opted for the bolder gamble. He knew that Berlin and the military mission under Liman von Sanders could no longer be strung along. He must have been afraid that the new momentum of war with its great expectations, including financial benefits, was lost if Turkey forfeited its German friendship, or the war would end for good by Christmas 1914, as many still expected. Since August, he had banked on bringing the transformative power of the European war to the Caucasus and the Middle East. It is not true that the decision makers "simply tried to walk a neutral path for as long as they could" and that Enver alone wanted war. Churchill honestly admitted that he and most representatives of the Entente had wrongly believed in August 1914 "that Turkey had no policy and might still be won or lost." It is a fundamental misunderstanding to still suggest in recent scholarship that they lacked "war aims, which reflected national policy objectives." Yet to say that their war aims were not "finely tuned" is a true understatement.[65]

Loyal to his general approach since 1912, to the engagement of 11 October 1914 in relation to Wangenheim, and to a further development of warfare in the East, Talaat remained committed to Enver's plan of anti-Russian provocation on the Black Sea, even without the cabinet's backing. A full-bodied message by Enver to the chief of the Oberste Heeresleitung (German Supreme Army Command) of 22 October 1914 promised war against Russia and Great Britain at several fronts, and also possibly against Serbia and Greece. On the same day, Enver wrote an order to the German admiral Souchon, the German commander of the Ottoman navy, demanding that he attack the Russian navy once he was on the Black Sea and had (or could create) the opportunity to use arms.[66]

These messages were announcements of a total war by a megalomaniac junior who not only followed his own designs and interests but, put under pressure, also wanted to gain recognition from a German senior—the military representative of the foremost Great power in Continental Europe. Therefore, the psychological state of those in power and German responsibility must be considered.

In late October 1914, Talaat followed the naval development day and night, telephoning the General Staff where Colonel Ali İhsan Sâbis served. On 27 October the Ottoman navy sailed through the Bosporus. "At midnight, Talaat Bey called me at home to ask if there were news about the navy."[67] Before the morning of 29 October, Talaat could not get the news he expected, but the same day, having got it, he could frankly admit to US ambassador Henry Morgenthau "that they had decided to side with the Germans, and sink or swim with them." To a colleague in the parliament he joked that "this was a misfortunate incident, but it was good." Germany and Turkey and Talaat and Wangenheim were now bound together even more strongly. For Morgenthau, by 29 October 1914, the Germans had "succeeded and Wangenheim has won out. He has stirred up Egypt and controls the Black Sea."[68] Talaat, Enver, and Wangenheim were henceforth the strongmen in Istanbul—though Wangenheim wasn't for long, and Enver was never in the position to compete with or to replace Talaat.

True to his announcement, Cavid resigned from the cabinet after the Ottoman attack on Russia.[69] The grand vizier was "weak-minded," Enver "entirely ignorant in politics and infantile-minded," and Talaat "imagined that everything could be resolved by boldness." The rule of these men "plunged the country into evil," Cavid noted on 30 October 1914, at last strongly critical of Talaat and, foremost, Enver. He read Talaat's face and knew well that his committee brother had lied when he spoke of a Russian attack. Yet, in a kind of "Nibelung loyalty" (unshakable loyalty and blind faith), he continued to assist Talaat in the future. He did this out of, he believed, patriotic Ottoman duty. His diary reveals a schizophrenic situation from which writing gave him some distance, serving as an exercise in mental independence as well as a memory hook for daily affairs. Writing in private, he cultivated an individual *arrière-boutique* of his mind, as Michel de Montaigne put it in his famous sixteenth-century *Essays*.

Cavid was disturbed by and revolted against an attitude of all or nothing, victory or death, among members of the Central Committee. He argued that nobody had the right to expect others to join in suicide. Talaat was "the foremost partisan of war" for "whom and his disciples, this war was *tout ou rien* [all or nothing]," also notes the diary of Krikor Zohrab, Cavid's Armenian friend, on 3 November 1914. Both discussed in the late evening of 3 November 1914 what they considered a Germany-centered, fatal "war psychology of Talaat and his followers."[70] For these bright minds, two evil currents, Otto-man and German, joined together for an unfortunate war in late October 1914. According to them, Talaat could have used his preeminent influence to keep the cabinet and the commit-tee safe from war. Instead, he did the exact opposite, because his political mind obeyed war logics and psychology, acting in connivance with the "sectarian" éminences grises, who were prominently involved in SO warfare in the East.

Nâzım approached Cavid as the last of several committee brothers to persuade him to revisit his decision and not to resign. Cavid's diary reports Nâzım's statements: "If the Central Committee has appointed me [Cavid] for a post but I opposed it, . . . from now on, there could be given to any young man a revolver to kill Cavid Bey, because I was a fallen man for the fatherland, since my power was from the party . . . all people would now call me a 'treacherous Jew' (in a way he [Nâzım] justified them). . . . there was no more place for me in the coun-try." When Cavid retorted that he would not act against his con-science but was ready for future service to the country, Nâzım "made do with the vulgar saying 'in this war we will perish or overcome.'" Cavid spared only a few words: "Wretched mind, ill-fated country."

In the weeks after this encounter, Nâzım, himself from Dönme origin, defamed Dönme Cavid everywhere as a treach-erous Jew. Ridiculing him, he changed his name to "David" and even threatened to expel all Dönme because of Cavid's withdrawal. This, in fact, caused a rupture in the committee. Deep distrust vis-à-vis Nâzım henceforth pervades Cavid's diary. Talaat was saddened, as was Cemal, by the resignation of Cavid, whose intelligence refused the tale of Russian aggres-sion, Talaat's lies, and Enver's candid ignorance. Talaat himself, however, had chosen Nâzım's political orientation.[71] Cavid detested Nâzım as a hypocrite and a fanatical brute, whom he avoided whenever possible. Still, he was to remain committed to "patriotic duty" within the mental prison of the committee, though he could have easily defected while often traveling in Europe.

From November 1914, Talaat enjoyed true dictatorial power in the capital. A poisoned milieu and the context of war allowed him to maximally shape and adjust interactions, information, and decision making in favor of what he believed to be best for Turkey's future and his own position. It is by no means astonishing, therefore, that Talaat, "though intelligent," became an "instrument of evil."[72] His behavior in October 1914 and additional acts of distrust against Cavid in November prove that he did not hesitate to lie and to let trust perish. "When I see the ideas and the mentality of the government, I cannot trust it," Cavid wrote after a discussion with French diplomat Louis Steeg, who was to leave Istanbul. "Because in Talaat's eyes, there does not exist any illegitimate action if problems are to be solved."[73]

Talaat's circle wanted to use French and British citizens as human shields against naval attacks. "Talaat told me again to try and secure an assurance of nonbombardment of unfortified seaports or else they would stop the exit of the French and English," Morgenthau noted on 11 November. "When I told Talaat that Americans thought them too decent to carry out the threat of burning and massacre, he said, 'What shall we do to prove that we mean it?' And I saw he meant it."[74] He identified with radical action as he identified with jihad. This was the ultimate instrument of power for a Muslim state—although contemporary Wahhabi scholars considered Talaat's telegraphic invitation to a Saudi leader on 20 November 1914 to join the Ottoman jihad as a call of Turkish unbelievers.[75]

From November 1914, Talaat led within a framework of total war even more than before, amid irregularities, extortion, corruption, and chaos. This was the element in which he had to unfold, and he unfolded. Menaces, cheap promises, unreliable financial behavior, and ongoing mistrustful bargaining with Germany reflected the Ottoman lack of stamina and fundamentals but also the general political realities in the cataclysmic world of a general war. The Ottoman signature political animal held up a distorting mirror to Europe. It showed the worst yet nevertheless real sides of Europe, scaled up. Unconcerned by rules and ethics, arguing that he saw both broken numerous times by the European powers, he began to use the ruthless arms of a comparatively weak actor also wanting an empire: extortion and aggression toward weaker ones who could not fight back. Talaat mirrored not only the committee forces around him but also contemporary Europe, whose three decades of cataclysm and breakdown of public confidence Talaat heralded.

He applied ad hoc decisions in a cabinet abandoned by adversaries of the war policy. He depended on a stressful alliance with Germany and relied on a committee where radicals like Şakir, Nâzım, Kara Kemal, and Gökalp had a strong say. Comparatively more moderate senior figures still in the government—Grand Vizier Said Halim and Sheykhulislam Hayri—were marginalized and unable to cope. Cemal Pasha, still minister of the navy, was nominated to govern "Great Syria," including Lebanon and Palestine, and assigned to reconquer British-annexed Egypt. This was again as much a German as an Ottoman project, which galvanized the minds in the capital. Actually, "in those days" in late summer and autumn 1914, "the conquest of the Caucasus and of Egypt was the most popular currency," a contemporary acquaintance of Gökalp recalled. Cemal left the capital in late November. "This morning [21 November] Cemal came to bid farewell. He said that two days ago he was appointed for Egypt and that all plans were ready in his mind. If his strong conviction is based on knowledge, what a big strength. If, however, on ignorance, what a terrific thing," Cavid noted.[76]

Cavid's rich diary is far from all-embracing, since it concentrates on the fields of interest of its author. Yet it documents well how Talaat's war dictatorship started. At times a Jacobin-style radical and a fervent patriot, but not a chauvinist, Cavid was a unique figure at the margins of the CUP war regime. He preserved basic principles of conscience and human dignity, in contrast to most men serving Talaat. The CUP man with the most experience and insights in the international arena, he kept on assisting his political friend, although he was more than skeptical about the war, the alliance, so-called constraints, and German imperialism. In sympathy with him, old Huguenin helped him penetrate the back stage of Berlin, where likewise political confusion was growing. After the tale of rapid victory, Wangenheim preached that Berlin wanted "to make it a long war now, so as to settle everything and secure a long period of peace."[77]

Enver Pasha remained in Istanbul, without reaching a position that politically rivalled Talaat, even if he may have dreamed of becoming a Napoleon-like emperor. He gradually became a war minister who conformed to hawkish designs, in contrast to his predecessors Ahmed İzzet and Mahmud Şevket. Irreplaceable for Talaat, Enver spoke German, was liked by broad circles in Germany—including the court—and thus enjoyed a special relationship with the Germans, although the collaboration with the military mission and German officers assigned to the Ottoman armies was often strained. All in all, Talaat was much better connected in international Istanbul than Enver. He regularly met with diplomats and all kinds of representatives. In the arena of both interior and exterior politics, Enver depended more on Talaat than vice versa. This kind of relationship applies for the whole course of 1914–18, even if both remained pillars of the war regime.

Although a public hero of the 1908 revolution and husband of an Ottoman princess since spring 1914, Enver did not possess the politically relevant, still ascending, broad popularity of Talaat. The war minister and actual commander in chief needed the political backing of Talaat after the flop of the early Caucasus-Iran-Turan scheme, and, even more, after a full-fledged military campaign in late December 1914 catastrophically failed in the mountains of Sarıkamış, west of Kars. "Enver was greatly depressed and very retiring," when he came back to the capital before mid-January 1915, "until he saw that his defeat was not held up against him," Morgenthau observed.[78] Talaat could not reproach Şakir and Enver for a scheme that he himself had supported from the start. Enver was therefore welcomed and accepted, apparently without a critical assessment of what had gone wrong. The failure was seen as a natural outcome of gambling, not as an issue that demanded responsibility. Military successes at Gallipoli, in Iraq, and in the Galician and Romanian campaigns could strengthen Enver's position and his "military faction" in the CUP only temporarily. In late 1917, for Germans, Enver had become weak to such an extent that he survived "only thanks to us and the grand vizier" (by then, Talaat).[79]

Talaat's dictatorial grip was not top-down but depended on gambles, corruption, and the balance of factions. It was therefore never truly firm, never countrywide, and less strict than the rule of the European dictators after him, although these also relied on corruption. Under Talaat, strong governors had room to maneuver at a regional level, although not at their own discretion, as the example of Cemal Pasha in Syria demonstrates. Talaat, backed by the committee, was the boss when sensitive questions were at issue, such as those related to Zionism. As a rule, he made the decisions concerning the assignment of governors and other high civil functionaries.

Istanbul's general depression after military failure in early 1915, when antiwar placards spread in the capital and invasion was impending, could become dangerous for Talaat's position, and not less so regarding his psychology. At this moment, the audacious optimism and reliance of Enver helped him gain new courage and to persevere. Onstage was nothing less than the defense of the capital. Talaat had prepared it at the side of the German command in the aftermath of the first attacks in December 1914, when Enver had not yet returned from the Caucasus. Talaat desperately needed success in late winter 1915 so as not to lose the lead or lose himself to apathy or despair. As in earlier crises, he was to seek success in radical action.[80]

Depressed by Defeat, Galvanized by Gallipoli

Talaat and the CUP had profited from the new international situation and the alliance with Germany to suspend monitored reforms, abrogate the Capitulations, close down foreign postal services, obtain financial support and loans, and prepare territorial restoration and expansion. But war went badly for Turkey during winter 1914–15 on all fronts, from the Caucasus to Northern Iran, from Southern Iraq to the Suez Canal. The Ottoman war momentum was almost lost, and depression began to weigh down those in power in Istanbul. Moreover, epidemics and famine began to loom in parts of the empire. However, Talaat followed a multiple agenda that did not depend on military victories against exterior enemies alone. On 29 December, a day before he ordered vali Cevdet to erase Armenian militancy in Van, Talaat obtained a cabinet decision and decree of the sultan that practically abolished the reform plan of 8 February 1914, because it terminated the agreement with the inspectors general.[81] Within five months since August 1914, Talaat had completely reversed the outlook on Eastern Asia Minor.

The situation in the East was even more radically transformed by Enver Pasha's Caucasian campaign, undertaken by the Erzurum-based Third Army and the SO. This campaign deserves a closer look. "At last, we advance, God be praised. With God's help, we will . . . continuously and victoriously advance," Colonel Hafız Hakkı Pasha wrote on 18 December in his diary. Commander of the Third Army, Hasan İzzet resigned on the same day because he did not trust the project. He was replaced by Hakkı. Much has been written on the fatal campaign against an enemy that was numerically inferior but superior in strategic intelligence, which resulted not only in the loss of a whole army and the failure of the invasion but also in a typhus epidemic and general misery in the region. The press in Turkey and Germany denied or silenced the facts.[82] Both, Germany in particular, could have learned important lessons for the future. Gökalp's "idealism" was a significant component of the dysfunctional political thought that had been invested in the scheme of a conquest toward Turan as early as August 1914.

It is true that the committee hawks were pushed by German diplomacy and the military in the months after August 1914, yet Liman von Sanders, head of the German military mission, had been reticent and skeptical when asked by Enver to command the anti-Russian advance in early December.[83] Enver's hold on the army and the SO had made him a strategist of far-reaching ambitions, while Şakir and many other "idealists" had dreamed of glory in a Turan that soon turned into a deadly utopia. Evading any soul-searching on the disaster, Ambassador Wangenheim swiftly changed his arguments, now saying that "it would be best if Turkey did not conquer . . . Russian territory, as that would make adjustment [for peace] more difficult." He tried to play down the fiasco and was "very anxious to have Turkey keep on fighting with Germany to the end and not seek a separate peace." The treaty of 2 August and the additional conditions of 6 August had already closely bound the destinies of Germany and Turkey. The new, more general treaty of 11 January 1915, to be valid until 1920, further bound them and their expectations together.[84]

Talaat himself had identified with a risky but up-and-coming enterprise that should have rewarded the investment of several months of war preparations and conquest in the East. After failure, many saw him looking "very glum," in "bad humor," and "extremely depressed" in early 1915. "For the first time since the war began, I have seen Talaat in despair," Cavid noted on 14 February 1915, after news of Hafız Hakkı Pasha's death by typhus arrived in Istanbul.[85] Hafız Hakkı, already a member of the internal committee in 1907, represented the activist idealists of the CUP who had fervently believed in conquest in the East. "It is impossible not to weep on the loss of this our beloved brother, this always forgiving, active, and valuable man of the army. Yet we have to die in order to make the nation and the country live," Talaat wrote two days later to his brother-in-law Mustafa Abdülhalik (Renda), the vali of Bitlis (west of Van). Abdülhalik was another of Talaat's Balkan-born young and devoted men now working as functionaries in the East, and he later served Mustafa Kemal Atatürk.[86]

Campaigns with irregular forces led by Enver's brother-in-law Cevdet and Enver's uncle, General Halil, in Northern

Persia, strongly harmed Armenian and Syriac villages, but again failed in their anti-Russian military objectives. Finally, the invaders were decisively defeated in the mid-April 1915 battle of Dilman, in which Armenian general Andranik Ozanian's volunteer brigade participated. Similarly, in early February, Cemal informed Istanbul that he must abort his attempt at crossing the Suez Canal. Thus, restorationist and expansionist expectations, which had stimulated elites in the capital and young officers in the army, had turned to trauma. According to the Ottoman chief rabbi Haim Nahum, "all the Turks" were "somewhat depressed" in February 1915.[87]

In this situation and atmosphere, Talaat and the committee seriously risked losing authority and composure. In both a depressed and an aggressive mood, Muslim deputies left the parliament when the session was closed prematurely on 14 February. The notoriously anti-Christian Diyarbekir deputy Fevzi and many others threatened that no Christian would survive in the capital if foreign forces advanced. When the Entente navy began to heavily bombard the Dardanelles (the naval entrance to Istanbul) on 19 February, the committee regime was faced with the reality that the empire was on the defensive, definitively no longer in a dope-like dream of restoration and expansion. Pessimism reigned widely, not only at the fronts and in the capital but also among those Ottoman representatives and allies whom Cavid met in Vienna and Berlin in early March 1915. Among the foreign diplomats in Istanbul, "everybody" was "tremendously nervous and excited about the situation."[88]

As a consequence of the fiasco in the East, the civil administration and the military lost their grip on those border areas. Ottoman rule was put into question there, since the army was decimated. The SO's main function was now defensive. The Russian army had occupied small strips of Ottoman territory and made temporary advances with limited forces. To console and encourage SO leaders and governors, Talaat did not hesitate to make promises (which he later voided) of rapid military support from Istanbul, or even to tell euphemistic lies, such as the news of a Bulgarian invasion in ex-Ottoman Macedonia by a Bulgarian ally.[89] With his telegrams and circulars, this powerful minister of the interior largely framed what representatives of the regime in the provinces knew about current domestic and international affairs. Newspapers were rare and late in the eastern provinces, and censored according to committee requirements.

Leader Talaat was himself at a loss by February and early March 1915, even if he was an experienced gambler who used a panoply of legal and illegal means. He could refocus from Turan and flamboyant attempts at reconquest to realities in Asia Minor. The Dardanelles and the eastern front, in particular Van, were two main concerns. The committee leaders could, however, reasonably demonstrate confidence that Istanbul would sucessfully be defended. German generals led, and German experts and weapons, and some German units, supported the Ottoman troops charged with the defense. Still, the risk was high. Van's and the eastern provinces' case was more difficult, though it did not directly threaten the power center. Together with the hawks, Talaat had sowed the wind there and was now reaping the whirlwind; that is, misery, hate, and an endangered future.

Both despite and because of its sectarian politics, the regime forces there could not even secure the support of all nominal Muslims. Alevis in Dersim, who had always been alienated from the Ottoman sultanate-caliphate, sympathized with Russia and refused to join the Ottoman army. The (Sunni) Kurdish leaders Abdurrezzak and Kâmil Bedirhan sought an alliance with the

ARF, backed by Russia. As a consequence, Talaat impressed upon Cevdet the need to immediately arrest any Kurdish chief inclined to follow this line. Talaat's reaction against the Armenians was harsher, although he reproached them for similar misdeeds. It was also harsher than against "the seditious and intriguing Zionists," who, in the eyes of Cemal Pasha, were "trying to create a nation and [were] already using paper money and stamps" in Palestine. In January and February, the CUP press had still emphasized Ottoman Armenian patriotism and loyalty in the ongoing war and that any anti-Armenian suspicion among Muslims originated from evil manipulation.[90]

Yet managed publicity did not correspond to Talaat's actual assessment. It rather misled and disguised the imminence of a hardening domestic strategy, foreshadowed in late summer 1914. In a telegraphic circular dated 28 February 1915, Talaat drew the attention of the governors in Eastern Asia Minor to news of "Armenian bandits" in Bitlis, "Armenian acts of violence against the army in Aleppo and Dörtyol," and subversive documents in Kayseri that "proved a rebellion [was] being prepared by our enemies." He shared relevant correspondence on Armenians with Enver and insisted that those arrested in Dörtyol needed severe punishment. His circular on 28 February also mentioned the general disarmament of Armenian soldiers by Enver's order on 25 February and called the governors to be ready for further action.[91]

Talaat was particularly upset by messages from Van and by a detailed report of Van deputy Arshak Vramian, a former classmate of Cevdet's at Istanbul's Mülkiye (school for civil servants). This report, presented to Cevdet on 21 February 1915,[92] and several telegrams, also by ARF Van deputy Vahan Papazian, not only described atrocities committed in the region of Van by SO irregulars, but in a less than submissive tone, it also made suggestions for how to overcome the grave crisis, save Turko-Armenian relations, and resolve unrealized reforms, including a recent one proposed by former governor Tahsin. It thus strongly recalled alternative projects of rule in Eastern Asia Minor in the vein of the February 1914 reform plan, as opposed to the presently shaky rule that made Christians fair game. Vramian's report asked permission for self-defense. The Central Committee understood the report as a step toward Armenian autonomy. It interpreted it as an antigovernmental affront that required a harsh and comprehensive response. Not only was deportation a ready topic after the successful Rûm removal in June 1914, but new talk of salutary extermination of minorities was so frequent among officers that, from late 1914, it directly reached the ear of foreigners at different places. It was probably nowhere as entrenched as among officers and SO people in Erzurum after the defeat at Sarıkamış.[93]

In early March 1915, Talaat was not yet in the mood or position to proceed toward comprehensive action. Acts of rebellion (resistance against recruitment, repression, and espionage) had taken place in Dörtyol, province of Adana, and in Zeitun, province of Aleppo, two towns where Armenians were well organized and partly armed. A small group of Zeitun Armenians, among them deserters, hoped for a full-on rebellion in Cilicia but were crushed by superior forces of the Ottoman Fourth Army in late March 1915. On the initiative of Cemal, commander of the Fourth Army, the Zeitun Armenians were ousted and resettled far away in Konya, with Muslim migrants settled in their place. Writing in the name of Talaat from the Interior Ministry's Directorate for Resettlement of Tribes and Migrants, Ali Münif (Yeğenağa), a close contemporary of Talaat's, asked Cemal to consider the difficulties of the situation, because the rocky region was not ideal for the resettlement of muhacir. In late February, before the removal from Zeitun, the vali of Adana had resettled the Armenians from Dörtyol to other places in the same province, but not directly at the sea.[94]

Of crucial importance was the naval victory, and thus the successful defense of Istanbul, on 18 March 1915. On 19 March, Talaat, in an excellent mood, let Captain William Hall, the British director of naval intelligence, know that "many of the most influential citizens" in the Ottoman capital "would welcome an immediate break with the Germans and prayers were even being offered at mosques of the city for the arrival of the British fleet," thus misleading Churchill about Istanbul's military resilience and Talaat's and Enver's common determination to fight at Germany's side. In contrast to what Britain hoped, there was no rift between the top two CUP leaders—and even less of a chance of a coup by Talaat against Enver—but only a British lack of basic intelligence. At a British war council meeting that same day, Churchill believed that "it was time for us to make a clean sweep," and to divide "this inefficient and out-of-date nation," meaning Ottoman Turkey. Oscillating between under- and overestimation of Turkish-Muslim power, mixed with British imperial fear, Churchill had, a few weeks earlier, vented that "India is the target, Islam is the propellant, and the Turk is the projectile."[95]

The victory on 18 March gave Talaat the confidence he needed to conceive and operationalize a comprehensive policy whose exact character was yet to be determined. "Under different pretexts, Vramian sends telegrams to [our] ministry that criticize the rule of the government and that abound with defamations. This man must be expelled from Van and . . . handed over to the court-martial in Erzurum. Send your investigation quickly," he ordered Cevdet on 21 March. On the same day, he informed Tahsin that "the resignation of Venizelos in Greece [a consequence of the national schism between Venizelists and royalists] has brought a change in our favor. Triumph continues in the Bosphore."[96] Cevdet willingly obeyed Talaat and set a snare for his former classmate and friend Vramian. He arrested him shortly after the murder of Ishkhan, another ARF leader of Van, on the night of 16 April, to "send him to the court-martial." As a rule, this set phrase meant the subsequent death of the targeted Armenian on the road to trial, as was ultimately the case with Vramian.

Talaat urged action on 13 April 1915: "Is there still an obstacle to sending away the aforementioned [Vramian]?" From this point on, he personally followed many individual cases of hunted Armenians to the end. As a last strong sign of life, on 8 May Vramian sent a message from Bitlis to Istanbul urging Talaat "in the name of supreme interests" to extend a hand of reconciliation and stop a fratricidal war in Van. He or his colleague Vahan Papazian would be happy to deal with an emissary from Talaat and would surely succeed within three days. Both optimistic and next to despair, this message from an Ottoman Armenian deputy on the road to death stands as the last testimony of a will to peace and life. Yet Talaat remained fixated on demolition, revenge, and easy victory in a self-declared war against a domestic enemy, which his decision for war and polarization in the East had largely created.[97]

The date 18 March 1915 was a watershed for the CUP's retrieval from defeat and depression in general and the beginning of Talaat's overall anti-Armenian policy in particular. The first important military success in World War I against a naval breakthrough attempt by the Entente at the Dardanelles, pushed foremost by Churchill, galvanized the depressed rulers. The attackers suffered heavy losses. "This evening [of 18 March], we received the first good news. . . . This was glad tidings after

long days of anguish and worry that depressed us. The issue of
Çanakkale [Dardanelles] is not a near danger. We were deliri-
ous with joy," said Cavid. Even more than after the recovery of
Edirne, the committee members boasted about victory against
the naval world powers and demonstrated everywhere the "firm
conviction that Çanakkale could not be transgressed."[98]

They concealed or minimized the decisive contribution of
German commanders, experts, and technology. In contrast to
the Ottoman-led Third Army in the eastern provinces, accompanied only by a few German officers, the Ottoman army in
Istanbul and Western Anatolia stood under direct German
command. "These [CUP] men are absolutely intoxicated with
their apparent success and are already beginning to completely
underestimate the assistance that the Germans have rendered
them," Morgenthau wrote. Interestingly, Wangenheim acquiesced to the CUP's representation of the facts. He welcomed
with emotion this first important success of an ally, for which
he felt responsible, but which had formerly caused him a lot of
worry. As a result, the alliance was strengthened and Wangenheim was even more eager not to affront Talaat and Enver.[99]

For CUP circles, the victory of 18 March 1915 against France
and Britain was the birth of "a feeling of national identity in
the country," as Muhittin Birgen wrote. The regime regained
more than its self-assurance in late summer 1914. Its new self-
reliance was combined with a chauvinist stance against foreigners in general and Ottoman Armenians in particular, who were
now declared subversive aliens and causes of previous defeats.
Most vocal was Şakir, who made the Armenians responsible
for failure in the East, as did some German officers. Instead of
further conquest, the SO was forced to retreat in February 1915;
hence, Şakir's August 1914 plan of conquest had turned into an
obvious fiasco. Nevertheless, he and others "did not abandon

their blind ambition of invasion," although they had to put it on hold temporarily. "The conviction that the Turks [Muslims] in Russia must be connected to Turkey was entrenched to such an extent that the relevant programs remained on standby," former SO member Arif Cemil wrote in retrospect.[100]

When Şakir left Erzurum on 13 March 1915 and arrived a little later at the CUP headquarters in Istanbul, this biased vision, deep frustration, and the will to anti-Armenian action framed his mind-set. From August 1914 on, he had actively planted the seeds of violence with brutal cross-border raids and incitement to jihad toward Russian Muslims and now reaped what he had sown, including violence against Muslims at the front. The failed campaigns and the chaos at the long eastern front infuriated the leaders and made the local Armenian and Assyrian Christians, who hoped for a Russian advance and help, easy targets for the propaganda of jihad. For the SO and the CUP, angst and panic were added to their frustration, knowing that retreat might continue on the Ottoman side of the border; thus, another future could emerge in the East, one that was more in favor of local Christianity. Nâzım, himself an SO leader, although based in the capital, shared these views of his longtime CUP friend Şakir. The CUP archives are largely lost or missing, and thus detailed reconstruction is scarcely possible—pending full disclosure of archival material in private and military archives in Turkey. Yet it is safe to conclude that committee meetings with Talaat, Gökalp, Kemal, Şakir, Nâzım, Halil, Şükrü, and Cahid in the second half of March, or perhaps early April, determined the conceptualization and operationalization of Talaat's overall policy against Armenian citizens. The beginning of its implementation was a matter of days or a few weeks, depending on macrodevelopments and reliable suggestions by his men in the eastern provinces.[101]

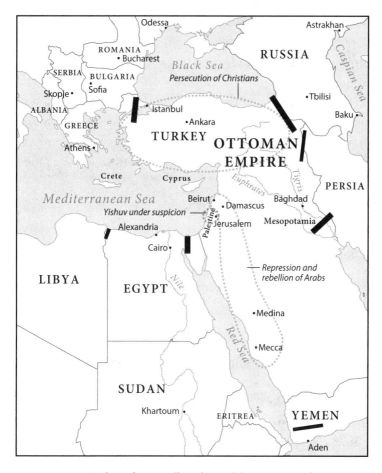

MAP 3: Total war, domestically and toward the exterior, as of 1915.

In a timely manner, the committee began implementing propaganda of victimization, atrocity, and revenge, such as that waged during and after the Balkan Wars, but this time it was more generally focused upon "our ill-fated religious and racial brothers in the Caucasus" and "the misdeeds done against all Muslims, not only the Ottomans." Simultaneously, the Foreign Ministry under the grand vizier Said Halim (now

little more than Talaat's and the committee's puppet), prepared a Red Book that collected military and civil documents
on "atrocities committed by Ottoman Armenians at the side
of the Russians" and—in an inversion of the intentions and
real-time sequence since late July 1914—on "aggressions and
attacks committed by the Russians before the start of the war
in order to modify the border." Correctly translated from propaganda language, this sentence confessed their own failed
agenda.[102]

Exploit: "The Armenian Question no longer exists"

Asymmetry, totality, and ethnoreligious specificity character-
ize the total war at home that Talaat started in April 1915. By
mid-July, he boasted that he had "accomplished more in three
months about crushing the Armenians than Abdul Hamid
could do in thirty-seven years."[103] This self-assessment confirms that by early April a comprehensive decision process for
the anti-Armenian policy had passed the critical threshold,
outmatching by far Abdulhamid's anti-Armenian efforts of the
1890s, in which tradition it stood. In his political philosophy,
Talaat had erased any last trace of the struggle for a constitution, for Turkish-Armenian cooperation, and against despotism, as before and shortly after 1908, when Abdulhamid II had
been considered a common adversary. He ultimately tainted
the judgment on his character by sending long-standing
Armenian companions and their entire population into brutal
deaths.

Euphoria over victory against the Entente's navy merged with
Şakir's and other political friends' vehemently anti-Armenian

stance, the initiation of removal-resettlement schemes in Dörtyol and Zeitun, and demands by militaries and valis for removal in the East, which gave Talaat the final compulsion to act comprehensively. He and Enver had already implemented several steps of repression against Armenian elites since September 1914. Yet in May and June 1915, it was Talaat—not Enver or anyone else—who designed the scheme of an almost total removal of Armenian fellow citizens from Asia Minor and European Turkey to places of death—not even camps—in the Syrian Desert.

The victorious defense at Gallipoli and the extermination of Armenians were not only simultaneous but also intrinsically connected, as was an immediate myth of heroic national triumph, which extinguished any soul-searching and healthy critique.[104] In April 1915, Talaat probably oscillated between a policy of removal focused on the huge area of Eastern Asia Minor and Cilicia and a countrywide exterminatory radicalism, suggested by the military doctors. The former policy was plausibly the least common denominator of the late March 1915 committee meetings, which lacked unanimity.[105] Cataclysmic radicalization emerged from this context and, driven by Talaat, transformed the countrywide persecution of Armenian elites initiated in April. The first regional removals were implemented in May and June, followed by an all-embracing removal from Asia Minor and Thrace in summer 1915. Planned massacre was inherent in the process of removal in the East, and removal generally developed into an overall dynamic of destruction that involved a multitude of perpetrators.

As the master of a policy that achieved more than Abdulhamid ever had, Talaat was proud and self-confident toward German diplomats in mid-June 1915. Wangenheim could no longer look the other way, as he had tried to do until then, because

Talaat's unmistakable policy was "to eradicate the Armenian race from the Turkish Empire" (wire of 7 July 1915 to the Reichskanzler Bethmann Hollweg). In late August 1915, Talaat announced to the German ambassador, "La question armé-nienne n'existe plus." The Armenian Question—the crucial center of the Eastern Question—no longer existed in Talaat's triumphant perception. He had fulfilled *Tanin*'s "prophecy" of the previous year.[106]

The anti-Armenian violence of the 1890s had targeted men and youths, if they did not convert. Talaat's policy of 1915 targeted potentially all members of the community, including those recently converted to Islam. In the East, it moreover unleashed anti-Christian violence beyond the explicit scheme of the Ministry of the Interior. In 1915–16 it therefore caused not only an Armenian but also an Assyrian genocide, emerging from radical regional representatives of the central regime and willing local Muslim perpetrators. In contrast to the massacres in the 1890s, conversion in Anatolia warranted survival in 1915–16 only if the Ministry of the Interior permitted it exceptionally or if it lacked the power to persecute targeted people. Conversion of religious identity and confession of faith were secondary to the ethnoreligious rationale of demographic engineering; or, as the governor of Trabzon put it at the beginning of July 1915, "an Armenian converted to Islam will be expelled as a Muslim Armenian."[107]

From April 1915, Talaat devised and coordinated the anti-Armenian policy in three main phases: (1) the countrywide arrest of Armenian political, religious, and intellectual leaders in April and May 1915; (2) from late spring to autumn, the removal of the Armenian population of Anatolia and European Turkey to camps in the Syrian Desert east of Aleppo, excluding Armenian men but also thousands of women and children in

Eastern and Central Asia Minor who were systematically massacred on the spot or on the road; (3) the starvation to death of most of those in the camps, except a large group resettled by Cemal, and the final massacre of those in the camps who still survived in 1916. Although Cemal governed in Syria, the camps in Northern and Eastern Syria, and the transfer of Armenians, were controlled by a directorate directly subordinate to the Ministry of the Interior.[108]

———

Incisive ciphered telegrams of 24 April 1915 (as alluded to in chap. 1, sec. "'On first impression'") to the provincial governors and to the army, with references to events in Van, Zeitun, and other places, defined the situation in Asia Minor as that of a general Armenian rebellion, of Armenians helping the enemy's war efforts, and of revolutionary committees that had long wished to establish Armenian self-determination and now believed they could achieve it, thanks to the war.

The main telegrams on 24 April, one to the army, the other to the civil administration, are nearly identical. They start with sweeping vocabulary in the vein of the 6 September 1914 circular. But their wording leaves little doubt that virtually all Armenians in the whole country, not only members of political organizations, were targeted, although the main verbal emphasis is on the latter, who were insinuated to have been conspiring collectively against Turkey "all along," and especially since August 1914. With the fatuous arrogance of an imperial revolutionist in power, Talaat presumed that any behavior except submission or clear-cut support for his regime was part of an overall conspiracy. In a long telegram to Enver, Talaat declared on 24 April 1915:

The efforts of the revolutionary and political organizations of the Armenian committees have long since proposed the establishment of an autonomy. Right after the declaration of war, the Armenian committee of Dashnak [ARF] bargained for the action of Armenians in Russia against us. Reckoning on the temporary weakness of the army, they decided on a full-fledged rebellion by the Armenians in the Ottoman Empire. They used every opportunity for impertinent acts of a treacherous campaign against the life and future of the country, now when the state is in the midst of war, as recent rebellious actions in Zeitun, Bitlis, Sivas, and Van have once more confirmed. All these committees, which basically have their headquarters in foreign countries and still today call themselves revolutionary, work with all kinds of means and reasons against the Ottoman government. Their final aim is the achievement of autonomy. The bombs discovered in Kayseri, Sivas, and at other places, the regiments of originally Ottoman volunteers who have joined the Russian army to attack the country along with the Russians, the campaign that Armenian committee leaders undertake and that thus threatens the Ottoman army from the back: All this has been verified by a great number of their publications and arrangements.[109]

Having fittingly framed a general situation according to his (imperially biased, revolutionist) perspective, Talaat enumerated the measures to be taken at this first stage to eradicate all political organizations. Thorough searches and arrests, not only of Dashnak and Hunchak members but also of "important and harmful Armenians known by the government," had to be realized. This wording involved the countrywide arrest of nearly the entire political, intellectual, religious, and economic elite. The circular for the governors of Bitlis, Erzurum, Sivas, Adana, and Maraş contained an additional sentence stating that the measures were directed only against the efforts of the committees. They should not, at that stage at least, trigger "killings between the Muslim population and the Armenian element."[110] This sentence shows that Talaat was perfectly aware of the murderous potential—well known since the 1895 and 1909 massacres—that could be ignited locally against the Armenians in general, especially when they were bereft of their leaders. Significantly, Talaat stated in an additional circular on 26 April 1915 that the general collection of arms did not concern the Muslim population.[111]

A short telegram by Talaat on 24 April 1915 taught Cemal that from then on, no Armenian should be sent to Konya, as had been done with a first group from Zeitun. If resettled there collectively, the Armenians would again be a unit and be able to act as such. From now on, the destination for removed Armenians was the desert region east of Aleppo between Urfa in the North and Der ez-Zor in the South.[112] Talaat's telegrams on 24 April spell out the new comprehensive strategy that he now followed. Yet its timing, implementation, and geographic dimension would still depend on the success of the first steps taken and on evolving contexts, in particular, concerning German reaction. On the night of 24–25 April, security forces began to arrest Armenian elites, starting with Istanbul, and to question, torture, and finally murder most of them. Provincial and military authorities, as well as CUP commissaries sent to the provinces, henceforth spread propaganda about treacherous Armenian neighbors who stabbed Muslims in the back and were therefore to be removed as soon as possible.[113]

Sources from observers on the ground, as well as published Ottoman army sources from the provinces during spring 1915, *do not* support the claim of a general uprising.[114] There were, as

we have seen, strong expectations in Tiblissi from August 1914
that the moment to liberate Turkey's Armenians had arrived,
and Armenians in Zeitun, Urfa, Şebinkarahisar (Sivas), Van,
and on the Musa Dagh set their hope on relief by the Entente
more than on desperate resistance in an inferior position at
home. Armenian alienation was largely the consequence of a
polarization that the radical politics of war, including the suspension of reform, and spoliation by requisition had caused in
the country from August 1914. There were instances of sabotage
and many desertions of both Muslims and non-Muslim young
men.[115] The reports for which Talaat asked the provincial and
military authorities in August 1915 as pieces of justification are
poor fabrications ex post facto. A recent study has analyzed in
detail a lengthy report written by Mehmed Reşid, the governor of Diyarbekir, and qualified the report's main arguments—
alleged Armenian conspiracy, circulation of secret plans, secret
mobilization, American missionaries leading an Armenian
revolt—as "little more than nonsense."[116]

In an interview in mid-May 1915, when the Armenian elite
had been largely suppressed, Talaat gave exalted statements.
They reflected the newly acquired self-confidence of an authoritarian demolitionist to whom victory at the Dardanelles had
given a decisive kick. "Today we are strong, we are stronger
than ever. See if there is still anybody among us who is not sure
that we and our allies will win. . . . War can continue as much
as it wants. Even the poorest man will not be hungry." (In Syria
alone, more than half a million Ottoman civilians starved to
death in 1915–19.) Talaat displayed no less misguided arrogance
with regard to urban development: "You admire the progress
that Istanbul shows since the last time you were in this town
that you've known for a long time," he said to a journalist.
"Come again in two years, and you will then understand how

much our town has improved. The obstacles that impaired our progress are now removed, that is, the old treaties. The Ottoman state can henceforth freely move its limbs."[117] By old treaties Talaat meant the Ottoman Capitulations, the Berlin Treaty, and the 1914 Reform Agreement.

The removal of the Armenians from Eastern Asia Minor mainly took place from May to September 1915, and from Western Anatolia and the province of Edirne in Thrace from July to October. As mentioned in chapter 1 (sec. "Fraught but in Top Form"), a provisional law of 27 May 1915—the parliament had been closed on 13 March—sanctioned repression and mass deportation if national security was an issue. In Eastern Anatolia, men and youths were mostly massacred on the spot, with those in the army, separated into unarmed labor battalions, also killed. At the Dardanelles and in Arabia, Armenian soldiers continued to fight in the Ottoman army. Removal from the West included men, and some of the deportees went by train. Women and children from Central and Eastern Asia Minor endured starvation, mass rape, and enslavement on their marches. In certain places, in particular, in the province of Diyarbekir, removal amounted to a prompt extermination of men, women, and children.

Extermination and robbery also struck more than half of Diyarbekir's Assyrian (Syriac) Christians and, in mid-June 1915, tens of thousands of Assyrians in the province of Bitlis. Altogether, Hakkâri included, about a quarter of a million died as victims of the Seyfo, the Assyrian genocide. As early as 26 October 1914, Talaat had ordered the governor of Van to remove the Assyrian population in Hakkâri near the Persian border. He could not, however, implement this early policy of removal and dispersal in late 1914 and never did transform it into a general, countrywide policy of removal and extermination, as he did in the case of the Armenians. In June 1915 a policy of destruction was nevertheless applied against the Syriac enclave in Hakkâri. In the case of the region of Hakkâri, two-thirds of about one hundred thousand Syrians perished, while the others managed to escape to Russian-held territory.[118]

Thus, most Christians, Armenian and Assyrian, were massacred in or removed from the East from late spring to autumn 1915, and all Armenian assets were transferred to the state or to the Muslim population. Armenian existence was extinguished, including culture, religion, and language. By July 1915, all Armenian newspapers (except in the capital) were forbidden, and the remaining Armenian-speaking people in Eastern Asia Minor had to do all their communication exclusively in Turkish.[119] Although Talaat's scheme of persecution and removal explicitly targeted the Armenians, it also unleashed widespread anti-Christian dynamics in the East. These tactics tied in directly with the polarizing war and jihad propaganda that began regionally in August 1914 and in a more general but relevant way with the Hamidian massacres of 1895.

———

Talaat led the overall scheme of removal and transfer of assets. All in all, he connived with, installed, or co-opted regional representatives of his regime in violent or illegally coercive action, and with perpetrators in mass murder. He did not or could not stop mass rape, slave markets, or widespread corruption. Head of a demolitionist, lumpen rule, he systematically promoted CUP radicals and deposed governors who opposed his lawless destruction.

Cemal alone, the governor-general of Syria, made plans for the resettlement of a large fraction of survivors and arranged punishment for a few manifest crimes against Armenian individuals. Even though Talaat appointed the so-called Commission of Mazhar in fall 1915 (led by the former vali Hüseyin Mazhar) to investigate unlawful conduct, there was not one officially filed case for crimes committed against Armenians, despite the commission's incriminating findings.[120] Talaat concentrated on cases of individual enrichment detrimental to the state—not on the basic crimes of murder and spoliation of the main Christian victims. He postponed even limited cases of prosecution to a future that never arrived in Turkey, since after Talaat's fall, the chance to take some steps of basic justice was missed in the turbulence of the war for Anatolia (1919–22).

Under Talaat, overstrung ambition met corruption and murder, and angst met illusion and hubris. Governors colluded with regional bullies, and party commissaries assumed arbitrary local rule. All of this was made administratively possible under Talaat's aegis, the first phase of the genocide in Asia Minor in spring through autumn 1915. He depended on compliant, and at times proactive, subordinates to implement the April–May scheme in the provinces. Particularly appropriate for the task were ambitious but pliable young men and senior functionaries with tarnished reputations who had to prove zeal and success. Where governors were less manageable, Talaat needed more time to implement the scheme. In very limited zones, he could not realize it at all, for example, in Kütahya, İzmir, and Dersim, or only slowly, as in Ankara.[121] Ali Mazhar Bey, vali of Ankara, refused Talaat's orders in spring 1915, explaining to the city council that his conscience forbade him to do so. Hence, the minister sent him a young emissary called Atıf Bey (Kamçıl), who announced "oral orders from the Ministry of the Interior concerning the massacre and the extermination of Armenians during their deportation. I thought, 'No Atıf Bey. I am a governor, not a bandit. I cannot do that, I can get up from this chair, [and] you can come and do it yourself!' I said."

In consequence, Talaat appointed Atıf as acting governor of Ankara Province. By an unusually direct and insinuating move, he attempted nevertheless to impose his will on Mazhar in a telegram on 22 June: "To Aleppo Governor Mazhar in Ankara: Considering the importance of the Aleppo Province because of the transfer and installation of Armenians, as well as your experience and knowledge of this province [Mazhar had served there before] and your agreement on the aforesaid subject [Talaat's imputation!], your designation in Aleppo has been agreed. Being convinced that you could not refuse this office on such a critical topic and at such an important moment, the ministry has not requested your prior approval." Mazhar, however, refused, preferring retirement instead, although he was only forty-seven years old. Afterward, Talaat defamed Ali Mazhar as a corrupt functionary, whereas Armenian survivors testified for "this law-abiding and truly conscientious government official" who had protected all Christians seeking shelter under his government, yet he was replaced by "a twenty-seven-year-old murderer named Atıf and a very young police chief of twenty-five years who was at least as strong a hater of Christians and as much full of greed for their property."[122]

Regarding the capital, where many international (foremost German) diplomats, merchants, and journalists lived, Talaat knew from the outset that a special proceeding was needed. He therefore made do with the arrest of Armenian elites and the deportation of Armenians who were not long-term residents.[123] Every region and province had its own characteristics. Deportations from Eastern Asia Minor included almost no men, because these were killed on the spot, in contrast to deportations from Western Asia Minor and Thrace that partly used the Anatolian Railway. The overall goal was the same—the eviction of the Armenians—as was a lawless and corrupt, yet brutal and efficient, operational style. In the memoirs of Talaat's high official Hamid Kapancızâde, Talaat's make-and-break style, which had older roots that this study connects with premodern imperial bias, caused the country's long-term decay.

Diyarbekir and its governor, Mehmed Reşid, are a case in point. Talaat knew well the former district governor of Karesi, who had become a Rûm-hater. He also knew well his capable collaborator Hamid, whom he had made the governor of Diyarbekir in early September 1914. Yet the problem with Hamid was his rationality, incorruptibility, and sense for justice. The February 1914 reform plan had caused "much excitement and alarm among the Islamic population" of Diyarbekir, according to a governor's report. CUP men affiliated with Feyzi Pirinççizâde proceeded to foment hatred against the local Christians, who were "in complete despair," according to Hamid's predecessor. The first step from hatred to violence took place on 19 August 1914, when the city's main market was burned down and Armenian merchandise looted. Hamid successfully began to establish security in the town and the province in autumn 1914. "I did not show friendship to the Armenians," he responded to reproaches, "nor enmity. There was no event that could [justifiably] have drawn hostility against this [Armenian] nation in my time [as governor]." Enver, however, ordered Hamid to send his unit of experienced gendarmes to Erzurum to join the war, although Hamid argued that he sorely needed them to maintain law and order in his province. "Rationality was, however, to no avail."[124]

In Diyarbekir, Hamid opposed widespread theft, committed under the guise of requisitions and war taxes, by officers, functionaries, and notables. He was therefore not only not favored by the local elite but also defamed as a person who vilified the army. Yet the main, though unwritten, argument against Hamid in early spring 1915 was that he would not implement anti-Armenian orders in the brutal and criminal way that was needed to achieve the goal intended by the imminent scheme. Reşid therefore replaced Hamid in late March 1915. "Crazy" Hamid was a rare high functionary in the state apparatus who, mentally almost free from imperial bias, did not lose his sober mind when his superiors did all they could to stigmatize the Armenians. This moral strength and close look at realities distinguishes him also from some high officers in the CUP who, though maintaining ethical standards and protesting partisan local government, still shared entrenched prejudices, notably against Armenian Christians.[125]

A year older than Talaat, and a cofounder of the CUP in 1889, Reşid was not an easy subordinate for Talaat. Moreover, he had become nervous, if not disordered, by late 1914, after Talaat had displaced him and his family several times. "Instead of the old poised character and calm [of before 1912], there was an appalling ambition and arrogance," wrote Süleyman Nazif, governor of Baghdad in late 1914. He had met Reşid there, whom he knew earlier. He then observed a disturbing lack of discipline among the latter's children, who destroyed, with their father's compliance, precious books and pictures in the house of an Englishman where Reşid's family temporarily stayed before he was sent to govern Basra. From there he informed Talaat how tribes and local forces were to be organized in order to "throw the enemies into the sea." Three months later, he was moved to Diyarbekir.[126]

Governor Reşid assured his superior in advance that he would take harsh action against the Armenians in Diyarbekir. In contrast to Hamid, he immediately fraternized after arrival with the local elite close to the CUP branch. At the same time, he affronted the Armenians, the other Christians, and even the Yezidis, all of whom were easy scapegoats. Since its origins in the late nineteenth century, the Diyarbekir CUP group despised the Yezidi minority in-line with entrenched religious prejudices. His message to Talaat on 17 April, in which he announced harsh measures against the Yezidis, began with the stereotypical set phrase, also used by Talaat against the Armenians and Assyrians: "Since ever the Yezidis [do this and that misdeed]."[127] Using slander, Reşid put the blame for the obvious irregularities during the requisitions on Armenian members of a commission dominated by the local CUP, then proceeded to implement a general purge of Armenian employees in the local administration. He had brought with him a loyal troop of about thirty (mainly Circassians) that had served him already in Karesi.

This strike force formed the core of his security forces and was joined by the local gendarmerie and a militia under Mustafa Cemilpaşazâde, a prominent member of the local CUP. Talaat wired him the important sum of five hundred Ottoman pounds for this actual "terrorist organization."[128] It was Reşid's main instrument in a repression that killed most Armenians and a majority of other Christians in the province of Diyarbekir in spring and summer 1915. Already on 16 April 1915, Reşid's forces surrounded the Armenian quarter, searched the houses, raped and plundered, and arrested several hundred men. Actually, Reşid anticipated measures that Talaat triggered in general only on 24 April. In-line with his radically anti-Christian mindset and the general religious polarization in the East, he largely

included the Assyrians in the repression. A cultural Muslim and
not pious at all, but a social Darwinist, Reşid argued strongly
against a "door of conversion" through which Armenians could
be saved.[129]

As Cavid privately assessed in summer 1915, Talaat basically
identified with "disordered ideas," though not only of "a few
idiots in the Central Committee" but, importantly, also of protagonists on the spot, such as Reşid, because Talaat mirrored
the forces around him as much as he managed them. This fundamental fact is to be kept in mind and not to be obfuscated
either by Talaat's at times deceiving (at other times blunt)
statements or by administrative correspondence or routines
that reflected only certain levels or instances of a more comprehensive real rule. When Reşid informed Talaat on 27 April
1915 about measures already taken and soon to be taken in the
whole province, concluding hopefully that in his province there
would "shortly be no question of the eastern provinces left," he
hit the mark of Talaat's preoccupation.[130] Both knew that the
extermination of the Armenians was meant.

Actively and proactively, local leaders and officials like Reşid
acted largely within the framework that Talaat had established
and whose evolution he accepted or determined in spring 1915.
This did not exclude harsh inquiry. Reşid was repeatedly made
to feel that he remained a subordinate despite the far-reaching
scope of a brutal, lawless, and undisciplined provincial lumpen
rule. Tarnished as he was already before arriving in Diyarbekir,
Reşid did all he could to prove his zeal, exhibit patriotic radicalism, and make aggressive proposals for neighboring Urfa as well
as Diyarbekir. His radicalism went hand in hand with an almost
hysterical mind-set. In the case of Urfa, he accused the authorities of passivity, threatening that "the Muslim people would
occupy the [local] government [building]." Like instigators

of the religiously tinted 1895 mob violence, he pointed to the Armenians, who would soon "impertinently attack and massacre the Muslims."[131]

Even if abuses, murders, and robbery happened in Diyarbekir, as he admitted to his superior, he assured him "with total honesty" that he had done all to prevent them, but that the local people had attacked the caravans of deportees like swarms of ants. In that point he was not wrong: there was predatory, murderous agency on the ground, just as Talaat was not wrong in pointing to mistakes made in the provinces. Yet in the end, national, regional, and local levels worked together willingly in a destruction whose main architect was Talaat. Reşid stated on 18 September 1915 that he had removed 120,000 Armenians from his province.[132] In the case of Diyarbekir, this meant death within the province for nearly all those "removed."

With all its self-praise, Reşid's discourse betrays a defensive, unconfident position. His correspondence with his superior thus always gave Talaat a lever to use on his uneasy subordinate, who proved as useful and efficient a collaborator in 1915 as he had at the beginning and during the Rûm removal in 1913–14. Even if Reşid's killing of Assyrians created problems with German diplomacy, in the end, the superior stood behind a governor who was neither able nor willing to protect non-Armenian Christians. For Reşid, they were all mentally "poisoned" and "turned against us by English [i.e., American] missionaries." Talaat did not back district governors, such as Hüseyin Nesimi and Ali Sabid, who, opposing Reşid's brutal orders, were killed by Reşid's death squad; nor did he enforce penal prosecution in such cases. Political convenience concealed criminality. Talaat backed those who acted within his fundamentally anti-Christian scheme of demographic uprooting and economic transfer in favor of the state and the

Muslims—even if funds taken from the Armenians were used for regional needs and not transferred to the central government's account, as Reşid did with the Abandoned Property Commission in Diyarbekir.[133]

Mirroring and Managing Anti-Christian Forces in the East

Reşid was proactive in the exterminatory repression of Ottoman Christians in his province (Diyarbekir) from late March 1915. In the province of Erzurum, the military command, the Special Organization (SO), and the governorate pioneered a murderous removal of the entire Armenian population from early May onward. From March, they had shaped Talaat's perception of the issue. All actors in the East cooperated closely with Talaat, who again mirrored—as much as he managed and coordinated—the forces on the ground, no less than those in the capital. SO head Bahaeddin Şakir and Governor Tahsin, both political intimates of Talaat's, were based in Erzurum, as was the headquarters of the Third Army under Mahmud Kâmil, the military commander in the eastern provinces.

Şakir had gone to Istanbul in March 1915 to brief the committee on "the Armenian and other issues." In communication with the neighboring provinces, Tahsin and Kâmil had "determined the line of action to pursue vis-à-vis the Armenians," as Tahsin wrote to Talaat in a message on 18 March. Tahsin called Vramian's complaints "nonsense" and opined that "for the moment," the assignment of the Armenian soldiers to disarmed labor batallions and measures against Armenian deserters were the appropriate line of conduct; "a domestic issue should not be aroused."[134] This language reveals that by mid-March in

Erzurum, different scenarios regarding the Armenians were considered. Discussions with Şakir in Istanbul incorporated such designs before he turned back in early April.

Correspondence between Talaat and Tahsin from late December 1914 to April 1915 documents how the upright Tahsin, a junior but influential governor who was respected by the Armenians in Van, caved under superior figures in Erzurum, step-by-step, into monstrous inhumanity. Yet his immature belief in conquest and readiness for radical policy had foreshadowed the risk of such a shift, as did imperial and anti-Armenian prejudices.[135] He was still on top of the world by the end of 1914 ("war continues with perfect success"), sobered but zealous by 10 January 1915 ("with full faith we will struggle and doubtless win"), and rather down in the dumps in a long telegram in late January, when the military catastrophe and its consequences, including typhus and thousands of Muslim refugees, had become manifest.[136]

Still, he escaped into illusion: "The war for Caucasus is a newborn baby that has got its name. . . . Let us not make it an orphan." There was "no house in Erzurum without tears. Misery and distress have reached a climax." The only possible cure "for the people in the province," according to Tahsin, was victory and revenge. By early March 1915, Tahsin's perception and language markedly altered. He referred to his exchange of information with the neighboring provinces and now described "the Armenians of the environs" as Russophiles who "had decided on a rebellion," to be started at "an appropriate moment," because of "many reasons and proofs." He begged Talaat "to turn to this issue by April." This language was in tune with that of Tahsin's close party brother Abdülhalik, governor of Bitlis, who, one and a half months later, in a telegram on 18 April 1915, went so far as to suggest to Talaat that "the extermination of these elements [Armenians in Bitlis], which had always been a threat to the state in these parts of the homeland . . . was a requirement for the security of the state." In agreement with CUP's social Darwinism, Abdülhalik expressed fear of Armenian dominance in the region, based on socioeconomic Armenian superiority and demographic developments detrimental to the Muslims, due to war. He answered his peer group's angst by suggesting to destroy the Armenians as such.[137]

A telegram by Tahsin on 22 April 1915 was another trigger for Talaat's 24 April orders. Tahsin first stated that he was often on the telegraph line with Cevdet and Abdülhalik. He then drew attention to a serious situation in Van, "in every sense a rebellion in favor of the Russians," that could, however, remain isolated if, "please God, [it was] quickly and violently suppressed," as Cevdet was attempting to do. If not, "a spread of rebellion to the other provinces" was "strongly to be expected." Tahsin then fell back into imperial language: "If Armenians attack Muslims, they logically will be subjected to mutual massacre; this is the pace of the matter. If the Sublime Porte now explains to the friendly states the political necessity [of this pace?], they will perhaps not hinder [us] in the near future." (Under Sultan Abdulhamid, official reports represented the mass murder of Armenians as mutual killings provoked by the latter.)[138]

This was important advice for Talaat. From the context, "political necessity" implied violent coercion, if not mass violence. This was, in fact, part of the April 1915 design, as Talaat himself conceded when writing in late August that additional atrocities were not needed because "the Armenian issue belonging to the eastern provinces is resolved." Military and civil intelligence from Erzurum in April 1915 with regard to the eastern provinces suggested regional Armenian rebellion.

This was, however, entirely on the level of suspicion, except for the locally limited defense of Van. A military report from the Third Army to Enver's headquarters on 14 April had explicitly denied any "serious and general rebellious movement," because those suspected of starting it "did not have the courage," even if the delicate situation was suitable to a rebellion. In any case, the governors and the army corps were instructed to severely suppress any suspicious Armenian activity. There was no insurgency in Erzurum, "but the Armenian population is alarmed and fears massacres," the German vice-consul Max Scheubner-Richter reported in late April. Like the Armenians, he still believed Tahsin to be friendly and moderate, as judged from his manners and the fame of his former office in Van.[139]

In reality, Tahsin was not only henceforth Talaat's willing executioner, as officially ordered in the 24 April orders, but remained proactive, made proposals, and gave information on the neighboring provinces as well.[140] He stood closer to his superior and was more self-confident than Reşid; still, he had to prove his devotion and his "idealism" (*mefkûrecilik*, that is, his nationalist creed in the vein of Gökalp) to CUP luminary Talaat. As usual in imperial communication, he did not stint on paying deference to his superior—"With perfect respect I kiss your hands"—again and again. Talaat's best trump in his interaction with subordinates and political friends was to have succeeded in making them all believe in his superior patriotism. This made him almost invulnerable, and capable of using the imperial administration to destroy the Ottoman social fabric.

Reacting to a specific military proposal, on 9 May Talaat ordered the governors of Van and Bitlis, Cevdet and Abdülhalik, assisted by the army, to deport Armenians "from places where they were concentrated, to the south." Since a part of the province of Erzurum was included, Tahsin was also informed of this first order to remove all Armenians of a region. "These efforts will produce very useful results," Talaat promised in his telegram. Removal from Van and Bitlis was actually retarded. The removals initiated by the Fourth Army in February–March for Dörtyol and Zeitun, and that by Enver's headquarters on 2 May for Van, had been limited. Talaat himself developed a scheme that concerned the whole country, made operational in May.[141]

Mid-May, Tahsin had begun to deport the first villagers but had not yet fully understood Talaat's design. "I did not think so far as [Der ez-]Zor. . . . Since there are no Armenians in Kastamonu yet [Northern Anatolia, west of Erzurum], I thought to send them there. Now, according to your order, I will send them to Urfa and Mosul."[142] Tahsin's correspondence with Talaat reveals how he organized deportation and followed Talaat's instructions, although he emphasized to the German vice-consul the demand of the Third Army, since military necessity was the only argument to be used before German diplomacy. General Kâmil's and SO chief Şakir's exterminatory radicalism strongly affected the scheme of global removal that started in Erzurum. Interestingly, there had been a last self-critical searching in Tahsin's soul: "There would have been no revolt at Van if we had not ourselves created [it], with our own hands, by using force, this impossible situation from which we are incapable of extricating ourselves, and also the difficult position in which we have put the army on the eastern front," he wrote to Talaat on 13 May 1915.[143]

Whereas Tahsin had displayed vivid emotions regarding Muslim refugees and to the tears of Muslims in Erzurum, he showed no compassion at all for Ottoman Armenians, even if they were slaughtered and died in the tens of thousands from starvation.[144] He wrote and acted now as a social Darwinist, eager to inform Talaat how successfully he had implemented his orders, and he was highly irritated to see Scheubner-Richter showing solidarity with the victims and investigating abuses: "Your behavior is a shame, while hundreds of thousands of Muslims are dying for our common interests." The German did not give in, however, when Tahsin complained to Talaat. "He said that he had taken an order from the embassy and will prepare a report on the killings." Talaat asked Tahsin for more information against Scheubner-Richter to present to Wangenheim.[145]

Communication from Tahsin to Talaat was intense:

> Shall the Armenians of Harput and Diyarbekir, and, above all, those from Sivas also be removed? In [the whole province of] Erzurum they have decreased to less than a half [of 135,000]. . . . In your excellent first order the necessity to action at densely populated places was emphasized. In this province they [the Armenians] have fallen to 4 percent [related to centers]. Shall we remove the very last Armenian individual? In the district of Hınıs, 3,000 men have been killed by Kurds. In general, now only women and children remain.

Interestingly, Talaat answered Tahsin that it wasn't necessary to deport the Armenians from Diyarbekir, Harput, and Sivas. Writing on 29 May, still before Wangenheim's explicit approval "to evacuate a few subversive families from centers of insurrection," he may have preserved a low profile vis-à-vis his subordinate. In a message on 23 May to Cemal, the military governor of Syria, he had, however, already defined a huge area composed of Erzurum, Van, Bitlis, Adana, Mersin, Maraş, Iskenderun, and Aleppo, from which, with a few exceptions, the Armenians were to be removed.[146]

Among many other sources, Tahsin's telegrams demonstrate that from the beginning of Talaat's global removal scheme, the state failed dramatically in protecting its civilians, although Tahsin wrote that he dispatched gendarmes at times. The governor may or may not have colluded in organizing SO massacres on a scale far beyond random local violence. Thanks to his efficiency and loyalty, as well as his relationship with Enver, Tahsin enjoyed great influence. This is reflected in his style of communication with Talaat that combined administrative directness with the "idealist" self-identification of a komiteci, audacious proposals, and insider allusions between the lines.

Talaat's removal-resettlement scheme gave the frustrated governors in the East a new goal and a feeling of imperial power, after they had experienced disillusionment, frustration, and impotence in the aftermath of a failed campaign for conquest. The thirty-six-year-old governor Tahsin embraced this with youthful enthusiasm. "If you can send 40,000 to 50,000 muhacir from Rumeli, they can be resettled quite nicely and receive subsistence," he wrote in a late May telegram that also demanded the rapid resettlement of muhacir in the district of Kığı, before "bandits from Dersim" could steal or destroy what was in the houses.[147]

Talaat's scheme started in Diyarbekir and Erzurum, making all of Asia Minor and Northern Syria an arena of mass crimes within months. A great number of villages and agricultural areas became fair prey and were offered to Muslim migrants, if others had not already served themselves. The deportees themselves, and what they possessed, were also considered fair prey. These civilians were spoliated, raped, abducted, and murdered en masse—without any protection and punishment of the offenders.[148] As a rule, the men were separated from the women and children before or at the beginning of the deportation and killed. By early summer 1915, the previously, seemingly promising, and enlightened vali Tahsin of Van had turned out to be a henchman who would do anything within Talaat's scheme. He "brotherly" (as he himself wrote) asked what to do with a number of employees and gendarmes involved in "shameful acts and corruption" but without further consequence. In a circular in mid-June, Talaat had asked governors "to protect the life of the ousted [Erzurum] Armenians en route according to the governors' possibilities." If violence was applied, "the [local] people should not be involved. Mutual killings between the elements, and thus events that leave an ugly impression to the outside world," should be prevented. The only point of concern was image and prestige.[149]

Since German vice-consul Scheubner-Richter continued to support victims in the province of Erzurum, Tahsin defamed him even more to Talaat and also denigrated him before Wangenheim, insinuating that he was a womanizer and ignorant of higher state interests. During a meeting of Tahsin and Scheubner-Richter with the German physician of the military hospital in Erzincan,[150] Scheubner-Richter argued against his compatriot in favor of Tahsin, saying that "if a nation undertook a similar rebellion in Germany it would immediately be wiped out."[151] This greatly impressed the thirty-one-year-old vice-consul, who still believed in Tahsin's moderation and humanity, and that only the militaries wanted "to entirely exterminate the Armenians," thereby establishing a postwar "Turkey without Armenians," as Kâmil said.[152] Upright but naive, Scheubner-Richter changed his opinion. "We are now entirely unanimous," Tahsin boasted to Talaat; Scheubner-Richter "consented that the proceeding of the government was justified." Tahsin proposed to the Ministry of the Interior that Scheubner-Richter be given a decoration. Even if Scheubner-Richter partly gave in, Tahsin exaggerated. Scheubner-Richter's "conversion" to social Darwinist radicalism did not take place then, and on Turkish terms, but after 1918. After returning to his hometown, Riga, which was soon occupied by Soviets, he went to Munich, where he became a radical antiminoritarian and, in particular, anti-Jewish fanatic. He was shot during the so-called Hitler Putsch of 1923 in Munich, at Adolf Hitler's side, being by then, in Hitler's dictum, Hitler's "right hand."[153]

Tahsin also denigrated and threatened the Alevi Kurds of Dersim, who feared facing the same fate as the Armenians. He reproached them for contributing nothing to "our holy war" and for having committed the perfidy of protecting thousands of Armenians. "They know that, faced with such ignominies, the government will not remain idle." Now no longer only imperially biased against minorities, in Erzurum Tahsin evolved into a fanatic who was gravely affected by mass crime and a utopia-dystopia of Turan. In late August 1915, the CUP-SO circle in Erzurum dreamed again of a new offensive. In the name of Tahsin, his deputy sent the following telegram of the SO-leaders Ömer Naci and Filipeli Hilmi: "This is for Talaat Bey and the Central Committee. . . . Hitherto, there was not the [necessary] seriousness, effort, and contribution to pursue vigilantly the road to Turan. I assure [you] that within two months Azerbaijan, including Tabris, can be occupied without any illusion."[154] CUP and SO executives shared the ongoing fixation on Caucasian conquest with other actors of genocide. At the Holiday of Sacrifice (Kurban Bayramı) in October 1915, Diyarbekir governor Reşid was telegraphically congratulated by a district vice governor "for having gained us the six [Eastern] provinces and [having opened up] access to Turkestan and to Caucasia."[155]

They all appeared galvanized by the anti-Armenian exploit and ready for a new campaign toward Turan. Tahsin was however deeply depressed a few months later by the capitulation of Erzurum. The same day that the provincial capital was captured

(16 February 1916), he sent for Şakir from neighboring Erzincan a telegram to Talaat saying that a specter was manifesting: "Eastern Anatolia—a Christian region." For the first time he felt compelled to ask for resignation, while simultaneously express-ing his "highest desire" to go back to the provincial capital "in order to take revenge for the [Muslim] people" of Erzurum. In April, he reassured Talaat that in all regions of the province from which the army had retired, no Armenian had been left. In July, finally, he wrote that the disasters that he had experienced over the past four years had overshadowed his mind. "I have done my duty. God is witness. I am an unfortunate person."[156] The man who had been responsible for mass murder now wal-lowed in self-pity.

In short, the correspondence from representatives in the East reflects a weltanschauung, according to which Islamic Turkdom and Christians fought an exterminatory war for territory. More characteristically, the correspondence details the collapse of a war of expansion, the recalibration of the aggression against a domestic enemy (or genocide as a war duty), the resump-tion of the former desire of conquest once the Armenians were "removed," and frustration, depression, and self-pity after the Russian breakthrough.

Benefiting from seeing the bigger picture than his subordi-nates, Talaat was able to refocus on the more realistic goal of a Türk Yurdu in Anatolia, although he did not give up the Cauca-sian dream. After the Russian breakthrough and the conquest of Erzurum and Trabzon, he concentrated on a new policy of deportation of Pontus Rûm at the Black Sea. Prudently at first, as long as Greece remained neutral, he strictly limited remov-als to zones of military importance where contact with Rus-sian ships was possible. But in autumn 1916, when the end of Greek neutrality appeared imminent as Entente troops entered parts of Greece, he then implemented his scheme generally. As a consequence, scenes of massacre, rape, and spoliation, similar to those in 1915, took place against tens of thousands of Pontus Rûm—men, women, and children. The same SO gangs as in 1915, the most notorious being that of Topal Osman, again took action. Trabzon governor Cemal Azmi, a main perpetrator who had enriched himself by plundering Armenians in 1915, assured his superior in a telegram on 27 June 1916 that, as in the Armenian case, he fully engaged in saving the holy fatherland from traitors.[157]

Governors in the East, such as Tahsin, Cevdet, Abdülhalik, Azmi, and Reşid, who had set their hopes on Caucasian conquest and had organized mass crimes and enriched themselves with plunder and power, remained gravely affected by the toxic mix of evil, misery, bad reputation, and unfulfilled ideological desire. The whole country, however, was badly affected already by summer 1915. When, after protracted negotiations in Berlin, an unsuspecting Cavid came back to Istanbul on 19 August 1915, he was surprised to find "a country very much decrepit materially and spiritually," as he noted on the day of his arrival. "Despite the [successful] defense at the Dardanelles, the morale is degenerate."[158]

Leading Assimilation, Plunder, Extermination, Nation Building

As much marked by, as having contributed to, a "degenerate morale" in the capital, from the very first stage, Talaat and his close political friends had inscribed mass crime into their project of an imperially connoted new Turkish nation building, the result of which were very distant, viable futures for Asia

Minor. Talaat's comprehensive effort at new nation building was, first, demolition and spoliation. This included not only mass removal, demographic engineering, and comprehensive looting but also starvation and systematic mass killing. Mass murder took on unspeakable dimensions when the concentration camps situated in Syria's desert, from Aleppo to Der ez-Zor, were liquidated in summer 1916. With the purpose of achieving an exclusive Turkish-Muslim unity in Asia Minor, Talaat's policy "replaced" the removed Christian population with Muslim migrants. Moreover, Talaat sought to "dilute" non-Turkish identities of Muslim groups and considered these groups fit for assimilation into the new nation of a "new Turkey," in contrast to Ottoman Christians.

Talaat's demolitionist domestic policy had started as a consequence of the Balkan Wars, and from spring 1914 the Rûm presence on the Aegean coast was erased. His policy reached an unprecedented extent with the Armenians in April 1915 by embracing its most ambitious and comprehensive scheme of erasure and demographic change. Talaat also engaged in the large-scale removal of Kurds from parts of the eastern provinces in 1916, because to him many Kurds appreared as unreliable elements. It was a prime moment for him to exploit the fact that thousands of Kurds had fled before the advancing Russian army. In an order to Mustafa Atıf (the governor of Diyarbekir and successor of Mehmed Reşid) on 2 May 1916, Talaat defined his policy. He forbade sending Kurdish refugees from the war zones to southern regions "because they would either Arabize or preserve their nationality there and remain a useless and harmful element." To be useful and acceptable elements of the new nation, Kurds, therefore, had to first lose their nationality (*milliyet*) and then be prevented from adopting others, like Arab or Armenian identities.

In a telegram to Mustafa Atıf on 2 May 1916, Talaat ordered:

1. To send Turkish refugees and Turkified townspeople to the
regions of Urfa, Maraş, and Anteb, and to settle them there.
2. To separate by all means the chieftains from the common people [among Kurds], and to send separately influential personalities and leaders to the provinces of Konya
and Kastamonu, and to the *sanjak* of Niğde and Kayseri,
in order to prevent Kurdish refugees from preserving their
tribal life and their nationality at the places where they have
gone. 3. To disperse the sick, elderly, lonely, and poor women
and children, who are unable to travel, in Turkish villages
and among Turks in [the province of Diyarbekir's] towns
of Maden and Ergani . . . [and] 4. Correspondence will be
conducted with the final destinations of the deportations.
The method of distribution, settlement procedures, and how
many deportees have been sent where and when will all be
reported to the ministry.[159]

In another important telegram on 4 May 1916 to governors
in Western Asia Minor, Talaat explained that nowhere should
the Kurdish proportion of the regional population rise above
5 percent. As in the case of other Muslim migrants, the Kurds'
needs should be supplied by Armenian assets (*emvali-metruke*,
or abandoned properties).[160]

Ahmed İzzet Pasha, the former war minister, and in 1916
commander of the Second Army (in 1917 of both the Second
and the Third Armies) at the eastern front, strongly opposed
the scheme of Kurdish removal, although, in the account of
his memoirs, he appears not to have understood that this was
Talaat's policy. He blamed regional actors for wicked, brutal,
and shortsighted rule, arguing that removal under the existing conditions was deadly, that Kurdish refugees from the war

zones could be settled close by, and that Kurds should not be sweepingly considered detrimental. Jakob Künzler, a Swiss medical missionary in Urfa and a rare foreign observer and reporter of the Kurdish removal, organized help for tens of thousands of Kurds who starved near Urfa in 1916, but most nonetheless died during the winter of 1916–17, because the management of the Kurdish removal by Talaat's ministry was utterly deficient. "The intention of the Young Turks was to keep these Kurdish elements from returning to their ancestral homeland. They should slowly become assimilated into Turkdom in Inner Anatolia," Künzler wrote. "In spite of a good harvest that year, almost all of the deported Kurds were victims of the famine."[161]

Kurdish mass deaths of 1916–17 were, to put it mildly, the result of irresponsibility and negligence, but never of massacre. This distinguishes them from the Armenians both in the first phase and, in particular, in autumn 1915 into 1916, the second phase of the genocide in the Syrian Desert camps.

———

Talaat's intent to kill Armenians en masse is already obvious in spring 1915 in the eastern provinces but unambiguous in the way he dealt with several hundred thousand Armenian survivors of the removal from Asia Minor who ended up in Northern Syria, most of them women and children. Although never himself on the spot during action, from the capital he closely led a whole range of actions through operatives of his ministry in order to reduce Armenian presence, in a sparsely habited zone outside Anatolia, below the level of 10 percent of the whole population. In plain language, this meant extermination.[162]

Talaat's operatives reversed the efforts of some benevolent governors and other functionaries on the ground who, from spring 1915, had taken seriously Talaat's deceptive plan of Armenian resettlement in Mesopotamia. These functionaries were removed, a modest resurgence of Armenian life in North Syrian exile was purposely destroyed, and surviving Armenians themselves were once again deported to the districts of Rakka and Der ez-Zor. Deliberate starvation was intended to kill, yet still many managed to escape and survive under unspeakable conditions. From March to October 1916, according to current research, more than two hundred thousand of them were finally massacred, burned alive, or drowned, most of them in August–September, east of Der ez-Zor. This annihilation followed the same Armenophobic political logic that accompanied the liquidation of the Armenian Patriarchate of Constantinople, the Patriarchate of Jerusalem, and the Catholicosate of Aghtamar in July 1916.[163]

Thanks to Khatchig Mouradian's recent in-depth research, Talaat's antiresettlement policy and his extermination of Armenian life in Northern Syria, which began in earnest in March 1916, is nakedly revealed. Talaat falsified his own statements of a few months earlier, although most contemporary people, including the victims themselves, lacked the insight to penetrate the Ministry of the Interior's thorough scheme for the genocide's second phase. This left Cemal Pasha, the governor of Greater Syria, little room for Armenian-saving action, although he agreed as a whole with his CUP brother's anti-Armenian policy, but only passively to the extermination of civilians.

Mouradian's research, added to that of a few scholars before him, reveals more clearly the agonizing yet still partly successful Armenian resilience under extreme hardship against extermination by a perverted state that, rather than protecting all of its citizens annihilated an entire group of them. Mouradian rightly observes that beyond a broad, contemporary phenomenon of internment, the Armenian case in Syria (as, on a smaller scale, that of the Herero in German South West Africa ten years earlier) points to a new genocidal world of concentration camps in which, as much as ever, possible victims were made subordinate perpetrators.[164]

Working through devoted operatives, Talaat was the mastermind of this genocidal universe in Northern Syria. From July 1915 he began impeding aid to surviving deportees, and by early fall he controlled all dealings with hundreds of thousands of deportees through trusted emissaries of his ministry. His purpose was the prevention and demolition of reconstituting communities of exiles. Since starvation did not decimate the survivors to the desired degree, in early 1916 he opted for active killing. In May, he replaced Der ez-Zor governor Ali Suat, who had tried to resettle at least part of the exiles according to the ministry's original guidelines, with Salih Zeki, a willing mass murderer. Moreover, Talaat could rely on an indoctrinated Muslim majority that was largely hostile toward the Armenian deportees, especially once Armenians were blamed for epidemics in the region. Although he often failed in this policy, he was keen to maintain the state's monopoly on anti-Armenian violence and loot.[165]

Significantly, Talaat had insisted on sending Zeki, who had proved to be an anti-Armenian hard-liner while governing the district of Develü, province of Kayseri. Enver would have preferred Şefik as most appropriate for the needs of the army, since Der ez-Zor was logistically important for supplying the Sixth Army with all kinds of goods, yet he gave in to Talaat, who had written him:

When Şefik Bey was the governor of the district of Hakkari, he deputized [vali] Cevdet Bey during the latter's absence from the center. During this time, when the ministry sent orders for the arrest of Vramian and his peers, he hesitated to act. Until Cevdet's return, he made unacceptable steps in order to appease the Armenians, who used the situation for bad subversion. Zeki Bey, in contrast, was a resolute and active governer of Develü. He perfectly executed the anti-Armenian measures and was therefore promoted to the post of a civil inspector [of the Ministry of the Interior]. We fully expect that he will very successfully execute his duties related to the army and Armenian goods in Der ez-Zor. Yet, if you are sure that Şefik Bey will not again hesitate when he must perform the measures against the Armenians, please let me know the arguments for Şefik Bey's appointment to the government of Der ez-Zor.[166]

Human resistance against murderous authorities was mostly led by Armenian long-term residents of Aleppo who, like those in Istanbul, Talaat did, at first, not dare to persecute. Yet he finally struck their leaders in fall 1915 before the eyes of a strong international colony that included several consuls. Those involved in resistance, above all, missionaries, helped the Armenian network to nonetheless succeed in a partial survival of the people who had been earmarked for death.

Talaat—the promising revolutionary leader of 1908 who had respected (though never fully accepted as equal) Armenian peers—became an obsessive anti-Armenian whose political hate included growing fear. He knew well his guilt, yet his belief in social Darwinism and a total war–jihad made the annihilation of civilians, including women and children, acceptable for him. Mixing political hate with a cultural and biological understanding of Armenians, Talaat increasingly apprehended the latter's survival outside Anatolia as a possible starting point for a reversal of his political "achievements" for the Türk Yurdu. This went on file when Matthias Erzberger, a German deputy who was responsible for propaganda abroad and thus influential in foreign policy, visited him in February 1916. Henceforth, Talaat tangibly feared that after the war, Armenian survivors would return to their homeland and that Germany, in Erzberger's words, would support them, as Talaat secretly wrote to Enver on 16 February.[167]

Active extermination in Northern Syria, beyond deliberate starvation, started in March 1916. In a circular to twenty-seven governerships, Talaat ordered that any employee who tolerated humanitarian help to Armenians by foreigners would be severly punished. Yet, as proved in many files of the Directorate of General Security in Talaat's ministry,[168] even after extermination was accomplished in fall 1916, he continued suspiciously tracking even individual Armenians, personally allowing (or not) conversions and prohibiting them to travel into Asia Minor or Istanbul.

Although claiming solidarity and principal consensus in his correspondence with Talaat, in 1916 Cemal nevertheless contributed to saving tens of thousands of targeted Armenians by (formally) Islamizing them and resettling them more to the south. To do this, he still referred to the clear decision of spring 1915 that Armenians had to be resettled, and they could not become a majority.[169] Cemal did this, however, with condescension. He largely employed Armenian slave labor and did not obstruct extermination as a whole in the northern part of his military governorate, where Talaat had the last say as far as Armenians were concerned. In contrast, he claimed the salvation of the "virtuous and heroic refugees" from Russian-occupied Erzurum, starving Muslims, to be "the religious and patriotic duty of every Turk."[170]

Beatrice Rohner, a Swiss teacher and member of a German Protestant mission, came from Marash to Aleppo in December 1915 in order to help Armenians to survive. With money from the United States, Switzerland, and Germany, and discreetly supported by the American and German consuls, she took responsibility for an underground network of help via messengers who brought letters and small sums of money to the camps, thus allowing the displaced to buy food and water from nomads (Pastor Hovhannes Eskidjian, the founder and leader of the network, died of typhus in March 1916). Rohner legally ran an orphanage for nearly a thousand street kids, mostly Armenian, in Aleppo, as agreed in a meeting in late December 1915 with Cemal Pasha and vali Abdülhalik (Renda), the former governor of Bitlis, a hard-liner and intimate of Talaat's. He had just arrived to take the position of the short-term vali Bekir Sami, who had replaced Aleppo governor Mehmed Celâl Bey in late June 1915.

Celâl, former vali of Erzurum and former minister of the interior, had helped the local Armenians, first of all, the Aleppo community, to assist deportees arriving in Northern Syria, beginning with those from Zeytun in May 1915. From July 1915, Talaat, however, intervened against help for survivors in camps, although Cemal had initially authorized this help.[171] In late July as well, Talaat set up a subdirectorate in Aleppo of his Directorate for Resettlement of Tribes and Migrants and made Abdulahad Nuri its head. In August, he dispatched Şükrü (Kaya), the directorate's head, to Aleppo to better oversee and organize his destructive treatment of the survivors. From October, all nonlocal Armenians were ordered to be redeported to Rakka and Der ez-Zor, Aleppo was to be cleared of them, leaders were arrested, and the Catholicos had to leave the city as well, in his case, to Jerusalem. Hence, terror pervaded the Armenian community of Aleppo in October 1915, and it feared that it would be removed as a whole.[172] (Şükrü was another of Talaat's docile young men who would occupy an important position during the Kemalist interwar period. He was the minister of the interior in 1927–37.)

Although Şükrü (Kaya) established administrative regulations in early October 1915, these and the Council of Ministers' (de facto, Talaat's) decree of 30 May and the guidelines of 10 June 1915 on Armenian resettlement proved entirely ineffective right from the start, except for their destructive edge. The same was true with the regulations of 10 June on Armenian property (see below). Making himself a liar, Talaat intended a complete and illegal transfer of Armenian property to Muslim owners. No funds were allocated for the resettlement of Armenian survivors in Northern Syria. Within a year, Mouradian dryly states, "most of the deportees would be 'settled' under the sands of the desert." Rohner, like any other foreign national or non-Muslim merchant, was prohibited to enter zones with Armenian camps from early 1916; in December 1915, she had visited camps. Lest the staggering truth be revealed, from September 1915, taking photographs of exiles was punished like photographing war theaters.[173]

The fragile but intrepid Rohner was only later able to report on her Gospel-inspired humanitarian resistance: "Never let us forget that the Pharaoh of Turkish hatred and the will to destruction [*Vernichtungswillen*] was after us and wanted at all costs to prevent a little people escaping his power. . . . How much we were disliked in Aleppo! Our simple presence was a permanent thorn in the flesh of those who were determined to destroy the remnants of the Armenian people. Every opportunity to scatter these children, the hope of the future, again, to ban me from Aleppo, to hunt my co-workers into the desert, would have been warmly welcomed,"[174] she wrote in post-1933 Germany, alluding to passages in the New Testament's letter to the Hebrews, thus unmistakably drawing lessons on how to face Nazi persecution.

———

Removal, starvation, murder, and mass robbery: Talaat's anti-Armenian policy had from the start an eminent material aspect for the state, local notables, and unashamed neighbors, yet, in particular, for the settlement of Muslims, that is, of nomads and all sorts of muhacir. Armenian assets were huge. They included private wealth, shops, businesses, concessions, and factories, as well as real estate and buildings of foundations and Armenian churches (Orthodox, Protestant, and Catholic). Not all assets were transferred during World War I; it continued in the interwar period and the second half of the twentieth century as well. Only the deaths of the legitimate owners made the spoliators—principally, the Ministry of the Interior, the army, and local notables—feel safe in the possession of fresh loot from 1915 to 1916. Talaat noted in his pocketbook around late 1916 a part of the spoils: more than 40,000 buildings, 90,000 *dönüm* farmland (a *dönüm* is an Ottoman measurement of little more than 1,000 square meters [1,094 square yards]), and 26 mining concessions.[175]

In a blanket and flimsy ideological accusation, Talaat and the CUP reproached the Ottoman Armenians for enriching themselves at the expense of the Turks under Ottoman rule. They thus mixed the political attack on the Armenians with economic arguments of a class struggle, copied from contemporary socialism and motivated by social envy and material need. Talaat's circle had partly used this tactic already during the Rûm removal and the pre-1914 boycotts.[176] The government developed a legalist argument to cover crime, as did Germany after 1933. At the same time, in contrast to Germany, Talaat and the CUP could connect the argument with recent practices, since the lives and assets of Armenians had already been regarded lawful Muslim prey during the massacres of the 1890s, two decades before the genocide. The state had proved unable and unwilling to restore such property, mostly land, after 1908.

Senator Ahmed Rıza alone spoke truth to power in the parliament in autumn 1915: "If there is a constitution in this country and constitutional rule, this [law on "abandoned property"] must not be. It is a crime. Strong-arm me, expel me from my village, then sell my property: this is never lawful. No Ottoman conscience or law can ever accept this." Rıza's statement had all the less impact as Talaat had intimidated him not to further press the issue. Yet, for posterity, the former spiritual head of the CUP testified clearly to the actual disruption and destruction of Ottoman bounds, conscience, and basic law. He implicitly condemned Talaat, who not only designed and operationalized the removal and material transfer, but also draped it in a legal cloak.[177]

From August 1914, military requisition had offered the opportunity for large-scale confiscations of (overproportionally non-Muslim) goods, which at times had nothing to do with military needs. What began in May 1915 with the Armenian removal was, however, an entirely new dimension of material transfer. The accompanying legal provisions, starting in May, were partly a legalist disguise for manifest plunder before parliament and public and partly an open break with constitutional law. The provisions also served as a means to cozen and silence both the representatives of a morally defeatist German ally and the victims themselves. This is true particularly for those

provisions in May through June that spoke of dislocations limited to sensitive zones, suggested only temporary removal, and
falsely promised restitution or full compensation and realloca-
tion of assets, all according to allegedly meticulous bookkeep-
ing by special commissions.

Talaat himself spun the web of fraud and lies designed to
shield the crimes. Successfully urging for cabinet decrees, in
late May 1915, he involved the whole government in his scheme.
The decisive step was his long letter on 26 May to the grand
vizier (see chap. 1, sec. "Fraught but in Top Form"). In the line
of his argument of 24 April, he emphasized that, due to Armenian treason, any further stabbing in the back of the Ottoman
army had to be prevented. Then he described the necessity of
removing Armenians from regions in Eastern and Southern
Asia Minor and proposed instructions for how to deal with
Armenian assets. These instructions made the false promises
just mentioned.[178] The Deportation Law of 27 May (a decree by
the cabinet) sanctioned limited removals of subversive families,
as had been realized already by the Third and Fourth Armies. In
general terms, it demanded "the annihilation of any resistance"
but did not give any instruction on expropriation or hint at an
overall removal. Said Halim and Enver had signed it, but not
Talaat. The cabinet decree of 30 May, however, was the consequence and sanction of Talaat's 26 May letter, from which it
copied large passages.[179]

Armed with both decrees, simultaneously with Wangenheim's approval of (limited) removals, from June 1915 Talaat
enjoyed the necessary backing and the opportunity to remove
and dispossess the most developed population group of the
late Ottoman Empire. He rapidly and radically exploited the
decrees, and the limited German approval, for comprehensive
measures. Protests did not fail to appear, but they were too late

and to no avail: by mid-June the destruction had already developed the comprehensive momentum desired by its designer. In further regulations of 31 May and 10 June 1915, Talaat gave detailed instructions that commissions for abandoned properties, directly subordinated to the Ministry of the Interior, were to be founded: Armenians were prohibited to make any transaction of assets, how these had to be registered, that those assets sold in auctions were to be deposited in the names of their owners, how the Armenians were to be resettled in small groups at their destination, how they would be provided with property according to their former situation, and that the new settlements had to be at least a 25-kilometer distance from the Baghdad Railway.[180]

Not only was the overall removal an anticonstitutional monstrosity, but all provisions for the protection of life and property were hollow promises from the start. Entirely malicious, they served as a temporary deception. It is by no means possible to interpret them as partly "well-meant" but failed efforts. In a few cases they only gave well-intended local governors the opportunity toward temporary resettlement of deportation survivors. A provisional law on abandoned possessions and debts of 27 September and correlated regulations of 8 November 1915 made it clear that, in contrast to what the provisions of May–June had suggested, any return of the removed people to their homes and properties was definitively excluded. The same law and its regulations gave the government full liberty concerning how to deal with Armenian goods. There was no possibility of appeal against any decision of the trial court.

In the eyes of social Darwinist adepts of Turkism, or of Islamists believing in legitimate killing and robbing of Christians, Talaat's move was again brilliant. It provided the war *ümmet*,[181] that is, the war-waging Istanbul-centered

Ottoman Muslim community (ummah) a very rich material "blessing." Ahmed Rıza called the law simply a crime, the German Embassy—quoting commercial circles in Istanbul— legalization of spoils. Everybody was aware of the mass plunder, but they were unable to do more than to protest. Germany remained captive to its original sin: moral defeatism built-in to the alliance to which it had committed itself in late July 1914.[182] Arthur Gwinner, the chairman of the board of the Deutsche Bank, who was one among several German representatives interested in refunding Armenian debts, succinctly summarized the law in a letter on 7 October 1915: "1. All Armenian goods are confiscated. 2. The government will collect the claims of the removed people and reimburse (or not reimburse) their debts."[183]

As already mentioned, Talaat did not fail to replace the district governor of Der ez-Zor, Ali Suad, who had taken seriously the resettlement of survivors and provided them, as far possible, with means to restart life—according to early instructions sent by Talaat—instead of extermination. Salih Zeki, his successor, rapidly implemented extermination in summer 1916. By late 1916, most Armenians—whether killed, alive but relocated, or among the few allowed to remain in towns of Asia Minor because economically needed—had lost their rights to former private property by order of the Ministry of the Interior. The main exception to this rule was Armenians who were native and long-term residents of a capital that still stood under international observation, and Armenians of a few other major towns like İzmir and Aleppo. Non-Armenian Christians, however, could keep their property, as far as the legal framework induced by Talaat was concerned.[184]

In 1917 in Beyoğlu, Emmanuil and his colleagues happened to encounter, in the entertainment area of Istanbul, a short,

young man about thirty to thirty-five years old, "whose appearance did not reveal any brutality. He told us that he was a Muslim. He had become rich as a governor of the Zor Desert [and]
had killed 60,000 Armenians and buried many children alive.
He appeared only rarely on the street because he did not want
to see human faces. He considered suicide." This man was Salih
Zeki. His and other teams of killers had been made to believe
that they fulfilled a religious duty.[185]

Although private enrichment and corruption, not only
the immediate needs of the state (including for the resettlement of Muslim migrants), used up a considerable amount of
Armenian assets, these still constituted an important material
basis of a so-called national economy (*milli iktisad*), that is, an
economy in the hands of Turks and Muslims. A great number
of local shops and large areas of highly developed agriculture
were part of a huge land transfer, to which Talaat's pocketbook again gives an idea. The mining industry in the province of Diyarbekir, for example, had depended on Armenians
and was entirely Islamized according to the terms of Talaat's
"national economy." The large and profitable cotton industry
in the Çukurova region, next to Adana, which had largely been
built up and possessed by Armenians since the second half
of the nineteenth century, was expropriated. An article titled
"O Turk! Become rich!" of late 1916 welcomed a general "economic revolution" and greatly appreciated that Muslim compatriots were now quick to involve themselves in commerce,
good affairs, and making money. Significantly, the destruction
of the Armenians remained completely unmentioned, not only
in contemporary articles but also in later Turkish histories of
economy.[186]

Talaat assured himself of the effects of his policy by inspection trips into an Asia Minor that had been terra incognita for

him until 1910, and actually remained so, as far as intimate, accurate knowledge beyond imperial rule was concerned. A journey in November 1916 led him to Ankara, Sivas, Diyarbekir, and again back to Konya, all in all, 2,000 km (about 1,243 miles) by car. Brass bands, applauding people, and children with Ottoman flags were organized in towns in order to duly welcome the real head of Ottoman politics. The political, economical, and human landscape was as much devastated as politically forced into line. Still, this komiteci from the Balkans looked at Anatolia through Macedonian glasses, that is, with satisfaction, seeing the Muslims now as masters at all points. Talaat was at pains to prove the rightness and success of his domestic politics, therefore, at every opportunity, he made a show of optimism despite manifest destruction.[187]

In a telegram on 5 December 1916 to Ali Haydar Pasha, the sharif of Mecca, a high religious dignitary, he stressed the benefits of the removal of the Armenians for "Islam" and "the Muslims." Faced with Arab rebellion, Talaat manifestly made an effort to pay Ali Haydar due deference, currying favor with him in the name of Islam and assuring him of his close relationship with the rulers in the capital. He therefore represented his Armenian policy as a successful Muslim empowerment. Only a short sentence in the middle of the message refers to an Arab publication on anti-Armenian oppression and atrocity (zulüm), written by a former district governor in Mamuretülaziz, Sheykh Faiz al-Huseyin, who was manifestly well known by Talaat and Haydar. Cemal had accused Faiz al-Huseyin of being an Arab autonomist and therefore sent him as a prisoner to Diyarbekir in 1915 where ex-governor Faiz al-Huseyin witnessed the local theater of extermination. He escaped the Ottoman realm in 1916 and wrote his booklet in the same year, which was later translated into English and German.[188]

Sublime Porte, Ministry of the Interior, Private Office. To His Excellence Ali Haydar Pasha Efendi, the Sharif of the venerable town of Mecca, [at present] in the enlightened Medina. Back from an inspection of the Anatolian provinces and *sanjaks* Konya, Ankara, Kayseri, Sivas, and Harput, I am proud to have seen closely, during my travels, the commitment shown by the Muslims. Seen from here [from Anatolia] it becomes evident how auspicious it was to remove the Armenians. The [Muslim] population [fleeing] from invaded places has entirely settled down. It has appropriated for itself the shops and assets of the Armenians, and started its commerce and trade, even if it lacked know-how. The declarations made by the bandit Hüseyin mention atrocity that we perpetrated against the Armenians. As soon as my budget has passed the parliament I will come to kiss your hands and implement the orders sent by Cafer Pasha and Seyyid Abdulvehâb. Cemal Pasha is on leave here [in Istanbul]. If there is any instruction from your side to be discussed with him, write me. He says that the campaign [in Arabia] depends on the supplies. The Romanian army has been defeated today around Bucharest. A few days later Bucharest will fall and we will divide the supplies of Romania, *inshallah* [hopefully, so God will]. This way, we will find a solution to the [notorious] problem of supplies. I kiss your hand, your Excellence, Pasha, and submit my respect to the Efendis Mecîd Muhiddîn and Mehmed Bey. Talaat.[189]

Sheykh Faiz al-Huseyin offered in his booklet an alternative, enlightened Muslim look at Talaat's Armenian policy. "Is it right that these imposters, who pretend to be the supports of Islam and the Khilâfat [caliphate], the protectors of the Moslems,

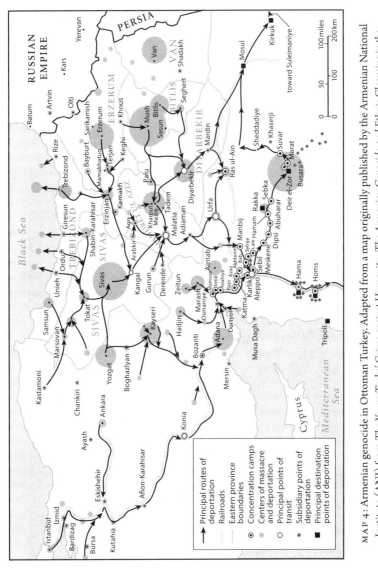

MAP 4: Armenian genocide in Ottoman Turkey. Adapted from a map originally published by the Armenian National Institute (ANI) from *The Young Turks' Crime against Humanity: The Armenian Genocide and Ethnic Cleansing in the Ottoman Empire* by Taner Akçam. Copyright © 2012 by Princeton University Press. Reprinted by permission.

should trangress the command of God, transgress the Koran, the Traditions of the Prophet, and humanity? Truly, they have committed an act at which Islam is revolted, as well as all Moslems and all the peoples of the earth, be they Moslems, Christians, Jews, or idolators."[190]

Victor, Noah, National Father: A Wide-Ranging Radiance

Sincere, though fragmentary, testimony stands in contrast to fraud, top-down lies, and exalted panegyric during genocide. A telling metaphor of such panegyric is the trill—a chilling war cry and joyful warble, used also during weddings—that women produced to cheer men on while the latter were spoliating, raping, and massacring in the towns or against defenseless caravans of deportees in the countryside.[191] They thus not only stimulated perpetration but also exorcised moral qualms—in 1915, in 1895, and on other occasions. Mehmed Talaat, the crafty, powerful "victor" over the Armenian problem, if not the whole Eastern Question, reaped adoration not only from those who enriched themselves in the process but also all those who saw Turkey saved and back on the track of victory—thanks to him.

On the opposite side stood those, including even a few in the service of the rulers, who witnessed and, indignant, put the facts down in writing, thus at least preserving honesty and independence of mind for themselves. Cavid in particular did so, privately bearing critical witness. He was, however, not willing or able to escape the political orbit of which he was a part. "Apparently, nobody has the power to open the mouth and say anything. . . . The Armenian issue is horrifying. Nobody can say anything." A totalitarian intimidation reigned, and Turkey's allies on the spot did little or nothing to overcome it. The senator Ahmed Rıza, former head of the Young Turks in opposition in Paris, had the courage to speak out. But Talaat sent for him and "told him that if he would persist in raising a rumpus about Armenians in the Senate, he would publish accounts of the doings of Armenians, which would rouse such a fanaticism among Moslems that the Armenians would receive much worse treatment than heretofore. Talaat told him if he really wished to benefit the Armenians, he better keep quiet," US ambassador Morgenthau noted on 1 October 1915.[192]

Talaat also used this pattern of threat toward German diplomacy, thus preventing any open discussion in the parliament or publicly. "The communication of atrocities committed by Armenians in Van would lead to excesses here [in Istanbul]."[193] This was a scarcely disguised threat of mob violence that could easily be provoked, as in 1895 and 1909, with false or exaggerated, sensationalist news. The potential for mob violence was real. Already, before the CUP, it had occasionally been an instrument of politics. (It did risk development of its own dynamic and producing backlashes.) Cavid, Talaat's close political friend, and Hamid, chief civil inspector and occupant of other high positions, agreed on the actual criminality not only *within* (Hamid's view) but *of* Talaat's administration (Cavid's feeling of August–September 1915).

When just back from Europe, Cavid began to realize that his leading political friends had implemented the "destruction not only of the political existence but the life itself of a whole [Armenian] people." Cavid deplored this "monstrous murder and enormous dimension of brutality that Ottoman history had never known before even in its darkest periods." He went further, concluding on the CUP's political project itself, that "[b]y these acts we have condemned everything. We have put an inextinguishable stain on the present administration. We have manifestly proved that we are a nation incapable of governing itself." He seriously feared for Turkey's future, also in economical terms. While "foolish people have a crazy joy," reasonable ones were saddened to see the destruction of learned manpower and functioning workshops for the sake of a pro-Turkish ethnoreligious class struggle.

The same was true for newly created, unproductive, and corrupt monopolies, as well as for a nationalist-corporatist radicalism against all those who produced on the basis of private initiative, and against all foreigners working in the country. "Enver and Talaat pretend to solve issues [of society and economy] that important thinkers in civilized countries could not yet solve," Cavid commented.[194] The committee was in fact "closely connected to certain Turkish-Mohammedan trade organizations that have contributed to the price rise alongside the mentioned Jewish merchants," Carl E. Wandel, the head of the Danish legation in Istanbul, reported. Petroleum, sugar, and other foodstuff had become unaffordable for many people. Wandel had previously alluded to "a rather strong ill-feeling" that had "lately arisen toward the rich Deunmés [Dönme] in Constantinople, those who at the moment dominate the capital's trade with a number of necessities, and who are being accused by the Turkish population of hoarding up a number of foodstuffs and necessities and of having made fortunes by forcing up the prices." Wandel predicted that the CUP government would "use the ill-feeling toward the latter to shift the blame for the steps taken away from themselves and solely to the Jews."[195]

The Armenian merchants were by then eliminated. As a matter of fact, Talaat's confidant Karasu, in charge of food distribution, had amassed a fortune.[196] Some Jews profited materially in that specific period, and not solely in the capital. Ahmet Refik, a liberal intellectual from Eskişehir and professor of history, was appalled by Muslim and Jewish profiteers who appeared in his hometown in August 1915, in order to benefit from Armenian assets sold at knocked-down prices. "Sir, this is very nice. . . . They go now, don't they? Farewell. What didn't they commit, what didn't they do against us Turks?!" The entirely innocent Armenians of Eskişehir, as Refik wrote, were brutally expelled from their houses, grouped together at the train station, and sent away on 14 August, crowded into railway cattle cars.[197]

In a long entry written in late summer 1915, Cavid gave room to conscience and emotions. He directly accused the committee in the privacy of his diary: "You are not only guilty, but also incapable. Of what quality is your conscience, when you accept that [Armenian] women, children, and elderly people, ousted from towns, are murdered at lakes and on mountains?" More than Hamid, Cavid understood that Talaat was "involved with full conviction," not only in the scheme, but he had also "embraced the underlying ideology." Cavid seems not to have grasped by then Talaat's overall leading role, but he knew to take the latter's talk of investigative commissions as evasion. He silently lamented that a "thoughtless and blindfold nationalist current has taken the place of Ottomanism. What becomes of the beautiful humanity in the hand of foolish butchers?" In fact, an unprecedented policy of demolition and xenophobia had definitively killed Ottomanity, enforced Islamist Turkism, and put the rule of law in shambles. "They did this in order to do away with the Armenians." Was this the birth of a nation, of a new Turkey? Had Talaat grafted evil right into the heart of his nationalist project? Cavid was next to despair, yet "despite all evils I do not want to give up my hope of a better tomorrow," he stated.

Hamid Kapancızâde, Talaat's collaborator in the ministry, again and again urged the government to act against crimes and political corruption, and dismiss illusions, although as an outsider to the CUP, his insights were limited. He actually succeeded in starting a few initiatives against lawlessness, but these resulted in little except some documentation. An administration that served mass crime to the extent of Talaat's ministry in 1915 could actually not save itself by pulling itself up by its bootstraps. In retrospect, before his death in 1928, Hamit concluded: "A reason for the decay of this country is that responsibility cannot take root, that theft, corruption, all ignoble crimes are blended into politics and left without punishment. The misdeeds of party members, who have reached a position of power by whatever means, are appreciated as extreme devotion and heroism." First and foremost a professional functionary and financial expert, Hamid did not read Talaat's character and know all sections of the ministry, yet his assessment of the minister's human resource policy is nonetheless pertinent:

> Talaat's patriotism and uprightness were out of question. Yet his worst deficit was his ingenuousness, which originated in his lack of experience and knowledge. He could not grasp that committee friends from yesterday would embrace abuse once they were in another field of activity. He could not appreciate that the same [komiteci] qualities and abilities could not succeed in various professions. He failed to anticipate that forcibly promoted creatures would not suffice in their office. In short, komiteci mentality and politics, which enforce de rigueur unity, outplayed the logic of [a good] administration.[198]

The point missed by Hamid is that Talaat needed precisely the collaborators whom he chose, because others would not have joined with him in his ruthless exploit. As a rule, employees in critical departments could only gain promotion if they entered the party. Thus, not to be shunted aside professionally and socially, they were compelled to involve themselves

personally into the single-party system. Cemil (Filmer), later
a well-known filmmaker in the Republic of Turkey, has shared
his experience. Eighteen years old, in late 1913 or so he had
found employment in the political division, Kısm-ı Siyasî, of
the security (police) department in Talaat's Ministry of the
Interior, where he processed Talaat's files. Forty killers (*fedai*)
belonged to his division, of which one part was for intelligence,
and another dealt with "Armenian affairs." After a while, he was
asked by Talaat to enter the CUP to be promoted. Though not
wealthy, his father insisted that his son abstain, thus Cemil
resigned from the well-paid post.[199]

Ismail Canbolad, a long-standing close committee friend of
Talaat's, expected a minimum of lawful management within
the Ministry of the Interior but felt entirely disillusioned. He
wrote Talaat an exasperated personal letter on 12 May 1916 saying that he saw no place for himself, either as a functionary of
the state or as a member of the CUP, ending: "Now I ask and
demand from you and the other friends only one thing, that
is: Do not pester me. With psychological pressure you prompt
me to commit suicide." Canbolad had resigned his leading post
both in the municipality and the management of the province
because of conflicts with corrupt trade organizations and the
intendant-general of the Ministry of War, İsmail Hakkı. He
refused Talaat's offer to become an undersecretary (*müsteşar*)
in his corrupt ministry. But even in this case, within a few days
after this letter, Talaat was able to sway his unwilling friend and
make him do what he had proposed.[200]

Talking about employment, corruption, and the prosecution of criminal functionaries, Talaat conceded to his political
friend Sheykhulislam Hayri that "our main mistake was that
we accustomed our friends to money. Many of them enriched
themselves . . . but this is not so important." Hayri wondered

why Talaat could not cleanse the administration of such bad elements, but he was far from interrogating the policy itself and scrutinizing Talaat's mind and soul.[201]

———

At the end of summer 1915, Paul Rohrbach, a subordinate collaborator of the German Foreign Office, wrote that "the *Ausmordung* [murderous eradication] of Armenia" had entirely broken the "moral neck" of Germany's alliance with Turkey, and that this also destroyed the dream of a strong and undefeated Ottoman Empire as a key to German world power.[202] Rohrbach's statement possessed the quality of a lone individual's testimony. Without Germany pulling its weight to stop the Armenian genocide, it must be complicit in the crime according to the logics of the war alliance, as Talaat had rightly calculated. The same is true for Austria, which conferred a First Class Order of Leopold in October 1915 to both Talaat and Halil (number one and number four among the CUP ministers).[203]

Apart from a few rare and fine undertones in Emil Ludwig's reports, panegyrics for Talaat and the other CUP leaders abounded in the German (not Swiss German) press from spring 1915. The same holds true from June 1915 for elaborate apologetics of CUP policy, political accusations against the Armenians in agreement with Talaat's wording of 24 April, and anti-Armenian denigrations on the levels of culture and race that markedly paralleled existing belle epoque anti-Semitism.[204] German censors worked hard not to allow any debate about the Armenian extermination into the country.[205] Debate took place only after Talaat's murder in Berlin in 1921. Then only did a larger part of the German public become well aware of the nature of Turkish nationalism and of what had happened to minorities in the realm of its former ally.

Enver's friend, the German naval attaché Hans Humann, echoed Turkish war hawks in the army when he stated in 1915 that "the Armenians had shown themselves disloyal in their Ottomanship and that anyone who has been in the Orient must realize that the two races cannot live together and that the weaker will have to succumb. . . . From the point of view of safety, the Turks were fully justified to destroy the Armenians."[206] Such language on and treatment of an ostracized ethnoreligious minority of citizens was to seminally impact an interwar Germany that envied Turkey's apparent political success despite world war defeat. Among German officers and a few civilians in Turkey during World War I, Humann was not exceptional. Among Germans in Turkey and generally, he was, however, clearly not yet in the majority.

German diplomacy focused principally on disclaiming any joint guilt while at the same time largely defending Turkey's attitude and discourse. Its overall reaction to "the greatest crime of the ages" (as Morgenthau and many others labeled it) was passive, self-righteous, and therefore dramatically insufficient. Generally speaking, Germany lost its (already frail) civic and political soul, disabling itself for decades from doing effective soul-searching and exerting moral authority. On many levels, the crime was seamlessly endorsed, for instance, during the ongoing genocide when officials sponsored a high-profile public meeting in Berlin that included German and Ottoman representatives, during which the ethnonationalist mantra of "Turkey belongs to the Turks" became respectable.[207]

Matthias Erzberger, German deputy of the Catholic Zentrumspartei (Center Party), reflected the prevailing German attitude on his 1916 trip to Istanbul where he met with Talaat and Enver. Although friendly to the Armenians, he expressed empathy for the CUP's repugnance of Armenian "nationalist ambitions," emphasized the loyalty of Catholic Armenians, and believed Talaat's promises that henceforth Armenians in general would no longer be persecuted. "A Turkish promise has no value," Erzberger felt compelled to state two years later in the Reichstag in June 1918. Talaat did not take soft verbal interventions by Germans seriously. He did take seriously the latter's expectation that Armenians should return to their homes after the war. "There has not been, until now, objection by the Germans against our Armenian policy and its consequences," Talaat wrote to Enver on 16 February 1916, shortly after Erzberger's visit, "and we understand that they consent.... Yet I felt, during recent interviews with German deputies, that they were committed to the return of the removed Armenians to their homes." To prevent any such unacceptable perspective, Talaat therefore proposed that Enver "profit from the present situation and ... bring the undertaken policy to an irreversible end."[208] This was the purpose of the Armenian genocide's second phase in Syria in 1916 and ongoing persecution elsewhere.

The German press and high officials praised the CUP regime and Talaat, its outstanding leader. Although this glorification smacked as war propaganda and untruth, many Germans bought into these presentations and thus were affected by their corrosive logic. A case in point was the detailed panegyric for the CUP rule by Alfred Nossig, a writer, sculptor, collaborator of the Foreign Office, and leader of the Allgemeine Jüdische Kolonisationsorganisation (AJK; General Jewish Colonization Organization). He founded this Zionist organization alongside the Zionist Organization (ZO) in the aftermath of the Young Turk Revolution (July 1908), hoping on full cooperation with the CUP for Jewish immigration. In contrast to Lepsius, who also arrived in Istanbul in summer 1915 but could only meet with Enver, Nossig was received by all of the important committee leaders, the sultan, and the German diplomats in August and September 1915.[209]

Laudatory newspaper articles and a whole book resulted from his visits. Nossig portrayed Mehmed Talaat as "the strongest man of Young Turkey," a "mature man," and a "man of will," a "unique and outstanding talent of statesmanship" who dominates "the whole state machine." Whereas "the sultan is a constitutional ruler, Talaat is an autocratic sultan," he quoted a contemporary bon mot from Istanbul. He did not allow any critical allusions, as Emil Ludwig did, but only one short rhetorical question: "'Usurper'? Nobody thinks of revolt against this man of will. One bows willingly to his authority and talent." Calling Talaat "the Turkish Bismarck," in early 1917 Nossig sculpted a portrait medallion of Talaat, then grand vizier and pasha, intending to offer him the accomplished work during the pasha's visit in Berlin in April 1917.[210]

AJK leader Nossig and Richard Lichtheim, ZO representative in Istanbul, wanted to achieve the best for their projects. Both profited from contacts with the German and American embassies, maintained contact with Ottoman Jewish leaders, and sought to persuade the CUP rulers. Yet Nossig flattered them most. To please the rulers, who did not want to see any "Jewish concentration" in Palestine, he transformed the original project of immigration in Palestine to a scheme of immigration of Eastern European Jews to the whole empire, including Asia Minor, to replace the Armenians. In Istanbul, he founded the Osmanisch-Israelitische Union (Ottoman-Israelite Union) and in Berlin, as a counterpart, the Deutsch-Osmanische Union (German-Israelite Ottoman Union) for the purpose of encouraging "intimate relations between Jews and Ottomans." He went so far as to approach US ambassador Morgenthau: "[A]s a brother Jew he begged of me [Morgenthau] to cease my

FIGURE 17: Nossig's portrait medallion (from *Der Orient: Zeitschrift für die wirtschaftliche Erschliessung des Orients*, July 1917, 14–15) and Georg Kolber's bust of Talaat Pasha (Archiv Georg Kolbe Stiftung, Poto: Margrit Schwartzkopf).

activities on behalf of the Armenians as it much displeased the Turks." Morgenthau refused.[211]

In a memorandum on 1 August 1916, Armando Moses adopted the idea of Jewish settlement in Eastern Asia Minor, replacing the Armenians. He was the Istanbul representative of the Bureau for German-Turkish Economic Questions (Auskunftstelle für Deutsch-Türkische Wirtschaftsfragen), an office established by the Turkish-German Society (Türkisch-Deutsche Vereinigung).[212] Founded in Berlin in April 1914 to promote German-Turkish friendship, the Istanbul branch of the Turkish-German Society was opened on 3 October 1915 with Enver as its president, and among its members were Wangenheim, Talaat, Said Halim, Halil, and Cemal. Talaat, Ernst

Jäckh, and others gave speeches. Paul Rohrbach, a member of the Turkish-German Society since its foundation in April 1914, resigned in a strong letter to board member Jäckh on 15 August 1916: "As long as the Turks do not atone [for the murder of the Armenians], the German name must remain reviled globally, and any good German conscience in the Occident and Orient is impossible. . . . I will draw the only possible consequence for me and stop being a German in a political sense [if German coercion toward Turkish atonement proves impossible]."[213]

Nossig was not alone in transgressing more than a fine boundary of human decency. A conceited and go-getting Zionist rival of the main ZO, Nossig made himself important in Istanbul and Berlin during war and exerted influence, therefore remaining a figure who could not be ignored. This is not only true with regard to European history until the Holocaust, when he was killed by partisans as a Nazi collaborator,[214] but also relates to a sometimes bitter history of Jewish attitudes toward late Ottoman Armenians from the late nineteenth century onward. Late Ottoman Jews tended to justify anti-Armenian violence in order to defend the government and prove loyalty, even if individually they may have helped their persecuted neighbors. (Contrary cases happened as well.) Armenians were envied because they excelled, moreso than the other minorities, in education, participation in public affairs, and often also economically. Only later experience clarified to many such Jews that submissive loyalty to, or "vertical alliances" with, the strongest authorities available (even if they were criminal), in exchange for privileges, proved an entirely wrong path. The second half of the twentieth century saw passionate discussions regarding this issue, in particular, in response to Hannah Arendt's assessment of the Hofjudentum and to her later writings based on this assessment.[215]

Lichtheim worried about Nossig and did all he could to prevent him from "talking stupidities," thus damaging Jewish interests. A comparable, though different, case was Moïz Kohen (Tekinalp), a Salonican Jew and productive writer for the cause of Turkism. He believed Turkism coincided with Ottoman Jewish interests. A fervent disciple of Ziya Gökalp and a CUP member, in his writings he largely identified with the CUP's anti-Christian stance, and in particular with the anti-Christian program of "national economy." Jacobson called him an "Over-turk" (*Übertürke*) who nonsensically defended Ottomanism being overcome by Turkism. A "piddling informer" (*kleiner Denunziant*), he could nevertheless damage the Zionist cause and must therefore be "called to order," possibly by the Jewish deputy Nissim Mazliah, who exerted influence on him.[216]

Where the suffering of the Armenians was concerned, ZO representatives and Ottoman Jewish leaders largely looked the other way, whereas young Zionists of the Netzah Yisrael Lo Yeshaker (NILI; "the Eternal One of Israel will not lie") espionage group in Palestine felt solidarity with the victims and sent reports to wake up the international community. They did this, they wrote, in the name of the prophets, of Jesus, and of their own humanity, asking prophetically, "When will our [the Jews'] turn arrive?" Spying for Britain, they were considered a danger, even a calamity, by a Yishuv (Jewish presence in Palestine) that not only disapproved of their subversive activities but feared to be associated, in any way, with the Armenians. Cemal Pasha worried that "Palestine might become a second Armenia" and want autonomy. NILI's commitment and sacrifice were critical for securing the Balfour Declaration.[217]

Morgenthau, contemporaries in neutral countries, and witnesses on the ground were "firmly convinced" that the murder of the Armenian nation was hitherto "the greatest crime of the ages." NILI group members believed that "the wholesale massacre of the Jews ordered by the Roman general Titus is the only record in history to be paralleled with the wholesale massacre of the Armenians. And now just as then, here just like there, it was a government scheme." Thanks to intra-Ottoman travels, NILI members were well informed and were not only aware of governmental (and hence Talaat's) direction of the genocide but also knew about the broad participation of the Muslim population and local agencies, including "real female markets" in all "agglomerations where the Armenians were driven through." Lewis Einstein, a member of Morgenthau's staff, concluded in late 1916 regarding the Armenian fate: "In all this war of horrors it must remain the crowning horror. Nothing has equaled the silently planned destruction of a race. . . . The Armenian race in Asia Minor has been virtually destroyed." Einstein came back to the seminal topic shortly before his death in 1967, emphasizing that these crimes, though on a smaller scale in numbers, "were like Hitler's anti-Jewish measures."[218]

―――――

With greater pathos, conviction, and rhetoric than the German panegyrics, it was Gökalp who lifted up Talaat as an exceptional statesman. Mehmed Talaat thus became the father and Noah of the Turkish nation amid a global tempest. Whereas Gökalp's poem for Enver of mid-August 1915 praised the charismatic and courageous hero who, always an example of hope, had faithfully begun the great jihad,[219] the poem for Talaat on 1 September 1915 went further by placing him at the center of the committee and the nation. In late summer 1915, after successful mass murder with robbery in Asia Minor, Talaat was actually stronger and more popular than ever before.

You are the spirit who unites the souls
In you the committee sees his conscience
If it [the committee] is a ship of salvation, you are Noah
You, if you were not, this nation would be orphaned . . .

You are of pure heart like a Turkish soldier
You are a hero free of arrogance and boasting
You are a statue of honesty as is Turkish history
You are an imperturbable heart . . .[220]

Talaat was the committee's and government's face domestically but also internationally. He was now strong enough to
deprive Said Halim of the Foreign Ministry, thus taking foreign affairs into his own hands and definitively marginalizing
the grand vizier. Halil, entirely dependent on Talaat, was foreign minister from 24 October 1915 onward. In mid-June 1915,
Talaat and the committee had already decided on this move. At
that time, Cavid had wanted Halil to intervene in what he considered base treatment of the Ottoman deputies Zohrab and
Vartkes, then sent to the court-martial in Diyarbekir. "Yet, in
this fellow [Halil] there is no vigor to insist." Cavid had immediately understood that "they [Talaat and the committee] had
not sent them from Istanbul to Diyarbekir only for interrogation," as they had pretended.[221]

From early June 1915, when he knew that the anti-Armenian
scheme had worked, Talaat's mood was self-confident and
satisfied. In this posture of winner and victor, he told the
US ambassador Morgenthau in early August 1915 that "they
[the committee and government] based their objections to
the Armenians on three distinct grounds: (1) that they have
enriched themselves at the expense of the Turks; (2) that
they wanted to domineer over them and establish a separate

state; (3) that they have openly encouraged their enemies, so that they [Talaat and the committee] have come to the irrevocable decision to make them powerless before the war is ended." Talaat added that they "want to treat the Armenians like we [Americans] treat the Negroes," thus once again justifying himself by referring to the sins of others.[222] Vis-à-vis German friends, Talaat openly welcomed "the annihilation of the Armenian people, because it was a political relief" for Turkey.[223] He thus displayed himself as perfectly justified in having committed genocide. The German ally lacked the will, the means, and the morale to face him and counter the enormity of the situation, having embraced moral defeatism in favor of military logics.

Talaat's war-specific arguments, as circulated in 1915 Istanbul, were that "the Armenians had thwarted all their plans of invading the Caucasus, that they were the cause of the Turkish defeat at Sari Kamish [Sarıkamış], and it was the Armenian volunteers who attacked and repulsed the Turkish troops in the Azarbaijan district," thus stopping the march toward Turan. The "reverses the Turkish troops had at Sari Kamish, Azarbaijan, and Van were all due to the Armenian volunteers and not the Russian troops." Therefore, "all their measures against the Armenians were perfectly justified," Talaat said to Armenian patriarch Zaven. At the same time he expressed "great resentment at Armenians having tried to secure European intervention to establish a proper government and introduce reforms in Anatolia." Talaat and the committee had been, the latter added, "just waiting for such a chance to punish the Armenians." By deporting the Armenians even from Rodosto (Tekirdağ, in European Turkey), Talaat pretended to avenge injustices against Muslims during the Bulgarian occupation of the First Balkan War.[224]

In a comprehensive report on 6 March 1916 on Urfa, written by Talaat or under his close supervision, and addressed to the Foreign Ministry, he derogatorily said that the Armenians were "able to maintain their national existence only as subjects under Ottoman governance."[225] Foreigners in the town of Urfa had reported on the brutal repression of Armenians in self-defense and the destruction of their quarters by artillery. The horrors of deportations had become more than obvious from spring 1915 on, since Urfa was a hub for deportees from the north, and those from Zeytun had already passed by in March. International observation and a capacity for self-defense were factors that explained why the Ministry of the Interior postponed the removal of Urfa's Armenians until October 1915.[226]

Since the Armenians had pursued the "dream of Armenian freedom," they had become "instruments of Russian, English, and French politics" and thus "a perpetual element of subversion for the Sublime State," the report reads. They thus finally lost their right to exist, Talaat implicitly but distinctly concludes. They had treacherously taken "the eve and the beginning of the General War as an opportunity to spark altogether rebellion and revolution." Their efforts of subversion had also intended to influence general public opinion and to persuade Muslims, but had, the latter's self-styled doyen pretended, only "provoked profound sentiments of hate among the loyal and submissive Muslim population." In his report Talaat even resented the grief expressed in Urfa's Armenian church when Ottoman forces had conquered Ardahan in late 1914 and actually massacred Christians. Embracing Hamidian imperial vocabulary and thus disloyal to the Young Turk language of 1908, he called the large-scale massacres of 1895 "Armenian events" linked to "a rebellious movement" and opined that Armenian komiteci had abused the aftermath of the Young Turk Revolution to organize themselves in Urfa.

To justify genocide, Talaat framed a whole discourse and set of arguments, so that the self-righteous justification for murder and destruction remained entrenched in later memoirs, politics, and historiography.[227] Repeated statements by Talaat, Enver, Halil, and others during 1915 suggest a strongly anti-Armenian mind-set created from early spring. An entrenched anti-Armenian perpetrator trauma was therefore the founding moment of a negatively defined post-Ottoman, but pre-Kemalist, Turkish-Muslim nationalism. This mind-set implanted a deathly bias against Armenian Christians, and, more abstractly, destroyed what had remained of Ottoman conviviality. The Armenian genocide killed the late Ottoman utopia of a modern individual equality married to a recognized, unique plurality of regions, cultures, and religions. As long as it remained unrepented, the legacy of this crime condemned the political culture of the country to remain unfit for a true, that is, egalitarian, pluralism, the twin brother of truly democratic rule.

A biased historical perspective of World War I, as framed by CUP luminary and minister Talaat, and a corresponding degradation of the Armenians, served henceforth as the common denominator of modern nationalist coherence. Historically, this was not at all the first community based on the killing of human scapegoats. The binding force of a major crime jointly committed, denied, belittled, or justified, and—in any case— jointly concealed, is a fundamental issue of society. Any society remains captive to similar logic if not severely checked and challenged by universal standards—or by the experience of a catastrophe that finally leaves no back door. Public acknowledgment, then, is a part of healing and a catalyst for transformative recovery.[228]

Talaat, Palestine, and Zionism

Against the background of Theodor Herzl's foundational book *Der Judenstaat* (1896) and other basic texts, late nineteenth- to early twentieth-century Zionism intended explicitly (though not publicly) a separate political entity in a Palestine that was still part of the Ottoman Empire. Vladimir Jabotinsky's concept of a pure, island-like nation, as published in 1911 in Russian (*Race and Nationality* [English, 1939]), was far more separatist than any nationalist idea of ARF or Hunchak authors.[229] Important features, however, distinguished the Jewish and the Armenian national renaissances in the late Ottoman world, and fortunately protected the Yishuv, the Jewish presence in Palestine, from a fate similar to that of the Ottoman Armenians during World War I. Yet at times, such a fate seemed impending.

Zionist agencies were largely based outside the Ottoman realm, before the British Mandate for Palestine offered them a protective roof in Mandatory Palestine in the interwar period. Although transnationally and transimperially organized like the Zionists, Armenians had been much more involved in the Ottoman political fabric since the Tanzimat, and, above all, since the Young Turk Revolution, when the CUP and ARF cooperated in an election alliance. While Ottoman Armenians had no viable alternative to constitutional rule, Zionists did. Principal Armenian presence was in Asia Minor and thus in a core area of Turkish nationalism under Talaat's policy, in contrast to Palestine, where Western warships had easy access. Although they were also a potential target for sweeping expulsion and suffered occasional duress during war, the Jews on the whole enjoyed efficient protection by Germany, US diplomacy, and Talaat.

This protection largely relied, however, on the assumption of real or imagined Jewish domestic and global power, which the protagonists wanted to have on their side during war. Zionism had "become one of the main undercurrents of the political situation" in the Ottoman capital, British ambassador Gerard Lowther wrote as early as 1911 to British foreign minister Edward Grey. This was certainly true. Yet Lowther and his dragoman, Gerald H. Fitzmaurice, saw blanket specters of "Pan-Judaism," "Pan-Islamism," and a "Judeo-Masonic conspiracy"—allegedly promoted by Freemason Talaat and his partly crypto-Jewish Salonican friends—that could possibly undermine the Middle Eastern future. Thus, the most important representative of British world power in the Ottoman Empire, who Rambert considered a weak analyst (not without reason), had missed an accurate and proper assessment of the political hub of Istanbul in critical times.[230]

Talaat in no way sympathized with Zionism, though Islamists and others vocally reproached him for doing so, and both contemporary observers and later historians claimed that this was the case. Indeed, he assessed the domestic and international field of forces more craftily than others. Any comparable parallel scheme of destruction against Zionism and the Jews was therefore excluded when he frontally attacked the Armenians in 1915–16. Ahmed Cemal Pasha, the military governor of greater Syria, was at pains to accept that the CUP's anti-autonomist logic did not similarly apply to the case of Palestine. As he explained in a telegram on 16 March 1915 to Talaat, he wanted to "deal a major blow to Zionism," because he considered it to be "an enormous catastrophe for Palestine." Cemal was not, however, comprehensively against the Jews in Palestine and, a fortiori, not against Jews in the empire, nor did he propose any exterminatory scheme. In mid-March 1916, he asked for authorization to stop the immigration of Jews who were unwilling to take on Ottoman citizenship and respect Ottoman sovereignty, to prevent large Jewish colonies and new-old Hebrew names for places of new Jewish settlements, to inquire about and expel Jewish foreign nationals involved in Zionism, and to reject demands for naturalization by Zionists.[231]

Because he had applied harsh wartime measures and wanted to crush the Zionist "state within the state," Cemal henceforth counted as an anti-Jewish hard-liner and evildoer par excellence, in contrast to the allegedly accostable, moderate, and "real statesman" Talaat. It is true that Talaat enjoyed respect among many Jews in Istanbul after 1913. For Abraham Elmaliyah, a journalist for *Le Jeune Turc* and a profound admirer, Talaat was the real "hero of the revolution"—not Enver, who, in his eyes, Talaat excelled by far.[232] Yet this was utilitarian and ethnocentric, originating at times from admiration of revolutionary power in action by CUP sympathizers, including Parvus.

For those who knew better (like the young Zionists of the NILI group), Cemal was an imperially biased committee pillar who nevertheless refused blatant extermination of minorities, in contrast to some of his more exalted political friends. Many Armenians, including the 150,000 he saved from death or final massacre in the camps, cherished Cemal as a comparably clement regional autocrat in a time of extremes.[233] US ambassador Abram Elkus, the successor to Morgenthau, judged both Talaat and Cemal as, "on the whole, rather friendly to the Jews, but they distrusted the professed Zionists." The assessment of German ambassador Johann H. von Bernstorff (Kühlmann's successor, who had followed Wangenheim's successor Wolff-Metternich) was identical. In a similar vein, obeying Istanbul-centered imperial logic, Cemal and Talaat detested Arabists and reproached them for refusing centralist Ottoman rule. During wartime, they brutally repressed "treacherous" Syrian Arab notables, and Cemal hanged a number of them, but without being aggressive toward the entire Arab population in general or in certain regions. Cemal used the infamous Sevk ve İskân Kanunu (Relocation and Resettlement Law) of May 1915 to the letter, that is, to deport temporarily certain families whom he or his subordinates considered obnoxious. He did not use it in the perverted, exterminatory way Talaat did against the Armenians.[234]

The case of the Armenians was different. Since the international Reform Agreement, and even more so after the failed Caucasus campaign, Talaat not only hated their desire for autonomy but also the people themselves. He thus totally reversed a former political partnership, his admiration of model revolutionaries, and the recognition of the outstanding Armenian contribution to a constitutional Ottoman society. Talaat's dealings with Zohrab and Vartkes symbolized the collapse of his former respect and self-respect, his self-negation as a constitutional politician, his recanting of some revolutionary-leftist ideals that he had shared with the ARF, and his embrace of crime. The Armenians had become the scapegoats of a failed war and of failed imperial expectations, and thus targets of blame in the competition for a future in Asia Minor. They were henceforth the visible but little understood outcasts in the Ottoman realm. Even German and Austrian militaries had to stay away from them and not intervene in matters of their fate.

Armenians constituted a paradigmatic reality of European modernity but remained exotically distant and incomprehensible to contemporaries. Talking about a famous Istanbulian Armenian sent to the desert, an Austrian officer based in Turkey (the later author Moshe Y. Ben-Gavriêl) noted, in a phrase both dry and bewildered, that the only thing the victim had done wrong was to be born an Armenian. Entente and Jewish newspapers misinterpreted the historic dimensions of Talaat's crime, when, in spring 1917, after repressive measures and the evacuation of Jews from Jaffa, they put Jewish suffering on the same level as that of the Armenians or even pretended that "the massacre against the Armenians pales before the latest outrages" in Palestine.[235] This and other misrepresentations contributed to fatally inaccurate Jewish assessments of collective danger in the near future.

Anti-Jewish sentiment in Palestine was not solely the result of instigation by feudal landowners, as Zionists tried to portray it, but was attached to challenging questions of late Ottoman coexistence. Already by early 1915, some Zionists had given up Ottomanist coexistence for good, if ever they had seriously considered it, and disdained cohabitation on the ground. Vladimir Jabotinsky, David Ben-Gurion's main contemporary in the interwar period, recalled having said to Max Nordau (cofounder of the World Zionist Organization together with Theodor Herzl), "I remember one of your speeches in which you said: 'We are going to Palestine to extend the boundaries of Europe to the Euphrates. And the obstacle is: Turkey.' Now its end is nigh—shall we just sit back and do nothing?" In fact, in spring 1915 Jabotinsky cofounded what became the anti-Ottoman Jewish Legion, which caused the Zionist representation in Istanbul serious aggravation.[236] In CUP logic, Jews were no less traitors than Armenians, but they lacked priority and possessed more international power.

Ottoman Armenians were not less innocent or less clever than others, and thus easy targets, as many tended to assume in the 1910s, in the interwar period, and afterward. They were, indeed, the best educated and most agile, but they were also the most vulnerable group in the late Ottoman world, and as such many of them had been deeply committed to a reformed constitutional policy since the second half of the nineteenth century. They knew the real challenges of the late Ottoman world, which was much more their world than the Zionists' world. Yet this world collapsed in the 1910s. Imperial cataclysm and a particular combination of circumstances in the first months of the war made the Armenians an obvious target in the aftermath of frustrated conquests. Actors from the top and below, extremist ideas, entrenched prejudices, and material incentives colluded in the brute destruction. A little more than two decades later, in different but related and comparable contexts, Europe's Jews were to experience an analogous situation.[237] Talaat was not Hitler, but both leaders represented societies, states, and political parties that embraced radical domestic violence to overcome, as they believed, crises and defeat. Talaat pioneered genocidal patterns within twentieth-century Europe at large.

While there were compelling contemporary reasons to shirk solidarity with the victims of those pioneering patterns, including fear, prejudices, ethnocentrism, and an instrumental, sensationalist comparison with Armenian suffering, those who did so, or who misunderstood the patterns as "Asian" or "Oriental violence," missed recognizing in time what the future might be. When a district governor of Haifa threatened Jewish villagers (allegedly or not), saying that "if you do not hand over the spy [Yosef] Lishansky [of the NILI group], your fate will be similar to that of the Armenians, whose deaths I was personally involved in," he applied, in fact, terrifying propaganda along with the individual torture in which he had engaged. Cemal used this same rhetoric during the evacuation of Jaffa, as did others, to bring whole groups to heel. Neither Cemal nor the district governor, however, could in reality apply a scheme that Talaat had formerly ordered to implement only against Armenians.[238]

The discourse used by CUP men was not harmless. Cemal worried that "Palestine might become a second

Armenia."[239] His harsh but limited measures were still biased by an entrenched imperial centralism versus local self-rule. His focused anti-Zionism had the potential to lead to comprehensive anti-Jewish measures. In fact, he considered at times that all Jews were part of the Zionist movement,[240] just as Talaat, radicalized, had seen all Armenians as involved in insurrection. Moreover, Talaat, too, thought "that all the Jews work together," and once hinted humorously to Nahum about a total expulsion of Jews from Palestine.[241] In the Armenian case, too, initially, Talaat and his close friends had "only" wanted to prevent European-monitored reforms involving more regional self-rule for non-Muslims, but the war promoted in the East from early August 1914 created a context that allowed them to embrace overall removal and extermination.

By 1915, any development toward a free and disciplined egalitarian plurality was unacceptable. It would have dismantled an outdated pretense of centralist imperial rule that relied on the myth of premodern Ottoman power, refueled by Gökalp's modernist exaltation of Islamic Turkdom. Julius Becker, a journalist for the German *Vossische Zeitung* and a Zionist representative, put it this way after long interviews with Talaat and Cemal in late 1917: These imperial rulers had angst. They felt unable to manage up-and-coming, economically prospering, and self-reliant groups. In the end, they insisted only on external boundaries of the empire without embracing a viable and vital internal project. Even in peace, they would lack the potential for a "reasonable policy for [different] nationalities" and the wisdom "to renounce a pan-Turkism that Germany had contributed to nursing." German assistance could not change this, even after war.

Astutely, Becker added, Germany itself lacked the necessary wisdom. Germany wanted to appear internationally as being

friendly to the Jews, and asked for the accompanying press coverage to prove it, but this wasn't so in Germany itself, where
action in favor of the Jews in Palestine, if made public, could
"compromise" the authorities. Becker did not, however, believe
that the Jews would "face a 'fate of Armenians,' as many fear. The
Turks have seen that this does not work so easy with the Jews
as with the Armenians." He thus challenged the sensationalist
reporting in the US media.[242]

————

Like other organizations of minorities, Zionism had been very
hopeful after the Young Turk Revolution in 1908. Salonica, the
center of the CUP, a largely Ottoman Jewish town, proved a
tower of strength for Zionism, even if most Ottoman Jews were
not explicitly Zionist, because they feared to appear disloyal,
were simply not interested, or considered the Zionists a "hand-
ful of charlatans."[243] However, after Abdulhamid's tough restrictions, a liberal era promised better possibilities for immigration
to Palestine. The European Zionists and their Ottoman Jewish
and Dönme intermediaries avoided assiduously appearing as
autonomist or separatist, although many of their writings in
Europe were explicitly so.

Obeying a vertical logic of power, from 1908 Zionism settled
on privileged relations with the CUP, the strongest organization of the Young Turk movement, but not on the oppositional
movement of Sabahaddin, whose model of decentralization
allowed, in principle, a much better chance to establish autonomies, including Jewish autonomy in parts of Palestine. The
main intermediaries of Victor Jacobson, the unofficial representative of the Zionist Organization in Istanbul since 1908,
were Emmanuel Karasu (deputy of Salonica), Nissim Mazliah

(deputy of İzmir), and Rabbi Haim Nahum. They were all close acquaintances of Nâzım, Talaat, and Cavid in Salonica. Nâzım called the Jews the "most reliable element," and in early 1909 he welcomed the immigration of millions of European Jews, though only a fraction of them to Palestine, because, if too concentrated there, they would constitute "a danger" for the Ottoman government.[244]

In late 1909 Talaat received a memorandum from David Wolffsohn, the second president of the Zionist Organization, on the historical and religious attachment of the Jews to Palestine, but he left it without response, though he had asked for it. Since his visit in London in July 1909, Talaat repeatedly clarified that "the government could not fulfill the wishes" of the Zionists. He respected them, however, as potentially useful junior teammates in a competition for power and resources. As a result of public discussion, skepticism within the CUP became more articulate, while bad press and hostility toward Zionism among broad Islamist circles, in particular, increased. The crisis of Talaat and the CUP coincided with a fundamental debate in parliament in 1911 on Zionism and the Ottoman future (see chap. 3, sec. "Sobered, Disturbed, Depressed"). It revealed the deficit of common, operational goals of a constitutional patriotism. Except for the Ottoman Armenians, all were to possess more or less articulate alternative choices, for instance, an exclusive Turkism for Asia Minor, a separatist Zionism for Palestine, and Arab rule for Iraq and Syria.

After the brief interlude of the opposition in the second half of 1912, Zionists welcomed the CUP putsch of January 1913 and the ensuing dictatorship, in particular, the new cabinet of June 1913, after Mahmud Cevdet Pasha's assassination. In general, the close working relationship between the CUP and members of the Ottoman Jewish elite was reinforced, because the single-party regime now regarded other non-Muslim representatives, with whom the CUP had closely cooperated, as unreliable and potential traitors. Jews filled the gap. The German-Jewish newspaper *Die Welt*, the mouthpiece of the Zionist Organization, wrote in July 1913:

> The new grand vizier, Prince Said Halim, has repeatedly shown his benevolent attitude toward the Jews. Talaat Bey, the new minister of the interior, as is well known, has been educated at a Jewish school and has stood since then in friendly relations with many Jewish personalities. He speaks the Judeo-Spanish idiom very well and understands some Hebrew. Jestingly they call him "the Jewish minister." Another member of the cabinet, Halil Bey, president of the council of state, and former president of the parliament, excels also with a particularly Judeophilic attitude.

Die Welt flattered itself and its Jewish readership, though it exaggerated Talaat's knowledge of languages and, above all, reduced the whole issue of the Ottoman future to the question of (seeming) sympathy—or not—for Jews. It did not offer any hint of possible abysses that the dictatorial cabinet might lead the region into.[245]

Thanks to Salonican and other networks, Jews possessed a privileged access to Talaat. A sociable networker, he was susceptible to personal démarches, expecting, however, services in return, especially in the press and regarding financial matters. Most times, Talaat enjoyed good press, particularly good Jewish press, in Istanbul and abroad.[246] Still, he did not want to be associated too much with Jews and Zionism. "Zionism is for us a question of domestic politics and of the struggle between parties," he stated to Jacobson during a personal meeting on 6 January 1913, fearing that the opposition would profit from an open cooperation between the CUP and Zionists. "Talaat persists in negating nationalities . . . he is not a statesman, but a good party leader," Jacobson observed in turn. Talaat actually sought a closer relationship with the Zionists in early 1913 and contacted Jacobson a few times. Now, he also used Essad Pasha (Toptani), a CUP veteran, and Ahmed Agayev (Ağaoğlu), a leading CUP intellectual and professor at the University of Istanbul, as his middlemen.[247]

After the January 1913 putsch, there was "a great change of spirit now reigning" in the capital with regard to "the Zionist question and the Jewish question in general," according to Jacobson.[248] A trigger for the CUP's perceptible pro-Jewish turn, as already alluded to, was the more distanced, potentially broken relationship with the Armenians after the reform issue was internationally relaunched in late 1912. Nahum used the opportunity to demand the abolition of anti-Zionist restrictions that also partly afflicted Ottoman Jews in general. His memorandum to the Ministry of Justice on 10 February 1913 was published in the Istanbul-based *L'Aurore*, a Jewish newspaper financed since 1909 by the Zionists. An editorial praised the benefits of Jewish-Turkish cooperation in a vein that "might be styled an alliance between Pan-Judaism and Pan-Islamism in Turkey."[249] *L'Aurore* made a show of global Jewish financial, intellectual, and political power that "may direct all others" and thus help realize the dream of "a great Turkey" alongside "a powerful Jewry." Talaat was seduced by the idea of an Islamic-Jewish alliance of sorts opposite Europe, or at least found that it opened up an additional range of operation for him.

"Islam is decaying, it is going and must inevitably disappear if there is no support coming from the outside. We do not possess the intelligence, nor the know-how, nor the money. The Jews have got all this, but they lack the field of action. The Jews shall come to us to direct our affairs, forming an intimate alliance with us," Jacobson summarized the arguments that Agayev allegedly proposed, "according to the instructions of Talaat," during a meeting after mid-February 1913. This idea, in different forms, harkened back to premodern times and possessed anti-Western and anti-Christian ideas that Jacobson, however, did not endorse. He knew "how naive and even dangerous" this proposition was if taken by the letter, but it was very promising on the other side, insofar as "the Turks begin to envisage the Jewish question . . . as a question of eminent political interest for Turkey itself." Jacobson urged "a program of action appropriate to realize this Jewish collaboration in the reorganization of Turkey." He was happy to play the new game in 1913, and not utterly upset that after one of their meetings, Talaat had dubbed him a "dog, son of the dog," who was, however, "entirely right in all that he said." Other Zionists did not believe in the idea right from the start. "No, the Turks are not our 'brothers,' and even with the real Ismaelites [the Arabs], we have no spiritual connection," Jabotinsky, one of Zionism's best orators (not thinkers), said to Nordau. "We are, thank God, Europeans, and the builders of Europe for a millennium."[250]

From 1913, the Zionist Organization was ready to reward free immigration and removal of other restrictions, notably, purchase of land with "1. pro-Turkish manipulation of the European press, 2. winning over of certain financial circles," and third, Jewish experts.[251] In turn, Talaat made some promises, or well-measured small steps, that could be undone or differently interpreted or contradicted by the tacit orders that he gave to the local authorities. Still, he rarely failed to make his "goodwill" appear without changing much on the ground.[252] He abolished the so-called red slip (a discriminatory residence permit that was not functional in the way the government had intended it) but remained restrictive on land purchase and settlement, thereby accommodating Arab demands. These demands had become more vocal in the context of the Arab Congress of June 1913 in Paris. In contrast to Jacobson and Sami Hochberg (the Jewish editor of *Le Jeune Turc*), who were observers at the congress, the majority of congressional participants preferred the League of Private Initiative and Decentralization. In the League's line, it proclaimed solidarity with the Armenians and the ongoing Armenian demands of reform and egalitarian plurality. The Zionist, however, preferred the obvious benefits of a "vertical alliance" (direct access to power) to principles that determined futures in the long term.[253]

Although Talaat made only minor concessions to Zionism, corruption increased the opportunity for land purchases to foreign Jews despite legal restrictions. All in all, a "favorable atmosphere" continued to reign in Istanbul for Zionists. Richard Lichtheim had joined Jacobson in Istanbul in 1913 and was optimistic in early 1914. "The Great Rabbi [Nahum] who is very intimate with Talaat, said to me yesterday verbally, 'The Turks are very satisfied that the [new] American ambassador [Morgenthau] engages in Jewish questions.' This means, of course, that they expect material profits from America if they accommodate the Jews." Nahum, the representative of the Ottoman Jews, had hitherto been very cautious but was now a more open friend of the Zionist agents in Istanbul.[254]

Ottoman Jews collaborating with the Zionists went far in schmoozing the new rulers and the ruling ideology, including cultural unification in a way that betrayed basic Zionist ideals. B. Israil, a journalist for the Zionist-sponsored newspaper *Le Jeune Turc*, for instance, complained in a long open letter to Talaat in early 1914 that there were not only Ottoman people who did not know Turkish but also those who "spent their life in founding many small fatherlands within the father-land, and whose spirits all the time nurtured themselves with non-Ottoman literature." He himself, he confessed, had been "deprived of patriotic consciousness and faith." Praising himself as now possessing a patriotic ideal, he called on Talaat to found an Ottoman Academy that followed the example of the Acadé-mie Française, pointing to the "great Cardinal Richelieu" as a model to emulate. This Ottoman Jew confessed his desire for a corporatist Ottoman society in Gökalp's vein. "The individual belongs," he wrote, "with all its parts and members, with his whole mind, to the society. His worth and greatness depend entirely on allegiance to the society."[255]

The exalted embrace—at least verbally—of Gökalp's ideals by Jewish representatives certainly created some pro-Jewish goodwill among the rulers, yet without in any way changing the fundamental CUP refusal of any Zionist autonomy in Pales-tine. Some notes by Lichtheim in spring 1914 illustrate, for good reasons, a low level of confidence. At times, outright deception reigned. CUP representatives acted largely ad hoc. They and others appeared unworthy of the money that Zionists paid them. Words and promises lost their value rapidly. Restrictions were not lifted. Worse, a Zionist association in Istanbul, first welcomed, almost immediately faced a ban. "Agayev, for years a collaborator of *Le Jeune Turc* for what we pay him monthly [15 pounds], seems to have ... duped us. His meeting [in our favor] yesterday with Talaat ... was an invention."[256]

Money still bought some power. "Now is [an] opportune [time] to bribe Ali Kemal [editor in chief of the newspaper *Peyam*]. He is a great trickster, but [Dr.] Wellisch thinks that we can buy him for 5,000 francs annually. It is anyway urgent to act against the Arab press. I consider it really ridiculous that we do not shut up the [Arab papers] *Karmel* in Haifa and the *Filistin* in Jaffa for a few thousand francs." Lichtheim knew that actually, "the relationship to the Arabs is the key to the situation. If we have no difficulties on this side, we can reach everything, since the government is well disposed." Yet his methods obviously did not fit in with trust building on the ground or prevent fundamental future problems.[257]

Mobilization and world war put Zionism and Palestine in the political background for a while. The topic only reemerged in late 1914 when Cemal began to propose and partly apply to Palestine measures—already topical in regard to Eastern Asia Minor—of surveillance, arrest, and limited expulsion or removal. Regarding Palestine, however, the process never became a priority for Talaat. Still, it gave him a considerable international lever that he successfully used, notably to deflect attention from Armenia. It would be absurd to accuse Zionism for this, yet later there was a stain related to the former attitudes. Successors of those actively interacting with Talaat on a continuous basis supported the denial of the 1915 genocide.[258] This was, and is, an unethical opportunism that trivializes genocide denial. Beyond this issue, some renewed marriages of convenience with Talaat's successors might be considered an exigency of a realpolitik, which the state of Israel and its lobby groups had to manage after 1948.

———

Even if living daily on shaky ground with little confidence, and bitterly experiencing repression in Palestine, the Jews within the Ottoman realm, including those of foreign nationality, were comparatively lucky in World War I. In contrast to almost all other nationals of enemy countries, such as Russia, who were interned or expelled, most of them could remain in Palestine.

Moreover, Germany exempted the German Zionist representatives in Berlin, Istanbul, and Jaffa from military service; non-
German Zionists, including Russian Zionists, enjoyed German
support in Europe and in the Ottoman Empire.

Wangenheim was gratified that Talaat renewed "the fullest
understanding" of the importance of attracting global Jewish
sympathy in November 1914. He feared that Germany would
be held responsible for any act that qualified as anti-Semitism
in the press. He repeatedly expressed the desire that German
support be given publicity, and was annoyed by news concerning the harshness against Jews, especially if exaggerated. Talaat
in turn continued to expect that the Zionists would do all that
they could to suppress bad publicity about Turkey in the world
press.[259] Having obtained strong backing in Istanbul against a
first wave of repression in Palestine, Lichtheim therefore had
reason to be confident. He concluded his letter on 6 January
1915 to the Zionist headquarters in Berlin by saying that "never
since our movement has existed have we been so strongly supported." This efficient support included German and American
diplomacy and a comparatively well-disposed central government in the Ottoman capital.[260]

Zionists enjoyed a privileged, almost continuous access
to the German and American embassies but were only rarely
able to meet Talaat himself, who had the last word concerning
Palestine on domestic and diplomatic levels. Yet they enjoyed
several efficient intermediaries who continually presented their
concerns to the government. When Bahaeddin, Cemal's secretary and former district governor of Jaffa, "issued [on 25 January
1915] a statement that they would fight the seditious and intriguing Zionists who are trying to create a nation and are already
using paper money and stamps," Morgenthau was immediately
informed. He went to Talaat, who phoned Enver. Talaat then

assured Morgenthau that "that order was not authorized and would, if issued, be revoked." He additionally promised that "military service would not be exacted from Jews during the first year of their Ottomanship, and that, any refugees so desiring could return if they agreed to become Ottomans." In principle, foreign Jews had to nationalize in order to be permitted to stay.[261]

On the eve of his comprehensive domestic attack on the Armenians, Talaat appeared particularly keen not to allow harsh measures against Zionism in Palestine and thus to enjoy acceptable press on widely reported Jewish issues. In this vein, Arthur Ruppin, chief of the Palestine office of the Zionist Organization, experienced "a sudden and blatant change in Cemal Pasha's attitude" on 3 March 1915, induced by Talaat's orders.[262]

On 24 April, after Talaat had sent his decisive circulars and immediately before Istanbul's Armenian elite was arrested, the unsuspecting American ambassador invited Talaat and Nahum to dinner. They "sat around the table and talked about the Zionism matter," yet the conversation turned to a more acute issue. Morgenthau understood that "they have made up their mind to crush all possible attempts at revolution." Nahum was "evidently as much afraid of internal trouble as [of] the war." When asked about Armenians, Talaat "admitted that they had arrested a great many of them" (general arrests actually began a few hours later). "Turks seem to realize that they can only govern if they suppress all intellectuals."[263]

The situation remained volatile for any exposed group in Turkey's chauvinist and murderous spring and summer of 1915. Talaat "was determined to destroy all societies and combinations [nonsubmissive groups and organizations]. He said that he has been at the head of revolutionaries and knows what can be done. They want to stamp out every organization,"

Morgenthau noted on 26 April 1915. Wangenheim assured Morgenthau that "he would help Zionists but not Armenians."[264] Talaat made threats at times and had to be courted again and again, but he managed to contain Zionism without destroying it. To achieve this, he combined corruption, extortion, and psychological knowledge of his interlocutors. Via Nahum, he not only censored Morgenthau's public appearances after the latter's return to the United States, lest Jews had to face negative consequences, but even made him "give a Turcophile speech."[265]

This constellation did not change from 1915 to 1916—to the relief of Nahum, who was assured during an interview with Talaat in early 1916 "that there would be nothing done against the Jews," because "he [Talaat] did not want a Jewish Question at present, when they [the committee rulers] had an Armenian Question."[266] The fixation on the Armenians thus helped to deflect attention from—and protect—the Jews. This was still true a year later, and also, in its own way, with regard to the evacuation of Jaffa's Jews in April 1917. Later in the same year, the Russian Revolution and withdrawal from war, the Balfour Declaration, and the conquest of Jerusalem fundamentally changed the political constellation for both Palestine and Armenia-Caucasus.

The evacuation of Jews from Jaffa was preceded by the evacuation of Muslims from Gaza, farther south, in March 1917. Both evacuations anticipated battles with the advancing British troops, including Anzac troops (Australians and New Zealanders), and followed similar procedures, largely based in military reasoning. The evacuations involved many hardships and appeared threatening, especially for Jews, who were still a comparatively small minority in the country. Yet Conde de Ballobar, the Spanish consul of Jerusalem, inquired about the issue and reported that it was "not true that there have been massacres or persecution of Jews." This was also the opinion of the US consul.[267] Nevertheless, press propaganda made sensationalist news of the Jaffa evacuation, as did an ethnocentric historiography during the decades to come. This wronged those involved in the 1917 evacuations, but even more important, the memory of Armenian victimhood was used for sensationalist comparisons but not recognized in its own right.

———

What remained was therefore a problematic heritage in terms of historical honesty. This is poignantly true regarding the depiction of Talaat as a decent and friendly statesman who entertained good working relations with members of Jewish elites in Turkey and Germany and who fought off obstructing and close-minded fellows or an inimical populace. Talaat played well his trump card of allegedly being an almost solitary friend of the Jews or, along with Enver, of the Germans, to secure maximal backing from the addressees of such messages. Thus, he persisted in closely identifying primarily with his CUP friends, but he also knew how to deal with, and best benefit from, Jewish issues. He knew how to play this card even after the Balfour Declaration (see chap. 6, sec. "Imperialisms Face Utopia, Dystopia").

There was not only an ongoing, comparatively uncritical presentation of this powerful pioneer of domestic genocide during World War I in Jewish circles but also, as part of bargaining with him, open propaganda for him and CUP causes. Since this depiction was not critically reflected and revised after war, except by a few leftist and/or liberal voices, but continued into the late twentieth century,[268] it identifies a fundamental problem and historical flaw. It denotes shortcomings in analytically facing evil, and a misunderstanding of relevant historical nexuses in Europe at large. In Germany, it contributed to what this study calls "political schizophrenia." It is a bitter irony that early National Socialists (Nazis) blamed the "all-too-powerful Jewish Press" in Germany for siding not with the upright Talaat but his murderer and the latter's too liberal judges in 1921 (see chap. 6, sec. "Death—and Afterlife—in Germany and Turkey"). The "Jewish press" in Istanbul and beyond had sided well with Talaat during the critical years of his rule.

Finally, regarding Jaffa in spring 1917, we may say that the Armenian genocide contributed not so much to deflecting destructive CUP attention from the Yishuv, as it had in 1915–16, but rather, by its unique horror, to drawing protective global attention to the Yishuv and to the project of Zion, which was still highly vulnerable. Regarding Talaat's position and his relation to Cemal Pasha (the minister of the navy and commander of the Fourth Army), often represented as the third triumvir at the top of the CUP regime, the communication between both on sensitive issues in Palestine reveals that Talaat had the last say on all these matters even before he acceded to the grand vizierate. Besides, he had managed crucial interactions with foreign representatives in the capital by himself since summer 1913. In close relation with the Foreign Office, he assessed issues of foreign pressure, international image, and the vital relation with Germany. All this contributed to his clearly superior position long before he assented to the highest post in the Ottoman administration.

6

Triumph and Fall, Lies and Resilience (1917–21 and After)

IT APPEARS LOGICAL, even belated, that Talaat replaced Said Halim as grand vizier in early 1917. He had largely marginalized and excluded Halim from the close circle of decision makers surrounding him since October 1914 and had removed him from the Foreign Ministry in late October 1915. Said Halim had jointly headed this ministry with the grand vizierate. At last, in 1917, a man from the CUP core group, a thoroughbred komiteci, led the empire. The CUP press called for a new era in which, for the first time, the CUP insiders and power holders would entirely represent the government.

Having warmly welcomed his accession to the grand vizierate, the German and Austro-Hungarian press continued to flatter Talaat Pasha as a great, capable, and enviably energetic statesman. "German schizophrenia," as framed in this study, developed and revealed itself in fascinated, ambitious, and possessive ways, and at times shocked and alienated relations with the cataclysmic CUP, the late Ottoman Empire in general, and the new grand vizier in particular. Talaat knew how to maximally play his cards and how to use Enver's and Cavid's talents as well. If Ludwig wrote in the *Berliner Tageblatt* about a demo-niacally tempered Talaat (see chap. 1, sec. "'On first impres-sion'"), many readers must have picked up on the fascinated overtone for this ingenious, still somewhat exotic, but new and promising type of politician.

Even in his new position as grand vizier, Talaat remained stamped by the trenchant consequences of his anti-Armenian policy, as his main speeches of 1917 reflect. The 1915–16 policy of destruction had left the whole country domestically in not only a more precarious but also a manifestly unethical and lawless state. Large parts of the political class and the army remained marked by a "degenerate morale" (Cavid), nationally, regionally, and locally, corroded by unrecognized, hushed-up crimes. Talaat himself continued to closely monitor surviving Armenians. He continued to fear any eventuality of Armenian autonomy in the future. He proved his and the CUP's ongo-ing attitude once more when deciding in early spring 1918 to implement the violent decimation of the Republic of Arme-nia. Mortally threatened right from the start, this small state was founded from necessity after the Russian retreat from the Caucasus and the collapse of the short-lived Transcaucasian Federation.

Talaat's rise to dictatorial stature at the head of the empire since autumn 1914 had depended on war and on the alliance with Germany, which continued to empower the Ottoman ally. Germany believed this was in the interest of its global stand—although common ground was dramatically lacking. Apart from a few remarkable military achievements, the alliance stood on shaky ground and risked breaking up in spring 1918, as Otto-man forces advanced into the Caucasus beyond what Germany believed to have been agreed. Also, Talaat must have realized that Germany did not support a much-desired recovery of some territory in the Balkans. Still, propaganda liked to celebrate deep commonalities beyond concrete, common, anti-British, and anti-Russian causes. Premodern imperial backgrounds sustained powerful myths in both cases. As far as the modern challenge of egalitarian pluralism was concerned, the CUP and Wilhelminian elites shared, subliminally or openly, conceits of supremacy. Therefore, anti-Semitism paralleled a stance against oriental Christians that directed itself, above all, against Armenians. Among German elites, foremost officers, both very often coexisted.

CUP men and war-prone Wilhelminians reacted against transatlantic dynamics. They abhorred what they considered an unfair and suffocating Anglo-Saxon imperialism, allied with malicious domestic agents of change. Ideologically, the CUP was far ahead of German elites in conspiracy theory, *völkisch* (exaltedly ethnic) nationalism, and demographic engineering. It pioneered a modern, right-wing revolution that blended ethnoreligious conflict with class struggle and a modernizing, antiliberal, and anti-Western political agenda. Until 1918, Berlin connived at systematic mass crimes that its analysts largely failed or neglected to anticipate, and that its politicians refused to prevent and remained unwilling and impotent to stop. Only in spring 1918, in connection with serious tensions in the Caucasus, did politicians and the public in Germany become more alert.

Despite its flaws, the alliance achieved a crushing, though temporary, diplomatic and territorial success in the negotiations at Brest-Litovsk (from 9 December 1917 to 3 March 1918), which Talaat was keen to assume himself, to which followed the Treaty of Bucharest (7 May) with Romania, Russia's war ally since 1916. In the aftermath of the Brest-Litovsk Treaty, Turkey regained the provinces of Batumi, Ardahan, and Kars, which had been lost in the Treaty of Berlin in 1878. After decades of late Ottoman losses, for the first time it acquired territory, thus "proving forever the genius and patriotism of His Excellence" Talaat, as read a message of congratulation.[1] Turkey could now revitalize the expansive dreams of August 1914.

Moreover, Talaat had reason to believe that he would victoriously emerge from the war gamble and determine at least Asia Minor's and the Caucasus's future, thus shaping Turkey for another decade. Even if Syria and Iraq, where Entente troops were advancing, had been partly lost, the perspective was hopeful in late 1917. Talaat had reached the zenith of his career. He defied the secret Entente partition plans of spring 1916 and the Balfour Declaration of fall 1917, which had all gained publicity in late 1917. (Sean McKeekin has rightly emphasized that the well-known Sykes-Picot Agreement of 16 May 1916 must be considered in its close relationship to the simultaneous agreement with Sazonov.)[2] It might then seem that Talaat departed to new and bright horizons in a fresh and vigorous grand vizierate that was bound to better times of the Ottoman state. "Turkey welcomed with most sweet hopes the dawn of the year 1918," as Ottoman deputy Emmanuilidis put it.[3] Yet the domestic corrosion of CUP rule was too obvious to reasonably believe in such restoration.

Grasping Western and transatlantic dynamics only rudimentarily, Talaat understood, only in a painful process lasting from July to September 1918, that the world war was lost for the Central powers. Yet the CUP government had also fought the war on other front lines than the European powers. Losing the war gamble, Talaat therefore did not lose everything. In exile in Berlin, in a defeated Germany, he kept working for the "patriotic cause," the minimal goal of which was still a Turkish national home in Asia Minor, hopefully including parts of the Caucasus and Mesopotamia. Post-1918 Germany remained far more divided than Turkey. After a few months of confusion and initial soul-searching in postwar Turkey, but still imprinted with years of CUP indoctrination and war politics, large sections of the elites rapidly unified behind the call for an armed fight in favor of a Muslim sovereignty in Asia Minor. Although depressed and partly disoriented, and no longer master of all (post-)CUP networks and instruments of power, Talaat was the most authoritative and pragmatic among the top CUP leaders in exile.

General Mustafa Kemal, hitherto an inferior rival of Enver Pasha, but since late 1919 corresponding with Talaat from a superior position, started to inherit Talaat's political role, including his staff and, finally, his post-1918 organization of Turkish nationalism in European exile. Talaat rapidly sought contact with Mustafa Kemal (Atatürk), the new leader of the unifying movement, who managed a reorganization of power starting in the Ottoman eastern provinces. Not only did the Entente powers have scant access after Russia's withdrawal, but an intact Ottoman army was positioned there that enjoyed a large scope of action. Local notables, Sunni Kurdish chieftains in particular, refused to restore loot and land to returning Christian survivors, and were therefore receptive to Kemal's rhetoric of saving, in a joint effort, the sultanate-caliphate from foreign powers and foreign justice. Thus, from spring 1919, Kemal Pasha resumed, with ex-CUP forces, domestic war against Greek and Armenian rivals. These were partly backed by victors of World War I who had, however, abstained from occupying Asia Minor.

The war for Asia Minor—in national diction, again a war of salvation and independence, thus in-line with what had begun in 1913—accomplished Talaat's demographic Turkification beginning on the eve of World War I. Resuming Talaat's Pontus policy of 1916–17, this again involved collective physical annihilation, this time of the Rûm of Pontus at the Black Sea. Although renouncing pan-Turkism, early interwar Turkish nationalism was, against Cavid's repeated affirmations, the continuation of a world war nationalism that had by no means been temporary. It was still radically xenophobic in the broad meaning of the term: hostile and fearful vis-à-vis any forces and identities outside the Turkish-Muslim war ummah. Cavid's argument during World War I was utilitarian, of course, but still demonstrated his weak historical sense. The same is even truer for his silly argument in mid-June 1916 concerning Jagow, the German foreign minister, that even if badly handled in 1915, the Armenian issue was now finished for good, and not to be revisited in any way. Talaat's friend Cavid was again minister of finance from February 1917 onward.[4]

As Cavid had predicted in August 1915, when he learned about the anti-Armenian abomination, Mehmed Talaat was killed in Berlin in 1921 by an ARF-commissioned avenger. The Berlin trial against his killer not only publicized the abysses of 1910s Ottoman, but revealed a seminal polarization in German society and German understanding of history. Its verdict, the acquittal of the "avenger," was therefore controversial. The public discussion of a crime to be labeled as "genocide" by an attentive observer of the trial, the student of law Raphael Lemkin, was incisive but split. Within a few years, the nationalist "pro-Talaat current" won the political upper hand in Germany.[5]

Grand Vizier Talaat Pasha's "New Turkey"

The "new," "young" Turkey that Talaat and his acolytes declared in early 1917 was an imperial single-party regime in which Talaat openly held dictatorial power. He was now not only grand vizier but still minister of the interior and, shortly, finance minister—and also, de facto, foreign minister, because Nessimi Bey, the official foreign minister, was a weak politician. "With Talaat, who for a long time [held] the real power, the strongest and most important man of the Young Turk Party ha[d] become the leader of the Turkish state," the German ambassador Richard von Kühlmann reported. A special medal was coined in honor of the new grand vizier to praise him as a model of a successful Turk now at the head of the state: "The Turks owe their triumphs to their courage and pertinacity. Tal'at Paşa—grand vizier and minister of the interior—the Sublime Ottoman State."[6]

The new regime combined ongoing Muslim self-assertion with a resurgence of strong pan-Turkist tendencies since late 1917, yet it foreshadowed restricted polity, personality cult, and top-down cultural revolutions of the interwar period. "We have not the courage to freely express our thoughts," Cavid wrote on the eve of Talaat's inaugural address.[7] The new grand vizier presented to the parliament his cabinet and his program, written by Cavid and Cahid, on 15 February 1917, and the parliament gave its support without a dissenting vote. The applause lingered for several minutes when Talaat appeared. Many times, his speech reaped keen applause and interjections of "God, give success!" He ended it by saying that "we will continue to do our duty, relying on divine benevolence and the prophet's [Muhammad's] spiritual help."[8]

Grand Vizier Talaat's speech started, importantly, by narrating a history of national salvation. Plagued by chronic crises, the country had at last achieved peace in early 1914 after the Libyan and Balkan Wars, but had almost immediately been forced by World War I to perform unprecedented commitment and sacrifices in very difficult circumstances, thus "honorably purifying itself from all its humiliations." Self-pity met self-adulation, whose addressee was "the nation," but, implicitly, its foremost representative, the orator himself. The nation (*millet*, now in the sense of the Muslim Ottoman nation) succeeded in adding new heroism to an illustrious Ottoman history. The speech reached a peak, inducing emotional interjections, when Talaat evoked the specter of an enemy that had wanted to remove "us" from Istanbul and the Bosporus into Anatolia. But after his "ridiculous threats," the enemy had to flee before the face of "our heroic army" on land and sea. Thus, national salvation started in 1913 but clearly culminated at Gallipoli in 1915.

Immediately turned into a political myth, and as such used and celebrated by Talaat, Gallipoli was henceforth commemorated as the place where the modern Turkish-Muslim nation had succeeded in defending, as Talaat put it, its existence (*muhafaza-i mevcudiyet*), that is, "our right to live" (*hakk-ı hayatımız*), and thus exemplarily assured its survival, future, and perpetuation.[9] Though presenting the victory at Gallipoli as almost purely Ottoman, Talaat recognized the alliance with the Central powers as a "matter of death and life." He did not leave any doubt about the new cabinet's loyalty to the alliance.

Leading to the second part of his speech, he emphasized the government's "perfect will" to introduce reforms in accordance with European civilization and the needs of the "present age," but conceded that wartime problems did not yet allow for the envisaged "fundamental and profound actions and revolutions." Still, the government set on German and Austrian experts to enhance education, reform law, and build infrastructure, and sent "a great many youth to Germany and Austria for studies in science and art" (those in Switzerland risked, in contrast, reading uncensored press and coming in contact with the main opposition in exile residing there). He later said that he believed "only in one civilization in the world," and that Turkey, "to be

saved, must be joined to civilization." Talaat concluded the second part of his speech with the fervently applauded sentence,
"It is our greatest desire to implement law in the country," in a
country, as Cavid wrote in his diary, where lawless compulsion
was a plague.[10]

Thus the new grand vizier had declared the main goals of
his government: thorough reforms, including of the whole law
system; the implementation of the rule of law; and redressing
the economy. Qualified voices timely reminded him of the realities on the ground, and his trip into Anatolia in late 1916 had
shown him the catastrophic state of the country. Then—as in
his letter to Ali Haydar—and at other occasions, he cloaked
the realities with euphemism. As mentioned, in quoting his
collaborator Hamid Kapancızâde, Talaat fully squandered the
challenge of reestablishing the rule of law in 1917–18. Still, in
September 1917, the 1917 CUP Congress broached pioneering
reforms of law, including family law, which Atatürk's so-called
Law Revolution (*Hukuk Devrimi*) implemented in a more radical and comprehensive way, importing ready-made European
codes. Talaat also reformed the calendar, thus preparing for the
Kemalist adoption of the Western calendar. His modernization
included "employment of women as nurses and in charitable
activities, in army shops and in labor battalions behind the
front; . . . extension of the University of Istanbul; new institutions in architecture, arts, and music; translation of the Koran
into Turkish, and even conduction of the ritual in Turkish in a
few mosques in the capital."[11]

Annual congresses of the CUP had not taken place in 1914
and 1915. The 1916 Congress had been less unifying and more
turbulent than the Central Committee had hoped. Main issues
of discontent were the ongoing war instead of (a separate)
peace, scandals in matters of supply, and the abuses regarding

Armenian goods. Even more so than during his inaugural speech in February, at the 1917 Congress, Talaat demonstrated how much he entrenched himself in lies and wishful thinking. As during the 1916 Congress, he emphasized once more the Russian attacks in October 1914 as the reason for Turkey's siding with the Central powers and its entrance into war in November 1914. He used more than half of his address to explain that "in the name of humanity and justice," Ottoman atrocities against Armenians and others were propagandistic lies (after war defeat, he blamed the Germans, who "overruled" him while trying to prevent extermination).[12] He conjured the CUP's historical mission "to institute justice and freedom based on law," that is, to realize a state's basic duty. By far not the only international leader to resort to lies and wishful thinking in World War I, Talaat, before a particularly docile and intimidated public, was much more tempted than others to hide behind the veils of oblivion. His mantra read that "we are only fighting for our existence, our independence, our free [nationalist] development, and our progress."[13]

Back to Talaat's inaugural speech on 15 February 1917. Its third part dealt with economy, finances, and the supply of the country. This was a sensitive, even infamous topic because of large-scale deadly famine on one side and fabulous enrichment on the other. In late 1915 and at the 1916 Congress, it had already led to turbulent scenes within the CUP, and did so again, this time in the parliament, in autumn 1917.[14] Certain CUP men, or people whom the CUP favored, were involved in countrywide corruption. Talaat assured the deputies that the harvest was much better this year. He presided over a General Commission for Supply, now taking care of all the needs of the country. Yet people continued to perish from hunger, and there were attempts at cannibalism, for example, in Diyarbekir prison.[15]

The government would be disciplined in its expenses and take out foreign loans only as needed. The supreme goal of national industrialization, however, demanded foreign investment and help, as did progress in the educational system, in science and knowledge (*ilm ü irfan*). In its rhetoric and contents, the second part—and elements of the third part—of Talaat's inaugural speech could almost verbally be from Atatürk.

Paradigmatically and lastingly, Talaat blended the Ottoman imperial myth with Turkish nationalism and revolutionist innovation. "Nationalism," "revolution," and "European civilization" logically became the catchwords of his grand vizierate. They were attached to an early narrative of national salvation, independence, and revolution that the press and the intelligentsia close to the CUP willingly and vocally supported. This remarkable narrative was reproducible and adaptable. According to its 1917 version, national salvation and liberation started in 1913 and culminated in the grand vizierate of Talaat, one of the "most preeminent figures of our revolution."[16]

————

Quoting and echoing Talaat's speech and program, the main press in the capital announced a henceforth energetic building up of the "new Turkey." Moreover, the allies' press organs extensively joined in the chorus of admiration, reproducing the discourse of marvelous authoritarian, revolutionist liberation. This was attentively tracked in the Ottoman capital and served the enhanced self-image.[17] "The leaders of the committee have accomplished an Ottoman revolution and saved the Ottomans from a deathly bondage and perdition, and taken the destiny of the state into their hands. From that moment a new era, an exalted era began," Ahmed Ağaoğlu wrote. "They were so audacious as to assume full independence within the state, once the general war broke out. . . . During the war, they proved to the whole world that Ottomans inspired by the spirit of Union and Progress were capable of asserting themselves in a resolute and effective way. . . . His Excellence Talaat Pasha is doubtless the highest person emerging from the Ottoman revolution. His personality is the living proof of the Ottomans' and Turks' vitality and energy."[18]

For Yunus Nadi (Abalıoğlu), another leading intellectual and journalist (and afterward also under Atatürk), Talaat's program "translates the sentiments and opinions of the whole nation. The world may be assured that in this will and resoluteness the whole Ottoman nation stands behind the government of Talaat Pasha."[19] Ahmed Emin (Yalman), a leading Turkish intellectual still in the early second half of the twentieth century, emphasized the unique moment of unity in Turkey's political history after 1908. He saw the reign of unprecedented, mutual confidence and intimacy in the capital. The parliament and "the whole nation" offered the new cabinet well-merited, unanimous support. Ahmed Emin called it a "government of law and peace."[20] The rhetoric of a young, new, and modernizing Turkey covered the stern fact of the actual political abyss. Most members of the now full-fledged CUP cabinet had renounced the thorny path toward a modern social contract, sought war, and welcomed the destruction of—in terms of modernization— the most educated, industrious, and promising part of the Ottoman nation.

After his and the CUP's crisis in 1910–12, dismissing constitutional patriotism, Talaat had wed a revised, now authoritarian, concept of the CUP power organization with the myth of superior Ottoman state tradition, and embraced Gökalp's Turkism. Thus inspired, he allowed for combining ongoing CUP power concentration, closely tied to the state, with primordial Turkic-Muslim solidarity and a fantasy called "Turan." This symbol blended myth and modernity, exalting pan-Turkism and pan-Islamism.[21] A perhaps amusing but significant episode in Talaat's insouciant, strictly Turkey-focused dealing with major global currents and issues is the 1917 Socialist Peace Conference. To be convened by the Second International in Stockholm in summer 1917, this contested conference was prepared from spring 1917 by delegates from various countries. Although the ideology of his single-party regime had nothing to do with peace-seeking internationalist socialism, Talaat did not want to miss any diplomatic opportunities. He therefore prepared to send CUP intimates like Mazliah, Hüseyinzâde Ali, and Akil Muhtar, but in the end, the delegation from Turkey was not admitted. Talaat's preparation had included the makeup of a fake Turkish Socialist Party with its own seal.[22]

Talaat focused his new program ostentatiously on the restoration of law and order, although he continued his policy of Muslim Turkification in the economy and demography of Asia Minor, thus sealing his fundamental breach of constitutional law. "Chauvinism" (*şovinizm*) and "extremist nationalism" (*müfrit nasyonalizm*) reigned, as Cavid repeatedly noted, but he himself thought at times that temporary chauvinism served the Turkish position in dealing with Germany.[23] Despite strong reservations, Cavid accepted, out of an unequal friendship, the invitation to be Talaat's minister of finance and to act in many more dealings as Talaat's direct envoy. "Based on our brotherhood, I request your consent [to the ministerial post]," Talaat telegraphed to Cavid. A day later, on 4 February 1917, Cavid answered that "I accept [the post] as an act of friendship and self-sacrifice." At the expense of his personal and intellectual coherence, Cavid sentimentally overemphasized his bonds to

Talaat and "self-sacrifice." He now orbited even more around Turkey's strongman.[24]

Both were in daily communication and regularly sat down to discuss ongoing affairs for hours. Cavid perceived his leading friend, at times, as affected and sad, foremost in the context of corruption within the CUP. Faced with palpable dysfunction, Talaat often sought to save the communication among his political friends with a joke.[25] In such situations, Cavid felt both anger and pity toward Talaat but justified his own, renewed commitment by saying that his love and responsibility for the country went beyond everything else. "Without giving in to bad sentiments in contrast to them [to CUP "friends," notably Nâzım], I considered it a duty of conscience to try saving what could be saved from this ship [of state] that manifested cracks and fractures everywhere." Compared to Hamid (Kapancızâde), Cavid lacked the balance of emotional and intellectual distance. He contented himself with writing down his frustration in his diary, as shortly before entering the cabinet: "I have pity for Talaat. How much I had wished that in a cabinet, which for the first time is really ours, there [would be] nothing rotten and dilapidated. But what can I do? He does not want to give up his well-known evil principles and habits."[26]

Despite his lucid insights and deep emotions in August–September 1915, Cavid went as far as to actively back Talaat's and the CUP's will to abort any future Armenian autonomy. From spring 1917, he drew Talaat's attention to the fact that the treaties with Germany guaranteed the Ottoman territorial status quo, but did not prevent the possibility of Arab and Armenian autonomies and Armenian return. Thus, a stipulation must be added. Cavid had correctly understood German diplomacy's repeated emphasis, since summer 1915, that it would not be able to defend Turkey during postwar peace talks in matters regarding the Armenians; this was the only consistent and sustainable point that it made against the CUP's Armenian policy. In vain, Cavid hoped to add his point. Moreover, he was convinced and feared in November 1917 that "a democratic Russia will not conclude peace without having addressed the Armenian issue,"[27] yet, soon ceasing to become democratic, Soviet Russia sacrificed this issue.

Sadness was Talaat's strongest "weapon" to disarm Cavid, to show him some consensus, telling him what he wanted to hear and bringing him again to his line of thinking without actually changing anything. Talaat's charm was sometimes combined with a melancholy that mollified even angry people in his presence. After six months in the grand vizierate, Cavid strongly criticized his friend: "In contradiction to what we promised, we have not done anything to make law reign," thus losing honor and integrity. "These words [of mine] made the grand vizier sad. . . . He too has begun to be pessimistic."[28] Pessimism, however, turned to high spirits after the geohistorical changes of fall 1917.

Cavid himself remained unable to draw any consequences. He continued working in the CUP government, making do with writing about his despair, caused by characterless committee members; an almost total lack of rule of law; and Talaat, the head of all, who made him feel both pity and anger.[29]

———

"Our intellectual life is since many years imprisoned," read a line by the twenty-seven-year-old collaborator Necmettin Sadık in Ziya Gökalp's (and the CUP's) new opinion journal *Yeni Mecmua* (New Journal) in early 1918. Manifestly, in order to counter the widespread feeling of intellectual repression in his "new Turkey," Talaat joined a meeting of journalists, including Necmettin and Hüseyin Cahid, in early March 1918, where he underlined the need of freedom of press and where "his genuineness and plainness increased the deference vis-à-vis him." Talaat argued that "it can do its duty only if it is free. We depend on the unique support coming from the press." Yet he "feared something," Sadık observed, and the situation was odd. Cahid, senior journalist and member of the CUP Central Committee, declared to the assembly that from now on the government and the press were friends that would go hand in hand. Misunderstandings had been a matter of the past, the "butchers" (censors) would henceforth apply their "scalpels" with restraint.

But there was one condition: "Let us always all together with the government struggle against the worst enemy of the country, the political reaction . . . Against the intellectual political reaction, against the dark forces which cause this reaction, let us all intellectuals of the country ally." Inspired by Cahid and Talaat, Necmettin noted that the word "reaction" had now lost its old meaning of religious and conservative reaction (as in the April 1909 coup). "Political reaction means from now on a sorrowful attitude that does not even mention its topic, but that is buried in bitter memories of past times . . . That we feel from time to time the distress of a nightmare is the reaction caused by dark forces. This is what we all, and foremost the press, must fear." Such "struggle against reaction" excluded reckoning with, or substantial criticism pertaining to, recent history. "Freedom of press" depended on whole-hearted participation in a war against evil defined by the single-party regime. Those worried by soul-searching were stigmatized as part of a conspiracy made up by dark forces.

Necmettin Sadık—an upcoming journalist and very young professor of sociology at Istanbul University, and later foreign minister of Turkey—bought what senior journalist Cahid and "our great statesman [Talaat]" preached that evening of 6 March 1918. The government would soon offer all necessary freedom to the press association. For him, the ideal of a constructive collaboration with the state went along with a renewed embrace of the great ideal of Turan, as forcefully reminded by an (unnamed) orator at the meeting, and by Talaat, who had just returned from successful negociations at Brest-Litovsk.[30]

Defiant Revolutionists, Troubled Wilhelminians

In the course of war action and propaganda, Germany enmeshed itself more and more in contradictions, pipe dreams, and unhealthy assessments regarding its alliance with CUP Turkey. Or it was simply resigned to what intelligent minds recognized as a fatal imbroglio. Talaat, in turn, feared losing Germany or putting their relations at risk—as when the United States declared war against Germany and Austria but not the Ottoman Empire.[31] The German leadership and press considered Talaat a friend and warrantor of safe relations, and Emperor Wilhelm II honored him by bestowing upon him the highly prestigious Order of the Black Eagle, which Talaat received with "deepest and subservient gratitude." This conferring of an order contributed to Talaat's prestige, both in Turkey and in Germany, and was understood in Istanbul as a strong confirmation of German-Turkish friendship even beyond wartime.[32] The same is true for Kaiser Wilhelm's visit in the Ottoman capital in October 1917.

Many Germans regarded Talaat as not only a successful statesman but also an honest, kind, and admirable person. "No one could escape the charm of his sympathetic and attractive personality," Liman von Sanders, the chief of the German

FIGURE 18: Kaiser Wilhelm II in the Ottoman capital, 15 October 1917. *In front of him:* Sheykhulislam Musa Kazım Efendi. *Behind him:* Talaat. *On his left:* Sultan Mehmed V. *Behind the sultan:* Enver Pasha (akg-images, Berlin, Sammlung Archiv für Kunst und Geschichte).

military mission, confessed. A wide range of Germans, such as Ambassador Bernstorff (who succeeded von Kühlmann in July 1917), journalist Friedrich Schrader, and Carl F. Lehmann-Haupt, professor of history at the Istanbul University, shared this view. Casual impressions mingled with preconceived opinions inspired by the press, and some fascination by Talaat himself—his energy, self-representation, and witty-melancholic charm.[33]

Again and again, diplomats wishfully interpreted tactical concessions or good words in their communication with the Ottoman government as a promising change, although they were acquainted with its fundamental dysfunction. In this vein, von Kühlmann, Wolff-Metternich's successor in Istanbul (before becoming German foreign minister), emphasized the "entire victory of the Turkish-nationalist direction" within the CUP "from which the large-scale extermination of the Armenians" had resulted. "The atrocities of the anti-Armenian will at long sight press down on the Turkish name," besides degrading the whole country, he concluded. Yet, too rapidly, he suddenly believed or wanted to believe by mid-February 1917 that Talaat's inaugural speech, and his words on equality before the law, was a seminally new direction in Ottoman national politics.[34]

Many Germans had not understood, or did not want to understand, even at the end of war, that Talaat was the architect of the genocide, although Wangenheim's and Wolff-Metternich's reports did not leave any doubt on this point. They confused Talaat's at times "tragic mind" with humanity, identified with him as a heroic defender of nation and empire, or simply admired his loyalty and intelligence despite his lack of education. "We cannot find a more loyal friend of Germany than him," Ambassador Bernstorff wrote, calling Talaat an "unselfish patriot" and also, with blatant prejudice and pretension, "diligent, as far as this is possible in the case of an Oriental."[35] Liman von Sanders admitted that the Central Committee "has ever remained a mystery" to him. Independent of their rank, German representatives in Istanbul were scarcely accorded "a look into the interior of the Turkish government mechanism," not even a man as powerful as Liman von Sanders.[36]

On the turbulent eve of World War I, envisaging general war, Germany had merged its fate with a revolutionist committee at the head of an empire that neither its generals nor its diplomats understood. They had unknowingly fallen into hot water and were building on shaky ground: high officers wanted to make Turkey a "German Egypt," not less than those like Ernst Jäckh, who wanted to develop a strong and sovereign "Turkish

Turkey" as a key to German world power.[37] Whereas fear of domestic revolutions increased in European countries from 1916, particularly Russia but also Germany, the rulers in Istanbul did not need to dread organized resistance. The opposition was crushed since June 1913, the press entirely censured, the civil and military organizations in firm CUP hands, and the SO an additional instrument of control and terror during a permanent state of emergency. Deathlike silence reigned after genocide. Large parts of the remaining society were intimidated, while others had satisfied their greed of spoliation. Only in the last months of World War I did chronic, subliminal complaints against the administration publically surface. Power struggles, as usual in mobilized armies, though not harmless (see below for Yakub Cemil), remained under control.

Throughout his diary, Cavid accused Germany of having dragged Turkey into active war. At times, he exploited this half-true argument in his almost permanent negotiations on loans, the Baghdad Railway construction, and further issues. He and Talaat capitalized on the psychological fact that in July 1914, Germany had shown vulnerability. "Once it saw trouble ahead, it remembered us." If it had wanted the alliance before July 1914, there would be perfect trust, Cavid reiterated to German diplomat Frederic Rosenberg, secretary for Oriental Affairs in the Berlin Foreign Office. "Talaat and Enver stand and fall with us," according to Bernstorff.[38] Yet Turkey's alliance and interaction with Wilhelminian Germany was as crucial for both sides as it was problematic, having introduced the Eastern Question into the logic and dynamics of a total global war and jihad.

"The conclusion of the alliance, the work of Talaat Pasha and his companions, inscribed Talaat Pasha into world history," the Vienna *Freie Presse* aptly put it in May 1917, when the new grand vizier visited Berlin, Vienna, and Sofia. Foremost, it

DEUTSCHE LEVANTE-ZEITUNG

Organ

der Deutschen Levante=Linie, der Hamburg=Amerika Linie, der Mittelmeer=Linie Rob. M. Sloman jr., der Hamburger Vereinigung der Freunde Bulgariens, des Deutsch=Persischen Wirtschaftsverbandes, der Deutsch=Türkischen Vereinigung, des Deutsch=Bulgarischen Vereins und des Deutschen Balkan=Vereins.

Diese Zeitschrift erscheint am 1. und 16. jeden Monats und dient zur Förderung der Handelsbeziehungen mit den Ländern des Mittel=, Schwarzen und Roten Meeres, des Balkans, Marokko, Arabien und Persien. — Jahrespreis bei der Post in Deutschland Mk. 6.—. Im Auslande abonniert man bei den deutschen und ausländischen Postanstalten; unter Streifband direkt vom Verlag bezogen Mk. 10.— jährlich. In Griechenland nimmt die Buchhandlung Eleftheroudakis & Barth in Athen das Abonnement entgegen. Im Buchhandel kann Bezug durch die Firma Wilhelm Opetz, Leipzig, Brüderstraße 61, erfolgen. Anzeigenpreis für vierspaltige Nonpareillezeile oder deren Raum im Anzeigenteil Mk. 1.—. Aufschläge für Platzvorschriften: zweite und vierte Umschlagseite 50 %, dritte Umschlagseite und Fahrplan=Einlagen 20 %. Für Kleine Anzeigen: die viergespaltene Zeile 50 Pf. netto. Redaktion und Verlag: Hamburg I, Levantehaus. Telegrammadresse: Levantezeitung Hamburg. Fernsprecher: Im Fernverkehr: Fernamt Nr. 45; im Stadts und Vorortsverkehr: Gruppe 6, Nr. 4561–4567, 4697 und 4751. Sprechzeit der Schriftleiters: 12–1½ Uhr.

| Nummer 9 | Hamburg, den 1. Mai 1917 | 7. Jahrgang |

(Nachdruck aller Artikel, auch teilweiser, nur mit genauer Quellenangabe gestattet.)

Großwesir Talaat in Deutschland.

Unter lebhafter Anteilnahme und warmer Zustimmung der politischen Kreise in Konstantinopel hat der Großwesir TALAAT-Pascha seine Reise nach Deutschland angetreten. Ein doppelt bemerkenswerter Schritt, einmal als Zeichen für den Umschlag in den Anschauungen, wie sie bislang in der Türkei herrschend waren, und sodann aber als ein sichtbarer Ausdruck der Einheitlichkeit der Politik der Mittelmächte.

Wenn alle die Diplomatie der alten Schule im allgemeinen sich mit dem Mantel des Geheimnisvollen zu umgeben stets bemüht war, so hat sich die türkische Politik im besonderen immer bestrebt, Europäern jeden Einblick in ihre Absichten und Beweggründe zu erschweren und eine Welt für sich zu bilden. Am Goldenen Horn lebte man in seinen eigenen orientalischen Gedankengängen und Anschauungen, nicht zum Vorteil für das Land. Die Wirklichkeit fand viel zu wenig Berücksichtigung und der Spekulation ward ein viel zu großer Spielraum gewährt. Und so kam man in Europa zu dem Urteil, daß die Fähigkeit, reale Verhältnisse nüchtern zu erfassen, dem Orientalen überhaupt selten gegeben sei. Nicht daß man der türkischen Rasse ein besonderes Unvermögen hätte zuschieben wollen. Der orientalischen Psyche im allgemeinen gab man die Schuld, daß so oft und so wenig mit der Wirklichkeit gerechnet wurde. Freiherr VON DER GOLTZ hat dieses Hindernis 1913 in einer Schrift mit den Worten charakterisiert: »Der Mangel an Augenmaß für das Erreichbare, das Sichverlieren in phantastischen oder rein theoretischen Spekulationen ist keineswegs nur ein Bildungsfehler. Er scheint in der ganzen Disposition des orientalischen Geistes zu liegen; denn man findet ihn nicht bloß in der Armee, sondern auch auf andern Gebieten öffentlicher Tätigkeit wieder. Das Naheliegende, Einfache genießt kein Ansehen. Durchweg werden die Pläne zu groß, ohne richtigen Zusammenhang mit dem praktischen Bedürfnis und ohne sorgfältige Prüfung der gegebenen Bedingungen entworfen.«

Der Hauptfehler, unter dem die Türkei bisher gelitten hat, dürfte jedoch mehr darin liegen, daß die leitenden Kreise weder ihr eigenes Land, seine Kräfte und Bedürfnisse kannten, noch die Verhältnisse in der übrigen Welt zu übersehen vermochten. Das Effenditum, d. h. die Beamtenkaste, die aus jahrhundertlanger Überlieferung ein Vorrecht auf die Verwaltung des Landes für sich in Anspruch nahm, kam aus Konstantinopel und den übrigen türkischen Großstädten kaum heraus. Höchst zufrieden mit sich selbst, beanspruchte sie lediglich auf Grund der Beziehungen ihrer Verwandtschaft zum Regierungsstaat für sich das Recht zum Eintritt in das Beamtentum und zum Zutritt zur Staatskrippe, einerlei ob die nötigen persönlichen Fähigkeiten und Kenntnisse vorhanden waren, auch einerlei ob in der Staatsmaschinerie eine Lücke auszufüllen war.

In diesen Verhältnissen haben die Führer der jungen Türkei glücklicherweise Wandel geschaffen. Wie in den verschiedenen Städten des Osmanischen Reiches ganze alte, düstere Stadtteile niedergerissen wurden, um ihnen Licht und Luft zu gewähren, so macht auch die neue Verwaltung jetzt die Augen auf, um sich im heimischen Lande nach seinem Zustand und dem daraus erwachsenden Notwendigkeiten umzusehen und sich auch in der Fremde zu unterrichten, um Vergleichsmöglichkeiten und Verbesserungsanregungen zu finden. Man hat eingesehen, wie wenig es angeht, sich in eigenen Gedanken eine Türkei auszumalen, die fern ist von der Wirklichkeit, auch ist man sich darüber klar geworden, daß sich der alte Lieblingswunsch »La Turchia farà da se« nicht verwirklichen läßt. Dieser Erkenntnis Raum geschaffen zu haben, ist schon das wenigsten ein Verdienst von TALAAT.

Wohl dem Volke, dem große Zeiten große Männer gebären! In dem gewaltigen Kriege, in dem es schon um Sein oder Nichtsein der Türkei ging, ehe sie sich den alten Mittelmächten anschloß, waren für das Osmanische Reich Wirklichkeitspolitiker ebenso nötig wie ein tapferes Heer und hervorragende Führer. Denn der größte Augenblick türkischer Geschichte stand bevor. Der osmanische Staatsmann, der geschichtlich und politisch klar zu denken vermochte, mußte wissen, daß die Schicksalsstunde seines Landes gekommen war, daß es galt, alles zu sichern, was die Zukunft seines Vaterlandes und seines Volkes brauchte. Ein solcher Staatsmann war unsern türkischen Freunden in TALAAT beschert. Nicht beschwert durch das Effendidünkel der alten Zeit, hat er sich durch geistige Talente und sittliche Vorzüge zu seiner heutigen Stellung emporgearbeitet

---

FIGURE 19: The German-speaking (except Swiss) press praised Talaat as the savior of imperial Turkey, a model for progressive politics, and a pillar of the common war alliance (*Deutsche Levante-Zeitung*, 1 May 1917) (Staats- und Universitätsbibliothek Hamburg).

inscribed him and the Eastern Question into German and Austrian history. The alliance with the Central powers made Talaat
an internationally respected leader. He was considered a strong
imperial leader in the line of Sultan Abdulhamid II, however,
more modern and energetic, and thus more promising and
exemplary. During Abdulhamid's funeral in Istanbul in mid-
February 1918 at the latest, Talaat and his CUP fellows publicly
endorsed the legacy of this ruler whom they had demonized
before. They discovered themselves, surprisingly, serving similar logics of state power, though much more radically.[39]

The year 1917 had started well for the Quadruple Alliance
(Bulgaria was included since September 1915), as the Central
powers finished the conquest of Romania in January, thus
largely securing the Balkans on their behalf. The February Revolution weakened the Russian army and nurtured hope for a
separate peace.[40] Insofar as Russia, the formidable enemy in the
East, wanted peace for good after the October Revolution, and
promising negotiations began in Brest-Litovsk, 1917 also ended
well—despite domestic corruption that had again depressed
the general mood during the months before. In October 1917,
the conclusion of a military convention, planned for the postwar era according to the treaty of 11 January 1915, prematurely
amended the Turkish-German alliance to enhance military
cooperation. An additional treaty on 28 September 1916 had
precluded a separate peace. It completed the general treaty
of 11 January 1915 that had replaced the 2 August 1914 treaty.
Again prematurely, as it were, it wanted to maximally secure the
interests and advantages of both countries "according to their
sacrifices and efforts," once a general peace was concluded. It
emphasized that both countries "fight with all their means to
realize a common goal." Austria had joined the new general
treaty on 21 March 1916.[41]

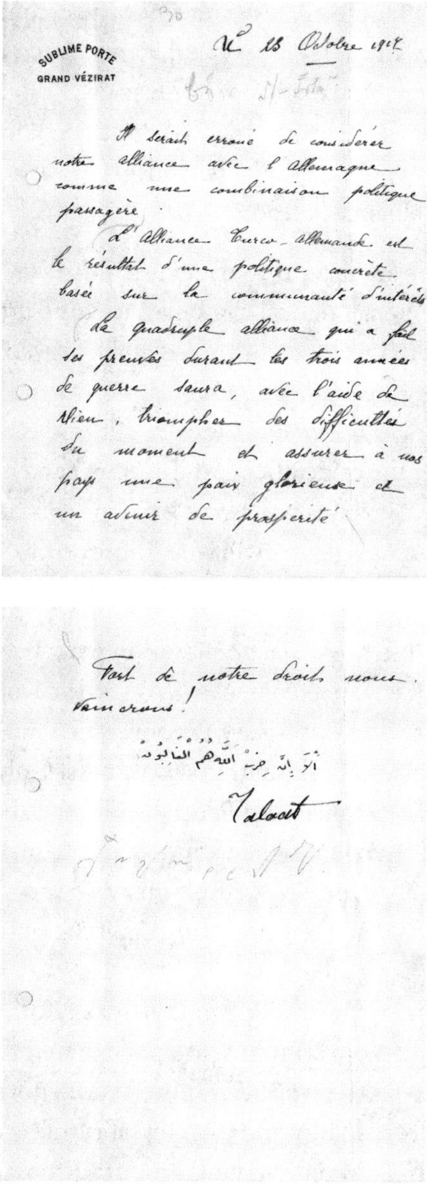

SUBLIME PORTE
GRAND VÉZIRAT

Le 23 Octobre 1917

Il serait erroné de considérer notre alliance avec l'Allemagne comme une combinaison politique passagère.

L'Alliance Turco-allemande est le résultat d'une politique concrète basée sur la communauté d'intérêts.

La quadruple alliance qui a fait ses preuves durant les trois années de guerre saura, avec l'aide de Dieu, triompher des difficultés du moment et assurer à nos pays une paix glorieuse et un avenir de prospérité.

Fort de notre droit, nous vaincrons!

ألا إن حزب الله هم الغالبون

Talaat

FIGURE 20: Talaat's notice of 23 October 1917 on the alliance with Germany, sealed by Surah 5:56 (Ernst Jäckh Papers, Yale University Library).

Five days after the military convention was concluded, on 23 October 1917, Talaat left a personal, handwritten notice, probably for Foreign Office collaborator Ernst Jäckh, but certainly to the attention of all German friends in politics. It may be read as a profession of political faith and concerned, significantly, only the German alliance partner:

> It would be an error to consider our alliance with Germany as an ephemeral political combination. The Turkish-German alliance is the result of a concrete policy based on the community of interests. The Quadruple Alliance has proved itself during three years of war; it will, with God's help, triumph over the difficulties of the moment and ensure for our countries a glorious peace and a prosperous future. On the strength of our right, we will win! Those on God's side will be victors [Surah 5:56, written in Arabic, the rest in French].[42]

It is plausible that Talaat believed in what he wrote in this informal notice. The reference to God and the Koran was obviously not part of a vocabulary for domestic purposes. Cavid's and Hayri's diaries confirm this seriousness. Only if Germany made a common cause with Russia would the alliance lose its validity for Turkey, Talaat had affirmed in late 1916. In any case, the CUP rulers expected that Germany "resigned freely and whole-heartedly on the [Ottoman] Capitulations," unilaterally abolished in September 1914.[43]

In retrospect, the young grand vizier's faith in a common Ottoman-German future might appear tragic and pathetic, as his last resort to save the empire, had he not combined it with a deathly ideology and a policy of ruthless crimes. Both elements—the systematic violation of Ottoman Christians and others, and his illusive outlook on a future alongside the Central powers—were, however, logically connected. Turan

FIGURE 21: Representatives of the Central powers at Brest-Litovsk,
early 1918: German general Max Hoffmann, Austrian foreign
minister Count Czernin, Talaat Pasha, and German foreign minister
Richard von Kühlmann (Generallandesarchiv Karslruhe).

was not a trivial fantasy but a significant, cogent element of the
CUP's imperially biased, territorially overstretched war ideol-
ogy. Talaat stood for faith in the right, might, and longevity of
the Central powers' new order of Europe, the Middle East, and
Russia, as endorsed by the alliance treaties and, foremost in
March 1918, the triumphant Brest-Litovsk Treaty.

Thanks to the reconquest of Erzincan, Erzurum, and Trabzon, and the reacquisition of Kars, Batum, and Ardahan, Talaat's
ministry enjoyed an outwardly strong position in spring 1918.
Many CUP leaders were, however, overconfident and lacked a
holistic view of the situation. "The Turks became triumphant
after the collapse of Russia," Bernstorff wrote in retrospect.
"They created increasing problems by running after annexations" beyond the agreements of the Brest-Litovsk Treaty.

FIGURE 22: Kaiser Karl's visit in the Ottoman capital; Talaat is in the foreground on the right, May 1918 (Wienbibliothek im Rathaus, Tagblattarchiv).

"They believed to have finished victoriously their war," overlooking the importance of the West front and the fresh will "of the Western powers to settle the Eastern Question according to their own will." In terms of a functioning domestic administration and of trust between the allies, things were unstable in Talaat's Turkey.[44]

Talaat's imperial "spirit of Brest-Litovsk" combined might and tradition, not only with a renewed pan-*völkisch* enthusiasm but also with the postulate of civilizational progress according to European lines. It welcomed selected cases of self-determination, as in Poland and the Ukraine, by the grace of hegemonic neighbors. Lacking principles, political viability, and global strategic intelligence, it was not rooted in democracy and basic human rights. Imperialist futures projected in the Entente's agreements in spring 1916 were, by contrast, at least publicly exposed, besides being challenged by the newcomer

United States and by revolutionary Russia. Britain attempted, at least, to achieve a minimum of justice for the Armenians, even if—in a fundamental analysis focused on the Levant—its imperial policy had lost its viability in the 1910s. This study contends that the Eastern Question in 1912–13 was its ultimate aporia, as personified by Talaat's contemporary Winston Churchill. Politics without a holistic approach under Churchill's leadership in the early 1920s led to purely functional approaches to a Levant that Churchill then conceptualized as the "Middle East." Even if it saved the empire in the short term, this "political pauperization" lacked vision for a vital future for all parts involved, especially for Middle Easterners themselves—except for Israel.

———

Germany and German-speaking Central powers and their presses joined in praising what they called highly promising "Turkish nationalists," that is, the CUP in power, and declared the CUP policy as concurring with their own interests, even if, as many felt, it was on shaky ground. The timeline of the leaders in Berlin was narrow and illusional even in the eyes of CUP man Cavid. "I was with Helfferich for lunch. Zimmermann and Rosenberg were also there. I saw them all being quite optimistic. When I stated that the war would continue for at least a year, they believed it would end before winter [1916–17]," Cavid noted in summer 1916. Vice-Chancellor Karl Helfferich held that a German victory would supersede a general peace conference, and the Central powers would obtain reparations, so that Berlin could pay back the loans it had made to finance war. Talaat trusted Helfferich's analyses and outlook on the contemporary world, but he distrusted Matthias Erzberger, the leader of the democratic forces since Germany's political July

1917 crisis, because Erzberger worried about the Armenians. After war, Helfferich became a leader of the German Far Right and a deadly adversary of Erzberger, his long-term competitor. Erzberger was murdered in 1921, after Helfferich had publicly targeted him. The case of foreign minister Walther Rathenau, assassinated in 1922, was similar.[45]

During war, imperial nationalists like Helfferich had their like-minded, already much more radical counterparts in Istanbul, who placed their faith in Germany, thus empowering one another in radical thinking. "This evening, the [Ottoman] [P]arliament has again witnessed the stupid thoughts of Bahâeddin Şakir. War must be declared against America; no American spy [missionaries, teachers, doctors] has to be left here," Cavid noted on 10 April 1917:

> It throws one into despair to see the destiny of the nation under the influence of men with such a mind. . . . Ziya [Gökalp] too opined that the nation had to take a resolute stance against America and to march together with Germany, as if Germany will provide for everything. There was again the old refrain [from 1914]: "If we must die, let us die. . . ." These wretched people do not know any relation with life outside Turkey and are unaware of what happens in the world. They imagine Germany to be as powerful as God.

The parliament decided to cut relations with America, as Talaat had stipulated, to please Germany. Cavid and Cahid were "voices in the desert crying out" against an interdependence with Germany that did not leave room for alternatives. Voiced in small circles and reaching his ears, such statements put the road that Talaat had chosen into question and made him visibly "feel sad." Yet, in consequence, he again convinced the "dissidents," in spite of it all.[46]

The German-speaking press unctuously praised the CUP men of action, their political style, and their policy and narrative of national salvation. The manner in which it celebrated the Turkish nationalists accustomed the German-speaking public (except for Switzerland) to have a positive outlook on protofascist features that the top elites in Berlin, however, did not embrace. Arthur Zimmermann, state secretary in the Foreign Office, expressed his sympathy with the solitary dissident Ahmed Rıza, "an idealist" who "left a good impression" during his visit in Berlin "for his belief in the [peaceful] unity of different peoples." Yet the rift had irreparably opened between ideals and what Berlin believed to be realpolitik (but that was actually unreal and illusionary, because it suppressed essential aspects of political life and society). In Cavid's ears, Kaiser Wilhelm's speeches during his mid-October 1917 visit in Istanbul were full of wishful thinking. Invited to a dinner in the house of banker Oscar Wassermann in Berlin in January 1918, Cavid utterly enjoyed conversing with Walther Rathenau, future foreign minister of the Weimar Republic, and writer Maximilian Harden, two men "who were not militarized," as was the German rule under the de facto dictator General Erich Ludendorff. The latter may be considered Talaat's German counterpart. Ludendorff, a social Darwinist with a narrowly militaristic, ingenious, tactical mind, built on sand even more than Talaat. After war, under the sectarian influence of his wife, this German counterpart resembled an enthusiast worshipping a racially German god Wotan.[47]

An anonymous author, probably close to Austrian foreign minister Czernin, well summarized Turkey-inspired political thought in Austria and Germany by spring 1918:

A new [CUP] regime has in a judicious tactic of rejuvenation introduced modern spirit, modern thought, and national feeling into the Orient . . . and ruthlessly forced [*durchge-drückt*] the success of the national direction. . . . Men head this movement who have acquired governmental positions not by birth but talent, men like Talaat Pasha . . . who have recognized in time the necessity of an alliance with the Central powers. The successful participation of Turkey at the Great War has naturally favored the nationalist direction. . . . The victorious resistance at the Dardanelles was an almost unique heroic deed in the middle of the present war's haunting events.

The same piece fully welcomed the restoration of Turkish rule on the former Ottoman territory of Caucasus, as determined in the Brest-Litovsk Treaty, and hopefully welcomed even a potential "Muslim republic of the Crimea under Turkish suzerainty." The article quoted Czernin as having coined the mantra "Triest-Damascus, and all the land that belongs to the Turks in Asia Minor" and culminated in conjuring "the great salvation" for Turkey's future with an economic and cultural alliance of "Central Europe [*Mitteleuropa*] and the Orient [the Ottoman Empire]." According to the article's author, both formed a holistic unity, possessed "one and the same goal and future," and had sealed with blood an eternal friendship.[48]

Faltering British Rule: A Matrix for Defiance

The multiple sources used for this biography point to the centrality of the alliance with Germany in Talaat's rise to might and political standing in 1910's Istanbul, and to his awareness of this fact, his loyalty, and his corresponding projection of a political future for the nation in whose name he claimed to act. That he began to learn German in the first months of the world war was more than a caprice. It is improbable that he seriously thought of a separate peace and, particularly, that he would commit a breach of the alliance agreements in 1917. Only serious tensions in the Caucasus and the reemergence of the Armenian issue, along with disillusionment about territorial recovery in the Balkans in spring and looming defeat in the West in summer 1918, made him lose international support and his faith in Germany for good. Together with Cavid, he certainly had done all he could to strengthen the Ottoman lever in negotiations with Germany.

Talaat may have used straw men to spread confusion or to sound out possibilities of negotiation regarding Britain in 1917, notably through his (in many British eyes) liberal friend Mustafa Rahmi, governor of İzmir. But even this is not certain. It is true that, like Britain itself, members of the dispersed opposition (but also a few CUP members) sought a separate peace. They were critical of the war policy or wanted to ensure their postwar positions early on. It is therefore tempting to take some British documents left by or relating to individuals such as J. R. Pilling, Basil Zaharoff, Mustafa Rahmi, Abdülkerim, or Fuad Selim at face value when they deal with thrilling plots. Yet insight into political life in the Ottoman capital under Talaat must be considered cautiously. It is true that, driven by self-interest or group interest, several smart people repeatedly claimed to speak for, or stand in contact with, high representatives, in particular Talaat, but this could only be partly true, or, more often than not, simply invented. There were chances to win influence and make money in a flourishing business of selling political contacts, information, and fake news. In this area, inexperienced Zionists had already made their own sobering forays in Istanbul in 1913 (see chap. 5, sec. "Talaat, Palestine, and Zionism").

There were two prominent cases of British prime minister Lloyd George's secret diplomacy with Turkey in the second half of the war. His "special envoy" in Switzerland in 1917, J. R. Pilling, left minor traces in the Ottoman state archives and merited a short entry in Cavid's diary (Cavid was sympathetic with the idea of taking some distance toward Germany) but elicited no direct reaction from Talaat Pasha himself. Pilling's second letter to Talaat on 22 May 1917 (conserved in the Ottoman state archive), sent from Bern, Switzerland, to Istanbul by the Ottoman legate Fuad Selim, was certainly not smart enough to strike a chord in Talaat's political soul or, at least, to provoke minor considerations. It was too bluntly anti-German, put too clumsily, falsely put all the blame for the alliance with Germany and the war policy on the former grand vizier Said Halim, and promised too much in the case of a separate peace. It was a fantasy, or a trial balloon, when he reported to Lloyd George that Talaat desired an independent Armenian buffer state between Turkey and Russia.[49]

The other prominent attempt of Lloyd George's secret diplomacy in Turkey, also beginning in spring 1917, sought to separate Enver from Talaat and the war, and even to push Enver into exile. There was—or was thought to be—a chain of contact from George via Basil Zaharoff and Abdülkerim to Enver. The weakest link in this case was Enver's relative Abdülkerim. Abdülkerim, a former diplomat and secretary under Abdulhamid II, was arms dealer Zaharoff's main contact person (superwealthy Zaharoff was a Turkish-speaking Rûm born in Asia Minor).[50] Abdülkerim's obvious motive, however, was to get money from his rich interlocutory; his detailed coordination with Enver—including the suggestion that Britain offer a luxury asylum to Enver, paid by Zaharoff—was most likely a lucrative lie, but he was clearly so smart that Western historians take him seriously in main points. Yet these awkward attempts of secret diplomacy are interesting for the light they shed on Lloyd George's disoriented outlook on the Middle East after the Russian February Revolution, and ultimately for Britain's aporia when faced with an unexpectedly costly war and the challenge of a postwar future in the Levant.[51]

Thanks to military successes in Gallipoli, Iraq, and (with Ottoman participation) Galicia and Romania, Enver had won more prestige. Yet he could not afford the loss of German backing and could not afford, in any case, the loss of his political friendship with Talaat. German ambassador Bernstorff judged him as "weak to such an extent that he survives only thanks to us and the grand vizier."[52] Enver's patriotic self-concept could only be insulted by Abdülkerim's fanciful offer of a British-sponsored life in luxury abroad. He was, however, shrewd enough, in accordance with Talaat, to plot any sort of deception, as in the case of the alliance offer to Russia in early August 1914. Lloyd George's experts and the British Foreign Office under foreign secretary Arthur Balfour, which were not informed about Zaharoff's attempts at getting in touch with Enver, correctly assessed the chances of a separate peace with Turkey as minimal in 1917.

The highest chance for brokering (a separate) peace was with Russia after the February Revolution, "but [these] peace hopes have expired," Cavid wrote mid-June 1917, shortly after the Zaharoff-Abdülkerim scheme, allegedly planned in Enver's name, had started (to last into 1918).[53] Neither Cavid nor Enver were in Switzerland when Abdülkerim pretended they were. During summer 1917, they were busy in Istanbul trying to get money from Berlin again and preparing to sign a military convention agreement; in January 1918 Enver deputized Talaat, who had gone to Brest-Litovsk, in Istanbul. What Aubrey

Herbert—an orientalist, captain, member of parliament, and agent for special contacts—had reported already in July 1917, from his more prudent and sober contacts with oppositional liberal Ottoman circles in Switzerland to his superiors in the Foreign Office in London, was that none "of the big forces in Turkey" were ready for negotiations, although Herbert then believed that Talaat was "the moving spirit in the feeler that has been put out."[54]

It is true, in conclusion, that Enver's attachment to and dependency on Talaat in political matters since 1908 seems to have suffered from the 1916 putsch attempt by Major Yakub Cemil (the killer of Nâzım Pasha in January 1913), along with SO Circassians who had been close to Enver, at least before 1916. Yet this and similar events proved, once more, that Talaat was smartest in the multidimensional game of power in the Ottoman capital. Cemil had wanted a separate peace and mentioned Mustafa Kemal as the man he apparently envisaged to replace Enver, the war minister. (If this "confession" was true and not fabricated, Talaat could certainly better deal with Enver than with the more independent-minded Mustafa Kemal.) Talaat suppressed the timely discovered group and executed Cemil in late summer 1916, when Enver was staying in Germany. By then, he had swiftly eliminated internal opposition and smartly navigated to "avoid discord with Enver." He had saved his web of high-level dependencies and successfully dealt with the protestation by the incorruptible CUP administrator Canbolad (see chap. 5, sec. "Victor, Noah, National Father") and with putschist officers (formerly) close to Enver. Apparently, there was also conflict between Enver and Talaat in early 1917 concerning a new recruiting law that went too far in Talaat's eyes. Rumor of another putsch attempt in late 1917 involved both Enver and Mustafa Kemal but was, again, short-lived.[55]

In his own apologetic words after war, Britain had been Talaat's first choice of foreign policy before 1914, but he had felt spurned and offended when Britain refused to provide inspectors general for reforms in the eastern provinces in autumn 1913. Serious alienation had started earlier, when Britain supported Kâmil Pasha's anti-CUP cabinet and positions during the Balkan Wars that CUP patriots could never accept. When Aubrey Herbert asked the exiled grand vizier in a long conversation in Cologne on 26–27 February 1921, "at what point friendly relations between ourselves and Turkey became impossible," Talaat answered, "at the time when [the British prime minister] Mr. Asquith made his speech on the question of Adrianople," demanding that it remain Bulgarian. He understood that Asquith was bluffing and thus lost respect. He then successfully defied Asquith's threatening statement and organized his hometown Edirne's (Adrianople) reconquest, implemented by Enver in late July 1913.

Although there is a clear apologetic strategy in the CUP argument of fatal rejection by British representatives, even before Cavid's letter to Churchill in 1911 (see chap. 4, sec. "CUP's Crises, Fall, and Radical Recalibration"), important aspects of Talaat's interaction with Britain must be considered. Rebellious defiance linked to a grudge over the refusal of recognition by Britain, which he had regarded the leading global power, characterizes Talaat's make-or-break approach from 1913 onward; his collaboration with Germany, entrenched in July 1914; his readiness to categorically put all blame on others; and his abandonment of differentiated approaches, notably regarding the Armenians and the future of Asia Minor. "You drove us into the arms of Germany. We had no alternative: anything else was political death and partition."[56]

Germany was already an attractive and obvious choice for Talaat and his friends before Britain refused companionship, as the development of relations from 1909 shows (see chap. 3, sec. "Sobered, Disturbed, Depressed"). German diplomats shared frustrations in view of the global system and had, since 1913, shown peculiar admiration and support for the CUP's struggle for a "new Turkey." Though there was British refusal on the level of diplomacy, CUP writers inflated it and used it as a far-reaching argument: the negative British behavior vis-à-vis sincere and hopeful CUP politicians and the British confiscation of Ottoman warships on 1 August 1914, authorized, in reaction, Turkey's radical measures and war at the side of Germany. In selective perception, the triumph at the Dardanelles and on Gallipoli in 1915, the British defeat in Iraq at Kut (southeast of Baghdad) in spring 1916, and the final collapse of Britain's Russian ally in the Caucasus all seemed to confirm Talaat's German strategy. The czar's overthrow mid-March 1917 had outweighed the depressing news of the fall of Baghdad, a former seat of the caliph, a year after the triumph at Kut.[57]

In detached analysis, the blame for squandered opportunities and missed compromises, which may have helped avoid a deadly geostrategic polarization, fell on both Turkey and Britain. Outwardly at its peak in the early twentieth century, imperial British rule certainly did not stand the tests of the twentieth century, based as it was on premodern royal prerogatives, race, and class mentality. Besides class distinctions, relatively democratic rule, including rule of law in Britain, differed fundamentally from the authoritarian and at times "lawless rule" of martial law by British governors overseas.[58] The exhaustion of its legitimacy and resources had become clear on the threshold of the twentieth century with the Second Boer War in dealing with Ireland and regarding the social question in Britain itself (pauperization, class cleavages, state-conducted transfer of children abroad). Faltering British behavior in Istanbul disabled possible initiatives of conflict resolution or mitigation regarding the Eastern Question.

Talaat's radicalization in the early 1910s interacted with British behavior, because he looked up to global power. A decade ago, the international press had broadly covered the Boer War, where the British military had introduced huge and deathly concentration camps. British discourse about humanity, democracy, and self-determination devalued itself significantly. Imperially biased racial, cultural, and Darwinist views appeared at the surface of political thought, also informing British philo- and anti-Semitism, after religious restorationism (the modern, mainly Protestant, current of faith in the restoration of the Jews to Palestine and to Jesus, a forerunner of current Christian Zionism) had largely vanished. Put pointedly, these views were contained only to distinguish oneself from ugly latecomer racisms in Continental Europe. Viewed from Istanbul, differences were gradual, not substantial. Racist treatment of indigenous people groups in Africa, Australia, and Asia by a respected power offered a strong but misleading justification to implement, or radicalize, anticonstitutional policies in their own Ottoman Empire.[59]

As already alluded to, the analyses provided by British diplomacy in the post-1908 Ottoman Empire lacked acumen and, after November 1914, direct access to important sources. Britain's diplomatic efforts had to make all sorts of interpolations, often based on mediocre intelligence. The representatives of the British Empire, the ambassadors Gerard Lowther and Louis Mallet, had been comparatively weak figures. Conspiracy theories pervade British post-1908 reporting from the Ottoman political hub (see chap. 5, sec. "Talaat, Palestine, and

Zionism"). Psychological capacity and proactive, constructive diplomacy in Istanbul would have been critical during those years. British-Russian compromise on a partial involvement of British experts in the reform scheme in 1913 would possibly have disarmed Talaat's defiance and saved posterity from the argument that the CUP had been forcibly driven into German arms. Britain may have squandered opportunities and failed to build a minimum of trust or, at the least, liability. It certainly lacked sustaining, constructive perspectives beyond its own faltering, imperial construction. Yet, fixated on the international game of power and the desire for sovereignty (i.e., CUP power), Talaat took British inconsistency as a reason and excuse for a radical, largely reactionary revolutionist attitude that only the alliance with Germany allowed him to act out.

Thus, apologetic right from the outset, Talaat played down his own responsibility for acts for which he was mainly responsible, as the archival track amply shows. "The Turks had virtually offered us Turkey, and we had refused it. We had thrown in our lot with the Russians, and they could not remain neutral. They [the Turks] took the only way that promised salvation. He [Talaat] excused himself for the Armenians, repudiating responsibility, and went into the possibility of an understanding with ourselves. Throughout these conversations, he was very friendly and rather cynical," Herbert noted in his diary on 3 March 1921. "I asked him what had been their relations with the Germans during the war. He laughed and said, 'detestable.'" Talaat's deceptive language in conversation with Herbert while he was in exile must, of course, be assessed on its own logic and according to the post-1918 context. It certainly did not change the fact that the synergy between Turan-loving revolutionists and Wilhelminians, who sought *Weltgeltung* (worldwide recognition and international standing) through world war, had set mental coordinates for history yet to come. Having read Herbert's report on his encounter with Talaat, a superior in the Foreign Office concluded insightfully that Talaat "found it difficult to co-operate with us since our policy towards Turkey for the last forty years has been essentially a negative one: hence its utter futility both as regards the Christian population in Turkey whom we wished to benefit as well as British interests."[60]

Winston Churchill rightly stated in his book *World Crisis* that there was "no great sphere of policy about which the British Government was less completely informed than the Turkish" and that it (including Churchill himself) wrongly believed in late summer 1914 "that Turkey had no policy and might still be won or lost." Churchill himself, and his ambivalence, mirrored a smug but confused attitude vis-à-vis the challenges of the late Ottoman world. For two decades, he oscillated between a liberal stance à la Gladstone, a conservative pro-Turkish line à la Disraeli, and a new current in the vein of German post-1908 Turkey fever. This current resulted in a strong sympathy with the CUP leaders, who it appreciated, identified with, and admired, as young and energetic representatives of a faltering empire who struggled to save their imperial stance. In Churchill's case, after a decade of decisive failures, this finally also meant, as early as November 1920, the will to friendship with (ex-CUP) Kemalist Turkey, at the cost of ethics and justice, for a short-lived imperial embrace of (mostly) Islamic territory ("to ease the [British] position in Egypt, Mesopotamia, Persia, and India"). Michelle Tusan recently concluded that the British incapacity "to fully prosecute Ottoman war crimes made visible the tension between nineteenth-century notions of moral responsibility and a universal standard of human rights by exposing a moralizing British Empire as a less than

legitimate voice of international justice mired in its own imperial struggles."[61]

Put shortly: The exhaustion of British rule in general, and
resources for conflict resolution as needed for the Eastern
Question in the early 1910s in particular, went hand in hand
with the rise of Talaat's Gökalp-inspired politics and served as
a self-righteous argument for such radicalism. World War I and
the alliance with Germany offered a fertile matrix for a pioneering political practice of young imperial revolutionists reacting
against the globally leading Entente powers. Against the historical background of Europe at large in the first half of the twentieth century, this practice might be understood and labeled
as protofascist. Yet it antecedes the rise of fascism, including a
more explicit religious factor, and was to transcend Continental European fascism. Pioneered by the CUP, the synergy of
Islamism and Turkish ethnonationalism, an aggressive pattern
of power concentration, did not die off after World War II, as
did National Socialism (Nazism) and other European fascisms.

Imperialisms Face Utopia, Dystopia: Sykes-Picot, Balfour, Brest-Litovsk

To defy Britain power in alliance with German might was a
feature that determined Talaat's political biography since 1913.
To this was added, since July 1914, the will not only to defy
and to contain but to destroy the Russian Empire. Once Russia
was revolutionized, Germany was defeated, and the Arab parts
of the empire were lost, Talaat in exile logically sought British
friendship again, as noted by Herbert, who met Talaat in Germany in early 1921. In this sense, the former grand vizier was a
pragmatist of power, or simply clung to power. Excepting (most

of) Asia Minor, he was again ready to deal with Britain after war, amply using the threat of what we might call an "antiliberal international of revolutionists," including CUP leaders in exile who were now heads of Islamist cells, to push his agenda forward (see chap. 6, "Antiliberal International of Revolutionists"). Yet the last year of World War I had offered him the viewpoint of a much more brilliant future.

Gökalp's Turan—the exalted, expansive, and lunatic politico-cultural utopia of Talaat's cohort—reemerged after its aborted late 1914 boom and again proved its deathly potential, as it went hand in hand with the will to partially (Talaat) or entirely (Halil Pasha, Enver's uncle) destroy the remaining Armenians in the Caucasus. At the same time (1917–18), the deportation of another Anatolian population group of Christians, justified for military necessity by German officers, again turned into genocide. This time, the target was the Rûm of Pontus—often called Pontus Greeks—at the Eastern Black Sea region (see also chap. 5, sec. "Mirroring and Managing Anti-Christian Forces in the East"). In spring 1918, Muslim voices in the parliament claimed that now the time had arrived that "the Rûm, our worst enemies [in the region of Trabzon], must depart."[62] As soon as he landed in Samsun on 19 May 1919, Talaat's heir, Kemal, was to continue the destruction of this Christian minority via gangs that had been involved in the slaughter of 1915–16. Led by Kemal's general Nureddin Pasha, a former CUP general and notorious fanatic, this was the first military action of the second, that is, post-1918 "Turkish war of salvation" (the first being the one starting in 1913 with the recovery of Edirne, although prefigured already by the domestic reconquest of power after the short-lived coup of April 1909) (see chaps. 3–4).

Talaat's grand vizierate marked the Ottoman context of the incisive 1917 to early 1918 projection of futures for Europe,

Russia, the Ottoman world, and globally. The plans agreed on by Sykes, Picot, and Sazonov in spring 1916 in Petrograd were partly realized after 1918, including the specific Sykes-Picot Agreement of 16 May 1916. Some of the projections of Talaat, the main leader of a still Ottoman Middle East and ally in a quadruple alliance of Central powers, however, determined the post-Ottoman Levant no less than did the secret Entente agreements of spring 1916, as well as the Balfour Declaration, which was added to them in late 1917. This is true for Asia Minor, the initial core of the agreements, where the plans of Sykes, Picot, and Sazonov entirely failed and the CUP's momentum, started for good in 1913, finally won over. Although defeat removed the longtime alliance with Germany, the international pillar of Talaat's policy, his core policy did not lose its momentum. It based a successful struggle for Asia Minor under Mustafa Kemal (Atatürk).

It is therefore accurate to consider two seminal moments and momentums regarding the Ottoman Levant in late World War I, even if only Sykes-Picot became a myth. The "Talaat Pasha moment" may be called Turkey's new momentum after the incisive recalibration of geostrategy in November 1917. This resulted from the Russian October Revolution, the British breakthrough in Palestine, the Balfour Declaration, German advances in Eastern Europe, and the publication of the secret Entente agreements. Talaat's political zenith, reflected in the Brest-Litovsk Treaty on 3 March 1918, was the outcome of negotiations that had started in December 1917. The CUP's self-confidence and scope of action in Eastern Asia Minor, the Caucasus, and beyond greatly increased. It was far from giving up the Arab parts of the empire. This went hand in hand with a German imperialism eager to ensure dominant influence—particularly, economical—in Turkey, preferably in cooperation

with Talaat's ministry, to continue after a general peace conference. German ambassador Bernstorff believed in early March
1918 that "several weeks of daily contact with European statesmen [in Brest-Litovsk, Berlin, and Vienna] had stimulated"
Talaat and permitted him "to catch up on the education that
he lacked." Yet Talaat's zenith was marked by simultaneous,
increasing domestic anger over corruption and the loss of his
confidence concerning German support for Turkey's imperial
restoration.[63]

To be accurate on competing futures, we must add a third
distinct momentum, built on more long-term confidence and
opportunity: the Balfour Declaration on 2 November 1917.
This was a small and short-lived but significant element next
to the copious and, later, largely dismissed arrangements for
the future based on military projections. This declaration, too,
centrally concerned the Ottoman world. It deserves a careful,
contextualized analysis. In a first approach, it was part of a British projection of a Middle Eastern future that responded, in
a timely manner, to fundamental geostrategic and ideological
changes induced by Russia's revolutionary transformation. It
set the Central powers into a difficult but revealing *zugzwang*
in Istanbul, Berlin, and at Brest-Litovsk. Jews in Eastern Europe
and Russia had until then generally sympathized with the Central powers, and the hate of Russia had contributed to a close
relation between CUP members and the Jewish Ottoman elite,
foremost since dictatorship was established in 1913 and during
World War I. Yet the Central powers were hardly capable of a
sound response to the Balfour Declaration, because they themselves were far from being progressive and consensual on matters of nationalities and self-determination.

A second approach to the Balfour Declaration, and a deeper
analysis of its contents, reveals more. The declaration not only

translated into diplomacy the centuries-old restorationist, decades-old Zionist demand of a Jewish home in Palestine, which went back to biblical prophecies, but also joined, if restrainedly, with the Ottoman 1908 constitutional framework of a fair coexistence, with equal rights, of different ethnoreligious groups in a modernized Middle East. Even if the declaration first attended to the Jewish desire of a national home, it also combined two main Levant-centered utopias of the modern era. These utopias stood entirely at odds with Talaat's post-1913 political spirit, and even more so as the declaration concurred with British government statements supporting a viable autonomy of Armenia.[64]

That World War I was a fundamental, groundbreaking cataclysm of larger Europe had become evident in 1917. Henceforth, for any modern-minded public with a minimal global consciousness, a convincing postimperial rule must unmistakably obey the principle of equality and democracy, regardless of ethnic and religious belonging, as both President Wilson and communist leader Lenin emphasized in their addresses to a global public in 1917–18. For those who appreciated the Bible, it must also take into account what the vital prophetic tradition had said for thousands of years about future forms of human cohabitation on Earth. This tradition insisted on basic human laws of equality and mutual respect, and thus evidently transcended premodern myths of religious, racial, cultural, or national superiorities, yet was stuck on the antique promise of a "restoration of Israel."[65]

Talaat reaffirmed his relevant position in correspondence with Cemal Pasha in early 1917. "I entirely agree with the opinion of Your Highness saying that the damaging agency and influence of Zionism against the supreme interests of the country must be erased. Yet, because the Zionists enjoy great political and economic power among our allies and the neutral states, I see it more appropriate [to achieve the same goal] to apply unambiguously the existing laws and to profit from the present situation, instead of enacting a new law that provokes international opinion. . . . I believe that we can destroy and erase Zionism, and thus preserve the holy interests of the country."[66] Cemal's temporary success in defending Gaza in the spring did not prevent the final fall of Jerusalem in autumn 1917. In early 1917, he had hoped to completely change the fortunes of war with a renewed Suez campaign, as he then wrote to Talaat. The sentimental, pious, allegedly patriotic, but egocentric and narcissistic language of this half-chimerical, half-tragic telegram of 6 January 1917 by a top actor might be read as the dead end of CUP imperialism on a linguistic level.[67]

Talaat's fundamental stance did not change after the loss of Palestine. He probably believed until summer 1918 that German power would, as the alliance contract stipulated, provide for the recovery of Ottoman territory during postwar peace negotiations. Even Cavid had opined, based on the stipulations, that Germany had to, if necessary, throw Belgium into the pot at the peace negotiations, in order to recover Basra, in the southern end of Iraq, from Britain.[68] Pressured by Bernstorff, Talaat accepted an interview with the Zionist representative Julius Becker on 12 December 1917, because the Central powers needed to counter the wave of pro-British sympathy among Jews engendered by the Balfour Declaration.[69] From its contents, the interview could be nothing other than a deception from a Zionist point of view. Talaat strictly stuck to imperial equalizing and strengthening of central government, and promised only within this framework a little more autonomy for municipalities, including those in Palestine. He emphasized inaccurately—as flimsy propaganda from several sides would repeat throughout the twentieth century—that "We do not have any Jewish Question," and "Turkey is the only land that does not know any anti-Semitism, present in all other countries."[70]

During his stay in the Ottoman capital in late 1917 to early 1918, Becker grasped the realities more accurately. Talaat, Cemal, and their political friends had hitherto not developed a promising domestic policy that could face challenges similar to that of the Jewish Question. Becker took it as a confession of political incapacity that they feared immigrating Jews as potential enemies, even if these brought capital and competence into the country, thus pointing to a systemic weakness of the empire. A cultured and upright German Zionist, however, he certainly overestimated Jewish goodwill, in the manner of Theodor Herzl's optimistic novel *Altneuland*, and underestimated the naked will of Zionists to rule over territory based on ethno-religious distinction or "maximalist" ideology, as represented by leaders from Eastern Europe (later explicitly criticized by him).[71] Still, Becker revealed main factors of CUP rule and psychology: fear and intimidation, along with defiance and the pretense of superiority, bound to feelings of inferiority vis-à-vis non-Muslims. These factors overlap with what this book calls a deep-seated, imperial Sunni Ottoman bias. "Why did we burn down İzmir [in 1922]?" Falih Rıfkı (Atay), Cemal's and later Talaat's assistant and Mustafa Kemal's close companion, asked rhetorically during the Interwar period.

> When the Armenians were deported, out of the same fear we have burned down all their still inhabitable quarters in the towns of Anatolia. . . . This was not by pure destructiveness, but an inferiority complex played a role. All that appeared to be European was like Christian and strange, and therefore strictly and fatefully not ours.[72]

The talk with Becker was not Talaat's last word to Zionists. Believing in the critical global power of the Jews, and therefore the need to bargain with them, Talaat met Zionist representatives in Berlin and Istanbul during and after the Brest-Litovsk conference, from January to August 1918, in view of ameliorated conditions for the establishment of a "Jewish center" in Palestine under Turkish rule. At Brest-Litovsk itself, neither the Central powers nor the young Bolshevik government could be convinced concerning stipulations favoring Jewish autonomy in Europe and/or Palestine, despite efforts by the Zionist executive branch in Berlin and Poale Zion (a movement of Marxist-Zionist Jewish workers). Berlin, however, was in favor, and Talaat gave the impression that he would do his best to look into the matter.[73]

On the road to Brest-Litovsk, Talaat met Nossig in Berlin on 5 January 1918 and (according to Nossig's optimistic reporting) promised to meet all Jewish wishes, praised Ottoman Jewish loyalty, emphasized the numerous Jewish friends he had himself, and authorized Nossig to call his CUP intimate Karasu from Istanbul for further negotiation. Karasu and Midhat Şükrü had been involved in Nossig's foundation of the Ottoman-Israelite Union in Istanbul in September 1915. Temporarily back from Brest-Litovsk, Talaat agreed to meet on 23 January 1918 with representatives of the German-Israelite Ottoman Union and the General Jewish Colonization Organization, joined by other Zionist spokespeople. He promised to accept immigration of a "large number of Jews," read Nossig's report. This was an important point for Berlin, because it would allow a reduction in Jewish immigration to Germany from Eastern Europe, which, as it seemed then, would remain under German rule.

In early 1918, after a widely pulicized statement from the German Foreign Ministry that refered to Talaat, German Jews saw a happy combination of Jewish, Ottoman, and German interests in favor of real equality and local government for Jews, both in Eastern Europe and in Palestine. The committee Pro Palästina, a "German committee for the promotion of Jewish settlement in Palestine," mirrored the (ephemeral) shining hour of German-Ottoman–supported Zionism that seemed to reach important goals quickly. The committee was founded in Berlin in spring 1918, with a broad coalition of prominent Jewish and non-Jewish German members. German-supported Ottoman-Jewish negotiations resumed at the end of June in Istanbul, led on the European Jewish side by Jacobson and on the Ottoman side by Mazliah and Nahum, as well as Şükrü, Gökalp, and Nâzım. The CUP's expectation from the Zionists was clear: not only sympathy but Jewish propaganda for Turkish rule in Palestine and imperial Turkey in general, implicitly including active denial of crimes against humanity.[74]

By mid-July 1918, when Talaat approved "the creation of a [religious] Jewish center in Palestine by means of a well-organized immigration and colonization," and the communiqué emphasized that "the Jewish ambitions could be well realized under Ottoman sovereignty and in the framework of the Ottoman Empire," the whole scheme rested politically on sand.[75] General defeat not only loomed, but there was also a lack of relevant political will and understanding in Istanbul, beyond Talaat's determination to hold the Jews on his side in an international power game that then quickly slipped away from him.

———

The plans of Sykes, Picot, and Sazonov had been published in late November 1917. Before, they had remained secret. By October 1916, Talaat had known about common French and Armenian efforts in view of the postwar order. In mid-November 1916, they had resulted in the establishment of a French Armenian Legion in view of a postwar order in-line with the Entente plans. Apparently, however (as concluded from the record in the Ottoman archives and the contemporary newspapers), these plans, once published in late 1917, did not attract much attention from the CUP government or the press. Talaat mentioned the Sykes-Picot Agreement later, in a letter on 22 December 1919, to Mustafa Kemal (Atatürk): "The treaty concluded by France and Britain in 1916 makes the Arab lands [of the Ottoman Empire] appear like a dissected bird, and leaves almost only desert for an autonomous Arabia." He then took this as an argument for the unity of Turks and Arabs during the peace negotiations and, to strengthen the bond, for emphasizing the caliphate.[76]

Russia's exit from the war and the Entente, and the negotiations at Brest-Litovsk starting in late 1917, seemed to offer the Ottomans a strong alternative to the Balfour Declaration and the secret Entente agreements of 1916. The Ottoman alternative banked on victoriously expanding Central powers, and the Central powers' subsequent strong position at a general peace conference. This would allow the CUP regime to end world war with territorial gains in the Caucasus and, hopefully, territorial recovery in the Balkans—and with a status quo regarding Arabia, thanks to the rescission of British conquests. Concluded after nearly four months of negotiations, the Brest-Litovsk Treaty on 3 March 1918 was a huge diplomatic victory for Turkey, since it opened the door to recovering three Caucasian provinces lost to Russia in 1878 (Article IV of the Treaty). The Treaty of Batumi, signed by Ottoman Turkey and the post-czarist states of Georgia, Armenia, and Azerbaijan on 4 June 1918, added even more territory. In the last third of May

Legend:
- Territory occupied by the Central Powers before the Treaty of Brest-Litovsk
- Territory occupied by the Central Powers after the Treaty of Brest-Litovsk
- Caucasian territory occupied by Turkey shortly after the Treaty of Brest-Litovsk
- Central Power satellites and occupied territories
- Territories in which Germany and Turkey vied for influence
- Claimed by Bulgaria from conquered Romania and Russia

MAP 5: Europe and the Caucasus after the Treaty of Brest-Litovsk, March 1918.

1918 and early June, the Ottoman army threatened Yerevan, the last remaining Armenian city, but was fought back by the ultimate effort of reorganized Armenian forces at Karakilise and Sardarabad.[77]

Talaat kept holding foreign policy in his hand and thus led the negotiations in person in Brest-Litowsk in January and February 1918. He identified with Ludendorff's policy of pressure and occupation of vast Russian territory. "We see this in accordance with the interests of the Ottoman state, since the Bolshevik program includes the idea of reviving, in another way, the old great Russia."[78] With the new independent Ukraine, negotiations were led separately and concluded earlier. The Ukrainian delegation expressed admiration for

Turkey's achievements during war and expected Palestine to also be Ottoman territory in the future.[79] Much more difficult than in Brest-Litovsk were—in the case of final victory for the Central powers—territorial gains in the Balkans. Negotiations with Bulgaria and Romania to recover former Ottoman territory failed. Yet undoing losses of the First Balkan War was an important matter of prestige and self-image for Talaat and the CUP. "Even small territorial gains" would be "useful for the standing" of his cabinet, he made known to German foreign minister Richard von Kühlmann in early March 1918—but was frustrated.[80]

A dark shadow over Talaat's brilliant early 1918 outlook was the Armenians. As in autumn 1914, Talaat and Enver again largely consented in matters that concerned Eastern Asia Minor and the Caucasus. They took seriously Entente statements on Armenian independence, followed closely analogous statements by the Bolsheviks, and knew Germany's sensitive stand as voiced by Erzberger in 1916 concerning the return of Armenian survivors and the restitution of their property.[81] In order to influence the negotiations, Enver informed Talaat during his stay in Brest-Litovsk of Armenian acts of atrocity and revenge against Muslims during the Russian retreat from Erzincan, Ezurum, and Kars; the arming of the Pontus Rûm; the creation of Muslim gangs; and Georgian-Armenian cooperation that led to the short-lived Transcaucasian Democratic Federative Republic. In early 1918, Enver made do in his letters by saying that if really, according to the principle of self-determination, the Armenians were to be considered, "this, of course, is to be applied not to our country but to regions [in the Caucasus] that belong to them and have no relation with us." Talaat warned in response that "if, God beware, we failed against the Armenians, this would be ugly in the eyes of the world and dangerous for our country"—not least because crimes would then be revealed and entail political consequences.[82]

In late spring 1918, the anti-Armenian stance of the CUP luminaries went far. "If in the future a small Armenia is established, it will take orders from America," Enver wrote to his general Vehib Pasha. From a few hundred thousand inhabitants, "it would become a country of millions and again for us a kind of Bulgaria in the East, and a more harmful enemy than Russia, because all Armenian interests and wishes are focused on our country." He concluded that "it is unacceptable to offer a [political] existence to the Armenians. It is necessary to do all in order to weaken them completely and leave them in an entirely destitute state so that their deprived life conditions prevent them from organizing themselves."[83]

Enver's uncle Halil, then the commander of a renewed campaign into the Caucasus, shouted even more bluntly his desire for global extermination: "I will not leave even one Armenian on the surface of the earth!"[84] As representative of a supposedly superior race and religion, he felt authorized to exterminate an "inferior" group that did not welcome Turkish-Muslim hegemony over Caucasia. General Otto von Lossow, military attaché at the embassy in Istanbul, reported in late May 1918 that "the aim of Turkish policy is the permanent occupation of the Armenian districts and the extermination of the Armenians. All of Talaat's and Enver's assurances to the contrary are lies. In Constantinople, the extreme anti-Armenian trend has gained the upper hand."[85]

In a hyperbolic reversion of reality typical for CUP discourse, Halil Pasha reproached the Armenians for their "campaign of annihilation" and "war of revenge" against the Turks in 1918. The CUP had conducted an exterminatory jihad against Caucasian and Ottoman Christians from the first year of World War I and

resumed it in the new context of Russian retreat in 1918. Galvanized anew by Turanist utopia, the CUP sought expansion far
beyond the imperial restoration of three Caucasian provinces,
subjecting the alliance with Germany to a serious stress test. In
German ambassador Bernstorff's words, the CUP leaders were
happy that atrocities in Caucasia in 1918 seemed to offer them
"a belated excuse for their prior sins." Massacres of Muslims,
including Alevis, by Armenian militias took place during the
retreat of the Russian army from Erzincan and Erzurum and
also in Baku on 31 March 1918, on the eve of Baku's communist
commune. In turn, in addition to former extreme mass violence, the advancing Turkish forces massacred the Armenians
of Kars and Ardahan, and—organized as the Islamic Army of
the Caucasus since July 1918—deliberately killed thousands
of Armenians when entering Baku mid-September 1915. The
Islamic Army of the Caucasus stood under the command of
Nuri (Killigil) Pasha, Enver's half brother.[86]

There are strong arguments that say that "Zion"—the place of
longing for generations of Jews and Christian restorationists—
stands for "utopia," whereas "Turan," in Gökalp's diction, the
Turks' "enormous and eternal fatherland," stands for "dystopia"
or a deathly utopia connected to the Great War of the 1910s and
to genocide. Zion and Turan (coupled with "Kızılelma") served
as a kind of abstract Messiah or Mahdi. Both Zionism and Turanism were political messianisms, though, from their substance,
at odds with each other. Both escaped from apparently over-
powerful imperialisms: Zion went beyond empire from its sheer
content—not least the salvation from, and repair of, defeat and
destruction once inflicted by the Roman Empire—whereas
Turan stood in explicit opposition to the British and Czarist
Empires. Although Turanism wanted European civilization
grafted into Turkdom (as did Kemalism afterward), it sought

escape from European power and supervision. As an exalted, overstretched irredenta, the Turanist escape was itself, however, imperialist: a nationalist expansion of the Ottoman Empire.

This is true even if in early 1918 certain authors (notably in Gökalp's new journal *Yeni Mecmua*) emphasized cultural, racial, religious, and economic—not political—unity. Still, Istanbul and Anatolia's Turkish polity was considered the "cultural center," "seat of the caliphate," and "national Kaaba" of a Turan composed of "40 million Turks and Muslims." Political ambitions were intertwined with cultural ones, political unity was envisaged as following cultural-religious unity. Gökalp persisted in his desire to see the "unity of [Turan's] Turks" form a "great Turkish nation" with a common "Turkish-Muslim ideal," because "this age only grants nations that are big in number the right to live." Once "saved," Turan would be, he prophesied, a great body politic or "organism" (*uzviyet*) of all Turks, their substates, and their strong joint armies in Asia Minor, the Caucasus, Central Asia, and so on. All would be Muslim, use the Turkish language of Istanbul, and be led by one charismatic, eschatological leader-commander (*reis, sahib-kırân, kumandan*). As a result, all Turks would be "organized top-down like an army" and form obedient members of one state and one solidary society. Dissent would be severely repressed, divergent opinions or ideals "killed." Indeed, Gökalp's early 1918 pamphlets look like blueprints for European fascism, yet they emphasize Islam.[87] Zion, the ideal of a small nation wanting to live, also escaped from contemporary Europe's social and political realities, including anti-Semitism. Moreover, it became a kind of trendy utopia for certain non-Jewish imperial elites in Britain and Germany, a utopia outsourced to the Levant by Europeans devoid of a utopian outlook. For Jews, it was to become a question of survival.

There existed, to conclude this section, not only Sykes-Picot, but two competing projections of the Ottoman world during World War I, both partly succeeding in the long term. Final victory of the Central powers seemed realistic after the recalibration of geostrategy in November 1917, and the Treaty of Brest-Litovsk of March 1918 opened the door to Ottoman reconquest in the South Caucasus and beyond. Grand vizier Talaat's regime won momentum, along with territorial recovery and the renewed idea of Turanic unity from Istanbul to Central Asia. The Balfour Declaration and its key notion of a "national home" went beyond the imperial projections, coinciding with the British promise of self-rule and justice for the Armenians. Both promises discriminated positively in favor of groups outside the centuries-old imperial Sunni hegemony in the Levant, but only one had the chance to succeed after war.

From a Summer in Denial in Istanbul to Truth in Berlin—and Resignation

Due to Ottoman re-expansion into the Russian Caucasus, Talaat enjoyed a strong position in early 1918, yet it failed to last, lacked a solid domestic construction, suffered heavy defeats at the other fronts, and finally, due to defeat in the West, lost Germany, its international cornerstone. Talaat came to understand the situation only belatedly, while visiting Berlin in September 1918 to discuss frictions in the Caucasus and coordination in view of peace negotiations.[88]

Before being confronted with the politically disintegrating German capital, he had refused to acknowledge facts that undermined the cornerstone of his war logic: his belief in Germany's might and support, and his faith in lofty alliance

treaties. With few gradual differences, almost all CUP leaders
had become *'nihai zafer'ci*, that is, mouthpieces for (and, mostly,
real believers in) ultimate victory. Any expression of doubt on
Endsieg (ultimate victory) was taboo; whoever looked pessimistic among the CUP people and in the Central Committee's
Nuruosmaniye headquarters was spurned as weak-spirited and
negative.[89]

Member of parliament and *Tanin* editorial writer Muhittin
(Birgen) had spent summer 1917 in Berlin, experienced Germany's political "July crisis," and made, as he wrote, alarming
observations. Back in Istanbul, he had shared them with Talaat.
Although still impressively strong and well organized in contrast to Turkey, Germany appeared deeply divided domestically. Muhittin had been in touch with representatives of the
Left and other democrats who wanted a state, including a kaiser
that was subordinate to the rule of the parliament. A nation that
had matured, they argued, could not be satisfied with a Reichstag reduced to budget inspection. Demanding peace without
annexation and the primacy of parliament against dictatorial
generals, Matthias Erzberger's seminal speech on 6 July 1917 was
backed by a majority of deputies and made Erzberger a new
democratic leader in a polarized political landscape. Chancellor Bethmann Hollweg must resign, vice-chancellor Helfferich
a few months later.[90]

Muhittin was appalled by the belief of German democrats
in "salvation not by force but politics, thus duping themselves,"
their will to rapid peacemaking with Russia, and their faith
in Britain's and France's readiness to peacefully compromise
once Germany became democratic. Writing in retrospect
under Atatürk's dictatorship (whom he praised in the same
breath with Hitler and Mussolini), Talaat's former collaborator felt sorry for those democrats in Germany who had gotten

into a predicament and, he believed, lost sight of the iron law of the "merciless struggle for life in international politics." When Muhittin, in September 1917, told Talaat his observations from Berlin, for the first time he noticed an expression of darkness in the leader's demeanor and eyes, whereas Gökalp, also present, remained utterly optimistic, refocusing on Turan in view of Russia's increasing collapse. Nine months later, in a long face-to-face interview in late spring 1918, Talaat questioned Muhittin again on the international situation. Before, during the five years of Muhittin's editorship, he had rarely felt the need to consult with him.

The young but experienced journalist discerned a worn, perplexed grand vizier, despite diplomatic triumph in March 1918. Talaat's usual habit of smiling and teasing during conversation was absent. Serious tensions with Germany, not only in view of the Caucasus but also of territorial reacquisitions in the Balkans, had emerged already by late March, thus "offending and depressing" Talaat. Thoughts of a separate peace or degraded relations with Germany then came to mind, according to Cavid. Cavid, in turn, added to the tension by pressuring Helfferich and Rosenberg to a full German relief of Turkey's debt. He overstretched the argument that preventing Turkey from financial collapse was in Germany's best interest. Secretary Rosenberg clarified to Cavid that the Reichskanzler was "saddened to see that the money which Germany had given us was used to annihilate Christians; [and that] this was part of the actual problem" between both governments.[91] An overcommitted patriot depending on Talaat, Cavid could not cope with unsettling truths, although he knew them.

Confirming Cavid's observation of an increasing laissez-faire in the supervision of the valis,[92] the grand vizier himself expressed disillusion, domestically and internationally, during a private talk in the Nuruosmaniye headquarters in July 1918, saying, "The war has broken the country's entire morale. Wherever you look, a great number of those involved in politics line their own pockets. . . . The Germans could not break through at the Western front; all hope we set in them has proved null and void." Talaat now trusted Ismail Canbolad (whom he had marginalized in spring 1916) with the Ministry of the Interior, but only until 2 October. "Hitherto, I still kept the Ministry of the Interior in order to avoid discord with Enver," he confided to Cavid; "now I want whatever discord exists to emerge in order to solve the problems."[93] Although again a hollow promise, this statement revealed the situation.

By July 1918, Talaat felt trapped amid three "fires," as he put it: Enver Pasha, now again a very unpredictable friend because he was newly galvanized and overly optimistic, thanks to Ottoman advance in the Caucasus, and ready "to fight to the last man"; the new sultan Mehmed VI Vahideddin, a critic of the CUP and a stronger personality than his predecessor; and enemies advancing from the West and the South. Talaat had lost his faith in the war dynamics, which he had enthusiastically embraced a few years ago, and with this the energy, drive, and self-confidence that had so much impressed German visitors during war. In Muhittin's words, "We had lost. Talaat was defeated. He himself does not yet believe and accept the defeat; he still expects the result of the repeated German offensives at the Western front. Yet he found himself defeated, although he was not yet conscious of it. His defeat implied the defeat of Turkey."[94]

Muhittin went to Berlin again in late July 1918 and met with Erzberger (the "man of the hour"), an utterly helpless Rosenberg, and other generally perplexed German representatives. He collected information for Talaat, who also had decided on a trip to the German capital. Muhittin was impressed by the pessimism and confusion reigning in the German capital and, most strikingly for him, by the topicality of the crimes against the Armenians among democrats from the Left and the moderate Right. The press abounded in relevant articles, "whereas we, in Istanbul, had not been aware at all of these kinds of publications." Yet he felt the democrats' strong point against the CUP regime as being comprehensively "against us [Turks]."

For Muhittin, the Ottoman Embassy in Berlin had been blind not to notice the emergence of a democratic coalition that explicitly took a different position than the ruling German establishment toward war, the CUP regime, and human rights. Hence, diplomatic reports had little to do with decisive realities. A crucial question for Talaat was about honoring agreements and coordination between the allies during the forthcoming peace negotiations. Muhittin asked this question during a private meeting with Erzberger in his hotel. Erzberger appreciated the issue but emphasized that the existing governments were military and political oligarchies that did not speak the political language of democrats and therefore could not be full partners.

The leader of democrats then went on, saying (in Muhittin's recollection), "Turkey has become a plague for us. You must indeed recognize that the publications on the murder of the Armenians in the French, English, and American press make us democrats ashamed. . . . Unfortunately, a huge opprobrium defiles Turkey, which we cannot defend, nor is it our duty to do so." He did not believe Muhittin's narrative of national self-defense against the Armenians, nor his argument that "our share of sin" was "slight and insignificant when compared to the Entente's share of sin and responsibility." Regarding the Armenians, Talaat's man, blinded, went so far as to state that "we Turks acknowledge ourselves as sinless."

The committee had known since summer 1915 that during postwar peace negotiations, German diplomacy would not be ready to defend Turkey regarding its Armenian policy. Since Erzberger's visit in Istanbul in early 1916, it feared the corollary conviction of German representatives that Armenian survivors must be resettled in their own homes and their property must be restored. Hence, from 1915 to 1916, despite moral defeatism in the main matter, there was a reasonably consistent argument of German diplomacy against Talaat's scheme, since Wangenheim, Germany's representative, had approved only a temporary removal of people from war zones in late spring 1915, and no spoliation. Although inconsequential, Cavid finally agreed that "the Armenians from the provinces of Anatolia" had "to come back to their homes," despite problems of restitution, partial destruction of homes, or the use of their properties by migrants and functionaries. He successfully defended this position in the parliament in mid-October 1918, after Talaat's resignation.[95]

Muhittin could not appreciate at all that "the Armenian issue was the whole reason" for German democrats to abandon Turkey in late summer 1918 in the name of humanity and a democratic future. (In his memoir, the murder of Erzberger and Germany's crises of the 1920s were the punishment for blindness and an unfaithful abandonment. In contrast to men like Erzberger, Adolf Hitler chose the right way, as the Turks had done in an exemplary manner before him, he opined.) Muhittin was Talaat's most intimate contact when Talaat arrived in Berlin in early September 1918. Cavid had left Berlin before and met with Talaat in the train between Budapest and Vienna on 5 September.[96] Talaat became grave when Muhittin reported to him about Germany's ongoing domestic collapse, Erzberger's statements, and the categorical language that Erzberger used in the name of democracy. Talaat still refused to accept a world war defeat that implied the defeat of his whole regime, reckoning with history and the urgent call of democracy.

In his negotiations with German foreign minister Paul von Hintze and General Lossow on 8 September 1918, Talaat turned his back on the pan-Turkist surge that parts of the CUP had been obsessed with since 1917. His new modesty translated into the formula of Caucasian "buffer states instead of Great power dreams," according to German protocol, and into renouncing annexations in Northern Iran. However, he left a door open to expansive influence by demanding "a new Mohammedan state in Turkestan" (east of the Caspian Sea with, according to Talaat, 14 million inhabitants). He demanded German arms and instructors for Turkestan in order to enable Turkestan's active participation in the war. Lossow answered that "we cannot send officers. We send, however, all the time [a lot of] arms. We do not need to control how Turkey uses them." On 13 September, Talaat was, according to Hintze, "very happy to be graciously invited [to the German military headquarters] by his Excellence" (the kaiser). In the German military headquarters, Talaat wished, in the words of Wilhelm von Stumm, undersecretary of state, "to comfort himself 'morally' by talking with his Excellence, the field marshal and general Ludendorff."[97]

In his repeated conversations with Muhittin in his hotel, Talaat finally became resigned to the reality that defeat in the world war was at his door. He began to focus on what he regarded as the main challenges in Turkey after defeat, after abandonment by Germany, and the fall of the CUP. It was evidently impossible, henceforth, to maintain any territorial status quo of the Ottoman Empire during the impending peace negotiations. Talaat and his German interlocutors agreed that the governments of the Central powers would each call for a peace based on US president Wilson's Fourteen Points. In his talks with Muhittin, Talaat welcomed, for the first time, a separation of the Arab domains, anticipating that negotiations could impose it. His main argument regarded Asia Minor, the focal point of his politics since 1913. From now on, there "remained no problem of minorities in any former sense and importance. . . . We may have done well or badly; in any case we have succeeded in transforming Turkey to a nation-state in Anatolia. Among us, the elements of disturbance and dissension have decreased." Although realizing world war defeat, Talaat thus reconfirmed what he believed to be the salutariness of his main exploit: the destruction of Ottoman minorities demanding equality— above all, the Armenians.

Talaat moreover admitted that, out of fear, the CUP had largely suppressed any opposition, and that in the future, a liberal and a conservative political pole should mutually check the political life in Turkey. Truly liberal forces remained excluded from the political thought of this first father of the nation-state. What he understood as "liberal" had nothing to do with the universal meaning of the word or with Ottoman liberals like Prince Sabahaddin and Krikor Zohrab, whom he had sent, as allegedly treacherous, to death. He reduced the label "liberal" to define a comparatively leftist faction within the CUP in contrast to another, more conservative one. He opined that "Union and Progress must be separated into two parts" in order to control future Turkey. A few years later, Mustafa Kemal Pasha failed twice in his attempts, as preconceived by Talaat, to introduce, top-down, an oppositional party.[98]

Before departing from Berlin and arriving in Istanbul on 27 September 1918, Talaat had practically decided to resign. The mood in the Ottoman capital had gone from bad to worse vis-à-vis the manifest corruption that badly affected infrastructure and supplies. Politically, Talaat had nothing to fear, but he had to deal with growing unrest in the parliament and in the CUP itself after everybody had understood that his grand vizierate could not keep its promise of ending corruption and undersupply. "All money that came from Germany or was already in the country coalesced in a few hands, whereas the big masses impoverish and starve," German ambassador Bernstoff had stated in early 1918. Only temporarily had the peace with Russia, the recovery of territory, and the revival of Turan saved the situation in spring 1918.[99]

"Istanbul has entirely become a place abounding in disgrace" (i.e., corruption, illegal enrichment, and ostentatious opulence of CUP circles alongside large groups living in misery), Lütfi Simavi, a leading official at the sultan's court and a privileged observer, wrote in an entry on 25 May 1918.[100] Complaints against the CUP rulers abounded. "This cabinet has no longer any right to survive. It failed in every challenge that it wanted to meet," said member of the cabinet Cavid, who was back in the Ottoman capital a week before Talaat, in late September 1918. He was angry about Talaat's travels, which in his eyes had not produced tangible results. He revolted against the waste of resources for conquest in the Caucasus, Enver's notorious and ill-placed optimism, and the death cult of sectarian committee members. "Doctor Nâzım pointed to national honor. 'Together with the Germans we will and are bound to die.'"[101]

FIGURE 23: Talaat Pasha in the moon of Kurban Bayramı
(Sacrifice Feast, 16–19 September 1918), from which peace
is expected (*Karagöz*, 27 September 1918).

Although his face looked extremely sad when he got off the
train at Sirkeçi station on 27 September 1918, on the same day, in
a press conference, Talaat drew a rosy picture of his Berlin visit
and the general situation. The collapse of the fronts in Bulgaria
and Syria were of minor importance, since "in the Caucasus
and Central Asia fresh forces were organized from [Turkes-
tan's] Turks and soon brought to the fronts, thus making up
the balance." Journalist and professor at the Istanbul University
Ahmed Emin (Yalman) could not find any comfort and sign
of hope in Talaat's "tired old refrains regarding the Caucasus."
When the grand vizier called him shortly after, he spoke an
entirely different language: "What I said to you all was to prevent sudden excitation and panic among the people. The truth
is that everything is finished. We have lost the war. . . . We have

committed a lot of mistakes. Yet you know that our love for the fatherland was strong, and that out of national fears we took a couple of risks and finally lost the thread."[102]

On 29 September 1918, two days after Talaat's arrival in the Ottoman capital, Bulgaria laid down its arms so that Turkey was isolated from Austria and Germany. "This news exploded like a bomb in Istanbul." Bewilderment and wretchedness reigned in the CUP Nuruosmaniye headquarters. Muhittin, Talaat's frequent companion in the last year of war and lead writer of the CUP paper *Tanin*, faced intellectual ruin. "How many years I have said so many things to the people. Everything has all at once collapsed."[103] Talaat's resignation was declared in the press on 13 October 1918. The new cabinet of Ahmed İzzet Pasha started on 14 October. Ahmed Tevfik Pasha, whom Sultan Vahideddin had first trusted to form a new ministry, had failed to succeed because Talaat had pressured him to include CUP men like Cavid and Hayri in the new cabinet.

Not everything had collapsed. Viewed from the CUP, the foremost organization of Turkish Muslim power since 1908 and the impetus of what this study calls "imperial war ummah," the time had now arrived to let CUP men who were not compromised by warmongering and direct anti-Armenian involvement—like İzzet, Hüseyin Rauf (Orbay), Mustafa Kemal, Mustafa Hayri, Kâzım Karabekir, and Ali Fethi (Okyar)—come into Turkey's limelight. They were all officers, except Hayri, and nearly the same age, except Hayri and İzzet. Moreover, Talaat's circle made sure that through a new organization called Karakol (Sentinel), based on CUP and SO members, there was a CUP-guided underground organization in and beyond Istanbul after the end of his rule.[104]

On 1 November 1918, Talaat delivered a farewell speech at the last CUP Congress in the Nuruosmaniye headquarters. A collaborator of Atatürk's, minister of education and Kemalist professor of history Yusuf H. Bayur (1891–1980), has detailed Talaat's "manifest lies regarding most important points," in his voluminous work *Türk inkılâbı tarihi*, written in the middle of the twentieth century. He notably elaborated on Talaat's wrong chronology regarding the genesis of the German-Ottoman alliance and his cleansed account of the anti-Russian Ottoman aggression in late October, both of which attenuated responsibility for the embrace of war. Not the expectant war-gambling from his and the CUP side but German pressure appeared, in his words on 1 November, as the main cause for Turkey's fatal entrance into war in 1914. "I absolutely intended to enter the war together with our allies," he stated, thus not denying his disposition toward war and the admission that he was convinced until 1918 of Germany's victory, but he pretended that he had wanted to postpone official entrance into war. Factual entrance into war must, however, be distinguished from official entrance in November 1914. The CUP had most willingly started irregular warfare at the eastern front in August; Gökalp had publicly, though unofficially, declared jihad on a road toward Turan. These sins of omission in Talaat's speech concerned crucial elements of total war and the matrix for genocide. Talaat could, however, not "deny evil deeds." Yet, again, he tried to evade primary responsibility by distorting narratives, suppressing facts, and relegating blame.[105]

Still, by fall 1918, large parts of the population stuck by Talaat and even loved him. They kept on believing in him as a little-educated but successful child from ordinary people like themselves. In their eyes, he stood for highly committed patriotism, national resurrection, and, in contrast to most others, incorruptibility. Once defeat was clear in October 1918, they expected from him at least a steadfast confession of what had gone wrong—in order to save their belief in him as a basically "good ruler." "They believed that ... he would stand up to justice and bravely accept any eventual judgment. This, however, did not happen," Lütfi Simavi wrote in his entry on 3 November 1918. He emphasized that the sad news of Talaat's, Enver's, and Cemal's flight exploded again like a bomb in Istanbul. There was still no answer from President Wilson by early November to the Ottoman proposal to accept peace according to Wilson's principles.[106]

German Asylum: Keeping on the Struggle

In the middle of the night on 1–2 November 1918, Talaat fled on a German vessel to Sevastopol on the Crimean Peninsula, together with CUP members Enver, Cemal, Nâzım, and Şakir. Grand Vizier Ahmed İzzet did not prevent the fugitives' flight yet asked for their extradition as soon as the court in Istanbul demanded it. Though victim of a plot in late 1913 that had made him resign from the war ministry in favor of Enver, İzzet did not seek personal revenge nor effective justice but acted within the limits that Turkish Muslim patriotism inspired him.

All three former ministers sent him short farewell letters that emphasized their unselfish commitment to state, nation, and fatherland. (These were rhetorical figures present in almost all "ego-documents" of the CUP cohort written in the first and second thirds of the twentieth century.) They asked for understanding for their flight at that critical time. Cemal underlined that he had not feared being arrested, "as you know better than anyone else," clearly pointing to the anti-Armenian crimes in which he had not been directly involved. Enver foregrounded his future commitment to Muslim independence in the Caucasus and that he would thus indirectly again fight for "my religion, my nation, and my sultan." Former grand vizier Talaat chose a personal language in his letter. His striking emphasis on honesty, modest property, and a limited amount of money, of which he would take half with him and leave the rest to his family, may suggest a strategic lie (if analyzed in the context of his numerous telic deceits). He may have taken important assets with him that allowed him to agitate in and from Berlin, as he was, in fact, to do.[107]

From Crimea, accompanied by Şakir and Nâzım, Talaat continued by train to Berlin, where he arrived on 10 November, one day after the German emperor Wilhelm II had himself fled the German capital. There, insecurity and a revolutionary atmosphere reigned. After the first difficult days in a hotel at the Alexanderplatz, then at other places, Talaat finally moved to a big flat that friends had found for him at the Hardenbergerstrasse 4, today's Ernst-Reuter Square, near the Zoologischer Garten railway station. Friedrich Ebert, the new chancellor from the Social Democratic Party, signed a paper that legalized Talaat's stay and travels in Germany. His wife, Hayriye, followed him in spring 1920.[108]

Old friends of the Foreign Ministry proved very helpful. Foreign minister Wilhelm Solf had written to the embassy in Constantinople that Germany would, of course, offer asylum to Talaat and Enver, loyal long-term allies, in contrast to those who, by leaving Turkey, wanted only "to elude responsibility for the persecution of the Armenians." He added—with doubled absurdity and simplemindedness—that "we must not retroactively become complicit in protecting perpetrators from punishment."[109] Oscar Wassermann (board member of the Deutsche Bank), Hanna Wangenheim (widow of the deceased German ambassador), and many others offered the former grand vizier and his companions hospitality. Talaat claimed lack of means in his letters, and Cavid's diary seems to confirm this situation. Yet he possessed the means to build up a center of agitation in Berlin and to travel extensively throughout Europe. In any case, he enjoyed support from wealthy friends like Wassermann, Strauss (a collaborator of the German Foreign Office and/or the Deutsche Bank), and Karasu and Mazliah, old party friends from Salonica and collaborators of the war regime, who repeatedly appear in his postwar correspondence.[110]

Talaat reemerged discreetly in Berlin under the name of Ali Sâî ("zealous worker"), a pseudonym he had already taken in autumn 1912 as a war volunteer, though he also used several other pseudonyms. In contrast to his show of patriotic defiance and his self-assured proclamation in summer 1912, when the CUP had also lost power and the deposed minister remained, nevertheless, in the capital, he decided now, in a more serious situation and deeper depression, for asylum in Berlin. He feared the revenge of political rivals and international, foremost British, justice. Above all, fear reigned regarding the "notorious topic" (Cavid), the crimes against the Armenians, so that the CUP decided all members clearly involved in these activities, for example, Diyarbekir deputy Feyzi or Anteb deputy Ali Cenani, go into hiding or at least disappear for a while from the Ottoman capital.[111]

Supported by the Turkish club in Berlin, and ordered to do so by Grand Vizier İzzet Pasha, the ambassador to Germany, Rifat Pasha, made efforts to extradite the high-ranking CUP asylum seekers to the justice of the Istanbul government.[112] Yet forces within the young Weimar Republic backed these exiles of the former ally and luminaries of the defunct single-party regime. Solf and many others German notables, still respectful of the CUP representatives, continued considering Talaat as an honorable and meritorious statesman, as German war propaganda had represented him for four years. More schizo-phrenically than naively, they missed coming to terms with Talaat's main share of the blame in the Armenian issue. Cavid (himself convinced of his friend's responsibility for the abomi-nation in 1915) wondered in late 1918 that Germans, although they believed that relevant orders had been given by Talaat and the CUP, could still absurdly seek others responsible behind the obvious playmaker Talaat.[113]

Initially, Talaat wished to return to Turkey as soon as possi-ble. Because of young officers and students in contact with left-wing Germans during the first weeks after World War I, parts of the Turkish club in the German capital were highly critical of the collapsed CUP regime. They planned to publish an article in the name of the Turkish colony in Berlin describing "how 800,000 Armenians had been murdered." Talaat denigrated all those who put the facts this way as ignominious. He started to organize the forces that shared his interests and understanding, including Islamists and Germans from the right wing.[114]

Even Hamdullah Suphi (Tanrıöver) made an impressive anti-CUP speech in the Turkish club on the crime against the Armenians. He was one of the most influential representatives of the Turkish Homeland (Türk Yurdu/Türk Ocağı) movement in Istanbul since 1912, and was sent to Berlin in autumn 1918 to inspect the Turkish students. The suspicious youth judged him, however, an opportunist and obstructed his leadership in the club. In-line with left-wing leader Rosa Luxemburg, who had protested persecution of Armenians already as a student in the 1890s, they were committed to a truly socialist attitude, including human and minority rights. Once back in Turkey, as historian of the Turkish Left Mete Tunçay concludes, "they started the first serious left-wing movement" of Turks (i.e., not predominantly composed of Ottoman Christians, as in the

decades before). It was soon brutally suppressed by the Kemalist regime.[115]

Since the former grand vizier and his friends enjoyed German protection from the top, as well as support in conservative
and nationalist papers, which rejected any notion of war crimes,
Rifat Pasha's efforts were frustrated, the self-critical momentum
among Turks in Berlin was lost, and the opportunity for a common soul-searching of Turks and Germans was squandered.
Next to his apartment, Talaat founded an "Oriental Club" (Şark
Kulübesi) where anti-Entente Muslims and their European
sympathizers met. They agitated and cultivated their ideas without fear of any censure or sanction. Right from the beginning of
his exile, Talaat was given the opportunity to agitate and even
to influence the German press again. Thanks to his relations in
Berlin, he was also able to organize a fake passport for Cavid.[116]

Talaat's acquaintance with well-disposed politicians and
diplomats, and a network of CUP sympathizers abroad, his
disguise (European dress, loss of weight, no mustache), and
a fake passport allowed him considerable mobility throughout Germany and Europe, although Britain and the Istanbul
government wanted him for trial. The courts-martial in Istanbul sentenced him in absentia to death on 5 July 1919, together
with Enver, Cemal, and Nâzım. Talaat's restless, subversive
diplomacy in 1919–20 included travels to meetings in Italy,
Switzerland, Sweden, Holland, and Denmark. Seen as a representative of a rapidly burgeoning Turkish resistance against
Entente plans, he reacquired stature, not only among Germans
and Bolsheviks but also for an Italy in quest of new influence in
the Balkans and the Levant. Many expected him to help them
financially.[117]

Agitation abroad, along with new dynamics in Anatolia itself, led within months to a broad Turkish nationalist

consensus in which the denial, trivialization, or relativization of major war crimes played a central role. Propaganda thus won momentum in nationalist circles in Turkey and its European diaspora, which presented Muslims, Turks, and Germans as the true and main victims of modern history and the world war. Many Germans shared this view. Yet in many ways, Germany remained deeply divided regarding its own war guilt and Turkey's war crimes. In constrast to flimsy, politically guided discourses of victimization, the first months after war saw, among many acts of soul-searching, a public memorial service in Berlin's big Hedwig Cathedral in May 1919 that paid tribute to the main victims of the Great War, referring to the massacre and starvation of "more than a million Armenians." It insisted that "Germany must carry with the suffering Armenian nation more pain than any other nation." Similarly, in 1919, Johannes Lepsius wrote in the preface of his reedited 1916 report *The Road to Death of the Armenian People*: "As bad as it looks in our own country, our misery cannot be compared to this genocide ["Völkermord" in the German original], which the Young Turks have on their conscience." Challenging his compatriot Jäckh, an unrepentant CUP enthusiast, the journalist Friedrich Schrader, a long-time resident in Turkey, also asked for German soul-searching (though with culturalist connotation): "Abroad, too, we shall not, as we have done, always stick by the party that aims for the violation of important cultural groups in favor of its own national hegemony. This will always revenge itself, as it did in Turkey. We should not have been more Turkish than the Turks."[118]

In mid-May 1919, once the Greek army occupied İzmir and its environments (where the CUP had organized the large-scale ethnic cleansing of Rûm in spring 1914), a self-righteous chorus based on Ottoman-Muslim resentment overpowered all self-critical voices. It literally perverted the vocabulary of genocide (murder of a nation and Völkermord in contemporary German diction) through a hyperbolic use of pamphletic notions, like "martyrdom of a nation" or "murder of a nation," exclusively related to defeated Turkey as treated by the victors. Hence, sincere and courageous Turkish attempts at honest history failed in late 1918 and early 1919, and was soon to be buried altogether.[119]

Turks joined not only a transnational Muslim chorus claiming that "final victory will be ours, because we are innocent victims," as read a declaration of the Union of Revolutionary Islamic Committees, a kind of SO successor organized by CUP members in exile, but they were also joined by leading voices of the German Far Right, which deeply believed in a "community of destiny" of Turkey and Germany. They shared a congruent view on contemporary history, saying that German politics with Turkey could in no way be blamed for the outbreak of the world war. A long-standing acquaintance of Talaat's, the sharp-minded, sharp-tongued Karl Helfferich in Berlin, considered it an "irrefutable historical truth" that Germany's neighbors had had "wishes that could only be realized by war." In this vein, both nations had, as loyal and committed allies, fought "a struggle for survival to the bitter end. The imposed Peace of Sèvres is the side piece of the Peace of Versailles, forced upon us."[120]

———

In seeking asylum, former grand vizier and party leader Talaat wanted not only to save himself and avoid humiliation but as a komiteci and signature political animal, he was soon busy organizing the European front of Turkey's post–world war struggle, and he wrote influential letters to friends in Istanbul and elsewhere. He encouraged them to resist and revolt in the name of

Turkish rule, pride, and national salvation.[121] He also penned
his memoirs and enjoyed a considerable audience in turbulent
post–World War I Germany. Militant right-wing circles, who
openly sympathized with the CUP fugitives, desired a putsch
against the Weimar Republic, although this had suppressed
left-wing revolutionists. In their eyes, the new republic was
much too compliant with the demands of the victors in Paris-
Versailles. When their Kapp putsch failed miserably in Berlin in
March 1920, the "master of revolution" (as Talaat was acknowledged) was seen and heard at the subsequent press conference.
He explained that "a putsch without a cabinet ready at hand was
just childish."

This advice came late for Hans Humann, a participant of
the Kapp putsch and long-standing acquaintance of Enver and
Talaat (see chap. 1, sec. "Relying on Germany" and chap. 5, sec.
"Victor, Noah, National Father"). This former attaché at the
German Embassy in Istanbul must have been in frequent touch
with Talaat. After the putsch, Humann began to publish the
Deutsche Allgemeine Zeitung in Berlin, a paper that besides the
Nazi papers focused mostly on Turkey, advocating "Turkish
methods" for "Germany's salvation." The expectant attention of
right-wing revolutionists began to turn to Asia Minor, where an
encouraging anti-Entente movement under Kemal Pasha was
rapidly emerging.[122]

Talaat had wanted to send the manuscript of his memoirs to
Istanbul for publication in autumn 1919 but renounced the idea,
perhaps because Cavid advised against it, seeing its assertions
as unreliable and its impact as counterproductive. Finished during his first year of exile, this text is a militant defense of his
and the CUP's position and policy. To Herbert he called it "a
memorandum on the Armenian massacres," thus once more
confirming the centrality of the Armenians in his political life.

Seeking anew good relations with Britain, Talaat had sent Herbert a letter after the Armistice "in which he declared that he was not responsible for the Armenian massacres, that he could prove it, and that he was anxious to do so." Talaat's young collaborator Hüseyin Cahid (Yalçın) noted retrospectively that "the situation and conditions" of Talaat's asylum in Germany "did not allow him to write true memoirs," and that Cavid had asked him to write memoirs during war already, but he had not wanted to do so then.[123] The young agitators in the diaspora loved the manuscript, but Talaat confessed in a letter to Cavid shortly before his death that, in the final analysis, he did not like it, and therefore he kept the manuscript under tight wraps.[124] Talaat himself probably recognized that his defensive text lacked persuasion and vision.

As a matter of fact, the leader of Ottoman Turkey in the 1910s remained in his written legacy defined by former arguments, far from introspection and, despite debacle, from new horizons. It is true that weighty constraints, malleable, often opportunistic behavior and possible multiple identities shape individuals. Talaat's apogee in the cataclysmic 1910s coincided with the birth of surrealism, (pacifist!) Dadaism, and the total questioning, in literature and beyond, of any unity of the person. Yet, how to conceive the human being other than as a potentially responsible individual, and thus take as fundamental Talaat's gift to respond to the questions and challenges of where he was, what he did, and where he moved? In any case, his memoirs are a telling contemporary ego-document. Starting his text, the author grieves over Europe's hollow talk about law, humanity, and its cruel international system, which had betrayed the Ottoman status quo, though the Berlin Treaty had warranted it. This served him by emphasizing Turkey's victimhood and the righteousness of CUP defiance.

His apologia identified with an imperial Turkey that he saw at risk of annihilation. He left no doubt that he considered only Muslims as Turkey's nationals and was at pains to prove himself a true Turk and Muslim (though on the same page he tried to reduce this identity matter—of critical importance for his politics—to an "issue of soul and feeling"). A war goal had been, he acknowledged, "creating a [Turkish Muslim] national sentiment, and rooting this sentiment in the spirit of the nation." The war at Germany's side had been popular, he asserted, because "the sultan, the crown prince, the senate and the parliament, the army officers, the population and the civil servants—all had come to believe that the country was now saved."[125] The author admitted some failures in politically sensitive matters—the treatment of the Armenians and wartime profiteering—yet he emphasized an honest, general patriotic commitment both domestically and at the fronts.

Barely disguised lies obliterate, however, true soul-searching in Talaat's apologia. Though rightly pointing to German pressure, Talaat described the situation of late October 1914 as if he and Enver had had no idea of Admiral Souchon's aggression, which triggered official entrance into war. In the same vein, he downplayed his proactivity in preparing the German-Ottoman alliance, as if Ambassador Wangenheim had taken the initiative. In the Armenian issue, he pretended having done all to slow down the application of deportation measures in the East, and then he asserted that a general uprising had demanded the actual removal from all of Asia Minor. The removal of the Armenians had "taken a disastrous shape," but Muslim civilians in the East suffered similarly. Evildoers had only been a few immoral individuals and savage Kurds. In matters of mismanagement and enrichment parallel to widespread domestic starvation, the former minister slandered Ali Mazhar, the righteous governor of Ankara. In any case, if ever, Mazhar, who had lost his income, stood entirely at the margins of a corrupted national war economy that Talaat and his men had implemented.[126]

From Europe, the author of the apologia expected high standards of justice as far as he and his cause were concerned but dismissed these standards as soon as others claimed them. In this logic, demanding justice for CUP war crimes with foreign help was "an assassination" of Turkish patriots that, he threatened, would be punished.[127] Talaat, in fact, literally called on the ghost of vengeful prosecution of all those who spoke truth on the mass crimes of World War I in Turkey after him.

———

In late 1918, Talaat was depressed by dizzy disillusionment after the high spirits that had reigned in spring. World war defeat and the imprint of an internationally and, in the first months after the end of the war, also nationally condemned CUP regime afflicted him. Yet in Berlin, he soon understood that European turmoil would protect him and allow for efficient agitation in-line with his former ideological choices. Familiar with defiant subversion, clandestine activities, conspiratorial networking, and allusive communication, he quickly found room to maneuver. By May 1920 he had established a propaganda office in Berlin with Arif Cemil (Denker) as his collaborator; had built up contacts with Turkish nationalist agitators in Lausanne, The Hague (La Haye), and Rome; and was the most authoritative figure of Turkey's militant networks abroad.[128]

Though in exile, Talaat maintained the militant "national spirit of war" that had inspired him since autumn 1912. He himself had been the main instigator and representative of an Ottoman "war ummah" that had been operating then. In contrast

to Abdulhamid's state-centered Islamism, with which it had
nevertheless joined, Gökalp's ideology galvanized Talaat and
culturally Turkish elites from the early 1910s until far beyond
World War I. "Turan" had been an expansive ideal, the Muslim Türk Yurdu in Asia Minor a minimal goal since the Balkan
Wars, and the focus of Talaat's politics in 1913–18. It became
the supreme goal of the post-1918 struggle led by Mustafa
Kemal. Although Talaat set much hope on Muslim militancy
in the Caucasus and Turkestan, he subordinated this hoped-for
dynamic to his paramount goal, the emergence of "an entirely
sovereign Turkey" in Anatolia, possibly confederated at last
with the Arabs.[129]

The contemporary victors named the Muslim struggle for
Anatolia in 1919–22 the War of Independence (İstiklâl Harbi).
For contemporary CUP adherents, from which the Kemalists
arose, it stood in agreement with a fight for sovereignty and
independence, starting definitively in 1913 and incarnated by
Talaat. Mustafa Kemal Pasha, a guerilla leader at Enver's side in
Tripoli against the Italians in 1911, and a general of fame since
the defense of Gallipoli in 1915, headed the Turkish War of
Independence in Anatolia from May 1919, and the subsequent
Ankara government. Politically ambitious, Kemal Atatürk had
been dissatisfied with the CUP leaders during the world war
but did not find, after the end of CUP rule in autumn 1918, the
leading place in a cabinet that he had sought—or been associated with—even before the end of the war.[130]

Instead of inspecting the army forces in Asia Minor to sub-
due them all to the Istanbul government in late spring 1919,
Kemal disobeyed and turned his mission into an organization
of revolt and war. Like the CUP luminaries before him, he pursued the goal of a sovereign and national Turkish-Muslim rule,
but now stripped from the overstretched attempt at territorial

restoration and expansion of the empire. Mustafa Kemal prepared the countergovernment in Ankara, where a parliament was inaugurated in April 1920. It was composed of delegates mostly elected by nationalist organizations, whose members had largely identified with the previous "war ummah," although they may have voiced occasional criticism of the CUP.

Significantly, Talaat's friend Ziya Gökalp also became a leading ideologist for post-1918 nationalism and Mustafa Kemal. Even more than the CUP luminaries, he now effusively extolled the leader and "great genius" Mustafa Kemal (Atatürk), who finally welcomed the former committee member in Ankara in 1922. "The whole world respects the name of the Gazi Mustafa Kemal Pasha," Gökalp wrote in 1921. "Beforehand, the Turkish nation had no right in Turkey. Today, all rights are theirs. The sovereignty of this country is the sovereignty of the Turk; in politics, culture, and economy the Turkish people reign."[131]

Which role did Talaat play in the post-1918 struggle for Turkish rule in Asia Minor? He understood rapidly the necessity to respect the new central position of Mustafa Kemal, as it crystallized in 1919. He had known better than most others the difficult relationship of this former subordinate of Enver's with his superior during war. Almost everything was in flux in 1919, but Talaat was alert enough to purpose in late 1919 full collaboration with Mustafa Kemal in an assisting role. He described himself as the head of underground diplomacy and networking abroad, eager to help Kemal's reorganization of power on Anatolian ground.[132] Logically, Kemal sought every reasonable support inside and outside the country in the fragile context of his beginning struggle in 1919. Lacking means, he even asked Talaat for an important sum of money. Lobbying was urgently needed in Europe, where the victors of war stood in conflict over how to deal with the defeated Ottoman Empire, and thus

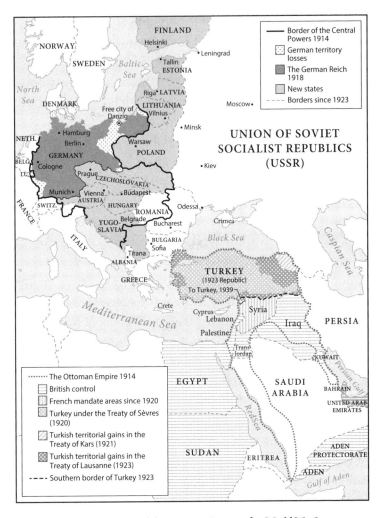

MAP 6: Europe and the Ottoman Empire after World War I.

sympathy and support could be won by propaganda and agitation, playing off one country against the other.

Mustafa Kemal had to conceal that his movement was mostly a continuation of the ill-reputed CUP and its circles across the country. Caution was therefore imperative in all contacts with former top leaders. Still, even if not on the luminaries, Kemal depended almost entirely on the former CUP networks, cadres, and know-how in Asia Minor. Moreover, the same war ummah and the same enemy images that had operated before autumn 1918—including the specter of returning Armenians demanding restoration of land and goods, and asking for justice— served as Kemal's popular, emotional, and ideological base for reorganizing an Anatolia-centered, post-CUP national governance (*millî teşkilat*). Significantly, in June 1920 Kemal's forces started an early military campaign against Armenian positions in the Southwestern Caucasus, forcibly preventing an Armenian home that would include former Ottoman territory, as the Treaty of Sèvres on 10 August 1920 stipulated. Kemal had already entirely identified with Talaat during war in refusing any return of Armenian survivors. In their eyes, these people had no right to come back to "Turkey's soil."[133]

Antiliberal International of Revolutionists

Reduced to life in exile, Mehmed Talaat bet again on the power of transnational revolutionary Islam, as he had done in August 1914, although he again proved that he had more sense for complex constellations and critical strategic developments than did his more passionate and illusionist fellow revolutionists. Still, he set considerable hope on Islamism and pan-Turkism, foremost on pro-Turkish dynamics among Muslims in the Caucasus. Most CUP luminaries not only fell back into their 1914 chimeras, which had revived after Russian revolutionary collapse in the Caucasus, but also their pre-1908 myths, when they had agitated underground. "Ongoing confusion and disaster in the Orient is a fatality, as long as there is no trust in the Turks." All would be better for everybody, if "as before, the Turks acted as guardians against trouble in the whole Orient," Talaat wrote to Cavid.[134]

From Berlin in late 1918, Talaat pursued hopes and efforts toward organizing militant Islamism in Egypt, India, Iraq, Afghanistan, and Turkestan, in cooperation with Enver, Cemal, Halil, and other CUP intimates. Communist fever after the Russian Revolution had reinspired revolutionary Islam. Anti-imperialism and the claim of victimhood united, and a heterogeneous, antiliberal international, composed by Bolsheviks, Islamists, the German right wing, CUP members, and Turkish nationalists, became partly operational. In the immediate aftermath of World War I, the Bolsheviks backed anti-Western Islamic and Turkish nationalist upheaval.

Transnational revolutionism did not impede Talaat's main focus on Asia Minor, in keeping with his long-lasting Ministry of the Interior and with Mustafa Kemal's struggle in Anatolia. Both considered Islam and Bolshevism, above all, as means to establish a politically and economically sovereign Turkey, and believed that the Western powers would give in, if the Turkish demonstration of power in Asia Minor was sufficiently sustained. Thus, both relied on support from Bolshevik Russia to counter British influence in view of the fight for the Türk Yurdu. "An alliance with the Bolshevists was purely a matter of expediency," Talaat told Aubrey Herbert. Full Turkish sovereignty in all of Asia Minor plus Eastern Thrace, Aleppo, and Mosul thus became the main principle of the National Pact (Misak-ı Millî),[135] agreed on by the parliament in Istanbul in early 1920. This National Pact also formed the basic agreement for the new parliament in Ankara, where several deputies fled after Britain had occupied the Ottoman capital in March 1920.

In autumn 1919, Talaat traveled to Holland, where he met Camille Huysmans, the secretary of the Second Socialist

International, whom he tried to influence on the Armenian issue; Switzerland, where he met Cavid and where an important Turkish-nationalist diaspora had already begun to agitate; and Italy, where Mustafa Kemal's anti-British movement enjoyed support in the highest quarters. Around mid-December 1919, Talaat organized a "congress" (or rather, meeting) of CUP sympathizers in Berlin. This event showed, as a contemporary observed, "cordial relations existing between the Turkish Nationalist organizations, the Bolshevik-Mussulman groups, and the Pan-German Nationalists!"[136] Talaat had in fact visited the communist leader Karl Radek several times in the Moabit prison, situated not far from the Zoologischer Garten railway station where Talaat lived. In his letter to Mustafa Kemal on 22 December 1919, he claimed that Radek, whom he knew from the Brest-Litovsk negotiations, was released from prison thanks to his efforts. Thus, Radek could also travel to Lenin in Moscow to work for good Turkish-Bolshevik relations in the interest of Germany.

Successful organization of power in the East against the victors of World War I required a collusion, or open cooperation, of Islamism, Turkish nationalism, and Bolshevism. This resulted in a collaboration of radical (Bolshevik) left-wing and markedly right-wing (ex-CUP and German nationalist) forces for which Germany served as a place of subversion. The Bolshevik flirtation with anti-Western Islamism revealed itself most during the Baku Congress of the Peoples of the East in September 1920, which was also attended by Enver. Six years after the German promotion of jihad (and sixty years before the CIA began to play the Islamist card and arm jihadists for good), the Comintern chief Grigory Zinoviev called upon Baku to wage a holy war against Western imperialism and was enthusiastically applauded by sword-raising listeners.

By 1920, centers of Islamic revolutionary committees were
established in many places and led by former CUP leaders,
including Berlin (Talaat), Baku (Bahaeddin Şakir), Afghanistan (Cemal), Anatolia (Küçük Talaat [Muşkara] and Nail), and
the Central Committee in Moscow (Enver and Nâzım). Enver
assured the Berlin center that, although working in good relation with the Bolsheviks in Russia, "we are not communists,
but pursue, within the limits defined by caliphate and sultanate, a policy that accepts the sovereignty of the people according to socialist principles."[137] Upon arrival in Kabul in fall 1920,
Cemal promised Talaat that he would organize huge Muslim
raids against British India.[138]

The saying "Les extrêmes se touchent" (extremisms join)
became true regarding revolutionism in postwar Turkey and
Russia, although not immediately. In the early working relationship of Bolsheviks with CUP leaders in exile and Kemal's
organization of nationalist power in Asia Minor, the Armenian
issue still played a critical role. Radek, back in Moscow, and
Georgy Chicherin, the Soviet responsible for foreign affairs,
still suggested in May 1920 that Turkey cede parts of the Ottoman eastern provinces to the Armenians, whereas, contrarily,
the Kemalists, foremost Kâzım Karabekir, their commander
at the eastern front, were at pains to content themselves with
the retention of the provinces of Kars, Batumi, and Ardahan,
acquired as a result of the Brest-Litovsk Treaty. Radek emphasized that Turkish responsiveness in this sensitive issue would
greatly improve Turkey's moral stand. Yet already in April
1920, Mustafa Kemal (Atatürk) had, in a letter to Lenin, displayed intransigence, stigmatizing the Armenian leadership as
an "imperialist government" to be attacked, because it sought
support from and shared values with the West.[139]

The Armenians, their fate, and their cause were well and
long known among Russian revolutionaries and in the Socialist

International, to which both the ARF and the Social Democrat Hunchakian Party belonged. Yet in favor of a common Turkish-Bolshevik move against designs of the "imperialist" Paris Peace Conference, by mid-1920 the Soviet rulers sacrificed an Armenian future in the former Ottoman homeland, after having first taken a different position loyal to common socialist bonds, the human solidarity with Armenian victims, and the Russian-backed reform plan of 1914. Gotthard Jäschke, a contemporary German area specialist, rightly emphasized the "total change of direction" by the Bolsheviks in 1920, induced by geostrategy.[140] Revolutionaries from the Left and the Right arrived then to join forces at the expense of the weakest and most victimized group of World War I, united in fundamental opposition to the peace treaties of Paris. The Europe-related Treaty of Versailles of 12 August 1919 was followed by the Levant-related Treaty of Sèvres on 10 August 1920. It was not a very long road from Armenia's denigration to the common revilement of Poland as "bastard of the Versailles Treaty" by both National Socialists and Soviets on the eve of common invasion in September 1939.[141]

––––––

Talaat had sent a long letter to Mustafa Kemal shortly after the Berlin meeting of mid-December 1919. This letter can be read as a full acknowledgment of Mustafa Kemal, the new hopeful leader of a Turkish power organization on Anatolian ground, and thus successor in a war of independence that had started in 1913.

Kemal's answer to Talaat on 20 February 1920 is a self-confident, though still tentative, acknowledgment of Talaat's principles, even if neither Kemal himself nor Kemalist historiography after him would ever have agreed with this reading. In his 22 December 1919 letter, Talaat had explained with great seriousness, and in most parts unpretentiously, his view of current affairs. He presented what he considered necessary for the reorganization of a sovereign "national governance" (or "national organization"; the term *millî teşkilat* appears frequently in both letters). Kemal and Talaat agreed on the essential points. Both believed in the operative power of Turkish and Muslim solidarity in and beyond Asia Minor, the propaganda force of the caliphate, and the need for Bolshevik support. Both proposed a "national" Muslim power reorganization in Asia Minor by a clandestine network of selected men under a supreme leader, that is, Mustafa Kemal, who was capable of waging war against the British-supported Greek forces that had landed in Izmir in May 1919. The leader had to exercise authoritative power behind a public facade, made up by a parliament, a cabinet, and a dominant party.

Both thus envisioned a fundamentally undemocratic governance in the post-1913 tradition of party leader and minister Talaat. Both shared the same animosity toward liberal citizens, whom they called "vile," "foolish," and traitors, because they put into question, in consensus with Entente voices, the recent past, including the nationalism promoted by the CUP since fall 1912. Liberals and others dared (most unpatriotically, as both agreed) to ask for justice for the recent crimes against non-Muslim compatriots. Mentioned in Mustafa Kemal's letter, and particularly targeted in this context, was, among many others, Ali Kemal, a mercurial journalist and minister of the Istanbul government in 1919. Nureddin Pasha, a CUP general who had been passed down to the Ankara government, let a mob kidnap and lynch Ali Kemal in 1922. A "severe fanatic and demagogue," in Falih Rıfkı (Atay)'s words, Nureddin was an expert in stirring up mob violence, thus personifying the continuity of extremist leadership on the ground. He brutally repressed the

Koçgiri rebellion of Alevi Kurds against the Ankara government and ordered the deathly removal of Pontus Rûm in 1921.
Leading the army that retook Izmir in September 1922 from the
Greeks, he was largely responsible for murdering civilians and
destroying the town by fire.[142]

Although he had, like so many others, uttered public criticism against the CUP regime right after the end of the war,
Mustafa Kemal identified himself in his very long letter on 20
February 1920 as largely in consensus with the former grand
vizier. He recycled patterns of Talaat's war discourse, foremost
the hyperbolic argument that the Entente had wanted to can-
cel "our right to exist." He assured Talaat that he, too, agreed
that the Ottoman Empire's participation in the world war on
Germany's side had been unavoidable and concluded that it
was absurd to persecute a few politicians for war guilt. He also
made clear that he was on Talaat's side regarding the Armenian
issue. He stressed again and again the "we" of an elite under his
crystallizing leadership, heading an Ottoman-Muslim nation in
Anatolia, and included, unmistakably, Talaat in this "we." In his
postwar letters, Talaat likewise repeatedly used this same "we."

In contrast to Kemal, Talaat stressed the makeup of a basic
power organization (teşkilat-ı esasiyye) abroad in a "wide Turkish world" and in a "Muslim world." He postulated "the unity
of the Turks" and the possible unity of Turks and Arabs. In
Turkestan and Afghanistan, Cemal and Enver had begun to
agitate. Talaat still counted on them, whereas Mustafa Kemal
was more reluctant. Yet Kemal built the main justification and a
compelling emotional rhetoric on the assertion that the sultan-
caliph was in the hands of the enemies, and that thus his fight
was in the name of a sovereign sultanate-caliphate.[143] He, too,
emphasized Islamic unity, working relations with anti-French
and anti-British forces in the Levant and the Caucasus, and,

in one of his friendly letters to Cemal, the utility of "striking Britain in India."[144] Kemal, too, addressed the possibility of a Turkish-Arab confederation that might even also include the Muslims of the Caucasus. The National Pact did not exclude confederative perspectives, although they remained secondary in the primary struggle for the Anatolian Türk Yurdu.

In his long letter to Talaat, the rising star of Turkish politics largely identified with the former grand vizier and CUP head. Thus, after Talaat had quasi-endorsed him in his letter as the incontestable leader on the ground, Mustafa Kemal approved in turn not only Talaat's current, "very satisfying efforts in Europe," but de facto also Talaat himself as Kemal's predecessor for a patriotic cause that, in spite of the mentioned differences, they both understood, essentially, in the same terms. Neither Enver and Cemal nor any other CUP leader played a comparable role. Eager to ensure Talaat's ongoing, supportive subordination to the Ankara government, Kemal continued to address him as a cooperative "brother," and Talaat apparently understood himself until his death as entrusted by Mustafa Kemal for diplomatic and propaganda duty in Europe. The very low profile of Kemal and Kemalism in acknowledging this cooperation does not abrogate the facts.[145]

After world war and defeat, Talaat had assessed, more realistically than most other CUP luminaries, Turkey's situation and its possibilities of reconcentrating post-CUP power. He thus became the first CUP top leader devoted to Mustafa Kemal, and ready to realize that, from 1920, the new national assembly and government in Ankara meant a new, post-CUP era in Turkey's political history. Enver never did so. He escaped to maniacal jihad in Turkestan and an anti-imperialist global struggle for Islam. For this purpose, he pinned his hopes on a new revolutionist committee grafted onto the SO, to be led by Turks and temporarily based on Soviet territory, which would allow him at the end to return victoriously to Anatolia. Talaat focused on power building in Anatolia, in concordance with his seasoned goal of a Türk Yurdu. He was therefore ready to compromise with Britain and to cooperate with Mustafa Kemal, although he knew that he would, perhaps, not be welcome in Ankara. In fact, an outspoken letter by Bekir Sami (Kunduh), the foreign minister of the Ankara government, had shown him his limits, but simultaneously emphasized that Ankara considered Talaat its representative for all of Europe (as opposed to the official legates of the Istanbul government).[146]

"The little educated telegraphist had . . . a holistic vision," Emil Ludwig had commented on Talaat's resignation in late October 1918, "yet overestimated the great energy he possessed. Nevertheless, this man is too strong, on the whole, to simply disappear. . . . Knowledge of human nature has a lot to commend that Enver will disappear, but Talaat will reemerge."[147] Biographer Ludwig, who combined historical with psychological analysis, proved right. This is true not only because of Talaat's agitation in exile or his possible reemergence in politics back home but because his overall legacy exerted posthumous influence in interwar Germany and, until today, in Turkey.

Death—and Afterlife—in Germany and Turkey

On the morning of Tuesday, 15 March 1921, at 10:45 a.m., Talaat left his home at Hardenbergstrasse 4 to buy gloves. Soghomon Tehlirian, a young Armenian, faced and recognized him, then advanced and turned, shooting the exile close from behind, in front of Hardenbergstrasse 27. Talaat died instantly, at the age of forty-seven. His companion Nâzım, who lived at Uhlandstrasse 194, a few minutes from where the assassination took place, arrived there shortly afterward, then went to Talaat's wife, Hayriye, at her home. At around 11:35 a.m., Ernst Jäckh, cofounder of the Turkish-German Society and propagandist of Turko-German world war, also arrived at Hardenbergstrasse 4. (Still a collaborator of the Foreign Office after the war, he continued to consider himself a "freelance ambassador" for friendship with a strong and independent Turkey.) Jäckh normally had an appointment with Talaat at 11:30. He and Nâzım went back to the scene of the murder.

For investigation by the murder commission of the police, the corpse was covered and left on the sidewalk until 1:00 p.m. Jäckh was agitated and argued with the patrolman that "the highest former official in allied Turkey . . . our loyal ally in the war," a "Turkish Bismarck," should not be left in a state of disrespect. At last, Jäckh and Nâzım got permission to transport the body to the nearby Charlottenburg mortuary. Jäckh told General Zeki Pasha and Nâzım wrote Cavid, relating what they knew about the event and what followed. Nobody could understand in Berlin at that time that Tehlirian had been assigned to his task by the ARF's secret operation "Nemesis," and that he had closely surveilled, since December 1920, the former Ottoman minister who was mainly responsible for the Armenians' agony. Talaat was number one on Nemesis's "list." Tehlirian enjoyed support by ARF members in Berlin, but his main handlers were stationed in Boston, among them Armen Garo, Talaat's former colleague in the Ottoman Parliament. (Garo had met Talaat a last time on 30 June 1914, when hate began to rule their relationship.) In early August 1914, Garo had escaped from Erzurum, where cross-frontier raids by the SO made up a matrix for genocide, before official war started (see chap. 5, secs. "For Turan's Sake," "Polarizing and Reframing the East," and "Embracing War").[148]

On Saturday, 19 March 1921, after a prayer in the home of the deceased, an impressive procession brought the corpse to the funeral at the comparatively nearby cemetery of Matthäi. Although invitations in the name of the Oriental Club and Hayriye had been sent to Talaat's broad circle, many more people than expected attended the funeral. Nâzım most appreciated the presence of High German officials who had stayed in contact with the assassinated former minister and grand vizier. During two hours, speeches in honor of the deceased were given by Bahaeddin Şakir in the name of the Turks, by Shekib Arslan and Sheik Abdülkadir for the Arabs, and by others for the Persians, the Azeris, and the Egyptians. In the name of the Germans, journalist Ernst Jäckh and the director of the Anatolian Railway, Franz Günther, exalted in their funeral orations the "great statesman and loyal friend" (as was also written on the wreath offered by the German Foreign Office). Şakir declared pathetically "in the name of the peoples of the Orient" that "the murder was not the product of personal or national revenge, but the consequence of imperialist politics against the Islamic nations. We will take revenge by breaking our chains and acquiring our independence."

Şakir thus deflected any concrete cause of the murder. Cavid dryly noted in his diary that they were wrong to believe that Britain or Greece had anything to do with the assassination. In his immediate reaction to Talaat's assassination, in the entry on 16 March 1921, he lamented that only Talaat's "iron hand had been capable of facing this [Turkey's] chaos that goes on for years." He revealed that "the only salvation for patriots loving their country, in order not to fall into despair because of all the corruption around them, had been to bring Talaat's ghost before their [spiritual] eyes." Talaat had, in fact, been Cavid's "attachment figure," although he had clearly suffered, not only under Talaat's disorganized and corrupt style but also, according to himself, under the undeniably evil aspects of Talaat's character.[149]

CUP friends intended to bring Talaat's remains back to Turkey, but for obvious political reasons, neither Istanbul nor Ankara wanted the body. It is remarkable that the newspapers in Ankara nevertheless eulogized the deceased grand vizier, lamented his death, and sharply condemned "the baseness of murdering a Turkish dignitary from behind." Like Şakir in Berlin, they pointed toward a British, not Armenian, conspiracy, because otherwise they would have drawn attention to a great open wound and Talaat's guilt regarding the Armenians. Papers in Entente-occupied Istanbul varied from harsh criticism of Talaat, notably by Ali Kemal, to paying homage to "the personality who [from 1908 to 1918] played the most important role in Turkey."[150] Most emphasized his extraordinary career from a mailman to a grand vizier. In contrast to those who exposed enrichment among CUP members, including Talaat, many articles provoked pity by writing that the pasha had been struck by poverty in exile. They also defended his anti-Armenian policy. A *Vakit* journalist stated rather critically that Talaat could now not render an account before the people, as he should have done, "being himself the key of the [Armenian-related] events."[151]

Journalist and deputy Celal Nuri (İleri) wrote right after Talaat's killing that "the era starting with the general war has not yet ended. Hence, we need to be cautious before giving a final judgment concerning this era. Even if Talaat Pasha had not become a grand vizier, history would have much to tell about him. More than a statesman, he was to be recognized as a revolutionary." He made a point by saying that "once the history of Talaat Pasha is written, the files of the Central Committee will have to say more than those of the Sublime Porte."[152] The daily

Joghovourti Tsayn of the independent Armenian socialist Dikran Zaven (who in the late 1890s had helped the CUP founders Cevdet and Sükûti publish *Osmanlı* in Geneva) struggled to come to terms with the enigmatic, all-too-ambivalent deceased. Now cursed by millions of victims, he had once "won even the trust of Rûm and Armenians through his democratic appearance." After getting power, Talaat and his circle "had wrongly believed that the history of Turkey, if not of the whole Middle East, restarted with them anew." Zaven hoped cautiously that "Turks aware of the true interests of their country will not count this former minister among their good statesmen."[153]

The German press, right-wing figures and officers, but also representatives of the Weimar Republic, paid respect to or openly identified with Talaat after his assassination. At the same time, they sympathized with Ankara's national countergovernment, which appeared enviable to them all, because it fought with growing success against accusations of war guilt and war crimes as determined by the Paris postwar treaties. Gustav Stresemann, leader of the national liberal German People's Party and later an internationally respected foreign minister, proposed to the Turkish-German Society in April 1921 that a public commemoration be held to honor the former grand vizier; he must have believed that this would gain merit in terms of popular sympathy.[154]

Yet despite broad German sympathies for him, Talaat proved divisive for the Weimar Republic when the trial against Tehlerian took place in June 1921. It clarified to a larger public that along with the assassination of a former high politician, crimes against humanity were at stake. Many journalists and doyens of public life underlined this relevance and took positions, and the tribunal itself pushed its scope of interpretation to the limit, to vindicate the killer, thus clearly condemning the former minister's great crime, which Germany had failed to stop during war or even connived in. People believing in universal values and circles close to the Armenians rejoiced at the manifestation of "another Germany than that of random and ruthless Turkophilia" (Ewald Stier). Others, like Heinrich Vierbücher or the leftist newspaper *Vorwärts*, welcomed Tehlirian as an "Armenian [William] Tell." More thoughtfully, Emil Ludwig concluded: "Only when a society of nations has organized itself as the protector of international order will no Armenian killer remain unpunished, because no Turkish Pasha has the right to send a nation into the desert."[155]

Satisfaction over Talaat's assassination was a bad substitute for real justice. Talaat and his close collaborators had been condemned to death in absentia by the judges in Istanbul.[156] Assassination perpetuated the sick relationship of a victim in quest of revenge with a perpetrator entrenched in defiant denial, instead of humble courage for the truth and redress. Repairing the relationship was impossible for many decades. The action of the Berlin court in 1921 was ambivalent, since it resorted to psychiatry to achieve the acquittal of Talaat's killer. It did not and could not discover the organization behind his act or refer to any established international norm for crimes against humanity to exculpate Tehlirian or, at least, put his deed into a wider legal context. There was an obvious lack of institutional justice appropriate to this grave and sensational case that attracted global media attention. The gap in institutional justice measures became particularly clear to two young students of law following the trial: Raphael Lemkin, the later pioneer of the UN Genocide Convention, and Robert M. Kempner, the later attorney at the Nuremberg trials.[157] Mustafa Kemal's movement had obstructed the prosecution of war criminals by the Istanbul tribunals, made British hostages, and in spring 1921, extorted the release of imprisoned suspects who had not fled in time, as had the main culprits. Lemkin was shocked by this failure of justice.

When other Nemesis operatives killed Bahaeddin Şakir and Cemal Azmi in Berlin on 17 April 1922, Ewald Stier saw less anti-Armenian reaction in the German press than the year before. Hence, he believed that "La vérité est en marche" (truth is on the move) and that, at long last, the pernicious "dream [of] Berlin-Baghdad is over."[158] This assessment was presumptuous. Not only did dreams of might keep their hold in Berlin minds, but because of Ankara's successes, Turkey, from Talaat to Kemal, became a major political role model for many Germans. "New Turkey" served as a paradigm for the radically nationalist "New Germany" that a large minority was calling for, taking power in 1933.

Hence, public condemnation of Talaat's, Şakir's, and Azmi's deeds remained weak and hesitant in interwar Germany, indicating a political culture that could become easy prey for comparable political thinking. Conservative and antidemocratic papers like the *Kreuzzeitung* mixed stereotypes, purportedly putting "adverse" characteristics of Jews on a level with those of Armenians. Sharply right-wing newspapers like the *Deutsche Allgemeine Zeitung* drummed into their readers the stab-in-the-back myth of provocative Armenian traitors against allies during war, whereas members of post-CUP exile organizations in Berlin reedited slightly updated anti-British and anti-Armenian propaganda material. Among these organizations was the Egyptian medical doctor Mansur Rifat, like Shekib Arslan, a collaborator of German intelligence during the war; both were active in early interwar Berlin. Rifat combined anti-British Egyptian nationalism with an intolerant pan-Islamist discourse.[159]

Not only contemporary German political thought in general, but even, concretely, the Hitler putsch of 1923, must be understood against this background, that is, beyond exclusive Eurocentric patterns of explanation of Europe's descent into fascism. Stefan Ihrig has shown in his recent studies that based on analysis of the contemporary German press, this "attempted seizure of power, contrary to current wisdom in historiography, was inspired much more by Mustafa Kemal and the events in Anatolia than by the example of Mussolini's 'March on Rome.'"[160] Alfred Rosenberg was a main ideologist of National Socialism and served as Hitler's deputy and leader of the National Socialist German Workers' Party when Hitler was imprisoned after the failed putsch of 1923. In Rosenberg's 1926 retrospect, the "Judenpresse" (Jewish press) alone had welcomed Tehlirian's acquittal. The argumentation is historically outlandish and lumpen intellectual, but it reveals Rosenberg's identification with Talaat and CUP discourse, including a reference to Mansur Rifat, a member of Talaat's circle in Berlin:

> In 1921, the former Turkish minister Talaat Pasha was murdered in Berlin. . . . Talaat Pasha was depicted as a bloodthirsty animal. . . . Anyone informed about the history of struggle between Turks and Armenians could easily ascertain that this was also a deliberately Jewish policy which had always protected the Armenians. Interests converged as England also used the Armenians to destroy the Ottoman Empire. At first came missionaries who baptized the Armenians, to separate them mentally more and more from the Turks. Then came bombs. Thus the almost successful [Ottoman] attempt of a peaceful coexistence was annulled. . . . Also during the world war, the Armenians have led the espionage against the Turks, similar to the Jews against Germany. This

forced the loyal ally of the German Reich, Talaat Pasha, to
sharp interventions, whereby some hardships were not to
be circumvented. (Read more in Dr. Mansur Rifat: "Das
Geheimnis der Ermordung Talaat Paschas.") After the collapse of 1918, Talaat Pasha lived in the capital of the country to which he had been faithful, and was murdered here.
The all-too-powerful press [Gross-Presse] of this country,
however, cursed him even after his death, protected his mur-
derers, and demanded his acquittal. And indeed, the Berlin
court discharged the Armenian Tehlirian. The Jew[ish] press
of all colors rejoiced and described the acquittal as the "only
possible" judgment.[161]

In Germany, identification with Mehmed Talaat and the
CUP version of World War I concurred with anti-Jewish and
anti-Armenian attitudes, and denoted German National Socialism right from its start.

Talaat's Long, Strong Shadow

In spite of dramatic turbulence after Talaat's flight from Istanbul and during the war for Asia Minor in 1919–22, CUP power
passed, all in all, rather seamlessly to the new capital Ankara and
the new strongman, Atatürk. Although a high military official
by profession, Kemal Pasha (Atatürk) was not Enver Pasha's
nor Cemal Pasha's heir but foremost that of Talaat Pasha, the
civilian at the top of CUP rule since 1913 who, since the pre-
1908 period, had also managed successful relations with military officers.

In contrast to his committee friends, Talaat had rapidly
grasped the fundamental changes in the climate and was
ready to contribute to a new organization of Turkish power

and polity, now under not his own but another's primacy. He may have been confident that his political legacy would seminally determine post-Ottoman Turkey, not least thanks to high offices offered to loyal young governors and employees in Ankara. Talaat's bloodstained young cadre—men like Tahsin Uzer, Şükrü Kaya, Abdülhalik Renda, Atıf Kamçıl, Celâl Bayar—soon occupied the highest positions again. Devoted aides, journalists, or students like Muhittin (Birgen), Falih Rıfkı (Atay), Necmettin Sadık (Sadak), Yunus Nadi (Abalıoğlu), and Reşit Saffet (Atabinen) built or rebuilt their careers in Ankara. (Talaat's committee brother Hüseyin Cahid [Yalçın] did this too, but less easily than others.)

To these immediate collaborators of Talaat must be added a whole circle of very young CUP and Turkish Home Society (Türk Yurdu/Türk Ocağı) members who were entirely loyal to CUP rule in the 1910s and who became Kemalist ministers, like Şükrü Saraçoğlu, Mahmut Esat Bozkurt, and Cemal Hüsnü Taray. Another case in point is Gökalp's cousin and CUP deputy for Diyarbekir Feyzi Pirinççizâde, twice a minister in the 1920s and the example for a personal and whole regional Pirinççizâde dynasty that had thrown in their lot with the CUP and Talaat's anti-Armenian policy; they were able to preserve their position and have influence even beyond the Kemalist single-party rule. Very similar to this is the case of CUP deputy for Anteb Ali Cenani, a leader of local anti-Armenian policy in 1915 and a deputy and minister in the 1920s.[162] All these men succeeded in making a quite seamless transition of power from Istanbul to Ankara after Talaat's flight to Berlin, thus perpetuating his patterns, practices, and principles of governance across the country, although idealist republican goodwill, foremost of people in the second and third ranks, must not be denied.

Most importantly, basic concepts remained the same despite structural changes in the 1920s. Summarized in a line of Mehmed Emin's poem of the mid-1910s, "I am a Turk / Great are my religion and my race," the ideas of Gökalp and related ideologues continued to sway the elites. They had consolidated from early August 1914 as an explicit "national *takbir*" (*millî tekbir*), or "Türk's Allahu Akbar" (*Türk'ün tekbiri*). That is the prayer and battle cry of "Allahu Akbar" in the service of empire and Turan.[163] For elites influenced by Gökalp, nation was based on common religion, culture, and race. The Gökalpian cohort of ideologues cultivated the idea of an organic and homogeneous, not a negotiated, plural and constitutional nation. They grafted it upon the old notion of an imperial Sunni "dominant nation" (*millet-i hâkime*). Although circles, names, and heads changed, this concept of nation allowed large parts of the politically dominant group in the Ottoman Empire—that is, Muslim Turks—to "save" themselves in a new era of republican rule if they "converted" to Turkism as their first doctrine. When an early Kemalist wrote that "I am no longer the servant of a prince, a sultan, or a lord / I am the son of a nation that prostrates before itself," he expressed the exaltation of a convert. Yet, though he converted from empire to Anatolia, as he put it, he still converted to a nation and a "Turkdom" in the sense of Gökalp.[164]

Thus, the spirit of Gökalp, Talaat's close friend and intellectual mentor, also pervaded Kemalism and Mustafa Kemal's personal thought. This is true, although Kemal attempted to suppress the role of Islam in Gökalp's system, based on the pillars of Turkism, Islam, and Western civilization. Even if every Western textbook writes that Atatürk, a moderate republican, renounced Ottoman imperialism and expansionist Turanism, nevertheless, elements of the fundamental excrescence present in Gökalp's thought of the 1910s found their place in Kemalism.

They solidified in the 1930s in a Turkish history thesis and a language theory that made Turkdom the ethnohistorical cradle of human language and civilization.[165] These speculations mirrored Gökalp's Turkist exaltation and could not provide the scientific foundation of a Kemalist nationalism beyond Islam. They lacked both serious scholarship and popular appeal.

Kemalism lost its fight against political Islam in the long term because Mustafa Kemal's political thought was based on the Gökalpian concept of an authoritarian-led Turkish-Muslim nation and on historic deeds going hand in hand with this concept. Kemal had defended it in the hottest hour of his struggle, during the "War of Independence," in a close fraternity with Islamism and a majority of Kurds, as had done the CUP. A large and overwhelming minority (not majority) organized in authoritarian structures dictated since 1913 politics and social life. Talaat's and Kemal's emphasis on an exclusively Turkish Muslim "national economy" betrayed the same coercive shadow. "The CUP members have therefore never found odd the hero of the new national movement. They all rallied around him [Mustafa Kemal] with a national spirit and a national discipline that they had acquired in the twelve years before [since 1908]," Talaat's intimate Muhittin Birgen wrote astutely in the 1930s. Birgen, in turn, had become a member of parliament and the head of the Directorate General of Press and Information under Atatürk. "All CUP people who had well begun to identify with Ziya Gökalp's ideas during World War I, which were published in the name of the CUP, easily and logically rallied around Mustafa Kemal Pasha, to defend these new and concrete principles."[166]

In his famous speech (*Nutuk*) of 1927, President Mustafa Kemal established a person-centered "self-narrative," or "ego-history," of Turkish national salvation.[167] We may take it as the proud and positive counterpart to Talaat's memoirs, which are a much more defensive narrative of a wounded but still assertive ego after world war defeat. Talaat claimed, like Kemal, to have selflessly served the renewal and self-assertion of the Turkish nation. Kemal's ego-history starts in May 1919, when he began to head rebellions in Anatolia against the postwar Istanbul government, and thus omits entirely the CUP's and Talaat's role before and also during the rebellion. Yet, significantly, it also excludes Talaat from the heavy criticism that he directs in his speech against other CUP predecessors and former comrades. Later, once his position was untouchable and a return or organization of former CUP leaders was no longer possible, Atatürk could, according to Jäckh, "frankly state that to a considerable extent his accomplishment 'rested on Talaat's shoulders.'"[168]

Kemalist historiography obeyed Atatürk's lines of the 1920s. Most Western twentieth-century Turkology followed on its coattails. Historiography remained trapped for decades by the concept of an outstanding, singular savior and modernizer, as many Atatürk biographies until the late twentieth century demonstrate. Scholarship was thus bereft of the first part—and the first part's critical determinants—of Turkey's foundational history.[169] With an emphasis on singularity and break, it long ignored the CUP legacy and Talaat's seminal political personality. The multifaceted continuity from him to Kemal, starting at the beginning struggle for Anatolia, remained unaddressed—and with it Gökalp's ideologemes in synergy with political strategy and activism.

Secular Kemalism abolished the caliphate in 1924, yet within three generations it lost its struggle against political Islam, because it had built on it in its war for Asia Minor, as had CUP rule from 1913, that is, during the Balkan Wars and World War I. Mustafa Kemal himself was proclaimed a *gazi*, a successful warrior in the name of Islam, by the Ankara Parliament in summer 1921. At that stage, he insisted on exclusive Muslim rights in Asia Minor and gave anti-Christian speeches in the provinces.[170] The principle of populism (*halkçılık*), which Kemalism soon adopted, was a substitute for real, negotiated democracy. It may sound harsh, but it is all too true that the same jihadist action of the "Islamic State" in 2014–17, occupied with discourse and extreme realities of violence and coercion, was performed in many regions under Talaat, Enver, and early Kemalist rule. Turkey never did openly cope with these realities in politics and public history; quite the contrary.

Talaat's successor Mustafa Kemal had well understood that a viable Turkey must demarcate itself fundamentally from the former regime and its blatant excesses if it wanted a future established on lasting ground. He therefore longed for fundamental departures. Kemal's "revolutions" aspired to the oblivion of the previous years and decades, foremost of political Islam and the pervasive realities of jihad in 1911–22. Notably, the "revolution of law"—the complete abolition of sharia and the adoption of the Swiss Civil Code and the Swiss Code of Obligations—was new and incisive, though it resumed Talaat's previous efforts. As a matter of fact, the new Civil Law of 1926 served for decades as a backbone of Turkish secularism. A recodification of this law today remains in force, although current Islamist trends, favored by the AKP government, threaten the validity of its letter and spirit in Turkey's society of the 2010s.[171]

Imposed, Kemalist policy failed to a large extent where Talaat—who initially had appeared as a democrat—had already failed: it fell short of an egalitarian social contract and the suppression of systemic corruption. It did not overcome imperial biases that evolved, inspired by Gökalp, into outspoken, ethnoreligious biases. Having endorsed undemocratic patterns and the results of previous CUP rule, it persisted in following Gökalp's idea of an organic, culturally homogeneous, and leader-centered nation.

———

Thus, even if it rhetorically broke with the late Ottoman period, the early Republic of Turkey followed lines predetermined by Talaat's political practice. Conspiratorial authoritarianism, refusal of a social contract, and disguised concubinages of convenience with Islamist and ultranationalist forces again played crucial roles, although expansionist neo-Ottoman ambitions remained largely excluded, at least before the early twenty-first century. To many contemporaries, foremost Western diplomats who economized on deeper analysis, Kemalism appeared for decades as a viable, even ultimate authoritarian model of Middle Eastern, if not Third World, modernization. In this vein, Talaat *and* Atatürk admirer Jäckh advocated American rapprochement to Turkey during and after the Second World War. At present, however, the explosive comeback of World War I issues in the Middle East goes hand in hand with a manifest exhaustion of this post-1945 order. In truth, it was labile right from the start, because it was geostrategically distorted and on shaky, undrained, post-Ottoman ground.

Inauspicious patterns of polity and governance originated from modernizers with antiegalitarian imperial biases, such as Sultan Abdulhamid and the late CUP. They might be excused for many of their shortcomings by the difficulty of the task and unfavorable circumstances related to European imperialism and nationalisms on the Balkans. Still, one must face the fact that they not only missed building up consensual egalitarian society, even if in rudiments, but even missed heading for the goal itself. Talaat's warmongering and make-or-break style, after he had given up on constitutional principles, is telling. In this mood, he became the CUP key leader, a master of power play, and a distinctive gambler in international affairs—the founding father of an Anatolian homeland exclusively based on Islam and Turkdom. Kemalism renounced empire, focused on domestic reconstruction, and longed, at times, for authentic democracy. Nevertheless, it did not acquire the stature to "overcome Talaat," that is, to clarify the legacy of the 1910s, although the former grand vizier remained disavowed in the early republic.

Yet his corpse came pompously back to Turkey on 25 February 1943, four years and four months after Kemal Atatürk's death, in a joint venture of Adolf Hitler's and İsmet İnönü's regimes. The prominently publicized transfer of Talaat's mortal remains from Berlin to Istanbul was not a revenant's manifestation in a dark hour of history but the official admission and affirmation of the basic truth that the republic owed Talaat a lot, and that this had to do with a common Turkish-German history during and after World War I (which Atatürk had not been eager to acknowledge). It thus gave up claiming distance from a legacy that was, in fact, built-in to Kemalism. Historically speaking, it surrendered to its failure to cope with the corrosion in the middle of this legacy.

In contemporary terms, it was a success: the true revolutionary Talaat, a patriotic child of the people and precursor of the Kemalist Revolution, had been forced to flee to Germany where he met neither friend nor justice, as journalist Orhan Seyfi wrote. "Today, however, Germany has expressed its respect toward the martyr, Talaat Pasha, and has acquitted itself of their old debt to him, and it is this that the Turks have waited for."

The senior journalist Yunus Nadi (Abalıoğlu), Talaat's mouth-piece in 1917, was very explicit that the Republic of Turkey was the heir of Talaat's and the CUP's efforts. The military victory of 1921 (Sakarya) was based on that of 1915 (Gallipoli), he wrote in the political biweekly *Ulus*. He insisted on historical continuity and justified the struggle against non-Turkish elements.[172] This was definitely relevant insofar as the *varlık vergisi* (property tax) during World War II induced again a disproportionate transfer of wealth from non-Muslims (Jews included this time) to the state, as had been done on a much larger scale during the anti-Christian genocide of 1915.

Only after Atatürk's death could the continuity from CUP to Kemalism be openly avowed. It relativized the achievements of the "Eternal Chief." The same development allowed, for the first time under the republic, publication of important CUP sources, such as Talaat's memoirs and Cavid's diaries—significantly, however, only in censored, sanitized versions. The crucial taboo was and remained the crime against the Armenians. After decades of complete suppression, this topic once again attracted international interest in the final third of the twentieth century. Thus, it also openly came back to Turkey.[173]

Abalıoğlu concluded his article in February 1943, submissively saying that the nation was "grateful from all of its heart to its beloved president and to the government of Saraçoğlu for allowing the remains of Talaat to return to rest in the bosom of his country." Hüseyin Cahid Yalçın gave the funeral oration on the Hill—and Monument—of Liberty (Hürriyet-i Ebediye Tepesi) where the military "martyrs" (*şehit*), fallen during the fight against the 1909 counterrevolution, had been buried, and after them other CUP heroes. Yalçın was another senior journalist and former CUP member who personified the continuity from the CUP single-party regime to the Republic of Turkey.

Ahmed Emin Yalman also attended the burial procession, at the side of German ambassador Franz von Papen and Turkish prime minister Şükrü Saraçoğlu (a 1910s member of the CUP-sponsored Türk Yurdu organization).

In 1996, Enver's remains were brought back from Tajikistan, and those of other CUP members followed, thus joining those of Talaat in the Monument of Liberty and definitively bringing all restless ghosts of the CUP and World War I back to Turkey. But they were not layed to rest. Despite some promising departures, neither the global transition period of the late 1940s nor that of the 1990s in Turkey became windows of opportunity for a true and lasting democratic beginning based on self-critical public history.

———

Mehmed Talaat began to be fully rehabilitated and installed as an outstanding and positive figure in public Turkish history when his body was brought from Nazi Germany to Istanbul. This was not, as one might assume, an ephemeral moment in the dismal times of Adolf Hitler and World War II but the start of a process that took place for good during Turkey's transition to a multiparty regime under the American aegis in the early Cold War, thus, when an ambivalent, shallow, geostrategically motivated Western orientation of Turkey began. The presumed reorientation could not therefore evolve into sustained democratization. There was no critical history and constructive soul-searching over divisive topics, supported and demanded by new friends and allies. The (theoretical) opportunity was squandered by American diplomacy.[174]

But the new liberties of the post-1945 era did serve to complete what had started as a Turkish-German joint venture in

1943: Talaat's rehabilitation, now also by various publications of former CUP members, foremost among them Talaat's own memoirs, published by his former collaborator and mouthpiece Hüseyin Cahid Yalçın. It was followed by the "coming-out" of many other unrepentant Unionists who, without fearing Kemalist admonition and repression, published their recollections of Talaat's long-suppressed era (many of them are referred to in this study). Though not ostentatiously, they nevertheless reminded their contemporaries of the pre-Kemalist preparation for the Turkish nation-state, and of a first "war of salvation" or "war of independence" starting in 1913. Well before the wars of 1919–22, they had struggled for unrestricted Turkish Muslim sovereignty in Anatolia.

Talaat's rehabilitation, triggered in 1943, was not seriously challenged in Turkey itself, either from the Left or the Right, nor the Islamic and Islamist circles that publicly reemerged in the new multiparty system, although some well-known criticism of the CUP by Kemalists (e.g., Yusuf Bayur) and from the opposite, Islamic side of the political spectrum took place. In the coming decades, many mosques, schools, and streets in Turkey were named after Talaat Pasha, Atatürk's predecessor. Atatürk himself nevertheless continued to enjoy unique veneration until the end of the twentieth century. The post-1945 departure to more prosperity and a more democratic system in Turkey was, right from the start, overshadowed by revenant ghosts of the last Ottoman decade.

Journalist and editor Hüseyin Cahid Yalçın and Enver Bolayır, publisher of Talaat's memoirs in 1946, lastingly framed Talaat's public image: "Talaat was a strong patriot, prepared to sacrifice everything, even his own life, for the salvation and well-being of the fatherland," Yalçın wrote at the beginning of his edition. He conceded, however, that when *Tanin* had earlier considered publishing the memoirs, Talaat's connection with "one of the most cruel events of that era" had restrained those responsible from doing so. Bolayır continued in his foreword of the same edition of memoirs that Talaat "was one of a few rare statesmen whom Turkish history produced. Among the Ottoman grand viziers, this great Turkish leader had reached his high position thanks to his patriotism, honesty, intelligence and assiduity. . . . By writing this book [memoirs], he defended himself, the party of Union and Progress, and the Turkish nation before global public opinion. Reading this book reveals nakedly how ugly and unfounded were the defamations that our contemporary enemies invented about us. Finishing my lines, I bow respectfully before the great presence of the late Talaat Pasha."[175]

Bolayır stands for many others who to this day remain respectfully bowed before Talaat's aura. Talaat's memoirs saw many reeditions in this same spirit. Far from Turkey, in the United States of the 1940s and 1950s, Ernst Jäckh became an important politico-academic voice in agreement with Talaat, to whom he had been very sympathetic in the 1910s, and remained so decades later. Emphasizing Turkey's geo-strategic uniqueness throughout the first half of the twentieth century into the 1950s, he was, since 1940, a professor of public law and government at Columbia University, where he founded its Middle East Institute in 1948. His advocacy of Turkish-American friendship was based on analyses in consonance with his former advocacy, marked by *Türkenfieber*. "The Young Turks' revolution had strange consequences," he wrote in 1944, after eulogizing Talaat and welcoming the transfer of his remains to Turkey. "It led . . . to a war of liberation and the realization of national independence. It may almost be said that the Young Turks' experience set the course of foreign policy which today places Turkey alongside the forces arrayed to defeat the Axis armies."

In Jäckh's line of thought, the leader-centered, Kemalist, single-party government was a "prodemocratic and peace-loving power." His acclaimed book *The Rising Crescent* (1944) was based on his German volume of 1911 with the same title (within two years a Turkish edition was published). In this book, he also reminisced about Tehlerian's trial of 1921, lashing out against "the denial of guilt by the jury" and the latter's alleged manipulation by the German government. "It was not in vain that the foreign minister [Friedrich Rosen] had seen to it 'that Germany never would have anything to do with Turkish friendship.' That was in 1921. In 1944 it is Turkey that will have nothing to do with German friendship."[176] The later exaggerated assertion revealed a flimsy argumentation: support for the Axis, though not at the top of the government, had been fervent in Turkey and had been built upon resilient ideologemes of World War I. Opportunism, once Hitler's fate was decided, along with fear of Stalin's self-interested reanimation of the Armenian Question, had turned Turkey to the West toward the end of World War II. Faith in and the will to democracy remained, from the start, relegated to the second rank from both sides.

Solid and constructive political science for the post-1945 order would have required more accurate historical scholarship than Jäckh's. New departures in the twenty-first century need, at long last, humble and humbling recognition of basic truths. "Making Turkey great again"—in the vein of the CUP's "New Turkey" and "Turkey for the Turks"—revealed itself as a dead end, even if Jäckh kept on arguing differently. But he slurred over the victims with the sovereignty of a Wilhelminian geostrategist who managed to convert himself to liberal America, and its quasi-imperial role after 1945, without much revision of his mental map. What, after all, remains the only constructive approach is, like more than a hundred years ago, making Turkey truly constitutional, even if different or smaller, and thus to honor the best spirits of the 1908 Ottoman spring and the best standards of the twenty-first century.

EPILOGUE

AFTER A HUNDRED years, it is high time to understand and conclude: Talaat Pasha and his Young Turk fellows failed to make a timely, healthy, painful break with the empire and its undefeated, built-in, premodern supremacy. Heading the Ottoman Empire, they not only drew out but fueled agony in the 1910s. Angrily and vengefully, they struggled for empire and the Turkish nation, their main identifications. What they missed was the fight for constitutional rule in a reduced territory that they could have reasonably preserved without resorting to extreme violence. A century later, one might be tempted to shrug off those failures—there were so many in that era!—if it were not for the lasting consequences that command precise and careful revisiting.

Pioneering radical nationalist revolutionism, that is—in this study's terminology—from the Right, Talaat's revolutionist cohort entered a temporary marriage of convenience with Bolsheviks after the end of World War I. It proved paradigmatic for larger Europe in the era of the world wars, though long and wrongly disregarded as peripheral or "oriental." Its unresolved (even if would-be solved) questions survived the global break of World War II and determine—modified—the convulsions of the present Middle East. Now visible for everyone, these old issues take center stage in global politics. Talaat and his cohort left behind wounds that even a century could not heal, and descendants of victims can neither forgive nor forget, because credible recognition—the precondition for such healing—is lacking. The hope voiced after Talaat's death by a close Armenian friend of the early Young Turks in opposition that "Turks aware of the true interests of their country will not count this former minister among their good statesmen" (see chap. 6, sec. "Death—and Afterlife—in Germany and Turkey") is still unfulfilled.

Although periods of relative prosperity and democratic openings were not absent in the post-Ottoman century, the Young Turk single-party leaders have, all in all, left dangerously divided societies behind them: prone to political violence and quasi-condemned to repeat patterns practiced during the Ottoman cataclysm. Because history remained unclarified and soul-searching was halfhearted—if it ever took place in the post-Ottoman states originating in that cataclysm of the 1910s—political culture failed to emancipate itself from unrepented, manifestly evil patterns. Kemalism benefited from what CUP extremism had achieved, but thus implicitly identified with it, without facing the built-in evil. Such historical summary related to Talaat is not uplifting, yet it is hopefully instructive: at long last, his legacy can today help us to better understand not only why certain politics went and still go wrong, but also, by excludability, even if after an end to terror, which directions must be taken.

This study has not intended to judge but to explore Talaat and even, under the aspect of eternity, to see him off. As a historian and "expert on the past," I know how to appreciate the worth and virtue of historical valediction. In the 2010s, Turkey has become post-Kemalist. It is at risk of losing not only its post–World War II orientation but also its new, more incisive, fundamental compass from the beginning of the twenty-first

century: accession to the European Union and implementation of the EU standards, allowing democratic ideals of the 1908
Ottoman spring to resume. In the aftermath of this recent loss,
Turkey is again, and perhaps more than ever, haunted by fatal
departures of a hundred years ago. In this sense, Talaat's ghost
is living on and has befallen Turkey's Justice and Development
Party (AKP), which had started so hopefully in the early 2000s.
Personal power, party interests, and ideology prevail over
democracy. As an analyst recently noted, this "remains one of
Turkey's main problems today. The AKP did not invent this
problem, of course, but it has been busy building on it, rather
than trying to turn Turkey into a genuinely democratic country
that is respected across the world."[1] A combination of power,
corruption, and imperially biased national-religious appeal
("neo-Ottomanism") has presently—in the late 2010s—made
politics sick again.

In scholarship and public history, Mehmed Talaat Pasha's
era, the first founding period of the Turkish nation-state, long
remained veiled. Unclarified or mystified, the period's actors,
ideologemes, and political practices lent themselves to incon-
siderate reuse and reidentification. Against this reality, their life
and policy decisions urge consistent historical deconstruction.
Besides being a study for erudition, the analysis of Talaat's political biography in this book has intended to serve this hopeful
purpose.

NOTES

Prologue

1. In Western languages, there is no biography at all. Two biographies in Turkish give interesting insights but lack critical distance and the indispensable variety of sources: Hasan Babacan, *Mehmed Talât Paşa, 1874–1921: Siyasi hayatı ve icraatı* (Ankara: TTK, 2005); Tevfik Çandar, *Talat Paşa: Bir örgüt ustasının yaşamöyküsü* (Istanbul: Imge, 2001 [1983]). The latter mirrors ongoing fascination for the "master of the [CUP] network" and does not give any references to sources. The former offers solid pieces of information based on Ottoman sources but is, however, narrowly state-centered. It lacks other perspectives, particularly for the years 1913–18.

2. Ernst Jäckh, *Rising Crescent: Turkey Yesterday, Today, and Tomorrow* (New York: Farrar & Rinehart, 1944, 90).

3. Critical sources for relevant insights are published diaries, newly disclosed Ottoman state documents, and foreign documents in and beyond Foreign Office archives, the German ones being most important. The existing literature generally presents Talaat as no more than a primus inter pares. For reference works on the CUP for 1908–14, see Feroz Ahmad, *The Young Turks: The Committee of Union and Progress in Turkish Politics, 1908–1914* (London: Hurst, 2010 [1st ed. 1969]). For the pre-1908 period, see M. Şükrü Hanioğlu, *The Young Turks in Opposition* (New York: Oxford University Press, 1995) and *Preparation for a Revolution: The Young Turks, 1902–1908* (New York: Oxford University Press, 2001). For studies on the continuity of Unionists (that is, CUP members) and Kemalists, and studies of certain aspects, see these studies by Erik Jan Zürcher: *The Unionist Factor: The Role of the Committee of Union and Progress in the Turkish National Movement, 1905–1926* (Leiden: Brill, 1984); *The Young Turk Legacy and Nation Building: From the Ottoman Empire to Ataturk's Turkey* (London: I. B. Tauris, 2010); and "Young Turk Decision-Making Patterns," in Conseil scientifique pour l'étude du génocide des Arméniens, *Le génocide des Arméniens* (Paris: Armand Colin, 2015), 15–32. A current meritorious textbook on Turkish foreign policy still presents Enver Pasha as politically leading; see William Hale, *Turkish Foreign Policy since 1774* (London: Routledge, 2013), 24–30.

4. Mustafa Aksakal, "The Ottoman Proclamation of Jihad," in Erik-Jan Zürcher, ed., *Jihad and Islam in World War I: Studies on the Ottoman Jihad on the Centenary Snouck Hurgronje's "Holy War Made in Germany"* (Leiden: Leiden University Press, 2016), 64.

5. Emil Ludwig, "Talaat und Enver," *Vossische Zeitung*, 26 October 1918, in Politisches Archiv Auswärtiges Amt (Archives of the German Foreign Office), PA-AA/R 13804-4.

6. Zafer Toprak, *Türkiye'de ekonomi ve toplum (1908–1950): İttihat-Terakki ve devletçilik* (Istanbul: Tarih Vakfı, 1995), vii.

7. *Talaat Paşa'nın hatıraları*, ed. Yalçın and Bolayır (Istanbul: Güven, 1946), 5–8.

Chapter 1: Istanbul, 1915

1. Max Grunwald, "Gespräch mit Talaat Bey," *Vossische Zeitung*, 28 December 1915. This multiple self-assertion still appears in Talaat's memoirs, written after his flight to Germany and finished in late 1919. No original manuscript remains of these memoirs, which are essentially an apology for Talaat's policies. The partial publication of the manuscript in the newspaper *Yeni Şark* in late 1921 offers insights via the original vocabulary, which later publications largely replaced (reproduced however in Talat Paşa, *Hatıralarım ve müdafaam* [Istanbul: Kaynak, 2008], 34). The American edition of 1921 is very far from reliable (Talaat Pasha, "Posthumous Memoirs of Talaat Pasha," *New York Times Current History* 15, no. 2 [November 1921]).

2. Aubrey Herbert, *Talaat Pasha*, typescript, Somerset Heritage Center, DD.DRU 56, 5-6.

3. On aspects of the CUP's political history in the 1910s, see Zürcher, *The Young Turk Legacy and Nation Building*. For an examination of committee activism (CUP and Armenian committees) in the context of contemporary military practices—insurgency and counterinsurgency—see Edward J. Erickson, *Ottomans and Armenians: A Study in Counterinsurgency* (New York: Palgrave Macmillan, 2013). For geographically limited to the Marmara region, but with more insight on armed gangs of the CUP and social issues, see Ryan Gingeras, *Sorrowful Shores: Violence, Ethnicity, and the End of the Ottoman Empire, 1912–23* (Oxford: Oxford University Press, 2009). On the approach to the late Ottoman world, see Efraim Karsh and Inari Karsh, *Empires of Sand: The Struggle for Mastery in the Middle East, 1789–1923* (Cambridge, MA: Harvard University Press, 1999): it is congruent with this biography in discarding views of peripheric, subaltern, and passive late Ottoman actors but lacks Ottoman insight.

4. Dikran Kaligian, *Armenian Organization and Ideology under Ottoman Rule, 1908–1914* (New Brunswick: Transaction, 2012); Bedross Der Matossian, *Shattered*

Dreams of Revolution: From Liberty to Violence in the Late Ottoman Empire (Stanford, CA: Stanford University Press, 2014).

5. See CUP member Emmanuil Emmanuilidis's insightful memoirs, *Osmanlı İmparatorluğu'nun son yılları* (Istanbul: Belge, 2014), 100 (original: Τα τελευταία έτη της Οθωμανικής Αυτοκρατορίας [Αθήνα: Τυπογραφείον Γ.Ν. Καλλέργη, 1924]); and İhsan S. Balkaya, *Ali Fethi Okyar (29 Nisan 1880–7 Mayıs 1943)* (Ankara: TTK), 60.

6. For more on this topic, see Krisztina Kehl, *Die Kizilbaş/Aleviten: Untersuchungen über eine esoterische Glaubensgemeinschaft in Anatolien* (Berlin: Klaus Schwarz, 1988); and Markus Dressler, *Writing Religion: The Making of Turkish Alevi İslam* (New York: Oxford University Press, 2013).

7. Baha Said, "Türkiye'de Alevî zümreleri: Teke Alevîliği-içtimaî Alevîlik," *Türk Yurdu*, September 1926 (transcribed ed., Ankara: Tutibay, 1999, xi, 105); Dressler, *Writing Religion*, 137–40.

8. Talat, *Hatıralarım*, 37. Cf. Mustafa Aksakal, *The Ottoman Road to War in 1914* (New York: Cambridge University Press, 2008), 153–82; and Zürcher's insightful comparative analysis, though based on secondary literature, "Young Turk Decision Making Patterns."

9. Emil Ludwig, "Zwei Audienzen," *Berliner Tageblatt*, no. 201 (21 April 1915).

10. Herbert, *Talaat Pasha* (on a separate sheet before the typescript). Herbert Aubrey had a reputation, though little regarded in Talaat's circle, as a "friend of the Turks." Entry of 23 February 1913, in Cavid Bey, *Meşrutiyet Rûznamesi* (Ankara: TTK, 2014–15; henceforth "Cavid diary"), 1:586; cf. entry of 3 January 1914, 2:434.

11. For an example regarding Cavid, see Emmanuilidis, *Osmanlı İmparatorluğu'nun son yılları*, 275.

12. Ali F. Türkgeldi, *Görüp işittiklerim* (Ankara: TTK, 2010 [1949]), 124, 138, 143.

13. Contemporaries called this at times the *Türkenfieber* (Turk fever). Stefan Ihrig has recently explored this relevant topic in *Atatürk in the Nazi Imagination* (Cambridge MA: Harvard University Press, 2014).

14. To his political friend Halil (Menteşe) in June 1915 (Halil Menteşe, *Osmanlı Mebusan Meclisi Reisi Halil Menteşe'nin anıları* (Istanbul: Hürriyet Vakfı, 1986, 216). One of the first general histories of World War I prominently uses the explanatory paradigm of social Darwinism (Samuel Zurlinden, *Der Weltkrieg: Vorläufige Orientierung von einem schweizerischen Standpunkt aus*, 3 vols. [Zürich: Orell Füssli, 1917–19]).

15. *Arşiv belgeleriyle Ermeni faaliyetleri 1914–1918*, ed. T. C. Genelkurmay Başkanlığı (Ankara: Genelkurmay Basım Evi, 2005), 1:424–25 (a collection of Ottoman sources from the Military Archive, ATASE); Taner Akçam, *The Young Turks' Crime against Humanity: The Armenian Genocide and Ethnic Cleansing in the Ottoman Empire* (Princeton, NJ: Princeton University Press, 2012), 186–87. The latter is an insightful recent study on the Armenian genocide, largely based on Ottoman documents.

16. Cf. Matthew S. Anderson, *The Eastern Question, 1774–1923* (New York: St. Martin's Press, 1966).

17. Kemal M. Ahmed, *Birinci dünya savaşı yıllarında Kürdistan* (Ankara: Berhem, 1992; 1st Kurdish ed., Bagdat, 1975), 62–64, 86.

18. An up-to-date biography of Abdulhamid is François Georgeon, *Abdulhamid II: Le sultan calife* (Paris: Fayard, 2003), 356–61. Relevant insights into Abdulhamid's reign, based on Ottoman sources, are provided by Selim Deringil, *The Well-Protected Domains: Ideology and the Legitimation of Power in the Ottoman Empire, 1876–1909* (London: I. B. Tauris, 1998).

19. Henry Morgenthau, *United States Diplomacy on the Bosphorus: The Diaries of Ambassador Morgenthau, 1913–16*, ed. Ara Sarafian (Princeton, NJ: Gomidas Institute, 2004; henceforth, "Morgenthau diary"), 24 April 1915, 215; 27 April 1915, 217. Morgenthau was a well-informed international observer-actor in 1914–16 Istanbul. His correspondence and diary are instructive and mostly appropriate sources.

20. *Arşiv belgeleriyle Ermeni faaliyetleri*, 1:235–81. Many Ottoman sources are today available in Latin transcript of the Arabic original, in print or online. The latter is an eight-volume collection of Ottoman army sources. A selection of Ottoman state sources on the Armenians in World War I can be accessed at the site of the Başbakanlık Osmanlı Arşivi (BOA), http://www.devletarsivleri.gov.tr/1915 -olaylari. The access to the military archives in Ankara (Askeri Tarih ve Stratejik Etüt Başkanlığı Arşivi) is restricted, and the selection and release of documents at the discretion of the archive. BOA is more liberal; it remains, however, uncertain how far sensitive documents are accessible.

21. Grigoris Balakian's firsthand testimony offers several examples: Grigoris Balakian, *Armenian Golgotha: A Memoir of the Armenian Genocide, 1915–1918* (New York: Vintage Books, 2009). Although not comparable to the distortion of Talaat's memoirs in their first American edition (see fn. 1), this edition of Balakian's *Armenian Golgotha* is problematic insofar as it again adapts a memoir to the supposed expectations of an American public, instead of leaving to emotions and religion their authentic place. There are unmarked cuts, in order, as the translator argues, to spare the reader "editorializing and sermonizing passages" (Balakian, *Armenian Golgotha*, xxviii–xxix).

22. Quoted in Raymond Kévorkian, *The Armenian Genocide: A Complete History* (London: I. B. Tauris, 2011), 252–53. This is the fullest history of the Armenian genocide to date, largely based on Armenian sources but including a multitude of others.

23. Krikor Zohrap, *Collected Works*, ed. Albert Sharurian (Yerevan, 2003), 6:312 (in Armenian).

24. An Armenian scholar delving into that synergy is Stephan Astourian, "Modern Turkish Identity and the Armenian Genocide: From Prejudice to Racist

Nationalism," in Richard G. Hovannisian, ed., *Remembrance and Denial: The Case of the Armenian Genocide* (Detroit: Wayne State University Press, 1998), 23–50.

25. Mustafa Nermi, "Türkismus und Kant," *Nord und Süd: Eine deutsche Monatsschrift* 173 (1920): 169–72; August Fischer, *Aus der religiösen Reformbewegung in der Türkei: Türkische Stimmen verdeutscht* (Leipzig: Harrassowitz, 1922), 5–7. Richard Hartmann, "Ziya Gökalp's Grundlagen des türkischen Nationalismus," in *Orientalistische Literaturzeitung* 28 (1925): 578–610 (quotation is on p. 610); Marie Bossaert, "La part arménienne des études turques," *European Journal of Turkish Studies* 24 (2017), http://ejts.revues.org/5525. Still instructive on Gökalp is Uriel Heyd, *Foundations of Turkish Nationalism: The Life and Teachings of Ziya Gökalp* (London: Harvill, 1950).

26. Emil Ludwig, "Unterredung mit Talaat Bei, dem Minister des Inneren," *Berliner Tageblatt*, no. 268 (28 May 1915).

27. "Glanures," *Journal de Genève*, 9 January 1915, front page.

28. Joseph Pomiankowski, *Der Zusammenbruch des Ottomanischen Reiches: Erinnerungen an die Türkei aus der Zeit des Weltkrieges* (Zürich: Amalthea-Verlag, 1927), 154–62. This is a sober and insightful account of Ottoman World War I by a privileged observer.

29. Morgenthau diary, 18 July 1915, 279.

30. Tahrirat of 16 May 1915, BOA BEO, 326465, quoted in Ahmet Efiloğlu, *İttihat ve Terakki azınlıklar politikası*, doctoral dissertation, University of Istanbul, 2007, 106. Talaat's notebook: *Talat Paşa'nın Evrak-ı Metrûkesi*, ed. Murat Bardakçı (Istanbul: Everest, 2008).

31. Talaat, "Mukaddime," in Karl Helfferich, *Harb-i Umûmî'nin menseileri* (Istanbul: Fratelli Hayim Matbaası, 1915), 8. The translation is by Talaat's, later Atatürk's collaborator Reşid S. Atabinen; the original's title is *Die Entstehung des Weltkriegs im Lichte der Veröffentlichungen der Dreiverbandmächte* (Berlin: Georg Stilke, 1915). Reception in Berlin on 27 April 1917, Österreichisches Staatsarchiv, K. und k. Ministerium des Äusseren, Departement 5, Zeitungsarchiv, Karton 86, Akte 3.

32. John G. Williamson, *Karl Helfferich, 1872–1924: Economist, Financier, Politician* (Princeton, NJ: Princeton University Press, 1971), 89–96.

33. Talaat (from the Interior Ministry's Directorate for Resettlement of Tribes and Migrants) to the grand vizier, 26 May 1915, BOA BEO, 4357-326758.

34. "Deportation Law" published on 1 June 1915 in the official gazette (*Takvim-i Vekayi*); in French on 2 June in *La Turquie*, reproduced in Arthur Beylerian, ed., *Les grandes puissances, l'Empire ottoman et les Arméniens dans les archives françaises (1914–1918): Recuil de documents* (Paris: Publications de la Sorbonne, 1983), 40–41.

35. *Armenians in Ottoman Documents (1915–1920)*, ed. Directorate of Ottoman Archives (Ankara, 1995), 34–35.

36. Contemporary English version in *United States Official Records on the Armenian Genocide, 1915–1917*, ed. Ara Sarafian (London: Gomidas, 2004), 29. On Talaat's reaction to this declaration, see Yusuf H. Bayur, *Türk inkılâbı tarihi* (Ankara: TTK, 1991), part 3, 3:39. Bayur's (1891–1980) work represents an instructive professional strand of Kemalist historiography, however marked by the social Darwinist zeitgeist and an absolute vision of one's own ethnonation. Bayur's work therefore bowed to Talaat's anti-Armenian prefiguration of national historiography, but was still critical of Talaat, and aware of the fatal domestic and international gravity of Talaat's spring 1915 decisions. On the juridical term, see Daniel M. Segesser, "Die historischen Wurzel des Begriffs 'Verbrechen gegen die Menschheit,'" *Jahrbuch der Juristischen Zeitgeschichte* 8 (2006–7): 75–101.

37. *Armenians in Ottoman Documents*, 36–37.

38. Entry of 4 February 1917, diary of Mustafa Hayri, *Şeyhülislam Ürgüplü Mustafa Hayri Efendi'nin Mesrutiyet: Büyük Harp ve Mütareke günlükleri (1909–1922)*, ed. Ali Suat Ürgüplü (Istanbul: Türkiye İş Bankası, 2015), 394; henceforth, "Hayri diary" (this is an important source for insights into the CUP Central Committee and essential conflicts).

39. Hayri diary, 372, 29 April 1917; *Tanin*, 15 November 1914, quoted in Emmanuilidis, *Osmanlı İmparatorluğu'nun son yılları*, 116.

40. Muhittin Birgen, *İttihat ve Terakki'de on sene: İttihat ve Terakki neydi?* (Istanbul: Kitapyayınevi, 2006), 370; Ziya Gökalp, "Kızılelma," *Türk Yurdu*, 2:31 (23 Jan. 1913) (Ankara: Tutibay, 1999), 2:115–20. For a pertinent interpretation, see Uğur Ü. Üngör, *The Making of Modern Turkey: Nation and State in Eastern Anatolia, 1913–1950* (Oxford: Oxford University Press, 2012), 35. Ziya Gökalp, "İslamiyet ve asrî medeniyet," *İslâm Mecmuası*, 51–52 (1917, English), in Niyazi Berkes, *Turkish Nationalism and Western Civilization: Selected Essays of Ziya Gökalp* (New York: Columbia University Press, 1959), 214–23.

41. Birgen, *İttihat ve Terakki'de on sene*, 382. Journalist Munittin Birgen was Gökalp's disciple in the 1910s.

42. For example, see Deputy Governor Cemal in the name of Governor Tahsin of Erzurum to Minister of the Interior, 26 August 1915, BOA DH. ŞFR. 485-76.

43. For historical and biographical insights into genocide and Lemkin, see Dominik J. Schaller and Jürgen Zimmerer, eds., *The Origins of Genocide: Raphael Lemkin as a Historian of Mass Violence* (London: Routledge, 2009); Raphael Lemkin, *Totally Unofficial: The Autobiography of Raphael Lemkin*, ed. Donna-Lee Frieze (New Haven: Yale University Press, 2013). On the Istanbul trials, see Vahakn Dadrian and Taner Akçam, *Judgment at Istanbul: The Armenian Genocide Trials* (New York: Berghahn, 2011).

44. Wangenheim to Auswärtiges Amt (Foreign Office), Berlin, 31 May 1915, PA-AA/R 14086. Most German documents concerning the Armenians during

World War I are accessible online, ed. Wolfgang Gust, http://www.armenocide.de. If not mentioned differently, document references are from this Internet edition. On Wangenheim, see H. Kieser, "Botschafter Wangenheim und das jungtürkische Komitee," in Rolf Hosfeld and Christin Pschichholz, eds., *Das Deutsche Reich und der Völkermord an den Armeniern* (Göttingen: Wallstein, 2017), 131–48.

45. Bleda is Midhat Şükrü's family name in the Republic of Turkey. There are family names in Turkey since a law on family names in 1934.

46. Krikor Zohrap, *Collected Works*, 4:291–96; Kévorkian, *Armenian Genocide*, 533–34. Nearly 90 percent of the Ottoman Turkish vocabulary used in the Ottoman Empire had been borrowed from Arabic and Persian. It also differed from today's Turkish with regard to a few grammatical aspects.

47. Holstein to Botschaft Konstantinopel, PA-AA BoKon 169 (http://www .armenocide.de).

48. 15 June 1915, facsimile and quotation in Jürgen Gottschlich, *Beihilfe zum Völkermord: Deutschlands Rolle bei der Vernichtung der Armenier* (Berlin: Ch. Links Verlag, 2015), 197.

49. On this topic, see Stefan Ihrig, *Justifying Genocide: Germany and the Armenians from Bismarck to Hitler* (Cambridge, MA: Harvard University Press, 2016); Hans-Lukas Kieser and Dominik J. Schaller, eds., *Der Völkermord an den Armeniern und die Shoah* (Zürich: Chronos, 2002).

50. On this Christian and humanitarian activist and historian of contemporary history, see Rolf Hosfeld, ed., *Johannes Lepsius—Eine deutsche Ausnahme: Der Völkermord an den Armeniern, Humanitarismus und Menschenrechte* (Göttingen: Wallstein, 2013); Hans-Lukas Kieser, "Johannes Lepsius: Theologian, Humanitarian Activist and Historian of *Völkermord*: An Approach to a German Biography (1858–1926)," in Anna Briskina-Müller, Armenuhi Drost-Abgajan, and Axel Meissner, eds., *Logos im Dialogos: Auf der Suche nach der Orthodoxie; Gedenkschrift für Hermann Goltz (1946–2010)* (Münster: Lit, 2011), 209–29.

51. Morgenthau diary, 7 October 1915, 351. See also chapter 5, sections "Leading Assimilation" and "Talat, Palestine, and Zionism."

52. "Antrag zum Völkermord an Armeniern beschlossen," https://www .bundestag.de/dokumente/textarchiv/2016/kw22-de-armenier/423826.

53. On the strong appeal of Atatürk and the Turkish national revolution, see Ihrig, *Atatürk in the Nazi Imagination.*

54. Birgen, *İttihat ve Terakki'de on sene*, 164.

55. "Eine Unterredung mit Talaat Bey," *Berliner Tageblatt*, 21 August 1915.

56. Quoted and discussed in Hans-Lukas Kieser, "Dr. Mehmed Reshid (1873–1919): A Political Doctor," in Kieser and Schaller, *Völkermord*, 262 and 270.

57. Burçin Gerçek, *Report on Turks Who Reached-Out to Armenians in 1915*, International Raoul Wallenberg Foundation, published online in 2015, http://www

.raoulwallenberg.net/wp-content/files_mf/1435335304ReportTurkishrescuers
complete.pdf.

58. Cavid diary, 3:135–36.

59. Warren Dockter, *Churchill and the Islamic World* (London: I. B. Tauris, 2015),
83 (based on British archives, this is a very instructive study, yet at times inaccurate,
because lacking Ottoman insight).

60. "Die Erstarkung der Türkei," *Berliner Tageblatt*, 11 February 1916, evening edition by Ludwig; see also "Talaat Bey über die deutsch-türkischen Zukunftsbezie-
hungen," *Berliner Tageblatt*, 19 January 1916, evening; "Unterredung mit Talaat Bey,"
Vossische Zeitung, 18 February 1916; M. Grunewald, "Gespräch mit Talaat Bey," *Vossische Zeitung*, 28 December 1915; H. Behle, "Berlin-Konstantinopel," *Berner Tagblatt*
(n.d.; contains conversation with Talaat of late May 1916 clipping in Jäckh Papers,
Yale University Library). Emil Ludwig, born Cohn, left Germany in 1922, from
which, after foreign minister Walther Rathenau's assassination, he immigrated to
Switzerland. In 1933, when the Nazis burned his books, he understood that German
foundations were not as strong and different as he had thought in 1915–16.

61. Cavid diary, 3:524, 31 July 1918.

62. Johann H. Bernstorff, *Erinnerungen und Briefe* (Zürich: Polygraphischer Verlag, 1936), 126–27. Bernstorff to Chancellor von Hertling, 6 April 1918, PA-AA/N
1097, vol. 14, no. 102. This is a long report reacting to a devastating fact-finding report
by German deputies. Bernstorff belittles the genocide in his counterreport, praising
Talaat and Enver. I thank Margaret L. Anderson for the reference.

63. "Serbian Ghosts" is the title of the first chapter of Christopher Clark's *The
Sleepwalkers: How Europe Went to War in 1914* (London: Penguin, 2012). This
innovative history of World War I gives the Balkans its full right but stops short of
examining the political hub in Istanbul to shed decisive light on German-Ottoman
agency in July–August 1914.

64. Cf. Hans-Lukas Kieser, "The Ottoman Road to Total War," in Kerem Öktem
and Maurus Reinkowski, eds., *World War I and the End of the Ottomans: From the
Balkan Wars to the Armenian Genocide* (London: I. B. Tauris, 2015), 29–53; and Kieser, "The Destruction of Ottoman Armenians: A Narrative of a General History of
Violence," *Studies in Ethnicity and Nationalism* 14, no. 3 (Dec. 2014): 500–515.

65. The terms allude to Eric Hobsbawm, *Age of Extremes: The Short Twentieth
Century, 1914–1991* (London: Michael Joseph, 1995), and Elizabeth Wiskemann,
Europe of the Dictators, 1919–1945 (Glasgow: Fontana, 1985).

66. Kapancızâde Hamit, *Bir Milli Mücadele valisi ve anıları: Kapancızâde Hamit
Bey*, ed. Halit Eken (Istanbul: Yeditepe, 2008), 493–98. It is not surprising that
Hamid, a respected and capable civil servant dedicated to the state also used
imperially biased language when speaking of the "ungrateful [Armenian] nation
[millet]."

67. Recent biographies of Atatürk, though instructive and innovative in many ways, do little to elaborate on this aspect. See M. Şükrü Hanioğlu, *Atatürk: An Intellectual Biography* (Princeton, NJ: Princeton University Press, 2011); Klaus Kreiser, *Atatürk: Eine Biographie* (München: C. H. Beck, 2014); Andrew Mango, *Atatürk* (London: John Murray, 1999).

68. Carl Mühlmann, *Deutschland und die Türkei 1913–1914* (Berlin: Walther Rothschild, 1929), 6. Mühlmann, a German officer, had been in Istanbul on the eve and during World War I.

69. Reference literature on Talaat and his role within the CUP is comparatively rich for the period before 1912; cf. Ahmad, *Young Turks*, and Hanioğlu, *Young Turks in Opposition* and *Preparation for a Revolution*.

Chapter 2: Patriotic Rebellion and Networking against Sultan Abdulhamid II

1. Cf. Hanioğlu, *Atatürk*, 192.

2. Quoted in *Bahaeddin Şakir Bey'in bıraktığı vesikalara göre İttihat ve Terakki* (Ankara: 2001 [1934]), 434.

3. An insightful and instructive English read on the Ottoman Empire in general is Caroline Finkel's *Osman's Dream: The Story of the Ottoman Empire, 1300–1923* (New York: Basic Books, 2005). Focused on the "long last Ottoman century" (late eighteenth to early twentieth century) and largely based on Ottoman sources is M. Şükrü Hanioğlu's *Brief History of the Late Ottoman Empire* (Princeton, NJ: Princeton University Press, 2008). Unequaled in its analytical power, leading from the thirteenth century to the present, is Hamit Bozarslan, *Histoire de la Turquie: De l'Empire à nos jours* (Paris: Tallandier, 2013).

4. Christine M. Philliou, *Biography of an Empire: Governing Ottomans in an Age of Revolution* (Berkeley: University of California Press, 2011), 1 and 165.

5. Elke Hartmann, *Die Reichweite des Staates: Wehrpflicht und moderne Staatlichkeit im Osmanischen Reich 1869–1910* (Paderborn: Ferdinand Schöningh, 2016, 96); explicit laws of recruiting of 1855 and 1870, quoted on p. 61.

6. British ambassador Layard in Constantinople to the Earl of Derby, British foreign secretary, 21 January 1878, British Foreign Office FO 424/67, quoted in Bilal Şimsir, *Emigrations turques des Balkans*, vol. 1, *Un exode turc* (Ankara: Türk Kültürünü Araştırma Enstitüsü, 1968), 283.

7. "He speaks French moderately well," Ambassador Lowther reported to foreign minister Grey on 6 July 1909, FO 371/778 (Visit to London and Armenian Massacres, 1909), 4–5.

8. Emmanuilidis, *Osmanlı İmparatorluğu'nun son yılları*, 273; Babacan, *Talât*, 38; "Lebensgeschichte Talaat Bej," Jäckh Papers, Yale University Library; İbnülemin M.

İnal, *Osmanlı Devrinde Son Sadrıazamlar* (Istanbul: İş Bankası, 2013 [1950]), 1333; *Die Welt*, 4 July 1913, 856. Some data are conflicting, for example, the death year of Talaat's father.

9. Mehmed Reşid [Şahingiray], *Hayatı ve Hâtıraları*, ed. N. Bilgi (İzmir: Akademi Kitabevi, 1997), 60–61. Cf. Hans-Lukas Kieser, "From 'Patriotism' to Mass Murder: Dr. Mehmed Reşid (1873–1919)," in Ronald G. Suny, Fatma M. Göcek, and Norman Naimark, eds., *A Question of Genocide: Armenians and Turks at the End of the Ottoman Empire* (New York: Oxford University Press, 2011), 126–49.

10. Mustafa Ragıb (Esatlı), *Meşrutiyet'ten önce Manastır'da patlayan tabanca* (Istanbul: Bengi, 2007 [1935]), 47–49; Babacan, *Talât*, 45–47; Mithat Şükrü Bleda, *İmparatorluğun Çöküşü* (Istanbul: Remzi, 1979), 20.

11. Meropi Anastassiadou, *Salonique, 1830–1912: Une ville ottomane à l'âge des Réformes* (Leiden: E. J. Brill, 1997).

12. Hanioğlu, *The Young Turks in Opposition*, 88 and 361, letter 74–75 (Talaat to Ahmed Rıza, 16 April 1902).

13. Marc D. Baer, *Jewish Converts, Muslim Revolutionaries, and Secular Turkish Jewish Converts* (Stanford, CA: Stanford University Press, 2010), 60; *Ali Münif Bey'in hâtıraları*, ed. Tahat Toros (Istanbul: Isis, 1996, 91).

14. Bleda, *İmparatorluğun Çöküşü*, 20–21; Tevfik Çandar, *Talat Paşa: Bir örgüt ustasının yaşamöyküsü* (Istanbul: Imge, 2001), 65; M. Şükrü Hanioğlu, "Talat Paşa," in *Türkiye Diyanet Vakfı İslam Ansiklopedisi* (Islamic Arastirma Merkezi [ISAM], 1988–2013), 39:502–3; Hanioğlu, *Preparation for a Revolution*, 75 and 151; Ahmet B. Kuran, *İnkılap tarihimiz ve Jön Türkler* (Istanbul: Kaynak, 2000 [1945]), 313.

15. Robert Graves, *Storm Centers of the Near East: Personal Memories, 1879–1929* (London: Hutchison, 1933), 200–201.

16. M. Şükrü Hanioğlu, *Preparation for a Revolution: The Young Turks, 1902–1908* (Oxford: Oxford University Press, 2001), 212.

17. Anderson, *The Eastern Question*, 272.

18. Bleda, *İmparatorluğun Çöküşü*, 21; cf. Emmanuilidis, *Osmanlı İmparatorluğu'nun son yılları*, 29.

19. Hanioğlu, *Atatürk*, 37–39; Andrew Mango, *Atatürk* (London: John Murray, 1999), 61–71.

20. Hanioğlu, *Preparation for a Revolution*, 218, 279; Bleda, *İmparatorluğun Çöküşü*, 22–23; Çavdar, *Talât*, 70–73; İbrahim Temo, *İttihad ve Terakki Cemiyeti'nin kurucusu ve 1/1 no'lu İbrahim Temo'nun İttihad ve Terakki Anıları* (Istanbul: Arba, 1987 [1939]), 173, 185.

21. Hanioğlu, *Preparation for a Revolution*, 130–41, 213–29. According to Ragıb, *Meşrutiyet'ten önce*, 35, members beside Talaat, Hafız Hakkı, and Manyasizâde Refik were Midhat Şükrü, Cemal (later Pasha), and Mustafa Rahmi.

22. Bleda, *İmparatorluğun Çöküşü*, 40–41; Ragıb, *Meşrutiyet'ten önce*, 52–54.

23. *Bahaeddin Şakir Bey'in bıraktığı vesikalara göre*, 412.

24. Hanioğlu, *Preparation for a Revolution*, 109–14.

25. *Bahaeddin Şakir Bey'in bıraktığı vesikalara göre*, 443–44, 467–68, 483; Hanioğlu, *Preparation for a Revolution*, 222–23, 240–41; M. Şükrü Hanioğlu, "The Second Constitutional Period, 1908–1918," in *The Cambridge History of Turkey*, ed. Reşat Kasaba (Cambridge: Cambridge University Press, 2008), 4:64.

26. Bleda, *İmparatorluğun Çöküşü*, 26–27.

27. Ibid., 44; Bayur, *Türk inkılâbı tarihi*, part 1, 1:438; Ziya Şakir (Soku), *Yakın tarihin üç büyük adamı: Talat, Enver, Cemal Paşalar* (Istanbul: Kaktüs, 2010 [1943]), 21–23.

28. *Bahaeddin Şakir Bey'in bıraktığı vesikalara göre İttihat ve Terakki* (Ankara: 2001 [1934]), 435–36.

29. Hanioğlu, *Preparation for a Revolution*, 236.

30. Ibid., 265–66; M. Şükrü Hanioğlu, "İttihat ve Terakki Cemiyeti," in *Türkiye Diyanet Vakfı İslam Ansiklopedisi*, 23:480.

31. Georgeon, *Abdulhamid II*, 397–98; Bleda, *İmparatorluğun Çöküşü*, 47.

32. Bleda, *İmparatorluğun Çöküşü*, 34–40; Ragıb, *Meşrutiyet'ten önce*, 54–69.

33. Bleda, *İmparatorluğun Çöküşü*, 49.

34. Hanioğlu, *Preparation for a Revolution*, 266–78.

35. Bleda, *İmparatorluğun Çöküşü*, 52.

36. Leon Sciaky, *Farewell to Salonica: City at the Crossroads* (Philadelphia: Paul Dry Books, 2003), 224–25.

37. "Cemiyetin görünmeyen ve örtülü kalan yöneltici kuvvetleri," in the words of Yusuf H. Bayur, *Türk inkılâbı tarihi* (Ankara: TTK, 1991), part 1, 1:241.

38. For a demonstrative summary of this kind of scientism, see Hanioğlu, *Atatürk: An Intellectual Biography*, 48–67.

39. *Bahaeddin Şakir Bey'in bıraktığı vesikalara göre*, 370–71; Hanioğlu, *Preparation for a Revolution*, 158–60, 174 (November 1906 letter), 180.

40. Quoted in Hanioğlu, *Preparation for a Revolution*, 185–86.

41. Hamit Bozarslan, "Le Prince Sabahaddin (1879–1948)," *Schweizerische Zeitschrift für Geschichte* 52, 3 (2002): 287–301. Cf. Cengiz Aktar, *Ademimerkeziyet elkitabi* (Istanbul: Iletisim, 2014), 9–33.

42. Quotations in *Bahaeddin Şakir Bey'in bıraktığı vesikalara göre*, 350, and Hanioğlu, *Preparation for a Revolution*, 260, 297.

43. Dikran Kaligian, *Armenian Organization and Ideology*, 2–3. Cf. generally on the missed late Ottoman peace in Eastern Asia Minor, Hans-Lukas Kieser, *Iskalanmış Barış: Doğu vilayetlerinde misyonerlik, etnik kimlik ve devlet 1839–1938* (Istanbul: İletişim, 2013).

44. Hasan Ünal, "Young Turk Assessment of International Politics, 1906–1909," *Middle Eastern Studies* 32 (1996): 30–44.

45. *Bahaeddin Şakir Bey'in bıraktığı vesikalara göre*, 483; cf. Hanioğlu, *Preparation for a Revolution*, 207.

46. Hanioğlu, *Preparation for a Revolution*, 207–8; Şakir's letter of 28 March 1908, quoted on p. 207.

Chapter 3: A Komiteci and the Challenge of Parliamentarism

1. From the name İttihad ve Terakki, translated as "Union and Progress."

2. Bahaeddin Şakir, in *Şûra-yı Ümmet*, quoted in Hanioğlu, *Preparation for a Revolution*, 288.

3. Hayri diary, 184–85.

4. Ibid., 82.

5. *Mîzancı Murad Bey'in II: Meşrutiyet dönemi hâtıraları* (Istanbul: Marifet, 1977), 214. Cf. Temo, *İttihad ve Terakki Cemiyeti'nin kurucusu*, 222, 224–25.

6. Diary of Louis Rambert, Musée du Vieux Montreux in Montreux, vol. 35, 26 October 1909. The Régie Company was established after the Ottoman state bankruptcy of the 1870s as part of the Ottoman Public Debt Administration (Administration de la Dette Publique Ottomane). It possessed the monopoly over Ottoman tobacco production. A lawyer, cantonal leader, federal politician, and then a railway administrator, Rambert (1839–1919) had left Switzerland in 1891 to be a manager in both Ottoman and European services in Istanbul.

7. Hayri diary, 125.

8. Heyd, *Ziya Gökalp*, 31. Data diverge on the start of Gökalp's Central Committee membership; Heyd and others mention autumn 1909. Membership in 1912 is confirmed in Hayri's diary, 184. In any case, from autumn 1909 he was in close contact with Talaat and other main CUP leaders in Salonica.

9. Yusuf H. Bayur, *Türk inkılâbı tarihi* (Ankara: TTK, 1991), part 2, 1:69; Georgeon, *Abdulhamid II*, 404–7.

10. Kâzım Karabekir, *İttihat ve Terakki Cemiyeti* (Istanbul: YKY, 2014), 232–33.

11. Rambert diary, vol. 31, 28 August 1908; and vol. 39, 24 April 1911.

12. Kuran, *İnkılap tarihimiz*, 326–30; Babacan, *Mehmed Talât*, 35; Georgeon, *Abdulhamid*, 408–15.

13. Talat, *Hatıralarım ve Müdafaam*, 27; Doğan Çetinkaya, *The Young Turks and the Boycott Movement: Nationalism, Protest and the Working Classes in the Formation of Modern Turkey* (London: I. B. Tauris, 2014), 41–42.

14. Noémi Lévy, *Ordre et désordres dans l'Istanbul ottomane, 1879–1909: De l'état au quartier* (Paris: Karthala, 2013), 118–19; Bayur, *Türk inkılâbı tarihi*, part 2, 1:125–26.

15. Georgeon, *Abdulhamid*, 416–19; Babacan, *Talât*, 54–57; Kuran, *İnkılap tarihimiz*, 327.

16. Rambert diary, vol. 33, 17 March 1909.

17. Cavid diary, 1:34, 12 April 1909.

18. Rambert diary, Tuesday, 13 April 1909, evening, vol. 33, including press clipping. Rambert refers to the massacres in Istanbul in late August 1896.

19. Kévorkian, *Armenian Genocide*, 100; Ahmed Rıza, *Ahmed Rıza Bey in Anıları* (Istanbul: Arba, 1988), 37.

20. Rambert diary, 14 and 16 April 1909, vol. 33, including press clipping.

21. "Halife-i İslâm Abdülhamid Han Hazretlerine," *Volkan*, 23 Rebîülevvel 1327 (14 April), front page, transcribed and ed. M. E. Düzdağ (Istanbul: İz, 1992), 505.

22. "İnkılab-ı Şer'î," *Volkan*, 24 Rebîülevvel 1327 (15 April), front page, transcribed and ed. M. E. Düzdağ (Istanbul: İz, 1992), 510.

23. A graphic contemporary Armenian report, now translated from the Armenian, is Zabel Yessayan's *In the Ruins: The 1909 Massacres of Armenians in Adana, Turkey* (Watertown: AIWA, 2016).

24. Rambert diary, vol. 34, 6 May 1909.

25. Celâl Bayar, *Ben de yazdım: Millî mücadeleye giriş* (Istanbul: Sabah kitapları, 1997), 8:119–20; Kévorkian, *Armenian Genocide*, 71–96.

26. Mahir S. Pekmen, *31 Mart hatıraları: İsyan günlerinde bir muhalif* (Ankara: TTK, 2011), 172–98.

27. Kévorkian, *Armenian Genocide*, 72; Sina Akşin, *Jön Türkler ve İttihat Terakki* (Istanbul: Simge, 2001 [1980]), 196–98.

28. Georgeon, *Abdulhamid*, 420–21.

29. Rambert diary, vol. 34.

30. Türkgeldi, *Görüp işittiklerim*, 36–37; Babacan, *Talât*, 61–63; Georgeon, *Abdulhamid*, 424–25.

31. Türkgeldi, *Görüp işittiklerim*, 40–41; Babacan, *Talât*, 64–65.

32. Rambert diary, vol. 34, 12 and 19 May 1909. The grand vizier read the sultan's speech in the latter's presence on 20 May; cf. Emmanuilidis, *Osmanlı İmparatorluğu'nun son yılları*, 24.

33. Cavid diary, 1:44, 30 April 1909.

34. Rambert diary, vol. 34, 6 May; Cavid diary, 1:47–48, 5–7 May 1909; Babacan, *Talât*, 65–67.

35. Rambert diary, vol. 35, 22 August 1909.

36. *Jewish Chronicle*, 23 July 1909, quoted in N. J. Mandel, *Turks, Arabs and Jewish Immigration into Palestine: 1882–1914*, doctoral dissertation (Oxford: St. Antony's College, 1965), 192.

37. *Yeni Gazete*, 21 July 1909, quoted in FO 371/778 (Visit to London and Armenian Massacres, 1909), 16.

38. Rambert diary, vol. 35, 26 October 1909; Babacan, *Talât*, 67–68; "Lebensgeschichte Talaat Bej," Jäckh Papers, Yale University Library; Miquel to Auswärtiges Amt, 14 August 1909, PA-AA/R 13796.

39. Dikran M. Kaligian, *Armenian Organization and Ideology under Ottoman Rule, 1908–1914* (New Brunswick: Transaction, 2012), 82–84.

40. Kévorkian, *Armenian Genocide*, 97–117.

41. Quoted in Kévorkian, *Armenian Genocide*, 101.

42. Tahat Toros, ed., *Ali Münif Bey'in hâtıraları* (Istanbul: Isis, 1996), 51–56.

43. Talat, *Hatıralarım ve Müdafaam*, 25–26.

44. Published on 3 September 1909 in *Tanin*, reproduced in Esat Uras, *Tarihte Ermeniler ve Ermeni Meselesi* (Ankara: Yeni Matbaa), 584–85. Cf. Kaligian, *Armenian Organization and Ideology*, 47–49.

45. Jean Rodes, "Déclarations du grand-vizir et du ministre de l'intérieur sur la politique générale," *Le Temps*, 27 September 1909.

46. Rambert diary, vol. 35, 14, 15, and 28 October 1909.

47. Ibid., vol. 37, 17 April 1910.

48. Ibid., vol. 36, 23 March 1910.

49. Soku, *Yakın tarihin üç büyük adamı*, 29; Rambert diary, vol. 36, 13 Dec. 1909; cf. Hanioğlu, "The Second Constitutional Period," 74–75; M. Şükrü Hanioğlu, "İttihat ve Terakki Cemiyeti," in *Türkiye Diyanet Vakfı İslam Ansiklopedisi*, 23:482.

50. Rambert diary, vol. 36, 31 December 1909; 13 and 30 January 1910.

51. Ahmed İzzet (Furgaç), *Feryadım* (Istanbul: Timaş, 2017), 1:99–100; memoirs rich in insights, written in the 1920s, when İzzet Pasha was definitively sidelined by the Kemalist regime. Cf. Nathalie Clayer, *Aux origines du nationalisme albanais: La naissance d'une nation musulmane en Europe* (Paris: Karthala, 2007), 611–705; Soku, *Yakın tarihin üç büyük adamı*, 29.

52. Cf. Thomas Kühn, *Empire, Islam, and Politics of Difference: Ottoman Rule in Yemen, 1849–1919* (Leiden: Brill, 2011), 237–39.

53. Yuval Ben-Bassat, "Palestine's Population and the Question of Ottomanism during the Last Decade of Ottoman Rule," in Hans-Lukas Kieser, Kerem Öktem, and Maurus Reinkowski, eds., *World War I and the End of the Ottomans: From the Balkan Wars to the Armenian Genocide* (London: I. B. Tauris, 2015), 153; Mandel, *Turks, Arabs and Jewish Immigration*, 209–10.

54. *Neue Freie Presse*, 14 August 1912.

55. Rambert diary, vol. 36, 30 January 1910.

56. For a political assassination in early 1910 reported by Talaat's friend Tahsin, see Tahsin Uzer, *Makedonya eşkiyalık tarihi ve son Osmanlı yönetimi* (Ankara: TTK, 1999 [1920]), 304–5.

57. This was the impression of Muhittin Birgen, as he states repeatedly (*İttihat ve Terakki'de on sene*).

58. For this comparison, see Baer, *Dönme*, 109.

59. Rambert diary, vol. 36, 30 January 1910; vol. 38, 6 November and 4 December 1910. Babacan, *Talât*, 71–73. Meeting, 28 August 1910, Arthur B. Geary to G. Lowther, FO 371/779; analogous to the report of Austrian vice-consul Zitovsky, Manastir, to foreign minister Ährenthal, 14 October 1910, together with comments, in Marschall to Auswärtiges Amt, 20 October 1910, PA-AA/R 13197.

60. Talat, *Hatıraları ve müdafaam*, 52–56. Manifestly envying it, Talaat belittled the ARF membership in the Socialist International as "cosmetics to impress the European public."

61. The Danish orientalist Johannes Østrup claimed that Talaat said to him in autumn 1910, "You see between us and this people there is an incompatibility which cannot be solved in a peaceful manner; either they will completely undermine us, or we will have to annihilate them. If I ever come to power in this country, I will use all my might to exterminate the Armenians." Østrup, *Erindringer* (Copenhagen: H. Hirschsprungs Forlag, 1937), 118, quoted in Matthias Bjørnlund, "'When the cannons talk, the diplomats must be silent': A Danish Diplomat in Constantinople during the Armenian Genocide," *Genocide Studies and Prevention* 1–2 (September 2006), 197–224, here 201.

62. Karl Helfferich, *Die deutsche Türkenpolitik* (Berlin: Vossische Buchhandlung, 1921), 21–23; John G. Williamson, *Karl Helfferich, 1872–1924: Economist, Financier, Politician* (Princeton, NJ: Princeton University Press, 1971), 89–96; Walter Mogk, "Jäckh, Ernst," *Neue Deutsche Biographie* 10 (1974): 264–67; https://www.deutsche-biographie.de/gnd118711253.html#ndbcontent; the Churchill quote is from Dockter, *Churchill and the Islamic World*, 50.

63. Rambert diary, vol. 38, 6 November 1910; Cavid diary, 1:185.

64. *Ali Münif Bey'in hâtıraları*, 81–82 and 92.

65. Ayşe, mother of Enver, to Talaat, 12 July 1914, BOA DH. KMS 63-66.

66. Emmanuilidis, *Osmanlı İmparatorluğu'nun son yılları*, 143. Celâl had been a director of the school for civil servants in Istanbul in 1908 and was the minister of the interior from December 1911 to July 1912. Celâl Bey, "Ermeni Vakayi'i, Esbab ve Tesiratı," *Vakit*, 10, 12, 13 December 1918, transcription in *Agos*, 30 July 2010; cf. Hans-Lukas Kieser, "Réformes ottomanes et cohabitation entre chrétiens et Kurdes (1839–1915)," *Ruralité, urbanité et violence au Kurdistan* (Études Rurales 186), 2010, 53; Kaligian, *Armenian Organization and Ideology*, 82–84.

67. Marschall to Reichskanzler Bethmann Hollweg, January 1910, PA-AA/R 13796-3.

68. Quoted in Bedross Der Matossian, *Shattered Dreams of Revolution: From Liberty to Violence in the Late Ottoman Empire* (Stanford, CA: Stanford University Press, 2014), 177–78.

69. Rambert diary, vol. 36, 4 March 1910; vol. 38, 4 December 1910.

70. MMZC, first session period, 3:331–37, session of 1 March 1911; 3:553–74, session of 16 May 1911; "Die türkische Märzdebatte," *Die Welt: Zentralorgan der zionistischen Bewegung*, weekly, Köln, 10 March 1911, 211–14; cf. Mandel, *Turks, Arabs and Jewish Immigration*, 240–46; Hasan Kayali, *Arabs and Young Turks: Ottomanism, Arabism, and Islamism in the Ottoman Empire, 1908–1918* (Berkeley: University of California Press, 1997), 103–5; Louis Fishman, "Understanding the 1911 Ottoman Parliament Debate on Zionism in Light of the Emergence of a 'Jewish Question,'" in Yuval Ben-Bassat and Eyal Ginio, eds., *Late Ottoman Palestine: The Period of Young Turk Rule* (London: I. B. Tauris, 2011), 111–19.

71. Cavid diary, 1:62, 7 February 1911; Rambert diary, vol. 38, 1 March 1911; Menteşe, *Halil Menteşe'nin anıları*, 250. For an assessment of Cavid, see Emmanuilidis, *Osmanlı İmparatorluğu'nun son yılları*, 283.

72. Cf. Bayar, *Ben de yazdım*, 2:91, 2:141; Emmanuilidis, *Osmanlı İmparatorluğu'nun son yılları*, 143.

73. MMZC, first session period, 3:559–62.

74. Minutes of the Fifth General Assembly, session 37, 2 September 1909, in *Materials for the History of the ARF* [in Armenian] (Beirut: Hamazkayin Press, 2010), vi, 78; session 50, 11 September 1909, ibid., 110.

75. Second Salonica accord, 26 March 1911, and letter of Occidental to Oriental Bureau, 15 April 1911, in *Materials for the History of the ARF* [in Armenian] (Beirut: Hamazkayin Press, 2010), 8:154 and 8:160.

76. Minutes of the Sixth General Assembly, session 19, 29 August 1911, in *Materials for the History of the ARF*, viii, 60; Lowther to Grey, 16 May 1911, FO 371/1244 (General Correspondence), 14934.

77. Ziya Gökalp, *Türkçülüğün esasları*, ed. Salim Çonoğlu (Istanbul: Ötüken, 2014; 1st ed. Ankara, 1339 [1923]), 28.

78. Birgen, *İttihat ve Terakki'e on sene*, 363–64.

79. Gökalp, *Türkçülüğün esasları*, 28–29.

80. Quoted in Enver B. Şapolyo, *Ziya Gökalp: İttihat ve Terakki ve Meşrutiyet tarihi* (Istanbul: Güven, 1943), 135, 169.

81. Hanioğlu, *The Young Turks in Opposition*, 120.

82. Selçuk A. Somel, "Melekler, vatanperverler ve ajan provokatörler: Mutlakiyet devri Diyarbakır okul gençliği, bürokrasi ve Ziya Gökalp'in idadi öğrenciliğine ilişkin soruşturma kayıtları (1894–1895)," Sabancı University 2014, http://research.sabanciuniv.edu/24852/; Hamit Bozarslan, "M. Ziya Gökalp," in *Modern Türkiye'de siyasi düşünce: Tanzimat ve Meşrutiyet'in birikimi*, 315–19.

83. "Felsefi vasiyetler (2): Hocamın vasiyeti," *Küçük Mecmua* 1, 18 (15 October 1922): 4.

84. "Kızılelma," *Türk Yurdu*, 2:31 (23 Jan. 1913), transcribed ed. (Ankara: Tutibay, 1999), 2:115–20; poem "Turan," *Altın Armağan*, supplement of *Türk Yurdu*, 1:24, 17 October 1912; transcribed ed., 1:418.

85. Gustave Meyrier, *Les massacres de Diarbekir: Correspondance diplomatique du vice-consul de France 1894–1896* (Paris: Edition l'inventaire, 2000), 196, telegram, 21 May 1896.

86. Meyrier, *Les massacres de Diarbekir*, 55–58. Cf. Owen Robert Miller, *Sasun 1894: Mountains, Missionaries and Massacres at the End of the Ottoman Empire*, PhD thesis, Columbia University, New York, 2015.

87. Meyrier, *Les massacres de Diarbekir*, 170.

88. Ibid., 130–36, 185.

89. *Bahaeddin Şakir Bey'in bıraktığı vesikalara göre*, 159–61.

90. Latin transcription in Şevket Beysanoğlu, *Diyarbakır tarihi* (Ankara: Irmak, 1998), 727–29; English translation in Jelle Verhej, "Diyarbekir and the Armenian Crisis of 1895," in Joost Jongerden and Jelle Verheij, *Social Relations in Ottoman Diyarbekir, 1870–1915* (Leiden: Brill, 2012), 124–26.

91. Joost Jongerden, "Elite Encounters of a Violent Kind: Milli Ibrahim Paşa, Ziya Gökalp and Political Struggle in Diyarbekir at the Turn of the 20th Century," in Jongerden and Verheij, *Social Relations in Ottoman Diyarbekir*, 55–84; Hilmar Kaiser, *The Extermination of Armenians in the Diarbekir Region* (Istanbul: Bilgi University, 2014), 23–35. The latter is an accurate and instructive piece of research largely based on BOA documents.

92. Hanioğlu, *The Young Turks in Opposition*, 121.

93. Sabine Adatepe, "'Das osmanische Muster': Das frühe Ideal des M. Ziya (Gökalp) anhand ausgewählter Artikel in der Wochenschrift Peyman," in Hendrik Fenz, ed., *Strukturelle Zwänge—persönliche Freiheiten: Osmanen, Türken, Muslime; Reflexionen zu gesellschaftlichen Umbrüchen: Gedenkband zu Ehren Petra Kapperts* (Berlin: Walter de Gruyter, 2009), 31–45.

94. "İslamiyet ve asrî medeniyet," *İslâm Mecmuası*, 51–52 (1917), English in Niyazi Berkes, *Turkish Nationalism and Western Civilization: Selected Essays of Ziya Gökalp* (New York: Columbia University Press, 1959), 214–23. There is, however, no reference to Max Weber's relevant essay on "The Protestant Ethic and the Spirit of Capitalism."

95. Poem in Gökalp, *Yeni hayat* (Istanbul: Yeni Mecmua, 1918), 1, quoted in Hanioğlu, "The Second Constitutional Period," 71.

Chapter 4: Alignment toward War and Dictatorial CUP Power

1. Rambert diary, vol. 47, 1 January 1914.

2. Babacan, *Talât*, 73.

3. Rambert diary, vol. 38, 1 March 1911; Hayri diary, 30, 31 March 1911; André N. Mandelstam, *Le sort de l'Empire ottoman* (Lausanne: Payot, 1917), 35.

4. Cavid diary, 1:107 and 1:113, 20 April 1911. For an assessment of Sadık's ambitious personality, see the Lord High Chamberlain Lütfi Simavi's *Son Osmanlı sarayında gördüklerim* (Istanbul: Örgün, 2004; first ed. 1924), 135–38.

5. Rambert diary, vol. 38, 18 March 1911; cf. vol. 39, 1, 5, 7, 12 May and 24 September and 4 October 1911.

6. Ibid., vol. 39, 11 September 1911; Cavid diary, 1:156–57, 12 September 1911.

7. Rambert diary, vol. 39.

8. Ibid., vol. 39, 28 September, 9:00 p.m., 4 October; Cavid diary, 1:161, 27–29 September 1911.

9. Charles D. Haley, "The Desperate Ottoman: Enver Paşa and the German Empire—I," *Middle Eastern Studies* 30, no. 1 (Jan. 1994): 2.

10. Cavid diary, 1:186, 29 October 1911; 1:190, 1:195, 1 and 25 November 1911; Bayur, *Türk inkılâbı tarihi*, part 1, 2:83; Dockter, *Churchill and the Islamic World*, 58–62; cf. Kieser, *Iskalanmış Barış*, 333.

11. Rambert diary, vol. 39, 12 October; vol. 40, 15 October and 15 November.

12. Ibid., vol. 40, 10 December.

13. Cavid diary, 1:183, 25 October 1911.

14. Ibid., 1:168–69 and 1:174, 16 and 18 October 1911.

15. Hans-Lukas Kieser, *Türklüğe İhtida* (Istanbul: İletişim, 2008), 102–8.

16. Rambert diary, vol. 40, 12 and 15 December 1911; cf. Ali Birinci, *Hürriyet ve İtilâf Fırkası: II, Meşrutiyet döneminde İttihat ve Terakki'ye karşı çıkanlar* (Istanbul: Dergah, 1990), 48 and 113–15.

17. Rambert diary, vol. 40, 18 and 23 January 1912; Cavid diary, 1:217, 24 December 1911, 18 January 1912. Talaat was accustomed to having a look at encoded governmental telegrams in the years before 1908 (Babacan, *Talât*, 17).

18. Rambert diary, vol. 40, 18 February 1912; vol. 41, 19 April and 25 May.

19. Ibid., vol. 41, 14 April 1912; Cavid diary, 1:285–86, 27 March 1912.

20. Rambert diary, vol. 41, 24 May 1912.

21. Cavid diary, 1:424–30, 7–13 July 1912; Hayri diary, 128, 9 July 1912; cf. 163–64, 16 August 1912; Bayur, *Türk inkılâbı tarihi*, part 1, 2:270.

22. Simavi, *Gördüklerim*, 214; Birinci, *Hürriyet ve İtilâf Fırkası*, 164–79.

23. Cavid diary, 1:444, 27 July 1912.

24. Rambert diary, vol. 41, 7 August 1912; Hayri diary, 142–45, 25–29 July.

25. Quoted in Bayur, *Türk inkılâbı tarihi*, part 1, 2:277. Cavid diary, 1:428, 12 July 1912.

26. *Sabah*, no. 8208, 26 July 1912, 2.

27. Talat, *Hatıralarım ve müdafaam*, 159.

28. Cavid diary, 1:442–43, 22–23 July 1912 and 1:442, 7–31 August 1912; Rambert diary, vol. 41, 7 August 1912; Hayri diary, 153, 4 August 1912.

29. Kaligian, *Armenian Organization and Ideology under Ottoman Rule, 1908–1914* (New Brunswick: Transaction, 2012), 122–39.

30. Hayri diary, 171, 23 August; Bayar, *Ben de yazdım*, 2:153.

31. Hayri diary, 179, 30 August 1912; Rambert diary, vol. 42, 6 September 1912.

32. Rambert diary, vol. 42, 2 October 1912.

33. Cavid diary, 1:460, 19–30 September 1912.

34. Ibid., 1:463, 4 October 1912; Dr. Cemil Pasha's eyewitness account, quoted in Ahmet Reşit Rey, *Gördüklerim–Yaptıklarım* (Istanbul: Türkiye Yay., 1945), 156 (Cemil narrates slightly differently and puts the event on Saturday, which may point to a second manifestation on 5 October in front of the Dolmabahçe Palace); Mustafa Ragıp Esatlı, *İttihat ve Terakki tarihinde esrar perdesi* (Istanbul: Hürriyet, 1975), 143.

35. Cavid diary, 1:463, 3–4 October 1912; cf. Rambert diary, vol. 42, 7 October. Hüseyin Cahid quoted in Ryan Gingeras, *Fall of the Sultanate: The Great War and the End of the Ottoman Empire, 1908–1922* (Oxford: Oxford University Press, 2016), 80.

36. See "fougueux Talaat," Rambert diary, vol. 42, 7 October.

37. Hayri diary, 192, 5 October 1912.

38. Rambert diary, vol. 42, 7 October.

39. Bayur, *Türk inkılâbı tarihi*, part 1, 2:393–406; Kévorkian, *Armenian Genocide*, 135–36.

40. Rambert diary, vol. 42, 8 October 1912; Cavid diary, 1:466, 8 October 1912; Esatlı, *İttihat ve Terakki*, 147.

41. Bayur, *Türk inkılâbı tarihi*, part 1, 2:413.

42. Cavid diary, 1:468–69, 12 October and 1:509, 10 November 1912. Cf. Hayri diary, 177–78, 29 August 1912.

43. Rambert diary, vol. 42, 4 and 10 October 1912.

44. Rey, *Gördüklerim*, 157.

45. Hanioğlu, "The Second Constitutional Period," 73; Cavid diary, 1:478, 24 October 1912.

46. Cavid diary, 1:512, 10 November 1912.

47. Rambert diary, vol. 42, 3–4 November 1912; vol. 43, 10–17 December 1912; Max Rudolf Kaufmann, "Erlebnisse in der Türkei vor 50 Jahren," *Zeitschrift für Auslandsbeziehungen 1962*, 240–41 (thanks to Jochen Schrader for this reference).

48. Talat, *Hatıralarım ve müdafaam*, 28.

49. Ibid. Rambert diary, vol. 42, 8–9 November 1912 (quotations from here); Cavid diary, 1:471, 15 October 1912.

50. Uzer, *Makedonya eşkiyalık tarihi*, 320.

51. This is the opinion of Hüseyin Kazım (Kadri), who was among the arrested (Hüseyin Kazım Kadri, *Meşrutiyet'ten cumhuriyet'e hatıralarım* [Istanbul: İletişim, 1991]), 134.

52. This is the opinion of Tahsin (Uzer), district governor and police director of Beyoğlu after the putsch, see Uzer, *Son Osmanlı yönetimi*, 320.

53. Hayri diary, 202, 5 November 1912; 213–18, 21 November 1912; 225, 29 November 1912; Cavid diary, 1:475, 20 October 1912; 1:524, 14 November 1912; Rambert diary, vol. 43, 15, 17 and 23 November 1912; Babacan, *Talât*, 76–77.

54. Rambert diary, vol. 43, 24 November and 6 December 1912; Richard C. Hall, "Balkan Wars, 1912–1913," *1914–1918: International Encyclopedia of the First World War*, http://dx.doi.org/10.15463/ie1418.10009.

55. Rambert diary, vol. 43, 22 December 1912.

56. Cavid diary, 1:537–46, 23 December–1 February 1913.

57. Ahmed İzzet, *Feryadım*, 1:159. Cf. Metin Ayışığı, *Mareşal Ahmed İzzet Paşa: Askerî ve siyasî hayatı* (Ankara: TTK, 1997), 60–65.

58. Reports of the Deutsche Bank, 11 January and 1 March 1913, OR 1322, Historical Archive of the Deutsche Bank, Frankfurt.

59. Rambert diary, vol. 44, 22–23 January 1913.

60. Jacobson, 4 January 1913, CZA, Z3-45, 00281; confirmed on 6 January 1913, Z3-45, 00274.

61. Babacan, *Talât*, 78–82; Hayri diary, 252, 23 January 1913.

62. Uzer, *Son Osmanlı yönetimi*, 320–21.

63. Türkgeldi, *Görüp işittiklerim*, 78–79.

64. Wangenheim to Auswärtiges Amt, 28 January 1913, PA-AA/R 13192-5.

65. Whole telegram in Wangenheim to Auswärtiges Amt, 23 January 1913, PA-AA/R 13192-2.

66. Bayur, *Türk inkılâbı tarihi*, part 2, 2:270; Rey, *Gördüklerim*, 206; Cemal Pasha, *Erinnerungen eines türkischen Staatsmannes* (München: Drei Masken Verlag, 1922), 7.

67. The minister of the interior had prepared a list of two hundred CUP members to be arrested, imprisoned, or expelled (Rambert diary, vol. 44, 9 March 1913).

68. Emmanuilidis, *Osmanlı İmparatorluğu'nun son yılları*, 36. On Emmanuilidis, see Vangelis Kechriotis, "On the Margins of National Historiography: The Greek İttihatçi Emmanouil Emmanouilidis; Opportunist or Ottoman Patriot?," in Amy Singer, Christoph Neumann, and Selçuk A. Somel, eds., *Untold Histories of the Middle East: Recovering Voices from the 19th and 20th Centuries* (London: Routledge, 2011), 124–42.

69. *Zeit*, 28 January 1913, Österreichisches Staatsarchiv, K. und k. Ministerium des Äusseren, Departement 5, Zeitungsarchiv.

70. Cf. Rambert diary, vol. 44, 9 March 1913.

71. Ibid., 4 February.

72. Hayri diary, 257, 9 February 1913; 273–74, 6 March 1913; 284–85, 1 April 1913.

73. Rambert diary, vol. 44, 3, 7, 9 and 10 March 1913.

74. Ahmed İzzet, *Feryadım*, 1:166.

75. Diary of Lütfi Fikri, *Dersim Mebusu Lütfi Fikri Bey'in Günlüğü* (Istanbul: Arma, 1991), 64–67, 3–8 April 1913; 83, 2 May 1913; and 95, 31 May 1913. Cf. Ali Birinci, "Lutfi Fikri," in *Türkiye Diyanet Vakfı İslam Ansiklopedisi*, 27:233–34.

76. Nor was he plausibly involved in the assassination of the Greek king George I on 13 March 1913. Behiç Erkin, *Hâtırat* (Ankara: TTK, 2010), 118. See also Andrew Dalby, *Eleftherios Venizelos: Greece* (London: Haus, 2010); Thomas W. Gallant, *Modern Greece: From the War of Independence to the Present* (London: Bloomsbury, 2016), 173–220.

77. Hüseyin Cahid Yalçın, *Siyasal anılar* (Istanbul: Türkiye İş Bankası, 2000), 269–71. Cf. the same, *Talât Paşa* (Istanbul: Yedigün, 1943), 43.

78. Rambert diary, vol. 45, 9 May 1913.

79. Lütfi Fikri, *Dersim Mebusu Lütfi Fikri Bey'in Günlüğü*, 93, 30 May 1913.

80. Rambert diary, vol. 45, 27–28 April 1913.

81. Lütfi Fikri, *Dersim Mebusu Lütfi Fikri Bey'in Günlüğü*, 68, 9 April 1913; Rambert diary, vol. 45, 9 May 1913.

82. As proposed to the sultan on 11 June 1913 by the cabinet (Hayri diary, 317; Türkgeldi, *Görüp işittiklerim*, 100).

83. German translation of Said Halim's booklet of 1921 in Fischer, *Aus der religiösen Reformbewegung in der Türkei*, 15–39 (cf. Ahmet Şeyhun, *Islamist Thinkers in the Late Ottoman Empire and Early Turkish Republic* [Leiden: Brill, 2015], 164).

84. Wangenheim to Reichskanzler Bethmann Hollweg, 13 June 1913, PA-AA/R 13797-4.

85. Cemal, *Erinnerungen*, 18–22.

86. Cf. Bayur, *Türk inkılâbı tarihi*, part 2, 2:316–18; Temo, *İttihad ve Terakki Cemiyeti'nin kurucusu*, 225.

87. Rambert diary, vol. 45, 5 and 9 July 1913.

88. Hayri diary, 330–34, 18–19 July 1913; Ahmed İzzet, *Feryadım*, 1:169–71.

89. Bayur, *Türk inkılâbı tarihi*, part 2, 2:422–23; Türkgeldi, *Görüp işittiklerim*, 106–7; Rambert diary, vol. 45, 23 July; vol. 46, 26 July; Cemal, *Erinnerungen*, 44–46.

90. Türkgeldi, *Görüp işittiklerim*, 108–9; Babacan, *Talât*, 86.

91. Rambert diary 45, 23 July 1913; 46, 18 September 1913.

92. See 16 February 1914, in *Die internationalen Beziehungen im Zeitalter des Imperialismus: Dokumente aus den Archiven der Zarischen und der Provisorischen Regierung*, 1:1, 1:253–54.

93. Eyal Ginio, *The Ottoman Culture of Defeat: The Balkan Wars and Their Aftermath* (London: Hurst & Company, 2016), 249–58.

94. Simavi, *Son Osmanlı sarayında gördüklerim*, 285.

95. Stephen Lades, *The Exchange of Minorities: Bulgaria, Greece and Turkey* (New York: Macmillan, 1932), 18; text of the treaty passage regarding the exchange is quoted in Akçam, *The Young Turks' Crime*, 64.

96. Cemal, *Erinnerungen*, 51–57; Babacan, *Talât*, 87; secret military convention of 25 January 1914, *Dokumente aus den Archiven der Zarischen und der Provisorischen Regierung*, 1:1, 1:449–50.

97. Wangenheim to Auswärtiges Amt, 7 September, 1; 10 October, 1, 7; 15 November 1913, *Die grosse Politik der europäischen Kabinette 1871–1914: Sammlung der Diplomatischen Akten des Auswärtigen Amtes* (Berlin: Deutsche Verlags-Gesellschaft für Politik und Geschichte, 1926), 36:74–75, 36:105, 36:112–13, 36:116–18, 36:123–24.

98. Erickson, *Study in Counterinsurgency*, 112, 117–18. What largely lacks in this and other SO studies (partly due to censure and secrecy, thus scarcity of accessible relevant sources), is the assessment of the SO's role during the Rûm removal and the Armenian genocide. For crucial insight into this aspect of the SO, see Kaiser, *The Extermination of Armenians*; "Tahsin Uzer: The CUP's Man in the East," and "Operative for Genocide: Abdulkadir Bey, a Man for All Occasions," in *End of the Ottomans: The Genocide of 1915 and the Politics of Turkish Nationalism*, Hans-Lukas Kieser, Margaret L. Anderson, Seyhan Bayraktar, and Thomas Schmutz, eds. (London: I. B. Tauris, forthcoming [2018]). For a historical survey of the SO, see Odile Moreau, *La Turquie dans la Grande Guerre* (Saint-Cloud: SOTECA, 2016), 119–62.

99. Wangenheim to Auswärtiges Amt, 2 December 1913, 4 January 1914; Nadolny, delegate of the control commission for Albania, to Auswärtiges Amt, 3 January 1914; Ambassador Tschirschky, Vienna, to Reichskanzler Bethmann Hollweg, 7 January, *Die grosse Politik der europäischen Kabinette*, 38:315, 38:327, 38:329–30; Cavid diary, 2:107–8, 24 September 1913.

100. Take Ionescu, *Souvenirs* (Paris: Payot, 1919), 146.

101. Rambert diary, vol. 46, 7 August 1913.

102. Cf. ibid., vol. 46, 20 September 1913 and 3 October 1913.

103. Ibid., vol. 46, 19 November 1913.

104. Cavid diary, 1:554, 6 February 1913; *Die grosse Politik der europäischen Kabinette*, 38:43, Wangenheim to Reichskanzler Bethmann Hollweg, 21 May 1913.

105. *Die grosse Politik der europäischen Kabinette 1871–1914: Sammlung der Diplomatischen Akten des Auswärtigen Amtes* (Berlin: Deutsche Verlags-Gesellschaft für Politik und Geschichte, 1926), 38:131, Wangenheim to the Foreign Office secretary Jagow, 8 August 1913.

106. *Die grosse Politik der europäischen Kabinette*, vol. 38, Wangenheim to Reichskanzler Bethmann Hollweg, 21 November 1913.

107. Wangenheim to Reichskanzler Bethmann Hollweg, 20 June 1913, PA-AA/R 13797-4, 18-20. Halil had joined the new cabinet as president of the council of state. Cf. Wasti, "Halil Menteşe–the Quadrumvir," 95.

108. Cavid diary, 2:103–4, 23 September 1913.

109. Rambert diary, vol. 47, 12 December 1913.

110. Cf. Hans-Lukas Kieser, Mehmet Polatel, and Thomas Schmutz, "Reform or Cataclysm? The Agreement of 8 February 1914 regarding the Ottoman Eastern Provinces," *Journal of Genocide Research* 17, no. 3 (2015): 285–304; Roderic H. Davison, "The Armenian Crisis, 1912–1914," in the same, *Essays in Ottoman and Turkish History, 1774–1923: The Impact of the West* (Austin: University of Texas Press, 1990 [1948]), 180–205.

111. Cf. Kieser, "Johannes Lepsius," in Müller et al., *Logos im Dialogos*, 209–29.

112. Davison, "The Armenian Crisis," 186.

113. Kieser, Polatel, and Schmutz, "Reform or Cataclysm?," 290.

114. Rober Koptaş, "Zohrab, Papazyan ve Pastırmacıyan'ın kalemlerinden 1914 Ermeni reformu ve İttihatçı-Taşnak müzakeleri," *Tarih ve Toplum Yeni Yaklaşımlar* 5 (Spring 2007): 164–67; Zaven Der Yeghiayan, *My Patriarchal Memoirs* (Barrington: Mayreni, 2002), 22–24.

115. *Kapancızâde Hamit Bey*, 465–66.

116. Kieser, *Türklüğe İhtida*, 109–14; Y. Doğan Çetinkaya, "'Revenge! Revenge! Revenge!': 'Awakening a Nation' through Propaganda in the Ottoman Empire during the Balkan Wars (1912–13)," in Kieser, Öktem, and Reinkowski, eds. *World War I and the End of the Ottomans*, 77–102.

117. Çetinkaya, *The Young Turks and the Boycott Movement*, 39–159.

118. See my chapter, "Violence et dissidence à partir des marges de l'Empire ottoman tardif: L'idéologue Ziya Gökalp et le *komitacı* Mehmed Talat," forthcoming in 2018 in *Marges et pouvoir dans l'espace (post)ottoman XIXe-XXe siècles*, ed. Hamit Bozarslan (Paris: Karthala).

119. Kieser, Polatel, and Schmutz, "Reform or Cataclysm?," 292–93. Cf. Michael Reynolds, *Shattering Empires: The Clash and Collapse of the Ottoman and Russian Empires, 1908–1918* (Cambridge: Cambridge University Press, 2011), 58–70.

120. Cf. *Felâha Doğru, İslâmiyet'in Avrupa'ya Son Sözü* (İstanbul: Tanin, 1331). Nurettin Albayrak ("Hüseyin Kâzım Kadri," in *Türkiye Diyanet Vakfı İslâm Ansiklopedi*, 18:554–55) does not delve into these aspects, in contrast to Emmanuilidis who had experienced its contemporary impact (*Osmanlı İmparatorluğu'nun son yılları*, 76–78).

121. Hayri diary, 281–82, 1 April 1913.

122. Ibid., 286, 6 April, 290–91; 14–15 April 1913; 295, 27 April.

123. Zekeriya Türkmen, *Vilayât-ı Şarkiye Islahat Müffettişliği* (Ankara: Türk Tarih Kurumu, 2006), 33; Hayri diary, 299–300, 13 May 1913.

124. Mandelstam, *Le sort de l'Empire ottoman*, 224.

125. Austrian ambassador Pallavicini, Istanbul, to foreign minister Berchtold, 28 June 1913, *The Armenian Genocide* [in Austrian State Archives] (Munich: Institut für armenische Fragen, 1988), 104–5.

126. Cavid diary, 2:170, 22 October 1913; Pomiankowski, *Zusammenbruch des ottomanischen Reiches*, 163.

127. Wangenheim an Bethmann Hollweg, 19 November 1913, PA-AA/R 14082: 7105, quoted in Thomas Schmutz, *Die deutsche Rolle bei den armenischen Reformverhandlungen 1913–1914*, MA thesis, University of Zurich, 2014, 81.

128. Thomas Schmutz, "The German Role in the Reform Discussion of 1913–14," in Kieser, Öktem, and Reinkowski, eds. *World War I and the End of the Ottomans*, 195–96.

129. Graves, *Storm Centers of the Near East*, 287.

130. Cavid diary, 2:250–51, 13 November 1913; cf. 2:280–82, 20 November 1913; 2:366–67, 4 December 1913.

131. Birgen, *İttihat ve Terakki'de one sene*, 172.

132. Cavid diary, 2:340, 30 November 1913.

133. Ibid., 2:420, 26 December 1913.

134. Ibid., 2:426, 28 December 1913.

135. Krikor Zohrap, *Collected Works*, 4:356–57, and 4:363.

136. Cavid diary, 1:19–20, 8 March 1909.

137. Ibid., 3:136.

138. Schmutz, *Die deutsche Rolle bei den armenischen Reformverhandlungen*, 93.

139. Cavid diary, 1:770, 12 July 1913; 2:341, 30 November 1913. The argument that Enver was appointed against Talaat's resistance goes against the evidence, though it still is claimed in Polat Safi, *The Ottoman Special Organization—Teşkilat-ı Mahsusa: An Inquiry into Its Operational and Administrative Characteristics*, doctoral thesis (Ankara: Bilkent University, 2012), 244–45. Talaat was strong enough from late 1913 not to fear a risk of "military autocracy" by Enver and could also play Cemal against it.

140. Graves, *Storm Centers of the Near East*, 289; Ahmed İzzet, *Feryadım*, 1:89–90, 1:173–76; Ayışığı, *Mareşal Ahmed İzzet Paşa*, 111–12.

141. Rambert diary, vol. 47, 12 December 1913 and 8 January 1914. The notion of a triumvirate of Talaat, Enver, and Cemal has recently been reassessed as a continuous conflict of three CUP factions (M. Talha Çiçek, "Myth of the Unionist Triumvirate: The formation of the CUP Factions and Their Impact in Syria during the Great War," in *Syria in World War I: Politics, Economy, and Society* (New York: Routledge, 2016), 9–36. Factions existed, but were not equal. From 1913, Talaat was the political mastermind, and his loyal "young men" (governors and functionaries), with or

without years of service in Syria, later formed a backbone of Atatürk's administration and government.

142. Kieser, Polatel, and Schmutz, "Reform or Cataclysm?," 297.

143. Graves, *Storm Centers of the Near East*, 291.

144. Ionescu, *Souvenirs*, 147–49; Rambert diary, vol. 46, 14 November 1913.

145. Aksakal, *Ottoman Road to War*, 48.

146. Halil [Menteşe], *Anıları*, 165–66; similar figure (119, 938) given by the Rûm Patriarchate. The figure for all Rûm expelled in the first half of 1914 is ca. 250,000 (Emmanuilidis, *Osmanlı İmparatorluğu'nun son yılları*, 51 and 152).

147. Cavid diary, 2:103, 2:23, September 1913; 2:196, 1 November 1913; 2:410, 18 December 1913; 2:463, 21 January 1914; Rambert diary, vol. 47, 27 December 1913; Wangenheim to Auswärtiges Amt, 1 September 1913, in *Die grosse Politik der europäischen Kabinette*, 36:73; Secretary Jagow to German ambassador in Rome, 8 September 1913, ibid., 36:76; Wangenheim to Auswärtiges Amt, 13 September 1913, ibid., 36:87–90; chargé d'affaires in Athens to Reichskanzler, 14 November 1913, ibid., 125–26.

148. Halil [Menteşe], *Anıları*, 165; Rambert diary, vol. 47, 23 January 1914 and 3 February 1914; cf. entry of 16 January in the same volume and letter of Paul Weitz to Arthur Gwinner, 12 January 1914, archive of the Deutsche Bank, Frankfurt, OR 1322.

149. "One lives with a little, nearly nothing, but the experience shows that one lives nevertheless. No functionary has left his post. One expects better days, and the payment of even the most miserable salaries is welcomed like a feast." Rambert diary, vol. 47, 5 April and 14 April 1914.

150. Rambert diary, vol. 48, 9 May 1914.

151. Sergej D. Sazonov, *Fateful Years, 1909–1916: The Reminiscenses of Serge Sazonov* (London: Jonathan Cape, 1927), 137.

152. Birgen, *İttihat ve Terakki'de one sene*, 179.

153. Rambert diary, vol. 48, 14 May 1914; cf. Hayri diary, 4 May 1916, 384.

154. Cf. Hans-Lukas Kieser, "World War and World Revolution: Alexander Helphand-Parvus in Germany and Turkey," *Kritika: Explorations in Russian and Eurasian History* 12, 2 (Spring 2011): 387–410. An author (who openly displays radical Turkism and anti-Semitism) asserts that Cavid had called Parvus to write articles for the CUP press in Istanbul, and Moiz Tekinalp had introduced him into commerce (Attilâ Demirâl, *Türkiye'deki ve dünyadaki komünizm* [Istanbul: Son Kale, 1972], 1:57–78).

155. Rambert diary, vol. 48, 25 May and 6 June 1914.

156. Ibid., vol. 48, 8 and 19 June 1914.

157. Bayar, *Ben de yazdım*, 5:108–11. Mahmut Celâl Bayar (1893–1986) was the president of the Republic of Turkey in 1950–60.

158. For up-to-date research on the Rûm removal, see Emre Erol, "'Macedonian Question' in Western Anatolia: The Ousting of the Ottoman Greeks before World War I," in Kieser, Öktem, and Reinkowski, eds. *World War I and the End of the Ottomans*, 103–30; and Çetinkaya, *The Young Turks and the Boycott Movement*, 190–203. For a rich contemporary firsthand account, see Félix Sartiaux, "Le sac de Phocée et l'expulsion des Grecs ottomans d'Asie Mineure en juillet 1914," *Revue des deux mondes* 84 (Nov.–Dec. 1914), 654–86. Cf. Camilla Dawletschin-Linder, *Diener seines Staates: Celal Bayar (1883–1986) und die Entwicklung der modernen Türkei* (Wiesbaden: Harrassowitz, 2003), 37; this biography, however, lacks critical insight into Celal Bayar's most formative years. On Mehmed Reşid, see Hans-Lukas Kieser, "From 'Patriotism' to Mass Murder: Dr. Mehmed Reşid (1873–1919)," in Ronald G. Suny, Fatma M. Göcek, and Norman Naimark, eds., *A Question of Genocide: Armenians and Turks at the End of the Ottoman Empire* (New York: Oxford University Press, 2011), 126–49.

159. Hans-Lukas Kieser, "From 'Patriotism' to Mass Murder," in Suny, Göcek, and Naimark, eds. *A Question of Genocide*, 133.

160. Erol, "'Macedonian Question' in Western Anatolia," 119.

161. In both diaries, these months are not covered. Bayar, *Ben de yazdım*, 5:105.

162. Halil [Menteşe], *Anıları*, 166. Talaat's telegram from contemporary Greek sources, quoted in Fuat Dündar, *Modern Türkiye'nin Şifresi: İttihat ve Terakkki'nin etnisite ve mühendisliği (1913–1918)* (Istanbul: İletişim, 2008), 211. As Dündar notes, the Ottoman authorities denied the originality of the telegram, chillingly arguing that they would give such an order orally, not in written form.

163. Sartiaux, "Le sac de Phocée," 656; Erol, "'Macedonian Question' in Western Anatolia," 110. For a meeting of Talaat with Kuşçubaşı Eşref, a chief operative in the cleansing, and Talaat's "dual mechanism," see Taner Akçam's detailed account of the Rûm removal in Akçam, *Young Turks' Crime*, 85.

164. Andrew D. Kalmykow, *Memoirs of a Russian Diplomat: Outposts of the Empire, 1893–1917* (New Haven: Yale University Press, 1971), 258.

165. Rambert diary, vol. 48, 12, 16, 18, and 19 June 1914; Emmanuilidis, *Osmanlı İmparatorluğu'nun son yılları*, 266. Cf. Efiloğlu, *İttihat ve Terakki azınlıklar politikası*, 281.

166. Rambert diary, vol. 48, 12 June 1914; Babacan, *Talât*, 93.

167. Armen Garo (alias Karekin Pastermadjian), "My Last Encounter with Talaat Pasha," *Hayrenik* (monthly review, in Armenian) 1, no. 2 (1922): 39–45. Back on 29 June, see Lichtheim to Aktionskomitee der Zionistischen Organisation (so-called Engeres Aktions-Comité, EAC, that is, the Zionist executive in Berlin), 29 June 1914, CZA Z3-11.

168. Galip Kemali (Söylemezoğlu), Ottoman Embassy in Athens to Grand Vizier, 11 July 1914, BOA HR.SYS.1707-106.

169. Rambert diary, vol. 48, 25 August 1914.

170. *Meclis-i Mebusan Zabıt Ceridesi* (MMCZ), İçtima-ı Fevkalâde, period 2 (Ankara, 1991), 2:606–14, meeting of 6 July 1914 (23 Haziran 1330).

171. "Les déclarations de Talaat bey," *Le Jeune-Turc: Journal ottoman quotidien*, 8 July 1914, 1.

172. BOA DH. ŞFR 43/71. Cf. Bilgi, *Dr. Mehmed Reşid*, 22.

Chapter 5: Total-War Gamble, Domestic Demolition, Biased Nation Building

1. Rambert diary, vol. 48, 29 June, 5 July, and 1 August 1914.

2. Cf. Mehmet Beşikçi, "Domestic Aspects of Ottoman Jihad: The Role of Religious Motifs and Religious Agents in the Mobilization of the Ottoman Army," in Zürcher, *Jihad and Islam*, 95–113.

3. *Anıları: Kapancızâde Hamit Bey*, 497. Referring to early 1914, Graves describes Hamid in these words: "I now got to know and appreciate the chief Civil Inspector at the Ministry of the Interior, Hamid Bey, who proved a great standby during the first few months of my advisership [to the Ottoman government], and whose original character had earned him the name of 'Deli Hamid'—'mad' Hamid in the rather flattering sense of the word, due more to his fearless and independent spirit and scrupulous honesty than to some slight eccentricities of manner. A Liberal under the old regime, he had risen rapidly since the deposition of Abdul Hamid, but his position at the Ministry was already threatened owing to his lack of subservience to the Young Turk leaders" (Graves, *Storm Centers of the Middle East*, 290–91).

4. Explicit Austrian suggestion of an alliance with Turkey made to Germany, Jagow to Wangenheim, 14 July 1914, PA-AA/R 1913, no. 533; Wangenheim to Auswärtiges Amt, 16 July 1914, PA-AA/R 1913, no. 346. Cf. Aksakal, *The Ottoman Road to War*, 93–102.

5. Cavid diary, 3:128, 17 August 1915.

6. Wangenheim to Auswärtiges Amt, 19 July 1914, PA-AA/R 19866, no. 352; 21 July 1914, PA-AA/R 19866, no. 354; Pallavicini to Ministerium des Äusseren, 20 July 1914, *Armenian Genocide in Austrian Archives*, 165–66; Cemal, *Erinnerungen*, 114. See all relevant German documents of late July and early August 1914 on www .armenocide.de.

7. Cavid diary, 2:613–17, 2 and 4 August 1914; Talat Paşa, *Hatıralarım ve müdafaam*, 33; Efiloğlu, *İttihat ve Terakki azınlıklar politikası*, 307.

8. Cavid diary, 2:613–17, 4 August 1914; Mühlmann, *Deutschland und die Türkei*, 44–45; Wangenheim to Auswärtiges Amt, 6 August 1914, PA-AA/R 1913, no. 438; Aksakal, *Ottoman Road to War*, 127. Cf. Ulrich Trumpener, *Germany and the Ottoman Empire, 1914–1918* (Princeton, NJ: Princeton University Press, 1968), 28.

9. Quoted in Erol Köroğlu, "Propaganda or Culture War: Jihad, Islam, and Nationalism in Turkish Literature during World War I," in Zürcher, *Jihad and Islam*, 137–47; Cavid diary, 2:621, 16 August 1914; Sâbis, *Harb hatıralarım*, 1:69–70, 1:136–41; Erol Köroğlu, *Ottoman Propaganda and Turkish Identity: Literature in Turkey during World War I* (London: I. B. Tauris, 2007), 63–75; Emmanuilidis, *Osmanlı İmparatorluğu'nun son yılları*, 93.

10. Erickson, *Study in Counterinsurgency*, 128–29; Yüksel Yanıkdağ, *Healing the Nation: Prisoners of War, Medicine and Nationalism in Turkey, 1914–1939* (Edinburgh: Edinburgh University Press, 2013), 16–20; Emmanuilidis, *Osmanlı İmparatorluğu'nun son yılları*, 92–101.

11. Wangenheim to Auswärtiges Amt, 2 August 1914, PA-AA/R 1913, no. 407; Aksakal, *Ottoman Road to War*, 103–18; Yiğit Akın, "Building Up the Ottoman Home Front," in Kieser, Öktem, and Reinkowski, eds. in *World War I and the End of the Ottomans*, 54–73; Hans-Lukas Kieser, "The Ottoman Road to Total War," in *World War I and the End of the Ottomans*, 29–53.

12. Quoted in Dockter, *Churchill and the Islamic World*, 67.

13. Cf. Efiloğlu, *İttihat ve Terakki azınlıklar politikası*, 375. In İzmir, from early August 1914, Governor Rahmi prepared the destruction (by arson) of the city in case of an attack. Although seen as liberal by many contemporary foreigners, and a relatively independent mind during the war, Rahmi shared Talaat's radicalism and warmongering attitude. "His Excellency [Rahmi] said that he considered the entire destruction of a city to prevent it falling into enemy hands a most natural measure; and that to his way of thinking if Turkey were victorious, she could recoup herself for the destruction of Smyrna from the enemy's war of indemnity, while if Turkey were crushed, then the razing of Smyrna to the ground would mean so much blood lost for the conquerors. Rahmi Bey is a standing danger to the Christian population as long as he remains here as Governor General. He is pleasant to talk to, active-minded, energetic, quite fearless and of no little intelligence; but on certain points, and notably in his anti-Greek and Pan-Islamic bias, I say with a full responsibility for the words that he is little other than a dangerous maniac possessed by an *idée fixe*. This opinion is shared in many Turkish circles," the British consul-general C. E. Heathcote-Smith reported to Ambassador Louis Mallet on 20 August 1914, FO 371/2143 (General Correspondence, 1914, 60266), 283.

14. Cavid diary, 2:619, 14 August; 2:625, 19 August; Birgen, *İttihat ve Terakki'de on sene*, 184; Kévorkian, *Armenian Genocide*, 175–76.

15. Rambert diary, vol. 48, 25 August 1914. There was some early British intelligence from Athens on the German-Ottoman alliance from the Greek queen consort Sophie, the sister of German emperor Wilhelm II; cf. Erskine to Grey, 5 August 1914, quoted in Dalby, *Venizelos*, 57.

16. Cavid diary, 2:620, 15 August; 2:645, 6 September; Ionescu, *Souvenirs*, 150–53; Wedel to the Auswärtige Amt, 24 July 1914, PA-AA/R 1913, no. 130; Russian ambassador in Paris to Sazonov, 27 August 1914, *Dokumente aus den Archiven der Zarischen und der Provisorischen Regierung*, 2:6.1, 2:124.

17. Rambert diary, vol. 48, 7 September 1914.

18. Wangenheim to Auswärtiges Amt, 9 September 1914, PA-AA/R 1914, no. 764; Cavid diary, 2:647–49, 9 September 1914; "L'abrogation des Capitulations," *Le Jeune-Turc*, 11 September 1914, 1.

19. Cf. Auswärtiges Amt to Wangenheim, 10 September 1914, PA-AA/R 1914, no. 650.

20. Cavid diary, 2:642–43, 2:645, 6 September 1914; Wangenheim to Auswärtiges Amt, 8 September 1914, PA-AA/R 1914.

21. Letter to William Peet, archives of the American Board of Commissioners for Foreign Missions (ABCFM), Bible House Istanbul, cited in Hans-Lukas Kieser, *Der verpasste Friede* (Zürich: Chronos, 2000), 336.

22. Telegram of 16–17 September 1914, BOA DH.EUM. 2. Şb. 1-52 (also, originally, DH. ŞFR. 441-23); Tahsin to Talaat, 23 September 1914, DH. ŞFR. 441-119; cf. Tahsin to Talaat, DH.EUM. 2. Şb. 1-31, 25 August 1914.

23. Talaat to province of Van, 1 April 1914, DH. ŞFR. 39-144. Cf. Kieser, *Iskalanmış Barış*, 516; Mahir Aydın, "Savaşın bitirdiği doğu açılımı: Tahsin (Üzer) Bey'in Van valiliği (1913/1914)," in Hedda Reindl-Kiel and Seyfi Kenan, eds., *Deutsch-türkische Begegnungen / Alman Türk tesadüfleri* (Berlin: EB-Verlag, 2013), 539–70.

24. "Siyâsiyyât: Şark Meselesi," *Tanin*, 7 September 1914, 1.

25. For files regarding the Special Organization and Talaat in the ATASE, see Ahmet Tetik, *Teşkilat-ı Mahsusa (Umûr-i Şarkıyye Dairesi) tarihi* (Istanbul: Türkiye İş Bankası, 2014).

26. Jagow, Auswärtiges Amt, to Wangenheim, 3 August 1914, PA-AA/R 1913, no. 305; Arif Cemil, *I. Dünya Savaşı'nda Teşkilât-ı Mahsusa* (Istanbul: Arba, 1997 [1934]), 9–11; Cavid diary, 2:618–19, 10 and 14 August 1914.

27. Wangenheim to Auswärtiges Amt, 6 August 1914, PA-AA/R 19881, no. 438.

28. Idem, 31 July 1914, PA-AA/R 1913, no. 286.

29. Quoted in Erickson, *Study in Counterinsurgency*, 119.

30. Quoted in Der Yeghiayan, *Memoirs*, 39.

31. Meeting with Russian ambassador Giers, Cavid diary, 2:669, 26 October 1914.

32. Tahsin to Talaat, 11 September 1914, BOA DH. ŞFR. 440-50; 17 September 1914, ŞFR. 441-22; Cemil, *Teşkilât-ı Mahsusa*, 48–49, 73, 80. On the SO Caucasus mission in general, see Mehmet Bilgin, *Teşkilât-ı Mahsusa'nın Kafkasya misyonu ve operasyonları* (Istanbul: Ötüken, 2017); on Talaat's preeminent role for the SO and this mission, as revealed in the BOA files, see 115–16.

33. Cemil, *Teşkilât-ı Mahsusa*, 58–60.

34. Tahsin to Talaat, 23 September 1914, BOA DH. ŞFR. 441-119.

35. This was probably in response to British reactions on the Ottoman closure of the Dardanelles on 27 September 1914, and also to the British confiscation of the Ottoman warships. Tahsin to Talaat, 29 September 1914, BOA DH. ŞFR. 442-77.

36. *Kafkasya İhtilâl Cemiyeti*; Moreau, *Turquie dans la Grande Guerre*, 129.

37. BOA DH. ŞFR. 44-200, to the provinces of Edirne, Erzurum, Adana, Bitlis, Van, Hüdâvendigâr, Haleb, Sivas, Mamuretülaziz, Diyarbekir, and the *sanjaks* of İzmit, Canik.

38. Pomiankowski, *Zusammenbruch des ottomanischen Reiches*, 162.

39. Erickson, *Study in Counterinsurgency*, 146.

40. BOA HR. SYS. D.2402 G.79, quoted in Tetik, *Teşkilat-i Mahsusa*, 168.

41. Sazonov's letter to Prime Minister Ivan Goremykin, in *Dokumente aus den Archiven der Zarischen und der Provisorischen Regierung*, 2:6.1, 2:144–45; Reynolds, *Shattering Empires*, 113 and 117.

42. Der Yeghiayan, *Memoirs*, 33.

43. Gurgen Mahari, *Burning Orchards* (Cambridge, UK: Black Apollo Press, 2007; Armenian original Yerevan, 1966), 395, 410.

44. Tahsin to Talaat, 3 October 1914, DH. ŞFR. 443-11.

45. Talaat to province of Van, BOA ŞFR. 47-78, facsimile and transcription in Fuat Dündar, *Modern Türkiye'nin şifresi: İttihat ve Terakki'nin etnisite mühendisliği (1913–1918)* (Istanbul: İletişim, 2008), 492–93.

46. Cf. Kieser, *Iskalanmış barış*, 517–18; Hilmar Kaiser, "A Deportation that Did Not Occur," *Armenian Weekly*, 17–18 April 2008.

47. Clarence D. Ussher, *An American Physician in Turkey* (Boston: Houghton Mifflin, 1917), 226.

48. For contemporary reports of Armenian prelates of Erzurum and neighboring regions, see Der Yeghiayan, *Memoirs*, 39–48. Cf. Hilmar Kaiser, "'A scene from the inferno': The Armenians of Erzerum and the Genocide, 1915–1916," in Kieser and Schaller, *Völkermord*, 130; David Gaunt, "The Ottoman Treatment of the Assyrians," in Ronald G. Suny, Fatma M. Göçek, and Norman M. Naimark, eds., *A Question of Genocide: Armenians and Turks at the End of the Ottoman Empire* (New York: Oxford University Press, 2011), 249; Kévorkian, *Armenian Genocide*, 225.

49. Der Yeghiayan, *Memoirs*, 50–51.

50. Morgenthau diary, 14 November 1914, 129–30; Arshavir Shiragian, *The Legacy: Memoirs of an Armenian Patriot* (Boston: Hairenik, 1976), 2–3.

51. Circular, 11 November, quoted in Tekin Alp (Moiz Kohen Tekinalp), *Türkismus und Pantürkismus* (Weimar: G. Kiepenheuer, 1915), 53; *Tanin*, extensively quoted in Emmanuilidis, *Osmanlı İmparatorluğu'nun son yılları*, 113–16.

52. Pamphlet cited in Kévorkian, *Armenian Genocide*, 220–25.

53. Sabis, *Harb hatıralarım*, 2:98–99 and 2:120. Sabis quotes a lot of archival material. Entry of 21–22 November 1914 in Hafız Hakkı's diary, *Hafız Hakkı'nın Sarıkamış günlüğü*, ed. Murat Bardakçı (Istanbul: Türkiye İş Bankası, 2014), 75–77.

54. Rahmi Apak, *Yetmişlik bir subayın hatıraları* (Ankara: TTK, 1988), 95.

55. Cemil, *Teşkilât-ı Mahsusa*, 139.

56. A few meritorious recent in-depth studies focus on security issues, largely dismissing ideology, thus missing the specific conjuncture of autumn 1914. They rightly take seriously a whole complex of security-related logics and mechanisms of realpolitik. Simultaneously, they take "the state" and its security needs for granted, although the latter was being fundamentally transformed. A holistic assessment includes at least basic questions, such as: Security for whom (which group of citizens), within which framework? In favor of what kind of new order? Based on which principles? Fueled by which ideology? Cf., for example, Erickson, *Study in Counterinsurgency* (2013); Arslan Ozan, *Les faits et les buts de guerre ottomans sur le front caucasien pendant la Première Guerre mondiale*, doctoral thesis (Montpellier: Université Paul Valéry, 2011).

57. Kévorkian, *Armenian Genocide*, 220–26; Johannes Lepsius, *Der Todesgang des Armenischen Volkes: Bericht über das Schicksal des armenischen Volkes in der Türkei während des Weltkrieges* (Potsdam: Missionshandlung, 1919), 77; Candan Badem, "The 'War before War' at the Caucasus Front: A Matrix for Genocide," in Kieser, Anderson, Bayraktar, and Schmutz, *End of the Ottomans: The Genocide of 1915*.

58. Cf. Erickson, *Study in Counterinsurgency*, 153–54.

59. Talaat to Cevdet, 30 December 1914, BOA ŞFR. 48-220 (1).

60. Rafael de Nogales, *Vier Jahre unter dem Halbmond: Erinnerungen aus dem Weltkriege* (Berlin: Reimar Hobbing, 1925), 44–55; Kieser, *Iskalanmış barış*, 522.

61. Rambert diary, vol. 49, 12 October 1914.

62. Talat, *Hatıralarım ve müdafaam*, 37.

63. Wangenheim to Auswärtiges Amt, 10 October 1914, PA-AA/R 22403, no. 702; 11 October 1914, PA-AA/R 1914, no. 1022; Cavid diary, 2:668, 12 October 1914.

64. Cavid diary, 2:671–78, 29–31 October 1914; Rambert diary, vol. 49, 15 November. Cf. Aksakal, *Ottoman Road to War*, 153–82.

65. Erickson, *Study in Counterinsurgency*, 137; Winston Churchill, *The World Crisis, 1911–1918*, quoted in Dockter, *Churchill and the Islamic World*, 70.

66. Reproduced in Mühlmann, *Deutschland und die Türkei*, 101–2.

67. Wangenheim to Auswärtiges Amt, 24 October 1914, PA-AA/R 1914, no. 1094; Sâbis, *Harb hatıralarım*, 2:44–50.

68. Morgenthau diary, 115, entry of 29 October 1914; Emmanuilidis, *Osmanlı İmparatorluğu'nun son yılları*, 105.

69. Cavid diary, 2:675, 30 October 1914.

70. Diary of Krikor Zohrap, in *Collected Works*, 4:401–2; Cavid diary, 2:684, 3 November 1914.

71. Cavid diary, 2:682–84, 3 November 1914; 2:687, 5 November. Cf. Cavid diary, 3:21, 30 November 1914; 3:22, 1 December; 3:141–42, 22 September 1915.

72. Ibid., 2:673, 29 October 1914; 2:689, 9 November 1914; 2:692, 13 November 1914.

73. Ibid., 3:15, 23 November 1914; cf. 3:15–23, until 24 December 1914.

74. Morgenthau diary, 11 November 1915, 127.

75. Telegram and response referred to in M. Şükrü Hanioğlu, "Ottoman Jihad or Jihads," in Zürcher, *Jihad and Islam*, 126–28.

76. Cavid diary, 3:12, 21 November 1914. Two recent instructive books on Cemal, largely based on Ottoman documents, are M. Talha Çiçek, *War and State Formation in Syria: Cemal Pasha's Governorate during World War I, 1914–1917* (London: Routledge, 2014); Nevzat Artuç, *Cemal Paşa: Askeri ve siyasi hayatı* (Ankara: TTK, 2008). For the acquaintance of Ziya Gökalp, see Yahya K. Beyatlı, quoted in Köroğlu, *Ottoman Propaganda*, 70.

77. Morgenthau diary, 16 December 1914, 151; 26 January 1915, 172.

78. Morgenthau to US foreign minister Lansing, 18 November 1915, in *United States Official Records on the Armenian Genocide, 1915–1917*, 370.

79. Bernstorff to Gwinner, 1 January 1918, in Bernstorff, *Erinnerungen und Briefe*, 138. Enver left Erzurum on 9 January 1915 (Sabis, *Harb hatıralarım*, 2:153).

80. Morgenthau diary, 23–24 February 1915, 184–85; Cavid diary, 3:28, 18 December 1914; Istanbul police chief Bedri to Morgenthau, 8 January 1916, Morgenthau diary, 432.

81. İrade-i Seniyye, 29 December 1914 (copy of 30 December 1914, DH.İD. 186-72).

82. *Hafız Hakkı'nın Sarıkamış günlüğü*, 91; Sabis, *Harb hatıralarım*, 2:132–33, including Hasan İzzet's telegram of resignation. On 10 January 1915, Hafız Hakkı replaced Hasan İzzet Pasha. For aspects of military history, see William E. D. Allen and Paul Muratoff, *Caucasian Battlefields: A History of the Wars on the Turco-Caucasian Border, 1828–1921* (New York: Cambridge University Press, 2011), 240–92; for a description of the general misery by an Ottoman Kurdish military veterinarian stationed in Erzincan, see Nuri Dersimi, *Hatıratım* (Stockholm: Roja Nû, 1986), 73–76.

83. Sabis, *Harb hatıralarım*, 2:120; Liman von Sanders, *Five Years in Turkey* (Annapolis: United States Naval Institute, 1927), 39.

84. Morgenthau diary, 9 January 1915, 163; 19 January 1915, 168; 8 March 1915, 191; Mühlmann, *Deutschland und die Türkei*, 46–47, 98–99.

85. Morgenthau diary, 18 January 1915, 167; 23 January 1915, 170; 22 February 1915, 183; Cavid diary, 3:36, 14 February 1915.

86. Talaat to Abdülhâlik, vali of Bitlis, 16 February 1915, facsimile and transcription in *Hafız Hakkı'nın Sarıkamış günlüğü*, 118. For a similar telegram to Şakir, see Cemil, *Teşkilât-ı Mahsusa*, 140–41.

87. Morgenthau diary, 23 February 1915, 184; Kévorkian, *Armenian Genocide*, 227.

88. Morgenthau diary, 1 March 1915, 188; Cavid diary, 3:14, 3:36–41, 21 February 1915; Artuç, *Cemal Paşa*, 224–25; Emmanuilidis, *Osmanlı İmparatorluğu'nun son yılları*, 129.

89. Cemil, *Teşkilât-ı Mahsusa*, 205–6.

90. For example, see "Osmanlı Ermenilerinin vatan-perverliği," *Tanin*, 18 January 1915, 1; Talaat to Cevdet, 14 March 1915, BOA DH. ŞFR 51-14 (1); Nuri Dersimi, *Kürdistan tarihinde Dersim* (Aleppo: Privately printed, 1952), 94–98; Dersimi, *Hatıratım*, 77–79; Morgenthau diary, 175, quoting a statement of Bahaeddin, secretary of military governor Cemal, 2 February 1915.

91. Talaat to several provinces and *sanjaks*, 28 February 1915, BOA DH. ŞFR 50-127.

92. Published as "Rapport de Vramian, député de Vaspourakan (Vilayet de Van), à la Chambre ottomane, présenté à Talaat Bey, Ministre de l'intérieur," in *La défense héroïque de Van* (Geneva: Ed. Drochak, 1916), 13–33. Cf. Der Yeghiayan, *Memoirs*, 60; Kévorkian, *Armenian Genocide*, 228–30.

93. On the harsh response, see the explanation of Halil to Morgenthau on 12 November 1915, Morgenthau diary, 381. See a sweepingly anti-Armenian report that uses exterminatory language, from Hasankale to the Military Command, dated 22 February (perhaps begun at that date as an answer to serious accusations in a memorandum of the patriarch to the government of early February, but dated as a whole from late April, because it refers to telegrams on 20 and 21 April), ATASE, in *Arşiv belgeleriyle Ermeni faaliyetleri 1914–1918*, 420–21; cf. Der Yeghiayan, *Memoirs*, 55). Among early foreigners who got wind of the extermination talk were the Austrian military attaché Pomiankowski, the German missionary Johannes Ehmann in Mamuretülaziz, and the Swiss hospital director Jakob Künzler in Urfa.

94. Ali Münif to Cemal, 14 April 1915, BOA DH. ŞFR. 52-51, in *Armenians in Ottoman Documents (1915–1920)*, 25; Wali Ismail Hakkı to Talaat, 26 February 1915, ATASE, in *Arşiv belgeleriyle Ermeni faaliyetleri 1914–1918*, 341; Aram Arkun, "Zeytun and the commencement of the Armenian Genocide," in Ronald G. Suny, Fatma M. Göçek, and Norman M. Naimark, eds., *A Question of Genocide: Armenians and Turks at the End of the Ottoman Empire* (New York: Oxford University Press, 2011), 231–36. Cf. Kévorkian, *Armenian Genocide*, 591–92.

95. Quoted in Dockter, *Churchill and the Islamic World*, 76–77.

96. Talaat to Cevdet, 21 March 1915, BOA DH. ŞFR 51-58 (1); Talaat to Tahsin, 21 March 1915, BOA DH. ŞFR. 51-77.

97. Talaat to Cevdet, 13 April 1914, BOA DH. ŞFR 51-169; Kévorkian, *Armenian Genocide*, 232–33, 823. "S[on] E[xcellence] Talaat bey, Consple [Constantinople] /

au nom intérêts supérieurs, deux races supplie[nt] votre excellence terminer question Van amiable / combattants arméniens poussées seulement par désespoir / si vous commandez fonctionnaire Bitlis portant vos ordres / et Papazian effendi en mai possible arriver Van / dans trois jours et faire arrêter guerre fratricide / attendant arrangement final / Vramian" (BOA DH.EUM. 2. Şb. 56-40, this file includes a second similar message from Vramian from Bitlis only in Ottoman). According to a telegram of Talaat to Cevdet, 13 June 1915, Vramian had not yet been killed; this expectation stood, however, written between the lines (BOA DH. ŞFR. 51-169).

98. Cavid diary, 3:47–51, 18–30 March 1915.

99. Birgen, *İttihat ve Terakki'de on sene*, 221; Cavid diary, 3:79, 3:98. In a retrospect of the first year of war in Istanbul, Morgenthau to Lansing, 18 November 1915, in *United States Official Records, 1915–1917*, 370; Alexander Krethlow, "The Armenian Genocide and the German Military," paper read at the conference *Witness to a Crime of the Century: The German Empire and the Armenian Genocide*, Deutsches Historisches Museum Berlin, 3 March 2015; cf. Krethlow, "Deutsche Militärs und die Armenier: Demographische Konzepte, Sicherheitsmassnahmen und Verstrickungen," in Rolf Hosfeld and Christin Pschichholz, eds., *Das Deutsche Reich und der Völkermord an den Armeniern* (Göttingen: Wallstein, 2017), 149–71.

100. Cemil, *Teşkilât-ı Mahsusa*, 236, 240, 261–63; Birgen, *İttihat ve Terakki'de on sene*, 222.

101. Sabis, *Harb hatıralarım*, 2:192; David Gaunt, *Massacres, Resistance, Protectors: Muslim-Christian Relations in Eastern Anatolia during World War I* (Piscataway, NJ: Gorgias Press, 2006), 63. Cf. Kévorkian, *Armenian Genocide*, 243–49.

102. "Harb ve vahşet," *Tanin*, 2 April 1915. Cf. Foreign Ministry to Ministry of the Interior, 7 March 1915, regarding a message of the Ottoman Embassy in Tehran about anti-Muslim atrocities in Russian Kars and Ardahan, BOA DH.EUM. 2. Şb 5-31, transcribed in *Osmanlı Belgelerinde Ermenilerin sevk ve iskanı (1878–1920)* (Ankara: Osmanlı Arşivi Daire Başkanlığı, 2007), 117–18; *Arşiv belgeleriyle Ermeni faaliyetleri 1914–1918*, 380–87 (quotations 381 and 384, messages of 23 and 25 February 1915, explicitly for the Red Book).

103. Caleb C. Gates, president of the Istanbul Robert College since 1903 (before, he was president of the Euphrates College in Harput-Mamuretülaziz where he had seen the 1895 Hamidian massacres); Morgenthau diary, 18 July 1915, 279. Cf. Kieser, *Der verpasste Friede*, 199–202.

104. Cf. Hans-Lukas Kieser, "Join the Dots between Gallipoli and the Armenian Genocide," in *The Conversation*, 23 April 2015 and "Der Mythos Gallipoli," *Neue Zürcher Zeitung*, 15 April 2015, 7.

105. Cf. Hüseyin C. Yalçın, *Talât Paşa* (Istanbul: Yedigün, 1943), 43; the same, *Siyasal anılar* (Istanbul: Türkiye İş Bankası, 2000), 313–18.

106. Wangenheim to Reichskanzler, 17 June 1915, PA-AA/R 14086, no. 372; 7 July 1915, PA-AA/R 14086, no. 433; Hohenlohe (ambassador in extraordinary mission) to Bethmann Hollweg, 4 September 1915, PA-AA/R 14087, no. 549.

107. German consul in Trabzon, Bergfeld, to the Reichskanzler on July 9, 1915, PA-AA/R 14086. Cf. Akçam, *Young Turks' Crime*, 296–301.

108. Cf. Kévorkian, *Armenian Genocide*, 285–696; Taner Akçam, *Young Turks' Crime*, 158–93; Hilmar Kaiser, "Shukru Bey and the Armenian Deportations in the Fall of 1915," in *Syria in World War I*, 169–236. The most recent, most comprehensive research on the second phase of the genocide in Syria is Khatchig Mouradian's thesis, *Genocide and Humanitarian Assistance in Ottoman Syria, 1915–1917* (Worcester: Clark University, 2016).

109. Talaat to Enver, 24 April 1915, ATASE, *Arşiv belgeleriyle*, 1:423–25.

110. BOA DH. ŞFR. 52-96, 97, 98, transcribed in *Osmanlı belgelerinde*, 125–26; English translation, except special sentence, in Akçam, *Crime*, 186–87.

111. Talaat to several provinces, 26 April 1915, BOA DH. ŞFR. 52-188, quoted in Akçam, *Young Turks' Crime*, 188.

112. Talaat to Cemal, 24 April 1915, BOA DH. ŞFR. 52-93.

113. For example, in such different towns as Eskişehir (Ahmed Refik [Altınay], *İki komite, iki kıtal* [Ankara: Kebikeç, 1994], 28–46); Urfa (Jakob Künzler, *In the Land of Blood and Tears: Experiences in Mesopotamia during the World War, 1914–1918* [Arlington, VA: Armenian Cultural Foundation, 2007; German original 1921], 16 and 21); and Aintab, see Kurt Ümit, *Destruction of Aintab Armenians*, 82.

114. For example, explicitly, see a message from the Third Army in Hasankale (Erzurum) to the Military Command, 14 April 1915, ATASE, *Arşiv belgeleriyle*, 1:79.

115. Mehmet Beşikçi, *The Ottoman Mobilization of Manpower in the First World War: Between Voluntarism and Resistance* (Leiden: Brill, 2012), 247–309.

116. Kaiser, *Extermination of Armenians in Diarbekir*, 217. A similar piece of retrospective justification is a report of the General Headquarters (*Arşiv belgeleriyle*, 1:27–121).

117. Interview with the Istanbul correspondent of *Die Neue Freie Presse*, in "Tal'at Beyin beyânatı," *Tanin*, 19 May 1915, 2.

118. David Gaunt, "Relations between Kurds and Syriacs and Assyrians in Late Ottoman Diyarbekir," in Jongerden and Verheij, *Social Relations in Ottoman Diarbekir*, 263; Gaunt, *Massacres*, 188; Kévorkian, *Armenian Genocide*, 379–80. For a sober, but moving, eyewitness account of the Bitlis killings from the diary of an officer on the Ottoman side, see Rafael de Nogales, *Vier Jahre unter dem Halbmond*, 89–90.

119. Talaat to several governorates, 1 July 1915, BOA DH. ŞFR. 54-261.

120. Kaiser, *Extermination of Armenians in Diarbekir*, 406. Hüseyin Mazhar is not to be confused with Ankara vali Ali Mazhar. After war, Hüseyin Mazhar led

the investigation of CUP crimes. Cf. Gerçek, *Report on Turks Who Reached-Out to Armenians in 1915*, 52–53.

121. Gerçek, *Report on Turks Who Reached-Out to Armenians in 1915*. On the Atıf quote right below, see Akçam, *Young Turks' Crime*, 195. For a more detailed analyses of proactive forces in the provinces in concert with Talaat, see chapter 5, sec. "Mirroring and Managing Anti-Christian Forces in the East" and the chapters on Angora, Aintab, and the eastern provinces by Mehmet Polatel, Ümit Kurt, and Hilmar Kaiser in Kieser, Anderson, Bayraktar, and Schmutz, *End of the Ottomans: The Genocide of 1915*.

122. Cf. Talat, *Hatıralarım ve müdafaam*, 41. All quotations, including telegram DH. ŞFR. 54-94, 22 June 1915, from Gerçek, *Report on Turks Who Reached-Out to Armenians in 1915*, 51–52. Cf. Hilmar Kaiser, "Between Massacre and Resistance: Officers, Bureaucrats, and Muslim Notables in Angora Province," in Kieser, Anderson, Bayraktar, and Schmutz, *End of the Ottomans: The Genocide of 1915*.

123. Kévorkian, *Armenian Genocide*, 540–43. This comprehensive study offers, from chapter to chapter, a detailed regional approach. For deportation from Istanbul, see also Akçam, *Young Turks' Crime*, 399–406.

124. *Anıları: Kapancızâde Hamit Bey*, 476; Uğur Ü. Üngör, "Disastrous Decade: Armenians and Kurds in the Young Turk Era, 1915–25," in Jongerden and Verheij, *Social Relations in Ottoman Diyarbekir*, 273–74.

125. Cf. Ahmed İzzet, *Feryadım*, 1:180, 1:220–29.

126. Reşid to Talaat, 6 December 1914, DH. ŞFR. 452-60; Süleyman Nazif, "Doktor Reşid," *Hadisat* of 8 February 1919, reproduced in Şahingiray, *Hayatı ve Hâtıraları*, 167–71.

127. BOA DH.EUM. 2. Şb 16-26.

128. This is the term that Hilmar Kaiser uses in *Extermination of Armenians in Diarbekir*, 149, 154–55, 165–67; letters of the American physician Floyd Smith, based in Diyarbekir until May 1915, to James Barton, 25 August, 18 and 20 September 1915, ABCFM archives, Houghton Library Boston, ABC 16.9.7.

129. Reşid to Talaat, 25 June 1915, BOA DH. ŞFR. 477-14. Talaat had ordered him to disperse converted people within the province (Talaat to several provinces, 22 June 1915, DH.ŞFR. 54-100).

130. Reşid to Talaat, 27 April 1915, BOA DH. ŞFR. 468-146.

131. Ibid., 24 June 1915, BOA DH. ŞFR. 477-11.

132. Reşid to the Ministry of the Interior, 18 September 1915, BOA DH.EUM. 2. Şb 68/71 (published in *Armenians in Ottoman Documents, 1915–1920*, 105). Cf. Reşid to Talaat, 16 July 1915, DH. ŞFR. 480-40; Talaat to Reşid, 27 July 1915, DH. ŞFR. 54-A-117; 2 August 1915, DH. ŞFR. 54-A-248, and Reşid to Talaat, 4 August 1915, DH. ŞFR. 482-83 (comparison with ants in this letter).

133. Reşid to Talaat, 16 July 1915, BOA DH. ŞFR. 480-40; Kaiser, *Extermination of Armenians in Diarbekir*, 287.

134. Talaat to governorate of Erzurum, 5 April 1915, BOA DH. ŞFR. 51-215; Tahsin to Talaat, 18 March 1915, BOA DH. ŞFR. 465-81.

135. He used, for example, the sweeping expression "a treacherous Armenian" in a short message to the Ministry of the Interior on 23 December 1914, BOA DH. ŞFR. 454-145.

136. Tahsin to Talaat, 24 December 1914, BOA DH. ŞFR. 455-40; 31 December 1914, BOA DH. ŞFR. 456-17; 10 January 1915, BOA DH. ŞFR. 457-26; 26 January 1915, BOA DH. ŞFR. 459-38.

137. Tahsin to Talaat, 3 March 1915, BOA DH. ŞFR. 463-82. Cf. German vice-consul Scheubner-Richter, Erzurum, to Wangenheim, 3 March 1915, PA-AA/BoKon/168, which confirms "sharp measures by the military authorities" against the Armenians. Abdülhalik to Talaat, BOA DH. ŞFR 467-120, quoted in Mehmet Polatel, "The State, Local Actors, and Mass Violence in the Province of Bitlis," in Kieser et al., *End of the Ottomans: The Genocide of 1915*; see also, in the same volume, Hilmar Kaiser, "Tahsin Uzer: The CUP's Man in the East."

138. Tahsin to the Ministry of the Interior, 22 April 1915, BOA DH. ŞFR. 468-66.

139. Talaat to governorate of Ankara, 29 August 1915, BOA DH. ŞFR. 55-290; 14 April 1915, ATASE, *Arşiv belgeleriyle*, 1:79; Scheubner-Richter to Wangenheim, 26 April 1915, PA-AA/BoKon/168. Cf. ibid., Scheubner-Richter to Wangenheim, 15 May 1915.

140. In a telegram of 5 May he informed the Ministry of the Interior of his according deeds, BOA DH. ŞFR. 469-132.

141. Talaat to Cevdet and Abdülhalik, 9 May 1915, BOA DH. ŞFR. 52-282. Cf. Akçam, *Young Turks' Crime*, 189–90.

142. Tahsin to Talaat, 19 May 1915, BOA DH. ŞFR. 471-114; Scheubner-Richter to Wangenheim, 16 May 1915, PA-AA/BoKon/168.

143. Quoted in Kévorkian, *Armenian Genocide*, 231 and 867n236.

144. Cf., already, Tahsin to Talaat, 25 May 1915, BOA DH. ŞFR. 472-71.

145. Tahsin to Talaat, 24 June 1915, BOA DH. ŞFR. 477-20; Talaat to Tahsin, 5 July 1915, BOA DH. ŞFR. 54-293. For Scheubner-Richter's report, see below.

146. Tahsin to Talaat, 25 May 1915, BOA DH. ŞFR. 472-71; Talaat to Erzurum governorate, 29 May 1915, BOA DH. ŞFR. 53-129; Talaat to the Command of the Fourth Army (Cemal Pasha), 23 May 1915, BOA DH. ŞFR. 53-94.

147. Tahsin to the Ministry of the Interior, 29 May 1915, BOA DH. ŞFR. 472-145; Tahsin to Talaat, 12 June 1915, BOA DH. ŞFR. 475-29; further praise of "beautiful and productive places" for muhacir from Rumeli in Tahsin to Talaat, 26 July 1915,

BOA DH. ŞFR. 480-45 (Tahsin's brotherly question regarding criminals among employees and gendarmes is also in this message).

148. For a detailed report on Erzurum, see Scheubner-Richter to Wangenheim, 5 August 1915, PA-AA/R 14088.

149. Tahsin to the Ministry of the Interior, 10 July 1915, BOA DH. ŞFR. 479-89; Talaat to the governorships of Diyarbekir, Mamuretülaziz, and Bitlis, 14 June 1915, BOA DH. ŞFR. 54-9.

150. Cf. Theodor Colley to German Embassy, 21 June 1915, PA-AA/BoKon 96/ Bl. 20-22.

151. Tahsin to the Ministry of the Interior, 28 July 1915, BOA DH. ŞFR. 481-68.

152. Scheubner-Richter to Wangenheim, 28 July 1915, PA-AA/BoKon/170; Stange to German military mission, 23 August 1915, PA-AA/BoKon/170.

153. On this part of Scheuber-Richter's life, see Michael Kellogg, *The Russian Roots of Nazism: White Émigrés and the Making of National Socialism, 1917–1945* (Cambridge: Cambridge University Press, 2005).

154. Tahsin to the Ministry of the Interior, 9 August 1915, BOA DH. ŞFR. 483-40; Defterdâr (financial director) Cemal in the name of the Erzurum governor, to Talaat, 26 August 1915, BOA DH. ŞFR. 485-76.

155. Telegram of Halil Edib, reproduced in Reşid, *Hayatı ve Hâtıraları*, 29.

156. Tahsin to Talaat, 16 February 1916, BOA DH. ŞFR. 509-98; 13 May 1916, BOA DH. ŞFR. 520-45; 20 April 1916, BOA DH. ŞFR. 516-88; 17 July 1916, BOA DH. ŞFR. 525-91. I thank Taner Akçam for help on telegrams sent from Erzurum.

157. Cemal Azmi to Talaat, 27 June 1916, BOA DH. KMS. 40-12, quoted in Efiloğlu, *İttihat ve Terakki azınlıklar politikası*, 412. On the Pontus Rûm in 1916–17, see ibid., 407–46 (from a state perspective, based only on BOA sources). More generally, see Stefan Yerasimos, "Pontus Meselesi," in *Toplum ve Bilim*, 43–44 (1988–89), 35–76; Ayşe Hür, "Pontus'un Gayri Resmi Tarihi," *Taraf*, 14 March 2010, http://arsiv.taraf.com.tr/yazilar/ayse-hur/pontusun-gayri-resmi-tarihi/10452; in sympathy with the "Pontus ideal," with rich sources: Sait Çetinoğlu and Dara Cibran, "Pontus Sorunu," January 2007, www.peyamaazadi.org/foto/PdfDosyalari /Pontos_Sorunu.pdf . For an analysis of memory cultures, see Erik Sjöberg, *The Making of the Greek Genocide: Contested Memories of the Ottoman Greek Catastrophe* (New York: Berghahn, 2016).

158. Cavid diary, 3:128, 19 August 1915.

159. BOA ŞFR. 63-172, transcribed in Fuat Dündar, *İttihat ve Terakki Müslümanları iskân politikası (1913–1918)* (Istanbul: İletişim, 2001), 73; cf. Üngör, *The Making of Modern Turkey*, 110–11. Cf. also Serhat Bozkurt, *Bir toplumsal mühendislik kurumu olarak "Aşâir ve Muhâcirîn Müdîriyyet-i Umûmiyyesi,"* Yüksek Lizans Tezi (Istanbul: Mimar Sinan Üniversitesi, 2013).

160. BOA ŞFR. 63-188, transcribed in Dündar, *İttihat ve Terakki Müslümanları iskân politikası*, 144.

161. Ahmed İzzet, *Feryadım*, 1:278–79, refered to also in Dündar, *İttihat ve Terakki Müslümanları iskân politikası*, 139; Künzler, *Land of Blood and Tears*, 67–68.

162. In consensus with Walter Rössler, German consul in Aleppo during World War I, the author of this biography has come to the conclusion that the testimony of Naim Bey, a functionary of the Aleppo Sub-Directorate of the Ministry of the Interior's Directorate for Resettlement of Tribes and Migrants, is largely pertinent, despite questions regarding the authenticity and accuracy of documents that he sold to the Armenian author and researcher Andonian (published as *Documents officiels concernant les massacres arméniens* [Paris: Turabian, 1920]). These show Talaat's explicit will to exterminate (however manifest, as explained in this chapter, also without these documents). Cf. Lepsius to Rössler, 13 April 1921, and Rössler to Lepsius, 25 April 1921, PA-AA/NL/Rössler, vol. 1. Cf. Kai Seyffarth, *Entscheidung in Aleppo: Walter Rössler (1871–1929); Helfer der vefolgten Armenier* (Bremen: Donat, 2015), 208–13; Taner Akçam, *Naim Efendi'nin Hatıratı ve Talaat Paşa Telgrafları: Krikor Gergeryan Arşivi* (Istanbul: Iletisim, 2016). For a detailed research into the 10 percent rule, see Akçam, *Young Turks' Crime*, 242–63.

163. Number given by Mouradian, *Genocide and Humanitarian Resistance in Ottoman Syria*, 237. The Catholicos of Sis in Cilicia, newly based in Jerusalem, was appointed the head of all remaining Ottoman Armenians (Mouradian, *Genocide and Humanitarian Resistance in Ottoman Syria*, 10–11, 136–40). On Cemal and his correspondence with Sahag II Khabayan, Catholicos of Cilicia, see Ümit Kurt, "A Savior, an Enigma, and a Perpetrator: Cemal Pasha," in Kieser et al., *End of the Ottomans: The Genocide of 1915*.

164. Ibid., 14–21, 128–30.

165. Ibid., 199–200, 275. Cf. Raymond H. Kévorkian, *L'extermination des déportés arméniens ottomans dans les camps de concentration de Syrie-Mésopotamie (1915–1916): La deuxième phase du génocide* (Paris: Bibliothèque Nubar, 1998); Hilmar Kaiser, *At the Crossroads of Der Zor: Death, Survival, and Humanitarian Resistance in Aleppo, 1915–1917* (Princeton, NJ: Gomidas Institute, 2002).

166. Talaat to Enver, 19 May 1916, BOA DH. KMS 39-13. Thanks to Candan Badem, who has drawn my attention to this document.

167. Talaat to Enver, 16 February 1916, *Arşiv belgeleriyle Ermeni faaliyetleri*, 8:104 and 8:253.

168. See 3 April 1916, DH. ŞFR. 62-234. Cf. Talaat to Cemal, 11 April 1917, DH. ŞFR. 74-273.

169. Cemal to Talaat, 20 July 1916, DH. ŞFR. 526-20; Cemal to the Ministry of the Interior, 1 August 1916, DH. ŞFR. 527-19. For Mouradian's reappraisal of Cemal, see *Genocide and Humanitarian Resistance in Ottoman Syria*, 110–20.

170. Cemal to the governorship of Aleppo, 24 November 1916, DH.EUM. 4. Şb. 24-17.

171. Telegram, 22 July 1915, quoted in Mouradian, *Genocide and Humanitarian Resistance in Ottoman Syria*, 55.

172. Mouradian, *Genocide and Humanitarian Resistance in Ottoman Syria*, 69–82 and 93–97.

173. Guideline on resettlement and supply of 10 June, *Arşiv belgeleriyle Ermeni faa-liyetleri*, 1:429–31; Şükrü's guidelines in Şükrü to Talaat, 8 October, BOA DH.EUM. 2. Şb. 68-88, quoted in Mouradian, *Genocide and Humanitarian Resistance in Otto-man Syria*, 122; the Mouradian quotation is on page 47. Order on photographs from the Interior Ministry on 13 February 1916 is quoted in Mouradian, *Genocide and Humanitarian Resistance in Ottoman Syria*, 11; Cemal's ban of photographs is quoted in Consul Rössler to Embassy, 27 September 1915, PA-AA/BoKon/170.

174. "Pfade in grossen Wassern," *Sonnenaufgang* 36 (1934): 38 and 54, quoted in H. Kieser, "Beatrice Rohner's Work in the Death Camps of Armenians in 1916," in Jacques Sémelin, Claire Andrieu, and Sarah Gensburger, eds., *Resisting Genocide: The Multiple Forms of Rescue* (London: Hurst, 2011), 367–82.

175. Talaat's pocketbook is not dated. Still in private hands, it has only recently been published: Murat Bardakçı, ed., *Talat Paşa'nın Evrak-ı Metrûkesi* (Istanbul: Everest, 2008), 90–103; cf. Ara Sarafian, *Talaat Pasha's Report on the Armenian Genocide* (London: Gomidas, 2011), 69–70. Research on confiscation has much improved in the last years but is by far not comprehensive; see Mehmet Polatel and Uğur Üngör, *Confiscation and Destruction: The Young Turk Seizure of Armenian Property* (London: Bloomsbury, 2013); Taner Akçam and Ümit Kurt, *Kanunların ruhu: Emval-i metruke kanunlarında soykırımın izini sürmek* (Istanbul: İletişim, 2012) [*The Spirit of the Laws: The Plunder of Wealth in the Armenian Genocide*, trans. Aram Arkun (New York: Berghahn, 2015)]; Ümit Kurt, *Destruction of Aintab Armenians and Emergence of the New Wealthy Class: Plunder of Armenian Wealth in Aintab*, doc-toral thesis (Worcester: Clark University, 2016).

176. Parvus's articles in the CUP press in 1912–14 had represented the Turkish peasants as the truly exploited class, and as the Turkish protonation to be led by the CUP, while the author Moïz Cohen Tekinalp had depicted Ottoman Christians as early as 1912 as spongers who lacked patriotism, thus approving of imperially biased Turkism. See Monsieur Risal (alias Tekinalp), "Türkler bir rûh-i millî arıyorlar," *Türk Yurdu*, 5 September 1912, 1:350–53. Cf. Morgenthau diary, 8 August 1915, 297–98; Kieser, "World War and World Revolution," 398–400.

177. MMCZ, period 3, 1:134–35, session of 13 December. Cf. Erdal Kaynar, *Ahmed Rıza (1858–1930): Histoire d'un vieux Jeune Turc*, doctoral thesis (Paris: EHESS, 2011), 788–95.

178. Talaat (from the Interior Ministry's Directorate for Resettlement of Tribes and Migrants) to the grand vizier, 26 May 1915, BOA, BEO. 4357-326758.

179. *Armenians in Ottoman Documents (1915–1920)*, 34–35.

180. *Arşiv belgeleriyle Ermeni faaliyetleri*, 1:426–38.

181. For the use of the term "war *ummah*" (*ümmet* in Ottoman) to designate the combined reality of central politics and social dynamics in the latest Ottoman period, foremost during World War I, see Kieser, *Iskalanmış barış*.

182. German Embassy to Ottoman Foreign Ministry, and German Embassy to Reichskanzler, 5 October 1915, PA-AA/BoKon 99/Bl. 9-12.

183. Gwinner to German Foreign Office, 7 October 1915, PA-AA/R 14088, including a French translation of the provisional law. Cf. Akçam and Kurt, *Kanunların ruhu*, 32–47.

184. Kaiser, *Extermination of Armenians*, 287. This finding with regard to Diyarbekir is also true for most other places in Asia Minor.

185. Emmanuilidis, *Osmanlı İmparatorluğu'nun son yılları*, 146.

186. "Ey Türk! Zengin ol!," *İkdam*, 29 December 1916, 1, quoted in Zafer Toprak, *Türkiye'de milli iktisat 1908–1918* (Istanbul: Doğan, 2012; original ed. 1982), 768; cf. Zafer Toprak, *Türkiye'de ekonomi ve toplum*. For a case study on Diyarbekir and Çukurova, see Üngör and Polatel, *Confiscation and Destruction*, 107–64.

187. Cf. Cevâd, Ottoman Embassy in Stockholm, to foreign minister Halil, 10 January 1917, including the translation of an instructive article from the semiofficial Russian newspaper *Novia Veremia*, 3 January 1917, HR. SYS. 2429-60.

188. Faiz al-Huseyin, Bedouin notable of Damascus, *Martyred Armenia*, trans. from the original Arabic (New York: George H. Doran, 1918).

189. DH. ŞFR. 70-180 and 180-1, 5 December 1916.

190. Al-Huseyin, *Martyred Armenia*, 15.

191. For graphic eyewitness accounts, see, for example, Künzler, *Land of Blood and Tears*, 25–32; Balakian, *Armenian Golgotha*, 95, 135–36, 143–46; unpublished report *Cinq ans d'exil, de 1914 à 1919*, by Franciscans of Urfa (Soeurs de Lons-le-Saunier), with a passage on 5 October 1915: "Les femmes, du haut des terrasses, font entendre leurs 'lilis' stridents, cris de joie sauvage en l'honneur des braves qui viennent anéantir les 'Gaours.'"

192. Morgenthau diary, 346; Cavid diary, 3:135–37.

193. Note of Mordtmann in Jagow to Wangenheim, 9 November 1915, PA-AA/BoKon/170.

194. Cavid diary, 3:136–37.

195. Wandel to foreign minister Erik Scavenius, 19 September 1915, RA-UM/Gruppeordnede sager 1909–1945. 139. D. 1, "Tyrkiet-Indre Forhold" Pakke 1, til 31 Dec. 1916, published on www.armenocide.de by Matthias Bjørnlund.

196. Feroz Ahmad, "The Special Relationship: The Committee of Union and Progress and the Ottoman Jewish Political Elite, 1908–1918," in Avigdor Levy, *Jews, Turks, Ottomans: A Shared History, Fifteenth through the Twentieth Century* (Syracuse, NY: Syracuse University Press, 2002), 216–17.

197. Ahmet Refik (Altınay), *İki komite, iki kıtal* (Ankara: Kebikeç, 1994), 35, first published in Istanbul in 1919. Cf. Kévorkian, *Armenian Genocide*, 565.

198. *Anıları: Kapancızâde Hamit*, 478, 494–95.

199. Cemil Filmer, *Hatıralar: Türk Sinemasında 65 yıl* (Istanbul: Emek, 1984), 34–37. I thank Hilmar Kaiser for showing me this source.

200. Entry of 18 May 1916, Cavid diary, 3:183–84. Canbolad's letter in Murat Bardakçı, ed., *İttihadçı'nın sandığı* (Istanbul: Türkiye İş Bankası, 2014), 416.

201. Hayri diary, 189, 30 August 1916.

202. Paul Rohrbach's remark about the broken neck is in a letter on 21 September 1915 to Ernst Jäckh (Jäckh Papers, Yale University Library). The project of Central European– and Near East–based German world power is described, for example, in Rohrbach's propagandistic article in the New York *Evening Mail* in August 1915 (copy in the Archive of the Deutsche Bank, OR 1388).

203. "Ta'lika Ruhsat," *Tanin* no. 2484, 15 October 1915, 1.

204. For a recent analysis of the German press on this topic, see Ihrig, *Justifying Genocide*, 163–89.

205. Jagow to Wangenheim, 9 October 1915, PA-AA/BoKon/170.

206. Morgenthau diary, 17 August 1915, 305.

207. "Türkiya Türklerindir," *Tanin*, 14 December 1915, 4. "Projet de démenti," Jagow to Wangenheim, 9 October 1915, PA-AA/BoKon/170, no. 1918.

208. Talaat to Enver, 16 February 1916, published in *Arşiv belgeleriyle Ermeni faaliyetleri*, 8:104 and 8:253; Erich Matthias, ed., *Der interfraktionelle Ausschuss 1917/18* (Düsseldorf, 1959), 2:410. Cf. Hans-Lukas Kieser, "Matthias Erzberger und die osmanischen Armenier im Ersten Weltkrieg," in Christopher Dowe, ed., *Matthias Erzberger: Ein Demokrat in Zeiten des Hasses* (Karlsruhe: G. Braun, 2013), 103–19.

209. Cf. Elmar Plozza, *Zwischen Berlin und Konstantinopel: Die diplomatischen Aktivitäten Alfred Nossigs für das zionistische Projekt*, unpublished (Lizentiatsarbeit: University of Zurich, 2004). Nossig cofounded the Berlin Jewish Publishing House (Jüdischer Verlag) on the eve of the Fifth Zionist Congress in Basel.

210. Alfred Nossig, *Die neue Türkei und ihre Führer* (Halle: Otto Hendel, 1916), 30–35. Photo of the medallion and report in *Der Orient: Zeitschrift für die wirtschaftliche Erschliessung des Orients*, July 1917, 14–15. Comparison to Bismarck in *Berliner Lokal-Anzeiger*, no. 606 (Nov. 1916), quoted in Dominik J. Schaller, "Die Rezeption des Völkermords an den Armeniern in Deutschland, 1915–1945," in Kieser and Schaller, *Völkermord*, 529.

211. See 17 September 1915, Morgenthau diary, 332. Wangenheim must have gotten the idea to replace the removed Armenians with Eastern European Jews from Nossig, cf. Morgenthau diary, 351, 7 October 1915, and 368, 28 October 1915; Jehuda Reinharz, ed., *Dokumente zur Geschichte des deutschen Zionismus 1882–1933* (Tübingen: Mohr Siebeck, 1981), 178.

212. Isaiah Friedman, *Germany, Turkey, and Zionism, 1897–1918* (New Brunswick: Transaction, 1998 [1977]), 268–69. On Armando Moses, cf. Mustafa Gençer, *Bildungspolitik, Modernisierung und kulturelle Interaktion: Deutsch-türkische Beziehungen (1908–1918)* (Münster: Lit, 2002), 216; on the society, see Lewis Melville, "German Propagandist Societies," *Quarterly Review* (July 1918): 76–77.

213. Enclosed in Jäckh to Rosenberg, 24 August 1916, PA-AA/R 14093; Morgenthau diary, 347, 3 October 1915.

214. From 1940 Nossig belonged to the Warsaw Judenrat and was killed in 1943 by Jewish partisans. Cf. Mitchell Hart, "Moses the Microbiologist: Judaism and Social Hygiene in the Work of Alfred Nossig," *Jewish Social Studies* 2, no. 1 (Autumn 1995): 72–97.

215. Cf. Hannah Arendt, "Privileged Jews," *Jewish Social Studies* 8, no. 1 (Jan. 1946): 3–30. A specific part of painful late Ottoman Armenian-Jewish history started with the large-scale pogrom in Istanbul late August 1896, when several local Jews led killers to the houses of Armenians and participated in looting (other Jews, however, helped Armenians). See *Sephardi Lives: A Documentary History*, ed. Julia P. Cohen and Sarah A. Stein (Stanford, CA: Stanford University Press, 2014), 134–39; Stanford J. Shaw, *The Jews of the Ottoman Empire and the Turkish Republic* (Basingstoke: Macmillan, 1991), 210 and 294 (quoting contemporary reports of the Alliance Israélite Universelle).

216. Lichtheim to Jacobson, 11 August 1915, CZA Z3-64, 00121; Jacobson to Lichtheim, undated carbon copy (first page missing), CZA Z3-64, 00073; Jacobson to Lichtheim, 18 July 1915, Z3-53, 00088-00089; Jacob M. Landau, *Tekinalp: Turkish Patriot* (Istanbul: Nederlands Historisch-Archaeologisch Instituut, 1984), 287–88.

217. Report of Avshalom Feinberg to Henrietta Szold, October 1915, quoted in Yair Auron, *The Banality of Indifference: Zionism and the Armenian Genocide* (New Brunswick: Transaction, 2000), 162. On NILI and the Yishuv, see Friedman, *Germany, Turkey, Zionism*, 367–73. Tamara Zieve, "Ex-Mossad Chief: Jewish Spies Were Instrumental in Balfour Declaration," *Haaretz*, 24 July 2017.

218. Morgenthau to Lansing, 18 November 1915, in *United States Official Records, 1915–1917*, 372; Aaron Aaronsohn, memorandum presented to the War Office in London, 16 November 1916, in Auron, *The Banality of Indifference*, 384; reference to a flourishing slave market also in Al-Huseyin, *Martyred Armenia*, 34; Lewis Einstein,

"The Armenian Massacres," *Contemporary Review* (1 Jan. 1917): 494. Einstein to Lawrence E. Gelfand, 27 March 1965, quoted in Lewis Einstein, *Inside Constantinople: A Diplomat's Diary during the Dardanelles Expedition*, ed. Ara Sarafian (London: Gomidas, 2014), xi.

219. "Enver Paşa," *Tanin*, 13 August 1915, 2.

220. "Tal'at Bey," *Tanin*, 1 September 1915, 2.

221. In spring through summer 1915, Cavid stayed mostly in Berlin for negotiations. Cavid diary, 3:84–85, 3:14–15, June 1915; 3:89, 24 June 1915; Babacan, *Talât*, 142. For a general assessment of Halil and of his moral failure vis-à-vis Zohrab, see Emmanuilidis, *Osmanlı İmparatorluğu'nun son yılları*, 284.

222. Morgenthau diary, 8 August 1915, 297–98.

223. Ernst Jäckh, chief of the Zentralstelle für Auslandsdienst, to Zimmermann, undersecretary of the Foreign Office, 17 October 1915, PA-AA/R 13750.

224. Morgenthau diary, 10 July 1915, 273, 7 October 1915, 350, and 18 October 1915, 358; Der Yeghiayan, *Memoirs*, 80–81.

225. Talaat to Foreign Ministry (Halil), 6 March 1916, transcribed in Ergünoz Akçora, "Talat Paşa'nın Urfa isyanı raporu," *XI: Türk tarih kongresi; Kongreye sunulan bildiriler* (Ankara: TTK, 1994), 5:1785–94.

226. Among the observers and humanitarian actors on the ground was the couple Jakob and Elisabeth Künzler of the Swiss hospital. Jakob Künzler managed to send contemporary reports to Germany and Switzerland. See his sober overall report in *In the Land of Blood and Tears* (translated from this 1921 book).

227. Anti-Armenian apologetics fill many pages of Talaat's, Cemal's, Halil's, and other CUP members' or sympathizers' memoirs. For a broad treatment of this topic, see Fatma M. Göçek, *Denial of Violence: Ottoman Past, Turkish Present, and Collective Violence against the Armenians, 1789–2009* (New York: Oxford University Press, 2015).

228. Scholars like René Girard and Jacques Sémelin have anthropologically elaborated on this topic on which the Bible tells a lot with regard to sin, sacrifice, scapegoat, responsibility, and revelation through catastrophe. Cf. Jacques Sémelin, *Purifier et détruire: Usages politiques des massacres et génocides* (Paris: Editions du Seuil, 2005). Cf. also Hans-Lukas Kieser, "Patterns and Politics of Public Violence in the Late Ottoman Empire and the Post-Ottoman Levant," *Cambridge World History of Violence*, vol. 4, forthcoming.

229. Vladimir Jabotinsky, *Race and Nationality* (Russian 1911; English 1939), quoted in Oskar K. Rabinowicz, *Vladimir Jabotinsky's Conception of a Nation* (New York: Beechhurst Press, 1946), 28–29.

230. See 7 March 1911, FO 371-1245-9105, no. 146, quoted in Mandel, *Turks, Arabs and Jewish Immigration*, 239. For an early, penetrating analysis of a British pre–World War I mind-set in the Ottoman capital inclined to conspiracy theories regarding

imagined Jewish omnipotence, see Elie Kedourie, "Young Turks, Freemasons and Jews," *Middle Eastern Studies* 7, no. 1 (Jan. 1971): 89–104, including lengthy quotations of sources.

231. Cemal to Talaat, 16 March 1915, BOA. DH. ŞFR., 465-19, reproduced and translated in Yuval Ben-Bassat, "Enciphered Ottoman Telegrams from the First World War concerning the Yishuv in Palestine," *Turcica* 46 (2015): 283–84. The same telegram is also referred to and translated in Çiçek, *War and State Formation in Syria*, 80–81.

232. Quoted in Isaiah Friedman, *Germany, Turkey, Zionism*, 211. Friedman himself adopted a positive view because he also sweepingly separated Cemal's, the local governors', and other functionaries' behavior from Talaat's policy, which he did not grasp (211–13).

233. Cemal's detailed telegram to Talaat on 3 November 1916 is telling proof of his harsh, social technologist, and imperially biased but nonexterminatory attitude. He demanded "humane [demographic] transfers" (DH. ŞFR. 541-120) and forcibly converted tens of thousands, thus saving them (Cemal to Talaat, 1 August 1916, DH. ŞFR. 527-19). In his letters during the war, and still in his memoirs written afterward, Cemal fraternizes with Talaat (e.g., "That God bless the country through your services. I kiss your cheeks"; 10 August 1916, DH. ŞFR. 519-63; similarly, "my brother," from both sides, 10–11 April 1916, DH. ŞFR. 62-294).

234. Abram I. Elkus, *The Memoirs of Abram Elkus, Lawyer, Ambassador, Statesman* (London: Gomidas, 2004), 84; Bernstorff to Hertling, 25 January 1917, quoted in Friedman, *Germany, Turkey, Zionism*, 385; Falih Rıfkı (Atay), *Zeytindağ* (Istanbul: Bates, 1981; 1st ed., 1932), 78; Dündar, *İttihat ve Terakki Müslümanları iskân politikası*, 92–107. Cf. Çiçek, *War and State Formation in Syria*, 41–43.

235. See the nonfiction novel by the Austrian officer Eugen Hoeflich, based on his 1917 diary: Moshe Y. Ben-Gavriêl, alias Eugen Hoeflich, *Jerusalem wird verkauft*, ed. Sebastian Schirrmeister (Wuppertal: Arco, 2016), 37, 45, 54; first Hebrew ed. 1946; "Allies to Capture Jerusalem in June," *Sun* (New York), 16 May 1917, 1.

236. Quoted in Michael Stanislawski, *Zionism and the Fin de siècle: Cosmopolitanism and Nationalism from Nordau to Jabotinsky* (Berkeley: University of California Press, 2001), 241. On Jabotinsky-related worries, see, for example, Lichtheim to Zionistisches Zentralbureau, 7 August 1916, CZA Z3-60, 00171-00175; communication to the Ottoman government, 17 August 1916, Z3-66.

237. In the life of the couple Lehmann-Haupt, we encounter a personal journey from Talaat's Istanbul to Hitler's Austria; see H. Kieser, "Armeniermord, Shoah und das Ehepaar Lehmann-Haupt: Eine Kontextualisierung," in Sebastian Fink, Klaus Eisterer, Robert Rollinger, and Dirk Rupnow, eds., *Carl Friedrich Lehmann-Haupt: Ein Forscherleben zwischen Orient und Okzident* (Wiesbaden: Harrassowitz, 2015), 95–108.

238. Inquiry by Talaat to governorship of Beirut, 24 November 1917, BOA DH. ŞFR. 81/233, telegram reproduced and translated in Ben-Bassat, "Enciphered Ottoman Telegrams from the First World War," 281–82; Atay, *Zeytindağ*, 61–63; Ali Fuad, quoted in Robert Mazza, "We will treat you like the Armenians': Djemal Pasha, Zionism, and the Evacuation of Jaffa, April 1917," in Çiçek, *Syria in World War I*, 99.

239. Lichtheim, 2 January 1917, quoted in Friedman, *Germany, Turkey, Zionism*, 279.

240. Çiçek, *War and State Formation in Syria*, 81, 84.

241. Lichtheim to Zionistisches Zentralburau, 11 August 1916, Z3-60, 00148; Morgenthau diary, 332, 17 September 1915.

242. "Reisebericht von Dr. Becker," early January 1918, CZA Z3-11. Similarly, cf. Lichtheim to Zionistisches Zentralbureau, 2 April 1917, CZA Z3-66.

243. Newspaper "Stamboul," 2 March 1911, quoted in Mandel, *Turks, Arabs and Jewish Immigration*, 243.

244. Jacobson to Wolffsohn, 8 and 12 February 1909, quoted in Friedman, *Germany, Turkey, Zionism*, 144–48. Cf. Esther Benbassa and Aron Rodrigue, *Sephardi Jewry: A History of the Judeo-Spanish Community, 14th-20th Centuries* (Berkeley: University of California Press, 2000), 121–23.

245. "Das neue türkische Kabinett und die Juden," *Die Welt*, 4 July 1913, 856. Cf. Ahmad, "The Special Relationship."

246. This is true for Jewish papers like *Jüdische Rundschau*, *Die Welt*, *Der Orient*, and even more for the Istanbul-based and Zionist-sponsored newspaper *Le Jeune-Turc*. Examples of long, flattering articles on Talaat include: "Le voyage de Talaat bey [to Livadiya]," *Le Jeune-Turc*, 9 May 1914, 1; "Le voyage de Talaat bey [to Bucharest]," 27 May 1914, 1. Examples of disinformation in the service of Talaat (denial of oustings and crimes against Rûm in spring 1914) include: "Déclaration de Talaat bey," 9 June 1914, 1; "Déclarations de Talaat bey sur son voyage à Carassi," 10 June 1914, 1; "L'arrivée de S. E. Talaat bey et la situation: De notre correspondant particulier," 22 June 1914, 1. Despite its pro-CUP attitude, *Le Jeune-Turc* was temporarily suspended in spring–summer 1913, when censorship became extremely strict (see Neufach to Zentralbureau, 22 July 1913, CZA Z3-46, 00052).

247. Jacobson, 6 January 1913, CZA Z3-45, 00274-00275.

248. Letter of Jacobson to Henri Frank, 28 February 1913, CZA Z3-45, 00160-00162.

249. In the words of the British ambassador, 17 March 1913, FO 371/1794/16925, no. 218, including cutting from *L'Aurore*, quoted in Mandel, *Turks, Arabs and Jewish Immigration*, 333–34.

250. Quoted in Stanislawski, *Zionism and the Fin de siècle*, 241.

251. Jacobson to Paul Nathan, Hilfsverein der Deutschen Juden, 2 March 1913, CZA Z3-1640.

252. J. Neufach, Istanbul, to Zentralbueau Berlin, 22 July 1913, CZA Z3-46, 00052. Cf. also the other pieces in this file of May–August 1913; Mandel, *Turks, Arabs and Jewish Immigration*, 384, 468.

253. Mandel, *Turks, Arabs and Jewish Immigration*, 380, 388.

254. Lichtheim to the Actionscomité der Zionistischen Organisation, 23 January 1914, CZA Z3-48, 00197-00203.

255. "To His Excellence the Minister of the Interior Tal'at Beyefendi," *İçtihâd*, no. 95 (12 March 1914): 2132–34.

256. Lichtheim to Zionistisches Zentralbureau Berlin, 12 April 1914, CZA Z3-48, 00052-00053.

257. Ibid., 14 March 1914, CZA Z3-48, 00103-00104.

258. See several examples in Rifat N. Bali, *Devlet'in örnek yurttaşları (1950–2003)* (Istanbul: Kitabevi, 2009); related to memory politics in late twentieth-century United States, see Edward T. Linenthal, *Preserving Memory: The Struggle to Create America's Holocaust Museum* (New York: Columbia University Press, 1995), 263.

259. Wangenheim quoted in Friedman, *Germany, Turkey, Zionism*, 209, 226; Lichtheim to E.A.C., 6 January 1915, CZA Z3-51, 00284-00292.

260. CZA Z3-51, 00292.

261. Morgenthau diary, 175, 2 February 1915. Cf. Mazza, "Djemal Pasha, Zionism, and the Evacuation of Jaffa," 92.

262. Arthur Ruppin, *Arthur Ruppin: Memoirs, Diaries, Letters*, ed. Alex Bein (New York: Herzl Press, 1972), 156.

263. Morgenthau diary, 215–16, 24 April 1915. This was not the only common dinner shared by Talaat, Nahum, and the American ambassador. For several dinners with Morgenthau's successor Elkus, see Göppert, Pera, to Bethmann Hollweg, 3 January 1917, PA-AA/R 13837; Lichtheim to Zionistisches Zentralbureau, 6 January 1917, Z3-66.

264. Morgenthau diary, 217–18, 26–27 April 1915; cf. 393, 23 November 1915.

265. Lichtheim to Zionistisches Zentralbureau, 7 August 1916, CZA Z3-60, 00168 and 31 August 1916, 00108.

266. Morgenthau diary, 431, 6 January 1916.

267. Yuval Ben-Bassat and Dotan Halevy, "A Tale of Two Cities and One Telegram: The Ottoman Military Regime and the Population of Greater Syria during WWI," *British Journal of Middle Eastern Studies* (4 Nov. 2016), http://dx.doi.org /10.1080/13530194.2016.1246240; Robert Mazza, "Djemal Pasha, Zionism, and the Evacuation of Jaffa," 96–97. Cf. Conde de Ballobar, *Jerusalem in World War I: The Palestine Diary of a European Diplomat*, ed. Eduardo Manzano and Moreno and

Roberto Mazza (London: I. B. Tauris, 2011). I owe insights to Dotan Halevy's and Yuval Ben-Bassat's contributions on Jaffa in 1917 during the conference *Ottoman Cataclysm: Total War, Genocide and Distant Futures in the Middle East (1915–1917)* at the University of Zurich, 28–31 October 2015.

268. This is true even of a meritorious scholar like Isaiah Friedman; see Friedman, *Germany, Turkey, Zionism*.

Chapter 6: Triumph and Fall, Lies and Resilience

1. Ottoman consul-general in Budapest, 8 March 1915, HSD.AFT. 6-57.

2. See Sean McKeekin, *The Ottoman Endgame: War, Revolution, and the Making of the Modern Middle East, 1908–1923* (New York: Penguin Press, 2015), 288.

3. Emmanuilidis, *Osmanlı İmparatorluğu'nun son yılları*, 327.

4. Cavid diary 3:194, 13 June 1916. On temporary nationalism, see Cavid vis-à-vis Oscar Wassermann, then Frederic-Hans Rosenberg, 16 December 1916, Cavid diary, 3:305 and 3:307.

5. Ihrig, *Justifying Genocide*, 270–98.

6. Ambassador Kühlmann to German Foreign Ministry, 5 February 1917, PA-AA/R 13801-1, 75-99. For the medal, see SALT, ANUDM00380.

7. Cavid diary, 3:360, 14 February 1917.

8. MMZC, first session period, 3:2, 3:181–82, session of 15 February 1917. Cf. "Hayât-ı teşrîyye Meclis-i Mebûsân'da," *Tanin*, 16 February 1917, 3.

9. See the 1918 special edition of *Yeni Mecmua: Çanakkale özel sayısı 18 Mart 1918* [Special Gallipoli issue]. In this, the secretary of the Central Committee, Küçük [Little] Talaat (Muşkara), and several CUP intellectuals celebrated the victory at the Dardanelles on 18 March 1915, and afterward on Gallipoli, as an "eternal joyful message of the Orient's salvation," a "gift offered by Anatolia's Muslims to a humanity trusting in courage, justice and honor." See transcribed ed. (Istanbul: Yeditepe Yay., 2006), 13–14.

10. Cavid diary, 3:361, 14 February 1917; Talaat to Aubrey Herbert in February 1921, in Aubrey Herbert, *Talaat Pasha*, typescript, Somerset Heritage Center, DD.DRU 56, 15; Cf. "1917 (1333) Kongresine sunulan raporda 'kavanin ve nizamatın ıslâhına' ilişkin kısım," in Tarık Z. Tunaya, *Türkiye'de siyasal partiler* (Istanbul: İletişim, 1998), 1:155–57; Gencer, *Bildungspolitik, Modernisierung und kulturelle Interaktion*; Hans-Lukas Kieser, *Vorkämpfer der "Neuen Türkei": Revolutionäre Bildungseliten am Genfersee* (Zürich: Chronos, 2005), 75–82.

11. See chapter 5, sec. "Leading Assimilation," and commander of the Second Army İzzet Pasha to the minister of the interior Talaat, 16 July 1916, DH. ŞFR. 532-33; Jäckh, *Rising Crescent*, 96; Osman B. Gürzumar, "Die Übernahme westlichen

Rechts in der Türkei vor 1926," in H. Kieser, A. Meier, and W. Stoffel, eds., *Revolution islamischen Rechts: Das Schweizerische ZGB in der Türkei* (Zürich: Chronos, 2008), 43. The new calendar, to be used in the administration, was valid beginning on 14 March 1917; it followed the Gregorian scheme and started the year with the month of January (not March, as is the previous Maliyye calendar); see Emmanuilidis, *Osmanlı İmparatorluğu'nun son yılları*, 244–45.

12. "He himself had always been against the attempted extermination of the Armenians. . . . He had twice protested against this policy, but had been overruled by the Germans," as he told Aubrey Herbert in February 1921. Herbert, *Talaat Pasha*, 3.

13. "Memo on Turkish Attitude Towards Peace," 20 December 1917, FO 371/3381 (General Correspondence), 239; M. Beau, French ambassador in Bern, to Aristide Briand, French foreign minister, "Annexe [report of a CUP member], Turquie—situation politique," 7 November 1916, *Documents Diplomatiques Français—1916* (Bern: Peter Lang, 2017), 5:1036–46 (many thanks to Claire Mouradian for drawing my attention to this document). Cf. Kévorkian, *Armenian Genocide*, 699–702.

14. Cavid reports that Talaat, who "never loses composure," did so, however, after a caucus on this topic. Cavid diary, 3:163, 12 December 1915; 3:446–47, 25 October 1917.

15. Birgen, *İttihat ve Terakki'de on sene*, 406.

16. "Şu'ûn-ı dâhiliyye," *Tasvîr-i Efkâr*, 7 February 1917, 1. Cf. "Yeni kabine ve ıslahât," *Tanin*, 17 February 1917, 1.

17. For example, see the review of the foreign press coverage of Talaat and his travels to Berlin, Vienna, and Sofia in *Servet-i Fünun*, 23 May 1917.

18. "Hâl ve atî," *Tercüman-ı Hakikat*, 5 February 1917, 1.

19. *Tasvîr-i Efkâr*, 17 February 1917, 1.

20. *Sabah*, 16 February 1917, quoted in Babacan, *Talât*, 138.

21. The symbol is important in terms of context but is about another history in terms of impact and legacy, which contemporary ex-Ottoman Christians then also nurtured in projects tied to premodern myths, for instance, of imperial Byzantium or Hellenism, and based on ethnic solidarity. Cf. Bernard Heyberger and Anastassios Anastassiadis, eds., "Voisinages fragiles: Les relations interconfessionnelles dans le Sud-Est européen et la Méditerranée orientale 1854–1923; Contraintes locales et enjeux internationaux," *Archives de sciences sociales des religions* 172 (2015): 241, http://assr.revues.org/27272.

22. Mete Tunçay, *Türkiye'de sol akımlar 1908–1925* (Istanbul: Iletisim, 2009), 65–66.

23. Cavid diary, 3:174–75, 23 February and 2 March 1916; 3:304–7, 15–16 December 1916; 3:355, 4 February 1917.

24. Ibid., 3:350, 3 February 1917; 3:356–57, 4 February 1917. Cf. 3:360, 11 February 1917.

25. For example, see Cavid diary, 3:173, 17 February 1917, and 3:179, 22 April 1917; 3:304, 16 December 1916; 3:313, 29 December 1916.

26. Ibid., 3:352 and 3:356, 3–4 February 1917.

27. Ibid., 3:377–89, 11 April–6 May 1917; 3:416, 5 September 1917; 3:449, 5 December 1917. Besides the record in the German archive (PA-AA), this German position is present in Ottoman documents, clearly voiced again and again to CUP interlocutors. Wangenheim, for example, did so again to Cavid shortly before his death (Cavid diary, 3:147, 26 September–18 October 1915, no precise date); Wolff-Metternich did so in İzzet Pasha's house on 5 January 1916 (Cavid diary, 3:169).

28. Cavid diary, 3:407, 25 August 1917. Muhittin Birgen also points several times to Talaat's melancholy, in particular with regard to summer–fall 1918 (*İttihat ve Terakki'de on sene*).

29. For example, see 22 September 1917, after a meeting of committee and government members in Talaat's house; Cavid diary, 3:433.

30. Necmettin Sadık (Sadak), "Sulh müjdesi," in *Yeni Mecmua*, no. 21, 14 February 1918, 101, and the same, "İrtica aleyine . . ." in *Yeni Mecmua*, no. 34, 7 March 1918, 141. A selection of articles of the first forty-five numbers of *Yeni Mecmua* are transcribed in Erdal Baran, *Yeni Mecmua üzerine bir inceleme*, thesis of Yüksek Lisans (thesis between MA and PhD), University of Niğde, 2009. On Sadak's Nazi sympathies, his foreign ministry, and his turn to the United States, see John M. VanderLippe, *The Politics of Turkish Democracy: İsmet İnönü and the Formation of the Multi-Party System, 1938–1950* (Albany: SUNY Press, 2005).

31. Cavid diary, 3:372, 7 April 1917.

32. Kühlmann to Foreign Office, 22 March 1917, PA-AA/R 13801-2, 66-90.

33. Liman von Sanders, *Five Years in Turkey*, 4. Cf. Bernstorff, *Erinnerungen und Briefe*, 126–30 (in retrospect, Bernstorff understood Talaat's assassination as a punishment for "his involvement in the Armenian sin"); Friedrich Schrader, *Eine Flüchtlingsreise durch die Ukraine: Tagebuchblätter von meiner Flucht aus Konstantinopel* (Tübingen: J.C.B. Mohr, 1919; many thanks to Jochen Schrader for drawing my attention to this publication of his great-grandfather), 22–23; Hans-Lukas Kieser, "Armeniermord, Shoah und das Ehepaar Lehmann-Haupt," in Dirk Rupnow et al., eds., *Carl Friedrich Lehmann-Haupt: Ein Forscherleben zwischen Orient und Okzident* (Wiesbaden: Harrassowitz, 2015), 95–107.

34. Kühlmann to Bethmann Hollweg, 16 February 1917, PA-AA/R 14046.

35. Bernstorff to German Foreign Ministry, 30 July 1918, PA-AA/R 13804-2, 77-78. Bernstorff's pretension is also manifest in his attitude toward Cavid and his intention to topple this intractable negotiator (Bernstorff to Kühlmann, 4 December 1917, R 13803-1, 73-75). On the role of the "tragic mind" in the history of violence, see Hamit Bozarslan, *Violence in the Middle East: From Political Struggle to Self-Sacrifice* (Princeton, NJ: Markus Wiener, 2004).

36. Liman von Sanders, *Five Years in Turkey*, 8 and 38.

37. Jäckh to von Weizsäcker, 9 November 1917, in Jäckh, *Rising Crescent*, 268.

38. Cavid to Wassermann of the board of the Deutsche Bank, 4 July 1916, and to Rosenberg, 12 July 1916. Cavid diary, 3:205–6 and 211–12. Bernstorff to German Foreign Ministry, 20 June 1918, PA-AA/R 13804-2, 44-45; Cavid diary, 3:353, 3 February 1917. Cf. Winfried Becker, ed., *Frederic von Rosenberg: Korrespondenzen und Akten des deutschen Diplomaten und Aussenministers 1913–1937* (München: R. Oldenbourg, 2011).

39. Cf. German ambassador Bernstoff's observations during this funeral in Bernstorff, *Erinnerungen und Briefe*, 21. *Freie Presse* quoted in *Servet-i Fünun*, 10 May 1917, 347–48.

40. As soon as 8 February 1917, the Ottoman Foreign Ministry was informed of an imminent revolution (that actually started in early March) and considered the salutariness of a separate peace with Russia. See letter in the name of foreign minister Halil to the Ministry of the Interior (e.e., Talaat), 8 February 1917, BOA DH.EUM. 5. Şb. 33-14.

41. Treaties reproduced in Mühlmann, *Deutschland und die Türkei*, 78–101, cf. 47–50.

42. Informal handwritten note dated 23 October 1917, on paper with the header "Sublime Porte, Grand Vézirat," in the Jäckh Papers, Yale University Library.

43. Cavid diary, 3:307, 16–17 December 1916. Cf. 3:330, 17 January 1917.

44. Bernstorff, *Erinnerungen und Briefe*, 129; cf. Bernstorff to Erzberger, 30 March 1918, in *Erinnerungen und Briefe*, 145.

45. Cavid diary, 3:224, 30 July 1916. Cf. Williamson, *Karl Helfferich*, 111–50, 365–73; Dowe, *Erzberger: Demokrat in Zeiten des Hasses.*

46. Cavid diary, 3:375–76, 10 April 1917; 3:382, 18 April 1917.

47. Ibid., 3:220, 25 July 1916 (Zimmermann was then Unterstaatssekretär [undersecretary of state], and from autumn 1915 Staatssekretär [secretary of state]); 3:437, 15 October 1917; 3:480, 19 January 1918. Cf. Manfred Nebelin, *Ludendorff: Diktator im Ersten Weltkrieg* (München: Siedler, 2010); Bettina Amm, "Die Ludendorff-Bewegung im Nationalsozialismus," in Uwe Puschner and Clemens Vollnhals, eds., *Die völkisch-religiöse Bewegung im Nationalsozialismus* (Göttingen: Vandenhoeck & Ruprecht, 2012), 127–48.

48. "Der türkische Bundesgenosse," *Belgrader Nachrichten*, 16 May 1918, 1, in BOA HR. SYS. 2453-5.

49. BOA HR. SYS. 2434-63; Cavid diary, 3:392, 15 June 1917; Jonathan Schneer, *The Balfour Declaration: The Origins of the Arab-Israeli Conflict* (New York: Random House, 2012), 258.

50. Ottoman representatives in Geneva seeking a separate peace were, in general, liberal dissidents; Abdülkerim apparently made them appear as if they were linked to CUP circles. Cf. Kieser, *Vorkämpfer*, 78–79, 168.

51. Cf., according to British archives, on Pilling, Rahmi, Fuad Selim, Zaharoff, Abdul Kerim, and Enver's involvement in separate peace efforts: Keith Hamilton (trans. Mete Tunçay), "'Zedzed' in çikolatası," *Radikal 2*, 17 April 2005, www.radikal .com.tr/radikal2/zedzedin-cikolatasi-872507; Joseph Maiolo and Tony Insall, "Sir Basil Zaharoff and Sir Vincent Caillard as Instruments of British Policy towards Greece and the Ottoman Empire during the Asquith and Lloyd George Administrations, 1915–18," *International History Review* 34, no. 4 (2012): 819–39; Schneer, *Balfour Declaration*, 253–62, 291–300, and 347–61; David French, "Failures of Intelligence: The Retreat to the Hindenburg Line and the March 1918 Offensive," in Michael Dockrill and David French, eds., *Strategy & Intelligence: British Policy during the First World War* (London: Hambledon Press, 1996), 87–91.

52. Bernstorff to Gwinner, 1 January 1918, in Bernstorff, *Erinnerungen und Briefe*, 138. Cf. Talaat's counselor Muhittin Birgen's observations on Enver's weak position, *İttihat ve Terakki'de on sene*, 404–7.

53. Cavid diary, 3:392, 15 June 1917.

54. Minutes by G. Clerk and R. Graham, 31 July 1917, FO 371/3057 (Separate Peace Talks 1917), 148986. Cf. Herbert diary, 5:5–11, 22 July 1917, DD/HER/70/1-3, Somerset Heritage Centre.

55. Cavid diary, 3:249, 9 September 1916; 3:458–60, 15–19 December 1917; 3:544, 5 September 1918; V.G.W. Kell to R. H. Campbell, 31 January 1917, enclosing "a report from a reliable source," FO 371/3048 (Talaat Quarrel with Enver), 27296; Babacan, *Talât*, 168–70; Beau, Bern, to Briand, "Annexe, Turquie—situation politique," 7 November 1916, *Documents Diplomatiques Français—1916*, 1036–46. On the "Yakup Cemil event" in 1916, see also Falih R. Atay, *Mustafa Kemal'in ağzından Vahdettin* (Istanbul: Pozitif, 2013), 18–19; Benjamin C. Fortna, *The Circassian: A Life of Eşref Bey, Late Ottoman Insurgent and Special Agent* (London: Oxford University Press, 2016), 176–77.

56. Herbert, *Talaat Pasha*, 8. Cf. Ünal, "Young Turk Assessment of International Politics," 31.

57. Cf. Emmanuilidis, *Osmanlı İmparatorluğu'nun son yılları*, 325–26.

58. Cf. Lyndall Ryan and Amanda Nettelback, "Frontier Violence in the British Empire," *The Cambridge World History of Violence*, vol. 4 (Cambridge: Cambridge University Press, in preparation). Thanks to the authors for sharing drafts with me.

59. Kieser, "Johannes Lepsius," 211–14. The newest in-depth study of the Boer War is Martin Bossenbroek, *Tod am Kap: Geschichte des Burenkriegs*, trans. from the Dutch by Andreas Ecke (Munich: C. H. Beck, 2016). On the assimilation of social Darwinism by young Turkish academics in the 1910s, see Kieser, *Türklüğe ihtida*, 184–91.

60. Aubrey Herbert diary, 9:4, DD/HER/70/1-3, Somerset Heritage Centre; Herbert, *Talaat Pasha*, 9; W. Tyrell, Foreign Office, to Herbert, 22 March 1921, DD/DRU 56, Somerset Heritage Centre.

61. Michelle Tusan, "'Crimes against Humanity': Human Rights, the British Empire, and the Origins of the Response to the Armenian Genocide," *American Historical Review*, February 2014, 69. The Churchill quote is from Dockter, *Churchill and the Islamic World*, 70 and 98.

62. Emmanuilidis, *Osmanlı İmparatorluğu'nun son yılları*, 329.

63. Bernstorff to German Foreign Ministry, 22 December 1917, PA-AA/R 13803-2, 11-13; 11–14 February 1918, PA-AA/R 13803-3, 7-25; 3 March 1918, PA-AA/R 13804-1, 2; Cavid diary, 3:494, 28 March 1918.

64. Schneer, *Balfour Declaration*, 261.

65. This was not only true for all versions of contemporary Zionism but also all modern Christian-Zionist currents hoping on and working for a "restoration of the Jews to Palestine and Jesus." Cf. Hans-Lukas Kieser, *Nearest East: American Millennialism and Missiona to the Middle East* (Philadelphia: Temple University Press, 2010).

66. Talaat to Cemal, 31 January 1917, BOA DH. ŞFR. 72-129, answering Cemal to Talaat, 26 January 1917, BOA DH. ŞFR. 544-29.

67. Cemal to Talaat, 6 January 1917, BOA DH. ŞFR. 456-100. Cf. Talaat to Cemal, 10 April 1917, BOA DH. ŞFR. 74-273. He congratulated Cemal and wished him "from God's side" successful continuation.

68. Cavid diary, 3:296, 9 December 1916, in a meeting with Rosenberg. Cf. ibid., 3:455, 11 December 1917, after the fall of Jerusalem.

69. Cf. Klaus J. Herrmann, "Political Response to the Balfour Declaration in Imperial Germany: German Judaism," *Middle East Journal* 19, no. 3 (Summer 1965): 303–20.

70. "Reisebericht von Dr. Becker," including interviews with Talaat (12 December 1917) and Cemal (1 January 1918), early January 1918, CZA Z3-11.

71. By 1919, then based in Geneva. See Becker's article "Maximalistischer Zionismus," *Neue Jüdische Monatshefte* 3, no. 13 (10 April 1919): 255–65.

72. Falih R. Atay, *Çankaya* (Istanbul: Pozitif, n.d.), 375–76.

73. Cf. Matityahu Minc, "The Zionist Movement and the Brest-Litovsk Negotiations in January 1918," *Jahrbücher für Geschichte Osteuropas, Neue Folge* 28, no. 1 (1980): 31–61, in particular, 39. Friedman, *Germany, Turkey, Zionism*, 382–413.

74. Reinharz, *Dokumente zur Geschichte des deutschen Zionismus*, 23–24; Friedman, *Germany, Turkey, Zionism*, 404–12.

75. Draft communiqué about Talaat's meeting with Jewish representatives in Istanbul on 14 July 1918, reproduced in Friedman, *Germany, Turkey, Zionism*, 427–28.

76. The Sykes-Picot Agreement was first published in Russian, then in the *Manchester Guardian*, 26 November 1917 (see facsimile of the latter on Wikipedia). Talaat to Foreign Ministry (Halil), 21 October 1916, asking for further investigation, after he had received intelligence based on two articles in August 1916, in Armenian, in the

journal *Armenia*, BOA HR. SYS. 2284-14 (1). Eliezer Tauber, "La Légion d'Orient et la Légion arabe," *Revue française d'histoire d'outre-mer* 81, no. 303 (1994): 171–80; Andrekos Varnaka, "French and British Post-War Imperial Agendas and Forging an Armenian Homeland after Genocide: The Formation of the Légion d'Orient in October 1916," *Historical Journal* 57, no. 4 (2014): 997–1025. İlhan Tekeli and Selim İlkin, "Kurtuluş Savaşı'nda Talât Paşa ile Mustafa Kemâl'in mektuplaşmaları," *Belleten* 44 (April 1980): 317.

77. Allen and Muratoff, *Caucasian Battlefields*, 468–77.

78. Talaat, Brest-Litovsk, to Enver, 1 February 1918, quoted in Tülay Duran, "Dünya Savaşı sonunda Türk diplomasinin ilk başarısı: Brest-Litovsk harzırlıkları," *Belgelerle Türk Tarih Dergisi* 12, no. 70 (1973): 31–32.

79. Long telegram from Talaat, Brest-Litovsk, to Foreign Ministry, Istanbul, 1 February 1918, BOA DH. SYS. 2295-2. Cf. also, reproducing many transcribed Ottoman documents, Duran, "Brest-Litovsk harzırlıkları," *Belgelerle Türk Tarih Dergisi* 12, no. 67–68 (1973): 43–49; no. 69, 22–26; no. 70, 31–34.

80. Becker, ed., *Rosenberg: Korrespondenzen und Akten*, 58–59; Cavid diary, 3:494, 28 March 1918.

81. Cf. "L'autonomie de l'Arménie," *Gazette de Lausanne*, 16 January 1918, BOA HR. SYS. 2295-2.

82. Talaat, Brest-Litovsk, to Enver, 1 February 1918, quoted in Duran, "Brest-Litovsk harzırlıkları," *Belgelerle Türk Tarih Dergisi* 12, no. 70 (1973): 31; and Enver to Talaat in Brest-Litovsk (sent via the Ottoman Embassy in Berlin, 29 January 1918), BOA HR. SYS. 2876, 3-1 (this file contains several letters of Enver to Talaat).

83. Enver to the commander of the Third Army Vehib Pasha, 9 June 1918, facsimile in Reynolds, *Shattering Empires*, between 166 and 167.

84. Halil Kut, "Eylül 1918'de Erivan ve Ermeniler," in *Ermeniler Hakkinda "Makaleler-Derlemeler"* (Erzurum: Erzurum Universitesi Yay., 1978), 147–65, quoted in Hamit Bozarslan, "L'extermination des Arméniens et des juifs: Quelques éléments de comparaison," in Kieser and Schaller, eds., *Der Völkermord an den Armeniern und die Shoah*, 322–23.

85. In Bernstorff to Foreign Office, 23 May 1918, PA-AA/R 14100, English translation from www.armenocide.de.

86. Halil Kut, *Kutül-Amare kahramanları: Halil Kut Paşa'nın hatıraları* (Istanbul: Timaş, 2015), 175; Bernstorff to Erzberger, 30 March 1918, in *Briefe und Erinnerungen*, 144; cf. Richard G. Hovannisian, *Armenia on the Road to Independence, 1918* (Berkeley: University of California Press, 1967), 94–227; Ronald G. Suny, *The Baku Commune, 1917–1918: Class and Nationality in the Russian Revolution* (Princeton, NJ: Princeton University Press, 1972); Thomas de Waal, *The Caucasus, an Introduction* (Oxford: Oxford University Press, 2010), 60–67.

87. Ziya Gökalp, *Rusya'daki Türkler ne yapmalı?* (Istanbul: Tanin Maatbası, 1918) and, "İçtimaiyat 'Turan' Nedir?," in *Yeni Mecmua*, no. 31 (8 February 1918): 82–84; Necmettin Sadık, "İrtica aleyine . . . ," in *Yeni Mecmua*, no. 34 (7 March 1918): 141; Reşid Safvet (Atabinen [secretary of the Turkish delegation at the conference of Lausanne]), "Kafkas etekleri Türk ticaret yolları," in *Yeni Mecmua*, no. 43 (9 May 1918): 325.

88. Cavid diary, 3:538, 29 August 1918.

89. Birgen, *İttihat ve Terakki'de on sene*, 395–435.

90. Williamson, *Karl Helfferich*, 218–55; "Die Krise auf dem Höhepunkt" and "Der Wortlaut der Kriegserklärung," *Frankfurter Zeitung*, 14 July 1917, 1.

91. Cavid diary, 3:494–96, 28–29 March 1918; 3:511–15, 9–20 July 1918; 3:524, 31 July 1918; 3:541, 31 August 1918.

92. Ibid., 3:504–5, 1–22 June 1918.

93. Ibid., 3:544, 5 September 1918; Bernstorff to German Foreign Ministry, 15 July 1918, PA-AA/R 13804-2, 69; 2 October 1918, R 13804-3, 80.

94. Birgen, *İttihat ve Terakki'de on sene*, 395–435, quotations 395, 427–28.

95. Cavid diary, 3:581–82, 16 October 1918.

96. Ibid., 3:542, 5 September 1918.

97. PA-AA/R 13804-3, 50-62.

98. Cf. Ahmet Demirel, *Birinci meclis'te muhalefet: Ikinci grup* (Istanbul: Iletisim, 2007); Erik J. Zürcher, *Turkey: A Modern History* (London: I. B. Tauris, 2004), 176–81. Birgen, *İttihat ve Terakki'de on sene*, 440–67 and 490–92, quotations 441, 449, 452, 460. Talaat's seminal and lasting legacy was a partisan and personalized governance; see below.

99. Cavid diary, 3:559, 21 September 1918; Waldburg, Pera, to German Foreign Ministry, 30 September 1918, 1918, PA-AA/R 13804-3, 77-78; Bernstorff, *Erinnerungen und Briefe*, 167–68.

100. Simavi, *Gördüklerim*, 256.

101. Cavid diary, 3:558–64, 20–29 September 1918.

102. Ahmed E. Yalman, *Yakın tarihte gördüklerim ve geçirdiklerim* (Istanbul: Yenilik Basımevi, 1970), 1:305–6.

103. Simavi, *Gördüklerim*, 285; Birgen, *İttihat ve Terakki'de on sene*, 500.

104. Babacan, *Talât*, 186; Mango, *Atatürk*, 186–87 and 203; Göçek, *Denial*, 377; Tunçay, *Türkiye'de sol akımlar*, 261.

105. Bayur, *Türk inkılâbı tarihi*, part 4, 3:774–79. The most detailed version of this speech is in Yalman, *Yakın tarihte gördüklerim*, 1:307–11.

106. Simavi, *Gördüklerim*, 297; cf. Birgen, *İttihat ve Terakki'de on sene*, 549; Cavid diary, 3:579, 14 October 1918.

107. Ahmed İzzet, *Feryadım*, 2:34–35 and (letters) 287–88.

108. Arif Cemil (Denker), *İttihatçı şeflerin gurbet maceraları* (Istanbul: Arma, 1992), 17–18 (this text was first published by the newspaper *Tevhid-i Efkâr* [Istanbul, May–July, 1922]); Birgen, *İttihat ve Terakki'de on sene*, 552, 559.

109. Solf to embassy in Constantinople (Bernstorff), 30 October 1918, quoted in Seyffarth, *Entscheidung in Aleppo: Walter Rössler*, 326.

110. Hüseyin C. Yalçın, *İttihatçı liderlerin gizli mektupları* (Istanbul: Temel, 2002 [1944]), 143–223; Birgen, *İttihat ve Terakki'de on sene*, 553–54. On Strauss, see Cavid diary, 4:305; cf. 4:258 (probably the same Strauss as referred to in Christian Gerlach, "Nationsbildung im Krieg," in Kieser and Schaller, *Armenian Genocide and Shoah*, 382, 415).

111. See 12 and 21 January 1919, Cavid diary, 3:649 and 3:662; Babacan, *Talât*, 191–204.

112. İzzet to Rıfat, 5 November 1918, "Très urgent—confidentiel," in Ahmed İzzet, *Feryadım*, 2:289–90.

113. See 23 November 1918, Cavid diary, 3:627.

114. Talaat (alias Hamdi) to Enver (alias Abbas), 29 November 1918, Enver Pasha documents, Türk Tarih Kurumu, Ankara.

115. Tunçay, *Türkiye'de sol akımlar*, 785–92.

116. Yalçın, *İttihatçı liderlerin gizli mektupları*, 143 and 199.

117. Babacan, *Talât*, 186; Talaat to Cavid, 16 October 1920, in Yalçın, *İttihatçı liderlerin gizli mektupları*, 165; Fabio L. Grassi, *İtalya ve Türk sorunu 1919–1923: Kamuoyu ve dış politika* (Istanbul: YKY, 2003), 138–40.

118. Schrader, *Eine Flüchtlingsreise*, 112–13; Lepsius, *Todesgang des armenischen Volkes*, xxviii. Invitation to the service quoted in Axel Meissner, *Martin Rades "Christliche Welt" und Armenien* (Münster: Lit, 2010), 263; Denker, *İttihatçı şeflerin gurbet maceraları*, 14–30; Sabine Mangold-Will, *Begrenzte Freundschaft: Deutschland und die Türkei 1918–1933* (Göttingen: Wallstein, 2013), 41–54. A relevant analysis of the contemporary German press is in Ihrig, *Atatürk in the Nazi Imagination*, 33–35.

119. Kieser, *Türklüğe ihtida*, 134–73; Safi, *Ottoman Special Organization*, 280.

120. Helfferich, *Deutsche Türkenpolitik*, 3 and 32; cf. Yalçın, *İttihatçı liderlerin gizli mektupları*, 201 and 307.

121. Birgen, *İttihat ve Terakki'de on sene*, 617.

122. Ihrig, *Atatürk in the Nazi Imagination*, 68, 102–3; Ihrig, *Justifying Genocide*, 227.

123. Herbert, *Talaat Pasha*, 1 and 21; *Talat Paşa'nın hatıraları*, ed. Hüseyin Cahid Yalçın and Enver Bolayır (Istanbul: Güven, 1946), 5; Yalçın, *Talât*, 8.

124. See 27 October, 26 November, and 27 December 1919, Cavid diary, 4:35, 4:44, 4:53; Talaat to Cavid, 18 February 1921; cf. Talaat to Cemal, 21 December 1920, Yalçın, *İttihatçı liderlerin gizli mektupları*, 182 and 187. The memoirs were posthumously published.

125. Talat, *Hatıralarım ve müdafaam*, 34, 42.

126. There was an abusive commerce with wagons (*vagon ticareti*). It is another question if and how Mazhar was involved in this commerce. Talaat had dismissed Mazhar because he had refused anti-Armenian orders in June 1915; see chap. 5, sec. "Exploit: 'The Armenian Question no longer exists.'" Talat, *Hatıralarım ve müdafaam*, 82.

127. Talat, *Hatıralarım ve müdafaam*, 46.

128. Talaat to Cavid, 1 May 1920, in Yalçın, *İttihatçı liderlerin gizli mektupları*, 152.

129. Talaat to Cavid, 21 December 1919 and 6 January 1920, in Yalçın, *İttihatçı liderlerin gizli mektupları*, 145–47.

130. Cavid diary, 11 November 1918, 3:636. Cf. 17–19 December 1917, 3:459–60. Cf. Mango, *Atatürk*, 185–286.

131. Gökalp, *Türkçülüğün esasları*, 30–31; cf. Heyd, *Gökalp*, 37–39.

132. The correspondence between Talaat and Kemal was first published in İlhan Tekeli and Selim İlkin, "Kurtuluş Savaşı'nda Talât Paşa ile Mustafa Kemâl'in mektuplaşmaları," *Belleten* 44 (April 1980): 301–45, Talaat's letter of 22 December 1919 is on pp. 315–21; Kemal's letter of 20 February is on pp. 312–30.

133. Atay, *Vahdettin*, 44–45; Kreiser, *Atatürk*, 118–20.

134. Talaat to Cavid, 2 December 1920, in Yalçın, *İttihatçı liderlerin gizli mektupları*, 170.

135. Ibid., 14 July, 9 August, and 19 December 1920, in ibid., 156–58, 162, 172–73; Herbert, *Talaat Pasha*, 18. Cf. Kâzım Karabekir, *İstiklâl harbimizde Enver Paşa ve İttihat ve Terakki erkânı* (Istanbul: YKY, 2010); Artuç, *Cemal paşa*, 324–82. The Misak-ı Millî is online on the Turkish Historical Society website, http://www.ttk .gov.tr/index.php?Page=Sayfa&No=244.

136. See 20 October–24 December 1919, Cavid diary, 4:33–52; Talaat's letters to Cavid, 27 September 1919–6 January 1920, in Yalçın, *İttihatçı liderlerin gizli mektupları*, 143–47; Kieser, *Türklüğe ihtida*, 149–73; Gregor Alexinsky, "Bolshevism and the Turks," *Quarterly Review* 239 (June 1923): 183–97, quotation on p. 190. On Alexinsky, a friend of Georgi Plekhanov, see David Shub, "Fact or Fiction on Lenin's Role: A Letter from David Shub Defending His Biography of Lenin," *New International* (March–April 1950): 86–91, https://www.marxists.org/history/etol /newspape/ni/vol16/no02/shub.htm.

137. Quoted in Tunçay, *Türkiye'deki sol akımlar*, 280.

138. Cemal to Talaat, 30 October 1920, in Yalçın, *İttihatçı liderlerin gizli mektupları*, 258.

139. Letter to Lenin, 26 April 1920, quoted in Tunçay, *Türkiye'de sol akımlar*, 263; Kâzım Karabekir, *İstiklâl harbimizde Enver Paşa ve İttihat ve Terakki Erkânı* (Istanbul: YKY, 2010), 12–17.

140. Gotthard Jäschke, "Der Weg zur russisch-türkischen Freundschaft," *Die Welt des Islams* 16 (1934): 31.

141. *Neue Zürcher Zeitung* (183–44), 14 January 1962, 9, referred to in Corsin Zander, *Wie Tageszeitungen Geschichte schreiben: Der Einfluss der Massenmedien auf die Erinnerungskultur am Beispiel der Berichterstattung der NZZ über das "Massaker von Katyn"* (1943–2017), MA thesis (Zurich: University of Zurich, 2017), 68–69.

142. Atay, *Çankaya*, 375–76; Elise Massicard, "The Repression of the Koçgiri Rebellion, 1920–1921," *Violence de masse et Résistance, Réseau de recherche* (2009), http://www.sciencespo.fr/mass-violence-war-massacre-resistance; Mango, *Atatürk*, 330–31. Cf. Ali Kemal's incisive article on the crucial but distorted topic of perpetration and victimhood (in contrast to contemporary abuse of such notions by Turkish nationalist propaganda): "Zâlimler, Mazlûmlar," *Sabah*, no. 10427, 9 November 1918, 1. On Nureddin Pasha, there are a few nationalist publications that include sources: Necati Fahri, *Nureddin Pasa ve tarihi gercekler* (Istanbul: Nehir, 1997; on Ali Kemal's killing, 208–12), and Mustafa Balcıoğlu, *İki isyan: Koçgiri, Pontus/Bir paşa: Nurettin Paşa* (Ankara: Nobel, 2000).

143. Cf. Kemal's letters, aimed at winning over notables in the provinces, and the relevant *fetva* of the Ankara government, signed by seventy-six mufti, alluded to in Edip Servet to Cavid, 19 May 1920, Yalçın, *İttihatçı liderlerin gizli mektupları*, 192; Kemal Atatürk, *Nutuk: Vesikalar* (Ankara: Atatürk Kültür, Dil ve Tarih Kurumu, 1991).

144. Kemal to Cemal, 1 October 1920, Yalçın, *İttihatçı liderlerin gizli mektupları*, 363.

145. Mustafa Kemal to Talaat, 7 November 1920, and Talaat to Cavid and Câmi, 2 February 1921, Yalçın, *İttihatçı liderlerin gizli mektupları*, 178 and 220.

146. Letter, 18 [*sic*] August, referred to in Talaat to Cavid, 9 [*sic*] August 1920, Yalçın, *İttihatçı liderlerin gizli mektupları*, 162–63, and in Cavid diary, 4:263–72 (April 1921 on Enver's and Talaat's self-understanding and policies). Cf. Birgen, *İttihat ve Terakki'de on sene*, 697–703, 741–46.

147. Emil Ludwig, "Talaat und Enver," *Vossische Zeitung*, 26 October 1918, in PA-AA/R 13804-4.

148. Dr. Nâzım, Berlin, to Cavid, n.d. (ca. 20 March 1921), Yalçın, *İttihatçı liderlerin gizli mektupları*, 105–8, referred to in Cavid diary, 4:258, 28 March 1921; Jäckh to Zeki, 17 March 1921, in Jäckh, *Rising Crescent*, 269–70; Meissner, *Martin Rades*, 199. Insider insights into Operation Nemesis in Shiragian, *The Legacy*; MacCurdy et al., eds., *Sacred Justice: The Voices and Legacy of the Armenian Operation Nemesis* (Piscataway, NJ: Transaction, 2015); detailed narratives in Rolf Hosfeld, *Operation Nemesis: Die Türkei, Deutschland und der Völkermord an den Armeniern* (Köln: Kiepenheuer & Witsch, 2005), and Eric Bogosian, *Operation Nemesis: The Assassination that Avenged the Armenian Genocide* (New York: Little, Brown, 2015).

149. Cavid diary, 4:246.

150. *Vakit*, no. 1175, 18 March 1921, 1. Cf. Babacan, *Talât*, 214–17.

151. *Vakit*, no. 1217, 27 March 1921, 2.

152. *İleri*, no. 1128, 19 March 1921, 1.

153. *Joghovourti Tsayn*, quoted in *İleri*, no. 1128, 19 March 1921, 1. Cf. Kieser, *Türklüğe İhtida*, 78.

154. Mangold-Will, *Begrenzte Freundschaft*, 166.

155. Emil Ludwig, "Ein weltgeschichtliches Urteil," *Die Weltbühne* 27 (7 July 1921): 65; Vierbücher quoted in Schaller, "Die Rezeption des Völkermords," 532; *Vorwärts*, quoted in Ihrig, *Germany and the Armenians*, 267; Stier quoted in Meissner, *Martin Rades*, 266. On the trial, see Schaller, "Die Rezeption des Völkermords," 531–38; Meissner, *Martin Rades*, 264–66; Ihrig, *Germany and the Armenians*, 234–69; *Der Prozess Talaat Pascha: Stenographischer Prozessbericht*, preface by Armin T. Wegener (Berlin: Deutsche Verlagsgesellschaft für Politik und Geschichte, 1921).

156. Cf. Dadrian and Akçam, *Judgment at Istanbul*, 101–7; Giovanni Bonello, "The 'Malta Trials' and the Turkish-Armenian Question" in *Histories of Malta: Confessions and Transgressions* (Malta: Fondazzjoni Patrimonju Malti, 2000), ix, 180–228.

157. Lemkin, *Totally Unofficial*, 20; Schaller, "Die Rezeption des Völkermords," 537–38.

158. Quoted in Meissner, *Martin Rades*, 266–67.

159. For example, three works by Mansur Rifat: *Das Geheimnis der Ermordung Talaat Paschas: Ein Schlüssel für das englische Propagandasystem* (Berlin: Morgen- und Abendland-Verlag, 1921); *Talaat Paschas Prozess—sein Verlauf und sein Ende: Ein letztes Wort zur armenischen Frage* (Berlin: Morgen- und Abendland-Verlag, 1921); and *Die Ahmadia-Sekte* (Berlin: Morgen- und Abendland-Verlag, 1923). Cf. Meissner, *Martin Rades*, 120; Schaller, "Die Rezeption des Völkermords," 536; Mangold-Will, *Begrenzte Freundschftaft*, 73.

160. Ihrig, *Atatürk in the Nazi Imagination*, 68.

161. Alfred Rosenberg, "Mörder und Mörderschutz," *Der Weltkampf*, July 1926 (reprinted in A. Rosenberg, *Kampf um die Macht. Aufsätze von 1921–1932* [München: Zentralverlag der NSDAP, 1938], 435–36).

162. See Ümit, *Destruction of Aintab Armenians*; Üngör, *The Making of Modern Turkey*. This significant study is focused on Diyarbakır throughout the twentieth century.

163. Mehmed Emin (Yurdakul), 1869–1944, nationalist poet and spiritual brother of Gökalp, quoted in Hanioğlu, *Atatürk*, 66; Ziya Gökalp, "Türkün tekbiri," 9 August 1914, quoted in Köroğlu, "Propaganda or Culture War," 147; Rauf Yekta, "Millî tekbir hakkında," *Yeni Mecmua: Çanakkale özel sayısı 18 Mart 1918*, transcribed ed. (Istanbul: Yeditepe, 2006, 175–76).

164. Abdurrahman Hâmid, "Mefkûre," *Türk Yurdu* 15 (February 1925), transcribed ed. (Ankara: Tutibay, 1999), viii, 198. The poem was written in Ankara on 27 December 1922.

165. Hans-Lukas Kieser, "Türkische Nationalrevolution, anthropologisch gekrönt: Kemal Atatürk und Eugène Pittard," *Historische Anthropologie* 1 (2006): 105–18.

166. Birgen, *İttihat ve Terakki'de on sene*, 697–98.

167. Cf. Hülya Adak, "National Myths and Self-Na(rra)tions: Mustafa Kemal's *Nutuk* and Halide Edib's *Memoirs* and *The Turkish Ordeal*," *South Atlantic Quarterly* 102, no. 2/3 (2003): 509–27.

168. Jäckh, *Rising Crescent*, 90; Kemal Atatürk, *Nutuk: 1919–1927* (Ankara: Atatürk Kültür, Dil ve Tarih Kurumu, 1989).

169. See notes in the foreword and in chapter 1, section "Married with a Cause" for more recent, critical literature, including Zürcher, *Unionist Factor*.

170. Cf. *Gazi Mustafa Kemal Atatürk, Atatürk'ün Söylev ve Demeçleri* (Ankara: Atatürk Kültür Dil ve Tarih Yüksek Kurumu, 1997), 2:130; Gingeras, *Fall of the Sultanate*, 287–89.

171. Cf. H. Kieser et al., *Revolution islamischen Rechts*.

172. Orhan Seyfi of the daily *Tasvir-i Efkâr* of 18 February 1943, and Yunus N. Abalıoğlu quoted and summarized in Robert W. Olson, "The Remains of Talat: A Dialectic between Republic and Empire," *Die Welt des Islams* 26 (1986): 47–49; Jäckh, *Rising Crescent*, 8, 95.

173. In this context, to defend him and his legacy, a "Talat Pasha Committee" was founded in the early twenty-first century by Doğu Perinçek, the leader of a minuscule party connected with Turkey's deep state since the 1980s, and Rauf Denktash, former president of Northern Cyprus. At odds with Perinçek in the first years of its rule, the AKP regime of the 2010s largely endorsed him and his position. "'Talat Pasha Organization' to Protest against Recognition of 'Armenian Genocide' in Germany," *Today.az*, 16 February 2006; "Talat Pasha Committee Holds Genocide Conference," *Hurriyet Daily News*, 16 April 2007; Alan Cassidy, "Dogu Perinçeks sonderbare Welt," *Tages-Anzeiger*, 3 January 2017.

174. Cf. Kieser, *Nearest East*, 124–30.

175. *Talat Paşa'nın hatıraları*, ed. Yalçın and Bolayır, 5–8.

176. Jäckh, *Rising Crescent*, 8, 96, 270.

Epilogue

1. Semih Idiz, "Turks Have Mixed Emotions about This Anniversary," *Turkish Daily News*, 18 July 2017.

BIBLIOGRAPHY

Archives

Başbakanlık Osmanlı Arşivi, Istanbul (BOA, Ottoman State Archives)

Central Zionist Archives, Jerusalem (CZA)

Deutsche Bank, Historical Archive, Oriental Affairs, Frankfurt

Foreign Office Archives, London (FO)

Genelkurmay Askerî Tarih ve Stratejik Etüt Arşivi, Ankara (ATASE, Military Archive)

Musée du Vieux Montreux, Montreux, diary of Louis Rambert

Österreichisches Staatsarchiv, Vienna (Austrian State Archives)

Politisches Archiv des Auswärtigen Amtes, Berlin (PA-AA, Political Archive of the Foreign Office)

SALT Research, Istanbul (http://saltresearch.org)

Somerset Heritage Center, Aubrey Herbert Papers

Türk Tarih Kurumu, Ankara, Ismail Enver Pasha Papers (TTK; Turkish Historical Society)

Yale University Library, Ernst Jäckh Papers

Published Source Collections

Armenians in Ottoman Documents (1915–1920). Ed. Directorate of Ottoman Archives. Ankara, 1995.

Arşiv belgeleriyle Ermeni faaliyetleri 1914–1918. Ed. T. C. Genelkurmay Başkanlığı. Ankara: Genelkurmay Basım Evi, 2005–8.

Der interfraktionelle Ausschuss 1917/18. 2 vols. Ed. Erich Matthias. Düsseldorf: Droste, 1959.

Der Völkermord an den Armeniern 1915/16: Dokumente aus dem Politischen Archiv des deutschen Auswärtigen Amts. Ed. Wolfgang Gust. Springe: Zu Klampen, 2005.

Die grosse Politik der europäischen Kabinette 1871–1914: Sammlung der Diplomatischen Akten des Auswärtigen Amtes. Ed. Johannes Lepsius, Albrecht Mendelssohn

Bartholdy, and Friedrich Thimme. Berlin: Deutsche Verlagsgesellschaft für Politik und Geschichte, 1922–27.

Die internationalen Beziehungen im Zeitalter des Imperialismus: Dokumente aus den Archiven der Zarischen und der Provisorischen Regierung. 11 vols. Ed. Otto Hoetzsch. Berlin: Hobbing, 1931–43.

Documents diplomatiques Français, 1914–16. 5 vols. Ed. Jean-Claude Montant. Bern: Peter Lang, 2002–17.

Dokumente zur Geschichte des deutschen Zionismus 1882–1933. Ed. Jehuda Reinharz. Tübingen: Mohr Siebeck, 1981.

Emigrations turques des Balkans. Vol. 1: *Un exode turc.* Ed. Bilal Şimsir. Ankara: Türk Kültürünü Araştırma Enstitüsü, 1968.

Frederic von Rosenberg: Korrespondenzen und Akten des deutschen Diplomaten und Aussenministers 1913–1937. Ed. Winfried Becker. München: R. Oldenbourg, 2011.

İttihadçı'nın sandığı. Ed. Murat Bardakçı. Istanbul: Türkiye İş Bankası, 2014.

Les grandes puissances, l'Empire ottoman et les Arméniens dans les archives françaises (1914–1918): Recuil de documents. Ed. Arthur Beylerian. Paris: Publications de la Sorbonne, 1983.

Materials for the History of the ARF [in Armenian]. Vols. 6–9. Beirut: Hamazkayin Press, 2010–11.

Meclis-i Mebusan Zabıt Ceridesi (MMCZ). 7 vols. Ankara: Türkiye Büyük Millet Meclisi, 1982–92.

Talat Paşa'nın Evrak-ı Metrûkesi. Ed. Murat Bardakçı. Istanbul: Everest, 2008.

The Armenian Genocide [in Austrian archives]. Munich: Institut für armenische Fragen, 1988.

Memoirs, Ego-Documents, Memorial Texts

Ahmed İzzet (Furgaç). *Feryadım.* 2 vols. Istanbul: Timaş, 2017.

Ali Münif. *Ali Münif Bey'in hâtıraları.* Ed. Tahat Toros. Istanbul: Isis, 1996.

Apak, Rahmi. *Yetmişlik bir subayın hatıraları.* Ankara: TTK, 1988.

Atatürk, Kemal. *Gazi Mustafa Kemal Atatürk, Atatürk'ün Söylev ve Demeçleri.* 2 vols. Ankara: Atatürk Kültür Dil ve Tarih Yüksek Kurumu.

———. *Nutuk: Vesikalar.* Ankara: Atatürk Kültür, Dil ve Tarih Kurumu, 1991.

Atay, Falih Rıfkı. *Çankaya.* Istanbul: Pozitif, n.d.

———. *Mustafa Kemal'in ağzından Vahdettin.* Istanbul: Pozitif, 2013.

———. *Zeytindağ.* Istanbul: Bates, 1981.

Balakian, Grigoris. *Armenian Golgotha: A Memoir of the Armenian Genocide, 1915–1918.* New York: Vintage Books, 2009.

Ballobar, Conde de. *Jerusalem in World War I: The Palestine Diary of a European Diplomat*, ed. Eduardo Manzano and Moreno and Roberto Mazza. London: I. B. Tauris, 2011.

Bayar, Celâl, *Ben de yazdım: Millî mücadeleye giriş*. 8 vols. Istanbul: Sabah kitapları, 1997.

Bernstorff, Johann H. *Erinnerungen und Briefe*. Zürich: Polygraphischer Verlag, 1936.

Bleda, Mithat Şükrü. *İmparatorluğun Çöküşü*. Istanbul: Remzi, 1979.

Cemal (Djemal) Pasha. *Erinnerungen eines türkischen Staatsmannes*. München: Drei Masken Verlag, 1922.

Dersimi, Nuri. *Hatıratım*. Stockholm: Roja Nû, 1986.

———. *Kürdistan tarihinde Dersim*. Aleppo: Ani Matbaası, 1952.

Der Yeghiayan, Zaven. *My Patriarchal Memoirs*. Barrington: Mayreni, 2002.

Einstein, Lewis. *Inside Constantinople: A Diplomat's Diary during the Dardanelles Expedition*. Ed. Ara Sarafian. London: Gomidas, 2014.

Elkus, Abram I. *The Memoirs of Abram Elkus, Lawyer, Ambassador, Statesman*. London: Gomidas, 2004.

Emmanuilidis, Emmanuil. *Osmanlı İmparatorluğu'nun son yılları*. Istanbul: Belge, 2014.

Faiz al-Huseyin. *Martyred Armenia*. Trans. from Arabic. New York: George H. Doran, 1918.

Filmer, Cemil. *Hatıralar: Türk Sinemasında 65 yıl*. Istanbul: Emek, 1984.

Graves, Robert. *Storm Centers of the Near East: Personal Memories, 1879–1929*. London: Hutchison, 1933.

Hafız Hakkı. *Hafız Hakkı'nın Sarıkamış günlüğü*. Ed. Murat Bardakçı. Istanbul: Türkiye İş Bankası, 2014.

Hayri, Mustafa. *Şeyhülislam Ürgüplü Mustafa Hayri Efendi'nin Mesrutiyet, Büyük Harp ve Mütareke günlükleri (1909–1922)*. Ed. Ali Suat Ürgüplü. Istanbul: Türkiye İş Bankası, 2015 (referred to as the Hayri diary).

İbrahim Temo. *İttihad ve Terakki Cemiyeti'nin kurucusu ve 1/1 no'lu İbrahim Temo'nun İttihad ve Terakki Anıları*. Istanbul: Arba, 1987.

Ionescu, Take. *Souvenirs*. Paris: Payot, 1919.

Kadri, Hüseyin Kazım. *Meşrutiyet'ten cumhuriyet'e hatıralarım*. Istanbul: İletişim, 1991.

Kalmykow, Andrew D. *Memoirs of a Russian Diplomat: Outposts of the Empire, 1893–1917*. New Haven: Yale University Press, 1971.

Kapancızâde Hamit. *Bir Milli Mücadele valisi ve anıları: Kapancızâde Hamit Bey*. Ed. Halit Eken. Istanbul: Yeditepe, 2008.

Karabekir, Kâzım. *İstiklâl harbimizde Enver Paşa ve İttihat ve Terakki Erkânı*. Istanbul: YKY, 2010.

———. *İttihat ve Terakki Cemiyeti*. Istanbul: YKY, 2014.

Künzler, Jakob. *In the Land of Blood and Tears: Experiences in Mesopotamia during the World War, 1914–1918*. Arlington, VA: Armenian Cultural Foundation, 2007.

Kut, Halil. *Kutül-Amare kahramanları: Halil Kut Paşa'nın hatıraları*. Istanbul: Timaş, 2015.

Lemkin, Raphael. *Totally Unofficial: The Autobiography of Raphael Lemkin*. Ed. Donna-Lee Frieze. New Haven: Yale University Press, 2013.

Lütfi Fikri. *Dersim Mebusu Lütfi Fikri Bey'in Günlüğü*. Istanbul: Arma, 1991.

Lütfi Simavi. *Son Osmanlı sarayında gördüklerim*. Istanbul: Örgün, 2004.

Mahari, Gurgen. *Burning Orchards*. Cambridge, UK: Black Apollo Press, 2007.

Mehmed Cavid Bey. *Meşrutiyet Rûznamesi*. Vols. 1–4. Ankara: TTK, 2014–15.

Menteşe, Halil. *Osmanlı Mebusan Meclisi Reisi Halil Menteşe'nin anıları*. Istanbul: Hürriyet Vakfı, 1986.

Meyrier, Gustave. *Les massacres de Diarbekir: Correspondance diplomatique du Vice-consul de France 1894–1896*. Paris: Edition l'inventaire, 2000.

Mîzancı Murad. *Mîzancı Murad Bey'in II: Meşrutiyet dönemi hâtıraları*. Istanbul: Marifet, 1977.

Morgenthau, Henry. *United States Diplomacy on the Bosphorus: The Diaries of Ambassador Morgenthau, 1913–1916*. Ed. Ara Sarafian. Princeton, NJ: Gomidas Institute, 2004 (referred to as the Morgenthau diary).

Nogales, Rafael de. *Vier Jahre unter dem Halbmond: Erinnerungen aus dem Weltkriege*. Berlin: Reimar Hobbing, 1925.

Pekmen, Mahir S. *31 Mart hatıraları: İsyan günlerinde bir muhalif*. Ankara: TTK, 2011.

Pomiankowski, Joseph. *Der Zusammenbruch des Ottomanischen Reiches: Erinnerungen an die Türkei aus der Zeit des Weltkrieges*. Zürich: Amalthea-Verlag, 1927.

Rey, Ahmet Reşit. *Gördüklerim-Yaptıklarım*. Istanbul: Türkiye Yay., 1945.

Ruppin, Arthur. *Arthur Ruppin: Memoirs, Diaries, Letters*. Ed. Alex Bein. New York: Herzl Press, 1972.

Sâbis, Ali İhsan. *Harb hatıralarım*. Vols. 1, 2, and 5. Istanbul: Tan matbaası, 1943.

Şahingiray, Mehmed Reşid. *Hayatı ve Hâtıraları*. Ed. by N. Bilgi. İzmir: Akademi Kitabevi, 1997.

Sanders, Liman von. *Five Years in Turkey*. Annapolis: United States Naval Institute, 1927.

Sazonov, Sergej D. *Fateful Years, 1909–1916: The Reminiscences of Serge Sazonov*. London: Jonathan Cape, 1927.

Sciaky, Leon. *Farewell to Salonica: City at the Crossroads*. Philadelphia: Paul Dry Books, 2003.

Shiragian, Arshavir. *The Legacy: Memoirs of an Armenian Patriot*. Boston: Hairenik, 1976.

Talat Paşa. *Hatıralarım ve müdafaam*. Ed. Atatürk'ün Bütün Eserleri çalışma grubu. Istanbul: Kaynak, 2008.

————. *Talat Paşa'nın hatıraları*. Ed. Hüseyin Cahid Yalçın and Enver Bolayır. Istanbul: Güven, 1946.

Türkgeldi, Ali F. *Görüp işittiklerim*. Ankara: TTK, 2010.

Yalçın, Hüseyin Cahid. *Siyasal anılar*. Istanbul: Türkiye İş Bankası, 2000.

Yalman, Ahmed E. *Yakın tarihte gördüklerim ve geçirdiklerim*. Istanbul: Yenilik Basımevi, 1970.

Selection of Studies (and Some Other Works, including Online Publications and Unpublished Doctoral Theses)

Adak, Hülya. "Identifying the 'Internal Tumors' of World War I: *Talat Paşa'nın Hatıraları*, or the Travel of a Unionist Apologia into 'History.'" In *Räume des Selbst: Selbstzeugnisforschung transkulturell*, ed. Andreas Bähr et al., 151–69. Wien: Böhlau, 2007.

————. "National Myths and Self-Na(rra)tions: Mustafa Kemal's *Nutuk* and Halide Edib's *Memoirs* and *The Turkish Ordeal*." *South Atlantic Quarterly* 102, no. 2/3 (2003): 509–27.

Adatepe, Sabine. "'Das osmanische Muster': Das frühe Ideal des M. Ziya (Gökalp) anhand ausgewählter Artikel in der Wochenschrift Peyman." In *Strukturelle Zwänge–persönliche Freiheiten: Osmanen, Türken, Muslime; Reflexionen zu gesellschaftlichen Umbrüchen: Gedenkband zu Ehren Petra Kapperts*, ed. Hendrik Fenz. Berlin: Walter de Gruyter, 2009.

Ahmad, Feroz. *The Young Turks: The Committee of Union and Progress in Turkish Politics, 1908–1914*. London: Hurst, 2010.

Ahmad, Kemal M. *Birinci dünya savaşı yıllarında Kürdistan*. Ankara: Berhem, 1992.

Akçam, Taner. *The Young Turks' Crime against Humanity: The Armenian Genocide and Ethnic Cleansing in the Ottoman Empire*. Princeton, NJ: Princeton University Press, 2012.

Akçam, Taner, and Ümit Kurt. *The Spirit of the Laws: The Plunder of Wealth in the Armenian Genocide*. Trans. Aram Arkun. New York: Berghahn, 2015 (translation of *Kanunların ruhu: Emval-i metruke kanunlarında soykırımın izini sürmek*. Istanbul: İletişim, 2012).

Aksakal, Mustafa. *The Ottoman Road to War in 1914*. New York: Cambridge University Press, 2008.

Aktar, Cengiz. *Ademimerkeziyet elkitabi*. Istanbul: Iletisim, 2014.

Allen, William E. D., and Paul Muratoff. *Caucasian Battlefields: A History of the Wars on the Turco-Caucasian Border, 1828–1921*. New York: Cambridge University Press, 2011.

Altınay, Ahmed Refik. *İki komite, iki kital*. Ankara: Kebikeç, 1994.

Anastassiadou, Meropi. *Salonique, 1830–1912: Une ville ottomane à l'âge des Réformes*. Leiden: E. J. Brill, 1997.

Anderson, Matthew S. *The Eastern Question, 1774–1923*. New York: St. Martin's Press, 1966.

Arkun, Aram. "Zeytun and the Commencement of the Armenian Genocide." In *A Question of Genocide: Armenians and Turks at the End of the Ottoman Empire*. Ed. Ronald G. Suny, Fatma M. Göçek, and Norman M. Naimark, 231–36. New York: Oxford University Press, 2011.

Artuç, Nevzat. *Cemal Paşa: Askeri ve siyasi hayatı*. Ankara: TTK, 2008.

Auron, Yair. *The Banality of Indifference: Zionism and the Armenian Genocide*. New Brunswick: Transaction, 2000.

Ayışığı, Metin. *Mareşal Ahmed İzzet Paşa: Askerî ve siyasî hayatı*. Ankara: TTK, 1997.

Babacan, Hasan. *Mehmed Talât Paşa, 1874–1921: Siyasi hayatı ve icraatı*. Ankara: TTK, 2005.

Baer, Marc D. *Jewish Converts, Muslim Revolutionaries, and Secular Turkish Jewish Converts*. Stanford, CA: Stanford University Press, 2010.

Bahaeddin Şakir. *Bahaeddin Şakir Bey'in bıraktığı vesikalara göre İttihat ve Terakki*. Ankara: Alternatif 2001.

Bali, Rifat N. *Devlet'in örnek yurttaşları (1950–2003)*. Istanbul: Kitabevi, 2009.

Bayur, Yusuf H. *Türk inkılâbı tarihi*. Vols. 1–3. Ankara: TTK, 1991.

Benbassa, Esther, and Aron Rodrigue. *Sephardi Jewry: A History of the Judeo-Spanish Community, 14th–20th Centuries*. Berkeley: University of California Press, 2000.

Ben-Bassat, Yuval. "Palestine's Population and the Question of Ottomanism during the Last Decade of Ottoman Rule." In *World War I and the End of the Ottomans*, ed. Hans-Lukas Kieser, Kerem Oktem, and Maurus Reinkowski, 149–65. London: I. B. Taurus, 2015.

Ben-Bassat, Yuval, and Eyal Ginio, eds. *Late Ottoman Palestine: The Period of Young Turk Rule*. London: I. B. Tauris, 2011.

Ben-Gavriêl, Moshe Y. *Jerusalem wird verkauft*. Ed. Sebastian Schirrmeister. Wuppertal: Arco, 2016.

Berhe, Simona. "Il fronte meridionale della Grande guerra: la Libia come teatro del primo conflitto mondiale." *Nuova rivista storica* 101, no. 3 (2017): 797–828.

Berkes, Niyazi. *Turkish Nationalism and Western Civilization: Selected Essays of Ziya Gökalp*. New York: Praeger, 1959.

Beşikçi, Mehmet. *The Ottoman Mobilization of Manpower in the First World War: Between Voluntarism and Resistance*. Leiden: Brill, 2012.

Birgen, Muhittin. *İttihat ve Terakki'de on sene: İttihat ve Terakki neydi?* 2 vols. Istanbul: Kitapyayınevi, 2006.

Birinci, Ali. *Hürriyet ve İtilâf Fırkası: II, Meşrutiyet döneminde İttihat ve Terakki'ye karşı çıkanlar*. Istanbul: Dergah, 1990.

Bjørnlund, Matthias. "'When the Cannons Talk, the Diplomats Must Be Silent': A Danish Diplomat in Constantinople during the Armenian Genocide." *Genocide Studies and Prevention* 1–2 (September 2006): 197–224.

Bozarslan, Hamit. *Histoire de la Turquie: De l'Empire à nos jours.* Paris: Tallandier, 2013.

———. "Le Prince Sabahaddin (1879–1948)." *Schweizerische Zeitschrift für Geschichte* 52, no. 3 (2002): 287–301.

———. *Violence in the Middle East: From Political Struggle to Self-Sacrifice.* Princeton, NJ: Markus Wiener, 2004.

Bozkurt, Serhat. *Bir toplumsal mühendislik kurumu olarak "Aşâir ve Muhâcirîn Müdîriyyet-i Umûmiyyesi."* Thesis of Yüksek Lizans. Istanbul: Mimar Sinan Üniversitesi, 2013.

Çandar, Tevfik. *Talat Paşa: Bir örgüt ustasının yaşamöyküsü.* Istanbul: Imge, 2001.

Cemil, Arif. *I. Dünya Savaşı'nda Teşkilât-ı Mahsusa.* Istanbul: Arba, 1997.

Çetinkaya, Doğan. *The Young Turks and the Boycott Movement: Nationalism, Protest and the Working Classes in the Formation of Modern Turkey.* London: I. B. Tauris, 2014.

Çiçek, M. Talha, ed. *Syria in World War I: Politics, Economy, and Society.* New York: Routledge, 2016.

———. *War and State Formation in Syria: Cemal Pasha's Governorate during World War I, 1914–1917.* Oxon: Routledge, 2014.

Clark, Christopher. *The Sleepwalkers: How Europe Went to War in 1914.* London: Penguin, 2012.

Clayer, Nathalie. *Aux origines du nationalisme albanais: La naissance d'une nation musulmane en Europe.* Paris: Karthala, 2007.

Cohen, Julia P., and Sarah A. Stein. *Sephardi Lives: A Documentary History.* Stanford, CA: Stanford University Press, 2014.

Dadrian, Vahakn, and Taner Akçam. *Judgment at Istanbul: The Armenian Genocide Trials.* New York: Berghahn, 2011.

Dalby, Andrew. *Eleftherios Venizelos: Greece.* London: Haus, 2010.

Denker, Arif Cemil. *İttihatçı şeflerin gurbet maceraları.* Istanbul: Arma, 1992.

Deringil, Selim. *The Well-Protected Domains: Ideology and the Legitimation of Power in the Ottoman Empire, 1876–1909.* London: I. B. Tauris, 1998.

Der Matossian, Bedross. *Shattered Dreams of Revolution: From Liberty to Violence in the Late Ottoman Empire.* Stanford, CA: Stanford University Press, 2014.

Dowe, Christopher, ed. *Matthias Erzberger: Ein Demokrat in Zeiten des Hasses.* Karlsruhe: G. Braun, 2013.

Dressler, Markus. *Writing Religion: The Making of Turkish Alevi İslam.* New York: Oxford University Press, 2013.

Dündar, Fuat. *İttihat ve Terakki Müslümanları iskân politikası (1913–1918).* Istanbul: İletişim, 2001.

————. *Modern Türkiye'nin Şifresi: İttihat ve Terakki'nin etnisite ve mühendisliği (1913–1918)*. Istanbul: İletişim, 2008.

Duran, Tülay. "Dünya Savaşı sonunda Türk diplomasinin ilk başarısı: Brest-Litovsk harzırlıkları." *Belgelerle Türk Tarih Dergisi* 12, no. 67–68, 43–49; no. 69, 22–26; no. 70, 31–34 (1973).

Efiloğlu, Ahmet. *İttihat ve Terakki azınlıklar politikası*. Doctoral dissertation, University of Istanbul, 2007.

Erickson, Edward J. *Ottomans and Armenians: A Study in Counterinsurgency*. New York: Palgrave Macmillan, 2013.

Esatlı, Mustafa Ragıp. *İttihat ve Terakki tarihinde esrar perdesi*. Istanbul: Hürriyet, 1975.

————. *Meşrutiyet'ten önce Manastır'da patlayan tabanca*. Istanbul: Bengi, 2007.

Finkel, Caroline. *Osman's Dream: The Story of the Ottoman Empire, 1300–1923*. New York: Basic Books, 2005.

Fischer, August. *Aus der religiösen Reformbewegung in der Türkei: Türkische Stimmen verdeutscht*. Leipzig: Harrassowitz, 1922.

Friedman, Isaiah. *Germany, Turkey, and Zionism, 1897–1918*. New Brunswick: Transaction, 1998.

Gaunt, David. *Massacres, Resistance, Protectors: Muslim-Christian Relations in Eastern Anatolia during World War I*. Piscataway, NJ: Gorgias Press, 2006.

Gençer, Mustafa. *Bildungspolitik, Modernisierung und kulturelle Interaktion: Deutsch-türkische Beziehungen (1908–1918)*. Münster: Lit, 2002.

Georgeon, François. *Abdulhamid II: Le sultan calife*. Paris: Fayard, 2003.

Gerçek, Burçin. *Akıntıya Karşı: Ermeni Soykırımında Emirlere Karşı Gelenler, Kurtaranlar, Direnenler*. Istanbul: İletişim Yayınları, 2016.

————. *Report on Turks Who Reached-Out to Armenians in 1915*. International Raoul Wallenberg Foundation, published online 2015. http://www.raoulwallenberg.net/wp-content/files_mf/1435335304ReportTurkishrescuerscomplete.pdf.

Gingeras, Ryan. *Fall of the Sultanate: The Great War and the End of the Ottoman Empire, 1908–1922*. Oxford: Oxford University Press, 2016.

————. *Sorrowful Shores: Violence, Ethnicity, and the End of the Ottoman Empire, 1912–1923*. Oxford: Oxford University Press, 2009.

Ginio, Eyal. *The Ottoman Culture of Defeat: The Balkan Wars and Their Aftermath*. London: Hurst, 2016.

Göçek, Fatma M. *Denial of Violence: Ottoman Past, Turkish Present, and Collective Violence against the Armenians, 1789–2009*. New York: Oxford University Press, 2015.

Gökalp, Ziya. *Türkçülüğün esasları*. Ed. Salim Çonoğlu. Istanbul: Ötüken, 2014.

Gottschlich, Jürgen. *Beihilfe zum Völkermord: Deutschlands Rolle bei der Vernichtung der Armenier*. Berlin: Ch. Links Verlag, 2015.

Grassi, Fabio L. *İtalya ve Türk sorunu 1919–1923: Kamuoyu ve dış politika*. Istanbul: YKY, 2003.

Gürzumar, Osman B. "Die Übernahme westlichen Rechts in der Türkei vor 1926." In *Revolution islamischen Rechts: Das Schweizerische ZGB in der Türkei*, ed. H. Kieser, A. Meier, and W. Stoffel, 35–47. Zürich: Chronos, 2008.

Hale, William. *Turkish Foreign Policy since 1774*. London: Routledge, 2013.

Hanioğlu, M. Şükrü. *Atatürk: An Intellectual Biography*. Princeton, NJ: Princeton University Press, 2011.

———. *Brief History of the Late Ottoman Empire*. Princeton, NJ: Princeton University Press, 2008.

———. *Preparation for a Revolution: The Young Turks, 1902–1908*. New York: Oxford University Press, 2001.

———. *The Young Turks in Opposition*. New York: Oxford University Press, 1995.

Hartmann, Elke. *Die Reichweite des Staates: Wehrpflicht und moderne Staatlichkeit im Osmanischen Reich 1869–1910*. Paderborn: Ferdinand Schöningh, 2016.

Helfferich, Karl. *Die deutsche Türkenpolitik*. Berlin: Vossische Buchhandlung, 1921.

———. *Harb-i Umûmî'nin menseileri*. Istanbul: Fratelli Hayim Matbaası, 1915. Ottoman translation by Reşid Safvet [Atabinen] of *Die Entstehung des Weltkriegs im Lichte der Veröffentlichungen der Dreiverbandmächte*. Berlin: Georg Stilke, 1915.

Heyd, Uriel. *Foundations of Turkish Nationalism: The Life and Teachings of Ziya Gökalp*. London: Harvill, 1950.

Hobsbawm, Eric. *Age of Extremes: The Short Twentieth Century, 1914–1991*. London: Michael Joseph, 1995.

Hosfeld, Rolf. ed. *Johannes Lepsius-Eine deutsche Ausnahme: Der Völkermord an den Armeniern, Humanitarismus und Menschenrechte*. Göttingen: Wallstein, 2013.

———. *Operation Nemesis: Die Türkei, Deutschland und der Völkermord an den Armeniern*. Köln: Kiepenheuer & Witsch, 2005.

Hosfeld, Rolf, and Christin Pschichholz, eds. *Das Deutsche Reich und der Völkermord an den Armeniern*. Göttingen: Wallstein, 2017.

Hovannisian, Richard G. *Armenia on the Road to Independence, 1918*. Berkeley: University of California Press, 1967.

Ihrig, Stefan. *Atatürk in the Nazi Imagination*. Cambridge, MA: Harvard University Press, 2014.

———. *Justifying Genocide: Germany and the Armenians from Bismarck to Hitler*. Cambridge, MA: Harvard University Press, 2016.

İlkin, Selim, and İlhan Tekeli. "Kurtuluş Savaşı'nda Talât Paşa ile Mustafa Kemâl'in Mektuplaşmaları." *Belleten* 44 (April 1980): 301–45.

Jäckh, Ernst. *Rising Crescent: Turkey Yesterday, Today, and Tomorrow*. New York: Farrar & Rinehart, 1944.

Jäschke, Gotthard. "Der Weg zur russisch-türkischen Freundschaft." *Die Welt des Islams* 16 (1934): 23–38.

Jongerden, Joost, and Jelle Verheij. *Social Relations in Ottoman Diyarbekir, 1870–1915.* Leiden: Brill, 2012.

Kaiser, Hilmar. *At the Crossroads of Der Zor: Death, Survival, and Humanitarian Resistance in Aleppo, 1915–1917.* Princeton, NJ: Gomidas Institute, 2002.

———. *The Extermination of Armenians in the Diarbekir Region.* Istanbul: Bilgi University, 2014.

———. "Shukru Bey and the Armenian Deportations in the Fall of 1915." In *Syria in World War I,* ed. M. Talha Çiçek, 169–236.

Kaligian, Dikran. *Armenian Organization and Ideology under Ottoman Rule, 1908–1914.* New Brunswick: Transaction, 2012.

Kasaba, Reşat. *The Cambridge History of Turkey.* Vol. 4. Cambridge: Cambridge University Press, 2008.

Kayali, Hasan. *Arabs and Young Turks: Ottomanism, Arabism, and Islamism in the Ottoman Empire, 1908–1918.* Berkeley: University of California Press, 1997.

Kaynar, Erdal. *Ahmed Rıza (1858–1930): Histoire d'un vieux Jeune Turc.* Doctoral thesis. Paris: EHESS, 2011.

Kechriotis, Vangelis. "On the Margins of National Historiography: The Greek *İttihatçi* Emmanouil Emmanouilidis—Opportunist or Ottoman Patriot?" In *Untold Histories of the Middle East: Recovering Voices from the 19th and 20th Centuries,* ed. Amy Singer, Christoph Neumann, and Selçuk A. Somel, 124–42. London: Routledge, 2011.

Kedourie, Elie. "Young Turks, Freemasons and Jews." *Middle Eastern Studies* 7, no. 1 (Jan. 1971): 89–104.

Kellogg, Michael. *The Russian Roots of Nazism: White Émigrés and the Making of National Socialism, 1917–1945.* Cambridge: Cambridge University Press, 2005.

Kévorkian, Raymond. *The Armenian Genocide: A Complete History.* London: I. B. Tauris, 2011.

———. *L'extermination des déportés arméniens ottomans dans les camps de concentration de Syrie-Mésopotamie (1915–1916): La deuxième phase du génocide.* Paris: Bibliothèque Nubar, 1998.

Kieser, Hans-Lukas. *Iskalanmış Barış: Doğu vilayetlerinde misyonerlik, etnik kimlik ve devlet 1839–1938.* Istanbul: İletişim, 2013. Revised and enlarged translation of *Der verpasste Friede: Mission, Ethnie und Staat in den Ostprovinzen der Türkei.* Zurich: Chronos, 2000.

Kieser, Hans-Lukas. *Nearest East: American Millennialism and Mission to the Middle East.* Philadelphia: Temple University Press, 2010.

———. *Türklüğe İhtida: 1870–1939 İsviçre'sinde Yeni Türkiye'nin öncüleri.* Istanbul: İletişim, 2008. Revised translation of *Vorkämpfer der "Neuen Türkei": Revolutionäre Bildungseliten am Genfersee.* Zürich: Chronos, 2005.

Kieser, Hans- Lukas, and Dominik J. Schaller, eds. *Der Völkermord an den Armeniern und die Shoah*. Zürich: Chronos, 2002.

Kieser, Hans-Lukas, Mehmet Polatel, and Thomas Schmutz. "Reform or Cataclysm? The Agreement of 8 February 1914 regarding the Ottoman Eastern Provinces." *Journal of Genocide Research* 17, no. 3 (2015): 285–304.

Kieser, Hans-Lukas, Kerem Öktem, and Maurus Reinkowski, eds. *World War I and the End of the Ottomans: From the Balkan Wars to the Armenian Genocide*. London: I. B. Tauris, 2015.

Koptaş, Rober. "Zohrab, Papazyan ve Pastırmaycıyan'ın kalemlerinden 1914 Ermeni reformu ve İttihatçı-Taşnak müzakeleri." *Tarih ve Toplum Yeni Yaklaşımlar* 5 (Spring 2007): 159–78.

Köroğlu, Erol. *Ottoman Propaganda and Turkish Identity: Literature in Turkey during World War I*. London: I. B. Tauris, 2007.

Kreiser, Klaus. *Atatürk: Eine Biographie*. München: C. H. Beck, 2014.

Kühn, Thomas. *Empire, Islam, and Politics of Difference: Ottoman Rule in Yemen, 1849–1919*. Leiden: Brill, 2011.

Kuran, Ahmet B. *İnkılap tarihimiz ve Jön Türkler*. Istanbul: Kaynak, 2000.

Kurt, Ümit. *Destruction of Aintab Armenians and Emergence of the New Wealthy Class: Plunder of Armenian Wealth in Aintab*. Doctoral thesis. Worcester: Clark University, 2016.

Ladas, Stephen. *The Exchange of Minorities: Bulgaria, Greece and Turkey*. New York: Macmillan, 1932.

Landau, Jacob M. *Tekinalp: Turkish Patriot*. Istanbul: Nederlands Historisch-Archaeologisch Instituut, 1984.

Levy, Avigdor. *Jews, Turks, Ottomans: A Shared History, Fifteenth through the Twentieth Century*. Syracuse: Syracuse University Press, 2002.

Lévy, Noémi. *Ordre et désordres dans l'Istanbul ottomane, 1879–1909: De l'état au quartier*. Paris: Karthala, 2013.

Mandel, N. J. *Turks, Arabs and Jewish Immigration into Palestine: 1882–1914*. Doctoral dissertation. Oxford: St. Antony's College, 1965.

Mandelstam, André N. *Le sort de l'Empire ottoman*. Lausanne: Payot, 1917.

Mango, Andrew. *Atatürk*. London: John Murray, 1999.

Mangold-Will, Sabine. *Begrenzte Freundschaft: Deutschland und die Türkei 1918–1933*. Göttingen: Wallstein, 2013.

McKeekin, Sean. *The Ottoman Endgame: War, Revolution, and the Making of the Modern Middler East, 1908–1923*. New York: Penguin Press, 2015.

Meissner, Axel. *Martin Rades "Christliche Welt" und Armenien*. Münster: Lit, 2010.

Miller, Robert. *Sasun 1894: Mountains, Missionaries and Massacres at the End of the Ottoman Empire*. PhD thesis. Columbia University, New York, 2015.

Moreau, Odile. *La Turquie dans la Grande Guerre*. Saint-Cloud: SOTECA.

Mouradian, Khatchig. *Genocide and Humanitarian Assistance in Ottoman Syria, 1915–1917*. Doctoral thesis. Worcester: Clark University, 2016.

Mühlmann, Carl. *Deutschland und die Türkei 1913–1914*. Berlin: Walther Rothschild, 1929.

Nebelin, Manfred. *Ludendorff: Diktator im Ersten Weltkrieg*. München: Siedler, 2010.

Nossig, Alfred. *Die neue Türkei und ihre Führer*. Halle: Otto Hendel, 1916.

Philliou, Christine M. *Biography of an Empire: Governing Ottomans in an Age of Revolution*. Berkeley: University of California Press, 2011.

Plozza. Elmar. *Zwischen Berlin und Konstantinopel: Die diplomatischen Aktivitäten Alfred Nossigs für das zionistische Projekt*. Unpublished. Lizentiatsarbeit: University of Zurich, 2004.

Polatel, Mehmet, and Uğur Üngör. *Confiscation and Destruction: The Young Turk Seizure of Armenian Property*. London: Bloomsbury, 2013.

Rabinowicz, Oskar K. *Vladimir Jabotinsky's Conception of a Nation*. New York: Beechhurst Press, 1946.

Reindl-Kiel, Hedda, and Seyfi Kenan, eds. *Deutsch-türkische Begegnungen / Alman Türk tesadüfleri*. Berlin: EB-Verlag, 2013.

Reynolds, Michael. *Shattering Empires: The Clash and Collapse of the Ottoman and Russian Empires, 1908–1918*. Cambridge: Cambridge University Press, 2011.

Şapolyo, Enver B. *Ziya Gökalp: İttihat ve Terakki ve Meşrutiyet tarihi*. Istanbul: Güven, 1943.

Sartiaux, Félix. "Le sac de Phocée et l'expulsion des Grecs ottomans d'Asie Mineure en juillet 1914." *Revue des deux mondes* 84 (Nov.–Dec. 1914): 654–86.

Schaller, Dominik J., and Jürgen Zimmerer, eds. *The Origins of Genocide: Raphael Lemkin as a Historian of Mass Violence*. London: Routledge, 2009.

Schneer, Jonathan. *The Balfour Declaration: The Origins of the Arab-Israeli Conflict*. New York: Random House, 2012.

Schrader, Friedrich. *Eine Flüchtlingsreise durch die Ukraine: Tagebuchblätter von meiner Flucht aus Konstantinopel*. Tübingen: J.C.B. Mohr, 1919.

Sémelin, Jacques. *Purifier et détruire: Usages politiques des massacres et génocides*. Paris: Editions du Seuil, 2005.

Seyffarth, Kai. *Entscheidung in Aleppo: Walter Rössler (1871–1929); Helfer der vefolgten Armenier*. Bremen: Donat, 2015.

Şeyhun, Ahmet. *Islamist Thinkers in the Late Ottoman Empire and Early Turkish Republic*. Leiden: Brill, 2015.

Shaw, Stanford J. *The Jews of the Ottoman Empire and the Turkish Republic*. Basingstoke: Macmillan, 1991.

Sjöberg, Erik. *The Making of the Greek Genocide: Contested Memories of the Ottoman Greek Catastrophe*. New York: Berghahn, 2016.

Soku, Ziya Şakir. *Yakın tarihin üç büyük adamı: Talat, Enver, Cemal Paşalar.* Istanbul: Kaktüs, 2010.

Somel, Selçuk A. "Melekler, vatanperverler ve ajan provokatörler: Mutlakiyet devri Diyarbekir okul gençliği, bürokrasi ve Ziya Gökalp'in idadi öğrenciliğine ilişkin soruşturma kayıtları (1894–1895)." Sabancı University, 2014. http://research .sabanciuniv.edu/19474.

Stanislawski, Michael. *Zionism and the Fin de siècle: Cosmopolitanism and Nationalism from Nordau to Jabotinsky.* Berkeley: University of California Press, 2001.

Suny, Ronald G. *The Baku Commune, 1917–1918: Class and Nationality in the Russian Revolution.* Princeton, NJ: Princeton University Press, 1972.

Suny, Ronald G., Fatma M. Göcek, and Norman Naimark, eds. *A Question of Genocide: Armenians and Turks at the End of the Ottoman Empire.* New York: Oxford University Press, 2011.

Tekin Alp (Moiz Kohen Tekinalp). *Türkismus und Pantürkismus.* Weimar: G. Kiepenheuer, 1915.

Tetik, Ahmet. *Teşkilat-ı Mahsusa (Umûr-i Şarkıyye Dairesi) tarihi.* Istanbul: Türkiye İş Bankası, 2014.

Toprak, Zafer. *Türkiye'de ekonomi ve toplum (1908–1950): İttihat-Terakki ve devletçilik.* Istanbul: Tarih Vakfı, 1995.

———. *Türkiye'de milli iktisat 1908–1918.* Istanbul: Doğan, 2012.

Trumpener, Ulrich. *Germany and the Ottoman Empire, 1914–1918.* Princeton, NJ: Princeton University Press, 1968.

Türkiye Diyanet Vakfı İslam Ansiklopedisi. 44 vols. Islamic Arastirma Merkezi (ISAM), 1988–2013.

Türkmen, Zekeriya. *Vilayât-ı Şarkiye Islahat Müffettişliği.* Ankara: Türk Tarih Kurumu, 2006.

Ünal, Hasan. "Young Turk Assessment of International Politics, 1906–1909." *Middle Eastern Studies* 32 (1996): 30–44.

Üngör, Uğur Ü. *The Making of Modern Turkey: Nation and State in Eastern Anatolia, 1913–1950.* Oxford: Oxford University Press.

Uras, Esat. *Tarihte Ermeniler ve Ermeni Meselesi.* Ankara: Yeni Matbaa, 1950.

Uzer, Tahsin. *Makedonya eşkiyalık tarihi ve son Osmanlı yönetimi.* Ankara: TTK, 1999.

Varnaka, Andrekos. "French and British Post-War Imperial Agendas and Forging an Armenian Homeland after Genocide: The Formation of the Légion d'Orient in October 1916." *Historical Journal* 57, no. 4 (2014): 997–1025.

Wasti, Syed Tanvir. "Halil Menteşe—the Quadrumvir." *Middle Eastern Studies* 32, no. 3 (1996): 92–105.

Williamson, John G. *Karl Helfferich, 1872–1924: Economist, Financier, Politician.* Princeton, NJ: Princeton University Press, 1971.

Yalçın, Hüseyin Cahid. *İttihatçı liderlerin gizli mektupları*. Istanbul: Temel, 2002.

———. *Talât Paşa*. Istanbul: Yedigün, 1943.

Yanıkdağ, Yüksel. *Healing the Nation: Prisoners of War, Medicine and Nationalism in Turkey, 1914–1939*. Edinburgh: Edinburgh University Press, 2013.

Yeni Mecmua: Çanakkale özel sayısı 18 Mart 1918. Transcribed ed. Istanbul: Yeditepe Yay., 2006.

Yessayan, Zabel. *In the Ruins: The 1909 Massacres of Armenians in Adana, Turkey*. Watertown: AIWA, 2016.

Zohrap, Krikor. *Collected Works*. Ed. Albert Charourian. Yerevan, 2003; in Armenian.

Zürcher, Erik Jan, ed. *Jihad and Islam in World War I: Studies on the Ottoman Jihad on the Centenary Snouck Hurgronje's "Holy War Made in Germany."* Leiden: Leiden University Press, 2015.

———. *The Unionist Factor: The Role of the Committee of Union and Progress in the Turkish National Movement, 1905–1926*. Leiden: Brill, 1984.

———. "Young Turk Decision-Making Patterns." In Conseil scientifique pour l'étude du génocide des Arméniens, *Le génocide des Arméniens*, 15–32. Paris: Armand Colin, 2015.

———. *The Young Turk Legacy and Nation Building: From the Ottoman Empire to Ataturk's Turkey*. London: I. B. Tauris, 2010.

Zurlinden, Samuel, *Der Weltkrieg: Vorläufige Orientierung von einem schweizerischen Standpunkt aus*. 3 vols. Zürich: Orell Füssli, 1917–19.

INDEX

Muslim Ottomans, in general, did not have family names. They are in this index alphabetized by personal name: "Talaat," "Enver," "Cavid"; and, where more than one personal name were usual: "Ali Rıza," "Ziya Gökalp" (not "Rıza, Ali," "Gökalp, Ziya"). Little-used first personal names are given together with the frequent one in brackets, and generally used titles are added: "Talaat (Mehmed Talaat) Pasha." Those Muslim Ottomans who survived into the Republic of Turkey and adopted a family name by the mid-1930s, as required by the newly introduced Swiss Civil Code, are alphabetized by family name: "Atatürk, Mustafa Kemal," "Uzer, Hasan Tahsin." To facilitate identification, at times the index makes cross-references, mentions alternative spellings, and includes titles or functions.

Abalıoğlu, Yunus Nadi, 326, 412, 419

Abandoned Property (Emvali-i Metruke), 15, 248, 260, 269–72; abuses with 323–24; Commission for, 248, 271; laws on, 269, 271–72

Abdulahad Nuri, 266

Abdülhalik. *See* Renda

Abdulhamid II, Sultan, 3–4, 9, 14, 16, 35–55, 58–59, 71, 336, 417; anti-Armenian violence under, 95, 102–3, 200, 232–33, 250; in 1908, 61, 65, 68; in 1909, 71–74; biography of, 432n18; exile in Salonica, 74; friend of Germany, 14, 148, 151; funeral of, 336; state-centered Islamism of, 392; against Zionism, 84, 302

Abdülkadir, Sheik, 405

Abdülkerim, 345–47, 479n50

Abdullah Cevdet, 100, 104, 131, 407

Abdurrahman Nesib, 118

Abdurrezzak Bedirhan, 156, 224

Action Army (Hareket Ordusu), 73–74

Adana, 139; during World War I, 226–27, 273, 276; 1909 massacres in, 8, 64, 71–72, 76–79, 92, 106, 154; CUP branch in, 71

Adıvar, Halide Edib, 113

Adom (Harutyun Sharigian), 92, 97

Adrianople. *See* Edirne

Afghanistan, 296, 398, 401

Africa/Africans, 111, 172, 263, 351

Agayev/Ağaoğlu, Ahmed, 305–6, 308, 325–26

Ahmed Cemal Pasha. *See* Cemal

Ahmed İzzet Pasha, 83, 132, 137–38, 143, 149, 162–63, 170–71, 218, 442n51;

Ahmed İzzet Pasha (*continued*)
grand vizier, 379, 381–83; against
Kurdish removal, 260; criticism of
Machiavellian politics by, 83
Ahmed Muhtar. *See* Muhtar Pasha
Ahmed Niyazi. *See* Niyazi
Ahmed Refik. *See* Altınay
Ahmed Reşid. *See* Rey
Ahmed Rıza, 44, 46, 49, 59, 62, 68–70,
96, 343; president of the parliament,
68; speaking truth to power, 269,
272, 278
Ahmed Midhat, 68
Ahmed Tevfik Pasha, 71, 74, 379
Akçam, Taner, 431n15
Aknuni (Khachadour Malumian), 70
AKP (Justice and Development Party),
99, 416, 427, 488n173
Albania/Albanians, 50–51, 54–55, 63,
90, 146–47, 150, 163, 174, 450n99;
Albanist movement in, 82–83; mak-
ing of as an Islamic state, 140, 146;
insurrection in, 118; independence
of, 83, 131
Aleppo, 103, 396; during World War
I, 225–26, 234, 237, 242, 253, 259,
264–67, 272, 276, 467n162
Alevis/Alevism, 4, 19, 91, 154, 204, 224,
367; CUP approach to, 4; Kurdish
Alevis, 224, 256, 401. *See also* Dersim
Ali Cenani, 383, 412
Al-Fath (surah), 16
Ali Haydar Pasha, 274–75, 323
Ali Kemal, 308, 400, 406, 486
Ali Mazhar, 241–42, 390–91, 463n120
Ali Münif. *See* Yeğenağa
Ali Sâi (pseudonym). *See* Talaat Pasha
Ali Sabid, 247
Ali Suat, 263, 272
Alliance Israélite, School in Salonica, 42

Altınay, Ahmed Refik, 279–80
American missionaries, 238
Anatolia. *See* Asia Minor
Anatolian Railway, 14, 80, 88, 243, 280
Andonian, Aram, 467n162
Anglophilia: Kâmil Pasha's, 69; Sabahaddin's versus alleged CUP's, 59–60
Ankara, 204; counterparliament in
anticipated, 72; during World War I,
204, 241–42, 274–76; Kemalist government in, 392–93, 396, 400–403,
406–7, 409; military archives
(ATASE) in, 432n20; transition of
power from Istanbul to, 31, 68, 411–12
anti-imperialists/anti-imperialism, 29,
59, 317, 402
anti-Jewish discrimination, 95. *See also*
anti-Semitism
anti-liberal International, 396
anti-Semitism, 20, 40, 279, 283, 310, 351,
360, 368, 453n154; in parallel to anti-
(oriental-)Christian stance, 317; and
philo-Semitism, 351
Anzac, 312
Apak, Rahmi, 207
apologia. *See* Talaat, memoirs
Arab Congress (1913), 307
Arabs/Arabia, 75, 83, 112, 303, 306,
308–9, 328, 354, 356, 363, 376, 405;
deportation of, 298; against CUP,
231, 274, 297–98; unity or federation
of Turks and, 363, 392, 394, 401–2
Arabist movement, 297–98
Arda, Hacı Âdil, 45, 132, 133, 136
Ardahan, 40, 197, 208, 293, 317, 339, 363,
367, 398, 462n102
Ardanush, 208
Arendt, Hannah, 288
ARF. *See* Armenian Revolutionary
Federation

Arif Cemil. *See* Denker

Armen Garo (Karekin Pastermajian), 116, 178–79, 404

Armenia, 198, 202, 283, 309, 312; as a buffer, 346, 375; as a Bulgaria in the East, 366; denigration of, 399; to include parts of Eastern Asia Minor, 398; Ottoman, 159, 179; Republic of, 316, 363–64, 399

Armenian autonomy or independence, 7, 11–12, 79; CUP's specter of, 7, 226, 235–36, 293, 316, 328, 366; Entente statements on, 358, 365, 358; Bolsheviks and, 365

Armenian charity in Istanbul, 92

Armenian community (formed by Apostolic, Catholic and Protestant millet), 78, 234

Armenian conspiracy, theories of, 10, 19, 22, 103, 235–37, 301

Armenian deputies and ministers, 18–19, 73, 80, 94, 116, 122, 128

Armenian genocide. *See* genocide

Armenian goods. *See* Abandoned Property

Armenian Legion, 363

Armenian lobbying, 86–87

Armenian millet 105, 436n66; assembly of the, 152

Armenian Question, 8, 10, 12–16, 79, 99, 151–65, 195, 423; land question within the, *see* land question

Armenian Revolutionary Federation (ARF, Dashnaktsutiun), 3, 50, 59, 70, 72, 87, 92, 160–61, 236, 295, 399, 406–11; accord with CUP of, August 1909, 79; alliance with CUP, 3, 50, 295; alliance with Kurds, 224–25; ARF-CUP interparty commission (mixed council from 1910), 76, 97;

congress of, in Erzurum, 190–91, 198, 202; general assembly of, 1911, 97; junior partner of the 1908 revolution, 50–51, 58–59; end of alliance of with CUP, 122; in Van, 202

Armenians, 6–8, 11, 13–14, 19–23, 25, 28, 34, 50, 71–72, 79, 87, 91–92, 151–65, 180, 349, 352, 355, 360, 365–67, 374, 382–84, 386, 388, 390; for constitutional rule, 78, 91–92; in the Berlin Treaty, 41; and CUP, 57–60, 78; in Diyarbekir, 102–3; and Erzberger, 342, 373–74; and Jews, 95–96, 280, 295–14, 471n215; justice for, 341, 369, 395, 398–99; and Kurds, 97; in Sasun, 101–2; during Tanzimat, 40; in World War I, 181–316, 324

Arslan, Mustafa Rahmi, 45, 46, 47, 65, 70, 96, 157, 175–77, 345, 438n21, 456n13, 480n51

Asia Minor (Anatolia), xi–xiii, 22, 80; as constitutional core of a reduced Ottoman realm, 67, 84, 90–91, 116; conquest of Eastern, 4; origin of the Ottoman Empire in, 83; post-1918 war for, 18, 34, 319–20, 356, 392–93, 411, 414; as a Turkish-Muslim national home (Türk Yurdu), xii, xiv, 9, 17, 21, 28, 169, 257, 259, 376, 392, 402. *See also* Reform Agreement; reform plan

Asım (deputy), 96

Asquith, Herbert H., 349

association de salut public, 81

Assyrians, 154, 185, 203–4, 230, 245–47; militias of, 208

Astourian, Stephan, 432n24

Atabinen, Reşid Saffet (Safvet), 412, 433n31, 483n87

ATASE (Military Archive, Ankara), 196, 431n15, 457n25

Atatürk, Mustafa Kemal, xi, xii, xiv,
21, 30, 31–32, 54, 73, 379, 410; and
Armenians, 395, 398, 416; compared to Talaat, 31; and CUP after
1918, 393–95; in Damascus, 47; and
Enver, 319, 392–93; in Edirne, 145;
ego-history of, 415; heir of Talaat's
role and staff, 174, 195, 222, 267, 319,
326, 411–17; inspired by Ziya Gökalp,
393, 413–14; introducing opposition, 376; and Kurds, 319, 486n143;
leading post-1918 struggle for Asia
Minor, 18, 37, 356, 363, 388, 392–403,
410; letter to Lenin, 388; letters
to Talaat, 363, 399–403; in Libya,
112; nation-building under, 411–19;
obstructing prosecution, 408–9; on
Talaat's shoulders, 31, 356, 31, 411–17;
proclaimed gazi, 415–16; renouncing
pan-Turkism, 320; resuming Talaat's
Turkification, 319–20; revolutions of,
30, 323–25, 416; and separate peace,
348; starting his struggle in eastern
provinces, 319
Atay, Falih Rıfkı, 360, 400, 412
Athens, 44, 179
Atıf Bey. See Kamçıl
Austria(-Hungary), 39, 66, 131, 146, 155,
170, 174, 181, 183, 186–87, 283, 322, 331,
336, 343, 379, 455n4
Australia, 172, 312, 351
Axis, 423
Ayastefanos (Yeşilköy), 72; counter-
parliament (1909) in, 72–73
Aydın, 176
Azerbaijan, 186, 194, 200, 207, 256, 363

Baath Parties, 30
Babacan, Hasan, 110, 429n1
Babikian, Agop, 78

Bagdadbahn (Baghdad Railway), 88,
90, 198, 271, 334; dream related to,
409
Baghdad, 244; fall of, 350
Bahaeddin Şakir, 22, 36, 48, 49, 50,
55–60, 62, 64, 81–85, 96, 98, 157, 217,
342; at the Caucasus front, 198–99,
205, 207–8, 219, 229–32, 249; in exile,
381–82, 398, 405–6, 409; pamphle-
tism of, 56–57, 64, 92, 99
Baku, 367, 397–98; Congress of the
Peoples of the East, 397
Balakian, Grigoris, 432n21
Balfour, Arthur J., 347
Balfour Declaration, 289, 312–13, 318,
356–59, 363, 369
Balkan League, 124
Balkan Wars, 4, 27, 40, 173, 181, 231,
321, 349, 415; First Balkan War, 4,
83, 107–8, 124–30, 138, 165, 292, 365;
Second Balkan War, 3, 4, 137, 141–45
Ballobar, Condé de, 312
bankruptcy, Ottoman, 40
Basra, 244, 359
Batumi, 40, 197, 317, 339, 363, 398;
Treaty of, 363
Bayar, Mahmud Celâl, 174–75, 195, 412,
453n157
Bayur, Yusuf H., 380, 421, 434n36
Becker, Julius, 301–2, 359–61
Beirut, 155
Bektashis/Bektashism, 4, 38, 82; tekke
of, 4, 44
Bekir Sami. See Kunduh
Belger, Nihad Reşad, 141
Belgium, 359
Belgrade, 44
Ben-Gavriêl, Moshe Y. (formerly
Eugen Hoeflich), 298, 473n235
Berchtold, Leopold, 146

Berlin, 14, 18, 24, 76, 129, 137, 151, 192, 212, 218, 223, 284, 287–88, 334, 341, 343, 347, 357, 382–411; centre of Zionist Organization, 109, 310; Congress and Treaty of, *see* Berlin Treaty; Oriental Club in, 385, 405; Ottoman Embassy in, 201, 373; Pro Palästina founded in, 362; Talaat in, 2, 4, 14, 31, 76, 79, 283, 286, 318, 320, 361, 369–77, 382–406; trial of Tehlirian in, *see* Tehlirian, trial of; Turkish club in, 383–84

Berlin Treaty, 40–41, 66–67, 101–2, 129, 197, 239, 317, 389; Article 23 of, 126; Articles 61–62 of, 41, 59, 101–2, 152; violation of, 66–67

Bernstorff, Johann Heinrich, 24–25, 297, 332–34, 339, 347, 357, 359, 367, 377, 436n62, 478n33, 478n35

Beşiktaş, 41, 67, 130

Bethmann Hollweg, Theobald von, 234; resignation of, 370

Beyoğlu, 272

Bible, 48, 358, 472n228

Bieberstein, Adolf Marschall von, 84–85, 88, 92, 113, 148, 183

Birgen, Muhittin, 21, 98, 160, 170–72, 229, 370–76, 412, 414

Bitlis, 15, 90, 152, 163, 165, 203, 225, 228, 236–37, 249–53, 266, 276; killing of Assyrians in, 239

Black Sea, 5, 197, 202, 210, 212–14, 257, 276, 320, 355

Bleda, Midhat Şükrü, 18, 22, 46, 47, 48, 50, 53, 87, 116, 124, 130, 132, 143, 160, 230, 361–62

BOA (Başbakanlık Osmanlı Arşivi), 432n20

Boer War, 350–51

Bolayır, Enver, 421–22

Bolsheviks/Bolshevism. *See* Russia, Bolshevik

Bonaparte, Napoleon, 39, 137, 218

Bosnia-Herzegovina, 40; annexed by Austria, 66, 155

Boston, 404

boycotts, CUP-organized, 67, 155, 174, 179, 269

Bozarslan, Hamit, 437n3

Bozkurt, Mahmut Esat, 412

Brest-Litovsk negotiations and Treaty, 317, 336, 339, 344, 356–57, 361, 363–65, 369, 397; recovery of Batumi, Ardahan, and Kars after, 317, 363, 398

Britain. *See* Great Britain

Bucharest, 110, 275; Treaty of, 317

Bulgaria, 35, 40–42, 124–25, 131–32, 141–46, 224, 365, 366, 378–79; armistice with, 131; autonomy of, 40; agreement with, including population exchange, 145–46; inclusion of in Quadruple Alliance, 336; independence of, 66, 155; refusal of war alliance by, 191, 193

Bulgarians, 42, 45, 55

Cafer Pasha, 275

calendar, new, 323, 477n11

caliph/caliphate, xiii–xv, 112, 224, 275, 350, 368, 398; abolition of, 32, 415; rhetoric of caliphate, 319, 363, 398, 400–401; separation of government and, 58; sultan Abdulhamid II as caliph, 35, 71

Canbolad (İsmail Canbolad or Canbulat), 47, 49, 87, 282, 348, 372

Çandar, Tevfik, 429n1

Capitulations (Ottoman), 39, 239, 338; abrogation of, 187, 191–92, 220

Caspian Sea, 207, 231, 364, 375, 394

Catholicos: of Aghtamar, 262; of
Etchmiadzin (Kevork V.), 152; of Sis
(Cilicia), 266, 467n163
Caucasus, 8–9, 27, 40, 128; World War
I and its aftermath in the, 5, 9, 12, 17,
183–84, 190, 196–203, 207–8, 212, 217,
219–23, 249, 256, 258, 292, 316–18,
344–45, 350, 355–56, 363–72, 375,
377–78, 392, 395, 401–2, 457n32
Cavid (Mehmed Cavid) Bey, 22,
44–45, 57, 65, 80, 88–90, 92–94, 97,
98, 115–18, 123, 128, 130, 132, 136–37,
158–59, 169–70, 176, 189, 223, 258, 303,
316, 321, 323, 342–43, 345, 359, 371–72,
377, 379, 385, 388–89, 396–97; accus-
ing Germany for dragging Turkey
into war, 193, 334; and alliance with
Germany, 186–87, 191; and Armenian
genocide, 22–24, 277–80, 383–84;
and Armenian reforms, 158–62; and
Armenian return, 328–29, 374; on
chauvinism, 327; and Churchill, 90,
113, 182, 349; and coup of July 1912,
121–22; on Dardanelles victory, 229,
256; diary of, 23, 24, 62, 90, 94, 162,
214, 218, 419; and éminences grises
in CUP, 75; as seen by Emmanuilidis, 444n71; on Enver, 162, 186,
214, 486n146; and Halil, 291; and
Helfferich, 341–42; on Mehmed
Sadık, 110–11; minister of finances,
62, 75, 162, 320, 327–28; and Nâzım,
215–16; and Rambert, 69, 111, 118,
137; resignation of, 214; on separate
peace, 346–47; on Talaat, 139, 222,
246, 328, 338, 377, 388–89, 477n14,
486n146; as used by Talaat, 315,
327–28; on Talaat's assassination,
320, 404–6; as a target of reactionaries, 70; as teacher of economics, 44;

on Wangenheim, 148, 158, 192; war-
sceptical stance of, 125, 191, 211–15;
weak historical sense of, 320; and
Zohrab, 116, 161, 214–15
Celâl (Mehmed Celâl) Bey, 85, 91, 93,
154, 266, 443n66
Celâl. See Bayar, Mahmud Celâl
Celal Nuri. See İleri, Celal Nuri
Cem (satirical journal), 119–20
Cemal (Ahmed Cemal/Jamal) Pasha,
87, 96, 136, 164, 182, 187, 211, 215, 220,
226, 237, 253, 275, 411; anti-Zionists
and anti-Arabists, 225, 274, 296–300,
309–10, 358–60; Armenian survivors
resettled by, 235, 240, 262, 265;
anti-Armenin crimes punished by,
241; Becker on, 301; as an early CUP
member, 45, 65; commander of the
Fourth Army, 226; exile, 381, 385, 396,
398, 401–2; failed Suez campaign
of, 12, 220, 223, 359; fear of a second
Armenian, 289, 300–301; governor of
Adana, 78; memoirs of, 141; member
of the Turkish-German Society, 287;
military commander of Istanbul,
139–40, 143–49; military governor
of Syria, 108, 182, 217–18, 225, 253,
274, 289; minister of the navy, 162;
and Rambert, 147; and Rohner, 266;
and Talaat, 163, 314, 473n233; as a
triumvir, 163, 314
Cemal Azmi, 130, 258, 409
Central Asia, 197, 368–69, 378, 409
Central Committee of the CUP (Committee of Union and Progress),
xi, 2–3, 16, 18, 22, 55–56, 62, 66, 84,
112; conspirational, 30; guidelines
of, mid-November 1914, 206, 208;
institutional cult of, 29; members of,
1911, 123–24; secrecy also after 1908,

66; Ziya Gökalp as the ideological
master of, 36
Central Powers, 318, 322, 324–36;
expecting reparations, 341; new
world order projected by, 339,
363–64, 369. *See also* Triple Alliance;
Quadruple Alliance
centralization/centralism, 11, 79, 82,
84, 86, 99, 152, 154, 301. *See also*
decentralization
Çerkez Ahmed, 209
Cevdet. *See* Abdullah Cevdet
Cevdet (governor, Enver's brother-
in-law), 90, 205, 209, 221–22, 225,
227–28, 250–51, 258, 263–64
chauvinism: actionist, 148; CUP/
Turkish, 12, 116, 229, 311, 327;
French, 182
Chicherin, Georgy, 398
Chios, 131, 148, 150, 168–69
cholera, 129
Churchill, Winston, xii, 12, 23–24,
29, 88–89, 113–14, 182, 189–90, 212,
227–28, 341, 349, 353
Cilicia, 226, 233, 467n163
Circassians, 41, 245; of SO, 348
Club de Constantinople, 70
Club d'Orient, 149
Cold War, 420
Cologne, 349
Commission of Mazhar, 241
Committee of Progress and Union
(CPU, temporary name change of
CUP), 36, 49–58; external (Paris)
center of, 49–50
Committee of Union and Progress
(CUP, İttihad ve Terakki Cemiyeti),
xi, xiii, 2–3, 14, 28, 36, 49, 139; action
party inside, 186, 211; affinity of with
Germany, 76, 88, 113, 350; branch

of in Diyarbekir, 98, 100, 106, 245;
as Cemiyet-i mukaddese (Holy
Committee), 49, 62; circle of in
1890s Edirne, 42; commissaries of,
237, 241; congress of (1909), 81, 98;
congress of (1910), 86; congress of
(1911), 123; congress of (1912), 123;
congress of (1916), 323–24; congress
of (1917), 323; congress of (1918),
379–80; CUP-liberal cooperation,
116–17; files of, 406; foundation of,
42–43; and Great Britain, 59–60, 76,
350; identity of, 45; imperialism of,
359; initiation ritual for, *see* Ottoman Freedom Society; memoran-
dum of, May 1908, 52; pioneer of
right-wing revolution, 317; secretary
general of, 46; seeking Huguenin's
help, 122; as strongest Young Turk
organization, 62
comprador bourgeoisie, 174–75
concentration camps, 259, 261–68, 276,
351
Congress and Treaty of Berlin. *See*
Berlin Treaty
Congress of Ottoman opposition
parties (1907), 37, 49, 58, 60
conscription, 39
Constantinople. *See* Istanbul
constitution/constitutionalism, Ottoman, 3, 10–11, 27–28, 36, 40, 52, 58, 98,
104, 303, 326, 424; of 1876, 41, 105; of
1908, 54–55, 58, 64–68, 78–79, 90–92,
151, 154–55, 269, 295, 298; gospel of,
91–92, 358; dismissal of, 86, 92, 116,
118, 151, 327, 351, 413, 418, 425
constitutional period, second, xv, 19
conversion, 158; during genocide, 234,
246, 265; to Turkish nationalism, 9,
21, 99, 104, 413

cooptation, of regional lords and gangs, xi, 8, 41, 82, 86–87, 92, 240

counterrevolution of 1909. *See* coup, of April 1909

coup: of April 1909, 63, 70–74; of July 1912 (Halaskâr insurrection), 119–21; of January 1913, 3, 133–36, 305

courts-martial, Ottoman: during World War, 19, 228; after World War, 381, 385, 408

Crawford, David, 159

Crescent Committee. *See* Ottoman Freedom Society

Crete, union declared with Greece, 66, 155

Crimea, 170, 344, 381–82

crimes against humanity, 362, 407–8; first use of the term in high politics, 15

Çukurova, 273, 469n186

CUP. *See* Committee of Union and Progress

CUP Central Committee. *See* Central Committee of the CUP

Curzon, George, Lord, 75

czar. *See* Nicholas II

Czernin, Ottokar, 339, 343–44

Dadaism, 389

Damascus, 47, 344

Dardanelles, 12, 23, 189–90, 223–24, 239; closure of, 458n35; victorious defense at, 12, 89, 190, 227–29, 258, 344, 350, 476n9; German warships entering, 187

Darülfünun (Istanbul University), 125, 323

Dashnak/Dashnaktsutiun. *See* Armenian Revolutionary Federation

death cult among CUP radicals, 222, 342, 377

decentralization, 58, 302, 307. *See also* League of Private Initiative and Decentralization

demographic engineering, xi, 13, 25, 48, 155, 167–69, 178–79, 205, 234, 249, 319. *See also* genocide; population exchanges; Talaat, pioneer of demographic engineering

Denker, Arif Cemil, 230, 391

Denktash, Rauf, 488n173

Deportation Law (decree), 15, 270, 298

Der ez-Zor, 237, 252, 259, 262–67, 262, 273, 276

Der Judenstaat (by T. Herzl), 295

Dersim, 224, 241, 254; Alevi Kurds of, 224, 256

Der Yeghiayan, Zaven (Armenian patriarch), 11, 202, 205–6, 292

deserters. *See* World War I, deserters in

Deutsche Allgemeine Zeitung, 388, 409

Deutsche Bank, 14, 88, 272, 382

Deutsche Levante-Zeitung, 335

Develü, 263–64

Die Welt, 304, 474n246

Dilman, 223

Directorate for General Security, Ottoman, 201, 265, 282

Directorate General of Press and Information, 414

Directorate for Resettlement of Tribes and Migrants, Ottoman, 226, 235; subdirectorate of, in Aleppo, 266, 467n162

Disraeli, Benjamin, 353

Diyarbekir, 19, 22, 36, 64, 72, 96, 98–106, 152–53, 163, 193, 223, 238, 253–54, 256, 259–60, 274, 276, 291, 383, 412, 464n128, 469n186; Abandoned Property Commission in, 248; CUP branch in, 98, 104, 106, 245; during coup of 1909, 72; extermination in, 19, 239, 243–47, 253; mining industry in, 273; prison in, 324; rebellious youths in, 36, 99–101; telegram sent in 1895 from, 103

Dolmabahçe Palace, 41, 143, 447n34

Dönme, 44–46, 85, 215, 279, 302

Dörtyol, 225–27, 233, 252, 276

eastern provinces (of the Ottoman Empire), 8, 12, 41, 50, 85, 99, 103, 109, 142, 152–59, 163, 170, 198–99, 205, 224, 229, 243–58, 261, 319, 349, 398. *See also* Reform Agreement; reform plan

Eastern Question, 8, 37, 130, 142, 185, 195–96, 351, 354; made part of the general war, 183, 334, 336; quagmire of, 130, 142, 151; as a vengeance against Europe, 195

Ebert, Friedrich, 382

Edirne (Adrianople), 3, 35–38, 41, 51, 124, 131–32; concession of, 132, 134; fall of, 138; reconquest (recovery) of, 3, 4, 142–45, 182, 349; as start of a history of salvation, 145

Edremit, 175–76

Edward VII, king, 53

egalitarian pluralism, 27, 40, 60, 294, 307, 317; killed, 294, 301. *See also* constitutionalism

Egypt, 4, 33, 141, 182, 214, 217–18, 231, 333, 353, 394 396

Ehmann, Johannes, 461n93

Einstein, Lewis, 290

elections, to Ottoman Parliament: of 1908, 68; 1911 by-election, 117; 1912 sopalı seçim, 117; of April 1914, 172

Elkus, Abram, 297, 475n263

Elmaliyah, Abraham, 297

Emmanuilidis, Emmanuil, 125, 135, 179–80, 272, 318, 431n5

Emrullah Efendi, 94

Enis Pasha, 102–3

Entente, 12–15, 59, 113, 129, 156, 182, 184, 189, 192, 197, 212, 223, 228, 298, 319, 354, 365; agitation and reaction against, 31, 354, 373, 385, 388, 400–402; Anglo-Russian, 197; Armenian preference for, 202; breakthrough attempt at the Dardanelles by, 199, 223, 228, 232; declaration by, 25 May 1915, 15, 21; hoped for relief by, 238; invasion of Greece by, 257–58; Istanbul occupied by, 406; partition plans by, 318, 340, 356, 363

Enver (İsmail Enver) Pasha, xiii, 5, 7, 12, 14, 18–20, 23, 47, 87, 118, 141, 144, 164, 178, 218, 232, 243, 251–52, 270, 332; as attaché in Berlin, 77, 88, 112; in the Balkan wars, 131, 144; and Caucasus campaigns, 17, 196, 207, 210, 221–22, 365–69, 377; and coup in 1913, 133–37; disarming of Armenian soldiers ordered by, 225; early CUP member, 47, 49; and Edirne's recovery, 109, 144, 349; and entering World War I, 186–89, 191, 193, 201, 211–15; in exile, 381–82, 385, 396–98, 401–3; family of, 53, 90, 112, 194, 204, 355, 367, 443n65; Germanophile, 18, 19, 183; hero of the 1908 revolution, 5, 53–54, 108, 118; Graves on, 163; and Humann, 20, 284, 388; in Libya, 112, 141; minister of war, 162–63; and Mustafa Kemal (Atatürk), 319, 392–93; and Pomiankowski, 12; president of

Enver (İsmail Enver) Pasha (*continued*)
Turkish-German Society, 287–88;
remains brought to Turkey, 420; and
separate peace, 346–48; and Talaat,
xiii, 5, 14–15, 108–9, 133–34, 141, 176,
178, 182, 186, 193, 196, 199, 218–20, 227,
233, 235, 263, 265, 279, 285, 294, 297,
310, 313, 315, 334, 365–66, 372, 390,
396, 402–3, 411, 416, 429n3, 452n139,
480n52; and Tahsin, 194, 254; vice
commander of the Ottoman army,
7; and Wangenheim, 18–20, 148, 183,
186–87, 189, 211, 213, 229; and Ziya
Gökalp, 98, 290
equality, 27, 63, 91; demand by non-
Muslims for, 8, 153; refusal or post-
ponement of, 71, 86–87, 154
Erzincan, 72, 255, 257; reconquest of,
339; Russian retreat from, 365, 367
Erzberger, Matthias, 265, 284–85,
341–42, 365, 367, 370, 372, 374
Erzurum, 15, 72, 91, 198–99, 205–6, 243;
captured, 256; leaders in, pioneering
genocide, 248–58; reconquest of,
339; Russian retreat from, 365, 367
Eskijian, Hovhannes, 266
Eskişehir, 279–80
Essad Pasha. *See* Toptani
Eurocentric history, 25–26, 34, 110,
436n63
Europe: belle epoque of, 30, 32, 173, 181,
183, 189, 283; family of, 172; guarantee
and intervention of, 40, 45, 52, 103,
153; July Crisis of, 5, 178, 182, 186;
larger (Europe, Russia, and the
Ottoman world), xv, 30, 32, 178
European Union, 427
Evlad-ı Fatihan (sons of conquerors),
4, 27, 59

Faiz al-Huseyin, 274–77, 469n188
famine, 40, 220, 261, 324
fascism, 354, 368, 410
fedai, CUP, 50, 53, 70, 282
federalism, 59, 96, 99
Ferid Pasha, 74–75, 117
Fevzi. *See* Pirinççizâde Feyzi
Filipeli Hilmi, 198, 256
Filmer, Cemil, 282
Fitzmaurice, Gerald, 296
France, 14, 43, 59, 129, 133, 170, 182, 229,
363, 370
Franz Ferdinand, Archduke, 178, 181
Freemason/Freemasonry, 44, 97, 111,
296
French Revolution, 81, 138
Friedman, Isaiah, 473n232, 476n268
Fuad Selim, 345–46, 480n51

Galicia, 219, 347
Gallipoli: defense of, xv, 13, 219–20, 233,
347, 350, 392, 419; culmination of the
narrative of national salvation at,
322, 476n9
Garo. *See* Armen Garo
Gates, Caleb C., 462n103
gavur, 8, 175, 469n191
Gaza, 312, 359
General Jewish Colonization Organization, 285, 361
genocide, xi, 17, 34, 261, 333–34; actors
of, 256–57, 269, 276, 290; alleged protection during, 255; anti-Christian,
419; Armenian, 232–77; Assyrian,
234, 239–40; and deathly utopia of
Turan, 367; deceptive resettlement
during, 262–63; denial of, 309, 313,
324, 362, 386, 472n227; first phase of
Armenian, 241; German perception

of in Turkey, 19–20; justification of, 292, 294; and Lausanne Treaty, 28; panegyric during, 277; of Pontus Rûm, 257–58, 319–20, 355, 401; second phase of Armenian, 261–68, 285; role of SO in, 252–54, 450n98; term of, 17, 320, 386–87; war matrix for, 34, 185, 380, 404, 408; and the Yishuv, 314. *See also* Germany, and Armenian genocide

Germany, 7, 17–21, 88–89, 151–52, 182–84, 381–411; and Armenian genocide, 18, 24, 278, 283–84, 292, 328–29, 436n62; backing of Turkey in 1913–14, 151–52, 158–64; CUP's and Atatürk's appeal for, 407, 409, 435n53; defeatism of, 24, 269, 272, 283–84, 292, 374; democrats in, 370, 373–74; Far Right in, 387–88, 396–97; friend of Abdulhamid II, 14, 148, 151; July crisis in 1917, 370; military mission of, in Turkey, 162, 212, 218, 221, 332; protector of Jews, 10, 295–96; schizophrenia of, 24, 314–15, 384; supporting return of Armenian survivors, 20, 265, 285, 328, 365; at a threshold (1913), 151; Turkophilia of, 7, 11; refusal to defend Talaat's Armenian policy, 328–29, 373–74, 478n27. *See also* Committee of Union and Progress, and Germany; Orientpolitik; Wangenheim

Germany, alliance of, with Turkey. *See* World War alliance of Germany and Turkey

Ginio, Eyal, 145

Girard, René, 472n228

Gladstone, William E., 353

Goeben (battle cruiser), 189

George, Lloyd, 346–47

Georgia/Georgians, 199, 363, 365

Gökalp. *See* Ziya Gökalp

Graves, Robert, 45, 153, 159, 163, 165, 455n3

Great Britain, 14, 33, 59, 76, 129, 148, 155, 157–59, 198, 213, 229, 349–52, 354–55, 359, 368, 370, 402, 405; and Great Game, 197; imperial embrace of Middle East by, 363–64; jihad against, 200; liberalism of, 29; and NILI, 289; occupation of Istanbul by, 396; and Ottoman order of warships, 179, 189; and partition of Ottoman Empire, 129–30, 363; ; and Ottoman wish for alliance, 113, 349; and postwar justice, 341, 385, 389; and separate peace, 227, 345–47; support for Kâmil cabinet, 148, 349–50; support for Tanzimat, 40; and Talaat, xii, 29, 88–90, 133, 189, 341, 349, 355, 385, 389, 403. *See also* Entente

Great Game, 197

Greece, 66, 138, 146, 167, 185, 187, 191, 405; annexation of islands by, 179; conflict with Turkey over islands, 131–32, 134, 148, 167–69; commission of and Ottoman Turkey for population exchange, 187; conquest of Salonica, 43; haven for expellees and refugees, 13, 204; idea of greater Greece (Megali Idea), 175; independence of, 38

Greece during and after the Balkan Wars, 124, 131–32, 142, 146, 150, 167–69, 174–79, 185, 449n76

Greece during World War I, 191, 213, 257–58; end of neutrality (occupied by Entente), 257–58; national schism, 227–28

Greece during the war for Asia Minor, 319; occupation and loss of Izmir, 386, 400–401

Greek-Orthodox Ottomans. *See* Rûm

Grey, Edward, 75, 296

Gulkevich, K. N., 145, 163

Günther, Franz, 405

Gust, Wolfgang, 435n44

Gwinner, Arthur, 272

Hacı Âdil. *See* Arda

Hafız Hakkı (Pasha), 49, 207, 221–22

Hafız İbrahim Efendi, 42

Hagia Sophia, 2; being hanged at, 138

Haifa, 300

Hakkâri, 239–40

Hakkı Pasha. *See* İbrahim Hakkı Pasha

Halajian, Bedros, 80, 93, 124, 125, 128, 131, 160

Halaskâr insurrection. *See* coup, of July 1912

Halaskâr, 119, 123

Halide Edib. *See* Adıvar

Halil (Enver's uncle). *See* Kut

Halil Bey. *See* Menteşe

Hall, William, 227

Hamid (Kapancızâde Hamid), 30, 31, 153–54, 185–86, 243–44, 278, 280–81, 323, 328, 436n66, 455n3

Hamidian massacres, 8, 78–79, 87, 95–96, 101–2, 185, 247, 293; compared to 1915 genocide, 234

Hamidism, 36

Hamidian (Hamidiye) cavalry, 164

Hanioğlu, M. Şükrü, 46, 48, 56, 437n67

Harden, Maximilian, 343

Hardenbergstrasse (Berlin), 382, 403–4

Harput, 253, 275, 277, 462n103. *See also* Mamuretülaziz

Hasan Fehmi, 70

Hasan İzzet Pasha, 206–7, 221

Hayri. *See* Mustafa Hayri

Hayri Pasha, 53

Hayriye Bafralı, 1, 42, 90, 382, 404–5

Hedwig Cathedral (Berlin), 386

Helfferich, Karl, 14, 88–90, 341–42, 370–71, 387

Herbert, Aubrey, 6, 347–48, 349, 352–54, 388–89, 396, 431n10

Herero, 263

Herzl, Theodor, 295, 299

Hilmi. *See* Filipeli Hilmi

Hilmi Pasha. *See* Hüseyin Hilmi

Hınıs, 253

Hintze, Paul von, 375

hisb-i cedid (disaffiliation from the CUP), 110

Hitler, Adolf, 256, 290, 300, 370, 374, 418, 420, 422

Hitler Putsch, 256, 410

Hochberg, Sami, 307

Hoff, Nicolai, General, 165, 180, 194

Hoffmann, Max, General, 399

Hofjudentum, 288

Holstein, Walter (German vice-consul), 19

Holocaust, 288

Huguenin, Edouard, Pasha, 80, 88–90, 122, 134, 218

Humann, Hans, 18–20, 284, 388

Hunchak. *See* Social Democrat Hunchakian Party

Hürriyet ve İtilâf (Freedom and Entente party), 117–18, 122, 126–27, 138

Hüseyin Cahid. *See* Yalçın

Hüseyin Hilmi Pasha, 49, 69, 71, 74–75, 80, 82

Hüseyin Kâzım. *See* Kadri

Hüseyin Mazhar, 241

Hüseyin Nesimi, 247
Hüseyinzâde Ali, 116, 327
Huysmans, Camille, 396

İbrahim Hakkı Pasha (grand vizier), 82, 93, 112
Ihrig, Stefan, 410
İhsan (Palace secretary), 177
İleri, Celal Nuri, 406
Ilinden-Preobrazhenie Uprising (1903), 45–46
Imam Yahya, 83
Imhoff, Heinrich K.A., General, 84
imperial bias, xiv, 2, 29, 39, 57, 83–84, 93–94, 174, 194, 209, 236, 243–44, 256, 297, 301, 339, 351, 360, 416–17, 427, 436n66, 456n13, 459n56, 468n176, 473n233; British, 351; Russian, 209; notion of, 29
imperial rebels, 36
imperial restoration, 9
India, 227, 353, 396, 398, 402
Internal Macedonian Revolutionary Organization (IMRO), 45, 50
Ionescu, Take, 166–67
İnönü, İsmet, 418
Iran, Northern, 12, 183, 194, 197, 202; Ottoman invasion in, 204–6, 222–23
Iraq, xiii, 12, 30, 90, 180, 184, 219, 220, 303, 318, 359, 394; British defeat in, 347, 350; post-war Islamism in, 396
Ireland, 350
irtica/mürteci (Islamic reaction/reactionaries), 8, 63, 67–68, 78–79, 102, 106, 118, 121, 165; revolutionist attitude of, 352
İshâk Sükuti, 103–4, 407
Ishkhan (Nikoghayos Mikayelian), 228
Islamic Army of the Caucasus, 367

Islamism/Islamists, 28, 31, 40, 61, 64, 68–69, 99, 182; CUP's, 31, 48, 56, 60, 85, 92, 141, 156, 198; anti-Christian, 101, 106; exterminatory, 72; late nineteenth-century Ottoman, 155; and Kemalists, 414, 416–17; organization after 1918 of, 355, 384, 395–97; propaganda and rhetoric of, 8, 56–57, 184, 188, 206; reemerging in Turkey's multiparty system, 421; reformist, 11, 41; refusal of Zionism by, 296, 303; rise of, 40; state-centered, 392; and war ümmet, 271–72, xenophobic, 91. See also pan-Islamism
Islamist International, post-1918, 57
İslamlaşmak (booklet of Said Halim), 141
İsmail Canbolad. See Canbolad
İsmail Enver. See Enver
İsmail Hakkı Bey/Pasha (intendant-general), 116, 132, 136, 282
Ismail Qemali, 140
İsmail Yürükoğlu (or Yürükov), 42, 44
Israel, restoration of, 93
Israil, B., letter to Talaat, 307–8
Istanbul, 1, 51, 54; international hub and hotspot, xv, 26, 32, 110; occupied, 396; mobilizing the streets of, 126, 135, 141; state of emergency, 63, 73, 112, 122, 126, 138
Istanbul University. See Darülfünun
Italy, 13, 30, 33, 36, 111–13, 170, 212; and Aegean islands, 168; backing Albanians, 131; and Kemalists, 397; peace with, 127; Talaat in, 385, 397
ittihadcılık, 61
ittihâd-ı anasır (Ottoman union of different peoples), 128, 343
İttihad-i Muhammedi Cemiyeti. See Society for Muhammadan Unity

İttihad ve Terakki, 440n1. *See* Committee of Union and Progress
Izmir, 174–78, 241; CUP branch of, 174; occupied by Greece, 386; reconquered, 401
İzzet Pasha. *See* Ahmed İzzet Pasha

Jabotinsky, Vladimir, 295, 299, 306, 473n236
Jäckh, Ernst, 88, 287–88, 333, 338, 386, 404–5, 415, 417, 422–23
Jacobins, 138, 218
Jacobson, Victor, 133, 289, 302, 304–7, 362; and Talaat, 304–7
Jaffa, 309–10; evacuation of, 300, 312–14
Jagow, Gottlieb von, 197, 320
Japan, 47
Jäschke, Gotthard, 399
Jaurès, Jean, 181–82
Jerusalem, 75, 262, 266, 467n163; British conquest of, 312, 359
Jesus, 289, 351, 481n65
Jewish Legion, 299
Jewish Question, 305–7, 312, 360
jihad, 25, 48, 71, 183, 185, 188, 197, 216, 240, 380, 416; declaration (14 November 1914), 16, 189, 200, 206; domestic, 155; against Great Britain, 200; exterminatory, 366; hailed locally, 185, 230; imam as agents of, 183; proclaimed by Ziya Gökalp, 17, 183, 188; promoted by others, 397; propaganda and rhetoric of, 155, 208, 230, 240; Talaat identifying with, xiv, 216, 264; and total war, xiv, 13, 28, 188, 334; toward Turan, 183, 188, 197, 380; in Turkestan, 402; World War I as jihad, xiv, 290, 334

Kâbe-i hürriyet (Kaaba of liberty), 49
Kabul, 398
Kadri, Hüseyin Kâzım, 156, 448n51
Kaiser, Hilmar, 445n91
Kalmykow, Andrew, 177
Kamçıl, Atıf, 241–42
Kâmil Bedirhan, 224
Kâmil Pasha (grand vizier), 66, 69, 127–31, 134–36, 148, 152, 349; anglophile, 69
Kâmil Pasha (general). *See* Mahmud Kâmil
Kapp putsch, 388
Karabekir, Musa Kâzım, Pascha, 379, 398
Kara Kemal, 133, 217, 230
Karakilise, 364
Karakol organization, 379
Karasu (Carasso), Emmanuel, 93, 131, 279, 302, 361, 383
Karesi, 175, 243
Karl I (Charles I of Austria), 340
Kars, 40, 197, 219, 276, 317, 363–65, 367, 394, 398, 462n102
Kastamonu, 252, 260
Kaufmann, Max R., 128
Kaya, Şükrü, 266–67, 412
Kayseri, 225, 236, 260, 263, 275, 276
Kâzım (Captain), 141
Kâzım Karabekir Pasha. *See* Karabekir
Kemalists/Kemalism, xi, 31, 135–36, 367–68; losing against political Islam, 414–15
Kempner, Robert M., 408
Kevork V, 152. *See* Catholicos, of Etchmiadzin
Kévorkian, Raymond, 432n22, 464n123
Kığı, 254
Killigil, Nuri, 367
Kızılbaş, 4

Kızılelma, 100–101, 367; as a messiah (mehdi), 101, 367

Kocgiri rebellion, 401

komiteci/komitecilik, 3, 35–36, 63–64, 107, 138–40, 144, 165, 203, 254, 274, 294, 325, 387; and children, 90; government, 183; imperial, 25, 36, 147, 151; in Macedonia, 35; mentality of, 139, 281; method of, 61, 136, 138; rule of, 183, 281

Konya, 19, 204, 226, 237, 260, 274–75

Konyar, Nureddin İbrahim, Pasha, 355, 400–401, 486n142

Kör Ali, 67

Koran, 16, 277, 338; CUP's use of, 48; tied to standards, 72; superseding the Torah, 93; translation into Turkish of, 323

Kosovo, 37, 50

Kühlmann, Richard von, 297, 321, 332–33, 339, 365

Kunduh, Bekir Sami, 266, 403

Künzler, Jakob and Elisabeth, 261, 461n93, 472n226

Kurban Bayramı, 256

Kurds: killing Armenians, 253; nationalist movement of, 156; removal of, 259–61

Kut, Halil, 47, 222, 355, 366

Kut (near Baghdad), 350

Kütahya, 241

labor battalions, 239, 248, 323

Lake Urmiah, 210

land question (agrarian question), 83, 91, 96, 152–53

Land Code (1858), 103

larger Europe. See Europe

Lausanne, 391

Lausanne Peace Treaty (1923), 28, 34, 394; population exchange, 28, 34, 146

Lausanne Treaty (1912), 110

Layard, Austen H., 40

League of Private Initiative and Decentralization (Sabahaddin), 57, 59–60, 302, 307

Lebanon, xiii, 158, 191, 217, 394

Le Jeune-Turc (newspaper), 180, 297, 307–8, 474n246

Lehmann-Haupt, Carl F., 332, 473n237

Lemkin, Raphael, 17, 320, 408–9, 434n43

Lemnos, 131

Lenin, Vladimir I., 29

Lepsius, Johannes, 20, 151, 285, 386, 435n50

Lesbos (Mytilene), 131, 148, 150, 168–69

liberal party. See Osmanlı Ahrar Fırkası. See Hürriyet ve İtilâf

Libya, 33, 42; invaded by Italy, 111–13, 114–16, 146, 182, 231, 321

Lichtheim, Richard, 286, 289, 307–10

Lishansky, Yosef, 300

Livadiya, 170, 182

loan. See Ottoman loans

London, 89, 93–94, 131, 135, 348, conference and peace treaty (1913) of, 110, 131, 135, 137, 141, 144; Talaat's visit to, 75–76, 113, 303

Lossow, Otto von, General, 366, 375

Lowther, Gerard, 296, 351

Ludendorff, Erich, 343, 364, 375

Ludwig, Emil, 5–6, 7, 12, 13, 14, 16, 22, 24, 85, 283, 286, 316, 403, 408, 436n60

lumpen rule, 240, 246

lumpen intellectual, 410

Luxemburg, Rosa, 384

Lütfi Fikri, 138–40

Lütfi Simavi, 119, 377, 381

Macedonia, 9, 35, 44, 50, 60, 69, 127,
142, 179, 224; CUP branches in, 51,
54; CUP specter of autonomy in, 52;
fight for autonomy in, 45; finances
of, 46; guerilla war in, 50–51; officers
in, 47; "new Macedonia" (for Armenia), 159; population exchanges in,
145–46; reform of, 52; Talaat in,
51–52; theater of revolution, 54, 61
Macedonian Question, 9, 52–53, 151;
as a metaphor for conflicts in Asia
Minor, 59, 109, 154–56, 159, 175, 274
Mahari, Gurgen, 202
Mahmud Bahri Pasha, 149
Mahmud Kâmil Pasha (general), 248,
252, 255
Mahmud Muhtar, 124, 127
Mahmud Şevket Pasha, 73, 74, 108, 133,
136, 137, 148, 157, 218, 303; assassina-
tion of, 140–41; Talaat and, 108, 118,
121, 133, 136, 137
Mallet, Louis, 351
Malumian, Khachatur, 60
Mamuretülaziz, 72, 96, 152, 163, 274,
461n93, 462n103; CUP branch in,
106
Manastir (Monastir/Bitola), 37, 49, 50,
54, 118; CUP meeting in, 86, 443n59
Mandelstam, Andrew N., 158
Mansur Rifat, 409, 411
Manukian, Aram, 202
Manyasizâde Refik, 49, 438n21
Mardin, 102, 193, 276
Marx, Karl, 2
massacres (anti-Armenian): in 1890s.
See Adana; Hamidian massacres, in
1909
Mazliah, Nissim, 75, 93, 289, 302, 327,
362, 383

McKeekin, Sean, 318
Mecca, 231, 274–75
Mechveret Supplément Français
(journal), 49
Medina, 145, 231, 275
Megali Idea (Great Idea), 175–76
Mehmed V (Reshad), Sultan, xiii, 7, 112,
143, 332; travel to Izmit and Bursa, 80
Mehmed VI (Vahideddin), Sultan,
372, 379
Mehmed Cavid. See Cavid
Mehmed Celâl. See Celâl
Mehmed Cevad, 76–77
Mehmed Emin, 413
Mehmed Kâmil Pasha. See Kâmil Pasha
Mehmed Reşid (Şahingiray, Dr.), 22,
43, 175, 180, 238, 243–48, 251, 256,
259; anticipating Talaat's measures,
245–48
Mehmed Rifat, 75, 137, 168
Mehmed Sadık, 110–11, 116, 118–20;
Cavid on, 110–11; Lütfi Simavi on,
446n4
Mehmed Said Pasha, 73, 112–13, 120
Mekteb-i Mülkiye, 46, 225, 443n66
Menteşe, Halil, 23, 93–94, 96, 116,
119–20, 140, 149, 160–61, 167, 168, 176,
186–87, 211, 230, 287, 304; evasive, 96;
failing vis-à-vis Zohrab, 291, 472n221;
foreign minister, 291; member of
the "action party," 186; member of
the Turkish-German Society, 287;
minister of the interior, 93–94; president of the Council of State, 149;
president of the Ottoman Assembly,
119; Talaat's close companion, 191,
211, 230, 283, 291, 294; in the Zionist
press, 304
Mersin, 72, 253, 276

Mesopotamia, 185, 231, 262, 318, 353
messianism, political, xi, 11, 17, 98, 101, 104, 367
Meyrier, Gustave, 101–2
Middle East, as conceptualized by Churchill, 341
Midhat Şükrü. *See* Bleda
Military School of Medicine, 42, 49
millet, 38–40; millet assemblies, 105; as Muslim-Ottoman nation, 322. *See also* Armenian millet
millet-i hâkime, 58, 413
Misak-ı Millî. *See* National Pact
Mohammed Arslan, Emir, 70
Montefiors, Francis, 75
Montenegro, 40, 124, 127, 131, 140, 150
Monument of Liberty, 419–20
Morgenthau, Henry, 10, 213–14, 216, 219, 229, 278, 284, 286–87, 289, 291, 307, 310–12, 432n19; and Talaat, 10, 213, 216, 278, 310–12
Moses, Armando, 287
Mosul, 19, 252, 276, 396
Mouradian, Khatchig, 262
müdafaa-i milliye. *See* national defense
muhacir (Muslim refugees or migrants), 27, 40, 128–29, 167, 177–78, 180, 249, 252; resettlement of, 13, 15, 40, 154, 180, 226, 254, 268, 273, 465n147
Muhammed (Prophet), xiii, 277, 321
Mühlmann, Carl, 437n68
Muhammed Ali, 141
Muhtar (Gazi Muhtar) Pasha, 120–21, 126–27
Mülkiye. *See* Mekteb-i Mülkiye
Munich, 256
Mürzsteg Agreement (1903), 46
Musa Dagh, 238, 276

Musa Kazım (sheykhulislam), 332
Muslim migrants and refugees. *See* muhacir
Mussolini, Benito, 29, 370; March on Rome of, 410
Mustafa Atıf, 259–60
Mustafa Cemilpaşazâde, 245
Mustafa Hayri, 16, 62, 63, 64, 82, 83, 110, 131, 133, 163, 176, 207, 217, 379; against war, 142–43; arrested, 131; central committee member, 62, 123; declaring jihad, 16, 200; diary, 434n38; minister of foundations, 113; and reforms for the eastern provinces, 157; resignation from ministry, 136; and Talaat, 16, 62–63, 136, 142–43, 282–83, 338; and Ziya Gökalp, 16, 64, 105
Mustafa Kemal. *See* Atatürk
Mustafa Rahmi. *See* Arslan
Muşkara, Talaat (called "Küçük Talaat"), 398, 476n9

Naciye Sultan, 112
Nahum, Haim, 223, 301–3, 305, 307, 311–12, 362, 475n263
Naim Bey, 467n162
national defense (müdafaa-i milliye): cabinet of, 138; Association of, 145
national economy (milli iktisad), 174–75, 273, 279, 289, 414
National Pact (Misak-ı Millî), 396, 402
national salvation, Turkish, xiii-xiv, 352, 370, 388; CUP, a ship of, 291; domestic war of, 169, 174; at Gallipoli, 233, 322; genocide included in, 352; Kemalist narrative of, 414–15, 421; Kemalist war of, 319; as narrated by Grand Vizier Talaat, 321–22, 325; new history of, 145; praised by German

national salvation (*continued*)
press, 343–44, 388; Talaat's narrative of, 321–22, 325; wars of, 175, 355, 421

nationalism: Turkish, 9, 11–12; wars of 1912–13 as a matrix of, 135–36, 155, 165, 167; negatively defined, 294. *See also* chauvinism; national economy

National Socialists/National Socialism, 19, 268, 288, 354, 399, 410–11, 418–20

Nâzım (Dr. Nâzım, Selanikli Nâzım), 22, 49, 50, 55–60, 62, 64, 70, 81–85, 98, 103, 116, 124, 125, 132, 215–17, 303; anti-Semite, 215; disregarding his Dönme origins, 85; in exile, 381–82, 385, 403–5

Nâzım Pasha (war minister), 131–32, 134, 140–41, 348

Necmettin Molla, 136, 157

Necmettin Sadık. *See* Sadak

Nemesis organization, 404, 408–9, 486n148

Nessimi Bey, foreign minister, 321

Nestorians. *See* Assyrians

Netzah Yisrael Lo Yeshaker (NILI), 289–90, 297, 300, 471n217

Nicholas II, czar, 53, 170–71, 350

NILI. *See* Netzah Yisrael Lo Yeshaker

Nissim Mazliah. *See* Mazliah

Niyazi (Ahmed Niyazi), 54, 118

Noah, 23, 291

Nogales, Rafael de, 209

Noradunghian, Gabriel, 82, 126, 128

Nordau, Max, 58, 299, 306

Nossig, Alfred, 20, 23, 285–89, 361–62, 470n209, 471n211, 471n214

Nubar, Boghos, Pasha, 152

Nureddin Pasha. *See* Konyar

Nuri Dersimi, 460n82

Nuruosmaniye, headquarter of the CUP central committee, 116, 370, 372, 379, 379

Okyar, Ali Fethi, 379

Olti, 208, 276

Ömer Naci, 46, 48, 49, 50, 60, 97, 125, 198–200, 256

Ömer Nâzım (Enver's brother-in-law), 53, 112

Orbay, Hüseyin Rauf, 379

order of Leopold, First Class, 283

Order of the Black Eagle, 331

Orientpolitik (German), 151–65; Wangenheim's, 198; and German Orient Mission, 151

Osmanlı Ahrar Fırkası, 66, 71

Østrup, Johannes, 443n61

Ottoman armies: in Istanbul and Western Anatolia, 229; in the eastern provinces (Second Army and Third Army), 197, 206, 221–22, 248, 251, 260, 270; in Iraq (Sixth Army), 263; in Syria (Fourth Army), 226

Ottoman Assembly. *See* Ottoman Parliament

Ottoman cataclysm, 32

Ottoman Freedom Society (or Liberty Committee), 36, 46–49; ritual of initiation to, 48–49; fusion with Paris committee, 49

Ottoman imperial language, 31–32, 435n46

Ottoman-Israelite Union, 361

Ottoman loans, 139, 142–43, 147, 168–70; during World War, 211, 325, 334

Ottomanism, undermined by centralization and chauvinism, 86, 92, 99, 280; neo-, 427

Ottoman Parliament: dissolution of, 122; during 1909 coup, 70; fundamental debate of March–May 1911, 93–96; and Rûm removal, 179–80. *See also* elections

Ottoman Public Debt Administration (Dette Publique), 63, 66, 440n6
Ottoman spring, 3, 65–69, 424
Ozanian, Andranik, 223

Palestine, 83–84, 95, 217, 306–9, 351, 358–59, 365; Ottoman Jewish center in, 361–62; as a second Armenia, 289; Mandate for, 295
Pallavicini, Johann Markgraf von, 186
pan-Islamism, Turkish-led, 57, 305, 456n13; British specter of, 296; czar seen as archenemy by, 171; Egyptian nationalism and, 409; mix of pan-Turkism and of, 199, 206, 327; primary references of, 59
pan-Turkists/pan-Turkism, xi, 17, 28, 101, 104–5, 301. See also Turkists/Turkism; Turan/Turanism
Papazian, Vahan, 225, 228, 462n97
Papen, Franz von, 420
Paris, 44; Arab Congress in, 307; opposition in exile in, 44, 49–52, 56, 58, 60, 278
Paris Peace Conference and Treaties (1919–20), 388, 399, 407
Parvus (Alexander Parvus, formerly Israil Lasarewitsch Helphand), 97, 173–74, 297, 453n154, 468n176
Patriarchate, Armenian, liquidation of, 262. See also Rûm, Patriarchate of
Pera, 206
Perinçek, Doğu, 488n173
perpetrator trauma, anti-Armenian, 294
Persia. See Iran
petitions, 84; writer of (arzuhalci), 84
Petrograd, 356
Phanariotes, 38–39
Pilling, J. R., 345–46, 480n51
Pirinççizâde Arif, 102–4

Pirinççizâde Feyzi, 96, 102, 104, 106, 223, 243, 383, 412
Plovdiv, 125
Poale Zion, 361
political Islam. See Islamism
Poland, 20, 340, 394; revilement of Armenia and, 399
population exchanges, 28, 34, 145–46, 167, 187
Pomiankowski, Joseph, 12, 158, 201, 433n28, 461n93
Pro Palästina, committee, 362
protofascism, 106, 343, 354
provisional law (decree) of 27 May 1915, 15, 239, 270
putsch. See coup

Quadruple Alliance, 336, 338, 356

Radek, Karl, 397–98
Rahmi. See Arslan, Mustafa Rahmi
Rakka, 262, 266, 276
Rambert, Louis, 63, 65–66, 69, 70–74, 80, 82, 84, 89–90, 109–14, 124, 128–33, 132–33, 169, 181, 191, 210, 440n6; and Cavid, 69, 111, 118, 137; and Cemal, 147; against European duress, 133; against war, 11, 137; for individual liberty, 118; for a neutral coalition, 191; on capitulations,192; on Rûm removal and anti-Greek revanchism, 177–79
Ramgavar, 152
Rathenau, Walther, 342–43, 436n60
reaction/reactionaries (Islamic). See irtica/mürteci
Red Book, 323
Red Cross, 128
Reform Agreement (of 1914), 8, 9, 15, 151–65, 239, 243, 298; annulled, 184, 191–92, 221

reform plan: of 1895, 102–3; of 1912, 152; of 1914, *see* Reform Agreement; for Macedonia, 52, 127

reforms: Ottoman, 38, 40–41; by Talaat, grand-vizier, 323–25; Turkish-nationalist, xi. *See also* revolution

Régie des Tabacs, 63, 66, 69, 72, 129, 137, 143, 440n6; concession agreement obtained by, 147

religion, freedom of, 41

Renda, Mustafa Abdülhalik, 195, 222, 249–51, 258, 266, 412; requiring extermination, 250

Reşid (Dr. Mehmed Reşid). *See* Mehmed Reşid

restorationism, 351, 358, 367; and Christian Zionism, 351, 481n65

Reval, meeting in, 53

revanchism, 165, 169; anti-Greek, 179

revolution: 1908 constitutional (Young Turk), *see* Young Turk Revolution; counter- (of April 1909), 63, 68–69; French, *see* French Revolution; Kemalist, 30; top-down cultural, 321

revolutionaries/revolutionists/ revolutionism: prototypical, 30, 36–37; left-wing, 60; right-wing, 2, 57, 60, 61–62, 64–65, 101, 105, 352; Young Turk, xii, 30. *See also* komiteci/komitecilik

revolutionary Islamic committees (post-1918), 387, 395, 398, 402–3

Rey, Ahmed Reşid, 127–28

Rifat Pasha, 383–84

Riga, 256

The Rising Crescent (by E. Jäckh), 88, 423

Rıza. *See* Ahmed Rıza

Rıza Tevfik, 75

The Road to Death of the Armenian People (by J. Lepsius), 386

Rodes, Jean (journalist), 80

Rodosto (Tekirdağ), 292

Rohner, Beatrice, 266–67

Rohrbach, Paul, 283, 288, 470n202

Romania, 150, 166–67, 191, 219, 275, 317, 347, 364, 365, 394; conquered, 336

Rome, 391; March on, 410

Rosen, Friedrich, 423

Rosenberg, Alfred, 410

Rosenberg, Frederic, 334, 341–42, 371–72, 476n4, 481n68

Rössler, Walter, 467n162

Ruhi al-Khalidi, 75, 93

Rûm (Greek-Orthodox Ottomans), 13, 117, 128, 185; contraband, 169; expulsion of, 13, 28, 167–69, 174–80, 185, 453n146, 454n158; Patriarchate of, 177; of Pontus, 257–58, 319–20, 355, 365, 401; as target of boycotts, 155. *See also* genocide, of Pontus Rûm

Rumelia (Rumeli, European Turkey), 50, 51, 52; loss of, 128, 139, 254

Ruppin, Arthur, 311

Russia, 21, 37, 39, 59, 85, 152–65, 186, 188, 191–93, 205, 209, 211–12, 309; Bolshevik, 396–400, 425; defeat of against Japan, 47; hypothetical alliance of, with Turkey, 171, 182, 202, 211; pro-Kemalist turn of, 399; revolutionary, 341

Russian revolutions: in 1905, 173; in February 1917, 336, 347; in November 1917 (October Revolution), 312, 356

Russo-Turkish (Russo-Ottoman) War of 1877–78, 40, 41

Saadetian, Sempad, 198

Sabahaddin (Mehmed Sabahaddin), prince, 37, 50, 57–59, 66, 79, 136, 138, 141, 302, 376

Sâbis, Ali İhsan, 213

Sadak, Necmettin Sadık, 329–31, 412, 478n30

Sadık. See Mehmed Sadık

Sahip Molla (sheykhulislam), 74; fetva of, 74

Said Halim, Prince, 14, 87, 129, 133, 140–45, 148–49, 163, 186–87, 211, 214, 217, 304, 346; foreign minister, 231–32; grand vizier, 140–41; losing foreign ministry, 291, 315; losing grand vizierate, 315; member of the Turkish-German Society, 287; and Talaat, 145, 163, 176–77, 217, 231–32, 291, 315

Said Pasha. See Mehmed Said Pasha

Sakarya, victory at, 419

Şakir. See Bahaeddin Şakir

Salih Zeki, 263–64, 272–73

Salonica, 36, 43–50, 53–55, 111–12; 1908 enthusiasm in, 54–55; a Jewish town, 302; military units from, 67, 69; center of CUP agitation (before 1910s), 42–55

salvation: national, see national salvation; of the Muslims, 56–57, 141; of the state, 16, 36; of the Orient, 476n9; by Zion, 367

Sanders, Otto Liman von, 162, 212, 221, 331–33; on Talaat, 331–32

Saraçoğlu, Şükrü, 412, 419–20

Sarajevo, 178, 181

Sardarabad, 364

Sarıkamış, 17, 184, 219, 226, 292

Sasun, resistance and massacre in, 101–2; on map, 277

Sazonov, Sergej D., 152, 162, 171, 201–2, 318, 356, 362

Scheubner-Richter, Max, 251, 253, 255–56

Schrader, Friedrich, 386

Şebinkarahisar, 238

second constitutional period. See constitutional period

Şefik (vali Cevdet's deputy), 209, 263–64

Selim I (Yavuz), Sultan, 3, 103, 189–90; as the CUP's patron saint, 4

Selim II, Sultan, 3–4; mosque of (Selimiye Mosque), in Edirne, 3, 144–45

Sémelin, Jacques, 472n228

Şemsi Pasha, 54

separate peace, ideas of, 336, 345–48, 371, 479n40, 479n50

Serbesti (newspaper), 70

Serbia, 40, 124, 131, 140, 142, 150, 183, 186–87, 191, 213, 364; ghosts of, 25, 436n63

Serengülian, Ohannes Vartkes, 92, 116, 160–61, 291, 298; speech in parliament, 94–96; sent to Diyarbekir, 291

şeriat. See sharia

Sevastopol, 364, 381

Sèvres Treaty, 387, 394–95, 399

Sevk ve İskân Kanunu (Relocation and Resettlement Law). See Deportation Law (Decree)

Seyfi, Orhan, 418

Seyfo. See genocide, Assyrian

Seyyid Abdulvehâb, 275

sharia, 31, 39, 67, 70–72, 78, 117–18, 416; vulgar understanding of, 208

Shekib (Shakib) Arslan, 405, 409

sheykhulislam, 16, 41, 74, 82, 183, 200, 207, 217, 282, 332

Sinai, 184

Sivas, 163, 253, 236–38, 253, 274–76

slave markets (of Armenian women and children), 103, 185, 290

single-party regime: of CUP, xiii, 25,
  62–63, 155, 281–82, 304, 330, 426;
  after April 1914 elections, 172–73;
  first of the twentieth century, 25;
  imperial, 320; Kemalist, 412, 423;
  and Weimar Republic, 383–84
Smyrna. *See* Izmir
SO. *See* Special Organization
social contract, 11, 28, 30, 416–17; refusal
  of 105, 417
social Darwinism, 7, 20, 28, 40, 173, 250,
  252, 255, 343, 351, 431n14, 434n36,
  480n59; mix of with Islamism and
  Turkism, 56, 61, 85, 246, 271; and
  world war and world revolution,
  173–74; and total war-jihad, 264
Social Democrat Hunchakian Party,
  152, 236, 295, 399
socialism, 2, 60; revolutionary, 85, xii.
  See also revolutionaries
Socialist International (Second), 97,
  396–99, 443n60; ARF memorandum at Congress in Copenhagen
  of, 86; Socialist Peace Conference
  (1917), convened by, 327
Society for Muhammadan Unity
  (İttihad-i Muhammedi Cemiyeti), 70
Sofia, 125
Solf, Wilhelm, 382–83
sopalı seçim (irregular election of
  1912), 117
Souchon, Wilhelm, Admiral, 213, 390
sovereignty (Turkish), xii, 27, 32, 46,
  51, 69, 143, 167, 191, 298, 319, 333,
  352, 398, 400, 421; centralized, 152;
  CUP's demand of full, 8, 21, 144, 155,
  160, 172; Jewish center in Palestine
  under Ottoman, 362; new domestic
  sovereignty (since August 1914), 191;
  paramount goal of Turkish, in Asia

Minor, 392–93, 396, 421; of sultanate-
  caliphate, 401
Special Organization (SO, Teşkilât-i
  Mahsusa), 5, 146, 379, 402; board
  of, 146; and Caucasus, 196–201,
  205–10, 221–26, 229–30, 404; role of
  in extermination, 252–54, 450n98;
  gangs related to, 13, 258, 355; start of
  in lost Rumeli, 146; and Talaat, 5,
  146, 199–200, 457n32
Stalin, Joseph W., 29, 423
Steeg, Louis, 216
Stier, Ewald, 408–9
stock exchanges and commerce, 127,
  132, 174, 181
Strauss, 383, 484n110
Stresemann, Gustav, 407
Stumm, Wilhelm von, 375
Sublime Porte, 1, 2, 41, 66, 112, 126–27
Suez Canal, 12, 220, 223, 359
Şükrü Pasha, 130
Sükuti. *See* İshâk Sükuti
Süleyman Askeri, 146
Süleyman Nazif, 131, 244
Sultanahmet Square, meetings on,
  125–26, 192
sultan-caliph/sultanate-caliphate. *See*
  caliphate
supply: General Commission for,
  324; mess and scandals related to
  (1914–18), 199, 279, 323–24, 485n126
Şûra-yı Ümmet (journal), 49, 56, 59,
  60, 71
Swiss Civil Code, 416
Switzerland, 25, 43, 266, 322, 343,
  346–48, 385, 397, 436n60, 440n6,
  472n226
Sykes-Picot Agreement, 318, 340, 356,
  362–63; and agreement with Russia's
  Sazonov, 318, 356, 362

Syria, xiii, 4, 14, 30, 33, 70, 108, 180, 182, 185; desert of, 233–34; Great, 217. *See also* genocide, second phase of Armenian

Syriac. *See* Assyrian

Tabris, 256

Tahsin. *See* Uzer

Taksim (square in Istanbul), 70

Talaat (Mehmed Talaat) Bey/Pasha: acknowledged CUP head by 1909, 63, 76; armenophobic, 30, 263; basic feeling of hurt, 43; birth, 35, 41; boasting with bravado and genocide, 134–35, 146–47; made colonel, 145; (twenty-first century) Committee for, 488n173; and coup attempts during World War, 348; crisis of, 63, 85–90, 93, 96, 107–8; demagogue, 125; deputy of Edirne, 68; dictator, 28, 63, 108, 216–20; education, 41–42, 44; (abandoning) equality, 63–64; father of a post-Ottoman Turkey, xi, 411–23; in German exile, 381–411; Germanophile, 193; in German eyes, 24; grand vizier, 315–20; herald of European cataclysm, 217; leading the 1908 revolution, 51–54, 61; leading the 1913 coup, 109, 133–36; leading diplomacy, 145–46; leading recovery of Edirne, 109, 142–45; learning German, 344–45; (seemingly) left-wing, 96–97; longing to enter the family of Europe, 172; minister of the interior, 62, 75, 140; minister of post and telegraph, 117; (a good) Muslim, 97; nation-building by, 33, 258–59, 280–81, 325, 403; natural authority, 47; notebook, 13, 268, 273, 468n175; pioneering a new political style, 147; populist, 54, 124–26, 135, 141; remains brought to Turkey, 418–20; and separate peace, 371; speech at meeting in Manastir (1910), 86; travel into Asia Minor (1909 and 1916), 80, 273–75; travel to London (1909), 75–76; and Turan, 224; a Turkish Bismarck, 179, 286, 404; vice-president of the parliament, 68; vilification of Armenians, 291–94; war-prone, 107–8, 124–26, 135, 142–43, 168, 193, 210–12, 380; weeping, 7, 30, 222; zenith of, 356–57

Talaat, Armenian genocide, 6–27, 232–94. *See also* genocide

Talaat, author of key documents: declaration in *Sabah* (July 1912), 121–22; decree of 30 May 1915, 15; letter of 26 May 1915, 14–15, 270; letters to Mustafa Kemal, 399–403; memoirs, *see* Talaat, memoirs; notice of 23 October 1917, 338; telegram of 6 September 1915 200–201; telegram of 24 April 1915, 235–37; telegram of 2 May 1916, 260

Talaat, family life: childless, 1, 2, 90; married to Hayriye, 1, 42, 90, 382, 404–5; moving with mother and sister to Salonica, 43; son of Ahmed Vasıf, 41;

Talaat, grand vizier: inaugural address of, 321–25; program of, 321, 327; wanting Europeanizing reforms, 322–23

Talaat, interactions of with: Abdulhamid II, 65, 72–74; ARF, 95–97; Atatürk, xiv, 31, 47, 174, 195, 222, 267, 319, 326, 356, 363, 399–403, 411–17, 437n67; Cavid, 23, 44, 94, 139, 162, 222, 246, 315, 320, 327–29, 338, 377,

Talaat, interactions of with (*continued*)
388–89, 404–6, 477n14, 486n146;
Cemal, 45, 65, 163, 314, 473n233;
Churchill, 89; Enver, xiii, 5, 14–15,
108–9, 133–34, 141, 176, 178, 182, 186,
193, 196, 199, 218–20, 227, 233, 235,
263, 265, 279, 285, 294, 297, 310, 313,
315, 334, 365–66, 372, 390, 396, 402–3,
411, 416, 429n3, 452n139, 480n52;
Helfferich, 14, 88–90, 341–42,
370–71, 387; Hüseyin Cahid (Yalçın),
138–39; İsmail Canbolad, 282;
Kaiser Wilhelm II., 375; Ludwig, 5,
6, 7, 12, 13, 16, 22; Mahmud Muhtar,
124–25; Mahmud Şevket, 118, 140;
Mehmed Reşid, 244–48; Mustafa
Hayri, 16, 62–63, 136, 142–43, 282–83,
338; Nâzım and Şakir, 51, 55–60, 64,
81–85; Special Organization, 5, 146,
199–200, 457n32; Zionists, 75, 93,
109, 220, 225, 295–314, 358–62; Ziya
Gökalp, 11, 60, 98–99, 108
Talaat, memoirs (apologia), 5, 67, 79,
86, 122, 129, 187, 211, 349, 388–91, 419,
421–22, 430n1
Talaat, more than a triumvir. *See*
triumvirate
Talaat, pioneer of demographic engineering and domestic genocide, xi,
25, 259, 300; anti-Armenian policy,
230–48; anti-Assyrian policy, 204–5;
Rûm removal, 109, 173–80. *See also*
genocide
Tanin (CUP newspaper), 23, 70–71, 88,
125, 139, 156, 160, 170, 188, 195, 206,
235, 379, 421
Tanrıöver, Hamdullah Suphi, 384
Tanzimat, 39–41, 101, 103, 105, 295;
constitutional patriotism originating
in, 98

Taray, Cemal Hüsnü, 412
Tbilisi, 201–2
Tehlirian, Soghomon, 18, 320, 403,
407–9; trial of, 18, 407–11, 423
Tekinalp, Moïz Kohen, 289, 468n176;
disciple of Ziya Gökalp, 289
Temo, İbrahim Edhem, 141
Tevfik. *See* Ahmed Tevfik
Teşkilât-ı Mahsusa. *See* Special
Organization
The Hague, 391
Thom, Daniel, 193
Thrace, 167, 178, 197
Tigris, 19
Titus (Roman), 290
Tokatlian, 206
Topal Osman, 258
Toptani, Essad Pasha, 140, 305
totalitarianism, Turkish version of, 37
Trabzon, 130, 155; reconquest of, 339
transfer of Armenian property, 240,
267–73. *See also* national economy
Transcaucasian Federation, 316, 365
typhus, 221–22, 249, 266
Triple Alliance, 186. *See also* Central
Powers
Triple Entente. *See* Entente
Tripolitania (Trablusgarb). *See* Libya
triumvirate, question of Young Turk,
xii, xiii, 163–64, 452n141
Trotsky, Leon, 85, 173
Tunçay, Mete, 384
Turan/Turanism, xi, 9, 12, 17, 188, 197,
207–8, 338–39, 352, 367–68, 413; campaign toward, 207–8, 256; gospel of,
36, 98, 101, 104, 221–22; jihad toward,
183, 188, 197, 380; revival of, 355–56,
367–68, 377; a sublation of Ottomanism and Islamism, 98; a utopia-dystopia, 256, 367. *See also* Ziya Gökalp

Türk inkılâbı tarihi (by Y. Bayur), 380,
434n36
Türkenfieber (Turk fever), 88, 422,
431n13
Turkestan, 256, 375, 378, 401
Turkey (late Ottoman and early
Republican: Talaat's world)
—*1870s: Traumatic war, faith in
Tanzimat's constitutionalism
exhausted.* Talaat's early childhood, 41; Russo-Ottoman War
(1877–78), losses in the Balkans
and the South Caucasus, Berlin
Treaty; Sultan Abdulhamid
II (r. 1876–1909) installs and
suspends first Ottoman constitution, thus ending the Tanzimat,
35–41
—*1880s: Abdulhamid's politics of
Islamic union,* 40, 155, 392. Talaat's
defiant youth, 41; foreign-
controlled Public Debt Administration after state bankruptcy,
Britain occupies Egypt, friendship of Ottoman Turkey with
Germany supersedes that with
Britain, 14, 148, 440n4; Committee of Union and Progress (CUP)
founded in Istanbul, in opposition to a sultan seen as weak and
reactionary, 42–43
—*1890s: Decade of repression.* Talaat
starts as a CUP activist; mass
arrest, flight and an opposition in
exile result from Abdulhamid's
repression of the CUP networks,
43–44; pogroms and massacres of
Armenians who demand reforms
according to the Berlin Treaty,
8, 101–4; after imprisonment,

Talaat becomes a subversive CUP
networker in Salonica, 43–46
—*1900s: Decade of hope, Young Turk
Revolution, eve and aftermath.*
Talaat becomes a mastermind of
the revolution in Salonica, 46–55;
and its political head in Istanbul
after 1908, 61–81; Young Turk
Revolution, 54–55; against European interference in Macedonia,
52–53; and Abdulhamid's style
(Hamidism), 36; Salonica, internal
center of subversion, merges with
the external center in Paris, 49–55;
allied to Armenian revolutionaries,
3, 50, 79; Ottoman spring: hope
in a democratic Ottoman Empire,
55, 65–69; reactionary coup and
anti-Armenian massacre in 1909,
70–74, 76–79; Cavid and Talaat are
first CUP ministers, 62, 75
—*1910s and early 1920s: Ottoman
cataclysm, imperial total war-jihad,
single-party regime and making of
a Turkish-Muslim national home.*
Frustrated from parliamentarism,
81–87, 110–21; Talaat becomes a
war-prone komiteci, 121–36; heads
an empire, 136–50; destroys the
Ottoman social fabric, 281–379;
then falls and agitates in exile,
379–403; his stratagemes and
Ziya Gökalp's ideologemes base,
despite defeat in 1918, Atatürk's
leadership from 1919, now reduced
to Asia Minor, 399–403, 411–17
—*1910–11:* CUP turn to Germany,
88; rebellion in Albania and
Yemen, 82–83; war in Libya,
111–13; personal and political crisis

Turkey (*continued*)
of Talaat, 85–87; his friendship
and synergy with Ziya Gökalp,
60, 98–99, 108
—*1912–13:* sopalı seçim (irregular
election of spring 1912), 117; coup
of July 1912 (Halaskâr insurrection), 119–21; CUP in opposition and crisis, 121–24; Balkan
wars, wanted by Talaat and CUP
(fall 1912), 124–30, 141–45; war
and muhacir misery, 128–29;
demand of reform of the eastern
provinces, based on Berlin
Treaty, reactivated by Armenians,
151–52; CUP coup of January 1913,
133–36; Grand Vizier Mahmud
Mahmud Şevket Pasha assassinated, 140–41; recovery of Edirne
and start of national salvation
narrative, 131–32, 145; Talaat leads
peace negotiations with Balkan
states and reform negotiations,
145–46, 157–65
—*1914:* revanchist, Talaat and other
CUP radicals keep on wanting
war with Greece, 167–69; expulsion of Rûm, 167–69, 174–80;
single-party regime consolidated
with April 1914 elections, 172;
war-prone group around Talaat
solicits during July Crisis alliance
with Germany (2 August 1914),
starts irregular war in the South
Caucasus, 196–203; abolition of
Capitulations, Lebanon's autonomy, and Reform Agreement for
eastern provinces, 191–92; official
entrance into World War I and

declaration of jihad (November
1914), 206
—*1915–16:* Enver Pasha's Caucasus
campaign ends in a fiasco at
Sarıkamış, 219–23; Cemal Pasha's
Suez canal campaign fails, 217–18;
Entente naval breakthrough at the
Dardanelles frustrated, 227–29;
deportation/extermination/
plundering of Armenians (in
eastern provinces also of other
Christians) starts in spring 1915 in
Eastern Asia Minor, ends 1916 with
the massacre of survivors in the
desert of Syria, 232–77; Quadruple
alliance includes Bulgaria, 336;
attack against British Egypt with
irregulars from Libya (late 1915)
fails, 231; in victorious defense of
Gallipoli (April–December 1915)
culminates henceforth Talaat's
national salvation narrative, 13, 233,
322; British defeat at Kut in Iraq
(spring 1916), 350; putschist Yakub
Cemil executed, 348; treaties with
Germany and Austria enlarged, 336
—*1917–18:* Talaat grand vizier, 321;
Cavid his minister of finances,
327–28; CUP talk of a "new
Turkey" renewed, 325–26;
overthrow of czar (mid-March
1917) outweighs bad news of
Baghdad's fall, 350; supply
scandals, famine, country-wide
corruption, and growing protests,
324–25; the October Revolution,
Russian collapse in the Caucasus,
and the Brest-Litovsk Treaty,
356–57, 363–65; open the door for

Ottoman recovery of Caucasian provinces, 317–18, 364; and—as Gökalps's circles believe—toward "Turan," 367–68; the grand vizier reaches the zenith of his apparent power in early 1918 and displays a comfortable outlook on general post-war peace conferences, 363; final disillusion during his visit to Berlin (September 1918), 371–76; harsh armistice (30 October), flight of the CUP top leaders after last CUP congress (1 November), and planning of continued struggle, 379–81

—*1919:* Paris conferences on post-World War order of victors, former CUP top leaders found "anti-imperialist" Islamist, pro-Turkish cells abroad, 395–99; Greek occupation of Izmir, 386; Kemal Atatürk's movement in Asia Minor reorganizes the former "war ummah," 393; fighting for a Turkey in Asia Minor for Muslims and Turks, against Greeks, Pontus Greeks (Rûm), Armenians, and Alevi Kurds, 392–95, 400–401

—*1920s: Making of the Republic.* Talaat supports Kemal Atatürk from his exile, 399–403; before being killed in Berlin (March 1921), 403–4; global interest for trial of Tehlirian, Talaat's killer, 407–11; National Pact (Misak-ı Millî), countergovernment (Grand National Assembly, Ankara), 396, 402; alliance with

Bolshevik Russia, 399; solidarity from German nationalists, 407; Kemalist victory in war for Asia Minor (1919–22) fought in the name of Islam, 414, 416; Lausanne Peace Treaty (1923), 28, 34, 146, 394; ends Ottoman cataclysm and replaces Treaty of Paris-Sèvres (1920), 387, 394–95, 399; caliphate abolished, 415; Kemalist "revolutions," 31, 416

—*1930: Zenith of Atatürk's single-party system.* It stands on Talaat's shoulders, though little avowed; the Kemalist successor single-party regime is more totalitarian, but territorially reduced and less corrupt and ware-prone than the CUP's, 37, 416–18; culmination of state-sponsored Turkism in politics, society and culture, Turkish History Thesis and language theory, 413–14

—*1940: Transition to multiparty regime.* CUP and Talaat are rehabilitated as patriots, their genocide remains censured and denied; strategic turn to the West and democratization after neutrality in World War II, yet weakly rooted, 420–21, 423–24; Talaat's remains brought back from Nazi Berlin to Turkey (1943), 418–20; his memoirs published (1946), 421–23

Turkish-German Society, 287–88, 404, 407

Turkish History Thesis, 414

Turkists/Turkism, 11, 16, 28, 56, 61, 86. *See also* pan-Turkists/pan-Turkism

Turkification, 86, 327; of Kurds, 179
Türk Ocağı (Turkish Hearth society),
    116–17, 384, 412
Türk'ün Tekbiri (Türk's Allahu Akbar),
    413
Türk Yurdu. *See* Asia Minor, as a
    Turkish-Muslim national home
Türk Yurdu (Turkish Home society),
    116–17, 384, 412, 420
Türk Yurdu (journal), 117, 173
Tusan, Michelle, 353–54

Ukraine, 340, 364–65
ulema, 82
ummah/ümmet (community of
    Muslims), 8; war ummah, 271–72,
    320, 379, 391, 393, 395, 469n181
United States, 27, 266, 312, 341; entrance
    of into World War I, 331; break of
    relations with Turkey, 342; Jäckh in,
    422; memory politics in, 475n258
Urfa, 72, 106, 237–38, 246, 252, 260–61,
    276, 293–94, 461n93
Ussher, Clarence, 205
Uzer, Hasan Tahsin, 96, 130, 133, 412; in
    Erzurum, 248–58; triggering Talaat's
    orders, 250–51; in Van, 194, 199–205,
    207, 226–27; wallowing in self-pity,
    257

Vahdetî (Naqshbandi sheikh),
    70–71, 73
Van, 15, 194, 202–3, 205, 209, 224–27,
    238, 251–52
varlık vergisi (property tax), 419
Vartkes. *See* Serengülian, Ohannes
    Vartkes
Vehib Pasha, 366
Venizelos, Eleftherios, 138, 175, 227
Versailles Treaty, 387–88, 399

Vienna, 44, 76, 223, 334, 357, 374
Vierbücher, Heinrich, 408
violence: anti-Christian, 234, 240; as an
    early CUP strategy, 51, 53; as alleged
    mutual killings, 237; ethnic cleans-
    ing, 386; extreme, 22–23, 28, 367, 425;
    as massacre, *see* massacre; of mob, 71,
    87, 106, 117, 247, 278; participatory,
    19, 247; as pogroms, 102; political,
    426; societal, 95; as substitutional
    revenge, 167, 294, 472n228
Vogorides, Stephanos, 39
Volkan (journal), 70–71
Vorontsov-Dashkov, Illarion, 201–2
Vorwärts (newspaper), 408
Vramian, Arshak, 178–79, 225–28, 248,
    264, 462n97
Vratzian, Simon, 198

Wandel, Carl E., 279
Wangenheim, Hans von, 10, 18–21,
    148, 168, 183, 186–87, 192–93, 197–98,
    211, 213, 218, 222, 229, 233–34, 255;
    admirer of CUP aplomb, 148; and
    alliance with Turkey, 20–21, 182–84,
    390; and Armenian reforms, 158–59;
    approval of evacuations by, 253;
    seeking Judeophilic image, 301–2,
    310, 312; Turkophile, 148
Wangenheim, Hanna, 382
wars: Balkan, *see* Balkan wars; Russo-
    Turkish War of 1877–78, *see* Russo-
    Turkish (Russo-Ottoman) War of
    1877–78; War of Independence, *see*
    Asia Minor, war for; World War I, *see*
    World War I
Wassermann, Oscar, 343, 382–83
Weber (Dr. Weber, German dragoman),
    134
Weber, Max, 445n94

Weil (manager of the Régie des Tabacs), 147
Weimar Republic, 383, 388, 405, 407
Weitz, Paul, 14, 88, 90
Weltgeltung, 18, 21, 352
Westenenk, Louis, 164
Wilhelm II, Kaiser, 187, 190, 382; visit of in Istanbul, 331
Wilson, Woodrow, 358; Fourteen Points of, 376, 381
Wolff-Metternich, Paul Graf, 34, 297, 332–33
Wolffsohn, David, 303
World War I (Ottoman): desertion in, 184, 204, 226, 238, 248; genesis of, 110 (see also World War alliance of Germany with Turkey); started in the Caucasus, 183, 190–210, 220–23, 249; linked to domestic agenda, 184; entrance into, 5, 211–15, 324; proactive policy of, 201; propaganda during, 184, 188; mobilization in, 188–89, 194, 196; requisition in, 184, 189, 194, 196, 238, 244–45, 269; sabotage in, 238; war taxes in, 244
World War alliance of Germany with Turkey, 5, 20–21, 182–84, 192, 222, 456n15; wanted and joined by Austria, 186, 336; treaties related to, 187–88, 336

Yakub Cemil, 134, 334, 348
Yalçın, Hüseyin Cahid, 70–71, 111, 123, 125, 130, 132, 136, 230, 330, 389, 419, 421; letter of, to Talaat, 138–39
Yalman, Ahmed Emin, 326, 378, 420
Yeğenağa, Ali Münif, 78, 90, 124, 125, 226
Yemen, 63, 132
Yeni Cami, 206

Yeni Mecmua (journal), 329–31, 368; Yeni Mecmua: Çanakkale özel sayısı 18 Mart 1918 (special journal issue), 476n9
Yezidis, 19, 245
Yıldız Palace, 41, 44; reception at (1908), 68–69
Yishuv, 289, 295–302; protected by Germany, USA, Talaat, 295–96
Young Turk Revolution (1908), 3, 39, 47, 88, 295
Young Turks, 3–4

Zaharoff, Basil, 345–47, 480n51
Zaven. See Der Yeghiayan
Zaven, Dikran, 407
Zeitun, 226–27, 233, 235–38, 252, 276
Zeki Pasha, 404
Zimmermann, Arthur, 159, 341–43
zimmi, 8, 95
Zinoviev, Grigory, 397
Zion, 314, 367–68; in contrast to Turan, 367
Zionists/Zionism, 10, 20, 58, 83–84, 94–96, 109, 111, 220, 225, 345; and CUP, 302–9, 358–62; English Zionist Federation, 75
Zionist Organisation (ZO), 285–86, 288–89, 299, 302–3, 306; Palestine office of the, 311
Ziya Gökalp, xi, 11–12, 16–17, 22, 23, 28, 36, 60, 64, 90, 98–106, 133, 141, 157, 217, 230, 308, 362, 368, 380; Central Committee member, 98; excrescence in thought of, 413–14; high school student in Diyarbekir, 99–101; ideal/idealism (mefkûre/mefkûrecilik) of, 2, 11, 100, 221, 251; identifying with Mustafa Kemal, 393; influencing Kemalism, 413–17; and Mustafa Hayri, 16, 64, 105;

Ziya Gökalp (*continued*)
panegyrist of rulers, 290–91;
interpreting Protestantism, 105;
refocusing on Turan, 371; refusing
social contract, 105; settled down
in Salonica, 98; subordinating individual rights, 106; suicide attempt
of, 100; supreme truth (hakikat-i
kübra), 100; Talaat's friend, 11,
60, 98–99, 108; as World War
propagandist, 188
ZO. *See* Zionist Organisation
Zohrab, Krikor, 10–11, 18, 19, 73, 78, 94,
124, 127, 152, 161, 214–15, 298; and
Cavid, 116, 161, 214–15; letter to Talaat
(1915), 19; sent to Diyarbekir, 291;
working for liberal-CUP cooperation,
116–18

A NOTE ON THE TYPE

This book has been composed in Arno, an Old-style serif
typeface in the classic Venetian tradition, designed
by Robert Slimbach at Adobe.